FLORIDA HO
John Rae

IT'S ALL ABOUT GUTS

****

WE SALUTE THE MEN

OF THE

135TH UNITED STATES COLORED TROOP

BY

JAY & AMY BAUER

PREFACE

The inspiration for authoring this book comes from years of research surrounding the men of the 135th United States Colored Troop, (Infantry). The information and background are found in historical documents but mainly at the National Archives in Washington, D.C., from the pension records of these forgotten soldiers. These men were previously slaves and enlisted in the Pioneer Corps in General William T. Sherman's Army in his March to the Sea and through the Carolina's. Once the Army reaches Goldsboro, North Carolina, there are enough ex-slaves who volunteered in the engineer corps, approximately 1,154, that the 135th United States Colored Troop is formed.

Of the over eleven hundred soldiers, we have been able to delve into approximately four hundred of their pension records. The documents in their files record just what the men, their spouses, and family members had to go through, to provide the proof required, to justify their service and entitlement for a pension. There are countless stories of the men suffering injuries and abuses during their service, in the pioneer corps building roads and bridges, to their time serving in the 135th United States Colored Troop. Some were even scarred for life.

What makes this story interesting is that each one of the pension records tells a life story of these ex-slaves, men of the 135th USCT, who volunteered in the service of their country. This was their freedom from slavery and a task they took on voluntarily, and prior to any knowledge of being able to draw a pension in years to come.

Of note is that during the process of going through the pensions of these men, we find that several of them testified that they marched through Washington, D.C., in what was the Grand Parade at the end of the war. Over the years it has become common knowledge that there were no colored troops that were allowed to march in the grand review however these men certainly indicate and memorialize in their declarations and depositions that they did. As a follow up, and going through official records, we find several documents that identify the marching order of the 135th United States Colored Troop in the Grand Parade on May 24, 1865. That being the case we have ascertained that this unit was the only USCT that marched in the grand parade in Washington, D.C., in front of the President, at the White House, at the end of the Civil War. This alone makes this book worth publishing.

"It's all about Guts" gives an insight into these soldiers, and the stories of their lives in service. It gives information on their backgrounds, where they came from, who they married, their wives, and the families of the men. Many lived to a ripe old age. The majority were born in the 1840s, some before, and they lived into the 1900s, 1910s, 1920s, and even 1930s.

What we have done with this book is to briefly tell some of their stories, "in their own words," as found in the files of their pension declarations and documents. This book includes copies of some of the papers from the files of the men as a backup to their story. It is a sample compilation of the various pension files that we have uncovered and as you will be able to see, some are extremely challenging to read, as the majority are handwritten and in cursive. You will be able to confidently conclude though, that these courageous men, demonstrating their valor, had GUTS!

DEDICATION

This book is dedicated to Amy Bauer's Godson, Michael George Kelly Brennan. Michael spent two years as an army consultant in Iraq and, at the time of his death, in 2016, was working as an intelligence analyst for the Defense Intelligence Agency. He served in the United States Army at Fort Drum, New York, and was an avid supporter of Civil War Preservation. Michael participated in Civil War Reenactments and living history demonstrations throughout Virginia, Maryland, West Virginia, and Pennsylvania as a drummer and fifer as a young man and later as an infantry soldier. He appears in the Manassas National Battlefield Visitors Center movie, "End of Endurance," as Sergeant Henry Ritter. Michael is buried at Arlington National Cemetery, in Virginia.

TABLE OF CONTENTS

CHAPTER 1

THE MARCH TO THE SEA AND THROUGH THE CAROLINA'S THE PIONEERS WHO BECAME SOLDIERS

General William Tecumseh Sherman's "March to The Sea," from Atlanta to Savannah, Georgia, in 1864, is important on several fronts. It is an incursion, with a philosophy of total warfare; an effort to break the fighting spirit of the Confederacy. "The "March to the Sea" had some strategic objectives as well. One was to totally disrupt the Confederacy by cutting off their supply lines, and the other was to psychologically break the fighting spirit of the people of Georgia. It is also the beginning of a recruitment drive, to enlist freed southern Black slaves, into a regiment of a trained Pioneer Corps. This Pioneer Corps would later amount to a United States Colored Troop, a full regiment, which would end up being one, if not the only United States Colored Troop, to march in the Grand Parade (Review), in Washington, D.C. on May 24th of 1865.

After General Sherman captured Atlanta on September 2nd, 1864, he had the opportunity to devote over two months to reorganizing and resupplying the armies under his command. He, along with Captain Poe, his chief engineer, employed a great deal of time calculating their coming tactical advance, that being a premeditated maneuver, to advance a force of over 55,000 infantry, 5,000 cavalry, along with the train of approximately 2,500 support wagons, 800 ambulances and artillery, on a south easterly crusade through Georgia. That passage would be his famous "March to the Sea," in his undertaking to capture Savannah. By November 15, 1864, the well-known "March to the Sea," by General Sherman's forces, was set in motion and thereby began the creation of the materialization of a unique Pioneer Corps. That pioneer corps would turn out to become the 135th United States Colored Troop. The troop would be composed of enlisted freed Black slaves primarily from Georgia, South Carolina, and North Carolina, and would become an element of General Sherman's army.

It is important to perceive at this point, and because of the Emancipation Proclamation, if a slave were to escape from the control of the Confederate Government or be set free by the advances of the Federal Troops the slave would in fact be free. The Emancipation Proclamation was communicated as an order to free all slaves in ten states that were under Confederate control. Lincoln issued a preliminary directive on September 22, 1862, warning that he ordered, by proclamation, the emancipation of all slaves in any state that did not end its rebellion against the Union by January 1, 1863. As such, not one of the Confederate states reverted back to the Union, and Lincoln's order was signed on January 1, 1863, as a result.

General W.T. Sherman and his staff were clearly aware of the importance of the Proclamation signed by President Lincoln in 1863. Also, he and his officers felt it worked to their advantage by recruiting the freed slaves as they made their trek through the south in unfamiliar territory. The Proclamation also ordered that suitable persons among those freed could be enlisted into the paid service of United States' forces and (the Proclamation), ordered the Union Army to "recognize and maintain the freedom of" the ex-slaves. As a result, it was determined that the recruitment of a pioneer regiment, made up of freed slaves, could work to their tactical advantage.

The importance of the pioneer force was key in facilitating the advance of a 60,000 plus man force, along with the train of wagons, across Georgia as there were numerous obstacles that had to be dealt with. The sizable forces had to navigate through an incredibly tough terrain, traversing swamps and forests under harsh weather conditions. Additionally, another challenge that stood in their way, other than the Confederate's forces, was the difficult task of establishing a stable supply line to manage the transportation of resources through enemy territory. As part of Sherman's total war philosophy, the destruction of infrastructure was essential in defeating the Confederate cause and had to be apportioned efficiently and effectively. One key important detail that needed to be dealt with was the destruction of the railroads, along with the tracks that the Confederates used for resupply. A figure of speech was coined, known as "Sherman's neckties," when describing what the torn up, twisted railroad tracks resembled. This was accomplished by piling up the railroad ties, starting large bonfires, and then heating the rails until they could be easily bent, twisting them in loops, often around trees, thus resembling a necktie. The twisted rails were also called Sherman's bow ties or Sherman's hairpins.

SHERMAN'S NECKTIES

Another crucial factor in deploying a 60,000-man army through Georgia and the South was the speed of their advance. In order to accomplish a rapid movement, it was necessary to have the workforce create a path the armies could follow that would not impede their progress and effectively slow them down. The army also had to be kept supplied. Since the Union army did not have the means to bring in supplies, in this enemy territory, foraging parties, and bummers were assembled and sent out daily to bring in necessary provisions to fulfill the army's needs.

It was the distinct job of the pioneer corps, to go in front of General Sherman's army, and pave the way so that they could advance rapidly with the least amount of interference or delay. To accomplish this, trees had to be felled, roads maintained, and roads corduroyed through swampy regions.

Typical example of building a corduroy road through the swamp

The corduroying of the roads was a challenging, dangerous, and fatiguing reality for the pioneers. This is evidenced in the years following when the men were applying for their pensions. The depositions unmistakably described the hardships these men experienced while they labored in the pioneer corps. It impacted their health and well-being, for many of them, for the remainder of their lives.

We must be cognizant of the fact Sherman's campaign through the South was accomplished during the winter of 1864 and well into 1865. There are stories in the pension records of the severe winter and coldness that the men had to deal with and building corduroy roads through the icy swamps, many times during the night, so the army could progress during the daylight hours. The men told of being injured by being run over by the wagon wheels or getting their hands smashed by large tree timbers building the corduroy roads and repairing the bridges. In any event, the life of a pioneer was arduous work but that which had to be accomplished.

In General Sherman's "March to The Sea," his army of the Mississippi was organized into several Army Corps.

General Henry W. Slocum, was appointed the commander of the left wing of Gen. William T. Sherman's famous "March to the Sea" from Atlanta to Savannah, through Georgia, and afterward turning north through the Carolinas. He commanded the 14th and 20th Corps, comprising the Army of Georgia. During this campaign, General Slocum captured Milledgeville, the then state capital of Georgia, and subsequently the Atlantic coast seaport of Savannah. In the Carolina campaign, Slocum's army saw victories in the battles of Averasboro and Bentonville in North Carolina. Sherman's "March to the Sea" and the Carolinas campaign were crucial to the overall Union victory in the Civil War.

General Jefferson C. Davis, separately commanded the 14th Corps.

General Alpheus S. Williams, commanded the 20th Corps. and later General Joseph A. Mower assumed command of the 20th Corps.

General Oliver O. Howard, commanded the right wing of Gen. William T. Sherman's Army in the "March to The Sea," The Army of the Tennessee, which consisted of the 15th and the 17th Corps. General Howard, who had lost his right arm in 1862 at the battle of Fair Oaks, was concerned about the welfare of the approximately four million slaves who had been freed as a result of the Civil War. Due to his concerns, President Andrew Johnson appointed Howard commissioner of the Bureau of Refugees, Freedmen, and Abandoned Lands, commonly known as the "Freedmen's Bureau." The Bureau was formed to rehabilitate former slaves. It was tasked to feed millions in need, build hospitals, provide direct medical aid, and negotiate thousands of labor contracts for former slaves. The bureau was instrumental in developing numerous schools and training facilities for Black people and as a result, as a founder, Howard University, in Washington D.C., was named in his honor. Not only did the bureau aid in their development, but they also provided the resources necessary for their survival such as food and clothing. Later Howard served as the university's third president.

General Peter J. Osterhaus was in command of the 15th Corps. in the "March to The Sea" and **General Francis P. Blair** commanded the 17th Corps. The 135th United States Colored Troop would eventually be mustered into service and be placed under the command of Gen. Blair in the 17th Corps. The 135th USCT commander was Col. John E. Gurley.

General Hugh Judson Kilpatrick, commanded the Calvary in the military division of the Mississippi in General Sherman's "March to The Sea." Sherman said of Kilpatrick, "I know that Kilpatrick is a hell of a damned fool, but I want just that sort of man to command my cavalry on this expedition." General Kilpatrick had a great deal of success raiding behind Confederate lines and tearing up their much-needed source of supplies, their railroads.

Captain Orlando M. Poe, a West Point graduate, was selected by General Sherman as his chief engineer in the destruction of Atlanta and continued in this capacity in the "March to the Sea" and the Carolina's. "Poe's engineering expertise was repeatedly called upon to survey the ground for attack, fortify Yankee lines, quickly build bridges for his men, and destroy the means of travel for the enemy." His planning and engineering were instrumental in dozens of river crossings, and numerous swamps negotiated, making poor or non-existent roads passable, repairing, and building bridges, and in the

placing of the pontoons to cross the rivers. He served with Sherman until the conclusion of the Carolina campaign. He was promoted to Colonel in Savannah and subsequently to Brigadier General at the end of the war. General Poe is responsible for documenting the routes of the march and developing the maps used by General Sherman during the "March to the Sea," the Carolina's campaign, and at the war's end.

We are now mindful that the speed of movement and the destruction of the Confederate supply lines were contributory to the success of General Sherman's "March to The Sea" and his philosophy of total warfare. Consequently, it was necessary for the recruitment of additional manpower; that being available volunteers from suitable ex-slaves that could be placed into the pioneer corps. These ex-slaves were recruited into the engineer force as "pioneers" building bridges and corduroy roads, as guides, foragers, and even spies for the Union Army. The versatility they provided to the army was unique and unparalleled. In the capacity they served, they were Sherman's secret weapon.

On November 15th, 1864 General Sherman made his way through Georgia in his "March to The Sea" to Savannah and captured the city on December 21st, 1864. He and his 60,000 man plus army, along with his 2,500 wagons, made the journey of approximately 250 miles in that six-week period, all the while living off the land and undermining the will of the people. In other words, ***"Making Georgia Howl."*** The army did this by splitting into several columns cutting a swath approximately sixty miles wide, all the while cutting the confederate rail lines used for their resupply and making sure they were not able to provide for their war machine.

Upon capturing Savannah, it being such a central phase of General Sherman's march, it resulted in him sending off a Christmas message to President Lincoln on December 22, 1864, and it read;

Savannah, Dec. 22, 1864

"To His Excellency,

President Lincoln,

I beg to present you as a Christmas Gift the City of Savannah with one hundred and fifty (150) heavy guns and plenty of ammunition, also about twenty-five thousand, (25,000) bales of cotton."

W. T. Sherman,

Maj. General

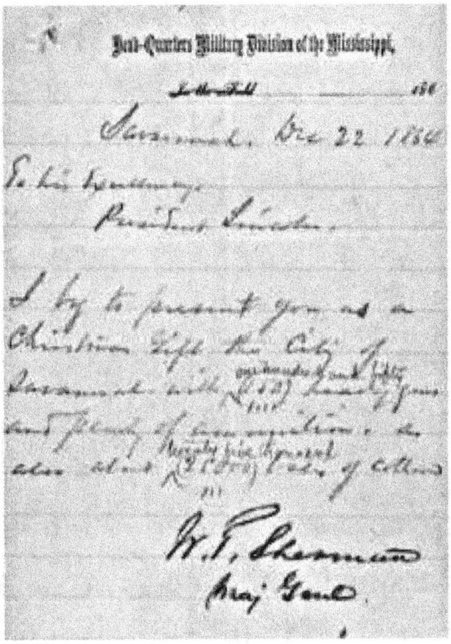
Head-Quarters Military Division of the Mississippi,

Savannah, Dec 22 1864

To his Excellency
President Lincoln

I beg to present you as a Christmas Gift the City of Savannah with one hundred & fifty (150) heavy guns and plenty of ammunition, & also about twenty five thousand (25000) bales of cotton

W. T. Sherman
Maj. Genl.

The capturing of Savannah was a significant objective because it was an essential base for supplying the Confederates with ammunition and cotton. On the other hand, General Sherman had barely started on his long and arduous campaign. True, he had succeeded in his "March to The Sea" mission, nevertheless he had many more challenges. On his march through Georgia, the army enlisted over two hundred ex-slaves into the Pioneer Corps. These men had been literally set free (as provided by the 13th Amendment), and they were willing to volunteer in the Union Army and work hard in the Pioneer Corps, for their future, their family's future, and their freedom. They were the original freedom seekers; little do they know that within months they would be enlisted into the 135th United States Colored Troop.

General Sherman's Army, the Army of the Tennessee, had time to rest up, get clothing, and re-supply while they spent several weeks in Savannah. They departed Savannah in January 1865 on their march to Columbia, the capital of South Carolina. The army received some resistance on the route mainly at the Salkehatchie swamp and Rivers Bridge at the beginning of February, although the delay to the movement of the army was barely two days. The main objective, however important, was Columbia, South Carolina which was the "Cradle of Succession." Needless to say, it didn't take long for General Sherman to move his forces to Columbia. The march was not without danger, however, due to the continuous skirmishes and as mentioned many times in the pension records the suffering due to the cold wet winter. The men told of working in the cold swamps at night so the army could move during the day and the freezing weather evidenced by the men having their wet shirts frozen to their backs. Once Columbia was reached, however, the Confederates evacuated the capital, and it was open to Sherman's army. The capital was seized on the 15th of February 1865.

Once the capital was taken the celebration was immense and there was plenty of drinking. General Slocum, in observance wrote, "A drunken soldier with a musket in one hand and a match in the other is not a pleasant visitor to have about the house on a dark, windy night." Although it is said that many of the fires had been set by retreating Confederate troops General Sherman wrote later;

"Though I never ordered it and never wished it, I have never shed any tears over the event, because I believe that it hastened what we all fought for, the end of the War."

General Sherman's next objective is the Confederate arsenal at Fayetteville, North Carolina. In retrospect, the number of pioneers enlisted on the march through South Carolina totaled another six hundred plus, making the added pioneer force, made up of ex-slaves, almost nine hundred. Those pioneers were a valuable force for the advancement of the army through the Carolina's as the army needed to pass through the low country and swamps of South Carolina, and the "quicksand's" of North Carolina, in the middle of winter. The roads required repairing and corduroying, the bridges needed repairing, new bridges had to be erected and the pontoons had to be placed across numerous rivers so the army, along with their train of wagons, could make the arduous crossings and continue the march.

It was now obvious of the importance of Captain Poe's engineering ability. His pioneering force was made up of seventy Black pioneers to every one hundred white pioneers in support of his engineers. Without critical planning and execution of the movement plan, Sherman's Army would not have been able to keep the rapid movement of his army or the Confederate forces off guard. There were constant skirmishes throughout the campaign as Confederate General Johnston was shadowing Sherman's movements. None of that caused a significant delay in their ultimate goal of reaching Goldsboro, North Carolina.

A major obstacle on the march to Fayetteville was the crossing of the great Pee Dee River at Cheraw. Although The Pee Dee provided for a minimal delay, Sherman's forces moved forward and captured Fayetteville, North Carolina, from General Johnston's army, on March 11, 1865, less than a month after his departure from Columbia. Subsequently, the Confederate arsenal (previously the United States Arsenal), at Fayetteville, a facility where Confederate weapons and munitions were made and stored, was successfully destroyed.

At this point, Sherman plotted his course for the march to Goldsboro, North Carolina. His departure from Fayetteville on March 13th gave the appearance he was headed directly to Raleigh. His army's movement, however, took the path to Averasboro where General Davis with the Fourteenth Corps and General Williams with the Twentieth Corps skirmished with Confederate General Hardee on March 16th, 1865. The battle lasted the day and the Confederate army departed to the north that night. As the Union army then moved toward Goldsboro General Slocum's fourteenth corps and twentieth corps were attacked by General Johnston at Bentonville on March 19th delaying that wing of General Sherman's army on his track to his Goldsboro objective. Sherman elected to send reinforcements at the battle of Benttonville and General Mower of the 1st Division of the Seventeenth Army Corps was ordered to attack the rear of the Confederate forces. Following sporadic skirmishes, General Johnston's forces retreated from the battlefield on the night of the 21st of March.

Although Confederate General Johnston delayed Sherman minimally at Bentonville, Sherman's army was able to unite in Goldsboro with General Schofield from New Bern and General Terry's troops from Wilmington, on the 21st of March 1865. Sherman's army covered 425 miles from Savannah in just 50 days, a tribute to the engineers and the pioneering forces. Also, the enlisted pioneer force of ex-slaves totaled over eleven hundred men, with over two hundred more recruits acquired in North Carolina.

General Sherman had now enlisted an adequate number of ex-slaves in the pioneer regiment to form a United States Colored Troop. Every one of them was required to be physically examined to qualify them for voluntary enlistment into a newly formed USCT. On March 27th, 1865, with physicals being completed, the 135th United States Colored Troop was formed in Goldsboro, North Carolina from the volunteered ex-slaves. The 135th USCT was formed with well over 1,100 men and their Commanding Officer was Colonel John E. Gurley. The unit was formed into ten companies and the able-bodied pioneers were encouraged to enlist in the service of the United States and to contribute their share towards maintaining their own freedom. Of interest is the following background information regarding Colonel Gurley from the record of the 22nd of March 1864:

"During the night and forenoon of the 22nd reports came in of noises, as of marching armies, heard in the woods and brush to the south and east. General Giles A. Smith, who commanded, did not believe it could be infantry, and that officer was considerably nettled over these reports. Finally, he sent Captain Gurley to make an examination and report. That officer did so; and, hearing the infantry marching in the woods, yet not seeing them, he mounted his horse, and, riding back to his command, ordered two regiments who lay to the east of the main body of the division into line of battle, ready to receive the enemy. He did this on his own motion, without orders from the general commanding. When he reached headquarters, the General and residue of the staff were mounted. He reported, "infantry in large numbers, and will be upon you in a few minutes." This the General did not believe, but felt sure it must be cavalry, and was quite angry when his attention was called to the fact that two of his regiments were falling into line of battle in obedience to a command from his subordinate officer, not directed by himself, and, turning to Captain Gurley, he said, "Captain, if they are infantry, you are all right, if not, you are a ruined man."

The General was afraid his military record might be injured by showing so much concern over cavalry, but the question was soon settled, as the enemy emerged from the brush and charged in the rear of the division, coming on double quick, several columns deep, filling the air with deadly missiles and that rebel yell. Turning to the General, Captain Gurley said, "Are they infantry?" To which he replied, "Yes, Captain, and lots of them; go take command of those two regiments, lead them into the fight, check the enemy for a few minutes, till I get our men in line, then fall back to the main body." Captain Gurley executed this order in the face of an overpowering foe and galling fire, then fell back as directed and fought with his comrades till night, maintaining their ground.

He lost one or two horses, shot from under him during the battle. For this act of ordering those regiments into line of battle, he, of course, received a court martial, but, as it was the means which saved the division from surprise and, doubtless, great loss of life, he was promoted to the rank of Colonel of the 135th United States Colored Troop Regiment as a reward of merit, in which capacity he served till the close of the war, marching from Atlanta to the sea, then to Washington, and back to Louisville, Kentucky, where he was mustered out in October of 1865." (from Find a Grave Col. John Gurley, memorial I.D. 34024896, 24 April 1838 - 2 April 1869).

Therefore, it can be said that his "reward" for his court martial was his promotion from Captain to Colonel and being given the command of a **United States Colored Troop.**

The toll that the war took on the soldiers is evidenced here in that "Colonel John E. Gurley, at the close of the war, returned to the practice of law at Platteville, Grant County, Wisconsin, forming a co-partnership with Paine & Carter, an established law firm in that town. Colonel Gurley was especially gifted as an advocate and orator, a man of great generosity, and he had many admirers. In the summer of 1868, he took a severe cold, and the effects of his army life consummated his demise, which occurred April 2nd, 1869, aged 30 years, unmarried."

Under the command of Colonial Gurley, in Goldsboro, North Carolina, the 135th USCT was incorporated as a regiment in General Sherman's Army. After spending several weeks in Goldsboro, the next route of march took the army to Raleigh, North Carolina, and the 135th USCT was camped out in tents at Page Station. At that point, in April of 1865, General Lee's Army was defeated, and he surrendered on April 9th, 1865, to General Grant. The larger southeastern force of General Johnston's army surrendered to General Sherman on the 26th of April 1865 at Bennett Place farm and homestead in Durham, North Carolina. Following General Johnston's surrender, and the Civil War being over, General Sherman's Army departed Raleigh on the 29th of April and moved north to Petersburg where several of the pension records indicated skirmishes occurring and a few of the men in the 135th USCT made a claim of battle injuries, one being shot in the head and another in the arm and leg. From there the march to Washington, D.C. continued, taking a good part of the Month of May. The army passed through Petersburg and two days later they reached Manchester which was on the south side of the James River.

Crossing the river and into Richmond Virginia, where many historic events took place, was their next point of the march, knowing full well their ultimate destination was the nation's capital. The army crossed the Pamunkey and Mattaponi Rivers and on through Fredericksburg and camped near the Rappahannock River. Following a short rest, the army moved northward and on into Alexandria covering a full three hundred miles in twenty days, arriving there on the 19th of May.

Rendering of Gen. Joseph Johnston surrendering to Gen. William T. Sherman at the Bennitt house. Originally printed in Harper's Weekly. Courtesy of the N.C. Office of Archives and History.

With the ultimate goal of reaching the nation's capital, Sherman's Army could celebrate by taking a break from the march for several days. On the 23rd of May General Grant's Army passed in review in front of the White House in Washington, D.C. That same night General Sherman's Army crossed the bridge from Alexandria and set up camp just before entering the streets of Pennsylvania Avenue. The following day they took their turn celebrating a pass in review in front of the President of the United States on the reviewing stand accompanied by General Grant and General Sherman. At nine o'clock the morning of the 24th of May 1865, the march down Pennsylvania Avenue began at the sound of a cannon shot. Although buried in history Sherman's Army of over sixty thousand soldiers along with the support wagons included the 135th UNITED STATES COLORED TROOP marching under their own flag as a regiment in the Army of the United States. We are told this in the many pension records reviewed and on file at the National Archives in Washington, D.C. This is also spelled out in the general orders for Order of March for the 24th of May 1865.

Clearly, the parade march through the capital and in front of the President of the United States was memorable for the men of the 135th USCT as mentioned so many times in their pension records. Following the march down Pennsylvania Avenue, the 135th USCT was sent out to camp at Fort Kearney to be on guard at one of the numerous forts surrounding the capital. They remained there for a couple of weeks prior to heading off to their next duty station which was Louisville, Kentucky. Their trip to Louisville took part not by marching, as they had done for so long, but by rail and boat. They departed Washington on the Baltimore & Ohio Railway to Parkersburg, West Virginia. Due to so many troops traveling they were put on flat cars, in box cars, and some in coach cars. At Parkersburg, and on the Ohio River, the troops were loaded onto river boats and barges on the next leg of their journey to Louisville. For many, this was their last leg prior to mustering out and returning home.

From the pension records of the men of the 135th USCT, we learned that while in Louisville and after being encamped for several weeks they were housed at Taylor Barracks. Some were assigned guard duty in and around Louisville, across the river in New Albany, in Jeffersonville, Indiana, and in Shepherdsville Kentucky.

Toward the end of October, it finally came time for the men of the 135th United States Colored Troop to muster out of service. On the 23rd day of October in the year 1865 the 135th USCT was mustered out of service, they received their final pay and were put on rail cars by their officers and sent on their way home. That, for many, was the beginning of a new life for those freemen who had honorably volunteered their service to the country.

Now that we have developed a snapshot of General William T. Sherman's "March to the Sea" and his "Carolina campaign," let us focus on some of the makeup of the 135th United States Colored Troop. Who were these men and what were their backgrounds? What are some of their stories and how do we know about them?

A good deal of research has been done at the National Archives in Washington, D.C., scouring through the pension records of the men of the 135th USCT. We also took on the task of searching for pictures of the recruits and officers of the men and have searched for their headstones. We were more successful in the headstone search than we were with locating pictures of the men however we were able to find a good many pictures of the men and have been able to locate many more of their headstones.

Just as an example, one of the men we have been able to document is Pvt. Holloway Crockett of Company "B" 135th USCT. Private Crockett was a civil war veteran from McDonough Georgia which is just south of Atlanta. Pvt. Crockett states in his pension record that he enlisted in Sherman's pioneer corps on the march between Atlanta to Macon Georgia on Sherman's "March to the Sea." That being the case he would have been one of the very first ex slaves to enlist in the Pioneer Corps later to become the 135th USCT. In his pension file, Holloway Crockett's death certificate shows that he was about 80 years old when he died on November 18, 1928, which would put his birth year at around 1848, making him about seventeen when he volunteered as a pioneer. We are fortunate enough to have two pictures of this veteran, we have a copy of his pension record, and we located his headstone and have a picture of that. As a footnote, we carry small American flags in our car and as we find the headstones of the men of the 135th USCT we place one of the flags for them in tribute.

Private Holloway Crockett, Veteran, 135th United States Colored Troop

In documenting the history of the 135th USCT we feel that the more intriguing aspect of the story of this unique Colored Troop was information from the many pension files of the men which are archived in Washington D.C. The unit had the difficult task of forging a path through harsh enemy territory which was why they faced unique challenges while constructing routes as well as foraging for resources. Despite such daunting obstacles, the 135th USCT showed exemplary determination and the desire for freedom, carving a name into history from their files. The records tell the story of these men, in their own words, and are documents preserved in time with stories yet unknown. You will find the most interesting accounts and facts about these freedom seekers in the coming chapters as you will now be exposed to the ***"rest of the story"*** directly from the pension records of these men and their lost troop.

CHAPTER 2

Journey to find "The Lost Regiment"

After over 30 years in Southern California, working in their careers, Jay retired and we decided to venture out of our comfort zone, we sold our house and moved to eastern North Carolina. Amy spent a couple of years searching for a place of interest to retire in and discovered Goldsboro, a small town with historic homes in need of restoration. One particular house of interest was a two-story Victorian home, in the historic district, that had been condemned several years earlier and was in desperate need of being brought back to life. Following some negotiations with the owner, Preservation North Carolina, Amy, and Jay came to terms with them and purchased the house.

We had to follow the Preservation North Carolina guidelines for historic preservation in renovating and rehabilitating the home. The house still had the original heart pine floors and a total of six fireplaces. We researched the history so that we would be able to bring the house back to its original glory. It took a couple of years to restore the house, and return it back to its beautiful self, and a wonderful addition to the historical community. In 2013 we were able to get a final inspection and we moved in for what we thought would be our retirement home. So, this was our introduction to the City of Goldsboro initially and researching the past in this historic town. You see Amy grew up in Savannah, Georgia surrounded by the history of the Civil War. She thoroughly enjoyed researching her family's genealogy as did Jay. We traveled the world to learn of our family's past. Amy's love of history and Jay being a Navy brat, and their love for travel propelled them down many roads in numerous states and even other countries. To effectively research our genealogy, we had to follow the paper trails. This was the way we found that primary sources were the key to learning the truth. As Amy once said, "remember you cannot change the true facts of the past, but you can only learn from them."

We were drawn to Goldsboro because we had the intrinsic desire to preserve the past and restore a part of history. The City of Goldsboro, along with United States Representative G. K. Butterfield were able to secure a grant to improve the historic district of downtown Goldsboro, to save the past with updates to the original downtown, which was complete with old buildings built in the late 1800's to the 1920's. It was done in phases over several years and was a considerable improvement to the downtown. The people that had grown up in the past had not been downtown center street in years. They now stroll through the greenbelt telling stories of their childhood, remembering shopping for Christmas presents and food for the holidays, and the annual buying of a new car at the corner of Center street and Mulberry. Recalling the next street over is where all the doctors' and lawyers' offices which were remarkably close to the beautiful courthouse.

Unfortunately, the grant monies to improve the downtown did not include the historic residential area. However, we did our part, in a grassroots effort, to improve the downtown residential portion of the historic district. This was something that we were very proud to do and did at great personal expense. We brought back to life the D.W. Davis house and it is once again part of the community.

Of interest in Goldsboro is that they love to honor their veterans. They have a veteran's park where the American flag flies and on Veterans Day, a ceremony is held, and a wreath laid in the park in honor of those lost. The beautiful city cemetery on the south side of town is well maintained and has gravestones that are marked from the early 1700's. The cemetery is just full of ancestors that tell stories of the past. Among the graves and headstones is an exceptionally large Confederate Monument where there is a mass burial mound where about eight hundred union and confederate soldiers.

There was another point of interest on center street, is an Oak tree that is dedicated to a POW from the Vietnam War. To save the tree, the roundabout was redesigned. The city of Goldsboro is prideful of its past and honors its Veterans. Our fathers were both in the Navy during World War II and both served in the south pacific. Jay served in the Army and was a pilot in the Vietnam War and Amy has found that her genealogy proves her ancestors served in the Revolutionary War. Amy's heart is filled with pride for all the veterans in the family that have served in the military.

Goldsboro is also home to the Wayne County Museum which we became affiliated with due to our love of history. It was one way we were able to learn the history of the town that we became invested in. The museum is dedicated to the history of the area and especially of Civil War history. On one occasion we attended a lecture and introduction to the history of the United States Colored Troops in the Civil War. It was told by a descendant of a colored civil war soldier and sponsored by the Wayne County Museum. Following the lecture, we were informed of the fact there was a United States Colored Troop formed in Goldsboro, in General William T. Sherman's Army and it was the 135th USCT. The librarian said that no one knew anything about it, and he would like to have pictures of the soldiers. This piqued our curiosity due to our love of history and experience in genealogy and research. We immediately said we would find them, and decided to take on the challenge

Our research on the 135th United States Colored Troop began in earnest by getting on the computer and doing a google search of the Regiment. We found that someone had put together a brief list of men that were in the 135th USCT and who were from North and South Carolina. We are now hooked on finding out about these men and solving the 150-year-old mystery. We started in Goldsboro, but not so fast, it's not that easy.

Since the 135th USCT was a unit formed in Goldsboro, North Carolina we felt Goldsboro would be a good place to begin our search. We discovered that the main cemetery in Goldsboro, Willow Dale Cemetery, had very few African Americans buried there. The primary cemetery for the Black population was the Elmwood Cemetery located on the outskirts of town and in the floodplain of the Neuse River. It is known that, whenever the Neuse River overflows its banks and floods the cemetery, caskets float to the surface. Also, many of the headstones in the cemetery have gone missing over the years. We found that the difference between the two cemeteries' (the one primarily for white people and the one for the Black people) is quite noticeable. That did not deter us from pursuing our research into the 135th USCT.

As we began our research into the 135th USCT we found it to be slow and arduous. We were not able to find much on the unit, even after searching through the library in town, and to our dismay it became more difficult than expected. First, we thought it would be fairly simple to locate some pictures of the soldiers of the 135th USCT, however that was not the case. Not one picture could be found. We began doing some genealogy of the men and we found that some had death certificates. The death certificates led to burial locations, so we started a search for headstones. This was also an arduous task as some of the burial locations could not be found.

There was a list of just over one hundred names of men who were in the 135th USCT that we were able to find on the internet. The list had the states the men came from and listed their ages, and most were from North Carolina. That being the case, it appeared that the Regiment was made up of North Carolina boys. Many questions needed to be answered.

We began searching out some of the names on the list of over one hundred. We were able to find one family, related to Jack Sherrod, who was a soldier in the 135th USCT. BINGO' the descendant was Paul Sherrod who lived in the Goldsboro area. In digging a little deeper into the soldiers' life we found that Jack Sherrod had a pension record, and it was located at the National Archives in Washington, D.C. To view the pension, we had to make the trip to the National Archives.

Here is where it got interesting as not just anyone can get into the National Archives and view the records there. The building is located on Pennsylvania Avenue in Washington, D.C. not far from the White House. To gain access requires a pass and one must review the necessary instructions, guidelines, rules and take a short test to receive their pass. This is done at a different location which is in Maryland and not at the Archives.

The National Archives opens at 8:00 am and there is a security guard on the outside of the building one must pass prior to entry. Once inside you must sign in and show your pass and if there prior to 8:00 am you can wait on a bench before they start letting people in. Everyone who enters after signing in MUST go through a metal detector, be screened by a guard, and pass their belongings through an x-ray machine. Once in, and if you are doing research you go to the room where the research is started, sign in, fill out all the necessary forms for who you are doing research on and submit them to the clerk. The forms are checked for accuracy and every hour the collected forms are sent to the archivists whose responsibility it is to pull the needed file or files. The process of doing this takes a couple of hours therefore there is a waiting period and research normally does not begin until after 10:00 am however, it took longer so our file was not pulled before 1:00 pm.

The actual viewing of the record is done in a room on the second floor. Waiting for the pension file was the hardest thing to do, but finally, our name was called to the pickup counter. After signing and dating the form we could sit down and read it carefully. No one in the room speaks and you can hear a pin drop. There are rules for touching the file, and a person watches over us like a nun with her ruler in hand. However, being able to hold the file reveals it was worth all the work and time to get there. It's a time capsule of the soldier's life in his own words.

Jack Sherrod had an interesting pension record and being the first one that we were able to open made it even more enlightening. The depositions in his record told the story of his time in the 135th USCT, it told of his wife and family, and where he lived. The file had depositions from several other people in his file and from other soldiers also. The most fascinating aspect of that pension file was finding an actual picture of Jack Sherrod. The picture had been taken years later, after his service, and as justification for him to receive a pension. It was quite compelling.

As we reviewed the pension record of Jack Sherrod, we began to wonder how many more of the men of the 135th USCT had a pension record. We decided to ask the archivist if they had any regimental records for the 135th USCT. After filling out the necessary paperwork for the clerk to do a search of the archives, the regimental rolls of the 135th USCT were subsequently produced. This original document listed all the men of the 135th USCT, by company, and by rank to include the officers and men of the unit and where they were from, and showing they were enlisted in Goldsboro, North Carolina on March 27, 1865. It showed about 250 men were from Georgia, about 600 from South Carolina and about 240 from North Carolina. These were the privates, who were ex-slaves, and who were recruited into the pioneer corps in Sherman's Army.

After the trip to Washington, DC and seeing the complexity of the task at hand to research the 135th USCT we enlisted the help of Margaret Oman, a genealogist from Omaha, Nebraska. She was able to put together an excel spreadsheet, listing all the men of the 135th USCT, with some of their vital information to include if they had submitted for a pension. This document turned out to be a main reference source relied upon for their years of research into the soldiers. As a matter of interest, and after over eight years we have been able to find and copy the pension records of over four hundred of the soldiers of the 135th USCT.

Researching through genealogy, family trees, and cemetery records, along with Find a Grave, and online, we found these sources to be extraordinarily successful tools looking into the men of the 135th USCT and discovering their families. We were able to actually find about one hundred and fifty descendant families of the soldiers, who had no idea their ancestor was a soldier in the Union Army in the Civil war, much less a soldier in the 135th United States Colored Troop.

Continuing with our research, we made numerous trips to Washington, D.C., and the National Archives. On one of our earlier trips, we found out about the African American Civil War Museum which was related to our subject of research. We were shown around the museum and met the reenactors and eventually met the director, Dr. Frank Smith, a good man from Georgia who was instrumental in putting the museum together. At the museum we noticed that they had just had their 20-year anniversary and on the very cover of the anniversary booklet, toward the bottom, it stated that there were no African American troops allowed to march in the grand review. This was an interesting declaration.

The research into the 135th USCT was becoming quite involved very quickly. We were finding ancestors and having discussions with them. We decided to form a non-profit organization so that we could continue with our extensive research. That being said, we started the 135th USCT Research Team, Inc. in 2016. Jay and Amy Bauer led the team, and Ms. Deborah Jones, a descendant of one of the soldiers, became a founding member.

At the library, we formed a Genealogical Study Group working on finding descendants of these soldiers. There is a question for the soldiers that have the same name, are they related by blood or by name? If he was a slave on a large plantation, his name would be the same. Is he blood related or is he just using the same slave owner's name? We all met for several years and found dozens of families and now are good friends. Each question compels us to keep looking for answers and we were determined to uncover the whole story and share with everyone this period of American history that was covered up. Does the public know the "GUTS" it took to join the Pioneer Corps and the 135th USCT, and the valor it took to finish the job given to them? They helped reunite the country and free their families.

As an educational event of the 135th USCT, we decided to hold a Living History Weekend in Goldsboro. The weekend held in 2018 included a symposium with experts on black civil war history and emancipation, and the 135th USCT in their own words. There was a pop-up museum downtown, an encampment in a large open field downtown with reenactors from the 35th USCT, 37th USCT, 135th USCT, and Battery-"B" 2nd Regiment USCT Light Artillery, who brought their cannon. Two rounds fired from the cannon on Saturday was quite a wakeup call. There was also a musical presentation on Friday evening, held at the Paramount theater, that featured the "Freedom Seekers Heritage Chorale," all descendants of slaves. On Saturday night a sold-out dinner that featured expert Hari Jones as the keynote speaker who was the highlight of the evening and weekend. Hari Jones was a writer, lecturer, historian, curator, motivational speaker, and the assistant director of the African American Civil War Museum who worked in conjunction with Dr. Frank Smith. Hari's talk was about the importance of the United States Colored Troops in the Civil War. The entire weekend was a complete success and brought a good deal of interest exposing the 135th USCT to Eastern North Carolina.

After the successful Living History weekend, we continued our extensive exploration into the 135th USCT. Our research continued all over the south, including Georgia, South Carolina, and North Carolina. We visited the North Carolina Museum of History in Raleigh where we met Earl Ijames, a curator, and a Black soldier historian. We told Earl we were doing research on the 135th USCT and wanted to pick his brain about the Regiment. Earl said we must mean the 35th USCT as he was not familiar with the 135th USCT. In time he ended up discovering there was a 135th USCT and after further meeting with him he turned out to give the unit more of his attention and has since been a valuable source of information. Earl was then welcomed to be on the Board of Advisors of the 135th USCT Research Team, Inc. The Board of Advisors is made up of professors and historians of the United States Colored Troops and the Civil War.

Over the years of researching the 135th USCT and the many trips to the National Archives, traveling all over the south we have been able to collect mountains of records to validate this Regiment. Of the many collectables discovered are the over ninety headstones of the men of the 135th USCT, all of which are pictured in this book. Jay searched many fields and backwoods to locate some of the headstones. Another of the discoveries is of the pictures of the men of the 135th USCT, the collection of which is also in this book. One of the pictures is a copy of an actual tin type that was in one of the pension records at the National Archives. The Archivists had no idea the picture was in the file as it was still inside of an envelope in the middle of the file from the 1920's.

As stated previously we have been able to copy and research over four hundred pension records of the men of the 135th USCT. The records tell the stories of the soldiers, how and when they joined up with Sherman's Army and what they experienced. It tells how most were initially put into the Pioneer Corps, and how they worked alongside the white Pioneers and Engineers building corduroy roads and repairing and building bridges. They were attached to different companies as they joined and never complained of the hard work or the long march.

One of the critical issues was to prove the men were not contraband or camp followers but they were recruited and enlisted into Sherman's Army. One weekend in Charleston, we went to Charleston College looking for more information and talked to the librarian who proclaimed that, "no Black soldiers ever marched with Sherman's army." She knew because she had written two books about Sherman. However, she came back to us a little bit later and told us that she found the original recruitment records out in Pasadena California at the Huntington Library. Well, God is on our side. This proves that they were regular soldiers, not just contraband. We flew to California and worked to get into the Huntington library and held the original recruitment contracts in our hands for Company, "I." The records have been in the library since 1959 after being in a trunk for years. This was a significant find and we were able to obtain copies of the documents. We feel we are now starting to put the bits and pieces together.

The records revealed that once General Sherman reached Goldsboro, North Carolina he had recruited a sufficient number of pioneers where he could form the 135th United States Colored Troop. At that point, the men tell of how they were stripped "naked," examined and if they passed the physical, they were placed in the company. The men revealed in their depositions how once enlisted in the 135th USCT, and after raising their right hand and taking the oath of service just as in today's army, they were able to discard their picks and shovels, were given their blue uniforms with the brass buttons and they began to drill and drill.

Of interest, and in a good many of the soldiers' depositions, they mention how they marched to Washington, D.C., at the end of the war. They camped prior to reaching the city and on March 24, 1865, the 135th USCT marched, through the city, in the Grand Parade, and in front of the President of the United States. They also mention how after that, they performed guard duty just outside the city for a couple of weeks and then rode on a train and then a boat to Louisville, Kentucky. There they performed guard duty, they had weapons, and performed other tasks before being mustered out on October 23, 1865. From there they had to find their way home. Most took the train however it only went as far as Augusta, Georgia and then they had to find their way home.

In 2022 a descendant (Cindy Pratt,) of one of the junior officers emailed our website. She informed us that, in a trunk in her grandmother's attic, she found a diary from Lieutenant John Auman, of Company "K," of the 135th USCT. The diary was written during his time in General Sherman's Army and included a good deal of information. In his diary it's stated that "we camped in the city of Savannah a few days, then moved down the river nine miles; here we started to organize our colored men into a Pioneer regiment, but we were not long at this camp to complete it. Captain John H. Davis of the Pioneer Corps was to be Colonel. On the 10th of January 1865, we moved to Beaufort, SC. While in camp here, John E. Gurley was sent to take command of our proposed pioneer regiment as Colonel. He reorganized the regiment. I was assigned first lieutenant of Company "A," but marching orders again interfered with perfecting the organization. We came to Thunderbolt Camp on the Savannah River to Beaufort, on an ocean steamer, which was a new experience for me, we were out 12 hours which was all I could stand without losing my breakfast." Cindy informed us she not only had Lieutenant Auman's diary but also his sword and scabbard. Pictures of these items are in the Apex of the book.

There are two other books written by members of the General Staff who also confirm the contents of Lieutenant Auman's diary. As General Sherman's Army left Beaufort, they began to recruit over six hundred freed Black slaves into the pioneer corps. The recruits would all tell the General, "the falsehoods of the rebels, and the papers never deceived them, but they believed that his 'retreat' was a victory; That they would serve the Union cause in any and all ways that they could, as soldiers, as drivers or pioneers."

"Indeed, the faith, earnestness, and heroism of the Black man is one of the greatest developments of this war." from the diary of Major General George Ward Nicholson 1866. The pension records from these soldiers and their widows are informative as to what camp life was like in the pioneer corps and the 135th USCT. The depositions go into the routes they took, and how bad the weather was in the winter in South Carolina. By the time they reached Goldsboro, many didn't have shoes anymore and their pants were ragged and there was no headgear to shade them from the warm spring weather in North Carolina. General Howard, of the right wing of the 17th Army Corps, quoted "South Carolina is a step into the jaws of destruction." At The first heavy skirmish at Rivers Bridge, they left behind three guns and had lost ten men. The first battle at the Salkehatchie swamp included the men of the 135th Pioneer Corps.

This project is a pragmatic tribute to those unwavering spirits in the face of the harsh realities of the Pioneer Corps and the 135th Regiment. Jay and Amy Bauer are sharing the story, the honor, and the sacrifices that in most cases followed them for the rest of their lives. They are true patriots exemplified by their actions. We feel it is a heartfelt honor to bring to light the struggles it took to find the truth about this Black regiment, which no one knew was part of General Sherman's army. After the dredge through Georgia and the Carolinas, the frozen winter, the pioneers became a regular Regiment in Goldsboro, North Carolina. They marched double time through Virginia mopping up at the end of the war. It was then found the 135th USCT was the only black regiment to march down Pennsylvania Avenue, on May 24th, 1865, in the Grand Review. They marched in front of the President of the United States at the White House, saluted by General Grant and General Sherman. Jay and Amy are immensely proud of these "Jewels" of the United States Army.

INTRODUCTION TO PENSIONERS

In the next ten chapters, the soldiers and their families unveil, "in their own words," an account of their lives as these ex-slaves become regular soldiers and beyond.

Our hundreds of hours spent at the national archives in Washington D.C. and libraries from coast to coast expose the hundreds of oral depositions that create their pension records. They describe their experiences as Black civil war veterans; they voice the circumstances of their young lives as slaves and their families.

Can you grasp the guts it took to join the pioneer corps in the Yankee army and become the regiment of the 135th United States Colored Troop? Along with the valor and endurance of the march, walking up to a thousand miles from Atlanta, Georgia, to

Washington, D.C., in extreme weather and circumstances of life on their journey to become regular soldiers representing over two hundred thousand Black soldiers in the Grand Review in front of the white house in Washington, D.C. to celebrate the end of the war and slavery. Though their service was not over, moving to Louisville, Kentucky, the home of the army of the west's largest arsenal, they spent months in the surrounding area on guard duty before mustering out.

Within their pension records and military orders, they continue to give their oral accounts of their lives. In applying for a pension which sometimes could take years to complete, due to the unique challenges to prove with a lack of written documentary evidence of their ages, births of their children, and marriages along with their scars of war. They struggle to verify these basic facts. In several of the applications, especially the older veterans, the bureau of pensions would send a special examiner to prove the information in the depositions and affidavits were correct, as some were fraudulent. Also, after 1890, congress dropped the requirement that a veteran of the civil war disability had to be service related.

Each pension record in the 135th USCT gave us another bit and piece of the puzzle in this unique regimental story, which was hidden from the moment they arrived back home, to one hundred and fifty years later when we were told about this exceptional group of ex slaves. No one knew anything about them, not even the North Carolina History Museum or Archives.

After eight years of searching for primary documentation to stay true to their words and experiences of General Sherman's Army, we are able to show the heroism and their common beliefs of family, God, and country for the rest of their lives.

George S. Shaw, the Regimental Chaplain, said "It seems like the good lord has opened the heavens and handed down the answers to my prayers."

There are a few things you need to remember when reading the pension records of the soldiers represented in this book.

They, for the most part, did not read, write, and did not know how to spell.

The applications in the pension records are oral and someone else did the written account of what they told in them.

The length of the process to get a pension is considerable, they lived on a farm outside of town, and they had to find someone who could write up the necessary paperwork, get witnesses, and people to do affidavits to verify who they were. They entered service using their slave owners' names, which made it more difficult to prove they were the soldiers who served in the 135th USCT.

A doctor or examination bureau must approve their injuries or disease, and scars after service up until 1890.

The age of the soldiers when they applied for the pension, in most cases, was between twenty and forty years of age. Later in life, memory comes into play.

So, with all of this said, the collection of pension records tell their stories *"In their own words"* and the way they remembered the experience of being a member of General Sherman's Army and how it affected their lives.

CHAPTER 3

THROUGH THEIR EYES YOU GET TO WITNESS THE HORRORS AND TRIUMPHS OF THESE YOUNG BLACK SOLDIERS THAT STARTED THE CHANGE OF AMERICA.

Greeting The Union Army and Freedom

COMPANY "A"

INCLUDED IN THIS CHAPTER ARE EXTRACTIONS FROM THE PENSION RECORDS OF;

GEORGE W. MASON

ISAAC THOMPSON

ANDREW NEWTON

AMOS WILLIS / COBB

LEWIS PETTIGREW

GEORGE WASHINGTON MASON

George W. Mason, Company "A," 135th United States Colored Troop, was born in Henry County Georgia in 1824. Henry H. Mason, the son of George W. Mason, applied for a pension as the guardian of the younger children. George W. Mason's story starts with the fact that he is the son of his slave owner, Larkin B. Mason. To tell his story you must start in 1889 when George Mason dies and leaves four children under the age of sixteen. Henry Mason, his son, applied for pension support as guardian of the children, along with several other people in the neighborhood such as Charlotte Roberts, who lived in Acworth, Cobb County, Georgia.

George W. Mason married Elmira Lemons, in 1843, in slave time as she was a slave belonging to Abraham Lemons. They had two children, Mariah, born in 1834, who died in 1924, and Wiley, no birth or death date given.

Elmira Lemons and George Mason lived as husband and wife for three years. Elmira Lemons was from Butts County, Georgia, and George Mason was from Henry County, Georgia. They ended up being separated which was brought on by trouble between their owners, Mr. Lemons, and Mr. Larkin

Mason. As a result of the tension between the two owners George was not permitted to visit Elmira any longer.

Wiley Mason was only eight months old when his mother and father were separated. In his written deposition, it is recorded that his father George can read and write and was accused of forging a pass for his brother-in-law. Because of the dispute between the two owners, Mr. Lemons prohibited George from coming into Butts County to see his wife. Mr. Mason, in an attempt to get Elmira and George together, attempted to buy Elmira from Mr. Lemons, however, she would not be sold. From then on, the two of them never lived together again.

Soon after Sherman's army started his March to the Sea the army came upon Henry County and began recruiting colored men for the Pioneer Corps. Among those recruited were George Mason, Livingston Mason, and two other ex-slaves from the Lemon plantation. George then became a soldier in the 135th USCT upon his enlistment in Goldsboro, North Carolina, March 27, 1865.

After being mustered out of service on October 23, 1865, George Mason returned home and married Francis Bradley. The two of them had nine children together during their marriage. Henry, one of the older sons, becomes the guardian of four of the youngest children who were under sixteen years of age.

Worth noting, we found that Larkin B. Mason ended up leaving ninety acres, "more or less," of land in his will to his son, George W. Mason.

PENSION NOV 28 1895 U.S. ... OFFICE

State Georgia } In the matter of the
County Cobb } Application of Henry
W Mason as the guardian of
Leanah, Fannie, and Eddie Mason
minor Children of George W Mason deceased for pension for
said Children and Mrs Charlotte
Robert, Colored a resident of Acworth,
Cobb Co, Ga appeared before me
a Notary Public in & for said
County and State, and on oath
deposes as follows:
My name is Charlotte Robert,
Wife of Jack Robert, I reside
in Acworth Ga & was well
acquainted with George W Mason,
the father of said minor Children during his life, I knew intimately said G W Mason before
and during the war and while
he was a slave, Before the war
said George W Mason married
or lived with a woman whose
name was Elmirah Lemon
in Butts County Ga. At that time
said George W Mason was the
slave of Larkin Mason who lived
in Henry Co Ga, Elmirah Lemon

was the slave of Abraham
Lemon who lived in Ruth.
County. I can not state the
year in which said Mason
and Elmirah Lemon were mar
ried but I know it was before the
war of the Rebellion, in slavery times
The said Elmirah Lemon was
my Cousin, At that time I was
a slave of Larkin Mason and
his mother, and lived with said
George Mason. Said George
Mason was my uncle, Said
George W Mason lived with said
Elmirah Lemon two or three
years, had two Children by her,
They the said Mason and Elmirah
Lemon were separated before
the war, The separation was
brought about by reason
of some trouble between the
said Larkin Mason and Abra
ham Lemon, Said George W Ma
son was not permitted by said
Abraham Lemon to visit his
said wife Elmirah Lemon,
After said George W Mason

and his wife were separated
as before stated he remained
in such state of separation and
single until she married
Francis Bradley in 1864
Affiant further says: the foregoing
affidavit was written by
J J Northcutt Notary Public
Cobb Co Ga in my presence
from my oral statement
just made to him and without
the aid or prompting of any
other person or of any written
or printed statement or recital
I dont know my age but am
between fifty and sixty years
old
Witness and attested by Charlott her x mark Roberts
John. Nichols
W. C. Rainey
I J J Northcutt Notary Public
in & for the County of Cobb and
State of Georgia do hereby certify that the foregoing affidavit
was read to Mrs Charlott Roberts
after having been written by
oral statement from her

General Affidavit.

State of Georgia **, County of** Cobb , **ss:**

In the matter of Emmy W. Mason guardian of Minor Children of Geo W. Mason Company K 138th Regt USC Infty

Personally came before me, a Notary Public in and for aforesaid County and State John O. Mason aged 34 years,

and ________________ aged ____ years,

citizen of the town of Acworth County of Cobb
(Post-office address)

State of Georgia well known to be reputable and entitled to credit, and who being duly sworn, declare in relation to aforesaid case as follows:

(Affiants should state how they gain a knowledge of the facts to which they testify.)

I am the son of Frances Bradly and was living with my said mother at the time of her marriage with said George W. Mason and at the birth of the Minor Children of said George W. Mason to wit, Leanah, Fannie and Eddie Mason. Frances Mason wife of said George W. Mason, died in presence of Affiant on the 16th day of March 188[illegible] at Acworth Ga. Said George W. Mason died in presence of Affiant at Acworth Ga on Dec 24th 1894, and from the time of the death of his said wife, Frances Mason, he remained single until his death. The precise date of the birth of said Minor Children was recorded at time of birth in the family bible, but said record was destroyed by [illegible] the children [illegible] in 1890. Affiant was living with said Frances & George W. Mason at the time of the birth of each of said Minor Children and knows the date of said births. Leanah Mason was born Aug 13th 188[illegible]. Fannie Mason was born March 1st 1884 and Eddie Mason was born May 14th 1886. The record of said births in said family bible does not now exist but affiant knows from memory the dates of said births. Said George W. Mason left one other minor child by his said wife Frances Bradly Mason under the age of sixteen years surviving him at the time of his death to wit, Lizzie Mason, she was born Aug 23rd 1880 but at the time of death of said Geo W. Mason said Lizzie Mason was living away from her father [illegible] and has been ever since maintaining herself. Said Lizzie Mason has no guardian. Said Geo W. Mason left no other children under sixteen years old at the time of his death, [illegible]. The foregoing affidavit was written by [illegible] Notary Public in my presence from my own statements [illegible] not aided or prompted by any other person or by any written or printed statement or evidence. All of said Minor Children are now living.

I further declare that I have no interest in said case, and am not concerned in its prosecution.

John O. Mason
Signature of Affiants.

NOTE.—In the execution of papers and evidence whenever a person or witness signs by mark (X), two persons who can write must attest the signature by signing their names opposite.
The official before whom papers are executed is *not a competent witness to a mark*.

DEPOSITION

Case of Henry H. Mason, No. 633.734

On this 13 day of December, 1898, at Acworth, county of Cobb, State of Ga, before me, A. B. Pooley, a special examiner of the Bureau of Pensions, personally appeared Wiley Mason, who, being by me first duly sworn to answer truly all interrogatories propounded to him during this special examination of aforesaid claim for pension, deposes and says:

I am 41 years of age, on 12th of next Jan; my post-office address is 1544 East Rock Street, Chattanooga, Tenn.

Occupation carpenter.

The claimant, Henry H. Mason, is said to be my half brother.

I am a son of George W. Mason by his first wife, Elmira Lemon. My father and mother were married years before freedom and had each other as slave man and wife for 8 or 10 years. They had two children, April older than I and myself. My mother belonged to Abraham Lemons of Butts Co. Ga.

When I was eight months old my father and mother were prohibited from having anything more to do with each other. My father was able to write and he was accused of writing a pass for his brother in law and he was prohibited from coming into the County (Butts) where my mother lived.

My father's master tried to buy my mother but Mr. Lemons refused to sell her to him.

After my father and mother were separated they never lived together again.

Page 1 Deposition 8

Some time after my father and mother were parted my father had a woman named Mary Wilson by whom he had one child. I'm not sure he ever claimed Mary as his wife. If so it was only a slave marriage and they had each other but a short time and were separated before freedom.

Some time during the war and before freedom my father and Frances Bradley were married and lived together until Frances died. About four years after freedom I went to live with my father and lived with him about a year. He was then living in Hampton Co. with Frances, and they had two or three children. Shortly after my mother and father were separated my mother married John Young with whom she is yet living near Hampton, Hampton Co. S.C.

Mary Wilson died in Campbell County many years ago but since freedom. Father never lived with her after freedom. I heard that. Father died about four years ago this Christmas. Frances died about 10 years ago. Father did not marry again after death of Frances.

Lizzie, Lexie, Fannie and Ed. were my father's youngest children. They were the only children under 16 years of age at the time of my father's death. I do not know dates of birth of children. They are all of record in the family Bible I think. [illegible] I have heard read the foregoing and the same is correct.

Wiley Mason

Deponent.

Sworn to and subscribed before me this 13 day of December, 1898, and I certify that the contents were fully made known to deponent before signing.

A. B. Pottle

Special Examiner.

94

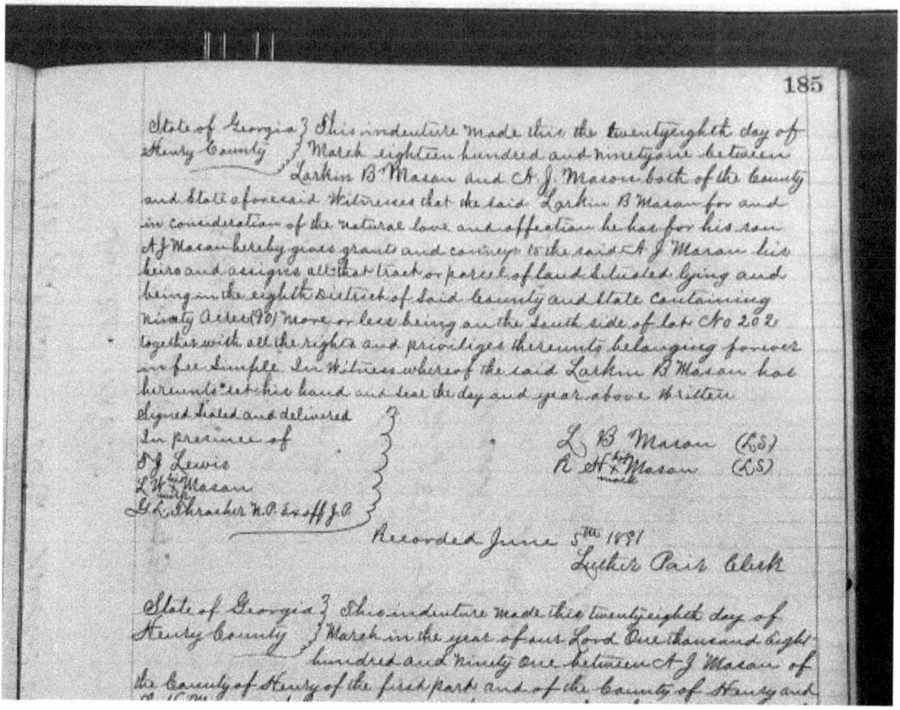

185

State of Georgia } This indenture made this the twentyeighth day of
Henry County } March eighteen hundred and ninetyone between
Larkin B Mason and A J Mason both of the County
and State aforesaid Witnesses that the said Larkin B Mason for and
in consideration of the natural love and affection he has for his son
A J Mason hereby gives grants and conveys to the said A J Mason his
heirs and assigns all that tract or parcel of land situated lying and
being in the eighth District of said County and State containing
ninety acres (90) more or less being on the South side of lot No 202
together with all the rights and privileges thereunto belonging forever
in fee Simple In Witness whereof the said Larkin B Mason has
hereunto set his hand and seal the day and year above written

Signed sealed and delivered
In presence of
S J Lewis
L W his mark Mason
G L Thrasher N.P. Ex off J.P.

L B Mason (L.S)
R H her mark Mason (L.S)

Recorded June 5th 1891
Luther Pair Clerk

State of Georgia } This indenture made this twentyeighth day of
Henry County } March in the year of our Lord One thousand Eight
hundred and Ninety One between A J Mason of
the County of Henry of the first part and of the County of Henry and

1859

RUNAWAY.

I WILL pay a reasonable reward to any person for the apprehension and delivery, in any safe jail where I can get him, of my Negro man, GEORGE, who left my plantation in Henry county, on the 25th of last month. Said Negro had on, when he left, a gray blanket overcoat, blue dress coat, black pants, black satin vest, black hat, and silver watch. He weighs about one hundred and sixty or one hundred and seventy pounds, five feet ten or eleven inches high, tolerable bright mulatto, straight hair, quick spoken. He is also left handed; aged about thirty five years, can read and write very well. I think that he will try to get to a free State. Any information in reference to said negro will be thankfully received. My address is Worthville, Butts county, Georgia.

jan11 c2m L. B. MASON.

ISAAC THOMPSON / FAISON

In his pension record it was noted that Isaac Thompson (also Isaac Faison) was just eighteen when he left behind his home to enlist in the 135th United States Colored Troop. Before joining Sherman's army, Isaac was a slave on the plantation of Curtis Thompson in Sampson County, North Carolina. He made his way to Wake County, North Carolina, where he enlisted on March 27, 1865, and then spent a few weeks at Goldsboro, North Carolina, before being mustered into the infantry as the Civil War was reaching its end. In April of 1865, Isaac was stationed at Neuse River, North Carolina, and then moved on to Ft. Kearney near Washington, D.C., in May and stayed through June. After Lee's surrender at Appomattox Courthouse in April of the same year, many troops were mustered out of their companies, with Isaac's honorable discharge happening on October 23, 1865.

Isaac was born and raised in Sampson County, North Carolina, on Mr. Curtis Thompson's farm. As a slave, Isaac adopted his master's last name, but following emancipation, he changed his last name to "Faison," the name of his slave father. Curtis Thompson, an old man at the time, was the first cousin to Thomas I. Faison. Thomas I. Faison was first cousin to William A. Faison, whose son Joseph F. Faison provided written testimony for Isaac Thomspon/Faison's pension file. Joseph recalled that before the Civil War, his father owned about a hundred slaves while his father's cousin, Thomas owned about two hundred slaves; Curtis Thompson also owned about a hundred slaves, and one, Joseph recalls, was an old man named Isaac who had children and lived there with his master even after the war for many years.

Joseph went on to recall a time when Sherman's army camped on Curtis Thompson's land on their way to Goldsboro, North Carolina. Isaac also recalled this story in his pension records:

"Some Yankee soldiers came by our place. They were all on horses and had guns and they had a mule cart with provisions which they had foraged, and they had a colored man driving the mule. They spent the night at my master's place my master was gone, but his wife, Virginia Thompson was there and the next morning they put me on this cart to drive the mule and let the other nigger go. I went with them, and they took me to Goldsboro, and there I was placed in Co. A 135th Pioneer Corps. It was called "Pioneer Corps" when I first went to the company and it kept that name till we were mustered in at some place near Raleigh, Wake County over three weeks after I joined the company."

Isaac told of how they camped in the woods and worked the roads, making corduroy roads for the wagons to travel until they were mustered in. They traveled from Raleigh, North Carolina, to Washington, D.C., stopping at Manchester before marching straight through Richmond and on to Washington, D.C. They marched through Washington to Ft. Kearney, just on the other side of the Capital. After spending about three weeks at Ft. Kearney they were placed on railway flat cars and taken to Parkersburg, West Virginia. In Parkersburg, they boarded boats to travel down the Ohio River and on to Louisville, Kentucky.

When Isaac was being interviewed for his pension file, he was asked and documented numerous questions about members of his outfit. In his statements, he can name those who deserted, those who had gotten sick, the men who died, and the names of his Sergeants and Officers. He clearly remembers his Colonel, John Gurley, Major Dixon, and several Sergeants. He spent the entire time of his enlistment with his Company, holding the rank of Private, with no unauthorized absence, desertion, or confinement listed in his records.

Isaac remembered that when he was mustered out in Louisville, Kentucky, he was given a discharge certificate and $72.50 "in money." He used that money to return directly to Sampson County, North Carolina, and his old master's home – he "rode part way and walked part way." Isaac remained on the Thompson homestead, working for Curtis Thompson and later his son William Thompson until the turn of the century. His reason for leaving was that "the white folks got to doing so bad I had to get away." Bands of white men were harassing the men who served in the Union Army to the point of beating and even shooting them. Isaac recalled being met by them one night as he was leaving, but after threatening to shoot him and taking his discharge certificate, the men let him go. From there, Isaac went to Edgecombe County, North Carolina, where he remained for the rest of his life.

Issac Thompson's pension record provides extensive details about his Company more than most including the officers, the men who died, the travel route of the Company, and, interestingly, the names of other men who also received pensions.

Case of Isaac Faison alias Isaac Thompson No. [illegible]

On this 10 day of November, 1921, at Tarboro county of Edgecombe, State of N. C. before me, H. A. Hales, a field examiner of the Bureau of Pensions, personally appeared Isaac Faison, who, being by me first duly sworn to answer truly all interrogatories propounded to him during this special examination of aforesaid claim for pension, deposes and says:

According to the information furnished me by my old master I was born on August 15, 1840, so I am now in my 82nd year.

My occupation has always been farmer and farm laborer.

P.O. address: Route #3, Tarboro, N.C.

I was born and raised in Sampson County North Carolina between Warsaw and Clinton, was about two (2) miles from Turkey, N.C. My mother was named Jane and she belonged to Curtis Thompson, and my father was named Guy and he belonged to Thomas Faison. These two men - Thompson and Faison - lived three miles apart. My old master was Curtis Thompson, I never belonged to Faison, but after I was discharged from the army and went back home I took the name of my father who was still living. Up to the time I enlisted and during the time I was in the army I was always called Isaac Thompson, never had been known or called by any other name, never was called by any nick name, just Isaac Thompson till after my discharge and then I took my father's name and since then have been known as Isaac Faison and have been known only by that name. I do not know when my mother died, I just barely remember having a mother and knowing her name. I had a brother named Peter Thompson who served in the same Regiment with me, but in a different company, he was in Co. B. Peter was the oldest one of my mother's children. My mother had 11 children and there were two younger than I was. One sister named Mariah who married Tom Davis in Sampson Co., N.C. but I do not know whether she is living, I have not seen her since I left Sampson County in 1866. One sister named Rachel who married Alfred Hines in New Hanover Co., N.C., have not seen her since 1866, do not know whether she is living or not. Do not know what her P.O. address was. Another sister Catherine who was not married when I left Sampson Co. I have not seen or heard from any of my relatives sine I left there in 1866. I had another brother named Wright Thompson who also served in the army in a Cavalry regiment but I do not

Page 4 Deposition A [illegible]

know the company or regiment. This brother immigrated from these parts in 18[illegible] and went to some of the Southern States and I have never seen him since. All the other children died before the war.

[illegible] OF SERVICE. At the time the civil war broke out I was living in [illegible] County, N.C. with my old master and lived there till one of his son's [illegible] David Thompson - and then my master sent me to work for this young master who lived in Duplin County, N.C. about two and half miles east of Mount Olive, N.C. [illegible] I used to be sent to Mount Olive pretty near every day for the [illegible] with this young master seven years. I made a mistake above [illegible] in Sampson County when the war started but had lived in that [illegible] was actually living in Duplin county when the war started and continued to live there until sometime in the spring of the year 1865, some Yankee soldiers came by our place, they were all on horses and had guns and they had a mule and cart with provisions which they had foraged, and they had a colored man driving this mule, they spent the night at my master's place - my master was gone, but his wife, Virginia Thompson was there - and the next morning they put me on this cart to drive the mule and let the other nigger go. I went with them and they took me to Goldsboro, and there I was placed in Co. A. 135 "Pioneer Corps." It was called "Pioneer Corps" when I first went to the company and it kept that name till we were mustered-in at some place near Raleigh, Wake County, N.C. over three weeks after I joined the company. We were camped in the woods and the best I remember is that Raleigh was the nearest town when we were mustered-in. From Goldsboro we had worked the roads, made corduroy roads for the wagons to travel over, up to where we were mustered-in. Very soon after I joined the company at Goldsboro they started on this road towards Raleigh, and after we were mustered-in we started on march for Washington City and the first place we stopped was at a place called Manchester which was on one side of the river and Richmond was on the other. We stayed in Manchester 3 days awaiting orders and then marched right through Richmond and on to Washington City and marched throug the city and to the further side and camped in the woods, if the camp had any name I do not know what it was. We were there about three weeks and then we were placed on flat cars for a place called Parkersburg and there we left the flat cars and went aboard a boat for Louisville, Ky. and on our arrival there we marched to a camp in a locust grove east of the town and we called the camp Locust Camp, and at this camp we were given arms, that was the first time [illegible]

Witness to mark:

[illegible] alias Isaac Thompson, No. 1687695

had been given muskets, before that all we had was our knap-sacks and tools to work with. While at this camp there at Louisville our regiment was "broke up" and my company, Co. A, was sent to a little place called "Badgetown", Ky. and there we went on "Progost" guard duty at night. Every night this guard left the camp and went to the town and would be there till relieved by another guard. We were camped in an old cotton factory outside of "Badgetown". I do not know how long we were there but it was several weeks and then the regiment got together again at Louisville and this time we were in Barracks and we remained there till we were discharged the last of November or first of December 1865.

Q. What happened at "Badgetown", did you get into any scraps there or did anybody get hurt or captured, tell me about what happened?

A. There had been some robbing going on there in the town and that is why we were sent there, and we tried to capture some fellows but they got away. No sir, we did not "ketch" anybody, no one was was captured that I know of, nor was any of our men captured or hurt.

Q. Were you at a place called Bardstown Junction any time?

A. I do not remember any junction, but we got to this place by RR.

Q. And you do not remember any man being captured?

A. No sir. Q. Did you ever hear of a man named William Newton?

A. Yes sir, he was a Corporal of my company? Q. What happened to him?

A. We lost him, somewhere on the RR between "Badgetown" and Louisville. I now remember this William Newton was one of some soldier's that were taking some prisoners from "Badgetown" to Louisville and sometime later it was reporte that he was found dead along the RR between "Badgetown" and Louisville, this was before we were mustered-out.

Q. How old were you when you enlisted? A. I do not know but I gave my age as 18. I did not know at the time how old I was, I learned the date of my birth after the war was over, my old master told me how old I was after I came home from the war. I was not examined when I first joined the regiment but when we were mustered-in we were all made to strip and were examined. do not know the name of the doctor.

Q. Were you sick or injured? A. No sir. Q. Were any men sick at Raleigh? A. Our "Top" Sergeant was sick at Raleigh and as I remember Daniel

Page

Walker was made "Top" Sergeant. I do not remember any other man sick at Raleigh of my company or of any being left there.

Q. Were any of your company left sick at Louisville?

A. I do not know sir.

Q. Did any of your company die in service?

A. Not to my rememberance, if they did I have forgotten it.

Q. Do you remember passing a place called Alexandria?

A. Yes sir. If any man died there I did not know it or have forgotten it.

Q. Did any of your company desert?

A. The first man to desert was John Stevens on the march to Washington but they caught him. And in Washington City a man named Granville Grimes who was from South Carolina deserted and we never caught him. Q. Did you have a man in the company named Granville Gregory? A. Dont remember that name. Now after thinking of it that is the same man I called Granville Grimes, that was my mistake for his name was Gregory, Granville Gregory. I do not now remember any other man deserting. Q. How about Louisville, did you lose any man while there? A. I do not remember any man deserting there, as near I can remember Granville Gregory was the last and he deserted at Washington,

Q. Did you ever know a man named Sains?

A. I remember a man named Thomas Singer, at least I called him Singer.

Q. What happened to him? A. I do not recall that anything happened to him if he deserted us I do not remember it.

Q. Did you have any real tall men or real short men in your company?

A. Yes sir: John Brown and George Wade were about as tall as we had. Both of these were from South Carolina but I do not know what place. Yes sir, I am sure the first names were as I give them, at least that is what I called them - John Brown and George Wade.

Q. Who was Washington Wade? A. I do not remember Washington Wade, I knew him as George Wade, of course his full name may have been George Washington Wade, but I do not remember the Washington part of it. This man Wade was our 5th Sergeant. No sir, I do not remember any Austin Brown, the John Brown I mention was a Private. Q. Give names of some other tall men?

A. Allison Howe was one. Q. Do you remember a man named Childs? or Shepard?

A. No sir, I do not remember any [illegible] named Childs but I do remember the name Shepard, his given [illegible] was Will[illegible] a tall man too, and I think he was from South Carol[illegible] Did [illegible] y man [illegible] bern, N.C.?

A. [illegible]

A. James Lawton was about as short a man as we had, he was from South Car. Butler Robinson was another, think he too was from S.C.. Can't think of any other short ones unless you take me for one, I was then among the short ones but I have grown some since then.

Q. Did you have a man named Walker?

A. Yes, there were two men named Walker in the company, think one was called Daniel Walker but I can't think of the other's name. Rather think they were both from South Carolina. Most of my company were Sputh Carolina men, think I was the only man from North Carolina. No, these men - Walker - were not brothers.

Q. Were all of the men in your company as dark as you?

A. No sir, the first Sergeant, George Mason, was a real bright man, yellow man; Arthur Dixon was the next yellowish man in the company; Andrew Newton was a bright colored man.

Q. Did you know a man named Simmons?

A. Yes we had a man named Simmons but I cannot think of his first name, he was a rather bright colored man, and of medium height.

OFFICERS: My Captain was Andrew Moore; 1st Lt. William Morse; 2nd Lt. Joseph Ray. Those were the white officers of my company. Yes sir, we had a Chaplain, a preacher, but his name has done gone clean out of my mind he done nothing but preach and teach school. George Mason was 1st Sgt. when I enlisted but he took sick and then Daniel Walker took his place, next Sgt. George Wade, Thomas Ringer, Henry Hanks was either a Sgt. or Corporal, Alson Howe was a Sgt., there were five Sergeants. Our Colonel was named John Gurley, and our Major was named Dixon, do not know where any of the officers were from. Our Lt.Col. was named Budlong, do not remember his given name. Do not remember the name of our Surgeon.

I had no sickness or medical treatment in the company.

AFTER SERVICE. When I was discharged at Louisville, Ky. I was given a discharge certificate and $72.50 in money, and I returned direct to Sampson Co. North Carolina to my old masters home - I rode part way and walked part way. I worked some on my old master's place and some for his son, William Thompson, stayed right there in the neighborhood where I was raised till latter part of

1865, when I had to leave there, the white folks got to doing so bad I had to get away, they went about in bands and got to shooting and beating everybody that would learn of who was in the union army, they met me one night on the RR between Faison depot and Goshen swamp and searched me and took my discharge certificate away from me and talked to me and told me they ought to shoot me but they finally let me go and I did not stay there any longer than I could get away from that section, and I came here to Edgecombe County N.C. and have been right here ever since. Q. What were these men called?

A. They were called "Scouts". No sir, they were not the Kuklux, that was a different set of men. No sir, the Kuklux never bothered me. I have not been bothered since I have been here. Have lived within 12 to 15 miles of Tarboro ever since I first came her e in 1866.

Q. When did you take the name Faison?

A. I took that name in latter part of 1865 right after I came from the army, that was my father's name and I have gone by that name ever since.

Q. Give me the names of your master's people and where they live or did live?

A. My old master was Curtis Thompson, his wife was Jane, their children were Willis Thompson, he was not married when I left there; Ivory Thompson, unmarrid lived with his father; Walter Thompson, unmarried, and Billy Thompson was the baby one, they all lived in Sampson County and their P.O. was either Warsaw or Clinton. There were two daughters, Ann married a Dr.Thompson, lived in same neighborhood; Sally Thompson married Owen Frye, also lived there on old place. Any of these, if they can be located would know that I served in the army as I have stated. I had relatiges who would know about my army service but I have not seen or heard from any of them since I left there.

Yes, I told people up here about being in the army, when I first came up here but all those people are dead.

Q. Who could testify that you are the same man who served as Thompson, or who knew you as Thompson? A. Nobody in this county would know me as Thompson because I have gone only by the name Faison around here, but if you could locate any of my old master's children above named they would know me by both names, I have been away from there so long it is hard to name others.

I have no attorney, Mr. Sam Clark has assisted me in filing this claim. I have not paid him anything nor promised to pay him anything. I understand that [illegible] the privilege [illegible] present during this [illegible]ation but I cannot [illegible] t and I w[illegible] [pr]ivilege.

1865, when I had to leave there, the white folks got to doing so bad I had to get away, they went about in bands and got to shooting and beating every-body they could learn of who was in the union army, they got me one night on the road between Faison depot and [illegible] swamp and whipped me and took my discharge certificate away from me and talked to me and told me they ought to shoot me but they finally let me go and I did not stay there any longer than I could get away from that section, and I came here to Edgecombe County N.C. and have lived right here ever since. Q. What were these men called? A. They were called "[illegible]". No sir, they were not the Kuklux, that was a different set of men. No sir, the Kuklux never bothered me. I have not been bothered since I have been here. Have lived within 10 to 15 miles of Tarboro ever since I first came here in 1866.

Q. When did you take the name Faison?

A. I took that name in latter part of 1865 right after I came from the army, that was my father's name and I have gone by that name ever since.

Q. Give me the names of your master's people and where they live or did live?

A. My old master was Curtis Thompson, his wife was Jane, their children were Willie Thompson, he was not married when I left there; Jerry Thompson, unmarried lived with his father; Walter Thompson, unmarried, and Billy Thompson was the baby one, they all lived in Sampson County and their P.O. was either Warsaw or Clinton. There were two daughters, Ann married a Dr. Thompson, lived in same neighborhood; Sally Thompson married [illegible] Pope, also lived there on old place. Any of these, if they can be located would know that I served in the army as I have stated. I had relatives who would know about my army service but I have not seen or heard from any of them since I left there.

Yes, I told people up here about being in the army, when I first come up here but all those people are dead.

Q. Who would testify that you are the same man who served as Thompson, or who knew you as Thompson? A. Nobody in this county would know me as Thompson because I have gone only by the name Faison around here, but if you could locate any of my old master's children above named they would know me by both names. I have been away from there so long it is hard to name others.

I have no attorney, Mr. [illegible] Clark has assisted me in filing this claim. [illegible] have not paid him anything nor promised to pay him anything. I understand that [illegible] the privilege [illegible] present during this [illegible] but I cannot [illegible] all I w[illegible] privileges.

[illegible]

[illegible]sition [illegible] Faison [illegible]tinued, sheet 4

[illegible] claim for pen[illegible] or other allowance?

[illegible] sir, [illegible] first claim [illegible] for anything.

[illegible] you say [illegible] years ago,

[illegible] around here are all

[illegible] Possibly

Witness to mark

3-289 b

Case of Isaac Faison alias Thompson, No. 1687698

Deposition of Isaac Faison, continued, sheet 4

Q. Did you ever file any claim for pension, back pay or other allowance?

A. No sir, this is the first claim I have ever filed for anything.

Q. You have not yet told me any old timer who knew you way back years ag

A. The people I worked for and with when I first came around here are al dead, cant name a single person now living who knew me way back. Possibly Richard Barlow, colored, has known me as long as any person I can name, he has known me since about 1868. He is about the only man I can name who is likely to know that I have years ago mentioned being in the army and possib he will remember that I said I served under the name Thompson. Cant name anyone else.

I have no complaint to make as to the conduct, manner or fairness of thi investigation so far as it has gone. Have heard the above read and it is all correct.

Witness to mark:

[illegible]

[illegible]

his
Isaac X Faison
mark.

Page

Page 14

Isaac Faison, he belonged to Curtis Thompson. None of Curtis Thompson's children are living now.

I have heard the above read and it is correct and is all I can tell about the matter. Isaac Thompson was a good bit older than I was, he was about grown when I last remember him.

her
Rachel X Gavin
mark

Witness to mark.

Q. Who was the mother of your mother?

A. My mother was named Maria and she belonged to Curtis Thompson, and her mother was named Jane and she too belonged to Curtis Thompson but I never saw her, she (my grandmother) was dead before I was born.

her
Rachel X Gavin
mark

Witness to mark.
[illegible]
only one witness available

Subscribed and sworn to before me this 22 day of November 1931, and I certify that the contents were fully made known to deponent before signing.

[illegible]
Field Examiner.
Authority: Veterans Administration Form 4505.

WAR DEPARTMENT

I certify that the records of the War Department have been searched in accordance with letters of reference and instructions herewith, (Exhibit A), for information relative to the above-named soldier, with the following results:

OLD FILES DIVISION, A.G.O.

File No. A.G.O. 1170917
Oct.4,1906 - Charles Parker, Rocky Mount, N. C., requested statement of service of ISAAC THOMPSON, Deceased, from Wilson County, N.C., who enlisted at Newbern, N.C. in the Civil War. No mother, father, or widow survives. Not desired for pension purposes.
Oct.5,1906 - Reply states service not identified.

No correspondence or other papers on file identified as relating to any ISAAC FAISON or ISAAC THOMPSON of N.C. in the Civil War, except that shown above, which might possibly relate to this claimant. More likely it relates to a white Confederate soldier. At any rate it could have no bearing on this pension case.

OLD RECORDS DIVISION, A.G.O.

"201 FILE"- CORRESPONDENCE FROM 7/1/17: None identified.

"CTF. IN LIEU" APPLICATIONS, 1930-1931: None identified.

GENERAL INDEX, U. S. COLORED TROOPS, CIVIL WAR.

No service by ISAAC FAISON or any other FAISON identified. Following is one of the many ISAAC THOMPSONS of record:

ISAAC THOMPSON, A, 135th U. S. Col. Inf.
Age 18; born Sampson County, N.C.; Farmer; Height 5ft 5in; Black hair, eyes, and complexion. Enlisted 3/27/65 Goldsboro, N.C., by Capt. A. J. Moore, 135th U.S.C.Inf. (Signed by mark). Examined by H. F. Parks, A.A.Surg.,USA. Mustered in 4/26/65 at Page Station N.C. to date 3/28/65, by Robert M.Woods, 1"Lt. 64 Ill.Vols,ACM, 4th Div. 17th A.C., for three years. Sworn in by D. Dixon, 1"Lt. 28 Ill. Inf.
(Whether formerly a slave, and if so, name of owner, not shown.)
(Jacket notes: "Phone to Mr.Patterson 3/3/31; S.O.1687698 4/4/31.)

/ts.)

STATIONS AND EVENTS, A, 135 U.S.C.Inf. (From rolls & morning repor/

The men comprising this Company and Regiment are shown to have been gathered from Sherman's line of march through Georgia, South Carolina, and North Carolina, and employed and paid as laborers by the Quartermaster Department, until March 27, 1865, when enlisted and formed into a regiment of Pioneers for the 17th Army Corps, at Goldsboro, N. C.
Mar.27,1865 - All members of Co. A enlisted at Goldsboro, N.C.
Apr.26,1865 - Mustered in at Page Station, N.C. to date 3/28/65.
May 27,1865 - Encamped near Ft.Kearney, Washington, D. C.
Jun. to Aug.1865 - Louisville, Ky.
Sep. 8,1865 - Sent to garrison Bardstown, Ky.
Sep.14,1865 - William Newton captured at Bardstown,Jct. Ky.
Oct. 8,1865 - Relieved at Bardstown, Ky. and rejoined Regt. at ((Louisville.

LEFT SICK AT RALEIGH, N.C. Wm.McEntyre, John Moore, & John Nelson

LEFT SICK AT LOUISVILLE, KY. Cato Stephens, and John Manning.

Page 5 Depositions B - C

ANDREW NEWTON

Andrew Newton was one of the early recruits of the 135th United States Colored Troop. He was from the small town of Oliver, Georgia, a little over 50 miles northwest of Savannah. His father's name was Henry Newton. We don't know his mother's name, but we do know she was born in Africa. Andrew had been a slave on the estate of Mr. Isaac Conner before leaving to join Sherman's Army during the infamous March to the Sea and, following the War, returned to his place of birth to become a farmer.

When the United States Pension Office interviewed Andrew in June of 1912, his sworn statement gave his birth year as 1841, though his mother told him he was born in 1842. After "freedom," Mr. George B. Conner, the son of Andrew's former slave master, confirmed that he was born in 1841. When he said as much to his mother, she agreed that Mr. George B. Conner was correct. By the time of his statement, both his mother and Mr. George B. Conner were dead, so he was unable to get a written statement from them, but he did believe he was born in May of 1841. In a statement from Mr. Ben Newton Conner, we learn that he and Andrew are close in age. Mr. Conner was born in 1846 and Andrew was married in 1862.

At the time of the interviews and statements, Andrew was an old man and sadly disabled. As part of the pension process, he was to be examined by a doctor, but of the few physicians he could have seen, one had died, and the other moved away. By the time of his statement on January 19, 1929, though, he had been disabled for about eight years, could hardly walk, and had very little use of his "limbs" without assistance. For the previous three years, he also required regular personal aid and the attendance of another person. Dr. H.E. Ezell, also from Oliver, Georgia, confirmed that Andrew was 86 years old, in feeble health, and unable to do any work. Another man, John Oliver, gave a sworn statement in which he also knew Andrew to be helpless and dependent for the past eight years. John was 54 years old and from the nearby town of Halcyondale, Georgia. He had known Andrew his entire life.

On April 16, 1930, Andrew gave another statement to the Pension Board, declaring he was sick and unable to do anything without a personal aide. He further explains that he had been in that state since 1920. He pursued claiming his rightful pension and recognition for his time in Sherman's army right up until his death on June 21, 1930, just a few months after his wife's death on February 9 of the same year. Soon after, he was buried in St. John's Cemetery in Oliver, Georgia. Following his death, Andrew's son, R.P. Newton, writes to request papers concerning the incident of his father's death. He wrote that he hoped his letter would not conflict with any other notice the Board may have had on hand but that he believed he was the proper one to write because his father was living with him at the time of Andrew's death.

When Andrew died in 1930, he had about twenty-five dollars and roughly 100 acres of land. Most of his land was in the woods and was considered very poor. According to one affidavit, the land was held by the Federal Land Bank and Guano Cos. Land, with a total encumbrance of about $300.00. In another affidavit, the Federal Land Bank held an encumbrance of approximately $200.00, and about $90.00 was due to the Screven Oil Mill, and another $60.00 to Oliver Trading Co. along with various doctors' bills owed. Oliver

Trading Co, Inc. issued a reimbursement request for expenses and approved charges. However, the Hon. Charles E. Edwards rejected the request on the grounds that the "pensioner left assets sufficient to meet the approvable expenses of his last sickness and burial."

There were other reimbursement requests and discussions following Andrew's death, all documented in his pension file at the National Archives in Washington, D.C. Sadly, these documents show that there were insufficient funds to pay all his debts, which included monies requested by his son R.P. Newton and daughter Corinthia Newton. In his final letter, the Director of Compensation acknowledges that he received recent correspondence related to the expenses of Andrew's final illness and states, "It is regretted to advise that there are no further benefits payable in this case." The letter is signed by George E. Brown, Director of Compensation.

Andrew Newton's records do not give much insight into the conditions he experienced or his work during his service with the 135th United States Colored Troop. Still, many others served in the Unit, and their records give remarkable details about their experiences in the Army during the Civil War.

State of Georgia Screven County

Before me W R Lee a Justice of the Peace in 259 G.M. Dist of said State and county, Personally come Ben. Newton Conner, who on his oath does swear that to the best of my belief and knowledge Andrew Newton to be between 70 and 71 years old, have known the said Andrew Newton all my life or since I could remember any thing, he Andrew Newton was borned and raised a slave of my father until grown and married, The said Andrew Newton being married in the year 1862, and have known him ever since to this day. I do further swear that said Andrew Newton being older than I am as he was large enough to nurse me when I could first remember. I do further swear that I Ben Newton Conner was born the 22nd day of November in the year 1845, and will be 67 years old the 22 day of November next. I do further swear that I have no interest in the foregoing what soever.

P.O. address Halcyondale Ga.

X Ben Newton Conner

Sworn to and subscribed before me this the 10th day of June Nineteen hundred (1912) and Twelve.

W. R. Lee Justice of the Peace of 259 G.M. Dist of Georgia Screven county.

U. S. [POST] OFFICE JUN 19 1912

My commission began the 24 day of Feb. 1910 and will Expire the 24 of Feb. 1914.

Georgia Screven County

Before me W R Lee a Justice of the peace in the 251 G.M. Dist of said State and County personally came Andrew Newton who on oath does Swear that to the best of his belief and knowledge he was born in the year 1841, I was first lead to believe by my mother that I was born in the year 1842, but may years after freedom I was told by Mr George Benson Connor my slave Masters son that I was born in the year 1841 whom was much older than my self, then I went to my mother and told to her what Mr George Benson Connor said then she my mother said the Mr George B Connor was correct, I do further swear that my mother and Mr George B. Connor have since died which is why I cant get the exact date of the month and year in which I was borned, But to the best of my knowledge I was borned in may.

P.O. Address Oliver Ga } Andrew Newton

Sworn to and subscribed before me this the 10 day of June - 1912

W R Lee Justice of the Peace of the in the 251 G.M Dist of Screven County Georgia. My commission commenced the 24th of Feb - 1910 and will expire the the 24th of Feb - 1914.

PENSION U.S. JUN 13 1912 OFFICE

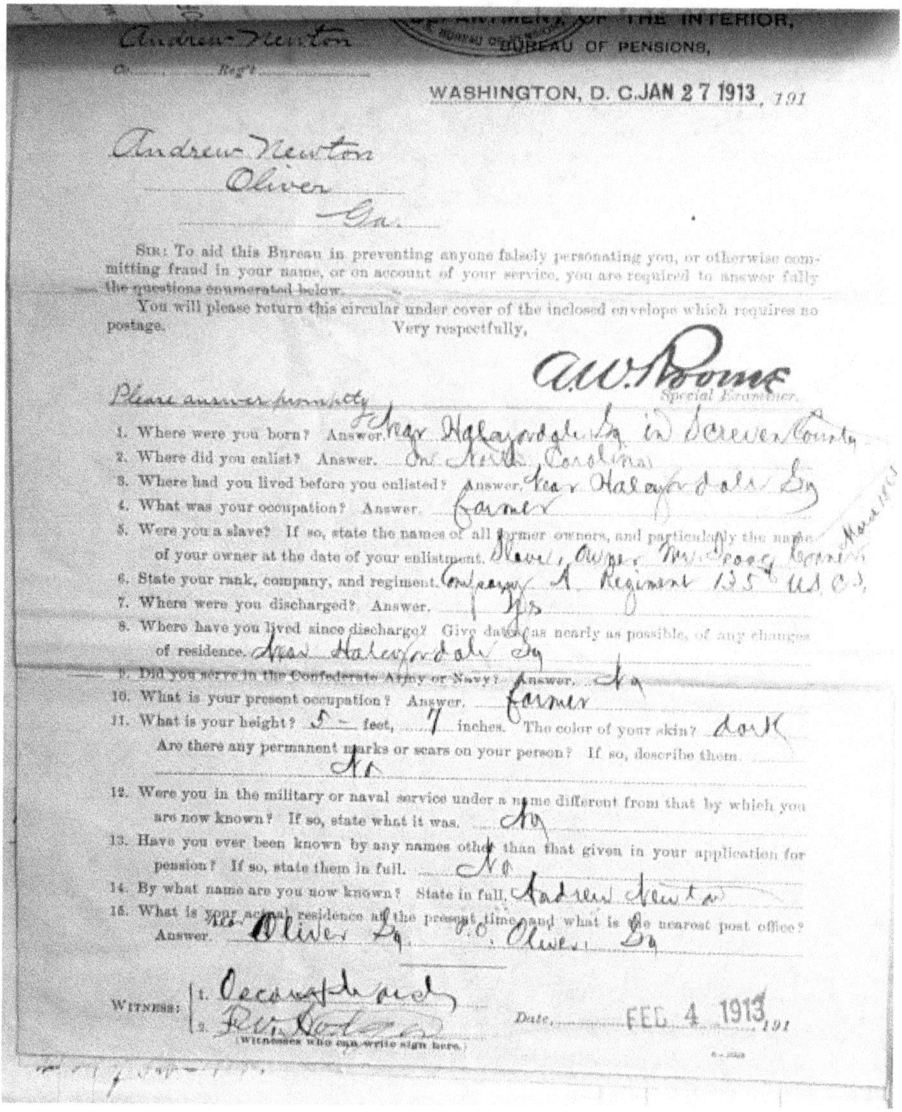
Andrew Newton

DEPARTMENT OF THE INTERIOR,
BUREAU OF PENSIONS,

Co. .... Reg't ....

WASHINGTON, D. C. JAN 27 1913, 191

Andrew Newton
Oliver
Ga.

SIR: To aid this Bureau in preventing anyone falsely personating you, or otherwise committing fraud in your name, or on account of your service, you are required to answer fully the questions enumerated below.

You will please return this circular under cover of the inclosed envelope which requires no postage.

Very respectfully,

A. W. Boone
Special Examiner.

Please answer promptly

1. Where were you born? Answer. Near Halcyondale Ga in Screven County
2. Where did you enlist? Answer. In North Carolina
3. Where had you lived before you enlisted? Answer. Near Halcyondale Ga
4. What was your occupation? Answer. farmer
5. Were you a slave? If so, state the names of all former owners, and particularly the name of your owner at the date of your enlistment. Slave, Owner Mr. [illegible]
6. State your rank, company, and regiment. Company A Regiment 135th U.S.C.T.
7. Where were you discharged? Answer. [illegible]
8. Where have you lived since discharge? Give dates, as nearly as possible, of any changes of residence. Near Halcyondale Ga
9. Did you serve in the Confederate Army or Navy? Answer. No
10. What is your present occupation? Answer. farmer
11. What is your height? 5 feet, 7 inches. The color of your skin? dark
Are there any permanent marks or scars on your person? If so, describe them. No
12. Were you in the military or naval service under a name different from that by which you are now known? If so, state what it was. No
13. Have you ever been known by any names other than that given in your application for pension? If so, state them in full. No
14. By what name are you now known? State in full. Andrew Newton
15. What is your actual residence at the present time, and what is the nearest post office?
Answer. Near Oliver Ga. P.O. Oliver Ga

WITNESS: 1. [illegible]
2. [illegible]
(Witnesses who can write sign here.)

Date, FEB 4 1913, 191

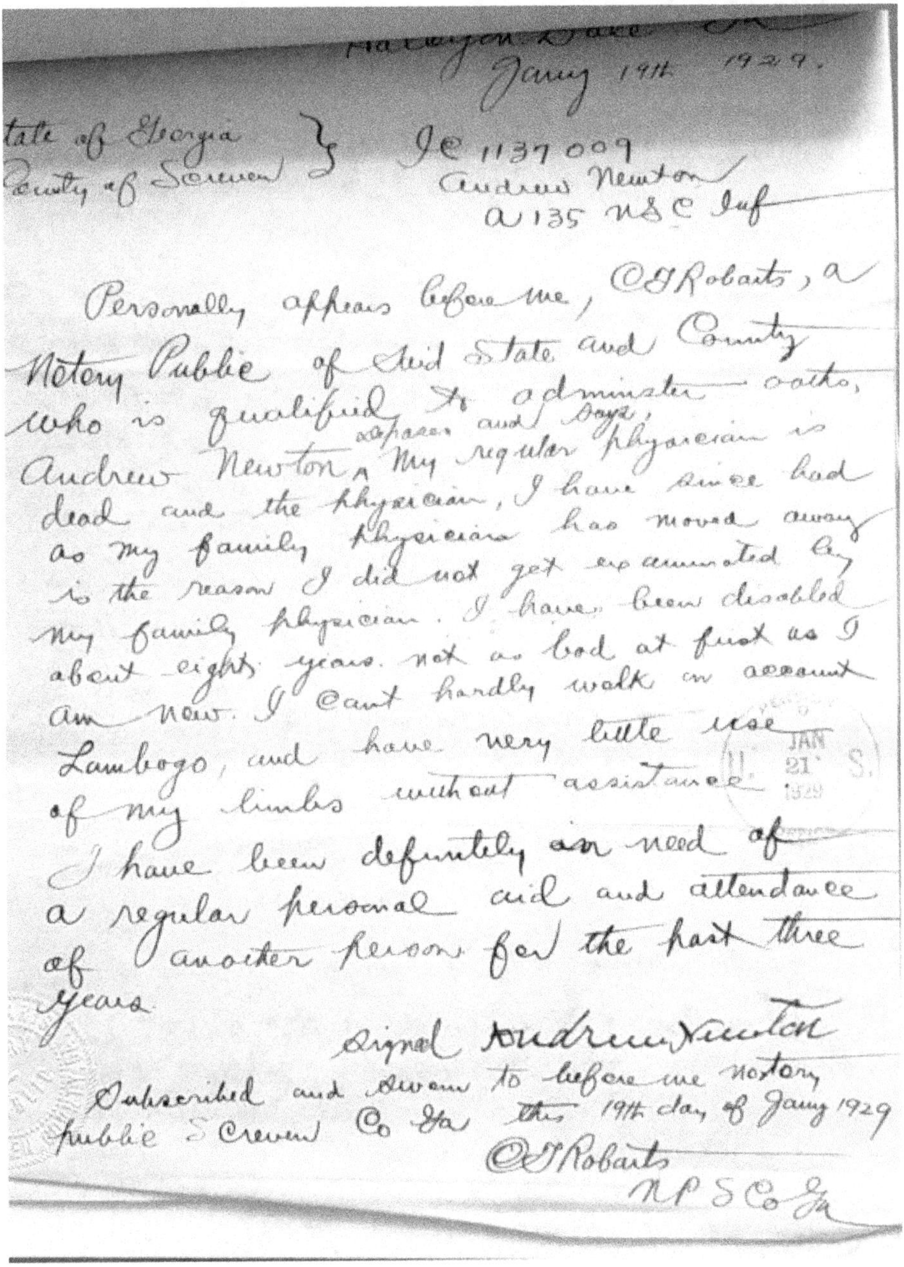
Halcyon Dale Ga
Jany 19th 1929.

State of Georgia }
County of Screven } IC 1137009
Andrew Newton
A 135 USC Inf

Personally appears before me, C J Robarts, a
Notary Public of Said State and County
who is qualified to administer oaths,
Andrew Newton, deposes and says, My regular physician is
dead and the physician, I have since had
as my family physician has moved away
is the reason I did not get examinated by
my family physician. I have been disabled
about eight years. not as bad at first as I
am now. I Cant hardly walk on account
Lumbago, and have very little use
of my limbs without assistance
I have been definitely in need of
a regular personal aid and attendance
of another person for the last three
years.

Signed Andrew Newton

Subscribed and sworn to before me notary
public Screven Co Ga this 19th day of Jany 1929
C J Robarts
N P S Co Ga

JAN 21 1929

Invalid Division

S.C. 1137008
Andrew Newton, Co. D. 135 U.S.C.
Inf.

This to certify that I, Andrew
Newton, a soldier of the interior
Department, do solemnly swear
and declare, that I am sick
and not able to do anything
without personal aid. Compel
to have the regular attendance
another person; I have been
in this helpless state since—
1920. Andrew Newton

Sworn to and Subscribed
before me This 16 day of
April 1930
E. H. Bennett
Notary Public
State of Ga at large.

HOUSE OF REPRESENTATIVES

WASHINGTON, D. C.

1988

Jany. 28th, 1931.

Re: SC 1137009-Andrew Newton, Oliver Ga. colored, deceased.

Pension Commissioner,
Washington, D. C.

Dear Sir:-

Please refer to your letter of 23d inst., addressed to the Oliver Trading Company, Oliver, Ga., declining this claim; and also note attached letter from the Oliver Trading Co., by Mr. Virgil P. Brewer, President, Oliver, Ga.

While the old colored man had someproperty, estimated at $236.97; you will note from the letter of the Oliver Trading Co., dated 26th, inst., that the property in question is encumbered for more than the property is worth. The Veterans Administration, in good faith, in my opinion, should pay the Oliver Trading Co., Oliver, Ga., for the deceased negro was in distress and they had to help him in his last illness. The Oliver Trading Company went to his rescue, arranged about nursing and medical attention and saw that he got a casket in which to be buried. It is hardly fair to leave the Oliver Trading Co., out in the cold, for they will never be able to realize a dime unless these expenses are paid by the Government. The enclosed letter from the Oliver Trading Co. is explicit on the subject and I will thank you to carefully read it and I hope it will be arranged for them to be reimbursed.

Thanking you, I am,

Yours truly,

Chas G Edwards

WIDOW DIVISION
JAN 29 1931
U. S.
BUREAU OF PENSIONS

JAN 29 1931

enc cge/bss

AFFIDAVIT SUPPORTING BURIAL CLAIM

(To be executed by next of kin, or other near relative, or friend of deceased)

1. (a) Full name of deceased Andrew Newton

(b) Rank and organization

(c) Date of enlistment Civil War (If dates of service can not be furnished, state war in which veteran served) (d) Date of discharge

(e) Age of deceased 90 (f) Legal residence at time of death Oliver, Ga.

(g) Date of death 6/21st.1930. (h) Place of death Oliver, Ga.

(i) Date of burial 6/22nd, 1930. (j) Place of burial Oliver, Ga.

(k) Name and address of undertaker Oliver Trading Co.Inc.Oliver, Ga.

2. Was deceased single, married, widowed or divorced? Widower

3. (a) All cash money left by deceased NONE.

(b) All amounts due and collectible from solvent debtors at date of death including accrued salary or commission

(c) Nature and value of all other personal property left by deceased About twenty five dollars.

(d) All real property owned by deceased at date of death about 100 acres. All this land is held by Federal land bank and Guano Cos. land mostly in woods and very poor land.

(e) Actual value thereof at date of death (If actual value can not be given state assessed value)

(f) Total encumbrances thereon About $300.00

(g) If property owned consists of house and land, state whether or not it was occupied or claimed as the home of the deceased at date of death Was his home.

4. (a) State total amount of all debts contracted and owing by the deceased at date of death exclusive of encumbrances on real property shown in 3 (f) above all debts including Dr. bills about $150.00. This also includes funeral expenses.

(b) Were the expenses of funeral, burial and transportation of the deceased entirely or in part paid by a state or other political subdivision, beneficial society, lodge, union, fraternal organization or national home for disabled volunteer soldiers? Nothing paid for by any one.

3—4565 (OVER)

VETERANS ADMINISTRATION
BUREAU OF PENSIONS
WASHINGTON April 14, 1931.

THIS LETTER REFERS TO
YOUR FILE NUMBER
FABB
801 NEWTON, Andrew 801
IN REPLY REFER TO:

Widow Division.
S.C. 1,137,009,
Andrew Newton,
A. 135 USC Inf.

The Director,
U.S. Veterans' Bureau,
Washington, D. C.

Dear Sir:

In reply to your inquiry of March 9, 1931, relative to the record of service of the above named pensioner, you are advised that a report from the War Department, on file in this Bureau, shows that Andrew Newton was enrolled March 27, 1865, in Company A, One-Hundred-Thirty-Fifth United States Colored Infantry and was mustered out with the Company October 23, 1865, as a Private.

This report shows that he was born in Georgia and at the time of his enlistment was twenty-two years ten-months old and five feet seven-inches in height.

Very truly yours,

E. W. Morgan

E. W. Morgan,
Acting Commissioner.

Z WC:ELN

AFFIDAVIT SUPPORTING BURIAL CLAIM

1. (a) Full name of deceased Andrew Newton.
   (b) Rank and organization Company A (Col.Int)
   (c) Date of enlistment ____ (d) Date of discharge ____
   (e) Age of deceased Above 90 (f) Legal residence at time of death Oliver, Ga.
   (g) Date of death June, 21st, 1930. (h) Place of death Oliver, Ga.
   (i) Date of burial June, 22nd. 1930. (j) Place of burial Oliver, Ga.
   (k) Name and address of undertaker Oliver Trading Co. Oliver, Ga.
2. Was deceased single, married, widowed or divorced? Widower.
3. (a) All cash money left by deceased NONE
   (b) All amounts due and collectible from solvent debtors at date of death including accrued salary or commission None collectable
   (c) Nature and value of all other personal property left by deceased Not more than $40.00
   (d) All real property owned by deceased at date of death XXXXXX about 100 acres. This is all tied up with Federal Land Bank and Screven Oil Mill. (These statements have been furnished to you by each concern.
   (e) Actual value thereof at date of death All very poor land and do not think it would bring more than the amts. due these two concerns.
   (f) Total encumbrances thereon Federal Land Bank about $200.00 and the Screven Oil Mill about $90.00.
   (g) If property owned consists of house and land, state whether or not it was occupied or claimed as the home of the deceased at date of death yes occupied by deceased.
4. (a) State total amount of all debts contracted and owing by the deceased at date of death exclusive of encumbrances on real property shown in 3 (f) above about $60.00 to Oliver Trading Co. and Drs. bills.
   (b) Were the expenses of funeral, burial and transportation of the deceased entirely or in part paid by a state or other political subdivision, beneficial society, lodge, union, fraternal organization or national home for disabled volunteer soldiers? funeral expenses never been paid.

CERTIFICATE OF DEATH

GEORGIA STATE BOARD OF HEALTH
Bureau of Vital Statistics

30-16958
STATE FILE NUMBER

N. B.—WRITE PLAINLY, WITH UNFADING INK—THIS IS A PERMANENT RECORD. Every item of information should be carefully supplied. AGE should be stated EXACTLY. PHYSICIANS should state CAUSE OF DEATH in plain terms, so that it may be properly classified. Exact statement of OCCUPATION is very important. Was death due to insanitary or dangerous conditions or occupations?

R. V. S.—Form 11.

1 PLACE OF DEATH
State—Georgia
County Screven Militia District No. 259 Registered No. 153
City or Town HALCYONDALE, GA. No. ____ St. ____ Ward
(If death occurred in a hospital or institution, give its NAME instead of street and number).

2 FULL NAME Andrew Newton
(a) Residence HALCYONDALE, GA.
(Usual place of abode, street and number)
Length of residence in city or town where death occurred ____ yrs. ____ mos. ____ ds. If NON-RESIDENT give city or town and state of residence.

PERSONAL AND STATISTICAL PARTICULARS	MEDICAL CERTIFICATE OF DEATH
3 SEX: Male · 4 Color or Race: Negro · 5 Single, Married, Widowed, or Divorced (write the word): Widowed	16 DATE OF DEATH (month, day and year) June 21st 1930
5a Name of Husband or Wife, if Married, Widowed or Divorced: Hagar Newton	17 I HEREBY CERTIFY, That I attended deceased from ____, 19__, to ____, 19__
6 DATE OF BIRTH (month, day and year) 1838	that I last saw h__ alive on ____, 19__
7 AGE: Years 92 · Months Don't Know · Days Don't Know · If LESS than 1 day ____ hrs. or ____ min.	and that death occurred, on the date stated above at ____ m. The CAUSE OF DEATH was as follows:
8 OCCUPATION (a) Trade, Profession or particular kind of work Farmer (b) General nature of Industry Business or Establishment in which employed (or employer)	Old Age No doctor Called
9 BIRTHPLACE (State or Country) Ga.	(duration) ____ yrs. ____ mos. ____ ds.
10 NAME OF FATHER Henry Newton	CONTRIBUTORY (Secondary) ____ (duration) ____ yrs. ____ mos. ____ ds.
11 BIRTHPLACE OF FATHER (State or Country) U. S. A	18 Where was disease contracted if not at place of death?
12 MAIDEN NAME OF MOTHER Don't Know	Did an operation precede death? ____ Date of ____ Was there an autopsy? ____
13 BIRTHPLACE OF MOTHER (State or Country) Africa	What test confirmed diagnosis? ____ (Signed) C. T. Robarts, M.D. (Address) HALCYONDALE, GA.
14 The Above is True to the Best of My Knowledge (Informant) J. M. Newton (Address) HALCYONDALE, GA.	19 Place of Burial, Cremation, or Removal: St. Johns, Oliver · Date of Burial 6/22 1930
15 Filed June 21st 1930 Registrar C. T. Robarts	20 UNDERTAKER None · Address ____

AMOS WILLIS / COBB

Amos Willis (aka Amos Cobb) was another member of the 135th USCT. Not much is known about where Amos came from or even details about his time in the service, but his pension record showed that he joined Sherman's army on March 27, 1865, mustering into Co. "A" of the 135th USCT regiment in North Carolina.

Along with Amos were Buddy Leach and Colon McKellin, both of whom enlisted at the same time as Amos. They testified in their affidavits to seeing him daily during their service together and then seeing him "very often, sometimes as often as once a week" following their discharge at Louisville on October 23, 1865. Also in their company were Cain McNair and Daniel McNair, who knew Amos Willis as Amos Cobb. Cain also claims to have seen Amos at least once a year following their mustering out.

Amos's file contains medical affidavits and requests for pension increases. From these, we learn that after the "War of Rebellion," as it's called in the documents, Amos lived for a while in Rowland, North Carolina, where he applied for an updated pension under the Act of February 6, 1907. That increased his pension payments from $8/month under the Act of June 27, 1890, to $12/month under the new Act. There was one claim for a pension that required medical documentation. According to the affidavit of Dr. H.L. Byrns it's documented that on November 20, 1900, Amos was "incapacitated for the performance of manual labor to the extent of three fourths." He cited Amos's maladies as rheumatism of the left leg, dyspepsia (indigestion), and "sluggish action of the heart," with a pulse of only about 60 beats per minute.

William S. Cobb filed for Accrued Pension Reimbursement following Amos's death. This request was "Rejected for the reason that the Pension left net assets sufficient to cover the costs of expenses incurred for the last sickness and burial." More documents reveal the appeal of this decision with claims of additional outstanding burial costs mentioned in a letter to William Cobb dated March 5, 1936. Sworn testimony from S.F. Latimer, Jr tells us Eventually, Amos made his way to Geneva, Alabama, where he purchased 80 acres, a mule, wagon, harnesses, and other farming equipment from Mr. Latimer on October 1, 1930. Following Amos's death on April 22, 1933, Mr. Latimer repossessed these purchases "due to default in the payment of certain installments due on said land, and for the mule, wagon, and harness."

Like many others, Amos Willis was a name that history nearly forgot, but we now remember. Though not much is known about his life, it appears that, like many others, he was faced with obstacles and health challenges following his service and denied a hard-earned pension for far too long.

Rowland, Robeson Co N.C.
September [illegible]th 1897.
Mr Taber & Whitman.
Dear Sir,
Before I en listen in the ware I went in the name of
A Mos Cobb and I toled them my name wos Amos Cobb they questioned of what my father when I told them he wos a Willis then they said I would haft to go by my fathers name so I dont no what name they gave me. You will please look on the recorde and see if you will find Amos Cobb

over

And If You do You will find
what I have Riten You
Cor es Pond ing with every
thing that I have
Riten You.
Please An Swer As
Soon As You have look
upon the record for
Amos Cobb. You request
ed of what my Capt name was
the short time that I was
in the war I never did learn his
full Sig Nature All I learn
wos Capt Moore he wos
a North ern Man.
Please send me a
Dupli Cate Yours truly
AMos Willis

SOUTH DIV

GENERAL AFFIDAVIT.

State of N C
County of Robison } ss:

In the matter of claim for Pension No 1194133 of Amos Willis
(Character and number of claim.)

alias Cobb Co A 135 U S C T
(Full name and relationship of claimant, and name and service of soldier.)

Personally came before me, a Notary Public in and for
(Justice, Notary, Judge, Clerk or Deputy Clerk.)

aforesaid County and State, Cain McNeill, aged 58 years,

residing at Wakulla, County of Robison, State

of N C, and Daniel McNair, aged 65 years,

residing at Maxton, County of Robison, State

of N. C., who, being duly sworn, declare in relation to the aforesaid case

as follows: Cain McNeill that he was a member of Co G 135 U S C T from the 27th day of March 1865 to the 23d day of October 1865. That during all of said time he was personally acquainted with the applicant and knew him as Amos Cobb, That he has seen him at least once each year since their discharge at Louisville Ky on the 23d day of October 1865 to the present time and knows him to be the identical Amos Cobb who served in Co A 135 Regt U S C T

Daniel McNair that he was a member of Co F 135 Regt U S C T from the 27th day of March 1865 to the 23d day of October 1865 That he knows the applicant to be the identical Amos Cobb who served during said time in Co A in said Regiment

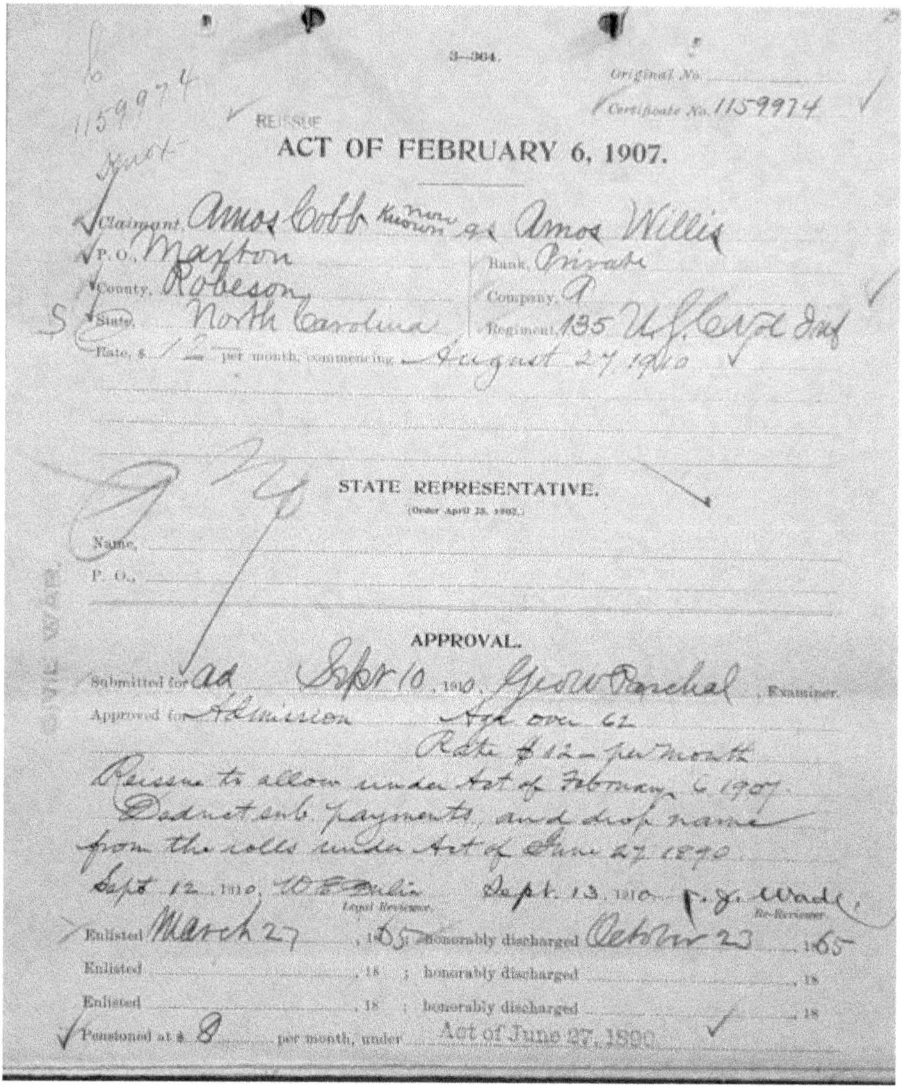

3—304.

1159974

Original No.

Certificate No. 1159974

REISSUE

ACT OF FEBRUARY 6, 1907.

Claimant, Amos Cobb known as Amos Willis

P.O., Maxton — Rank, Private

County, Robeson — Company, A

State, North Carolina — Regiment, 135 U.S. Col. Inf.

Rate, $ 12 per month, commencing August 27, 1910

STATE REPRESENTATIVE.

(Order April 23, 1902.)

Name,

P. O.,

CIVIL WAR.

APPROVAL.

Submitted for ad Sept 10, 1910, Geo W Paschal, Examiner.

Approved for Admission Age over 62

Rate $12 — per month

Reissue to allow under Act of February 6 1907.

Deduct sub. payments, and drop name from the rolls under Act of June 27 1890

Sept 12, 1910, W. E. Butler, Legal Reviewer. Sept. 13, 1910 J. J. Wade, Re-Reviewer.

Enlisted March 27, 1865; honorably discharged October 23, 1865

Enlisted ..., 18 ; honorably discharged ..., 18

Enlisted ..., 18 ; honorably discharged ..., 18

Pensioned at $ 8 per month, under Act of June 27, 1890

DECLARATION FOR PENSION

ACT OF MAY 1, 1920

The Pension Certificate Should Not Be Forwarded With the Application

State of Alabama, County of Geneva, ss:

On this 7th day of May 1925, personally appeared before me, a Notary Public within and for the county and State aforesaid, Amos Willis who, being duly sworn according to law, declares that he is 78 years of age, and a resident of Geneva, Ala. county of Geneva, State of Alabama; and that he is the identical person who was ENROLLED at Fayetteville, N.C., under the name of Amos Willis on the ... day of ... 18..., as a Private in Co. A 135 Regiment United States Colored Inf. (Here state rank, and company and regiment in the Army, or vessels if in the Navy) in the service of the United States, in the Civil (State name of war, Civil or Mexican.) war, and was HONORABLY DISCHARGED at Louisville Ky. (Discharge has been lost) on the ... day of ... 18...

That he also served ... (Here give a complete statement of all other services, if any.)

That his personal description at enlistment was as follows: Height 6 ft. feet ... inches; complexion dark; color of eyes Black; color of hair black; that his occupation was farming; that he was born Robertson County, N.C. at ...

That he requires the regular personal aid and attendance of another person on account of the following disabilities:

Rheumatism (State in this space the nature of any and all disabilities.)

Can hardly walk; can do no work of any kind

That since leaving the service he has resided at Geneva County, Alabama.

and his occupation has been farming. That he has ... applied for pension under original No. ... That he is a pensioner under Certificate No. 1,169,974

That he makes this declaration for the purpose of being placed on the pension roll of the United under the provisions of the Act of May 1, 1920.

(Attesting and identifying witnesses.)

(1) O. A. Mickey (Signature of first witness.)

Wathie Burghard (Address of first witness.)

(2) Geneva, Ala (Signature of second witness.)

Amos his x mark Willis (Claimant's signature in full.)

(Claimant's address in full.) Geneva, Ala. Route #1

OFFICE (Official character.)

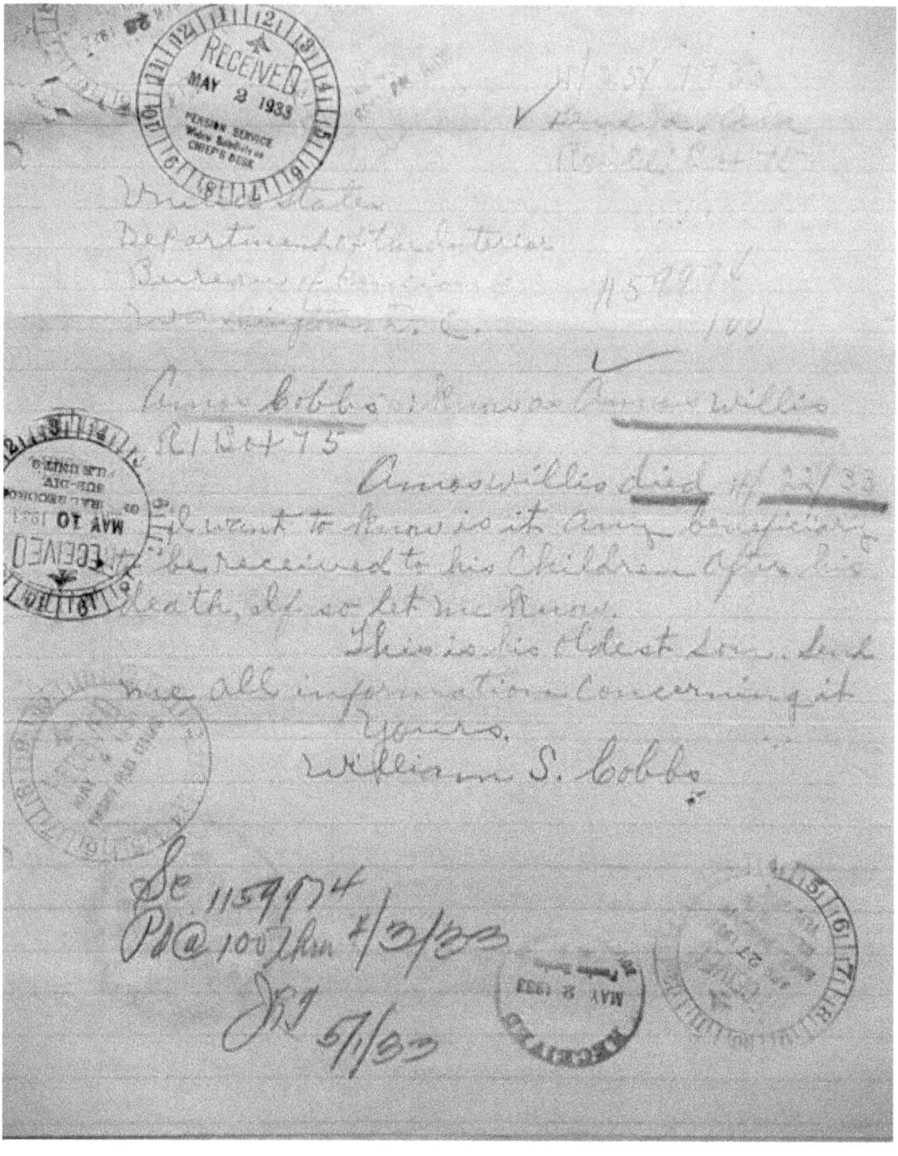
RECEIVED
MAY 2 1933
PENSION SERVICE
CHIEF'S DESK

United States
Department of the Interior
Bureau of Pensions
Washington D.C.

1159974
100

Amos Cobbs ... Amos Willis
R1 Box 75

Amos Willis died 4/22/33

I want to know is it any benefition to be received to his Children After his death, If so let me know.

This is his oldest son. Send me all information concerning it

Yours,
William S. Cobbs

Sc 1159974
Pd @ 100 thru 4/3/33
JKI 5/1/33

RECEIVED
MAY 10 1933

RECEIVED
MAY 2 1933

VETERANS ADMINISTRATION
Pension Form 5645
Rev. Dec., 1922

No. [illegible]

REIMBURSEMENT

ACCRUED PENSION

Claimant [illegible]	Pensioner [illegible]
Street and No. [illegible]	Class [illegible]
P. O. [illegible]	Law
State [illegible]	Section

Rate, $ .... Last paid to .... at $ ....

Last illness commenced .... Date of death [illegible] Accrued pension, $ ....

Amounts claimed			Charges approved		Deductions		
Physician's bills	$ 21	00	$		State aid	$	
Medicine	5	00			Assets [illegible]	1300	00
Board					Insurance		
Nursing and care	2	00			Amount waived		
Rent							
Living expenses for pensioner							
Undertaker's bill	84	00					
Livery							
Cemetery charges					Total	1300	00
Other expenses					Summary		
Cement & Material	4	00			Charges approved	$ 116	00
					Deductions	1300	00
					Amount approved	—	—
Totals	116	00					

Approved for Rejected for the reason that the Pensioner left net assets sufficient to cover the cost of expenses incurred for last sickness and burial

Jan. 11, 1934. [illegible]
Reimbursement Claims Adjudicator.

1-12-34 [illegible]
Reimbursement Claims Aud

U. S. GOVERNMENT PRINTING OFFICE 14—389

STATE OF ALABAMA, †††

GENEVA COUNTY. †††

Before me, R.H.Phillips a Notary Public in and for said State and County personally appeared S.F.Latimer Jr. who is 31 years of age, and Oscar Hightower, who is 46 years of age, and who being first duly sworn deposes and say:

We are citizens of Geneva, Geneva County, Alabama, and were acquainted with Amos Willis, alias, Amos Cobb during his lifetime; that on or about October 1st, 1930, deponent S.F.Latimer Jr. executed a bond to convey title to 80 acres of land in Geneva County, Alabama to the said Amos Willis; that at the same time deponent Latimer sold to the said Amos Willis a mule, wagon andharness and other farming implements; deponents say that or or about April 22nd 1932 Amos Willis departed this life, and due to default in the payment of certain installments due on said land, and for the mule, wagon and harness, said S.F.Latimer Jr. repossessed all of said personal property and land that was ageeed to be conveyed;

Deponents say that they are informed and believe that this was all the property, either real or personal that was owned by the said Amos Willis at the time of his death.

S F Latimer Jr

Oscar Hightower

Sworn to and subscribed to before me on this the 14th day of September 1935.

R H Phillips

NOTARY PUBLIC.

LEWIS PETTIGREW

In 1902 Lewis Pettigrew applied for a pension where he and his wife lived at 609, 10th Street West, Savannah, Georgia. He was a soldier during the war in Company "A" 135th United States Colored Troop. He started his service in the Pioneer Corps in Savannah Georgia however was born in Screven County, Georgia. Lewis belonged to Edward Jones, his father was Louis Jones and his mother, Mary, were both slaves of Edward Jones. Lewis had a half-brother named William Castle and a half sister Mrs. Nora Lewis.

In 1867 when Lewis was asked about his name, he replied that he went by Lewis Jones during slavery, but his father's name was really Pettigrew and that was the name he used to enroll in the service.

Lewis said that in the service he was paid $16.00 a month and performed the duties of a soldier. They listed him as 5' 9" tall and he was given a uniform when he enlisted. Since the war, he said that "I have been a member of the free masons of the Mariah Lodge in Savannah, Georgia." He said he married Amanda Miner in Savannah in 1867 and has a marriage license but never had any children.

Lewis died October 20, 1910, and was buried by the Mason Lodge, in Laurel Grove Cemetery, Savannah, Georgia. His wife applied for a widow's pension in 1910.

OFFICE OF
COMMISSIONERS OF CHATHAM COUNTY.
GEORGIA.

Commissioners
Augustus B. Moore, Chairman
Oliver T. Bacon, Vice Chairman
Albert Wylly
Jos. M. Dixon
John Wood Motte

G. Reubert Butler, Clerk

Savannah, Ga., 1/26/11. 191

Mr. J. L. Davenport,

Commissioner Bureau of Pensions,

Washington, D. C.

Dear Sir:-

Referring to your letter of October 31st., addressed to Honorable Chas. G. Edwards, M. C., Savannah, Ga., in reference to the application for a pension for Amanda Pettigrew, colored, widow of the late Lewis Pettigrew. I am enclosing you herewith form of application sent in the letter referred to above. You will notice that there is certain information which relates to the enrollment and etc. of Pettigrew, which his widow is unable to furnish, this information though I think is on file in your office with the original application of Lewis Pettigrew.

Will you kindly advise me if the application is all right and if the woman will receive the pension formerly allowed by her husband. As I wrote Mr. Edwards my interest in this matter is that the woman is an old family servant of ours and I would like to see her get whatever she may be entitled to. I would appreciate it if you would communicate direct with me, as it is useless for her to have to pay for the services of a lawyer if it can be avoided.

Respectfully,

Reuben Butler

PENSION N JAN 28 1911 U. S. OFFICE

ARP

3-1066

a. J. R.

DEPARTMENT OF THE INTERIOR

BUREAU OF PENSIONS

WASHINGTON March 3, 1911.

Civil War Division.
Wid.Orig. 957,194.
Amanda Pettigrew,
Lewis Pettigrew,
Co.A, 135 U.S.C.Vol.Inf.

Mrs. Amanda Pettigrew,

Savannah, Georgia.

Madam:

You are advised that the above-entitled claim for pension requires testimony of two credible witnesses who have personal knowledge, showing whether you and the soldier lived together from the date of your marriage to his death, and, if not, whether you were divorced, as the testimony of Reuben and Clara V. Butler is not satisfactory, it failing to show how long affiants knew you and the soldier.

The claim also requires the testimony of credible witnesses who knew you and the soldier from the time each became of marriageable age, showing whether either had been married prior to your marriage to each other, and, if so, how and when such marriage or marriages terminated.

Very respectfully,

J. L. Davenport,
Commissioner.

PENSION K MAR 27 1911 U. S. OFFICE

Savannah, Ga., June 27, 1902.

Hon. Commissioner of Pensions,

Washington, D. C.

Sir:

Herewith I have the honor to return, with report, the papers in pension claim No.1,281,001, of Lewis Pettigrew, late private, Co. A, 135th U. S. C. Vol. Inf. Post-office address, #609 10th Street, Savannah, Georgia.

This is one of the W. E. Moore claims referred to the field for special examination under Law Division letter dated May 17, 1902.

It appears that Moore had very little, if anything, to do with the prosecution of this claim. I have been unable to find anything irregular upon the part of any one in connection with this claim. I submit herewith the best obtainable testimony bearing upon the question of claimant's identity with the soldier of record. The claimant gives a good history of the regiment and its movements, corresponds well with the soldier of record, and is identified by one comrade of good reputation. I have no doubt whatever but that claimant is the soldier of record. Claimant gave me the name of another witness, A. Lucas, who he stated could identify him but later returned and stated that he had seen Lucus but that he had stated that he knew nothing about his service. Under these circumstances I did not deem his deposition necessary.

I recommend that the papers in this claim be referred to the Chief of the Law Division for consideration.

Very respectfully,

W. B. Parkey

N. B.—Examiners should be particular to have affiants sign on the line next below the closing words of their depositions, so as to leave little or no space between their signatures and the end of their depositions.

3-290.

DEPOSITION A

Case of Lewis Pettigrew, No. 1,281,001

On this 28 day of June 1902, at Savannah, County of Chatham, State of Georgia, before me A. B. Parker, a special examiner of the Bureau of Pensions, personally appeared Lewis Pettigrew, who, being by me first duly sworn to answer truly all interrogatories propounded to him during this special examination of aforesaid claim for pension, deposes and says: I am 58 years of age; my post-office address is 1607 10th Street west, Savannah, Georgia. Am a carpenter.

I am the identical person who served during late war as a private in Co. K 135th U.S.C. Vol. Inf. I do not know the date of enlistment but I became a Pioneer as Sherman came through during the fall of 1864 and kept with the army until during the spring of 1865 when I enlisted. I was discharged during October 1866 at Louisville Kentucky. I served under the name of Lewis Pettigrew. I had no other service than as above in the U.S. Army and never served in the U.S. Navy or Marine Corps.

I was born near Oliver, Screven County, Georgia, and was reared at same place. I was a slave of Edward Jones. I was born his slave and was yet owned by him at the time of emancipation. My father was named Fin Jones. Mother was named Mary. Both were slaves of Mr. Jones. I have a half brother, William Castle. I have a half sister, Mrs. Nora Lewis. Father and mother are dead. Half brother is about 23 years of age and half sister is about 50 years of age.

Page 3 Deposition A

I was on the plantation of my owner when Sherman's army came through, I fell in with the army. I do not remember any one now who left the plantation with me. Andrew Newton, dead, left with me. He was a member of the same company. I went by the name of Lewis Jones during slavery. My father was really named Frank Pettigrew, though his owner called him Frank Jones. When the soldiers asked me my name I stated that my father's name was Pettigrew so that is the name under which I enrolled. I have had the name of Lewis Pettigrew ever since. I was mustered into service here at Savannah. We went from here to Beaufort and on through South Carolina thence through North Carolina to Richmond and Washington City. We were sent from Washington to Louisville, Kentucky where we were discharged. Immediately after discharge I returned to the old home in Screven County. Only remained there a short time when I came here, where I have ever since resided.

I think Turley was the name of our colonel. My captain was Andrew J. Moon, do not recall name of lieutenant. I do not recall the sergeants or corporals.

Andrew Newton and Billy Newton, both dead, were tentmates. I am unable to give you the name of a single private in my company. Sharp Carter of the co. served in Co. I of my regiment. He is the only person here or elsewhere that I know who served in the regiment. I have heard you read the list of comrades. I do not recall any of them with the exception of Captain Moon and

Lieutenant Ray &c. I do not remember
Austin L. Frank, alias Brown or Shepherd
Mingo. Never knew them before service and
have not seen either of them since
discharge. I was paid $16 per month
as a soldier. I had a gun, a uniform, and
performed duty just as the other soldiers.
There was no other Pettigrew in my company.
I was 21 years of age when I enlisted.
I am now 5 ft. 9½ inches, and black;
born in Barnes County, Georgia. I was
a farm laborer at and prior enlistment.
I was not a mason at enlistment or
before, and had never been a stone or
brick mason. Since the war I have been
a free mason, or a member of Mount
Moriah Lodge of this city.
I had a discharge certificate but it was
lost about 1882. I had sent it to Mr. R. B.
Lester with a view to procuring some bounty
and during the correspondence ~~corres-~~
~~pondence~~ with Mr. Lester the discharge
certificate was lost. It was a brown
paper with the picture of an eagle and
U.S. flag on it.
I never filed a pension claim until
last February. I went before Notary H.
Kuecker and made out the declaration.
W. L. Moore had written to Fisher & Whitman
about me but Moore had nothing

Lewis Pettigrew
Deponent.

Sworn to and subscribed before me this 24th day of June 1904, and I certify that the contents were fully made known to deponent before signing.

A. B. Parker
Special Examiner.

Page 5 Deposition A

3—289.

DEPOSITION A

Case of Lewis Pettigrew, No. 1,281,001

On this 21 day of June, 1902, at Savannah, county of Chatham, State of Georgia, before me, A. B. Parker, a special examiner of the Bureau of Pensions, personally appeared Lewis Pettigrew, who, being by me first duly sworn to answer truly all interrogatories propounded to him during this special examination of aforesaid claim for pension, deposes and says:

to do with filing the claim. Moore did not even see the blank application sent me by the Washington attorneys. Richard Simpkins and R. H. Reese were my identifying witnesses. Myself and witnesses were each before Kimble and were properly sworn to the declaration. Kimble done all the writing in the claim. No one else has had anything to do with the claim. My name has always been signed by mark while in the army. None of my white people are living who were old enough to know anything about me being in the army. The most of the colored people who knew me prior to me coming here since freedom and they are all dead.

I have only been married one time. The name of wife is Amanda. Her maiden name was Amanda Miller. She and I were married in this city during Aug. 1867. I became acquainted with wife here after I came out of the army. Wife had no prior marriage. Wife and I have lived together ever since our marriage. We have never been separated or divorced from each other. Our marriage ceremony was performed by Rev. Wm. J.

Page 6 Deposition A

Page 7

applied. We had licensed wife and I have never had any children.

I claim pension on account of asthma and shortness of breath. Have had this trouble since the year 1873, due to cold which I then contracted. Asthma is not due to vicious habits. I had no sickness while in the army.

I do not know of any person by whom I can prove my identity with exception of Sophie Carter and a man named A. Lucas at Thunderbolt. Have no small picture of myself. Have heard read the foregoing statement and my answers have been correctly recorded.

Lewis Pettigrew
Deponent

Deponent.

Sworn to and subscribed before me this 25th day of June, 1908, and I certify that the contents were fully made known to deponent before signing.

A. D. Parker
Special Examiner.

CHAPTER 4

EXTRAORDINARY JOURNEY OF RESOLUTE BLACK SOLDIERS.

New Recruits

COMPANY “B”

INCLUDED IN THIS CHAPTER ARE EXTRACTIONS FROM THE PENSION RECORDS OF;

JERRY HUBBARD / RIVERS

CATO HOPKINS

DENNIS ISHAM / FAISON

NICODEMUS JONES

REUBEN FORT

SOLOMAN FAISON

JERRY HUBBARD / RIVERS

Jerry Hubbard, also known as Jerry Rivers after the Civil War, was in Company "B" of the 135th United States Colored Troop. He was from Bennettsville, Marlboro, County South Carolina where he enlisted in the Pioneer Corps when General Sherman's Army came through. The 1880 federal census shows him, along with his family, in Brightsville, Marlboro County South Carolina. It's shown that he was thirty-five years old at the time and his wife, Violet, was twenty-seven. They listed six children ages 11, 9, 6, 5, 4, and ½ years old.

The interesting part of his pension application is he referred to being shot in the face and hip while in service. Jerry Hubbard said that one morning they were on guard duty in Louisville, Kentucky guarding about seventy-two horses. He was with Joe Gates, who he claimed was dead at the time he made his application. So, he, Joe and Henry Moore who were also present, were approached by a "white man in citizen clothes on horseback." The man on the horse had a shotgun and he went in amongst the horses, and he saw the three of them guarding the horses and the white man raised his gun and fired it at them.

Jerry claimed that one of the buckshot struck him in the middle of his chin and another of the buckshot hit him in the left groin and hip. He ended up going to the hospital and the doctor extracted most of the buckshot, however, he was not able to remove it all. When he made his application for pension, he said that the shot in his hip and groin area burned at times, he had difficulty walking, and it gave him problems while sitting down for any length of time. Interestingly he mentioned, in the record, that the Doctors in the area were prejudiced against the colored men who were in the U.S. Army, and they wouldn't give them a fair deal or examination as they were against them getting a pension.

Jerry Hubbard applied for his pension in 1889. Years later Jerry was visited by his physician on June 19, 1902, and he claimed that Jerry died that same night. His wife, Violet, applied for her widow's pension in 1902 following her husband's death.

(3—118)

DEPOSITION 4

Case of Jerry Hubbard, No. 699640

On this 17 day of April, 1895, near Bennettsville, County of Marlboro, State of S.C., before me, J. G. Gibbes, Jr., a Special Examiner of the Pension Office, personally appeared Jerry Hubbard, who, being by me first duly sworn to answer truly all interrogatories propounded to him during this Special Examination of aforesaid pension claim, deposes and says: My age is about 52 years. My occupation is farm laboring when I am able to work. I live on Alfred W. Moore's place 5 miles from Bennettsville S.C. which is my P.O. address. Some call me Jerry Rivers but Hubbard is my business and army name. I am the identical Jerry Hubbard who served in Co. B, 135 U.S.C.T. I enlisted in this county and joined Potter's raid. I

Jerry Hubbard, who, being by me first duly sworn to answer truly all interrogatories propounded to him during this Special Examination of aforesaid pension claim, deposes and says: My age is about 52 years. My occupation is farm laboring when I am able to work. I live on Alfred W. Moore's place 5 miles from Bennettsville S.C. which is my P.O. address. Some call me Jerry Rivers but Hubbard is my business and army name. I am the identical Jerry Hubbard who served in Co. B, 135 U.S.C.T. I enlisted in this county and joined Potter's raid. I

joined for 5 years or sooner discharged. I was put right into Capt Whitney's Co. B 135th. The 1st Lt. was Westfall - 2nd Lt. "Sol Polly" - Oglesby was 3rd Lt. Ord. Sgt was Rix Brown - Geo Petty, Nat Campbell, Jesse Williams were sergeants - Bacchus Miller & Hop Potts were Corporals. Aaron Baventine, Henry Moore & myself volunteered at the same time. The Dr was Sparks and he had us to strip and he examined us to see if we were sound. The regiment went into North Carolina from there & we went to Goldsboro in the same month I enlisted i.e. March 1865. From Goldsb

name. I am the identical Jerry Hubbard
who served in Co. B, 135. U.S.C.T. I enlisted
in this County and joined Potter's band. I
joined for 3 years or sooner discharged.
I was put right into Capt Whitney's Co. B, 135.
The 1st Lt was Westfall – 2nd Lt Sol Petty –
Oglesby was 3rd Lt. Ord Sgt was Rix Brown.
Geo Petty, Nat Campbell, Jesse Williams
were sergeants – Bacchus Miller & Hop Potts
were Corporals. Aaron Barrentine, Henry
Moore & myself volunteered at the same time.
The Dr who Sparks and he had us to strip
and he examined us to see if we were sound.
The regiment went into North Carolina
from there we went to Goldsboro in the same
month I enlisted i.e. March 1865. From Goldsboro
we went to Raleigh N.C. then Petersburg Va &
then Richmond. We went then to Alexandria
then to Washington. We camped near Washington
for about a month and about June 1st we started
for Kentucky on the train. I was a sound
man until we reached Ky. The first sickness

Page 6 Deposition N

I had was in July 1865 at Louisville Ky. I was
at that time taken down with typhoid pneumonia
Dr Sparks the regimental surgeon, and Dr
Sparks the asst surgeon gave me treatment.
I was sent to the Hospital at Louisville Ky and
the Dr gave me medicine and applied mustard
plasters to my chest & sides. I recovered enough
to go back to the Company in July 1865 – the same
month I was taken down. I think
about the latter part of July Co B was ordered to
Lexington Ky to guard government property. We
staid there and guarded horses and other
property during the months of Aug & Sept. One
morning while on post guarding 72 horses
belonging to the government, I noticed a
white man in citizens clothes on horseback
in amongst our horses. Joe Gates (dead) and
Henry Moore were present and the man on
horseback raised his gun and fired on
me. One of the buckshot struck me on the

[illegible]
in amongst the horses. [illegible] and
[illegible] were present and the man on
horseback raised his gun and fired on
me. One of the buckshot struck me on the
middle of the chin and it glanced around
and now rests in the face. Other shots
struck me in the left groin and the Dr
took out some of them and there are more
in there yet. I can distinctly feel one now
and there may be others. The shot in my
thigh or groin itches me at times & burns
in cloudy weather and causes me to be
stiff in the left leg often and I have
difficulty in walking. It also gives me
trouble after sitting down long. I pass

Witness: A. C. Moore
Jerry (his X mark) Hubbard
Deponent

Sworn to and subscribed before me this 17 day of April
, and I certify that the contents were fully made known to deponent before sign

J. G. Grover Jr

I

(3—146.)

DEPOSITION B

Case of Jerry Hubbard , No. 699644

On this 19 day of April , 1895 Near Bennettsville , County of Marlboro
State of S.C. , before me, J. G. Grover Jr , a
Special Examiner of the Pension Office, personally appeared
Jerry Hubbard , who, being by me first duly sworn to answer
truly all interrogatories propounded to him during this Special Examination of aforesaid
pension claim, deposes and says: I am claimant.

In reply to your questions I will say that the
buckshot in my face does not continuously trouble
me now. It used to a few years ago give me
neuralgia to such an extent that I had to have
most of my jaw teeth taken out. In summer time
it gives me most trouble. It sometimes so pains
me till my cheek swells so I can hardly see.
The wounds in thigh have caused the rheumatism

buckshot in my face [illegible]
me now. It used to a few years ago give me
neuralgia to such an extent that I had to have
most of my jaw teeth taken out. In summer time
it gives me most trouble. It sometimes so pains
me till my cheek swells so I can hardly see.
The wounds in thigh have caused the rheumatism
with which I suffer, it is my belief. The doctors
in the army cut out some of the shot but they
did not dare to take out the one or two now
left in there as they said a big artery was too
close by. The wound itches me at times and
burns me sometimes. I have often expected the
shot to work out but it never has started to
do so yet. Yes sir, Dr Sholes probed all in
there and the scars are there now. I incurred
the wounds just as I described to you. I hear
now that Joe Yates who was shot at same
time, is dead.
The Drs in this part of the State are prejudiced
against a colored man who was in the U.S
Army. They won't give us a fair deal or
examination as they are against pensions.

Jerry his x mark Hubbard

CATO HOPKINS

Cato Hopkins was a private in Company "B," 135th United States Colored Troop. When he was mustered into service, he said "the doctor stripped me to see if I was sound then he thumped me around and this is all he did." He applied for his pension and gave a deposition stating he was born in Buford County South Carolina but left there when he was 4 or 5 years old. He was taken to McIntosh County Georgia and was a slave owned by Mr. Henry Mungen. Although he did not go into detail, his second owner was Mr. Octavas Hopkins, and said his father was Hector Scott. Prior to the war, Cato used Scott as his last name. After he enlisted, he then went by the name of Cato Hopkins. There is confusion in his file as to his place of enlistment as he gives Charleston, S.C., Hilton Head, S.C., and Buford, S.C., however, it was most likely the latter.

The date of Cato's original filing for pension was July 19, 1898, and at the time he was married to Delia Hopkins, his first wife. In his deposition for pension dated June 17, 1903, Cato was required to give a lengthy written testimony to justify his need for pension. In that filing, he claimed his wife died about a month prior to the filing and the record showed she died May 5th, 1903. He also gave his height at 5' 5" and his complexion, hair, and eyes black. He also stated that prior to enlistment he worked on the farm.

In a later filing on the 2nd of August 1912, when Cato requested to be placed on the pension rolls under the act of May 11, 1912, he gave his residence to be in Darien, Georgia.

Cato Hopkins died April 29, 1927, due to heart failure in Crescent, Georgia and his death certificate lists his wife at that time as Georgia Hopkins.

Following the death of Cato, Georgia Hopkins, who was his second wife, made a claim with the widow's division for the soldier's pension. There is sworn written testimony in June of 1928, giving statements as to the fact that Cato had married Georgia "some several years ago, probably 4 or 5 years ago," and that they lived together as husband and wife. In a later writing, from the director of pensions, the widow's pension is denied as the director writes "as you did not marry the veteran prior to June 27, 1905, and as his death was apparently not due to a disability incurred in the service or in line of duty, there is no law under which you may be granted a pension as his widow."

I was born in Beaufort Co. S.C. but I left there when a child of 4 or 5 years of age & was brought to McIntosh Co Ga. I was a slave and was owned by Henry Munger. My second owner was Tabby Hopkins. My father is Hector Scott. Cato Scott was my name before the War but after my enlistment I took the name of Cato Hopkins & I have gone under that name ever since.

Height 5 feet about 5 inches; complexion, hair & eyes black & says before enlistment that he worked on the farm.

I served during the War of the Rebellion in Co. B, 135 U.S.C. Vol. Inf., enlisting in Dec. 1864 at Beaufort S.C. and was discharged in "Kentucky Barracks" Oct 1865. I do not know in what state the Ky. Barracks are located unless it was located in the state of Ky.

After I enlisted at Beaufort they marched us to Orangeburg S.C. & from there to Raleigh N.C. & then to Wilmington & then we went up in

he worked on the farm.

I served during the War of the Rebellion in Co. B, 135 U.S.C. Vol. Inf., enlisting in Dec. 1864 at Beaufort S.C. and was discharged in "Kentucky Barracks" Oct 1865. I do not know in what state the Ky. Barracks are located unless it was located in the state of Ky.

After I enlisted at Beaufort they marched us to Orangeburg S.C. & from there to Raleigh N.C. & then to Wilmington & then we went up in
Va but I do not know where, & from there they took us to Wash. D.C. & then to Kentucky Barracks & mustered

Page Deposition

out. We were in the Barracks several mths before they mustered us out.

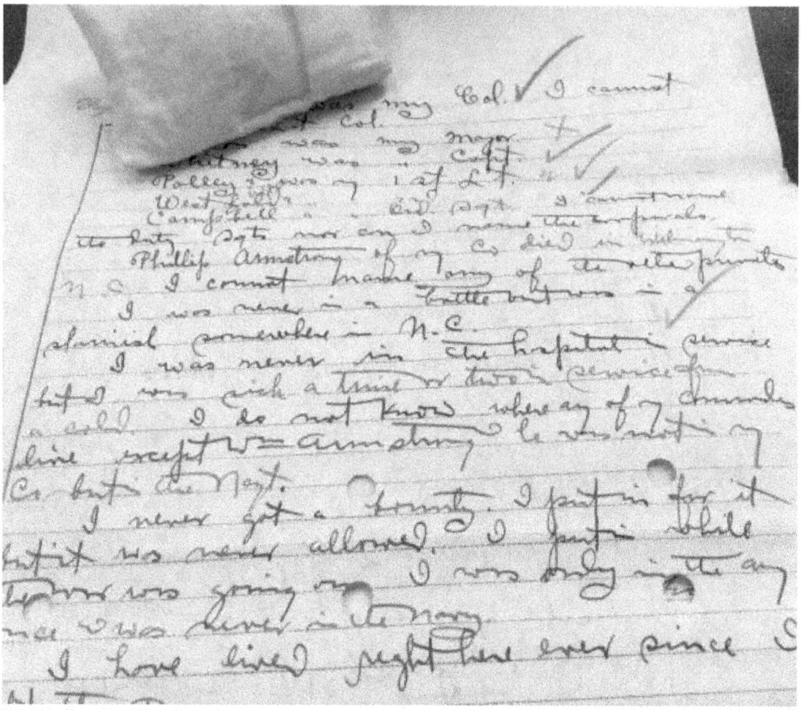
... was my Col. I cannot
... Col.
... was my Major
Whitney was my Capt.
Polley was my 1st Lt.
Westfall ... 2nd Sgt. I cannot name
Campbell ... Sgt. I cannot name the corporals
the Duty Sgts nor any ... of my Co died in Wilmington
Phillip Armstrong of my Co died in Wilmington
N.C. I cannot name any of the other privates
I was never in a battle but was in a
skirmish somewhere in N.C.
I was never in the hospital in service
but I was sick a time or two in service from
a cold. I do not know where any of my comrades
live except Wm Armstrong he was not in my
Co but in the Regt.
I never got a bounty. I put in for it
but it was never allowed. I put in while
the war was going on. I was only in the army
once I was never in the Navy.
I have lived right here ever since I

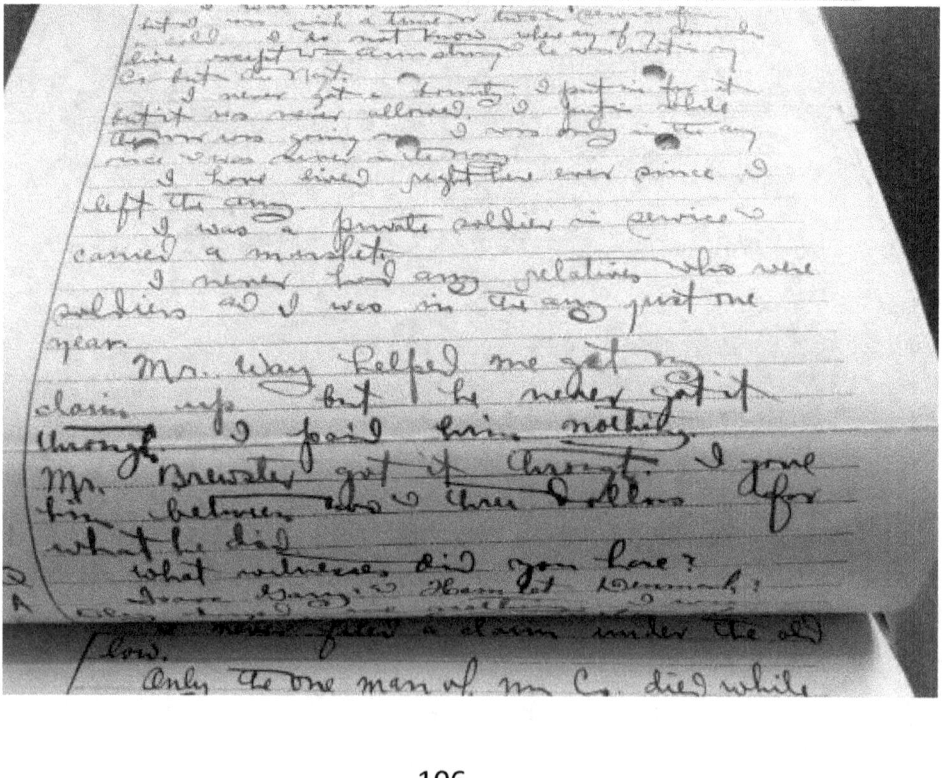
but I was sick a time or two in service from
a cold. I do not know where any of my comrades
live except Wm Armstrong he was not in my
Co but in the Regt.
I never got a bounty. I put in for it
but it was never allowed. I put in while
the war was going on. I was only in the army
once I was never in the Navy.
I have lived right here ever since I
left the army.
I was a private soldier in service I
carried a musket.
I never had any relatives who were
soldiers and I was in the army just one
year.
Mr. Way helped me get my
claim up but he never got it
through. I paid him nothing.
Mr. Brewster got it through. I gave
him between two & three dollars for
what he did.
What witnesses did you have?
Isaac Gregg & Hamlet Dennis?
...
I never filed a claim under the old
law.
Only the one man of my Co. died while

Only two men of my Co. died while we were in service.

The reason I cannot name any more of the comrades is because they were strangers to me all from N.C. & S.C. at enlistment & I have never been with them since I left the army.

I was only married once & my wife Welia died a month ago in two miles of here.

I have no children under 16 years of age.

I lost my discharge about 25 years ago. I then lost it by giving it to lawyer Way. He said he was going to get money for me but did not do it.

The reason I cannot name any more of the comrades is because they were strangers to me all from N.C. & S.C. at enlistment & I have never been with them since I left the army.

I was only married once & my wife Welia died a month ago in two miles of here.

I have no children under 16 years of age.

I lost my discharge about 25 years ago. I then lost it by giving it to lawyer Way. He said he was going to get money for me but did not do it.

I contracted rheumatism in my legs in service & have had it ever since. I never had it before enlistment.

When I was mustered in service the Dr. stripped me to see if I was sound & then he thumped me around. That was all that he did.

I was never treated by the Dr. in service.

I have my vouchers executed by Mr. Moretz. He charges me nothing. I have never promised

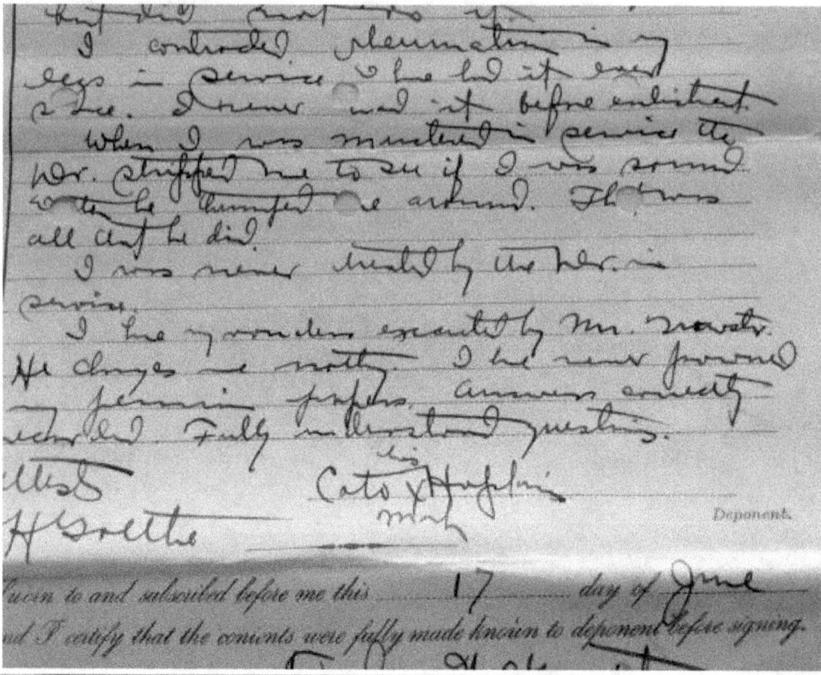
but did not [illegible]

I contracted rheumatism in my legs in service & have had it ever since. I never had it before enlistment.

When I was mustered in service the Dr. stripped me to see if I was sound & then he thumped me around. That was all that he did.

I was never treated by the Dr. in service.

I have my answers recorded by Mr. [illegible]. He charges me nothing. I have never [illegible] pension papers. Answers correctly recorded. Fully understand questions.

Attest
H. [illegible]

his
Cato X Hopkins
mark

Deponent.

[S]worn to and subscribed before me this 17 day of June
[a]nd I certify that the contents were fully made known to deponent before signing.

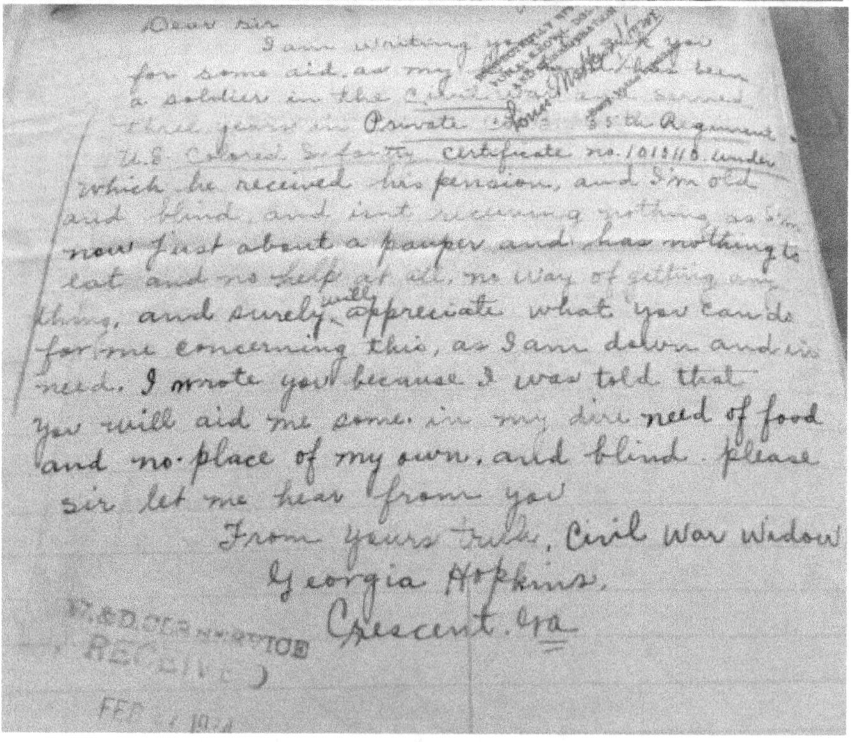
Dear sir

I am writing you to ask you for some aid, as my [illegible] has been a soldier in the Civil War [illegible] served three years in Private [illegible] 55th Regiment U.S. Colored Infantry certificate no. 1013118. under which he received his pension, and I'm old and blind, and isnt receiving nothing as I'm now just about a pauper and has nothing to eat and no help at all, no way of getting any thing, and surely will appreciate what you can do for me concerning this, as I am down and in need. I wrote you because I was told that you will aid me some. in my dire need of food and no place of my own, and blind. please sir let me hear from you

From yours truly, Civil War Widow
Georgia Hopkins.
Crescent. Ga

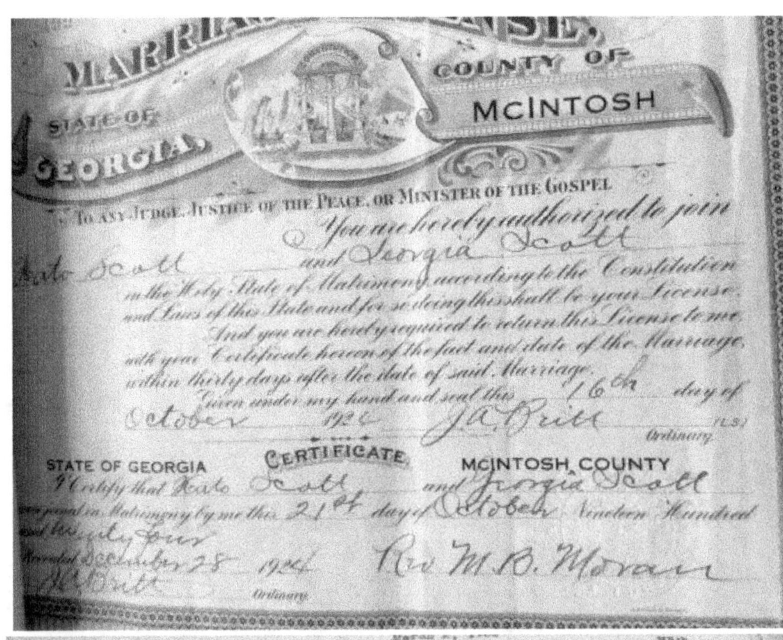

[illegible] SERVICE
RECEIVED
FEB [illegible] 19[illegible]

MARRIAGE LICENSE,

STATE OF GEORGIA, COUNTY OF McINTOSH

To any Judge, Justice of the Peace, or Minister of the Gospel

You are hereby authorized to join Cato Scott and Georgia Scott in the Holy State of Matrimony, according to the Constitution and Laws of this State and for so doing this shall be your License.

And you are hereby required to return this License to me with your Certificate hereon of the fact and date of the Marriage within thirty days after the date of said Marriage.

Given under my hand and seal this 16th day of October 1924

J. A. Britt (L.S.)
Ordinary.

STATE OF GEORGIA CERTIFICATE McINTOSH COUNTY

I Certify that Cato Scott and Georgia Scott were joined in Matrimony by me this 21st day of October Nineteen Hundred and twenty four

Recorded December 28 1924 Rev M. B. Moran

J. A. Britt
Ordinary.

NSS

Mrs. Georgia Hopkins
Crescent, Georgia

HOPKINS, Cato
W.O. 1,720,339

Dear Madam:

This is in further reply to your letter of January 12, 1934, addressed to President Roosevelt, relative to your pensionable status as the widow of the above named veteran, Cato Hopkins.

As you did not marry the veteran prior to June 27, 1905 and as his death was apparently not due to a disability incurred in the service in line of duty, there is no law under which you may be granted a pension as his widow.

It is regretted that this Service is unable to afford you any relief.

All communications relative to this case should bear the veteran's name and refer to the number W.O. 1,720,339.

Respectfully,

E. W. MORGAN,
Director.

DENNIS ISHAM / FAISON

Dennis Faison was about twenty-six years old when he joined Sherman's army in Company "B," 135th United States Colored Troop. He was ill throughout his tenure in the military and sadly passed away just eight short years after the war ended; his story is told through the depositions of family and friends, many who were in Company "B," with him.

In March of 1865, Sherman stopped near the small community of Faison Depot in Wayne County, North Carolina. John Hargrove, a boyhood friend of Dennis and one of six bunkmates in Company "B," with Dennis, remembered it was a Monday morning. With John, his cousin Solomon Faison, and another childhood friend, John Thompson, Dennis left Faison Depot to join the "Yankee army," as several men called it. Dennis was a slave on the plantation of Isham Faison, while Solomon's master, Billy Faison, owned the adjacent plantation. Curtis Thompson owned John Thompson on another nearby plantation, and John Hargrove was a slave on the plantation of "a Mr. Hargrove." The four knew Dennis well, each having grown up with him. John Hargrove said he was "well and unusually acquainted with Dennis Faison" and "knew him as well as I do one of my own boys." They all were bunkmates at one time or another, each claimed to have slept with Dennis and eaten with him, and he and John Hargrove even "wore one another's clothes."

Each man in their depositions recalled Dennis being ill almost from the beginning. According to Solomon, Dennis developed jaundice at Raleigh about a month after they mustered in and was unable to do his duty for about two months. He was "hauled on a wagon from Raleigh to Richmond," and then a month later, "he was taken down with rheumatism" in Orange County, Virginia. He went on to say that Dennis was hospitalized in Louisville, but Solomon did not know why because he was in Springfield and away from Dennis for about two months. He did say that Dennis went home sick and "never was hearty anymore." Both John Hargrove and John Thompson confirmed Dennis's illness early in their service, and both recollect his complaints of pain on his left side. Hargrove stated his "worst trouble seemed to be about his heart on his left side" and that he would complain of constant pain in that area. When Dennis first fell ill, Hargrove thought he might have had consumption, even though he never saw Dennis "spit blood." He went on to say that Dennis was "always kinda puny."

Though the name given to him by his father was Dennis, some friends and family would refer to him as "Isham." John Thompson claims that Dennis was "nicknamed Isham by us colored boys because he tried to talk something like his Master." Though he used the name Dennis throughout the service, this childhood moniker stuck, and after the war, Dennis Faison often went by the name Isham. Solomon also knew him by both names, while John Hargrove only knew him as Dennis. Henry Faison was also Dennis's cousin and a slave on Isham Faison's plantation; however, he was several years younger than Dennis. He remembered that Dennis "went north with the Yankee Army when they first came through" and said Dennis never returned to live with his Master. He recalls his cousin going by Dennis before the war and Isham after.

Dennis is described by John Hargrove as a "ginger cake," meaning he was "not as black as some colored men." He said he had black eyes, black curly hair, and a little mustache. John Thompson describes Dennis as having been a "pretty black colored man" who "did not wear any whiskers in the service." He also recalled that he and Dennis were close to the same age, but Dennis "was right smart smaller than I am." (John described himself as being 5'9" tall.)

Following the war, Dennis initially returned to Faison, but John Hargrove stated that Faison was "too hot" and Dennis "could not stay about here" so he left. Solomon confirmed that and explained the situation by saying he destroyed his discharge certificate after the war "as times was 'too hot' around here to keep such things." Because of the dangerous environment, especially for black Union soldiers, Dennis left Faison and eventually made his way back to Goldsboro where he married Florence, and together they settled in the city. Dennis and Florence had two children, Serena and Isham, with Isham being born about a month after Dennis's death.

George Everett, a blacksmith, met Dennis and Florence Faison just after they married. According to George, Dennis "had his soldier clothes on yet" and went by the name Isham. It was soon after the war when Dennis went to see George at the shop where he was shoeing horses for the Government, and after that, George would see him "about every day" as he lived across the street from the couple. He said that Isham was "always complaining about some misery inside his chest" that took him by spells, sometimes much worse than others. He recalled that Isham never had a cough until his last illness when he had both a cough and "hemorrhage of his nose." He claimed that the doctor treated Isham's nosebleed and "plugged it up," but Isham died soon after. George was there when Isham (Dennis) died and at his funeral, remembered it was sometime in the winter (January 12, 1874, according to other records). He also said Isham is buried in Robinson Graveyard, "back of the College" in Goldsboro.

Solomon, Henry, John Hargrove, and John Thompson visited Dennis at different times following the war, with Henry likely visiting the most. None of Dennis's companions had met Florence before their marriage, and none saw her after his death. Each of them remembered Dennis's declining health, though, with John Thompson recalling that Dennis was sick in Onslow and stayed with his sister Anne and Laura Thompson when John visited. John Hargrove saw Dennis several times after the war, and Dennis complained of his side, "the same thing he complained of in the army." Hargrove would say to him, "Dennis, you must be growing worse," to which Dennis would say, "Yes, it will be the death of me yet." Hargrove never lived near Dennis after the war and never knew Florence, but Dennis's other companions got to know her after Dennis and Florence were married, none having met her before then and none seeing her after Dennis's death.

Following Dennis's death, Florence Faison never remarried; instead, she worked to support herself and her two young children. At the time of her appeal for Widow's Pension, she lived in a bedroom that she paid fifty cents per week rent. She owned about fifteen dollars' worth of property, including two bed stands, five chairs, a trunk, a few bedclothes, one feather bed, and two mattresses. At the time of her statement in 1900, she had had no income since July 23, 1895, and had not collected any pension. Strangely, in her deposition, as well as that of her friend Lucy Sellars, she repeatedly claims that her husband served in Company "A," of the 135th USC Infantry, while all the men who served with him distinctly remember they were in Company "B."

Dennis "Isham" Faison was plagued by illness during his enlistment in Sherman's army, yet he remained until all their company was mustered out in late October of 1865. He built many lasting friendships before the war, and several of those friends served alongside him in Company "B," of the 135th USCT. All these men had their own stories, yet they are so intertwined that to tell one is to tell all.

N. B.—Examiners should be particular to have affiants sign on the line next below the closing words of their depositions so as to leave little or no space between their signatures and the end of their depositions.

3—200.

DEPOSITION B

Case of Florence Faison, No. 557391

On this 10th day of December, 1900, at Bowden, County of Duplin, State of N. C. before me, H. T. [illegible] a special examiner of the Bureau of Pensions, personally appeared Solomon Faison, who, being by me first duly sworn to answer truly all interrogatories propounded to him during this special examination of aforesaid claim for pension, deposes and says: I am 57 years of age; my post-office address is Bowden, N. C.

Occupation, farmer.

I served in Co. B, 135 U.S.C. Inf., from March 1865 to about Nov 28 1866, and was well and personally acquainted with Dennis Faison who served in my company. I was a private, and he was a private. We tented and ate together most of the time. I knew him since he was a boy about 13 or 14 years old, and we grew up as boys together. He belonged to Isham Faison who lived at Faison Depot, and I belonged to Kilby Faison who lived five miles from Faison. Dennis and I were first cousins. He and I enlisted at the same time at a near Raleigh N.C. We were in the Pioneer Corps before that building breastworks and repairing the road, and such things. His name was Dennis Faison when he enlisted, and he served under that name, and that was his name when they called the roll. He was about 26 years old and weighed about 150 lbs when he enlisted

Page 13 Deposition B

Page 4 was about 5 ft. 6 in. tall. He had no marks about him and wore a little mustache. He was a pretty black complexion, black eyes and black curly hair, and was a farmer when he enlisted. He was a sound healthy man when he enlisted, but was sick some in the service. He had the yellow jaundice when encamped at Raleigh about a month after he enlisted. He could not do duty for about two months and was hauled from Raleigh to Wilmington on a wagon train. About a month after that he was taken down with rheumatism at Orange C. H. Va. He did not go to a hospital but got medicine from a doctor that stayed with us all the time. He was sick at Louisville in Sept. 1865, but I don't know what was the matter with him then as I was at Springfield, Ky. about that time and away from him about two months. He was in a hospital at Louisville Ky. He came home sick and was hardly ever well again. He had a doctor after he came home at Goldsboro, but I don't remember who he was. I don't remember that he ever had any bowel trouble in the army. His full name was Simmons Isham Forbes, so named by his father but before the war he was called Isham, but after the war he was called Simmons Isham Forbes up around Goldsboro. He was called Isham after his old master. He never was married before the war or before he married the claimant. I think and am satisfied her name was Simmons, but I don't know she had

man I did not know her before
Dennis married her. I knew her 1st
husband was the same man that
served in our company and regiment under the name of Thomas
Frison. I can't read or write and don't
know how they spelled my name
on the rolls and I have not any discharge certificate. I destroyed it after the
war as there was "no use" to hold [illegible]
here to keep such things. I am sure
he served in Co B. 135 U.S.C. Inf. He
was never in any other service and
was never in Co A, 135 U.S.C. Inf.
I visited him pretty often after he
was up at [illegible] since the war,
and visited him [illegible] when he
was sick. He was living with
Florence then, but I don't recollect
seeing her since her death. John
Morgan was in our company. [illegible]
[illegible] Thompson (dead) John Thomas at
Henderson was also in the company and
[illegible] Dennis [illegible]. I don't know of any
others about here. I have understood
your questions and my answers
are correctly recorded in this deposition which has been read to
me before signing. I am 1st cousin of
soldier, but have no interest in the
claim

Witness:
[illegible] Frison
H. F. Shontz

his
Solomon X Frison
mark
Deponent.

Sworn to and subscribed before me this 10th day of December
1900, and I certify that the contents were fully made known to deponent before signing.

H. F. Shontz
Special Examiner.

Page 12 Deposition B

3-446.

DEPOSITION D

Case of Florence Faison, No. 557,391

On this 13th day of December, 1900, at Newbern, county of Craven, State of N.C., before me, H.F. Sheats, a special examiner of the Bureau of Pensions, personally appeared John Thompson, who, being by me first duly sworn to answer truly all interrogatories propounded to him during this special examination of aforesaid claim for pension, deposes and says:

I am 57 years of age; my post-office address is Newbern N.C. occupation: nothing, am unable to work.

I served as a private in Co. B, 135 U.S.C. Inf. from April 1865, when Gen Sherman came to Goldsboro, and was discharged sometime in November of the same year. Dennis Faison was a messmate of mine. We slept together, ate together and served together. He and I were acquainted ever since we were four or five years old, and were raised on adjoining plantations partly. There was not much difference in our ages, but he was right smart smaller than I am. I am 5 ft 9 in in height. He was a pretty black colored man, and did not wear any whiskers in the service. He belonged to Isham Faison, and was raised on his plantation near Faison depot. I belonged to Curtis Thompson and we were both raised near each other, and were together almost every day or night of the week. We both joined Sherman's Army at the same time and were in the same company and regiment, all through the service and came home together at

Page 1 Deposition D

No. 24

the close of the war. He came back to Goldsboro again and after a year he moved down to Onslow Co. N.C. and stayed there a while. He was sick down there and I went down to see him once. When he was there he stayed with his sister Annie, and Lucy Thompson. No, he was not living with any other woman when I was to see him.

Q. Did he ever have any other name?

A. No, not except Isham. He was nick-named Isham by us colored boys because he tried to talk something like his master, but his right name was Dennis and he served under the name of Dennis, while in the war, and that was the name they called on the roll. After the war I called him Dennis but I know some people did call him Isham. He married Florence Green, but I don't know what her master's name was. I got acquainted with his wife soon after they were married since the war. I have not seen claimant and Dennis very often since the war – came to see them once in a while. I lived in Goldsboro a short time after the war and then moved to Pitt Co. then to Nash Co. then Edgecombe, and then back to Duplin Co., about 2 or 3 miles from Warsaw where I lived until the 11th of last August, since which time Deponent

Sworn to and subscribed before me this 13 day of December, 190 , and I certify that the contents were fully made known to deponent before signing.

[illegible] Claimant

H. F. [illegible]

Special Examiner.

SPECIAL NOTICE.—The civil officer before whom this affidavit is executed should be careful to fill in all spaces both in the caption and jurat.

Claimant's ~~GENERAL~~ AFFIDAVIT.

State of North Carolina, County of Wayne, ss:

In the matter of Claim #557391 of Florence Faison widow of Isham Faison Co A 135 U.S.C.I.

ON THIS 5th day of July, A. D. 1899, personally appeared before me Hugh Humphrey U.S. Com. in and for the ~~aforesaid~~ Eastern District N.C. ~~County, duly authorized to administer oaths~~ Florence Faison aged 66 years, a resident of Goldsboro, in the County of Wayne, and State of N.C. whose Post-Office address is Goldsboro N.C. ~~and~~

~~aged~~ ~~years, a resident of~~

~~in the County of~~

~~and State of~~ ~~whose Post-Office address is~~

well known to be reputable and entitled to credit, and who, being duly sworn, declared in relation to aforesaid case as follows:

(Note.—Affiants should state how they gain a knowledge of the facts to which they testify.)

I am the Widow of Isham Faison late soldier Co A. 135 U.S. Colord Infantry. I have no property real or personal, except one bed stead, five chairs, one trunk & a few bed clothes one feather and one mattress, the value of fifteen dollars, have no income now, or since July 23. 1895, and there is no person legally bound to support me, and I earn my Scanty living by washing, earning about one dollar per week on an average.

My decd husband Isham Faison did not serve in the Military or Naval Service of the United States prior to March 27 1865, nor after October 23rd 1865, he only belonged & Served in Co A. 135 U.S. Col'd Infantry and no other.

PENSION U. S. JUL 21 1899 OFFICE

~~further declare that~~ ~~no interest in said case and~~ ~~not concerned in its prosecution.~~

J. L. Mayerberg
T. P. Parker
(If Affiant sign by mark, two witnesses who can write sign here.)

her
Florence X Faison
mark
(Signature of Affiant.)

NICODEMUS JONES

The pension declarations regarding Nicodemus Jones show that he was a soldier in Company "B," 135th United States Colored Troop and was known by that name since birth. He disclosed in the record that he was born in Burke County, Georgia, and was a slave of Madison Reynolds who was his owner. His father was Henry Jones and they enlisted in Charlotte, North Carolina when General Sherman's Army passed through the area towards the end of the Civil War. Nicodemus recalls that he and his father were both privates in Company "B," and he goes on to recollect that his father died when their unit was about forty miles from Richmond Virginia while on their way to Washington D.C.

The profile of Nicodemus in the record revealed that he was mulatto and being about 5' 5" tall, was a farm hand prior to his enlistment in the 135th USCT and suggests that he was never in any battles. Nicodemus did claim an injury during his service to his right ankle. That happened while crossing the Roanoke River on their way to Richmond Virginia, but he never spent time in the hospital and was carried in an ambulance wagon for about two weeks. He remembered being discharged in Louisville, Kentucky and from there he went to Augusta, Georgia, and lived and worked there for six or seven years after his honorable discharge.

The disposition of the pension for Nicodemus seems to be quite the story following his death. There is a good deal of controversy in the record regarding his marriage status to determine the rightful widow eligible for the widow's pension. The depositions showed Nicodemus initially married Georgiana Jackson with a license issued August 14, 1869, out of Richmond County, Georgia. Georgiana stated in the record that she was first married to William Henry Jackson "about the close of the Civil War." They lived together for about two years however she said that he went off with the "racehorse men," and he never came back. When he left, they had one child that she said was very small at the time. Within about six or seven months, after William Jackson left her, word came back that he had died.

There is testimony in the file that Nicodemus deserted Georgiana and eloped with Jannie Tilley about 1875 or there about. This is about 5 or 6 years after he legally married Georgiana Jackson. They were living in Augusta Georgia, and it was evident that Nicodemus was away at times doing work in Athens, Georgia where he met up with Jannie Tilley. This was about 1875 and Nicodemus led Jannie to believe he was a single man and never had been with another woman. In any case, it is shown in the record that Nicodemus deserted Georgiana and eloped with Jannie Tilley.

Jannie Tilley took up living with Nicodemus in Savannah, Georgia and they lived as husband and wife for some 30 or 35 years. They had one child together who was named Jackson, and he died when he was about thirty around 1910.

In searching the public records, (Ancestry), Nicodemus Jones was born on March 10, 1844, and died on September 12, 1913, in Savannah, Georgia, and is part of the African American Civil War Memorial.

Jannie filed her widow's Declaration for Pension, on October 1, 1913, just weeks after Nicodemus' death. This is where the problem with the application for widow's pension comes into play. There is an investigation that takes place due to Jannie having to prove she was in fact legally married to Nicodemus Jones. There are no records to prove their marriage, however, we find numerous fraudulent depositions claiming they were in fact married at Beach Island South Carolina. During the investigation, the Commissioner of Pensions finds no ceremonial record of the marriage of Jannie Tilley to Nicodemus Jones.

The Commissioner of Pensions ended up interviewing Georgiana Jones and discovered that they were in fact married and had children together, but he was informed that Nicodemus had left her without legally getting a divorce. Georgiana provided the Commissioner with the original marriage certificate which she was supposed to have properly filed with the courts; however, she didn't do so because she wanted to keep the original.

The investigation is incredibly involved and there are several witnesses, however in the end the determination made was that Georgiana Jones was the legal wife. Jannie Jones was not ceremonially married to Nicodemus, was not his lawful wife, and had no status as his lawful widow.

Wid. Orig. 1015154
Jannie Jones
Nicodemus Jones
Co. B, 135th U.S.C. Inf.

Record of Marriage

Marriage License issued to Nickedemos Jones and Georgania Jackson August 14, 1869, by Sam'l Levy, Ordinary, County of Richmond, State of Georgia.

(MARRIAGE CERTIFICATE)

I HEREBY CERTIFY, That Nicodemus Jones and Gorgiana Jackson were joined together in the holy bans of matrimony, by me, on the 15th day of August 1869.

(Signed) Emanuel Asberry
Pr W. J. W.

The above is a true copy of a marriage certificate this day returned to Georgiana Jones, 15th Street (near new Methodist Church), Augusta, Georgia.

John F. Kennan
CHIEF, CIVIL WAR DIVISION.

January 29, 1915.

The soldier in this claim died at Savannah, Georgia, September 12, 1913, and on October 1, 1913, this claimant filed a declaration for pension as his widow, in which she alleged a ceremonial marriage to soldier at Beach Island, South Carolina, August 17, 1875, and its subsistence until his death, and in the course of the prosecution of the claim she furnished the testimony of witnesses to corroborate her allegation of a ceremonial marriage, which in the course of the special examination was clearly shown to have been fraudulent, as was the claimant's allegation of a ceremonial marriage to the soldier. It is clear, however, from the testimony that the claimant lived with the soldier for many years and that she was known and recognized as his wife but the parties were never ceremonially married, which fact has been clearly demonstrated in the evidence.

The claimant appears to have been legally competent to contract marriage at the date of the inception of her relation with thesoldier. On the part of the soldier it is shown that he was first ceremonially married to one Georgiana Jackson under a license which issued out of Richmond County, Georgia, August 14, 1869, and which bears the certificate of the officiating clergyman which shows that the marriage was entered into August 15, 1869, and while this license was never returned to the Ordinary for the purpose of recording, it has been fully identified as having been issued by the Ordinary of the county at that time, and is competent proof of the fact of the marriage between the parties. Georgiana, the first wife of the soldier, was located by the special examiner, and in her deposition she admits her ceremonial marriage to the soldier and furnished the license evidence showing the fact thereof. She also admits that prior to her marriage to soldier, and about the close of the Civil War, she was ceremonially married to one William Henry Jackson, with whom she lived for a period when he left her to follow his vocation with race horses, and she further alleges that sometime after he left her she received information of his death, subsequent to which time she has never seen nor heard of him, and on the belief that Jackson was dead she was ceremonially married to the soldier, as above stated.

The evidence also shows that said Georgiana never remarried or lived with any man in the ostensible relation of husband and wife subsequent to Jackson's

As above stated we have no proof whatever to show that Georgiana's husband, Jackson, survived her marriage to the soldier. On the contrary, she alleges his death prior to that time and there is no evidence in rebuttal, and under the laws of the State of Georgia, she having entered into a formal ceremonial marriage with the soldier in 1869, said marriage is presumptively valid, and as it subsisted until the soldier's death she became his lawful widow at that time.

As to the claimant Jannie Jones, it is clear that she was never ceremonially married to the soldier; that the soldier deserted Georgiana and eloped with the claimant to Savannah, Georgia, where they lived ostensibly as husband and wife for many years; that her allegation of a ceremonial marriage was fraudulent and that she has filed fraudulent evidence in support thereof, and as the soldier's marriage to his first wife Georgiana subsisted until his death, the relation he sustained with the claimant, meretricious and adulterous at inception, so continued during its existence. She was never the soldier's lawful wife and has no status as his lawful widow.

Respectfully,

Case of Jannie Jones, *No.* 1015184

On this 8th *day of* October 1914, *191* , *at* Augusta, *county of* Richmond *State of* Ga., *before me,* Thos. H. Goethe *a Special Examiner of the Bureau of Pensions, personally appeared* Georgiana Jones, *who, being by me first duly sworn to answer truly all interrogatories propounded to h___ during this special examination of aforesaid claim for pension, deposes and says:*

Age, occupation and post office address, as before stated.

How many times have you been married?

Twice and only twice. No, I was not married three times. My first husband was William Henry Jackson. He married me about the close of the Civil War in this city and we lived together awhile and then he went off with the race horse men and word came back that he was dead and I think he died in Hancock Co, Ga. We were married by a white Minister of the Gospel named Cox. Mr. Cox left here and I never knew where he went to.

Q Can you prove the death of William Henry Jackson?

I was born in Burk County, Ga., and was a slave; was owned by Madison Reynolds. My father was Henry Jones and he died while he was in my company in service. We were both privates. He died about forty miles this side of Richmond, Va.

Personal description: Height five feet six inches; complexion; mulatto; hair and eyes, black and says prior to enlistment he was a farm hand.

I served during the war of the Rebellion in Co. B, 135th U. S. C. Vol. Inf., enlisting at Charlotte, N. C., just before the war was over and being discharged about a year and six months later at Louisville, Ky. The above was my only service in the army or navy of the U. S., and I was never in the Confederate service.

We were never in any battles. I had my right ankle thrown out of place while crossing the Roanoke River going to Richmond and I was not in the hospital but was carried in the ambulance for two weeks. That was the only sickness that I had while in service.

After enlistment at Charlotte we went to Washington, D. C., and from there to Louisville, Ky., and after we got there the regiment was split up and we were sent to take Government stock through, Ky. Finally we re-assembled in Louisville and then mustered us out. I was never in South Carolina or Georgia while I was a soldier.

After my discharge I moved to Augusta, Ga., and lived there some six or seven years and then I moved here where I have been

Richmond and I was not in the hospital but was carried in the ambulance for two weeks. That was the only sickness that I had while in service.

After enlistment at Charlotte we went to Washington, D. C., and from there to Louisville, Ky., and after we got there the regiment was split up and we were sent to take Government stock through, Ky. Finally we re-assembled in Louisville and then mustered us out. I was never in South Carolina or Georgia while I was a soldier.

After my discharge I moved to Augusta, Ga., and lived there some six or seven years and then I moved here where I have been ever since.

I was about twenty one or two when I enlisted.
Gurley was my Colonel.
Dixon was Lt. Col.
I do not recollect the name of my Major.
George W. Whitney was my Capt.
Westfall was my 1st Lt.
Polly was 2d Lt.
Brown was Ord. Sgt.
George Petty was a duty Sgt.
Williams (Jesse) was a Sgt.
Kelley was a Corporal.

5

Page_______ Deposition_______

RUBEN FORT

In 1924 a letter was sent from Washington DC to the heirs of Ruben Fort indicating that there was an accumulated pension of $700.00 due to him for his military service. Ruben Fort was from Sampson County, North Carolina, and enlisted at Goldsboro, North Carolina on March 27, 1865, in the newly formed 135th United States Colored Troop. He was promoted to Corporal in Company "B," on March 28, 1865.

As a result of his service in the 135th USCT Ruben Fort developed Chronic Diarrhea in Louisville, Kentucky after his several months in the Regiment. After he returned home, he married Edith with whom he had three children. Sydney was born in 1880, William born in 1883 and Minnie who was born in 1887. Unfortunately, Ruben died January 15, 1894, and his wife, Edith died a week later January 22, 1894, leaving the three children all under the age of sixteen.

Following the deaths of Ruben and Edith, Saul Parker became the guardian of the three Fort Children who had been orphaned. Now back to the $700.00 due to the heirs of Ruben Fort. There is a letter explaining the circumstances and it reads; ***"Ruben Fort, an old colored man died here several years ago, leaving three children, Sid, Minnie, and Pinkney Fort. The said William Fort deceased having presented some thirty or forty years ago and made a claim for a pension on account of military service, this being promised him at that time, but he has never received the same up until the time of his death, being an invalid for twenty or thirty years prior***

to the time of his death. A few years after his death one of the heirs received a letter sent from Washington, D.C. stating that there was an accumulated pension of something like $700.00 due to their father Ruben Fort on account of such military service. A few days after this letter was received the one to whom it was mailed to died and left one brother and one sister living, and some children." As a result, we found that there was no indication of whatever became of the $700.00 due.

(3—060.)

M. T.
Ie. DIVISION. E461

Department of the Interior,

PENSION OFFICE,

Feb. 12, 1880.

Respectfully requested of the ADJUTANT GENERAL U. S. A. a report of service and disability in the case No. 453.864, of

Reuben Fort

Co. B. 135 U.S.C.T.

Disabled by Chronic Diarrhoea, contracted at Louisville, Ky.

— — ——, 1865.

Discharged Oct. 23, 1865;

Please furnish full military history.

Wm. W. Dudley

Commissioner.

State of North Carolina
Sampson County

Personally appeared before me this day Chaney Fort who being duly sworn according to law doth depose and say. That she was the female attendant of Edith Fort at the birth of Sydney Fort and that she was born on the 15th day of January AD 1880. And she was also the female attendant of Edith Fort at the birth of Pinkney Fort and that he was born on the 20th day of December AD. 1883. and that she was the female attendant of Edith Fort at the birth of Minnie Fort and that she was born on the 10th day of March AD 1887. She further swears that this affidavit was written in her presence and only from her oral statements and that she was not aided or prompted by any written or printed recital or statement prepared or dictated by any other person.

Chaney her + mark Fort (Signature)

M. M. Hall
Bascom J Spell } Sworn & subscribed before me this 26th day of Oct 1895.
J. F. Owen Justice of the Peace

Roseboro, N. C.
Dec 23rd 1895.

Hon. William Lochren
Commissioner of Pensions
Washington. D.C.

Dear Sir:-

Replying to yours of 5th Inst. I have to say.

That I do not remember the date of the birth of Ruben Fort's minor children from record but from the date of my own children which I take from record I am able to remember the ages of Sydney Fort and Pinkney Fort.

As to the age of Marine Fort I remember it by the great earth quake and that I was staying with Mr Delaney Mathews wife at the time I was called to the wife of Ruben Fort and the age can be obtained by that.

I am confident that the month and years are given correctly. Hoping that this will be satisfactory.

I am

Writer Very Respectfully
Chaney Fort.

E. CROSWELL ROBINSON
ATTORNEY AT LAW

PHONE 10 STARLING BUILDING

ROSEBORO, N. C.
April, 3, 1924.

Answered May 1, 1924

The Commissioner of Pensions,
Department of Interior,
Washington, D.C.

Dear Sir;-

I have a letter before me from Senator Simmons with reference to a claim that I wrote him about a few days ago, and he refers me to your office.

The facts in the case are these. Ruben Fort an old colored man died here several years ago, leaving three children, Sid Boykin, Minnie Crumpler, and William Fort. The said William Fort deceased having presented some thirty or forty years ago and made claim for a pension on account of military services, this being promised him at that time, but he having never received the same up until the time of his death, and being an invalid for twenty or thirty years prior to the time of his death. A few years after his death one of the heirs received a letter sent from Washington, D.C. stating that there was an accumulated pension of something like $700.00 due their father Ruben Fort on account of such military service.

A few days after this letter was received the one to whom it was mailed died and left one brother and one sister living, and also some children.

PENSION OFFICE
APR 5 1924
U. S.

SOLOMAN FAISON

Soloman Faison's application for pension is one of the more unique pension applications as his slave owner Kilby Faison owned many slaves in Sampson County, North Carolina. There was an extensive list of all the slaves that were owned by Kilby Faison that his granddaughter provided after his death. The list of slaves was certified to be a true list by J.N. Bennett on November 27, 1909. Soloman's name is clearly entered on the list of names which gave his birth date certifying his age. He was born on September 2, 1843, as shown on the document. The granddaughter gave the entire record to Soloman. That list had a wealth of information for all those related to the Kilby Faison plantation in Duplin County, North Carolina.

Soloman said in his declaration that Mr. Kilby Faison raised him however he belonged to Mr. Alex Herring at the time of his enlistment. After his service, he returned to Bowden, North Carolina, and married Louisa Faison and they raised ten children together.

As spelled out in this soldier's pension record, due to the many miles of marching and his time on guard duty, it almost made him a person with disabilities. He had severe back problems and apparent kidney ailments therefore Soloman was awarded a small pension for his service in Company "B," of the 135th United States Colored Troop.

Mt Olive N C

Solomon Faison is dead
But his Company was B-135
Regiment U S C; V Inf.
This is the No. on his Pension
Papers. Hope to hear from
you soon. I remain very
truly Sallie. B. Faison
613 East Hillsboro St

WAR DEPARTMENT,
THE ADJUTANT GENERAL'S OFFICE,
WASHINGTON, SEP 27 1909

Respectfully returned to the
Commissioner of Pensions,
with the information that in the case of
Solomon Fazen
Co. B, 135 Reg't U.S.C. Inf.
the records show personal description as follows:
Age 21 yrs, height 5 feet, 8 inches,
complexion dark,
eyes black, hair black,
place of birth Sampson Co, N.C,
occupation laborer
Name of former owner
has not been found
Also borne as Solomon
Fazan

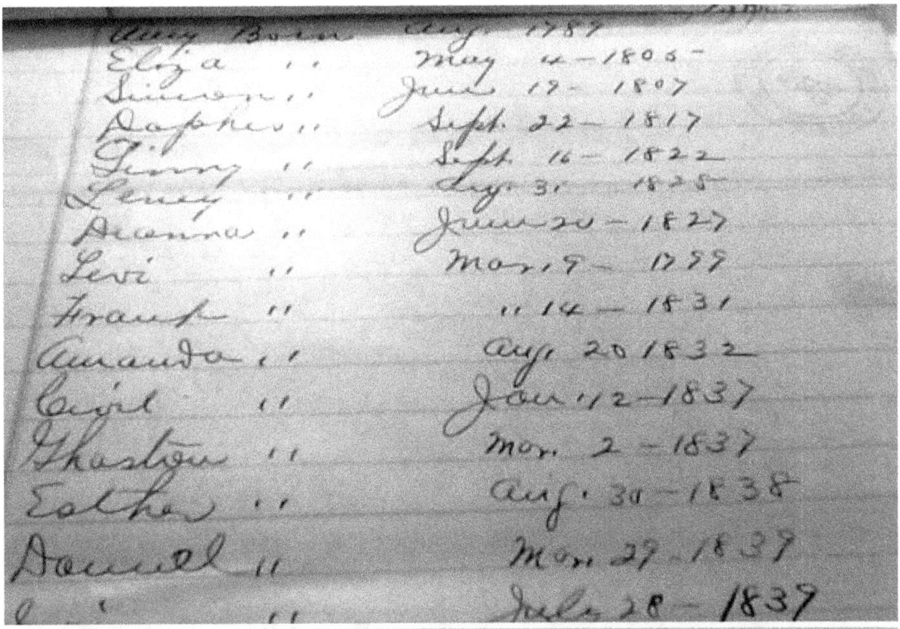
Amy Born Aug. 1787
Eliza " May 4-1805
Simeon " June 17-1807
Daphne " Sept. 22-1817
Ginny " Sept. 16-1822
Lemy " Aug. 31 1825
Arianna " June 20-1827
Levi " Mar. 9- 1829
Frank " " 14-1831
Amanda " Aug. 20 1832
Cyril " Jan. 12-1837
Ghaston " Mar. 2-1837
Esther " Aug. 30-1838
Daniel " Mar. 27-1839
" July 28-1839

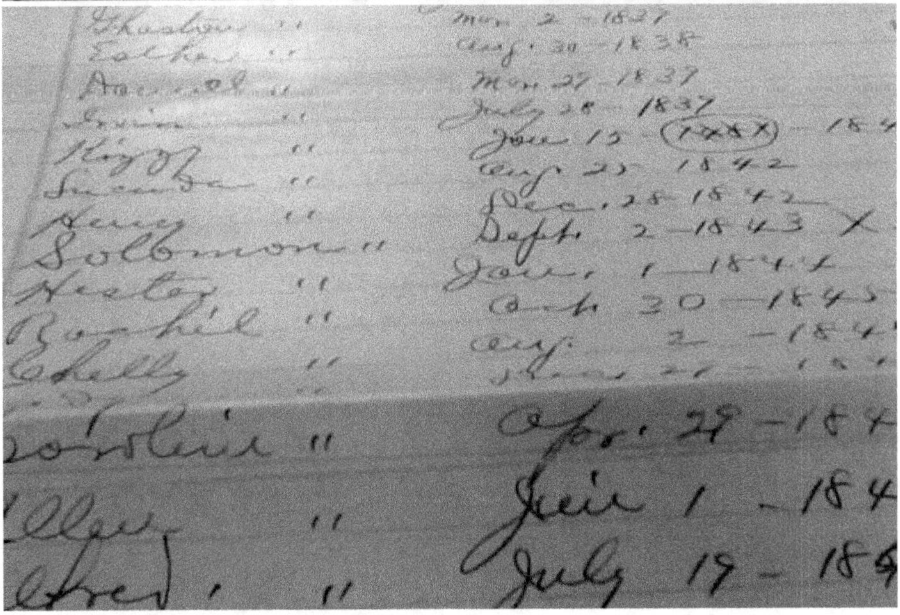
Ghaston " Mar. 2-1837
Esther " Aug. 30-1838
Daniel " Mar. 27-1839
" July 28-1839
Jan 15 (1888) 184
King " Aug. 23 1842
Amanda " Dec. 28 1842
Amy " Sept. 2-1843 X
Solomon " Jan. 1-1844
Hester " Oct. 30-1845
Rachel " Aug. 2-184
Shelly " June 2 184
" Apr. 29-184
" June 1-184
Alfred " July 17-184

The above is a true and accurate record of the ages of Negroes of the late Kilby Faison furnished to me by his grand daughter Miss Mary (Faison) McCullen of Faison N.C.
This the 27th day of Nov 1909
J. M. Bennett

North Carolina
Duplin County
Sworn to and subscribed before me this
day of November 1909.

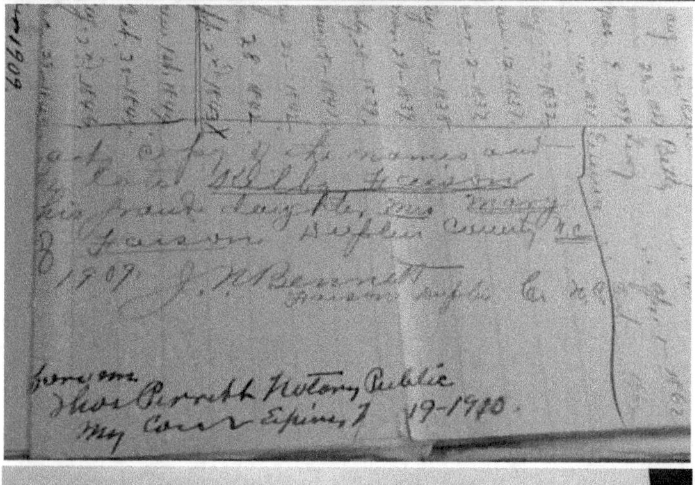
...ate copy of the names and ...
late Kilby Faison
his grand daughter Mrs Mary
Faison Duplin County N.C.
1909 J. M. Bennett
Faison Duplin Co N.C.
...fore me
Thos Perrett Notary Public
My Com Expires 7 19-1910.

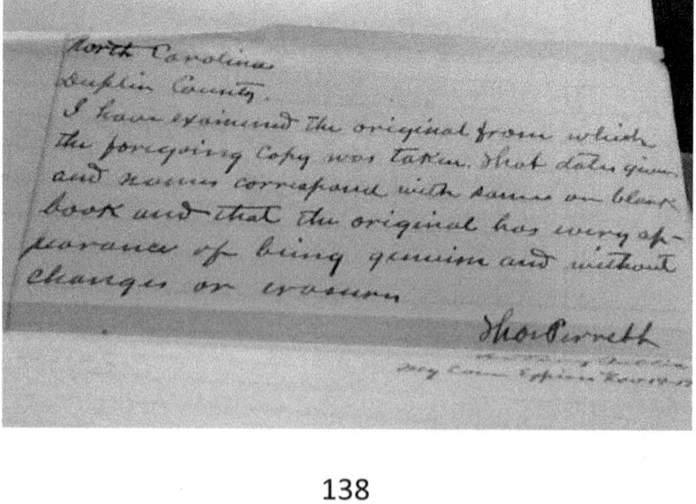
North Carolina
Duplin County.
I have examined the original from which the foregoing copy was taken. That dates given and names correspond with same on blank book and that the original has every appearance of being genuine and without changes or erasures

Thos Perrett
Notary Public
My Com Expires Nov

CHAPTER 5

THEIR UNWAVERING STRENGTH FOR FAMILY AND COUNTRY.

Building A Corduroy Road

COMPANY "C"

INCLUDED IN THIS CHAPTER ARE

EXTRACTIONS FROM THE PENSION RECORDS

OF;

ISHAM BREWER

FRANK KEITT / KENNERLY

EDMUND LAMAR / RANDALL

GABRIEL CLAY

ISHAM BREWER

The record showed that Isham Brewer served in Company, C. 135th United States Colored Troop, and was from Clinton, Sampson County North Carolina. Mrs. Sally Brewer owned him, hence his last name. He said that he was "just about grown" when he went away with the army to Goldsboro. He mentioned being mustered into service in Raleigh, North Carolina and from there they marched to Washington DC.

When Isham Brewer went away with the army he joined the Pioneer Corp. As they were on their way to Goldsboro they were in a skirmish and as they were fired upon, he was hit with a piece of shell and thought it had glanced off him. It didn't hurt much but took some skin off, however later it began to fester. He then ended up going to the doctor and the doctor opened the wound and took something out. After that, he was able to recover.

We find that the pension declaration was executed in May of 1897 before a notary, Mr. McClay. The claim had been rejected in June of 1899 on the grounds that there was no ratable degree of disability. The Department of the Interior forwarded the case thereafter for investigation due to the illegal acts of Mr. George P. McClay, notary public, who had been convicted of forgeries in connection with other pension claims. As a result, he had been sentenced to six years imprisonment in the penitentiary. It was found that, after the rejection of the claim, two declarations had been filed. One declaration purported to have been executed before Solomon M. Brown, who was thereafter under investigation, and the other purported to have been executed before William M. Molen, an insane person.

In due course, the investigations went in favor of the claimant. The medical referee held that after reconsideration of the individual, he was of the belief that the former adverse action should not be considered. The claim should be re-submitted and approved at $6.00 per month for general debility from the date of May 13, 1897. In September of 1903, the Department forwarded the case to Mr. Jennings for further investigation. In the end, the Bureau of Pensions certified a pension for Isam Brewer in the amount of $12.00 per month on the fifteenth of March in 1907.

I forward herewith the original papers pertaining to the claim of Isam Brewer, late of C 138th U.S.C.V.I., Orig. 911,197, together with two reports of Special Examiner Jennings relative thereto.

This is one of the cases which was forwarded to Charleston, S. C., for investigation in connection with the illegal acts of Geo. F. McClay, notary public, who was convicted of forgeries in connection with pension claims and sentenced to six years' imprisonment in the penitentiary. When this case was forwarded to Mr. Jennings for investigation the records show that it had been rejected June 6, 1899, on the ground that there was no ratable degree of disability, and that thereafter two declarations had been filed one purporting to have been executed before Solomon M. Brown, who is now under suspension of sentence, and the other purporting execution before William M. Molen, an insane person.

The testimony obtained by Mr. Jennings was deemed competent to show that the declaration filed July 27, 1900, was not executed as its jurat purports to show, hence is invalid, and the declaration filed Aug. 8, 1901, was held to be valid. Thereafter an appeal was taken from the action of the Bureau, and prior to forwarding the papers to the Interior Department on Sep. 17, 1902, the Medical Referee held that after reconsideration of the case, he was of the opinion that the former adverse action should not be adhered to, and that the claim should be re-submitted for approval at $6 per month for general debility from May 13, 1897. On Sep. 25, 1902, the Interior Department dismissed the appeal, instructing that action be taken in accordance with the opinion of the Medical Referee, and on the 11th inst., the Chief of Board of Review forwarded the papers to this Division for consideration as to whether the

as its jurat purports to show, [illegible] tion filed Aug.6,1901, was held to be valid. Thereafter an appeal was taken from the action of the Bureau, and prior to forwarding the papers to the Interior Department on Sep.17,1902, the Medical Referee held that after reconsideration of the case, he was of the opinion that the former adverse action should not be adhered to, and that the claim should be re-submitted for approval at $6 per month for general debility from May 13,1897. On Sep.25,1902, the Interior Department dismissed the appeal, instructing that action be taken in accordance with the opinion of the Medical Referee, and on the 11th inst.,the Chief of Board of Review forwarded the papers to this Division for consideration as to whether the declaration filed May 13,1897, which purports to have been executed before Mr. McClay can be accepted as a valid instrument. Inasmuch as the statute of limitations bars prosecution for any offenses which may have been committed by Mr. McClay in connection with the preparation of the declaration in question, and as ample testimony had been obtained to disbar and convict McClay(and as the cas[e] had beenrejected on the ground that no pensionable degree of dis- [illegible] testimony with [illegible] pending thereon when the case was in his hands.

You are requested to forward the papers to Special Examiner Jennings at Charleston, S. C.,with instructions to obtain all available testimony to show whether the declaration filed May 13, 1897, was executed as its jurat purports to show.

In view of the fact that the appeal has been dismissed the Department has instructed the Bureau to set aside the former adverse action,and it is requested that Mr. Jennings be instructed to take this case up at once and render a report at the earliest practicable date.

This letter should appear as an exhibit in the examiner's report.

Very respectfully,

S. W. Cuddy.

Chief of Law Division.

DEPOSITION

Case of [illegible], No. 9111[illegible]

On this 28th day of Nov., 190[illegible], at [illegible], county of Charleston, State of S. C., before me, E. R. Jennings, a special examiner of the Bureau of Pensions, personally appeared [illegible], who, being by me first duly sworn to answer truly all interrogatories propounded to h[illegible] during this special examination of aforesaid claim for pension, deposes and says:

[illegible]

Q Did you ever have Cesar Johnson as a witness to any paper in your pension claim?

A I don't know that I ever did.

Q Did you ever have Jack Small?

A No sir. I think not.

Q Did Mr. Clay ever make you touch the pen or hold up your hand?

State of S. C., before me, E. R. Jennings, a special examiner of the Bureau of Pensions, personally appeared [illegible], who, being by me first duly sworn to answer truly all interrogatories propounded to h[illegible] during this special examination of aforesaid claim for pension, deposes and says:

[illegible]

Q Did you ever have Cesar Johnson as a witness to any paper in your pension claim?

A I don't know that I ever did.

Q Did you ever have Jack Small?

A No sir. I think not.

Q Did Mr. Clay ever make you touch the pen or hold up your hand?

A Yes sir.

Q How often?

A Only once or twice.

Q Can you tell me when or what papers?

A He sent for me to come to his office & made me hold up my hand & touch the pen.

I don't know [illegible] what was to

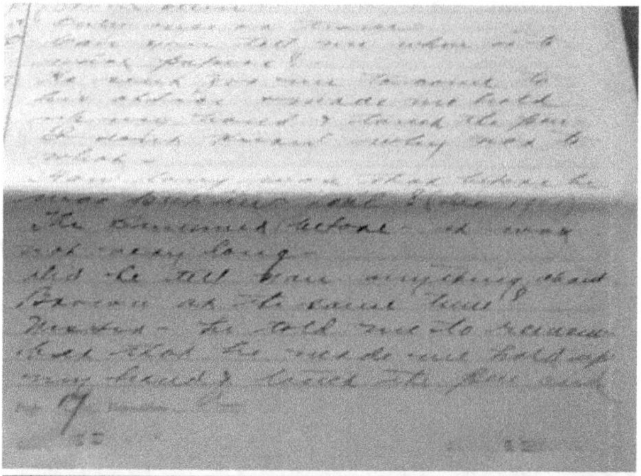

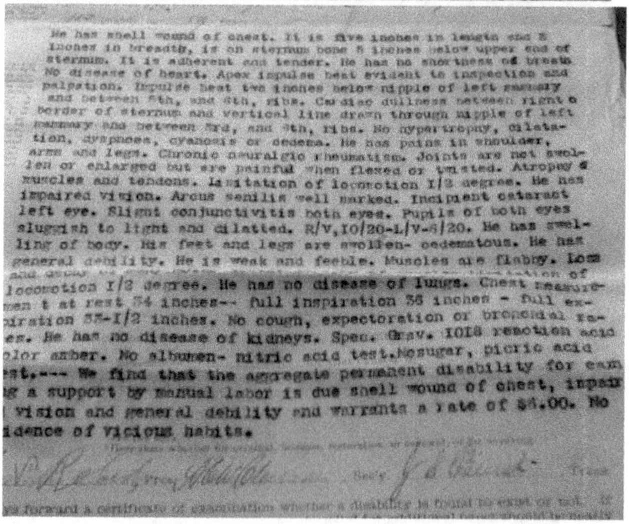

He has shell wound of chest. It is five inches in length and 5 inches in breadth, is on sternum bone 5 inches below upper end of sternum. It is adherent and tender. He has no shortness of breath. No disease of heart. Apex impulse beat evident to inspection and palpation. Impulse beat two inches below nipple of left mammary and between 5th, and 6th, ribs. Cardiac dullness between right border of sternum and vertical line drawn through nipple of left mammary and between 3rd, and 4th, ribs. No hypertrophy, dilatation, dyspnoea, cyanosis or oedema. He has pains in shoulder, arms and legs. Chronic neuralgic rheumatism. Joints are not swollen or enlarged but are painful when flexed or twisted. Atrophy of muscles and tendons. Limitation of locomotion I/2 degree. He has impaired vision. Arcus senilis well marked. Incipient cataract left eye. Slight conjunctivitis both eyes. Pupils of both eyes sluggish to light and dilatted. R/V,10/20-L/V-6/20. He has swelling of body. His feet and legs are swollen- oedematous. He has general debility. He is weak and feeble. Muscles are flabby. Loss [illegible] of locomotion I/2 degree. He has no disease of lungs. Chest measurement at rest 34 inches-- full inspiration 36 inches - full expiration 33-I/2 inches. No cough, expectoration or bronchial rales. He has no disease of kidneys. Spec. Grav. 1018 reaction acid color amber. No albumen- nitric acid test. No sugar, picric acid test.--- We find that the aggregate permanent disability for earning a support by manual labor is due shell wound of chest, impaired vision and general debility and warrants a rate of $6.00. No evidence of vicious habits.

FRANK KEITT / KENNERLY

Frank Keitt/Kennerly stated he was born June 3, 1844, in Orangeburg, South Carolina. He said that he was born and raised on the Keitt's plantation and had always lived in Orangeburg, South Carolina. He had one sister, Elizabeth Hoover, and his first wife was Bettie Hall and they had six children. He reported that he belonged to Bill Keitts who died before the war. Bill Keitts mistress, Nancy Keitts, died just before the close of the war. Ann Zimmerman, a white woman over ninety years of age, and a resident of Saint Matthews, Calhoun County, South Carolina is the daughter of Bill Keitts from a previous marriage. Frank believed she was still living and had living children. She was the sole survivor of the family of Bill Keitts. He said his brother and sister were also slaves of his master Bill Keitts.

Sherman's Army came through Orangeburg in February of 1865. His enlistment or what he thought was an enlistment, was into the Pioneer Corps, which from there he said they went to Goldsboro North Carolina, marching all the way. At Goldsboro, they enlisted into the 135th United States Colored Troop and were organized, and marched to Raleigh, North Carolina, where they were examined by the patrolling officers and sworn in. The examination consisted of having them all stripped and being passed through the patrolling officers who looked them over for any bruises or defects. If they looked alright, they were tapped with a little switch for approval.

In their blue uniforms, they marched from Raleigh, North Carolina to Welton, North Carolina, a small town just on the south side of Petersburg, Virginia, and is where they camped. They then passed Richmond, Virginia on the way to Washington, D.C. He mentioned that they remained in Washington, D.C., for about a week, then went on a train and then on a boat to Louisville, Kentucky. Frank said it was a big river and they passed Cincinnati, Ohio and then into the Mississippi River. They remained in Louisville until mustered out in October of 1865. He recalls that he started home on a Saturday, and traveled about a week by train, then partially by wagon, to get back home to Orangeburg, South Carolina.

In 1867, he voted under the name of "Frank Kennerly." He no longer had to use his slave name and he wished to have his father's name. His father's name was Joe Kennerly, and his mother was Susan.

Frank said that his second wife was Laura Ellis Kennerly, and he married her a year after his first wife, Bettie died. Frank Kennerly died June 22, 1925, and Laura died in 1928 and is buried in the Kremlin graveyard.

Case of Laura Kennerly , No. 1235216.

Deposition of Claimant , continued, sheet 2.

I have no attorney in my claim and I have paid nothing foer services in my claim except notary fees. I have no agreement to pay anyone anything.

I do not desire to be present or represented when witnesses are seen in my claim and I waive notice of further examination.

I have heard the foregoing read and it is correct.

her
Laura X Kennerly.
mark. Deponent.

W. W. Thompson
Witness to mark.
Only one available.

Subscribed and sworn to before me this 26 day of August 1926, and I certify that the contents were fully made known to deponent before signing.

E. F. Sewell
Inspector.

his death. He died here in this house about 28 years ago as well as I can recall. He is buried at the Thomas Sumner graveyard near here. After his death I lived here in this house until I married the soldier. I was married to the soldier, Frank Kennerly, here in this house, I do not know the date of the marriage but it was in January and I think it was 27 years ago, about a year after my first husband died. We were married by Rev. Sumter but he is dead. I had a marriage certificate but I lost it in some way. I had it in a trunk but it disappeared. There was a large crowd present at the wedding but there is only one person here now that was present. That is Sylvia Guistentanner, she was present and saw the ceremony performed. I lived with the soldier continuously from the date of our marriage to the date of his death. We were never separated or divorced. The two marriages that I have named are all the marriages I have ever had and I never lived with any man in the marital relation other than Christian Warner and Frank Kennerly.

Q. How many times was Frank Kennerly married before he married you?

A. Only one time before he married me. His first wife was Bettie Hall and I knew her. She had been dead about a year before I married him. She died out in the country form here and is buried

A. Only one time before he married me. His first wife was Bettie Hall and I knew her. She had been dead about a year before I married him. She died out in the country form here and is buried
out in the country near where she lived. That is the only wife he ever had before he married me as far as I ever knew or heard. The soldier was born and raised on the Kitt place in this county and he always lived here. He has one sister living somewhere but I have not seen or heard from her in years. Her name is Elizabeth Hoover, a widow. He has no brothers living.

I have had three children, all by my first husband Warner. They are all dead. I never had a child by the soldier. The soldier had a number of children by his first wife and I think six of them are living. Some of thse children live out in the country some where and some of them live in Columbia.

No member of my family served in the World War and I am not receiving nor have I applied for compensation on account of the service of any person in said war

W. W. Thompson

Witness to mark.
Only one available.

Laura her X mark Kennerly.
Deponent

3-289a

Case of Laura Kennerly No. 1735216.

On this 20 day of August, 1926, at Orangeburg county of Orangeburg, State of South Carolina before me, E. F. Fewell, an inspector of the Bureau of Pensions, personally appeared Laura Kennerly, who, being by me first duly sworn to answer truly all interrogatories propounded to her during this special examination of aforesaid claim for pension, deposes and says:

My age is about 70. Residence and mail address, Box 68, Orangeburg, S. C. I live just out of the city limits on Goff Avenue. I do general cleaning and housework and I make my living that way. I live here in this house which I own and no one else lives here except my adopted son, Claflin Kennerly, he is not my own child but I raised him from a baby.

My full name is Laura Kennerly and I am the same Laura Kennerly who is applying for pension as the widow of Frank Kennerly who served in the U. S. Army in the Civil war but I do not know in what Regiment he served. He served in the army under the name of Frank

burg, S. C. I live just out of the city limits on Goff Avenue. I do general cleaning and housework and I make my living that way. I live here in this house which I own and no one else lives here except my adopted son, Claflin Kennerly, he is not my own child but I raised him from a baby.

My full name is Laura Kennerly and I am the same Laura Kennerly who is applying for pension as the widow of Frank Kennerly who served in the U. S. Army in the Civil war but I do not know in what Regiment he served. He served in the army under the name of Frank
Keith but was always known here as Frank Kennerly. He died in June of last year. He died here in this house and I was with him when he died and I attended him all during his last sickness.

I was born on the George Sellers place in this county and I have lived here all my life. My father was named Jake Tribbell and my mother was named Fannie. My parents are both dead. I have no living sisters but I have two brothers. One is named George Tribbell and the other is named Niler Tribbell. Niler lives here in Orangeburg and George lives over the river somewhere but I do notknow just where. I lived with my parents out in the country from here up to the time I was first married.

Q. How many times have you been married?

... years. He died here in this house and ... he died and I attended him all during his last sickness.

I was born on the George Sellers place in this county and I have lived here all my life. My father was named Jake Tribbell and my mother was named Fannie. My parents are both dead. I have no living sisters but I have two brothers. One is named George Tribbell and the other is named Siler Tribbell. Siler lives here in Orangeburg and George lives over the river somewhere but I do not know just where. I lived with my parents out in the country from here up to the time I was first married.

Q. How many times have you been married?

A. Twice and no more. My first husband was named Christian Warner and I married him at the home of my father out in the country. I was only about 15 years old at the time I married him. We moved into town anf we bought the house in which I now live. I lived with him continuously from the date of our marriage to the date of

Page 5 Deposition A.

3-288.

DEPOSITION A.

Case of Frank Keitt *, No.* 83116.

On this 9 *day of* January 1912, *at* Orangeburg, *county of* Orangeburg, *State of* South Carolina *before me,* J. R. Bachelder, *a Special Examiner of the Bureau of Pensions, personally appeared* Frank Keitt, *who, being by me first duly sworn to answer truly all interrogatories propounded to h*im *during this special examination of aforesaid claim for pension, deposes and says:*

The name that I am now known by is Frank Kennerly. That is the way it sounds, not knowing how to read or write, I do not know how it is spelled. I am 67 years old, occupation farmer, and my post office address is Orangeburg, Orangeburg Co., S. C. I was born a slave in Orangeburg Co., S. C., June 3, 1844. My master was Bill Keitt, who died before the Civil War. My mistress was Nancy Keitt, who died just after the close of the Civil War. Ann Zimmerman, a white woman over 90 years old, and a resident of St. Matthews, Calhoun Co., S. C., is a daughter of Nancy Keitt by a marriage prior to that with Bill Keitt and I believe is still living. This daughter of Nancy Keitt is the sole survivor of the family of Bill Keitt. She has children living. I have a brother called Sam Williams, who resides in Columbia, Richland Co., S. C. I have a sister called Elizabeth Hoover, who resides in Lonestar, S. C. Both this brother and sister

... by a marriage prior to that with ...

lieve is still living. This daughter of Nancy Keitt is the sole survivor of the family of Bill Keitt. She has children living. I have a brother called Sam Williams, who resides in Columbia, Richland Co., S. C. I have a sister called Elizabeth Hoover, who resides in Lancaster, S. C. Both this brother and sister were slaves with me and belonged to my master Bill Keitt. No white neighbors of my old master, Bill Keitt, now survive, nor do any of their children who were old enough to remember me as a slave. I remained a slave to Bill Keitt until the coming of Sherman's Army in 1865, when I left my master and joined Sherman's Army in Feb. 1865, at a place about 8 miles from Orangeburg, S. C. This enlistment, or what I think was an enlistment, was into the Pioneer Corps. From here I went with the army to Goldsborough, N. C., marching all the way. At this place the 135 U. S. C. Inf. was organized and marched to Raleigh, N. C., where we were examined by the parolling officers and sworn in. This examination consisted in having us all strip and pass before the parolling officer who looked us over to see if we had any bruises or defects, and if we were alright we were tapped with a little switch which the officer had in his hand, and passed over to where those stood who had already been accepted. We then marched to Welton, a little town just the other side of Petersburg, Va., and there camped. We staid at Welton one night and the next morning marched to Richmond, Va. but did not stop at that place going on until we finally reached Washington, D. C., about June 1, 1865. We were in no battles or skirmishes on this march from Orangeburg, S. C. to Washington, D.C.

Page 3 Deposition A.

Page 4.

nor was I ever in any battle or skirmish while I was in the army. The only captain I ever had was called Mitchell. Lt. Ball was the only 1st. Lt. I ever had. Lt. Ferguson was the only 2nd Lt. I ever had. My only Ord. Sergt. was Frank Peppers from Georgia. Wilson Jones, Henry Greer, Abram Lamar and Meet Greer were with me in Co. C, 135 U. S. C. Inf. We remained in Washington, D. C. about a week and then took a train to a big river where we went on a boat and sailed down it to Louisville, Ky. This big river flows past Cincinnatti into the Mississippi River. We landed in Louisville, Ky. in June 1865, but I do not remember the day. Our first camp was called Locust Camp because it was in a locust tree grove. We staid there a week or so and then marched to Germantown, Ky., which we left about the last week of September 1865 and marched to a place called the "Barracks" about two miles from Germantown, Ky. Here we remained until we were mustered out, which I think was on a Friday, October 1865, and that we started home the next day which was Saturday. I travelled about a week, partly by train, partly by waggon, the railroad not being all finished, arriving in Orangeburg, S.C. I went first to my home in Jamison, S. C. and went to work for Eli Melton. I have lived here in Orangeburg, S. C. ever since. About 1867 I voted under the name, "Frank Kennerly". My reason for changing my name was because I was no longer a slave and did not have to take my master's name, and wished to have a last name like that of my father, which was, "Kennerly". My father's full

sissippi River. We landed in Louisville, Ky. in June 1865, but I do not remember the day. Our first camp was called Locust Camp because it was in a locust tree grove. We staid there a week or so and then marched to Germantown, Ky., which we left about the last week of September 1865 and marched to a place called the "Barracks" about two miles from Germantown, Ky. Here we remained until we were mustered out, which I think was on a Friday, October 1865, and that we started home the next day which was Saturday. I travelled about a week, partly by train, partly by waggon, the railroad not being all finished, arriving in Orangeburg, S.C. I went first to my home in Jamison, S. C. and went to work for Eli Melton. I have lived here in Orangeburg, S. C. ever since. About 1867 I voted under the name, "Frank Kennerly". My reason for changing my name was because I was no longer a slave and did not have to take my master's name, and wished to have my last name like that of my father, which was, "Kennerly". My father's full name was Joe Kennerly, my mother's full name was Susan Kennerly. I was about 19 years old when I enlisted, as I was told by my old people who are now dead. Being born a [slave], I know of no Bible or other record of my birth, and I do not think that there is one. I am well and generally known here in Orangeburg, S. C. by the name of Frank Kennerly.

I have heard the foregoing statement read, understood your questions, and my answers are correctly recorded therein.

Frank his X mark Keitt

Deponent.

The Commissioner of Pensions:

Herewith are returned all papers in the above cited claim for pension together with my report.

Claim was referred to the field to determine whether there was a ceremonial marriage of claimant and soldier, and if so, the date of same. The number of prior marriages of each should be shown, and the manner and date of dissolution of same. Did the claimant and soldier live together continuously from date of marriage to the date of his death? The claim came to this district for the initial examination.

The usual notice was served on the claimant and her rights and privileges fully and carefully explained to her, all of which she waived. She was not present when the witnesses were seen.

Claimant appeared to be telling the truth when she testified and she bears a good reputation for one of her race. She is well known in the section where she lives and owns considerable property. All the witnesses seen bear good reputations for truth and appeared to be entirely frank in testifying.

It appears from the testimony that claimant and soldier were married about January 1899. She syas the marriage took place in January 27 years ago and Sylvira Guisentanner says the marriage was before her husband died and he died in July 26 years ago. This is the only eye witness to the marriage that I could find but it is well known by a number of people that they lived together as man and wife for 25 years or more. There appears to be no doubt that they were married by ceremony and that they lived together continuously until soldier died.

Claimant was married once before her marriage to soldier and her first husband was Christian Warner with whom she lived until his death. He died about a year before she married soldier. She says she was only 13 years old when she married Warner and from what I could learn she is about right in that.

It appears that soldier was married once before he married the claimant and his first wife was Bettie Hall, Bettie Elizabeth was her full name so claimant says. Soldier has stated that he was married to Bettie in 1866. They lived together until her death and she died in the country about five miles from Orangeburg about a year before he married claimant. Sylvira Guistentanner says "they had hardly got through throwing dirt on Bettie before soldier was looking for another wife". Soldier was well thought of at Orangeburg and is what is locally known as a "white folks Negro"

EDMUND RANDELL / LAMAR

Edmund Randell/Lamar was from Etheridge, Jones County Georgia. In his oral deposition dated 1906, he stated that he gave his discharge papers to a man in Macon, Georgia, who was getting pensions for colored soldiers. He said "I have not seen it since. I think his name was Hill and I never found him again."

Edmund was born on the Lamar plantation four miles from Clinton, North Carolina. Mrs. Louisa Lamar owned him. He worked on her plantation until he went away with the Union Army. When he got out of the army, he came right back to the Lamar plantation as Louisa had been in the community ever since. "Senator Bacon's wife is the only one of the Lamar family that is living." The old plantation is now called "Cal Blonds Place."

When he went away as part of Sherman's army he cooked for them. He recalled that they went to Milledgeville first then to Augusta, Georgia. He said in his deposition "we were only there a day or two and then on to Savannah, Georgia. We were in Savannah about a month before starting on to Columbia, South Carolina." All that time he worked as a cook and a servant. In Goldsboro, North Carolina he was enlisted. The doctors examined him, stripped him, pounded his chest, felt him all over, asked him questions and passed him. He was sworn in before the doctors. They gave him a gun, a uniform composed of trousers, a blouse, an overcoat, a shirt, drawers, also shoes and a hat.

After becoming a soldier there was lots of drilling and building corduroy roads. "We marched to Washington, D.C. and camped out on the hill outside the city." He recalls from Washington, D.C., they went to Louisville, Kentucky by rail and then by boat, which was his first ride.

The first year after he was home from the war, he abandoned the name Lamar and took his father's name Randell. His mother told him his name was really Edmund, not Edward so he took the name Edmund Randell. He married in the first three or four years after the war to Mary Jane Faser. Preacher George Simmons married them. They were together until she died about seven or eight years after they married, they had seven children during that time.

About five years later he married Lattie Banney in the Bethlehem Church in Putnam County Georgia. He lived with her until she died several years after their marriage. Those are the only two women he married, but he had been with other women but did not marry them.

He was not legally married to Ceily Davidson. There was a ceremony performed by Reverend Louis Davidson. Edmund lived with her for fourteen or fifteen years and had four children. Once Ceily died he married Lattie, and she was his last wife who had seven children. She left Edmund and he thinks she lived in Macon, Georgia. When she left Edmund, he took up with Lucy Fallow, but he never married her. He lived with her for only about three months. Edmund Randell died on May 28, 1923.

ACT OF JUNE 27, 1890,
As Construed by Act of Congress, Approved July 1, 1902, and order of the Commissioner of Pensions made March 15, 1904.

DECLARATION FOR PENSION.

NOTICE.—This can be executed before a Notary Public, Justice of the Peace, or a Court of Record, or any officer duly qualified to administer oaths.

NOTICE—Officer executing this should notice instructions on this Declaration.

State of Georgia, County of Jones, ss:

ON THIS 10th day of Mch, A. D. one thousand nine hundred and Five personally appeared before me a Judge of County Court (Official title of officer executing this application) within and for the county and State aforesaid Ed Lamar (Name of claimant) aged 60 years, and was born on the 15th day of Oct 1844 a resident of Clinton, County of Jones, State of Georgia who, being duly sworn according to law, declares that he is the identical Ed Lamar (Name under which he served) who was ENROLLED as a private on the day of Mch, 1865 in Company C of the 135th Regiment of U S C I. Vols., (Company and Regiment, or vessel, if in the navy) in the war of the Rebellion and served at least ninety days, and was honorably DISCHARGED at Louisville Ky on the 23rd day of Oct, 1865

That he is partially (Partially or wholly) unable to earn a support by manual labor by reason of age (senility). For four or five years past a dislocated hip which grows worse (If under 62 years of age, state any injury or disability you may have.)

That said disabilities are not due to his vicious habits, and are to the best of his knowledge and belief permanent.

That he has applied for pension under application No. Certificate No. (If ever drew a pension the certificate number only need be given. If not, give the number of the former application, if one was made.)

That he has been employed in the military or naval service otherwise than as stated above (Here state what the service was, whether prior or subsequent to that stated above, and the dates at which it began and ended.)

and when ordered for examination desires to be ordered before the Board of Surgeons at Macon County of Bibb, State of Georgia

That he makes this declaration for the purpose of being placed on the pension roll of the United States, under act of Congress approved June 27, 1890, as Construed by Act of Congress approved July 1, 1902, and order of the Commissioner of Pensions made March 15, 1904. He hereby constitutes and appoints,

JOSEPH H. HUNTER, of Washington, D. C.,

his true and lawful attorney, hereby annulling and revoking all former powers of attorney, to prosecute his claim. That he hereby agrees to allow his said attorney the legal fee when the claim is allowed. That his Post Office Address is Clinton, County of Jones, State of Georgia

John Black
G L Barwell
(If claimant signs by mark, two witnesses must sign here)

Ed his x mark Lamar
(Signature of claimant.)

When executed return to JOSEPH H. HUNTER, Attorney, Washington, D. C.

ATTY FILED

MAY 31 1905 OFFICE

N. B.—Examiners should be particular to have affiants sign on the line next below the closing words of their depositions, so as to leave little or no space between their signatures and the end of their depositions.

3—230.

DEPOSITION A

Case of Edward Peeden, alias Edward Farmer, **No.** 1151681

On this 11 day of Oct, 1906, at Eldridge, County of Jones, State of Georgia, before me, L. A. Hulkins, a special examiner of the Bureau of Pensions, personally appeared Edward [illegible], who, being by me first duly sworn to answer truly all interrogatories propounded to him during this special examination of aforesaid claim for pension, deposes and says: I am 64 years of age; my post-office address is Clinton, Ga. Occupation farmer. I am the claimant in this case. I am the identical man who served in Co. G, 135 U.S. C. Inf. Two or four years after the war I gave my certificate of discharge to a man in Macon, Ga. who was getting pension for colored soldiers and I have not seen it since. I think his name was Hill. He moved after I gave him my paper and I have never found him. I enlisted at Goldsboro during the latter part of the war. It was during March or April but I do not remember the year. I was mustered out the same year during the fall. I got back home before Christmas. We were quite a while getting home from Louisville, Ky. where we were discharged. I only had the one service in the U.S. army and that was in the name of [illegible] of the [illegible]. [illegible] was my only name and was under the name of Edward Farmer.

I was born on the Farmer plantation [illegible] miles from here on the [illegible] of Mrs. [illegible] Farmer and [illegible] belonged to her and worked on her plantation

Page 6 Deposition A

until I went away to the army of the U.S. During all that time I was known as Edward Ramsey. I never had any other name until after the war. When I got out of the army I came right back to the same plantation and [illegible] since. I have not lived more than [illegible] miles from here any part of my life except while I was away with the U.S. Army. When I returned I worked the first year for Miss Ramsey and I have worked in this settlement ever since. Senator Bacon's wife is the only one of the Ramsey family that is living. The old Ramsey plantation is now called Col. Bacon's place. The first year I was home from the war I changed the name of Edward Ramsey and took my father's name Randall. My mother told me my name was Edmund instead of Edward so I took the name Edmund Randall and have been known as Edmund Randall ever since. I was Edward Ramsey before and during my military service and Edmund Randall since. I have no picture of myself taken at any period of my life. Never had a picture taken. I am about 5 feet 8 inches now and seem a little taller than when I was in the army and very a little heavier. I now weigh about 150. Otherwise I was black.

I went away when part of Sherman's army came through here. I just joined in with them and cooked for them. We went first to Milledgeville, Ga. was there one night and then went to Augusta.

We marched to Wilmington. We only stayed there a day or so and then marched to Greensboro, N.C. We remained there a month or so and then marched to Columbia, S.C. and probably remained about a week. We left there and went to Goldsboro N.C. All this time I was cooking and washing as a servant. When we reached Goldsboro I was enlisted. The doctors examined me I think. They [illegible] my [illegible] and [illegible] and asked me questions but I do not remember what. They passed me. I was sworn in before the doctors examined me I believe. They gave me a gun and uniform composed of trousers, blouse and overcoat and shirts and drawers, also shoes and a hat. I did not get a cap and only one suit and no gloves or mittens. I wore clothing [illegible] but not when I enlisted. After I became a soldier they drilled me. I think we were in Goldsboro a week or two. Then we went to Raleigh, N.C. and remained two or three weeks and drilled and did guard duty when it fell to my lot to guard. We were at Raleigh N.C. when President Lincoln was shot, and were held up there for orders. We marched from Raleigh to Wilmington N.C. and camped out on a hill outside the city. We were there quite a long time. I think it must have been a month. We had regular guard [illegible]. We went from Wilmington to Louisville Ky. by train and boat. That was the first I rode. We had marched all the time [illegible] to [illegible] Washington or Louisville, Ky. We camped outside of Louisville at a place called

Page 8 Deposition 9

N. B.—Examiners should be particular to have affiants sign on the line next below the closing words of their depositions, so as to leave little or no space between their signatures and the end of their depositions.

3—200.

DEPOSITION A

Case of Edward [illegible] & Fred Lanier, **No.** 115768(?)

On this 11 *day of* Oct, 1906, *at* [illegible], *County of* Jones(?), *State of* Georgia, *before me,* [illegible], *a special examiner of the Bureau of Pensions, personally appeared* Edward [illegible], *who, being by me first duly sworn to answer truly all interrogatories propounded to h*____ *during this special examination of aforesaid claim for pension, deposes and says: I am* ____ *years of age; my post-office address is* ____

Capt. was Bell. He was somewhat [illegible]. He was short, chunky and was middle aged. We had a Lt. named [illegible]. He was a white man(?), [illegible], tall and [illegible], and wore a mustache. Frank [illegible], colored, was first sergt. Jesse [illegible] ([illegible]) was a sergt and [illegible]. [illegible] was a Corp. Don't recall any other Corps. or Sergts. [illegible] was a sergt. Privates in my company: [illegible] Lanier, Floyd White, Jim Wilson, Jim Watson, Henry [illegible], [illegible]. That is all I recall just now. I do not know where any of these comrades. The only two that I know of now that were in my regiment are Baldwin(?) Miller and [illegible], who served as [illegible]. They were in my regiment but not in my company. They can identify me as the Edward Lanier who served in 13th U.S.C. Inf. They have known me all my life, during my military service and under both names. I cannot name any others who knew

Page 10 Deposition A

me during my service. Of the names you read I remember Geo. Inman and Whitterly as members of my Co. I do not recall the rest of them.

I married my first wife 3 or 4 years after the war. Her name was Mary Jane Travis. Preacher Geo. Simmons married us at this county and I had a license from this county. I lived with her until she died and had six children. It must have been 12 or 15 years after our marriage until she died. About 3 or 4 years after she died I married Nettie Ramsey. I had a license there from this county and was married by Jack Dufoy a preacher of Bethlehem Church in Putnam county just across from [illegible] Co. I lived with her until [illegible] probably 4 or 5 years. My first wife died at [illegible] and my second wife died on Town Creek Place near here. Those are the only women I have been married to. I have lived with other women but have not been married to them. I was not legally married to Alay Davidson. I did not get a license. There was a ceremony performed by Rev. Lewis Davis. I lived with her 12 or 14 years [illegible] and had four children. I have 11 children living. My first wife and the last woman I lived with are the mother of them all. I was mistaken when I said I only had four by the last woman. I believe there was 7 by my first wife and all the balance was by the last woman. I am not sure how many I had by the last woman. All the children by my first wife are over [illegible] up [illegible] my children. Snyder is the youngest [illegible]. He is about 5 or 6 years old. [illegible] is the next oldest. Bennie is the next oldest. [illegible] preceded Bennie and [illegible] is probably about 11 or 12. Cleveland preceded [illegible] and the next older than Cleveland is Bettie. I think Bettie is the oldest and is 16 years of age. [illegible] of their [illegible] and nobody [illegible] knows their age. The last woman I lived with and I separated. She has been gone two weeks. I think she will come back. If she returns we will live together again. I am not legally married to her. Her maiden name was [illegible]. The [illegible] woman who I lived with is dead.

I first married Mary Jane Turner. She died and I married Celey Brandon. She died [illegible] I married Bettie Banney who was a [illegible] during [illegible] hood. Bettie was my last wife. She left me and I think she lives in Macon. When she left I took up with Lucy [illegible]. I never was married to her. I lived with her about [illegible] months. My wife Bettie was married to Anderson Banney and he died in Macon before we were married. I married this Bettie Banney within the last year. We only lived together a short time. All my children are by my two first wives. My wife Celey died 2 or 3 months before I married the Banney woman who left me. This last statement about my wives is correct. I got them all confused at first. The only living woman

Page 13

who I ever was married to is Lettie formerly Mrs Barney and both as a widow. I married this Lettie about a years ago at Bethleham Church in Patterson Co. Got a license in this county and Jake Bryson a preacher married me. I have no child son by her.

I have heard this deposition read & have understood the questions and my answers are correctly recorded.

his
Edward X Randall
mark

Witness R. [illegible]

Mary Jane Randall

Deponent.

Sworn to and subscribed before me this 11 day of Oct 1906, and I certify that the contents were fully made known to deponent before signing.

S. H. Cutting
Special Examiner.

DJT

GABRIEL CLAY

In his deposition in support of Lucy Clay, the wife of Gabriel, in 1898, George Clay testified that he was raised in Toomsboro, Wilkinson County Georgia. He was the slave of Peyton Clay, lived on the Clay Plantation, and belonged to the Clay family from childhood to freedom. He was asked if he knew a slave named Gabriel and he responded that he did and that he and Gabriel were both slaves of Peyton Clay and that they were raised together. George said, ***"If I had as many dollars as Gabe had fights when we were young, I'd be a rich man."*** He added that he had heard that Gabriel was dead and that he was killed down in Coffee County. George said that Gabriel had a wife named Lucy and a son named Dennis.

Further in his deposition for Lucy, George was asked if Gabriel was in the war with the Yankees and he answered "I think he went to the Yankee war. He had money when he came back and we boys who stuck to the rebels didn't get any money." He also said that he didn't know what regiment Gabriel served in the Yankee war or how long he served, however, he said ***"just as soon as freedom Gabe and Lucy resumed their marriage relations and continued to live as man and wife until they left here for coffee county,"*** which was several years prior. George recalled that Gabriel and Lucy belonged to the Parker Hill Church and Gabriel finally became a preacher and preached at the Liberty Church.

In Gabriel Clay's Service Affidavit, he stated that he was a private in Company "C," 135th U.S.C. Inf. and his post office address was McDonalds Mill, Coffee County, Georgia. He enlisted in the Pioneer Corps on the 15th of October 1864 and was honorably discharged on the 16th of November 1865. Gabriel testified that his left hand was badly crushed by a sill against another sill in building a breastwork on the banks of the Oconee River, in Georgia, while working with Sherman's Army Corps. He didn't know the name of the surgeon who attended to him on that occasion. He also said that he wrenched his right arm while carrying logs through a slippery swamp to build the road for the Army and it was sometime after he recovered from his crushed hand. He also claimed he had heart disease that was caused by exposure and hardship endured during the service from October 1864 to November 1865, and the injuries got worse as he got older.

In the General Affidavit of Lucy Clay on March 27, 1895, she revealed that Gabriel Clay died on the 26th of January 1895, at McDonalds Mill, Georgia, and was killed by a Locomotive Engine. He was drawing a pension at the time of his death, and she was also entitled to the same pension. The Department of the Interior, Bureau of Pensions, investigated the widow's pension request of Lucy Clay and determined her "claim was of merit," and recommended for admission. The record showed that commencing February 20, 1895, a pension of $8.00 a month for Lucy is authorized along with an additional $2.00 per month for each of the three children listed under the age of sixteen, Franklin, Eddy, and Mary until they reach the age of sixteen. This document was issued September 16, 1898, and had the ending dates for payment of pension for each of the three children shown.

DEPARTMENT OF THE INTERIOR,

BUREAU OF PENSIONS,

Macon, Ga. March 30, 1898.

Hon. Commissioner of Pensions,

Washington, D. C.

Sir:

Herewith I have the honor to return, with report, the papers in the pension claim, No.609,151, of Lucy Clay, widow of Gabriel Clay, late private, Co. C, 135th U. S. C. Vol. Inf. Post-Office address, McDonald's Mills, Coffee County, Ga.

The papers in this claim were referred to the field to determine marriage and its legality under state law, continued cohabitation, dates of birth of children claimed for and whether they are living and dependance.

The papers came to me, with notice waived, for further examination as to marriage and dates of birth of children, Frank and Mary.

Of the witnesses referred to by the claimant, Bryant Bunyan, Isaac Hasten, Easter Jackson, Jerry Jackson and Wyatt Clay are dead.

This report is based upon the depositions of George Clay, Harriet Whittaker, Rose Caldwell and Samuel Parker. No more witnesses could be found who could state more, if endeed as much, as these witnesses.

The evidence now in the claim shows legal widowhood, that the children claimed for are living, dependence and the dates of birth are fairly well shown. It is almost positively shown that the date alleged is about correct as to Mary's birth.

I was informed by all the witnesses that the soldier was rather particular about keeping the dates of the births of his children as he was a kind of preacher and under all the circumstances I am of the opinion that the dates of births alleged can be accepted.

The claim is one of merit and I recommend the admission of the same.

2

Very respectfully,

(3—446.)

DEPOSITION L

Case of Lucy Clay, No. 609.151

On this sixteenth day of July 1897, at McDonalds Mills, County of Coffee State of Georgia, before me, J A Davis, a Special Examiner of the Pension Office, personally appeared Dennis Clay, who, being by me first duly sworn to answer truly all interrogatories propounded to him during this Special Examination of aforesaid pension claim, deposes and says: I am about 35 yrs. of age. A farmer & my post office address is McDonalds Mills, Ga.

I am the oldest son of the claimant, Lucy Clay. My father's name was Gabriel Clay. I was born in Wilkinson Co., Ga. & lived there until 1887 & then came here. I came here a little ahead of my father & mother. My father Gabriel Clay was killed by the cars. It was in 1895, Jany. the 26. At the time of his death there were only three children under sixteen years of age. They are still living with & supported by my mother. Their names are, Frank, Eddie & Mary. I do not know the dates of their births, not in my head. I cannot fix the dates by any of my children, or in any way by any circumstance I can think of. They were all born in Wilkinson Co. Ga. Mary was just a little bit of a baby, she was a suckling baby when my mother & father came here. I left Wilkinson Co. early in the year 1887 & my mother came here the same year, but I can't exactly recollect how it was. Mary was born after I left Wilkinson Co. & before my mother came down here. As near as I can remember Eddie is about a year & a half older than Mary. There is about the same difference between Frank & Eddie, as between Eddie & Mary.

My mother has 150 acres of land, I helped run it out. There is about 16 acres cleared & there is a four room unfinished log house on it. She has one horse, I do not know of any other personal property. The land & improvements I reckon would bring about

Page 26

three hundred Dollars. The horse may be worth about fifteen Dollars. I been trying to tend to the land & help my mother along & on an average she makes one light bale of cotton & between forty & fifty bushels of corn. The balance of the land is worth something for pasture, some of it & some is not worth anything. There is no timber on it of any value. It has been turpentined & used for saw mill purposes & also fire. There is nothing more to be got off from it. My mother has to work out a portion of the time for a living. I have no pecuniary interest in this claim. I think I was sworn once in this case by Mr Griffin. (Signature to affidavit B. J. Ex 6 shown to [illegible]). The signature shown to me I believe is in my handwriting.

I have fully understood all your questions. My answers have been correctly recorded.

Dennis Clay

Deponent.

Sworn to and subscribed before me this 16 day of July, 1897, and I certify that the contents were fully made known to deponent before signing.

J. A. Davis
Special Examiner.

(3—146.)

DEPOSITION K

Case of Lucy Clay, No. 609.151

On this sixteenth day of July 1897, at McDaniels Mills (Smoto Still), County of Coffee State of Georgia, before me, J. A. Davis, a Special Examiner of the Pension Office, personally appeared Mary Rew (now Mary Clay), who, being by me first duly sworn to answer truly all interrogatories propounded to her during this Special Examination of aforesaid pension claim, deposes and says: I am about 22 yrs of age. I am now the wife of Dennis Clay. My post office address is, McDaniels Mills, Ga. I lived with Lucy Clay the claimant about six years & I had known her here about four years before that. When I first knew her she was living with & known as the wife of Gabriel Clay. I knew Gabriel Clay was killed by the cars Jany 26 1894. I do not know the date of births of any of the children I know there were three children under sixteen years of age when Gabriel died. They are living with & taken care of by Lucy Clay. Their names are, Frank, Eddie & Mary. I have no interest in this claim. I remember swearing to a paper in this case before Mr Griffin. I cannot write my name. I have fully understood all your questions. My answers have been correctly recorded.

Mary (her X mark) Rew now Mary Clay

J. D. Wall } Witnesses
W. J. Cooney } to mark

Sworn to & subscribed before me this 16 day of July 1897 & I certify that the contents were fully made known to deponent before signing.

J. A. Davis
Special Examiner

Page 24 Deposition K

(3—146.)

DEPOSITION B

Case of Lucy Clay, No. 689.181
widow of Gabriel Clay

On this sixteenth day of July, 1897, at McDonalds Mill, County of Coffee, State of Georgia, before me J A Davis, a Special Examiner of the Pension Office, personally appeared Lucy Clay, the claimant, who, being by me first duly sworn to answer truly all interrogatories propounded to her during this Special Examination of aforesaid pension claim, deposes and says: I am about 54 yrs. old. I am the widow of Gabriel Clay. My post office address is, McDonalds Mill, Coffee Co. Ga.

I was a slave before the war and belonged to Ellick Heston. My name then was Lucy Heston. We lived near Toombsborough, Wilkinson Co, Ga.

I was married to Gabriel Clay right in the yard, right before master door. I was married a year before the war begun. We were married by Bryant Bangin, a Justice of the Peace. Gabriel belonged to Peyton Clay. They lived in the same locality about two miles from me. We lived together until Gabriel went in the Army and when he come home, or just before he went in the Army my boss died and we were all divided and scattered and I lived in Milledgeville Ga. Gabriel was still at Ellick Clays and he used to come to Milledgeville to see me and then the Yankees came through and Gabriel went off with them and I did not see him until the war ended. I was at Milledgeville when he came out of the Army and he came right to me then and we lived together from that time until his death. We went back to the Clay settlement near Toombsborough and lived there until we came to this place in 1887. I have heard Gabriel call the name of the Regt. and Co, he was in, but I have forgotten. He was drawing a pension when he died. When I made my claim I had his papers to go by. I had fifteen children by Gabriel and

Page 6 Deposition B

There are two living. Gabriel was killed by the cars. I do not remember the date. He has been dead three years next January. There were three children under sixteen years of age when he died. I do not remember the dates of their births. I had all the ages of my children, but the book got burned and my old man had the dates of the youngest ones set down. He had Frank's and Eddie and Mary's ages put down.

(The Bible produced by claimant was published in 1881 and contains the date of birth of eight children in the following order, of entry, viz:

Susie Clay, born March 1st 1880.
Elbert Whitley Clay " May 29th 1878
Jeffie Clay " March 1st 1874
David Clay " March 10th 1872
Eulie Ann " Jany 1st 1866
Thomas Clay " Sept 13th 1867
× Mary Magdalene " April 7th 1888
Alaminee Clay, daughter of J. T. & Eliz Clay born Nov. 10th 1887
× Frank Clay born Feby 18th 1883
× Eddie Clay " Dec 22nd 1885

Nearly all entries are in different handwriting and different colored ink and the entire record is a very crude combination by claimant) — J. A. Davis, Spl Examiner.)

That is the same record Mr. B. F. Griffin made a copy from (See B. J. Ex. 8.) Frank and Eddie and Mary are still living and in my care and custody. I claim a pension for myself as the widow and for Frank, Eddie and Mary as the three minor children of Gabriel Clay. I have 150 acres of land deeded to me by my father as a gift to

J. H. Hall
J. B. Cooper } Witness to Mark

Lucy her X mark Clay
Deponent.

Sworn to and subscribed before me this ______ day of ______, 189__, and I certify that the contents were fully made known to deponent before signing.

Special Examiner.

CHAPTER 6

CHRONICLING THEIR JOURNEY IN DEPTH.

From Civilian to Soldier

COMPANY "D"

INCLUDED IN THIS CHAPTER ARE EXTRACTIONS FROM THE PENSION RECORDS OF;

JOHN CHAVIS
RICHARD IHLY
BOSTON EARLY
MARSHALL GREEN
MARS EVANS

JOHN CHAVIS

On the 1901 oral deposition for pension, John Chavis told us that he was eighty years old. He was born in Virginia across the river from Norfolk. His oldest master was Billy Gregory. Tom O'Neal, Billy Gregory's son in law, married his oldest daughter. John went with them to O'Neal's plantation just a little back from the river, at a place called "Cohoke Mills." He was then sold to a slave trader, Speculator White, when he was ten years old. White was buying up slaves and taking them to Richmond. John was carried to Charleston, put in the broker's office, and sold to David McClure from Orangeburg, South Carolina. He stayed with him for four years. McClure then got into debt and sold John to Russel Keller, who he lived with until 1865 when he enlisted in the 135th Regiment. They stayed there one night, and then marched on to Columbia, South Carolina, then on to Goldsboro, North Carolina.

John stated that he remembered staying three weeks in Goldsboro, and they drilled there, and got their army clothes. From there they went to Raleigh, and then went to Petersburg, Richmond, Virginia, and Alexandria, just on that side of Washington, D.C., and that is when they attended the Grand Review. After the Grand Review he said they camped just outside the city. When they left there they took the railroad until getting to a big town on the Ohio River. From there they all boarded six or seven boats that took them to Louisville, Kentucky. John was assigned over to Indiana to guard the hospital in a small town, then sent back to Louisville to muster out in October of 1865. From there he went back home to Orangeburg, South Carolina.

When John volunteered, he was put into the Pioneer Corps, and he stated that he had no guns but had an ax. He recalls that they cut down trees and corduroyed the roads on their way up to North Carolina. He was then taken from the Pioneer Corps and put into Company "I," until he got to Washington and then put into Company "D," under Captain Fleming. He was asked if he was a carpenter but told them he was a farmer but said had built some homes for the colored people.

John went on and stated that he never got a gun or clothing until he got to Goldsboro, North Carolina, and was then a full soldier. The only people who knew John in the army were Alexander Scott and Ben Esau; they were in Charleston. He applied for a pension with Mr. H.A. Towles, Mr. Julius Cogswell, and Mr. J.M. Johnson, and the first pension money he got was $482.00. He didn't pay Mr. Towles or Mr. Cogswell any money for their help with his claim. He did pay Mr. Harris 50 cents. After about a year Mr. J.M. Johnson wrote a letter to his lawyer in Washington, DC wanting him to put in a claim under the old law. He went to Charleston to make out a claim and Mr. Johnson had a witness named Richardson; he was a man boarding with Mr. Johnson. John stated that he could not read or write. In Mr. Johnson's office, there was nobody but Mr. Johnson and John, and Mr. Johnson had John touch the pen and Mr. Johnson made the X on his application in 1901. John then got a voucher for $36.00 quarterly. He explained that he was receiving $17.00 a month for his left foot that had gotten frostbitten and for yellow Jaundice as he had been in the hospital while in Kentucky.

Special examiner Mr. John L. Harris started to talk to Mr. Johnson and James Richardson about John Chavis. He discovered that Mr. Johnson forged the witness statement and defrauded the government pension, but John received $914.47 from the pension office. They proved that there was a group of men in Charleston that defrauded the pension claimants. The investigation goes very deep and takes many years.

John Chavis's first wife Sarah Thompson had eleven Children who were all named in the pension file. It is recorded that Sarah died in 1921. John said his father's name was Paul Chavis. He owned ten acres and a house on John's Island, South Carolina. John died on September 23, 1912, and is buried at St. Stephens, AME Church yard on John's Island.

DEPOSITION A

Case of [illegible] Davis, No. 978,522

On this 18 day of December, 1901, at Charleston, county of Charleston, State of South Carolina, before me, J. M. Edmonds, a special examiner of the Bureau of Pensions, personally appeared Wm. Davis, who, being by me first duly sworn to answer truly all interrogatories propounded to him during this special examination of aforesaid claim for pension, deposes and says:

I am about 80 years of age so far as I can tell. I was born in Virginia across the river from Norfolk. My oldest master was Billy Gregory & Tom O'Neil married his eldest daughter and I went with her to O'Neill just a little ways from the river at a place called White Wells. I was sold when I was ten years old. I was sold to a speculator White, he was buying up slaves. I was taken to Richmond Va. I was then carried to Charleston & put in the Brokers office and sold to David McClure in Orangeburg Co. S.C. I stayed with him 4 years & he got in debt and I was sold to Russell Jolley and I lived with him until 1865 when I enlisted at Orangeburg in the 128th Regt U.S.C. Troops. From Orangeburg we went to Columbia

I was ten years old. I was sold to a speculator White, he was buying up slaves. I was taken to Richmond Va. I was then carried to Charleston & put in the Brokers office and sold to David McClure in Orangeburg Co. S.C. I stayed with him 4 years & he got in debt and I was sold to Russell Jolley and I lived with him until 1865 when I enlisted at Orangeburg in the 128th Regt U.S.C. Troops. From Orangeburg we went to Columbia
S.C. After I came in my regiment just out of Orangeburg, we stayed there one night and then we marched to Columbia and stayed one night. From Columbia we marched until we came to Goldsboro N.C. This is the first town I remember. We remained there three weeks on recruiting drill and there we got our army clothes. From Goldsboro we marched to Raleigh N.C. and stayed one night and then we marched to catch President Davis about a half days journey from Raleigh & a dispatch came that he was caught and we

Page   Deposition A

page 5

then marched back to Raleigh N.C. and laid
in camp 3 weeks and we then marched to Petersburg V.a and from there to Richmond Va. From
Richmond we marched to Alexandria just
in this side of Washington D.C. and then we
went on a straight road from Alexandria
towards Washington and camped for the
night and the next day we went to
Washington and attended the Grand Review
and then we went in camp and staid 3
weeks and then went into the City of Washington
and took the Railroad train untill we
got to a big town on the Ohio River we
got six or seven Government boats
there and went to Louisville Ky and
went into camp and staid in camp
for some time and then we went over
into Indiana to garrison the hospital
in some town. We then went back
to Louisville Ky and were mustered

in this side of Washington D.C. and then we
went on a straight road from Alexandria
towards Washington and camped for the
night and the next day we went to
Washington and attended the Grand Review
and then we went in camp and staid 3
weeks and then went into the City of Washington
and took the Railroad train untill we
got to a big town on the Ohio River we
got six or seven Government boats
there and went to Louisville Ky and
went into camp and staid in camp
for some time and then we went over
into Indiana to garrison the hospital
in some town. We then went back
to Louisville Ky and were mustered
out of service. The whole of our regiment was mustered out there. When
I went in to enlist at Lynchburg I was
put in the Pioneer Co. we had no guns but
we had axes and cut down trees and
corduroyed the roads. When we were
on the road up to North Carolina I was
taken out of the Pioneer Co and put in Co 2
and staid in Co 2 untill I got to Washington
and then I was put in the 13th U.S.

[illegible]
I took the Railroad train until we
got to a big town on the Ohio River we
got on a Government boat
there I went to Louisville Ky and
went into camp and staid in camp
for some time and then we went over
into Indiana to guarding the bridges
in some town. We then went back
to Louisville Ky and were mustered
out of service. The whole of our regiment was mustered out there. then
I went in to [illegible] [illegible] I was
put in the Pioneer Co. we had no guns but
we had axes and cut down trees and
corduroyed the roads. Then we were
on the road up to North Carolina I was
taken out of the Pioneer Co. and put in Co "G"
I staid in Co "G" until I got to Washington
and then I was put in Co "D" 13th U.S.C.
[illegible] and I staid in Co "D" until discharged
then I enlisted at [illegible] [illegible] Capt Fleming

Witness
[illegible]

his
John X [illegible]
mark

Sworn to and subscribed before me this 25th day of Dec [illegible]

RICHARD IHLY / ELY

Richard Ehly/Ely was born and raised on the Samuel R. Ely plantation in Buford County South Carolina. He said that he was always called Ely. He also mentioned that he can't spell and that his name comes from his master. His father's name was Boston Owens, and he belonged to the Owens family. Richard recalled that his father died when he was very young. Richard's mother's name was Rose Ely and he said that he had a brother who served, and his name was Boston Ely.

Richard claimed, "the federal army picked me up right near here, (Rivers Bridge) and put me in the Pioneer Corps where we corduroyed the roads and built the bridges across the rivers and creeks." He said that he got his uniform when they got to Goldsboro, North Carolina, but he didn't get a gun until he got to Louisville Kentucky. *"I was a regular soldier from that time on!"* he said. He went on and said they quit pioneering and put on a uniform in April. In Kentucky, they did guard duty and the same while in Murphysville, Tennessee. They were in Washington, D.C. but had no guns. They went from Goldsboro to Richmond, thence Petersburg then on to Washington. He said they were discharged in Louisville in October of 1865. He mentioned that he got his government pay and went straight home and had been there ever since.

He went on to recall that he "had a discharge paper and a man came around and took my discharge paper" to get him some more money "but never brought it back." His name was Dick Preacher and he claimed he was dead at the time of his statement. He said "the discharge paper was about a foot wide and fifteen inches tall."

Richard remembered that Gurley was his Colonel, Bud Long was the Lieutenant Colonel, and Dixon was the major, and Parks and Stewart were the doctors. John Clark was the captain, and John Stone and Joe Ware were the Lieutenants. Jim Grant was the first Orderly Sergeant; he was black, and he said that he was reduced in rank for a disorderly quarrel he had in Louisville Kentucky. He got cut up “mighty bad" and had to go to the hospital. Jim Hooper was the next Orderly Sergeant; he was a short man and ginger cake color. The Orderly Sergeant called the roll, formed the company, and went around to “intercede” to see that the camp was clean and detailed. The company was always formed with the tallest in front and then they dropped down from there. They had to dress/parade in the evening, and guard mount in the morning. “Taps” meant out all lights and to bed. Once “We had ***Columbia*** for a countersign.” It changed every night.

When Richard got home, he married Sarah Bostic in 1866, and they had ten children. His slave owner was General Samual R. Ely who was buried in Yaman’s graveyard on November 23, 1925.

The foregoing was from an oral deposition given by Richard Ely in 1904 found in his pension file.

(1-280)

DEPOSITION

Case of Richard Ihly Ctf. No. 799533

On this day of 190 , at
Continued county of
State of , before me, , a
special examiner of the Bureau of Pensions, personally appeared
Richard Ihly who, being by me first duly sworn to
answer truly all interrogatories propounded to h during this special
examination of aforesaid claim for pension, deposes and says:

black. He was reduced for a row he had in Louisville, Ky. He got cut up mighty bad and had to go to the hospital. Jim Hooper was our next. Or. Sergt. He was a short man ginger-cake color. He served until he was discharged. The Ord. Sergt. calls the roll, forms the Co. goes round to "intercede" to see the that the camp is clean and makes details. Our Co. formed with the tallest men in front and drop on down. We had dress-parade in the evening, guard-mount in the morning, "taps" means out all lights and to bed. On guard we were two hours on and four off. Only the regimental officers rode horses. We had "Columbia", "Quily" for countersigns. It changed every night. On inspection I placed the ramrod in my gun and the inspecting officer jumped it up and down and took it out and put the end on his hand to see if the gun was clean. Now about my name being down as Ihly, I cant explain it. I cant spell. I cant write. I have never had any U.S. service of any kind except Co. D-136-U.S.C.V.I. I was not in the navy. I never applied for but this one pension. I have been drawing a pension 8 or 10 years. (Pension voucher and Ctf. shown. Voucher OK. Ctf. shows: Orig.

Page 5 Deposition A

Page

Act of June 27, 1890 - No. 779533 - Richard Ihly, Private D 135 - U.S.C.I. Issued July 29, 1892 - at $8 a month to commence Aug 11, 1891.) I keep these papers at home. I have never pledged them for money or thing of value. A.C. Richard was my first Atty. I paid him nothing. They took it out at Washington. Calvert and Whitman are getting my increase. I have paid them nothing. Tom Williams is my local agent. I only pay him 25¢ a paper. If my claim is further examined I waive my right to be present or represented at such further examination. I have no more witnesses. I am satisfied with the way I have been treated by you. I have been married but once. I married Sarah Bostic in 1866. She had a slave husband but did not live with him after the war. I think his name was Caesar Henry. A preacher, Rev. Daniel Walker, married me and my wife. He is dead. We had no license. None was required. We have no Ctf. of marriage. We have had ten children. None are under 16. I have heard you read the foregoing statement. I fully understand it and it is entirely correct.

Richard his mark Ihly

Attest:

R F Keeran

Deponent.

Sworn to and subscribed before me this 17th day of May 1904, and I certify that the contents were fully made known to deponent before signing.

Don McClain
Special Examiner.

B-289.

DEPOSITION

Case of Richard Ely 6 Y. No. 797513

On this 17 day of May 1904, at Fairfax, county of Barnwell, State of S. C., before me, Wm. McClain, a special examiner of the Bureau of Pensions, personally appeared Tucker Williams, who, being by me first duly sworn to answer truly all interrogatories propounded to him during this special examination of aforesaid claim for pension, deposes and says:

I am about 60 years of age, P.O. Hampton, Hampton Co., S.C. I live 2 miles W. of my P.O. I am a farmer. I served as a private in Co. D. 135 U.S.C.I. during the war of the Rebellion. I recognize this man present here as Dick Ely. He served in my Co. and and Regt. during the war and he and I slept together a part of the time. I am as sure that this man was in my Co. as I am that I was in it. I have heard the foregoing statement read, have understood the same and you have recorded me correctly.

Attest: Tucker his mark Williams

R. J. Kearse

Page 7 Deposition B

3709

(Public-No. 628.)

WORLD WAR VETERANS' ACT, 1925.

Sec.201 (1). If death occur or shall have occurred subsequent to April 6, 1917, and before discharge or resignation from the service, the United States Veterans' Bureau shall pay for burial and funeral expenses and the return of body to his home a sum not to exceed $100, as may be fixed by regulation. Where a veteran of any war, including those persons who served honorably as Army nurses under contracts for ninety days or more during the Spanish-American War, who was not dishonorably discharged dies after discharge or resignation from the service and does not in the judgment of the director leave sufficient assets to meet the expenses of burial and funeral and the transportation of the body, the United States Veterans' Bureau shall pay the following sums: For a flag to drape the casket, and after burial to be given to the next of kin of the deceased, a sum not exceeding $7; also, for burial and funeral expenses and the transportation of the body (including preparation of the body) to the place of burial, a sum not exceeding $100 to cover such items and to be paid to such person or persons as may be fixed by regulations: Provided, That when such person dies while receiving from the bureau compensation or vocational training, the above benefits shall be payable in all cases: Provided further, That where such person, while receiving from the bureau medical, surgical, or hospital treatment or vocational training, dies away from home and at the place to which he was ordered by the bureau, or while traveling under orders of the bureau, the above benefits shall be payable in all cases and in addition thereto the actual and necessary cost of the transportation of the body of the person (including preparation of the body) to the place of burial, within the continental limits of the United States, its Territories or possessions and including also, in the discretion of the director, the actual and necessary cost of transportation of an attendant: And provided further, That no accrued pension, compensation, or insurance due at the time of death shall be deducted from the sum allowed.

Approved, March 4, 1925.

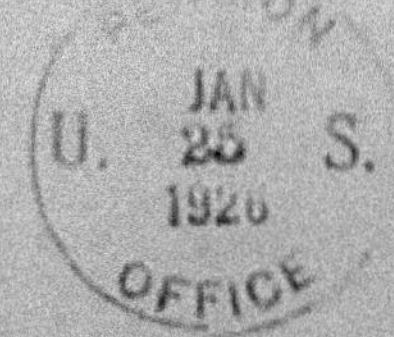

BOSTON EARLY

In 1891 the United States Congress made changes to the pension requirements for the veterans of the Civil War. This made it possible for any veteran of the Civil War to apply for a pension.

Boston Early, who was born in 1837 in Hampton County South Carolina, enlisted into Sherman's Pioneer Corps at Port Royal South Carolina in February 1865. Boston was a strong man who had worked timber in South Carolina and entered service as a healthy man at Goldsboro, North Carolina, He was enlisted in the 135th United States Colored Troop on March 27, 1865, and was discharged October 23, 1865, in Louisville, Kentucky.

After Boston returned home, he married his wife Rhina in 1867 and raised sixteen children with her. When Rhina applied for a widow's pension in 1911, she stated that when Boston came home from the war, he could not work full time all the time, and he suffered from rheumatism which he contracted in the army. He told her his suffering came from a falling limb off a tree on a road that they were corduroying. Rhina's slave master Mr. Ben Williams stated in the record that Boston was an old servant of his family.

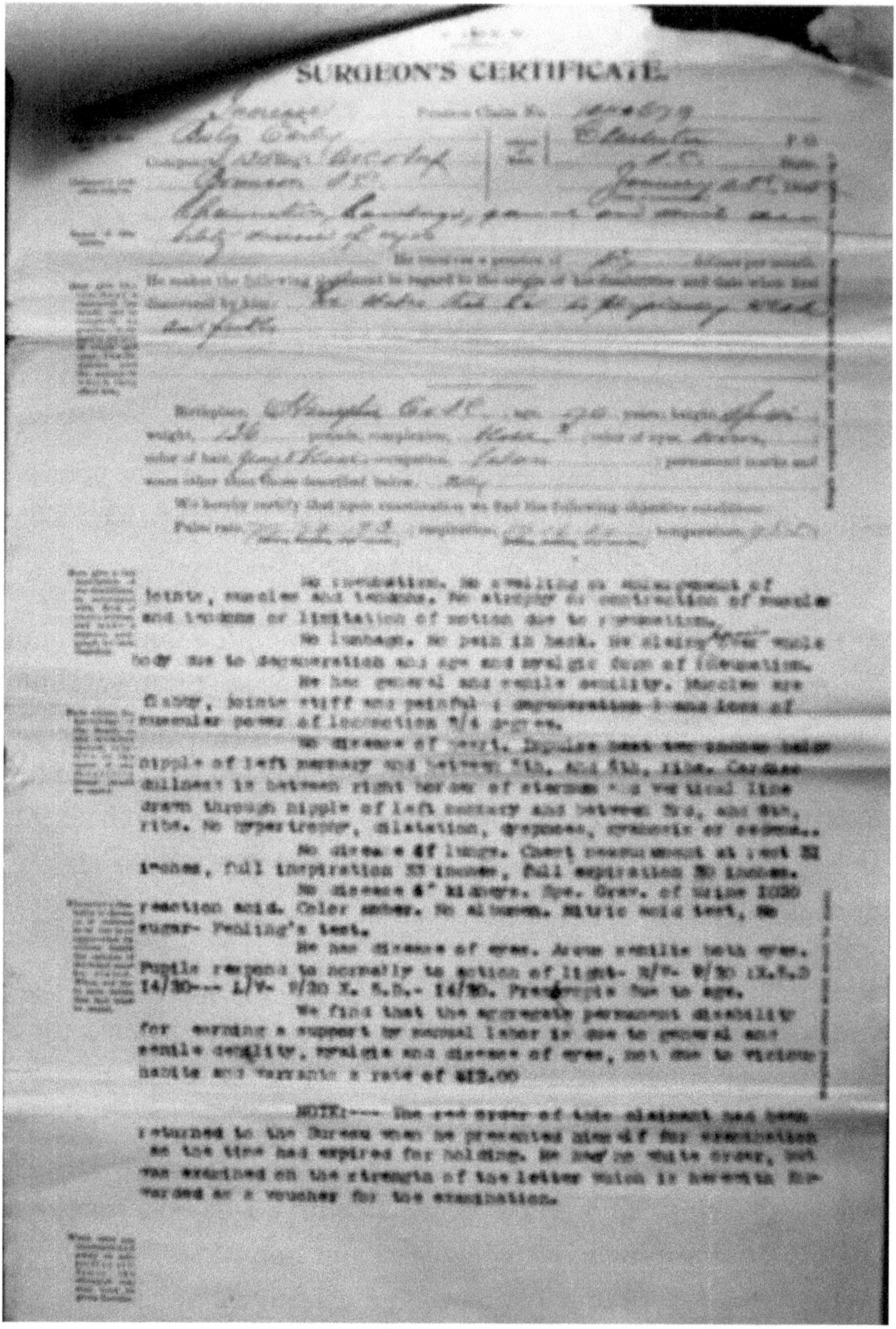
SURGEON'S CERTIFICATE.

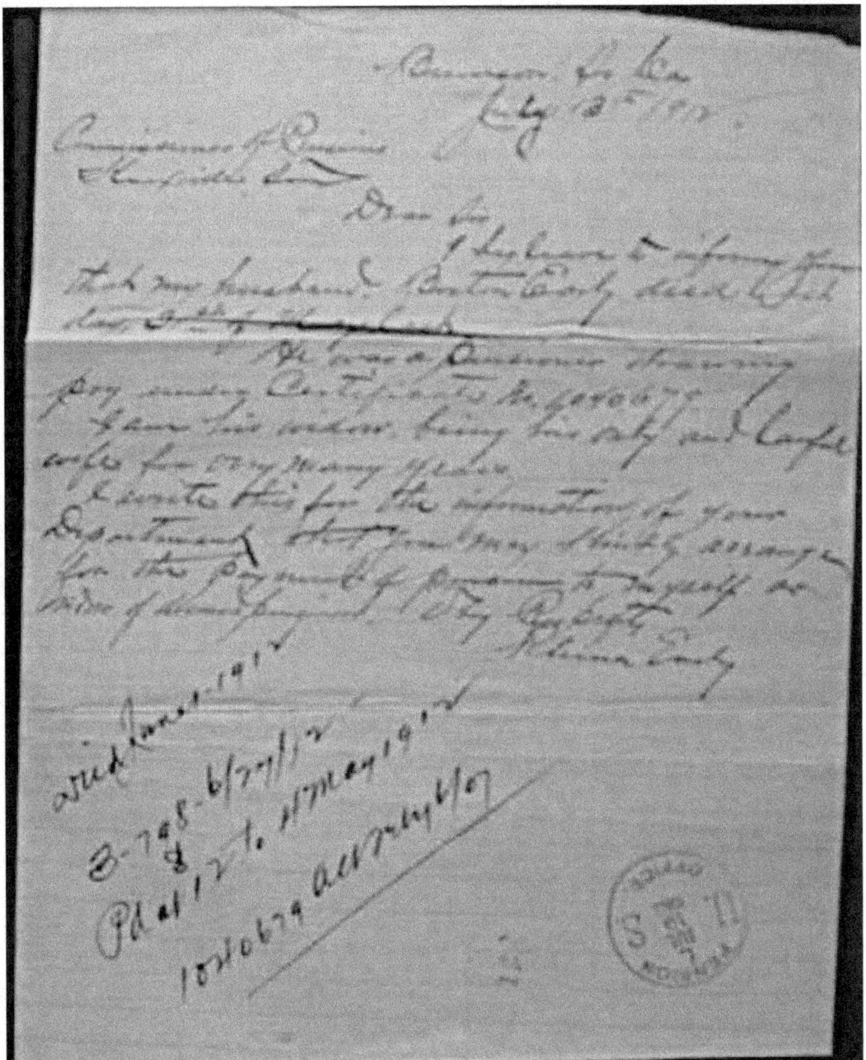

[illegible], Ga.
July 18th 1918

Commissioner of Pensions
Washington, D.C.

Dear Sir

I take pleasure to inform you that my husband Benton [illegible] died [illegible] day [illegible]

He was a Pensioner drawing pay under Certificate No. [illegible]

I am his widow, being his only and lawful wife for very many years.

I write this for the information of your Department that you may kindly arrange for the payment of pension to myself as widow of said pensioner. Very Respectfully,

[illegible]

died [illegible] 1918

3-788-6/27/12

Pd at 12 to [illegible] May 1918

1050679 [illegible] 6/07

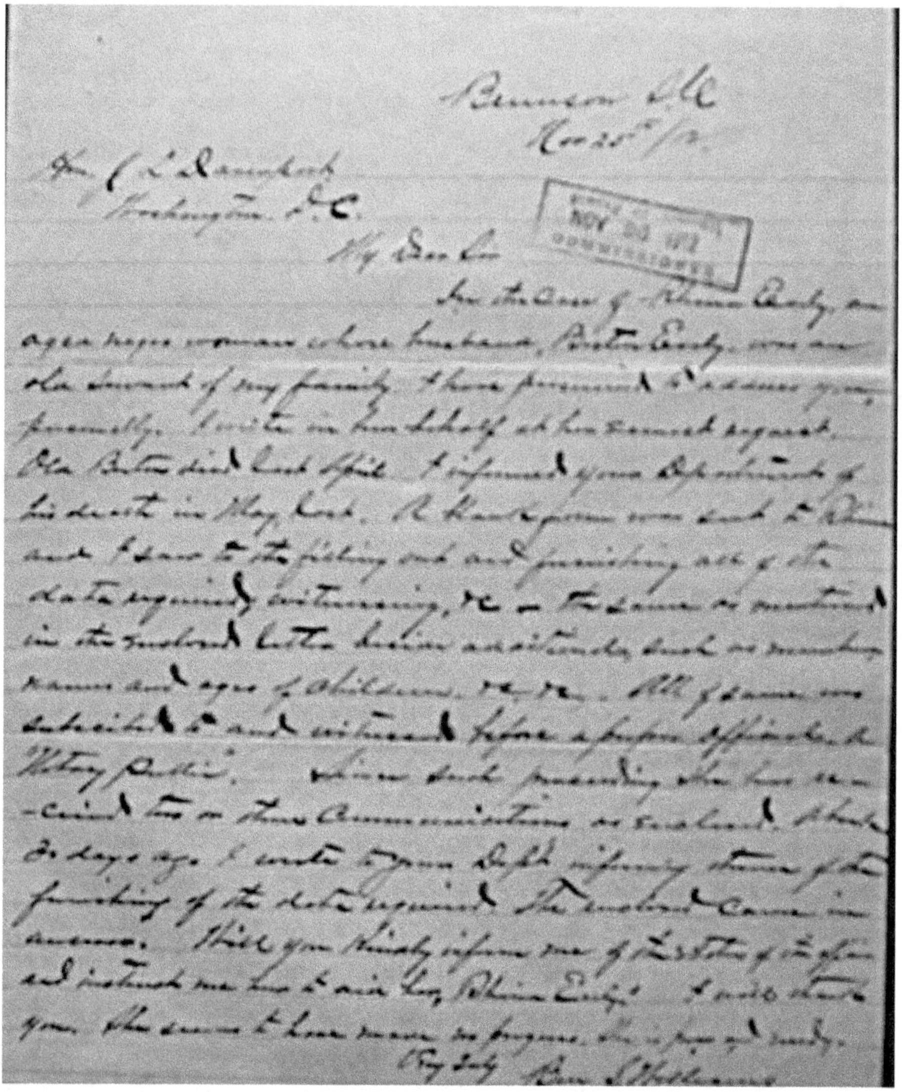

Benson N.C.
Nov 25th /92

Hon [illegible]
Washington D.C.

My Dear Sir

In the case of Rhina Early an aged negro woman whose husband, Preston Early, was an old servant of my family, I have presumed to address you personally. I write in her behalf at her earnest request. Old Preston died last April. I informed your Department of his death in May last. A blank form was sent to Rhina and I saw to the filling out and furnishing all of the data required, witnessing, &c — the same as mentioned in the enclosed letter besides additionals, such as marriage, names and ages of children, &c &c. All of same was subscribed to and witnessed before a proper official, a Notary Public. Since such proceeding she has received two or three communications as enclosed. About 30 days ago I wrote to your Dept informing them of the furnishing of the data required. The enclosed came in answer. Will you kindly inform me of the status of the affair and instruct me how to aid Rhina Early. I will thank you. She seems to have made no progress. She is poor and needy.

Very truly
Ben S. Williams

MARSHALL ROGERS / GREEN

Marshall Rogers/Green was born on February 15, 1837, in Hawkinsville Georgia. His mother's name was Eliza Rogers from Tennille, Georgia. He rose to the rank of First Sergeant in Company "D," 135th United States Colored Troop. His story only began after the war when he arrived home in Washington County Georgia. This was after marching in Sherman's army in both the Pioneer Corps and the 135th United States Colored Troop. From his home in Georgia to Louisville, Kentucky he marched over 1,000 miles while corduroying the roads, building the bridges over creeks and rivers that helped to move Sherman's Army along to end the war.

In Marshall's lifetime, he learned to read and write, and he was able to sign his pension application. He spelled out in his deposition that in the 135th Pioneer Corps in Savannah Georgia, the Pioneer Corps loaded and unloaded the vessels in port. He worked unloading both vessels and wagons that they moved over to South Carolina.

Though Marshall was old and physically worn out from laboring all his life, he could still take care of himself. He could dress and undress himself; he could also feed himself without much help. He paid his daughter Susie Pearl, his youngest, to buy his groceries. His son drove him to Dublin where he had family, and after his visit, he had no trouble getting on the train and going back home. People saw him in town talking to Lizzie Brown the prostitute and they heard he gave her money; some people seemed to think it was "shameful." Marshall was well known, and he always read his bible daily, and walked to town with a cane. All this after the hard life of being a slave, working in the fields and marching over 1,000 miles in Sherman's Army with the 135th United States Colored Troop.

Marshall died in 1938 in Hawkinsville, Georgia, at age 101.

The Pension Certificate Should Not Be Forwarded With the Application

State of GEORGIA, County of WASHINGTON, ss:

On this 4th day of Jan 19 36, personally appeared before me, a [illegible] within and for the county and State aforesaid, who, being duly sworn according to law, declares that he is 78 years of age, and a resident of TENNILLE county of WASHINGTON, State of GEORGIA, and that he is the identical person who was ENROLLED at SOUTH CAROLINA(in the woods) under the name of MARSHALL ROGERS on the 4th day of April 1865 as a 2nd sergant in Co."D" in the army (U.S.A.)
(Here state rank, and company and regiment in the Army, or vessels if in the Navy.)
in the service of the United States, in the CIVIL WAR
(State name of war, Civil or Mexican.)
war, and was HONORABLY DISCHARGED at LOUISVILLE, KY. on the 1st day of Dec. 1865

That he also served
(Here give a complete statement of all other services, if any.)

That his personal description at enlistment was as follows: Height [illegible] feet [illegible] inches, complexion [illegible] color of eyes [illegible], color of hair black (now gray), that his occupation was slave that he was born 18[illegible], at WASHINGTON CO. GA.

That he requires the regular personal aid and attendance of another person on account of the following disabilities: [illegible] [illegible], FEET AND ANKLES AND VERTIGO
(State in this space the nature of any and all disabilities.)

On this [illegible] day of [illegible], 19[illegible], at [illegible]

county of Laurens, State of Georgia before me, C. H. Collier, an inspector of the Bureau of Pensions, personally appeared Ulysses S. Johnson, who, being by me first duly sworn to answer truly all interrogatories propounded to him during this special examination of aforesaid claim for pension, deposes and says:

I have been practicing medicine for 18 years. I am a graduate of Meharry Medical College, am now 48 years of age, and my address is Dublin, Georgia.

Within the last three years I have treated the claimant Marshall Green about a half dozen times, and I last saw him about two weeks ago. Every time I have seen him it has been at my office. He was every time brought here in an automobile. When he has called at my office he has been lead in. I never saw him eat. His people have told me that he does not know water from milk and cannot tell one article of food from the other, and that someone has to help him eat. I doubt whether this claimant could put on all of his clothes, nor pull them off. I have never seen him try to, but have been told that they have to help him put them on.

off. I have never seen him try to, but have been told that they have to help him put them on.

I filed some affidavits in this claim. My statement as to whether the claimant is able to care for himself is based on the history of the case as given me by him and his relatives. I know from examining him that he is feeble and has poor eyesigh I tried him out on seeing if he could find his way down my office steps and found that he could not.

I am not related to this claimant.

Rev. C. H. Harris of Dublin is a nephew of this claimant. Rev. Harris lives here in Dublin.

I have no financial interest in this pension claim.

I have read the foregoing and it is correct.

Ulysses S. Johnson

Page 10 Deposition B

On this 13 day of September, 1926, at Chester county of Dodge, State of Georgia before me, C. H. Collier, an inspector of the Bureau of Pensions, personally appeared Marshall Green, who, being by me first duly sworn to answer truly all interrogatories propounded to him during this special examination of aforesaid claim for pension, deposes and says:

My address is Box 165, Tennille, Georgia. I am now at Chester, Georgia with my daughter Susie Green. I have been staying with my son Tom Green. I am pensioned at the rate of $65 per month, based on my service under the name of Marshall Rogers as a Sergeant in Company D 135 U. S. Colored Infantry. I enlisted in South Carolina April 4, 1865, and it was discharged at Louisville, Kentucky the last of November or the first of December, 1865.

I am able to go to the table and eat without any help, and what little I eat I eat without help. Nobody has to help me pull off my clothes when I go to bed, and I put on my clothes without any help. I travel alone. I came from Dublin to

without any help. I travel alone. I came from Dublin to Chester here on the train without any help last week. I walk along by myself and go to the village by myself. I don't need anybody to help me do these things. I am not to where I have to be waited on every day. Dr. Johnson made out the papers in my case, and he ought to have known better than to make out that I am helpless. I am not helpless and I am not blind. I can read, and was reading my Bible when you came up. I am not going to tell anything but the truth to the government, and I did not mean to swear that I am helpless, because I am not.

I am not a married man. My last wife was Ella Green. She died in September, 1920. I have only been married twice. My first wife was Elmira Green. She died years ago. I put both my wives away, and I know they are dead. My youngest child is Susie Green. She will be 25 her next birthday.

I have heard you explain what my privileges are in this

Page 8 Deposition A

...illie, ... in this [i]nvestigation, and made inquiry about the claimant. No one there [s]eemed to know when the claimant would return, or where he could [b]e found, so I took two depositions to avoid having to return [t]o Tennille after finding the claimant. At Dublin I was informed that the claimant had left there for Chester, Georgia, and since I was not certain that I would return to Dublin on the case I took the deposition of the BJ witness Dr. Ulysses S. Johnson before going to Chester to serve notice on the claimant.

At Tennille I was told by a dozen or more people, white and black, that the claimant regularly goes alone about town and travels alone. When I asked a group of negroes there about where the claimant could be found I was referred to one Lizzie Brown. This Lizzie Brown is a chocolate colored woman, said to be a prostitute. She did not know where the claimant was, but she knew what his plans were when he was last at Tennille. A number of people told me about the claimant associating with prostitute[s] and some of them complained about his dividing the money paid him by the government with them. His son Samuel Green, a [r]espectable negro farmer, seemed to regard the claimant's condu[ct] [a]s shameful. I never made any inquiry as to the claimant's [be]havior toward women of light affairs, and never questioned t[he] [cla]imant about it. The people who voluntarily mentioned his [con]duct to me seemed to be under the impression that somethin[g] [shoul]d be done about it, and it was suggested by claimant's

Case of Marshall Green , No. 1132531

Deposition of Summary , continued, sheet 2

he wished that he had listened to the Postmaster, and followed his advice. Dr. Johnson may have encouranged the claimant to send in his application, but very likely the claimant did not need much coaxing. He would be glad to receive more pension. A good part of that which he receives goes for flattery and adulation, and he knows that this will be to some extent commensurate with the amount which he can spend. There are few negroes in his section having incomes in excess of $65 per month.

When I came upon the claimant he was reading his Bible. In view of the testimony to the effect that he travels alone and goes about without aid I never made any effort to test his vision. His statement is that he could recognize a person 30 feet away. It would appear from the information which I obtained at Tennille that the claimant actually spends a good part of his daylight moving about, and to them it would seem queer to have someone leading him.

Recommendation It is recommended that the claim be sent to the Medical Division for consideration.

Respectfully submitted

Mr. George E. Brown, Director,
Veterans Claims Service,
Veterans Administration,
Washington, D. C.

C 2483537

Dear Sir:

RE: MCC-BG, Rogers, Marshall, alias Green, Marshall. C-2 483 573.

I received your letter of April 2nd, advising me that an award of $100. per month had been made in favor of this Veteran, commencing July 1st, 1933.

The Guardian advises me that up to date she has only received payments of $570.00 and $100.00.

As I wish to keep closely in behind this matter, and see that all funds received by her are properly deposited to her credit as Guardian, and legally paid out, I would thank you to advise me if this is the correct amount, and the approximate time when the remainder of the award will be paid to her, bringing the payments up to date. Kindly advise me the amount of payments made and the other information, and oblige,

Yours very truly,

MARS EVANS

Mars Evans was from Fayetteville, North Carolina, and claimed an injury from a fall that he sustained in Munfordville, Kentucky. The fall occurred in the fall of 1865 prior to being mustered out of his service in the 135th United States Colored Troop. In his pension record, he stated "I was hauling water with a horse and cart to the hospital about two miles. The horse bolted and crushed my leg and foot." What had happened was the horse lunged forward, Mars was thrown to the side and the cart ran over him.

As a result of his injuries Mars Evans was permanently disabled to do significant labor for the rest of his life. David Walker, in his declaration of fact, said that he was also in Company "D," and was aware of the injuries sustained by Mars to his leg and foot.

When Mars Evans returned home from the army, although he was obviously disabled because of his injuries, he had the fortitude to still go on to support his family. His wife, Rebecca stated in her deposition that Mars Evans passed away on September 28, 1904. At the time of his death, Mars left Rebecca with three children under the age of sixteen. Lula was the oldest child, Robert was next, and then there was Willie who she was not sure of his age. Rebecca indicated that she, at one time, had a record of their ages however she lost it. Rebecca was left a small house and a couple of acres of land upon her husband's death.

For Rebecca to receive her widow's pension she had to go on to prove that she and Mars were, in fact, married and that she had three children with Mars and that they were all under sixteen years of age. She had several people testify and give statements that Mars and Rebecca were in fact wed and had the children together. To justify her children's ages, she recalled that Robert was born in December. She didn't know the exact date, but it was at the beginning of the month. She went on to tell that Leslie Gray, who lived with George Newell, four miles from Fayetteville, had a boy who was three weeks older than Robert. Leslie had her boy's age memorialized in her family Bible. Rebecca went on to indicate that Lula was fifteen at the end of the previous July and she had been born on the tenth of the month and Henry Levy had a daughter who was three months younger than Lula. This was Rebecca's attempt to justify the ages of her children under sixteen years of age.

We do, however, find in the Declaration for Pension by Rebecca in October of 1904 that she did in fact list the birth dates of her three younger children who were under the age of sixteen.

At the time of his death, Mars Evans was drawing a pension of $12.00 a month from 1893.

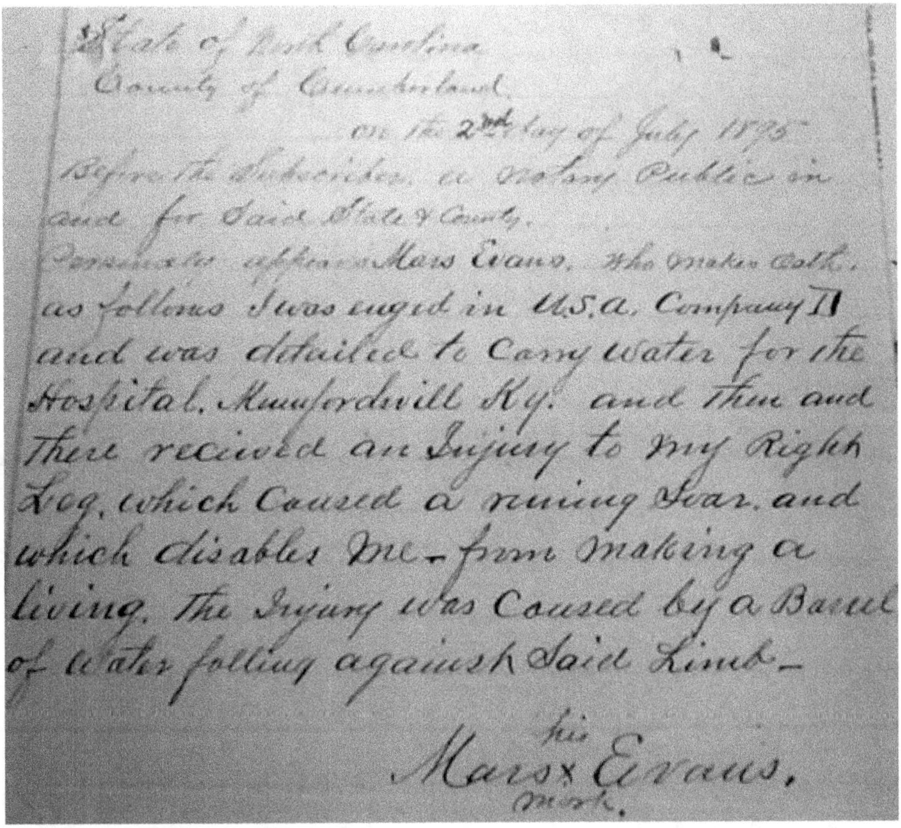

State of North Carolina
County of Cumberland
On the 2nd day of July 1895
Before the Subscriber, a Notary Public in
and for Said State & County.
Personally appears Mars Evans, who makes oath
as follows I was engd in U.S.A. Company II
and was detailed to Carry water for the
Hospital. Mumfordsvill Ky. and then and
there recived an Injury to my Right
Leg, which Caused a runing Soar. and
which disables me - from making a
living. the Injury was Caused by a Barrel
of Water falling against Said Limb -

his
Mars x Evans,
mark.

1-280.

DEPOSITION A

Case of Rebecca Evans, No. 814648

On this 24 day of March 1905, at near Fayetteville, county of Cumberland State of N. C., before me, T. H. Goette, a Special Examiner of the Bureau of Pensions, personally appeared Rebecca Evans, who, being by me first duly sworn to answer truly all interrogatories propounded to her during this special examination of aforesaid claim for pension, deposes and says:

I am about 63 years of age; housekeeping and washing and I live 2 miles from Fayetteville, N. C.

I claim pension as widow of Mars Evans who served during the Civil War in the Union Army but

I am about 63 years of age; housekeeping and washing and I live 2 miles from Fayetteville, N. C.

I claim pension as widow of Mars Evans who served during the Civil War in the Union Army but
I do not know the Co. or Regt., and who died Sept. 28, 1904. Hee was drawing a pension of $12 a month at time of his death.

Both my husband and myself were raised here, and we were married in Fayetteville. As well as I can recollect we were married about 34 years ago. Neither of us were ever married till we married each other and I have never remarried since his death. My maiden name was Rebecca Lomax and I married under that name. We were married by A. G. Thornton, Justice of the Peace. We lived together as man and wife, from our marriage

drawing a pension of $12 a month at time of his death.

Both my husband and myself were raised here, and we were married in Fayetteville. As well as I can recollect we were married about 24 years ago. Neither of us were ever married till we married each other and I have never remarried since his death. My maiden name was Rebecca Lomax and I married under that name. We were married by A. G. Thornton, Justice of the Peace. We lived together as man and wife from our marriage till my husband died and we were never separated or divorced. I own this little house and two acres of land. I don't think I could get fifty dollars for house and land. My only income is derived from washing. I own no property except what you see here.

Page 5 Deposition A

No. 6

At the time my husband died he left 3 children under 16, viz., Lula is the oldest, Robert is next and then comes Willie. Willie is the only one whose age I am sure of. I once had a record of their ages but lost it.

Willie was nine years of age on the 2nd day of last Nov.

Robert was born in Dec. and was three years old when Willie was born. I cannot tell you the date in Dec. but it was towards the first of the month. Sallie Gray who lives with George Newell 4 miles from Fayetteville has a boy that is three weeks older than mine. She has her boys age in her Bible.

Lula was 15 this last July past. She was born on the 6th. Henry Levy has a daughter 3 months younger than Lula. Her name is Carrie. Mr. Levy is educated and a teacher and can give you correct age. I have fully understood your questions and

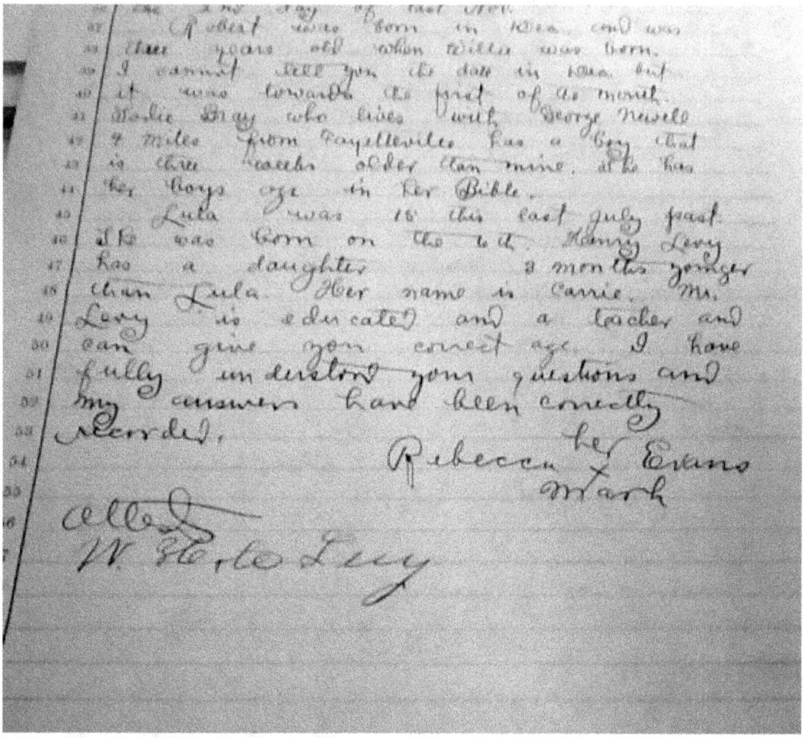

[illegible] day of last Nov.
Robert was born in [illegible] and was three years old when Willa was born. I cannot tell you the date in [illegible] but it was towards the first of the month. Nodie Gray who lives with George Newell 7 miles from Fayetteville has a boy that is three weeks older than mine. She has her boys age in her Bible.
Lula was 18 this last July past. She was born on the 6th. Henry Levy has a daughter 2 months younger than Lula. Her name is Carrie. Mr. Levy is educated and a teacher and can give you correct age. I have fully understood your questions and my answers have been correctly recorded.

Rebecca her x mark Evans

Attest
W. [illegible] Levy

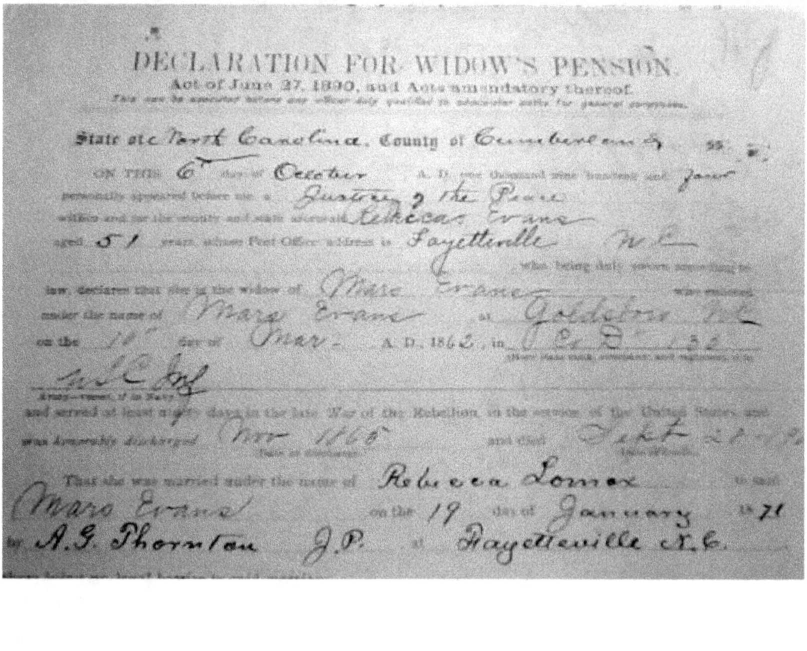

DECLARATION FOR WIDOW'S PENSION.
Act of June 27, 1890, and Acts amendatory thereof.
This must be executed before any officer duly qualified to administer oaths for general purposes.

State of North Carolina, County of Cumberland ss:

ON THIS 6th day of October A. D. one thousand nine hundred and four personally appeared before me, a Justice of the Peace within and for the county and state aforesaid Rebecca Evans aged 51 years, whose Post-Office address is Fayetteville N.C. who, being duly sworn according to law, declares that she is the widow of Marc Evans who enlisted under the name of Marc Evans at Goldsboro N.C. on the 16th day of Mar. A. D. 1862, in Co. D. 135 (Here state rank, company, and regiment, if in the Army; or vessel, if in Navy) U.S.C. Inf. and served at least ninety days in the late War of the Rebellion, in the service of the United States, and was honorably discharged Nov 1865 (Date of discharge) and died Sept 28 [illegible] (Date of death).

That she was married under the name of Rebecca Lomax to said Marc Evans on the 19 day of January 1871 by A.G. Thornton J.P. at Fayetteville N.C.

CHAPTER 7

THE WOODS RESOUND WITH THE MUSIC OF AXES AND THE CRIES OF THE PIONEERS AS THEY MOVE TIMBERS AND OTHER MATERIAL TO THE RIVER.

In The Salkehatchie Swamp

COMPANY "E"

INCLUDED IN THIS CHAPTER ARE EXTRACTIONS FROM THE PENSION RECORDS OF;

ANDREW MANNING
HARRISON STRANGE
ABRAHAM MCDANIEL
HUYCEN FORT

ANDREW MANNING

Andrew Manning in his deposition said, "I was born a slave to my old Master R. I. Manning on his plantation in Clarendon County South Carolina." He goes on to indicate there is no bible, slave, or other records as justification. The slave records were destroyed by fire with the destruction of the Master's house. The old Master died at the end of the civil war and Mistress Eliza Manning and four of the children are still living in Bishopville, South Carolina which is where Andrew was living.

He stated that he was a big boy, and his father was a slave of Manning too. His father was born in Virginia, and he recalled that his mother said that his old master bought her from the Burroughs Estate near Manning, South Carolina. Andrew said he had two living sisters, Emma Nelson, and Miss Harriett. Andrew clarified that shortly after the end of the civil war he changed his name to Andrew Gooden, which was the name of his father.

The record indicated also that when Sherman's army came through the Manning Plantation the old master and his brother took a lot of the slaves across the county to keep the Yankees from getting them. Andrew was among the lot taken and they were all captured but Andrew was able to escape.

Andrew then got with the Yankees, he enlisted and was examined by the doctors, sworn in, and given a blue uniform. He recalled being in Goldsboro, North Carolina, where they stayed for a few nights and then they marched to Raleigh, Richmond Virginia, and stayed three or four months. Then they went on to Washington, D.C., for a few weeks. He went to Louisville, Kentucky, and mustered out in October of 1865. He stated that he was in several battles at the following places: Goldsboro, North Carolina, Richmond, Virginia, and claims to have been in a battle at Bull Run.

As a result of a shell explosion Andrew was issued a pension because he was wounded in the right arm. He is an excellent example of how many pension records we need to see to get the whole story of these men. Every little piece of information is a piece of the puzzle that fits together to form the whole experience of the men and their service. It is a testament of the men living with the scars of service for the remainder of their lives. True GUTS!

Case of Andrew Manning . *No.* [illegible]

On this 27 *day of* February, 1912, *at* Bishopville, *county of* Lee, *State of* South Carolina, *before me,* I. R. Schneider, *a Special Examiner of the Bureau of Pensions, personally appeared* Andrew Manning *who, being by me first duly sworn to answer truly all interrogatories propounded to* him *during this special examination of aforesaid claim for pension, deposes and says:*

My name is Andrew Manning, but shortly after the close of the Civil War I assumed the family name of my father, who was Andrew Gooden, and I have been generally known as Andrew Gooden ever since. I was married under the name of Andrew Gooden and all of my contracts are under the name of Andrew Gooden, in fact, I transact all of my business other than that relating to my pension under the name of Andrew Gooden, and I solemnly swear that I, Andrew Gooden, and Andrew Manning who served in Co. E, 135 U. S. C. Inf., and is pensioned by the United States at the rate of $15. a month, are one and the same person, and that the only reason that I had for changing my name was in order to have my family name like that of my father. I was born a slave to my old master, R. I. Manning, on his plantation in Clarendon County, but I do not remember the date

fact, I transact all of my business other than that relating to my pension under the name of Andrew Gooden, and I solemnly swear that I, Andrew Gooden, and Andrew Manning who served in Co. E, 135 U. S. C. Inf., and is pensioned by the United States at the rate of $15. a month, are one and the same person, and that the only reason that I had for changing my name was in order to have my family name like that of my father. I was born a slave to my old master, R. I. Manning, on his plantation in Clarendon County, but I do not remember the date
of my birth, nor do I remember what town was nearest to us. There is no bible, slave or other record of my birth in existence, the slave record having been destroyed by fire when my old master's house at Gilman, S. C., was burned. My old master died just before the war closed. My old mistress was Eliza Manning, who died about two years ago. Their children still living are as follows: William Manning, Spartanburg, S. C.; Mrs. Daisy Boykin, Camden, S. C.; Mrs. Eliza Richardson, Sumter, S. C.; and R. I. Manning, Sumter, S. C., on whose place in Bishopville, S. C., I am now living. I was a large boy when these children's parents were married, but all of them were old enough at the time I was a slave to remember me as a slave. My father was a slave of my old master, R. I. Manning, having been born on the Manning estate, and was known during slavery as Andrew Manning, but on gaining freedom he took the name Andrew Gooden, which might have been the name of his father who was purchased by my old master from someone in Virginia, I believe. I think I heard my mother say that my old master bought her from the Burroughs estate, near Manning, S. C., but I do not know what her name was before she married my father. My

of my birth, nor do I remember what town was nearest to us. There is no bible, slave or other record of my birth in existence, the slave record having been destroyed by fire when my old master's house at Gilman, S. C., was burned. My old master died just before the war closed. My old mistress was Eliza Manning, who died about two years ago. Their children still living are as follows: William Manning, Spartanburg, S. C.; Mrs. Daisy Boykin, Camden, S. C., Mrs. Eliza Richardson, Sumter, S. C., and R. I. Manning, Sumter, S. C., ...

... children's parents were married, but all of them were old enough at the time I was a slave to remember me as a slave. My father was a slave of my old master, R. I. Manning, having been born on the Manning estate, and was known during slavery as Andrew Manning, but on gaining freedom he took the name Andrew Boyden, which might have been the name of his father who was purchased by my old master from someone in Virginia, I believe. I think I heard my mother say that my old master bought her from the Burroughs estate, near Manning, S. C., but I do not know what her name was before she married my father. My father and mother are now both dead. I have no brothers living to my knowledge, but have two living sisters: Mrs. Emma Nelson, Sumter, S. C., and Rica Harriett

Page 3 *Deposition* A

I was sworn in. We staid at Goldsborough for a fort-night and then marched to Richmond, Va. We staid at Richmond three or four months and then marched to Washington, D. C. I cannot remember all the places in between. We remained in Washington about a fort-night and then some of us were taken to Texas, I being one to go. We did not stay there long because there was no fighting but came back to Washington, where I staid a few days and then went to Louisville, Ky. and was mustered out. I then came home to Gilman, S. C., in the vicinity of which place I have lived ever since. I never had any service other than that in the 1st U. S. C. Inf. I was in battles at the following places: Goldsborough, N. C., and Richmond, Va. I was also in the battle of Bull Run. The only officers that I can remember are Lt. Johnson, Lt. Buck and Lt. Dixon. I do not remember if there were any changes among the officers while I was in the army, nor do I remember anything about the number of killed in any of the battles I was in. I do not know how old I am, my occupation is farmer, and my post office address is Bishopville, Lee Co., S. C. I have the foregoing statement read, understood your questions, and my answers are correctly recorded therein.

Witnesses:

[illegible signature]

his
Andrew X Manning
mark

Subscribed and sworn to before me this 27 *day of* February *[illegible]*, *and I certify that the contents were duly made known to deponent [illegible]*

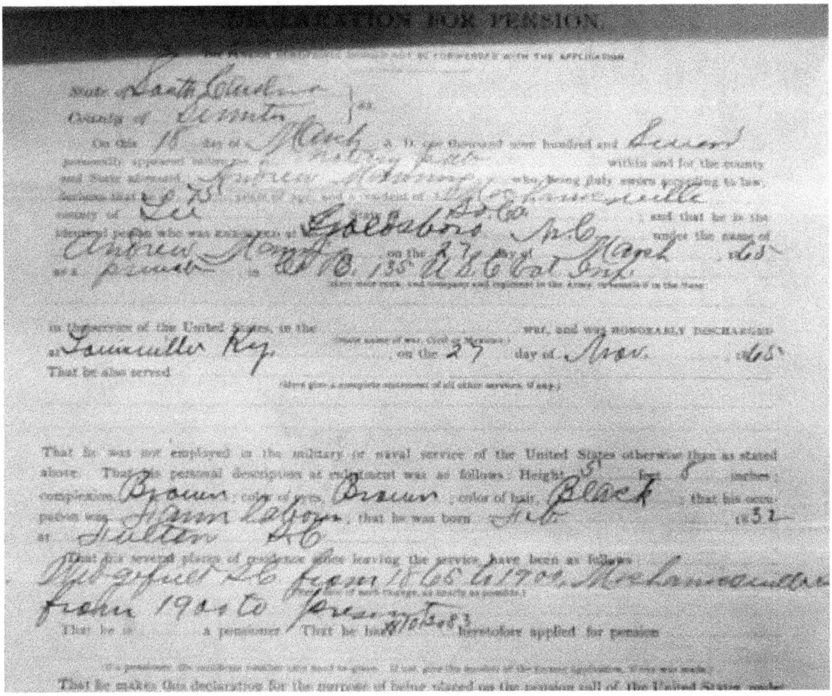
DECLARATION FOR PENSION.

State of South Carolina
County of Sumter } ss

On this 18 day of March, A. D. one thousand nine hundred and seven personally appeared before me a Notary Public within and for the county and State aforesaid, Andrew Manning, who, being duly sworn according to law, declares that he is 75 years of age, and a resident of Mechanicsville county of Lee State of S.C., and that he is the identical person who was enrolled at Goldsboro N.C. under the name of Andrew Manning on the 27 day of March 1865 as a private in Co B. 135 U.S.C. Col. Inf.

in the service of the United States, in the war, and was HONORABLY DISCHARGED at Louisville Ky. on the 27 day of Nov. 1865.

That he also served

That he was not employed in the military or naval service of the United States otherwise than as stated above. That his personal description at enlistment was as follows: Height 5 feet 6 inches; complexion Brown; color of eyes Brown; color of hair Black; that his occupation was farm laborer; that he was born Feb 1832 at Salter S.C.

That his several places of residence since leaving the service have been as follows: Mt... S.C. from 1865 to 1900, Mechanicsville from 1900 to present.

That he is a pensioner. That he has not heretofore applied for pension

That he makes this declaration for the purpose of being placed on the pension roll of the United States under

HARRISON STRANGE

Harrison Strange was from Oliver, Screven County Georgia. He was born in Washington County, Georgia, near Sandersville and enrolled in Honey Hill, South Carolina. He married Lucy Lockhart by the Reverend J.E. Holmes and he belonged to Bob Williams who had many slaves. Harrison was born in 1824 and died June 20, 1909.

So many people have said, as we work to find out the true story of this regiment, that the pioneers would be called just laborers, camp followers, or contraband. Through our research, however, we found that they were recruited into service, when Sherman's Army passed through where they lived, from the very beginning of the march to the sea from Atlanta. They were volunteers.

After Sherman's Army left Savannah, Georgia, and in Beaufort, South Carolina, the very first encounter with the rebels (confederate army) was at Rivers Bridge, South Carolina. Shortly thereafter Harrison Strange joined the Army and he was wounded at Salkehatchie swamp South Carolina, during their encounter with the rebels. He stated in his deposition that he was carrying ammo "down the line of fighting" and was wounded in the back of his head. He claimed to have recovered from his wounds in two days but when he was wounded, he had been "unconscious for a period of time."

Harrison stayed with the company and went along with them. He was struck by a shell which affected his head, ear, and lungs. He found himself back at camp with the doctors over him and the doctor told him that they had to take out bone however he was able to stay with the regiment.

We acknowledge that Harrison Strange is a man with "GUTS" as he stayed with the regiment and completed his military service with the 135th United States Colored Troop. As a result of his injuries, he suffered physically for the remainder of his life.

DECLARATION FOR INVALID PENSION.

Act of June 27, 1890.

This May be Executed before any Person Authorized by Law to Administer Oaths for General Purposes. The Certificate of the Clerk of the Court need NOT be attached, but will be procured hereafter if called for.

95
33

State of Georgia County of Screven ss:

On the date hereinafter mentioned, personally appeared before me, a Notary Public (Title of Magistrate) within and for the County and State aforesaid Harmon Stranger (Name of Applicant), aged 62 years, a resident of the ____ of Screven County of Screven, State of Georgia, who, being duly sworn according to law, declares that he is the identical Nelson (Name under which service was rendered) who was **ENROLLED** on the ____ day of January, 1865, in Co. E 135 U.S.C. Inf (Here state rank, company and regiment, in military service; or vessel, if in the Navy.) in the war of the Rebellion, and served not less than ninety days, and was **HONORABLY DISCHARGED** at Taylor Barracks, Ky, on the ____ day of Dec 1865. That he is to a material extent disqualified from earning a support by manual labor, by reason of wound in head resulting in affection of head and eyesight, neck and lungs (Here name all diseases, wounds or injuries from which disabled for manual labor.)

That said disabilities are not due to his vicious habits, and are to the best of his knowledge and belief permanent. That he has never served in the Army, Navy or Marine Corps of the United States, otherwise than as above stated, except no prior or subsequent service (State other service, if any.)

That he is not a pensioner, Has applied for pension by claim (If a pensioner, so state, giving certificate number; if not a pensioner, so state;) #1,050,451

(If a prior application is pending, so state, giving case number.)

Attention is invited to the outlines of the human skeleton and figure upon the back of this certificate, and they should be used whenever it is possible to indicate precisely the location of a disease or injury, the entrance and exit of a missile, an amputation, &c.

The absence of a member from a session of a board and the reason therefor, if known, and the name of the absentee, must be indorsed upon each certificate.

Original Pension Claim No. 1050 454

Harrison Sprangt Rank, Private

Company E 33 Reg't U.S.C.T. Savannah Ga State,

Hicks, Ga November 24 1915

I hereby certify that in compliance with the requirements of the law I have carefully examined this applicant, who states that he is suffering from the following disability, incurred in the service, viz: Wound of the Head, resulting in affection of the Head, eyesight, neck and lungs.

and that he receives a pension of ______ dollars per month.

He makes the following statement upon which he bases his claim for ______

In december 1865 or soon after, I was wounded at Salkehatchie, S.C. while conveying ammunition down the line in a fight; I was wounded in the back of the Head; I recovered in 2 days, and went on with the Company. During the first 3 years has had a swimming in the head; also for a few years past

Upon examination we find the following objective conditions: Pulse rate, 74 respiration, 18 temperature, 98¾ height, 5 feet 7 inches; weight, 190 pounds; age, 68 years.

This applicant is a fine looking, splendidly nourished negro of 68. Lungs perfectly sound. Heart somewhat irritated but not organic trouble. His hands are fairly rough, not as rough as a workman's however. He admits that he can do light work, ploughing and picking cotton, but claims that he cannot do a full man's work; I do no know where he draws the distinction as he looks like as if he could do the work which ought to be expected of an ordinary man! There is a well healed scar in the upper portion of the back of the head, running upwards and backwards at an angle of 45° from the point (tip) of the left ear and the same angle almost upwards and backwards from point of right ear (5 inches). This scar, is in my opinion, a cut from some instrument; He claims that his regimental surgeon cut down and elevated the bone, after he was struck, He don't know what he was struck with. He claims that his eye-sight is only affected when the attacks of vertigo occur. His vision is normal for 68 years. [illegible], which glasses remedy. No disease of the neck which I can find. Absolutely no lung disease. There is no depression of the bone nor anything about the alleged head injury which, would, in my opinion, interfere with manual labor. No other disability found to exist.

______ Pres. ______, Sec'y ______, Treas.

N. B.—Always forward a certificate of examination whether a disability is found to exist or not.

I am of the opinion that he is not entitled to any rating for alleged: Wound of the Head or any of the alleged results; E.H. Nichols, M.D.

State of Georgia, before me ..., a special examiner of the Bureau of Pensions, personally appeared Lucy Strange, who, being by me first duly sworn to answer truly all interrogatories propounded to her during this special examination of aforesaid claim for pension, deposes and says: I am about 69 years of age; my post-office address is Olive, Screven Co., Ga.

I am the widow of Harmon Strange who was a soldier in the Civil War. I do not know his company and regiment. He drew a pension. He died the third Sunday in June 1909 [June 20 Cont. Rl. E.] I do not know the date of my marriage to Harmon Strange because I kept no account of it. I can't say how many years ago it was but it was just [illegible] the [illegible] years ago. We were married by Rev. J. E. Holmes a colored preacher, and I have given the date of our marriage, it is doubtless correct. We were married about 2 miles from where I now live. My maiden name was Lucy Lockhart. I had never before been married. I was born in Bulloch Co. but lived here from the 2d year after the war. I had never been

received a pension. He died the third Sunday in June 1909 [June 20 Cont. Rl. E.] I do not know the date of my marriage to Harmon Strange because I kept no account of it. I can't say how many years ago it was but it was just [illegible] the [illegible] years ago. We were married by Rev. J. E. Holmes a colored preacher, and I have given the date of our marriage, it is doubtless correct. We were married about 2 miles from where I now live. My maiden name was Lucy Lockhart. I had never before been married. I was born in Bulloch Co. but lived here from the 2d year after the war. I had never been

married before I married the soldier. He had never before been married. I had known him for 6 or 7 years before I married him and am certain that he was never before married. If he had been I would have known or heard of it. He was known as a single man by all who knew him, before I married him. I never

Page 6 Deposition A

Page 7

had any children except one boy dead.
I have not remarried since the soldier's death.

I can prove that the soldier was never before married by James Carter, who lives about a mile from Hollygrovedale on Paul Elkins' place. Elmira Simmons, widow of Charles Simmons who lives at Clinton, Ga. is his sister. I don't know of any other relatives of the soldier, that I know of. No brothers of his are living. These are the only people who knew the soldier "way back".

Richard Lockhart my brother can testify that I was never before married. He also knew the soldier for a while before I married him. I have another brother in Emanuel Co

I do not know of any other witness who would know the facts in the case. The soldier & I lived together continuously from the time of our marriage until his death.

I do not desire to be present or represented by an attorney during the examination of my claim. I do not know of any witness who testify I did by them, either here or elsewhere other than those named herein. I do not desire to be present at any examination elsewhere and waive notice of further examination.

I have made no contract with any person to pay him a fee in my pension claim, nor have I paid any fee to any one.

I have understood the questions asked & my answers have been correctly recorded in this deposition which I have been read to me.

The words "that I know of" erased, line 35, before signing.

her
Lucy x Strange

ABRAHAM McDANIEL

Abraham McDaniel was born and raised in Flea Hill, Cumberland County, North Carolina on the plantation of John McDaniel. He married Tama Williams in 1855 or 1856 at the Joel Williams plantation. He would come to see Tama on Saturday and then leave on Monday every week. They had three girls and one boy and unfortunately, three of the children died very young and the last one died in 1865.

When Abraham left with the soldiers in Sherman's army in March of 1865 Tama left also and went to Beaufort, North Carolina. She was gone until June and then returned to the Joel Williams plantation. Tama's recollection is that Abraham was about twenty years old, one hundred and forty pounds, and 5' 6" tall when they were married. The record of births and marriages were destroyed when the house burned in 1864. Tama said the only complaint Abraham had before he left with Sherman's Army was that he had a yellow discharge coming from both of his ears.

Arron McDaniel was in the same company as Abraham and said that they camped outside of Washington, D.C., in May of 1865. At the time Abraham complained of having diarrhea in the company quarters, so he reported to sick call and was excused from duty. When the regiment departed Washington, D.C., Abraham, and the other soldiers who were sick were sent to the Alexandria, Virginia hospital. Arron stated in his deposition that "it was the last time I saw him." Warren Brauson who was at Alexandria Hospital came back to the regiment while they were at Louisville, Kentucky, and told them that Abraham McDaniel died November 1, 1865, of chronic diarrhea.

Tama's father was Jeffrey Williams and he lived with Tama and John Williams. Her brother lived on the same Joel Williams plantation. He, his mother, and younger brother were sold to John Manchester who was the son in law of Joel Williams. Prior to Abraham going off with the Union Army he was a laborer in the turpentine fields.

As a result of the death of Abraham McDaniel, Tama applied for her widow's pension in 1888.

DEPOSITION A

Case of Tamar McDaniel, No. 363522

On the 3 day of Aug, 1889, at Fayetteville, County of Cumberland, State of N C, before me, Orville A Ross, a Special Examiner of the Pension Office, personally appeared Tamar McDaniel, who, being by me first duly sworn to answer truly all interrogatories propounded to her during this Special Examination of aforesaid pension claim, deposes and says: That she is about 61 years of age. Occupation Housekeeper. Post Office address Fayetteville Cumberland Co N.C.

She was born a slave on the plantation of Joel Williams in Flea Hill township Cumberland County about eight miles from Fayetteville N.C and resided on said plantation until in March 1865 when Genl Sherman's army came to the County. She then went to Beaufort, Carteret Co N.C and remained there until about June 1st 1865 and she was always known up to this time by the name of Tamar Williams.

She has lived in Flea Hill twp Cumberland Co and in Fayetteville N.C from about June 1st 1865 until the present date and has been known by the name of Tamar Williams and Tamar McDaniel during that time.

She is the widow of Abram McDaniel deceased, late private Co E 135 Regt U.S.C Infty Vol, who is reported to have died at Alexandria Va during Nov 1865.

She was married in the hall of the house of her master in Flea Hill twp Cumberland Co N.C during the year 1855 or 1856, when she was about twenty nine years of age under the name of Tamar Williams to said Abram McDaniel by Joel Williams, her former master. There being

Page 5 Deposition A

Pg 2 no legal barrier to said marriage.

[illegible] Williams her former mistress and Uncle Toby Williams a slave were the only persons present at her marriage.

Her former Master and Mistress, her father and mother and Uncle Toby Williams are dead.

To the best of her recollection her late husband Abram McDaniel was about as old as she was, viz 20 years of age - was 5 feet 5 or 6 inches in height - weighed about [illegible] pounds - had oval face with broad forehead - eyes and hair black - and complexion dark at the time of their marriage.

She became acquainted with Abram McDaniel about the year 1853 or 1854 and he courted affiant regularly during two years prior to their marriage.

Her husband was a slave on the plantation of John McDaniel when she first made his acquaintance and he worked on said plantation until he went off with Genl Sherman's army in Mch 1865 and he was always known as Abram McDaniel.

The plantations of Joel Williams and McDaniel were five miles distant from each other and her late husband Abram would visit her nearly every week and sleep with her on each Saturday and Sunday night from the time of their marriage in 1855 or 1856 until in March 1865.

Said Abram McDaniel and Affiant cohabited together and lived with each other as was the custom of slaves who were married and residing on separate plantations - they acknowledged each other as man and wife and were recognized as such by their relatives, their masters' families and their fellow slaves from about 1855 or 1856 until in March 1865.

Neither she nor Abram McDaniel had been previously married - she was his wife at time of his death - she has remained his [illegible]

[illegible] [illegible] her [illegible] - three girls and one boy were born to her in wedlock with Abram McDaniel none of whom were surviving on Nov 1, 1880 the reported date of the death of their father.

She has been informed that all of the plantation records of her former Master Joel McDaniel were destroyed when Sherman's army came through the county and hence she can not state the exact date of her birth, of her marriage or of the births or deaths of any of her children.

She has not in any manner been voluntarily engaged in or aiding or abetting the rebellion in the United States - she has not cohabited with any man since the death of her late husband Abram McDaniel except with one Frank Elliott who had sexual intercourse with her about ten or fifteen times during the year 1864 - that a daughter named Mary Williams was born to her about 1865 as the result of her cohabitation with said Elliott - that her daughter said Mary Williams died during 1855 or 1856.

She has not lived in open, notorious adulterous cohabitation with any man nor lived in the quasi relation of man and wife with any man since the death of Abram McDaniel

By reason of being in such destitute circumstances shortly after the surrender so that she could scarcely obtain food enough to maintain life in her body she was persuaded by Frank Elliott, a colored man to have sexual intercourse with him at times during ten or twelve months and said Elliott then furnished her with provisions to eat.

Her menstrual discharges did not cease until about three years ago.

She is an applicant for pension under claim No 363522 as widow of Abram McDaniel, deceased, late private in U.S. -

Page [illegible] 35 Regt U S C Eighth Vol and who is reported to have died at Alexandria Va while in the service of the United States.

Her late husband Abram Mc Daniel was a stout, sound, able bodied man when he went off with Genl Sherman's army in March 1865 Having did not complain of or suffer from a diseased condition of any part or portion of the body at or prior to enlistment except a [illegible] [illegible] of [illegible] [illegible] from both ears.

Daniel Elliot a former witness is deceased.

She has been informed that her late husband Abram was a member of the same Colored Regt that Aaron Mc Daniel of Fayetteville N C.

Eliza Royals formerly Williams. John and Nathan Williams and J Marshall Williams of Fayetteville N C would know that Affiant and Abram Mc Daniel were married according to the custom of slave times. and were recognized by their fellow [illegible] as man and wife during eight or nine [illegible] prior to 1865.

J E Mc Daniel of Fayetteville N C would know that her late husband was a slave on the plantation of his Father John Mc Daniel prior to the war.

She has no knowledge as to what Company in the United States service her late husband served in, except that which is [illegible] in information obtained from the Bureau of Pensions.

She does not know the name or Post Office address of any soldier who belonged to the same Company that Abram Mc Daniel did.

Attest

[illegible]

[illegible]

her
Fannie X Mc Daniel
mark
Deponent

Sworn to and subscribed before me this 13 day of Aug 1890, and I certify that the contents were fully made known to deponent before signing.

Orville A Rea
Special Examiner

Page 3 Deposition A

Case of Fannie McDaniel. No. 363522

On this 13 day of Aug, 1880, at Fayetteville, County of Cumberland, State of N C, before me, Orville A. Ross, a Special Examiner of the Pension Office, personally appeared Fannie McDaniel, who, being by me first duly sworn to answer truly all interrogatories propounded to her during this Special Examination of aforesaid pension claim, deposes and says:

She can not furnish the testimony of any witnesses in her claim except those who are closely or remotely related to her except Mr J. M. Williams, the son of her former master, as the white people of the community usually knew but little about the association or relations of the slaves to each other.

She does not know the present residence or Post Office address of Rev David Williams.

She does not wish to be present or represented at the examination of any of the witnesses in her claim in Cumberland County N C or elsewhere.

She is well satisfied with the conduct and fairness of the examination of her claim thus far and she has been afforded ample time and sufficient opportunity to make a detailed statement of all facts and circumstances within her knowledge which have a material bearing on the merits of her claim.

She has never seen her late husband, Adam McDaniel, at any time since he left this vicinity with Genl Sherman's army in March 1865 and is reported to have enlisted in the United States service at Goldsborough N C.

She understands the questions asked her during the taking of her testimony

Page [illegible]

her answers thereto as read to her by the Special Examiner are correctly recorded in the foregoing deposition.

She may be mistaken in stating that she was 20 years of age and that her late husband was about 29 years of age when they were married in 1855 or 1856. She may have been about 0 years of age and her husband may have been about the same age when they were married.

She is an ignorant, unlearned colored woman. Can not read writing or printing. Can not write her own name and can not recollect dates or years.

Attest
D. M. Williams
J. C. Scurlock

her
Fannie x McDaniel
mark
Deponent

Deponent.

Sworn to and subscribed before me this 13 day of Aug

(3—146.)

DEPOSITION B

Case of Sarah McDaniel, No. 363522

On this 14 day of Aug, 1880, at Fayetteville, County of Cumberland, State of N. C., before me, Orville A. Ross, a Special Examiner of the Pension Office, personally appeared James F. McDaniel, who, being by me first duly sworn to answer truly all interrogatories propounded to him during this Special Examination of aforesaid pension claim, deposes and says: That he is 35 years of age. Occupation Farmer – Post Office address, Fayetteville, Cumberland County, N. C. – Residence six miles east of Fayetteville.

He is a son of John McDaniel Esq. deceased, who formerly owned the same plantation on which affiant now resides.

All of his Father's plantation records were destroyed by fire when Genl Sherman's army passed through Cumberland Co N.C.

He remembers quite distinctly a slave owned by his Father during the war and prior to the war who was known as Abram McDaniel.

He was informed by his Father that the slave Abram was married to some colored woman owned by Joel Williams Esq. and he remembers that Abram would be absent from the plantation during a couple of Sundays in each month and was believed to be visiting his wife.

Said Abram McDaniel left the plantation when Genl Sherman's army passed through Cumberland County N.C. and he has not seen said Abram McDaniel since March 1865.

He does not know the surname of the Williams woman to whom Abram McDaniel was said to have been married.

He has no personal knowledge of ...

Page 11 Deposition B

acquaintance with Duncan McDaniel or Duncan Williams the Claimant.

His best information is that Abram McDaniel was born a slave on the plantation of his Grand Father, John McDaniel, and was owned by the [illegible] by the McDaniel family from birth until he left Cumberland Co NC in March 1865.

He is not related to the Claimant and has no interest in the result of this claim.

His recollection is that Abram McDaniel was in fair physical health in March 1865 and was generally regarded as one of the best and strongest hands owned by his Father.

He understands the questions asked him during the taking of his testimony and his answers thereto are correctly recorded in the foregoing deposition.

The plantations of Joel Williams and his Father John McDaniel were about eight miles distant from each other.

[illegible] McDaniel
Deponent

Deponent.

Sworn to and subscribed before me this 12 *day of* Dec, 1890, *and I certify that the contents were fully made known to deponent before signing.*

Orville A. Ray
Special Examiner.

HUYCEN FORT / MELVIN

Huycen Fort joined the 135th United States Colored Troop in Goldsboro, North Carolina in March of 1865. He was doing both farming and turpentining in Cedar Creek Cumberland County, North Carolina. The name of his father was Henry Melvin and his mother's name was Maria Fort. His sister Charlotte Goddin said that they were first owned by John Fort and then they sold to Tom Fort in Bladen County North Carolina.

This veteran was a very tall man 5' 10" with bowed legs and large feet. He went with the Army for about a year and when he returned, he was wearing his blue uniform and had his discharge papers with him. His sister Charlotte remembers him telling "a heap" of stories about his time in the army.

In 1911 Huycen applied for his pension while in Florida and was granted a small one along with back pay from the time he applied. A man named Dempsey Parker prepared the necessary paperwork for the pension application as Huycen did not read or write and he relied on Mr. Parker to help him. In 1912 the special examiner filed a lawsuit against Dempsey P. Parker for violation of Section 4 of the act of June 27, 1890, for retaining an illegal fee of $400.00. Also, for keeping a $10.00 per month of Huycen's pension, in 1910 he kept $159.80 out of his first payment of $1,059.80 which was put in the Bank of Tampa. Dempsey also demanded that he be paid an additional $80.00 in cash from Huycen. At the time Huycen was about seventy-three years old and could not read or write. When the pension payment was received Dempsey and Huycen compromised and settled on a lump sum of $400.00 and soon after Dempsey arrived at the home of Huycen and demanded $525.00.

Huycen worked in the turpentine fields and complained to his supervisor about Dempsey Parker and what he had done to him. Also, the cashier at the bank provided testimony that he suspected that Dempsey Parker was trying to swindle Huycen out of his money. Huycen became afraid of Dempsey, left the turpentine camp, and moved to Plant City with his wife, Zilpha who was from Willacoochee Georgia.

Interestingly there is documentation in the pension file of Huycen Fort/Melvin stating that “It is shown by the Rebellion Records that an order was issued from Headquarters of the 17th Army Corps, Jones’ N.C. dated April 26, 1865, directing that the 135th, with other regiments, move back to Raleigh, N.C.," The document goes on and records that, “on May 22, 1865, the regiment, with others, were near Alexandria, VA., and participated in the Grand Review. When the claim is returned by the Special Examiner this statement should be attached to the face of this report.” This is further proof that we have uncovered that the 135th United States Colored Troop participated and marched in the Grand Review in Washington, D.C., on May 24, 1865.

WASHINGTON, D. C., January 2, 1915.

SIR: Please answer, at your earliest convenience, the questions enumerated below. The information is requested for future use, and it may be of great value to your widow or children. Use the inclosed envelope, which requires no stamp.

Very respectfully,

[illegible signature]

HUYCEN MELVIN,
SOCRUM FLA
1167558 ACT MAY

U. S. APR 26 1915 OFFICE

No. 1. Date and place of birth? Answer. Bladen Co. NC. June 12th 1850

The name of organizations in which you served? Answer. Company E. 135 Regiment

No. 2. What was your post office at enlistment? Answer. Cedar Creek Cumberland NC.

No. 3. State your wife's full name and her maiden name. Answer. Maria Evans

No. 4. When, where, and by whom were you married? Answer. Cumberland Co NC. By Rev. James Cain about 1872

No. 5. Is there any official or church record of your marriage? I dont know

If so, where? Answer.

No. 6. Were you previously married? If so, state the name of your former wife, the date of the marriage, and the date and place of her death or divorce. If there was more than one previous marriage, let your answer include all former wives. Answer. Never Married But one time

No. 7. If your present wife was married before her marriage to you, state the name of her former husband, the date of such marriage, and the date and place of his death or divorce, and state whether he ever rendered any military or naval service, and, if so, give name of the organization in which he served. If she was married more than once before her marriage to you, let your answer include all former husbands. Answer. My wife only married one time

No. 8. Are you now living with your wife, or has there been a separation? Answer. She is dead Died at Cedar Creek P.O. N.C., date not known.

No. 9. State the names and dates of birth of all your children, living or dead. Answer. the oldest child

At Jacksonville—First Monday in December.
At Ocala—Third Monday in January.
At Miami—Fourth Monday in April.
At Fernandina—First Monday in April.

Office of United States District Attorney,

SOUTHERN DISTRICT OF FLORIDA.

Jacksonville, Fla., Oct. 30/1912.

The Commissioner of Pensions,

Washington, D. C.

Sir:-

I have your letter F.E.P. of the 21st inst., giving certain information as to the present whereabouts of Dempsey P. Parker, for whose arrest a warrant has been issued in this District for an alleged violation of Section 4, of the Act of June 27, 1890, by obtaining an illegal fee of $400.00 for his services in assisting in the prosecution of the pension claim of one Hayeen Fort, now known as Hayeen Melvin, Co. E, 135th U.S.C. Inf., Ctf. No.1167558. This information has been given the Marshal, with the request that he use his efforts to locate and apprehend Parker.

Respectfully,

[illegible]

Acting U.S.Attorney.

16-217

PENSION OFFICE U.S. E NOV 1 1912

October 21, 1912.

Hon. John M. Cheney,

U.S. District Attorney,

Jacksonville, Florida.

Sir:

Referring to your letter of July 23, 1912, that you had made complaint before U.S. Commissioner for arrest of Dempsey P. Parker, for his violation of section 4, of act of June 27, 1890, by obtaining an illegal fee of $400. for his services in assisting in the prosecution of the pension claim of Huycen Fort now known as Huycen Melvin, Co. E, 135th U.S.C. Inf., Ctf. No. 1167538, this Bureau later received information from a special examiner that the U.S. Marshal could not locate and apprehend the accused.

I now enclose letter of 17th instant from Mr. P. L. Weeks of Enville, Fla. (for whom the accused formerly worked) tending to show that said Parker is now working for B. F. Powell in a turpentine camp on G.S. & F. R.R., just north of White Springs, Hamilton Co., Fla., and seems to receive mail at Genoa, Hamilton Co., Fla. It is suggested that the U.S. Marshal be advised of the whereabouts of the accused.

Very respectfully,

J. L. DAVENPORT.

Commissioner.

December.
At Ocala—Third Monday in January.
At Miami—Fourth Monday in April.
At Fernandina—First Monday in April.

Office of United States District Attorney,

SOUTHERN DISTRICT OF FLORIDA

R.P.M. Jacksonville, Fla., July 23/1912.

The Commissioner of Pensions,

Washington, D. C.

Sir:-

I beg to acknowledge receipt of your letter of the 20th inst., enclosing letter under date of the 13th inst. from P. L. Weeks, of Enville, Florida, tending to show the whereabouts of one Dempsey P. Parker, charged with violation of Section 4, of the Act of June 27, 1890, in connection with the claim of Huycen Melvin for pension, for which please accept my thanks. I had intended holding this matter for the Grand Jury, but as, in all probability, we shall not have a Grand Jury in session for some time, I have made complaint before Commissioner for the arrest of Parker.

Respectfully,

J. M. Cheney

U. S. Attorney.

U. S. PENSION OFFICE. JUL 25 1912

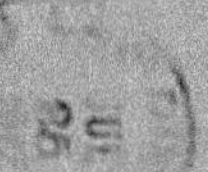

AND REFER TO INITIALS AND NUMBER

JCO

DEPARTMENT OF JUSTICE,

WASHINGTON, D. C.

162602-1

June 2[illegible], 1912.

The Secretary of the Interior,

Sir:

I have the honor to say that, in obedience to the recommendation made in your letter of the 15th instant, the United States Attorney at Jacksonville, Florida, has been instructed to institute proper criminal proceedings against Dempsey P. Parker, charged with having violated Section 4 of the Act of June 27, 1890, in demanding and retaining an illegal fee of about $400.00 for his services in the prosecution of the claim of Huycen Fort, certificate No. 1,167,558.

Respectfully,

For the Attorney General,

J. A. Fowler

Assistant to the Attorney General.

Fort

SOUTHERN JUDICIAL DISTRICT OF FLORIDA.

THE UNITED STATES	) FOR HIS SERVICES IN ASSIST-
V.	) ING IN THE PROSECUTION OF
DEMPSEY P. PARKER.	) THE PENSION CLAIM OF HUYCEN
VIOLATION OF SECTION 4,	) FORT, NOW KNOWN AS HUYCEN
ACT OF JUNE 27, 1890, IN	) MELVIN, CO. K, 135th U. S.
OBTAINING AND RETAINING	) C. INF., CTF. NO. 1,167,558.
AN ILLEGAL FEE OF $400	)

\- - - - -

STATEMENT OF FACTS.

Said pensioner filed original application for pension under the Act of June 27, 1890, on September 23, 1897. The prosecution of such claim appears to have been abandoned for some years, the claimant being unable to furnish evidence showing that he was identical with the soldier of record. In the year 1910, it appears that claimant resided in the vicinity of Enville, Hernando Co., Fla., and said Dempsey P. Parker assisted him in the prosecution of the claim by writing letters in his behalf, some of which are on file in the papers in the case, and claimant's address was given in said letters as c/o D. P. Parker (see B. J. 5 and pp. 16 to 31, S. E. Report No. 3).

In the summer of 1911, a special examination was instituted to determine the merits of the claim; this without cost or trouble to the claimant, and the evidence obtained thereby was deemed sufficient to show that said claimant was identical with the soldier of record, and the claim was allowed by certificate issued January 9, 1912, under the Act of June 27, 1890, at $6 per month from September 23, 1897, and $10 per month from December 7, 1910, which first payment amounted to $1,059.80. No attorney was recognized in the allowance of the claim and no attorney fee was paid, the full amount going to the pensioner by check numbered 655,615, drawn January 24, 1912, by the U. S. Pension Agent at Knoxville, Tenn. Said Dempsey P. Parker was advised of the fact that the pensioner had received his first check and intended going with him to Tampa, Fla., to have same cashed on January 29, 1912, but it is alleged that he did not catch the train in time. Claimant proceeded to Tampa, Fla., where he cashed said check in the First National Bank on January 29, 1912, and on that date deposited in said bank the sum of $900, retaining in his possession $159.80. On the following morning, to wit, on January 30, 1912, said Dempsey P. Parker called upon the pensioner at the latter's "shack" and demanded of him one-half of the pension allowance as payment for his services in assisting him in the prosecution of the claim. To such demand the pensioner demurred and paid said Parker the sum of $50 in cash and said Parker was not at all satisfied and demanded more. They compromised the settlement by pensioner

2

agreeing to pay said Parker the sum of $400, whereupon both proceeded to Tampa, Fla., where the pensioner drew from said First National Bank the sum of $320 and turned said amount over to said Parker. Said Parker deposited $100 of said amount in said bank on January 30, 1912, and on the same day deposited $200 in the American National Bank in said city, as will be mentioned hereinafter.

Some time shortly following this, the pensioner, being dissatisfied over the large amount he had been required to pay said Parker, complained of the matter to Mr. Peter L. Weeks, his employer at Enville, Fla., and the latter (Mr. Weeks) attempted to have Parker return the money to pensioner, but he refused to do so and soon thereafter left that place. It is reported that said Parker has two brothers still working for Mr. Weeks and that his wife's [illegible] at Willacoochee, Ga.; that that their name is Robertson or Robinson and that it is believed that said Parker can be readily located and apprehended to answer for the alleged offense.

EVIDENCE.

The certified copy from the Grand Roll of Pensioners is offered for use as evidence under the provisions of Section 882, R.S.U.S., to show the fact and date of allowance of pension in said case. The certified photographic copy of the original voucher is also offered for use as evidence under said Section; this with a view to corroborating the pensioner as to the allowance of the claim and as to the amount of the first payment made therein. The original check which is enclosed with envelope among the papers, speaks for itself and shows the endorsements thereon and that same was cashed January 29, 1912, at the First National Bank at Tampa, Fla.

Huyeen Melvin, of Plant City, Fla., testified May 2, 1913, before special examiner Don E. Clarke as follows: Age about 73 years. I live on E. Haines St., with F. G. Garvin, a shoemaker. I am not working now. I am the same person who was pensioned as Huyeen Fort, now known as Huyeen Melvin, on account of my service in Co. E, 135th U. S. C. Inf. My first check for pension amounted to $1,059.80. I had that check cashed at the First National Bank in Tampa and opened an account with $900. The bank charged me nothing to cash the check and I had $159.80 in cash, after I deposited $900. From that $159.80 I paid Dempsey F. Parker $80. I paid that money to said Parker at Mr. Weeks' turpentine still at Enville, the next day after I got the check cashed. No one was present but Parker and I when I paid him the $80. Parker was not with me the day I got the check cashed. He started to come with me, but got left at Enville, so I went on to Tampa alone and went back alone. Parker knew I had the check for he had seen and read it. The following morning after I had the check cashed in Tampa I paid Parker the $80 and then he and I went to Tampa that same day and I drew out $320 more for him and paid him that amount right there at the First National Bank. No other person went with us. I was with Parker at said bank when he opened an account with my money and he told me afterwards that he had put some of the money he had gotten from me in the American National Bank. He did not give me a written receipt for the money. He did not give me a note of any kind as security and he said nothing about paying back the whole or any part of such money. I never had borrowed any money from him and the only reason he had for getting money from me was because he had written letters for me in connection with my claim for pension. I had told him I would pay him for doing my writing, but we had no agreement as to how much I should pay him. He came to my "shack" the next morning after I had cashed my check at Tampa and wanted me to pay him $525, or one-half of what I had received. I paid him then $80 and we went to Tampa to get more. After I had paid Parker the money I told Mr. Weeks about it and asked him to try and get the money back for me and Mr. Weeks talked to Parker about it. That was a few days after I had paid Parker, but I cannot remember the exact date. I never borrowed any money from Parker in my life and never told him that I would pay him any money for anything except for the writing he had done for me in my pension claim. He never told me personally that he would harm me if I did not pay him any money, but there was a report around camp that he said he was going to take some money from me if I did not pay him. I was not willing and did not want to pay him $400, but he demanded $525 and I finally told him I could not pay him more than $400, and that I did not want to pay him that much.

R. J. Dinnicker, cashier, First National Bank, Tampa, Fla., testified April 19, 1912, before said examiner as to the bank's records showing that on January 29, 1912, an account was opened by Rhycen Melvin, colored, and that he was credited on that date with $900; that on the following day, to wit, January 30, 1912, there was drawn out of said bank the sum of $320, leaving a credit of $580, and embodied in the testimony is a full statement of said pensioner's account up to April 19, 1912, showing that he then had on deposit in said bank the sum of $130; also said statement shows that Dempsey P. Parker opened an account with said bank on January 30, 1912, and deposited therein on that date $100. It also shows the settlement of said account and that the last portion thereof was drawn out on March 23, 1912. Said cashier further testified that from his personal recollection he remembered both the pensioner Melvin and said D. P. Parker and that he remembered that both parties were in the bank on January 30, 1912, and recalled the fact that the pensioner withdrew the sum of $320 and that he suspected that said Parker intended to get money from Melvin.

Lee L. Buchanan, cashier, American National Bank, Tampa, Fla., testified on the same date before said examiner as to the account opened in his bank on January 30, 1912, by D. P. Parker, that he deposited therein on that date the sum of $200, and further shows the date and fact of the withdrawal of such amount in sums of $50, $26.05, and $123.95, leaving the account balanced.

Peter L. Weeks, of Enville, Fla., testified April 30, 1917, before said examiner as follows: Occupation turpentine operator; I am the same person who wrote a letter dated March 29, 1917, to the Bureau of Pensions, relative to Duncan Port, or Melvin, who was then living at Enville. He left here three or four weeks ago and it is reported that he is now in Plant City, Fla. His pension check came to Enville and was deposited by the pensioner at the First National Bank at Tampa. Dempsey P. Parker had been writing for the old man and claimed that he was the one who got the pension for him. The old man told me that he offered Parker $25 for his services, but he would not take it; that he then offered him $200 and Parker would not take it. Parker demanded, it seems, $400, and the old man told me that he paid Parker the money at a bank in Tampa. I understood that they went to Tampa together and that Parker got the money there. Some three or four days thereafter the pensioner came to me and told me he had paid Parker the money and asked me to try and get it back. It was some time before I saw Parker and he then acknowledged to me that he had gotten $400 from the pensioner, and I understood that Parker deposited some of the money in the banks at Tampa; I think in the American National Bank there, and also in the First National Bank; Parker made the charge by reason of assisting the old man in getting the pension. Parker stayed around the camp for about a month after he got the money and after I made the demand upon him to return the money to the pensioner. He then left and I understood he was going to Bradentown, Fla. I have not seen anyone who has seen him since he left camp. He has a wife and they are supposed to have gone together. She was called Zilpha and her people live at Willacoochee, Ga. Parker came from Whitesville, N. C. and has two brothers, Van and Mack D. Parker, who work for me. The old pensioner told me that Parker had beat him out of $400; that he did not want to pay him that money, but he said he was afraid that Parker would do him bodily harm if he did not pay him that amount of money.

Should the District Attorney deem it necessary to prove that letters were filed in the Pension Bureau in behalf of the pensioner, signed by Dempsey F. Parker, it is suggested that a subpoena be served upon the Commissioner of Pensions, directing him or some clerk of his Bureau, whom he may designate, who has handled there the original papers in the case, to appear in court and testify upon the point in question.

8

BUREAU OF PENSIONS
WASHINGTON, D. C. April 6, 1912.

Chief of
S. E. Division.

Sir:

Herewith are forwarded the papers in claim of Huycen Fort, now known as Huycen Melvin, Co. E, 135th U.S.C. Inf., Ctf. No. 1167558, which you are requested to transmit to a special examiner for immediate investigation of criminal features at Enville, Hernando Co., Florida, as hereinafter indicated. This claim was allowed last January and it is presumed that the first payment was made up to November 4, 1911, which would amount to about $1059.80. No attorney was recognized and no fee paid. Mr. P. L. Weeks, a business man of Enville, Fla., states in his enclosed letter of 29th ultimo that one D. P. Parker forced pensioner to pay him $400. from the amount of first payment for his services in the prosecution of the claim; that Parker has refused to return the money (Mr. Weeks says he tried to get it back, acting upon pensioner's request) and left there.

It is noted that said Parker wrote three or four letters for pensioner to this Bureau, therefore he was instrumental within the meaning of the law in the prosecution of the claim and should be held responsible for his wrongdoing if he has collected an illegal fee, as alleged. It is desired that the examiner first call on pensioner and obtain his sworn

...s 2, Ex 6.

statement showing the facts in the premises, and then act as developments shall warrant. If the charge is sustained all available corroborative evidence should be obtained, and in this connection all the details concerning the payment should be brought out, and if no one witnessed the actual transfer of the money the examiner should seek circumstantial evidence to show that the parties were together at the bank, or where ever the money was paid, and to show that Parker had $400., or some large amount immediately thereafter. Possibly, payment was made by bank check, and if so such paid and cancelled check should be obtained for use as evidence. Pensioner should be carefully questioned as to whether he owed Parker for anything except his work performed in connection with the claim for pension ? Did said Parker obtain the money as a loan and give security, real or pretended, therefor ? The examiner should endeavor to ascertain the present whereabouts of said Parker and whether he has any ties to bind him to any particular locality.

This letter should be returned as an exhibit in the examiner's report.

Very respectfully,

Chief of Law Division.

Approved

DEPOSITION G.

Case of Huycen Melvin. , *No.* 1167558.

On this 23nd *day of* May *191*2, *at* Plant City, *county of* Hillsboro *State of* Florida *before me,* DON E. CLARKE, *a Special Examiner of the Bureau of Pensions, personally appeared* Huycen Melvin *who, being by me first duly sworn to answer truly all interrogatories propounded to* him *during this special examination of aforesaid claim for pension, deposes and says:*

Age about 73 years. Live on East Haines St., Plant City, Fla. No number on house but live with F. G. Garvin, a shoe maker. Am not working now. I am the same person who is pensioned as Huycen Fort now known as Huycen Melvin on account of my service in Co. E. 135 U. S. C. Inf., and have heretofore made a statement before you. Ques. When your claim was allowed, what was the amount of the check you received? Ans. $1059.80 Ques. What did you do with that check? Ans. I had it cashed at the 1st National Bank in Tampa, and opened an account with $900. I do not think the Bank charged me anything to cash the check and I had $159.80 in cash left after making the deposit of $900. Ques. What did you do with the $159.80? Ques. I paid D. P. Parker $80. and I kept the balance. I paid that money to Parker at Mr Week's still at Enville the next day after I got the check cashed. Just me and him were present when I paid him the $80. Parker was not with me when I got the check cashed; he started to go with me but got left at Enville. I went to Tampa in the morning by myself and went back alone; Parker knew I had the check, he had seen and read it. It was the next morning after I had been to Tampa that I paid him the $80. and the same morning Parker and I went to Tampa, and I drew out $320. for him. I paid him the $320. right at the 1st National Bank. I gave him the $80. and $320. in cash, did not give him a check. Just Parker and I went to the Bank together, no other person went with us. I turned the $330. over to Parker before we went out of the Bank, and I was with him when he opened an account with my money. He told me afterward that he had put some of the money he had gotten from me in the American National Bank. He did not give me a written receipt for the money. No, he did not borrow that $400. from me, and he did not give me a note or any kind of security, and he did not say anything about paying back the whole

Page 8 *Deposition* G.

Page 9.

amount or any part of it. I never had borrowed any money from him, and the only reason he had for getting money from me was because he had been writing letters for me in connection with my claim for pension. I told him I would pay him for doing the writing but we did not have any agreement as to how much I should pay him. I could not do the writing myself so I got him to write for me. He came to my shack the next moring after I came back from Tampa and wanted some money. He wanted me to pay him $585. or half of what I got, and I gave I paid him $80. and we went to Tampa to get more. There was no other person present when he made the demand for money; there was nobody there but me and him. I did not say anything to Mr Pete Weeks about it before I paid the money to Parker, but I told Mr Weeks about it afterwards and told him to try to get the money back for me. Mr Weeks talked to Parker about it, and if Mr Weeks had gotten the money from Parker, I would have gotten it. I put the money in the bank on Monday (Jan. 29 DEC) and paid Parker on Tuesday (Jan. 30th. DEC) and I told Mr Weeks about it that same week, I do not recall what day I told him, but it was a few days after I had paid Parker. I left Enville in March, along toward the first part of the month, and came here. Parker was at Enville when I left, and I saw him in Tampa about a month ago. He was staying at Enville then, and I have not seen him since. He told me that if I did not come back to Enville before May I would not see him because he would be gone. He did not say where he was going except that it was up the road to work for some fellow. No, he did not tell me who he was going to work for or where the man was located. I never borrowed any money from Parker in my life, and never told him that I would pay him any money except for the writing he had been doing for me. He never told me personally that he would harm me if I did not pay him any money but there was a report around the camp that he said he was going to take some money from me if I did not pay him. I do not know whether he did say anything like that and I do not know whether he said anything like that to other people. I was not willing and did not want to pay

Attest:

his
Vincent X Melvin
mark
Deponent.

Sam

DEPOSITION a.

Case of Huycen Melvin., *No.* 1107558

On this .... *day of* ...., *191* , *at* Second Sheet., *county of* .... *State of* .... *before me,* DON E. CLARKE, *a Special Examiner of the Bureau of Pensions, personally appeared* Huycen Melvin, continued. *who, being by me first duly sworn to answer truly all interrogatories propounded to h... during this special examination of aforesaid claim for pension, deposes and says:*

him any $400. but he demanded $525. and I just told him that I could not pay him more than $400. and I did not want to pay him that much. No, I do not recall a single person who was present when he told me that I would have to pay him any money. I told him I was willing to give him $100. but he was not satisfied with that, and he was not satisfied with the $400. I have a slight recollection that you told me last year that if my claim was allowed that I was to watch Parker and not let him rob me; (Parker was called in as attesting witness to claimant's mark May 18, 1911. DEC) I have heard this deposition read; have understood all questions, and my answers are correctly recorded herein.

Attest:
J. J. Garner
Sam Williams

Huycen his X mark Melvin

Subscribed and sworn to before me this 22nd day of May 1912, and I certify that the contents were made known to deponent before signing.

Don E. Clarke
Special Examiner.

Page 10 *Deposition* a.

DEPOSITION B.

Case of Huycen Fort now Huycen Melvin. , *No.* 1167558.

On this 13th *day of* April 1912, *at* Brooksville, *county of* Hernando *State of* Florida *before me,* DON E. CLARKE, *a Special Examiner of the Bureau of Pensions, personally appeared* Peter L. Weeks *who, being by me first duly sworn to answer truly all interrogatories propounded to* him *during this special examination of aforesaid claim for pension, deposes and says:*

Am of legal age. Address Enville, Fla. Am a turpentine operator. I am the same person who wrote letter dated March 29, 1912 to the Bureau of Pensions, relative to Huycen Fort or Melvin, who has been living at Enville, but left about 3 or 4 weeks ago, and it is reported that he is in Plant City. He took up with a woman after he got his pension, and she was at the camp for a while. I do not know her name. The check came to Enville, and was deposited by the old man at the First National Bank at Tampa. Dempsey P. Parker had been writing for the old man and claimed that he was the one who got the pension for him. The old man told me that he offered Parker $25. but he would not take that. He then offered him $200. and he demanded $400. The old man told me that he paid the money to Parker at the Bank in Tampa, I think he deposited the check and drew out the $400. to pay Parker at that time. He did not say whether he drew more than $400. at that time or whether he gave Parker a check or cash. They went to Tampa together and I understood that Parker got the money the same day the check arrived. The old man told me 3 or 4 days after he had paid Parker the money and asked me to try to get it back. It was sometime before I saw Parker; I do not recall that he acknowledged that he had gotten $400. but he did not deny it. I do not know that any one that saw Parker with a big sum of money after the old man had gotten his check, but I understood that Parker deposited some money in the American National Bank at Tampa, and I think some at the First National Bank. The old man paid him that money for his services in connection with getting the pension; that was what Parker made the charge for. Parker stayed around the camp for about a month after he was said to have gotten the money, and after I made the demand for him to return the money, he left and I understood that he was going to Bradentown, Fla., but I do not know whether he went there or not. I have not seen any one who said they

Page 11 *Deposition* B.

had seen Parker since he left the camp. He has a wife who went away with him, or they were supposed to have gone together. She was called Alpha, and her people live at Willacoochee, Ga. I do not know her family name, but will find out and let you know. Parker came from Whiteville, N. C. and has two brothers, Van and Mack D. Parker, who work for me. That is the reason I did not want it known that I had written the letter, as I did not want to disturb them. When Parker left he owed me an amount of $100, more or less. Between the time the time the old man received his check and the time Parker left, he had been taking long trips. He came back from Jacksonville just a few days before he finally left. The old man did not let me know when the check came, but took Parker and went to Tampa. In a few days he came and told me that Parker had beat him outof the $400. and wanted me to get it for him. The old man said he was afraid that Parker would do him some bodily harm if he did not pay over the money. The money, as I understood, was paid over at the Bank at Tampa, and if any other men from the camp were present, I do not know it. Parker was not supposed to have had any money before he got that sum from the old man; he had been getting his supplies from me on credit and had been borrowing money from me occasionally. I have no doubt but that Parker got the money all right. It is a common report around the camp that he did get the money, but none of the men have told me that they saw him with the money. I have no financial interest in this matter. I have read this deposition; have understood questions, and my answers are correctly recorded herein, with the exception that it was a few days after the check arrived before Parker got the money, but it was the day the check was deposited, as I understood. This additional statement is correct.

Peter, L. Keeke.

I.C. 1,198,156
Huyson Fort,
alias Melville,
E, 135" U.S.Col.Inf.
Served from March 27, 1865
to October 23, 1865.

WASHINGTON January 24, 1911.

The following brief sketch of the organization in which claimant alleges service is taken from "Volunteer Army Register, 1861-1865" and other sources, and is given for the purpose of aiding the Special Examiners and Reviewers in determining whether the claimant and soldier are identical.

135" U. S. COLORED INFANTRY.

This regiment was recruited during the campaign through the States of Georgia and the Carolinas, and organized at Goldsboro, N.C., March 28, 1865, to serve three years. Mustered out October 23, 1865.

The principal officers were: John E. Gurley, Colonel; David H. Budlong, Lt. Col; David Dixon, Major. Hinton F. Parks and George A. Shorles were Surgeons. George S. Shaw Chaplain.

The following were Captains: Moore, Whitney, Mitchell, Klock, George W. Johnson (See claimant's statement in declaration) Hazen, Fleming and William Johnson.

Capt. Lloyd D. Pocock was dismissed the service October 20, 1865.

John Jackson was 1st. Lt.. Daniel Jackson does not appear to have been a commissioned officer.(See D.J. 4).

It is shown by the Rebellion Records that an order was issued from Headquarters of the 17th Army Corps, Jones' N.C., dated April 26, 1865, directing that the 135th, with other regiments, move back to Raleigh, N.C.

On May 22, 1865, the regiment, with others, were near Alexandria, Va., and participated in the Grand Review.

When the claim is returned by a Special Examiner this statement should be attached to the face of his report.

C.C. Stauffer
Chief Clerk.

CHAPTER 8

YESTERDAY AFTERNOON THE SOUTH CAROLINA SWAMPS WERE CONQUERED.

Train of wagons crossing a corduroyed road

COMPANY “F”

INCLUDED IN THIS CHAPTER ARE EXTRACTIONS FROM THE PENSION RECORDS OF;

DANIEL TOWNSEND

JAMES GREEN / HACKLE

JACOB FINLEY

EMANUEL WILSON

DANIEL TOWNSEND

Daniel Townsend was a member of Company "F," 135th United States Colored Troop and stated that he was born in South Carolina. His deposition and records show that he joined the 135th USCT in Raleigh, North Carolina. He was wounded in the left arm by the accidental bursting of his gun while firing at the enemy. This happened while on a picket, near Raleigh North Carolina. As such he had to have the lower portion of his arm amputated.

Records on file show that Daniel was admitted to L'Ouverture Hospital in the city of Alexandria, Virginia in May of 1865. The doctor's statement read: "I certify that I have carefully examined the said Daniel Townsend, Private of Captain E. Hazens "F," company, and find him incapable of performing the duties of a soldier because of Amputation of lower third of left forearm in consequence, he states of a gunshot wound received by accident while on picket and in the line of duty in April 1865." The diagnosis was of a total disability for Daniel.

Not all recruits of the 135th USCT claim to have been provided weapons prior to arriving in Louisville, Kentucky. However, there are a few of them that provided depositions on the record that they did, in fact, have rifles. Daniel Townsend is proof of that, and the fact that he was wounded by the weapon, and it is verified by hospital records. Daniel Townsend was discharged on September 10, 1865. He applied for his pension on January 22, 1902, and died in 1938 after living a long life.

No. 91152

ACT OF JULY 14, 1862.

War of 1861.

Vol. 3, page ______

Daniel Townsend

Cincinnati

Ohio

Pvt Co F 135 U.S.C.T.

Discharged Sept 10, 1865.

Claim abandoned

Jan'y 1885

ABANDONED.

Joseph H. Barrett

Commissioner.

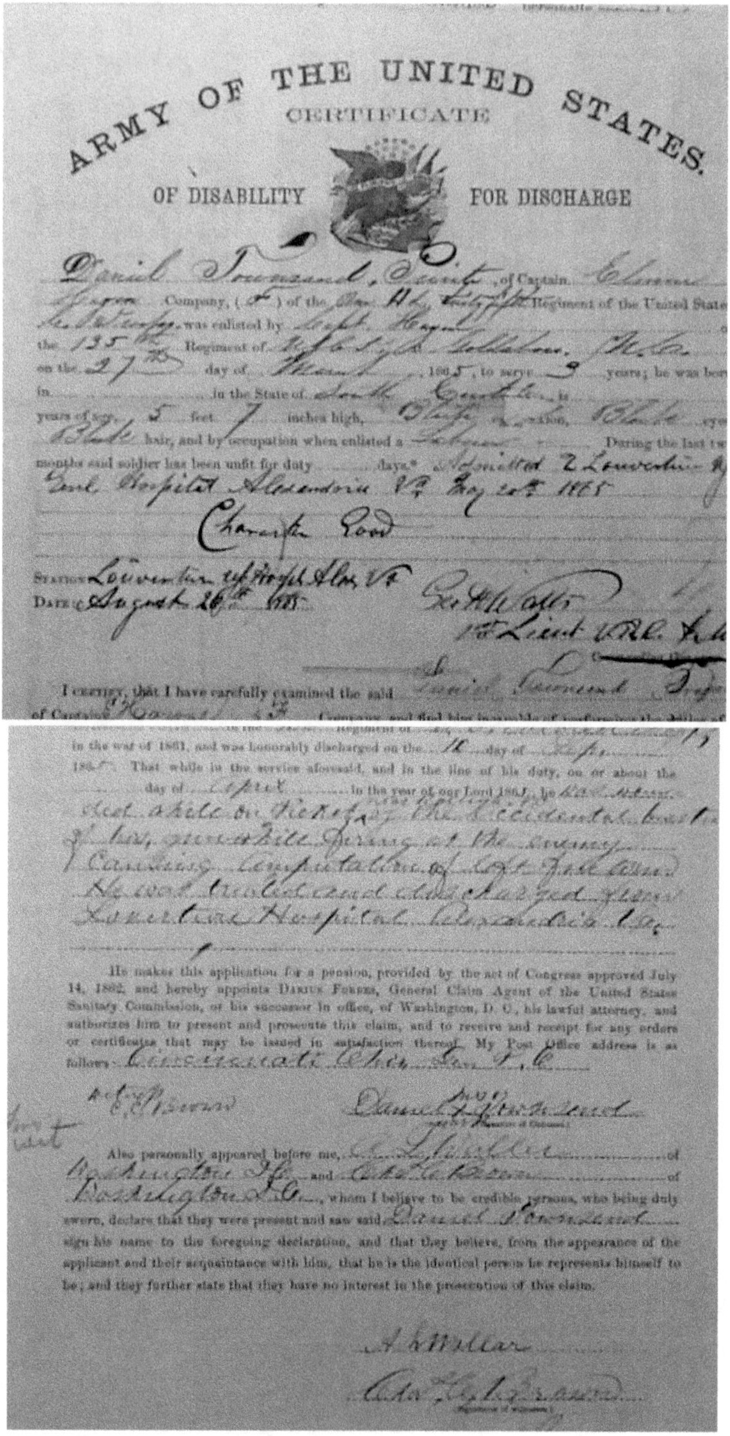

ARMY OF THE UNITED STATES.

CERTIFICATE

OF DISABILITY FOR DISCHARGE

Daniel Townsend, Private, of Captain Elmore Hagan Company, (F) of the One Hundred Thirty fifth Regiment of the United States Col'd Infantry, was enlisted by Capt. Hagan of the 135th Regiment of U.S. Col'd Volunteers, at N. Ca. on the 27th day of March, 1865, to serve 3 years; he was born in .... in the State of South Carolina is .... years of age, 5 feet 7 inches high, Black complexion, Black eyes, Black hair, and by occupation when enlisted a Laborer. During the last two months said soldier has been unfit for duty .... days.* Admitted 2 Louverture Genl Hospital Alexandria Va May 20th 1865

Character Good

STATION: Louverture U.S. Hospital Alex. Va

DATE: August 26th 1865.

Geo. H. Walls

1st Lieut. V.R.C. & ...

I CERTIFY, that I have carefully examined the said Daniel Townsend, Private of Captain Hagan's F Company, and find him incapable of performing the duties of ... in the ... Regiment of ... in the war of 1861, and was honorably discharged on the 10 day of Sept. 1865. That while in the service aforesaid, and in the line of his duty, on or about the .... day of April in the year of our Lord 1865, he was wounded ... shot while on picket by the accidental ... of his own rifle firing at the enemy causing amputation of left fore arm. He was treated and discharged from Louverture Hospital Alexandria Va.

He makes this application for a pension, provided by the act of Congress approved July 14, 1862; and hereby appoints DARIUS FORBES, General Claim Agent of the United States Sanitary Commission, or his successor in office, of Washington, D. C., his lawful attorney, and authorizes him to present and prosecute this claim, and to receive and receipt for any orders or certificates that may be issued in satisfaction thereof. My Post Office address is as follows: Cincinnati Ohio ... P. C.

Attest: C. H. Brown

Daniel Townsend (his mark)

(Signature of Claimant.)

Also personally appeared before me, A. L. Miller of Washington D.C. and Chas. H. Brown of Washington D.C., whom I believe to be credible persons, who being duly sworn, declare that they were present and saw said Daniel Townsend sign his name to the foregoing declaration, and that they believe, from the appearance of the applicant and their acquaintance with him, that he is the identical person he represents himself to be; and they further state that they have no interest in the prosecution of this claim.

A. L. Miller

Chas. H. Brown

(Signature of witnesses.)

JAMES HECKEL / GREEN

In 1927 they sent a special examiner to Summertown, Georgia to interview James Green and other people in his community.

James Green testified in his pension record that he owned a large amount of property in town and farms. Also, he said he got his property by working "hard and economically." He claimed he "did not fall into traps like most colored people and probably never bought a bottle of hair straightener in his entire life." He "didn't join lodges nor did he fall for insurance schemes." He said he "was a member of the church but didn't let himself be swept away by a rash of religion. His brother, Jesse Green was at one time in good shape financially, but his property got away from him." Another witness is Shade Allen from Waynesboro, Georgia, also in company "F." This veteran was 98 years old, and he didn't remember any comrade. Samuel Copeland from Olar, South Carolina was also mentioned. These Civil War veterans were all old men.

Lizzie O. Green was the widow of James's brother, Oseaola Green. James said he enlisted in Savannah, Georgia. He was put to work on the roads and worked with the same group of men under the same officers. He never married and was a slave of Ned McGar. As a young boy he was sent with Ned's daughter Susie Hackle, widow of John Hackle and Walker Hackle was her grandson.

James Green said, "when the Yankees came through, I didn't have the better sense than to go off with them," in the Pioneer

Corps. "I was first General Sherman's Road hand. All of us pioneers wore blue clothes just alike, and they paid us money. I worked the roads until we got to North Carolina, and at Raleigh, we were then considered regular soldiers. I remember my brother Ocle Green. He went with me, and he took the oath at the same time I did and stayed with me until we came home. His widow is Lizzy Green. We went from North Carolina to Virginia, then to the river at Alexandria, Virginia. We went to Maryland and went through Washington, D.C. ***We passed by some big men and had an inspection in Washington. I know I marched by the White House, and I think the president saw us. We walked until we got to Washington.*** We rode the train and then the Steamboat to Louisville, Kentucky. After Louisville, we came home and stayed here ever since. Elmo Hazen, my captain, was a heavy man. He had a black mustache; Johnny Cochran was Lieutenant for company "F.," Hazen was my ***overseer*** when I worked on the roads. Lieutenant Adams joined us in Kentucky. These officers were not young, they were older, 25 or 30 years old. Peter Blue is a corporal, black, and a little hard man. Shade Green was not kin. ***We colored people did not know about places or people. We were just like birds out of a cage.***"

"There is a picture of me after I got out of the army." Testified James, "A colored woman named Mrs. Johnson has it. She is known as Hannah Roberts. She lives down on the river not far from here. Brother Jesse Green is about 10 years younger than me. A few years after the Civil War, a colored lawyer from Boston was with the white man from Savannah, and they 'Conductin' things for a bounty for soldiers. They took my discharge paper and he never got money or paper."

He was asked "what became of your uniform?" He answered "The white people didn't wear the same clothes as us, we wore a blouse and coat. I could write at one time, but not now. I have Palsy.

I call on people sometimes to put on my clothes. I know that I served in the US Army in the 'winding up' of the Civil War. When I was discharged, they gave me over $100, and they never gave me a railroad ticket. I'm paid $8 per month and a bounty of $400.00. Ocie Greens, brother, had scars on his breast when he enlisted. Colonel Gurley was a redhead. I celebrate April 15th as my birthday. Jesse and Ben Green are my brothers. Louisa Carlton and Harriet Williams are my sisters. Shady Green, Abraham Green, and Ocie Green are in my company."

James Green died on September 30th, 1928.

DEPARTMENT OF THE INTERIOR
BUREAU OF PENSIONS
Augusta, Georgia

May 29, 1926

The Commissioner of Pensions:

<u>Caption</u> James Green, who is alleged to have served under the name of James Hackle in Company F of the 135 U. S. Colored Infantry, is claiming pension under I. O. 1589302. He resides in the country, not on a rural route, about five miles of Summertown, Georgia, which is his address.

<u>Reference</u> To determine whether the claimant is the person who served in Company F of the 135 U. S. Colored Infantry under the name of James Hackle.

<u>Notice</u> The usual formal notice of special examination was served on the claimant and his privileges were fully

<u>Reference</u> To determine whether the claimant is the person who served in Company F of the 135 U. S. Colored Infantry under the name of James Hackle.

<u>Notice</u> The usual formal notice of special examination was served on the claimant and his privileges were fully made known to him. The claimant did not wish to be present when witnesses were seen, and was not present at those times.

<u>Manner of testifying</u> The claimant testified in a frank and open manner, as did the witness Jesse Green. The witness Thomas Simms never understood the purpose of my call, and assumed the attitude of an old colored man trying to stay out of trouble. In his section when a white man comes about the place it usually means trouble of some kind, and as soon as this witness saw me he started thinking as fast as he could trying to find what to say and how much to know, and it seems that he never was convinced that my call did not spell grief for him. His manner was not frank and open.

Reputation The claimant and the witness Jesse Green bear a good reputation. The claimant is one of the best known colored men in his section, and I was told repeatedly by white people that he inspires more confidence than any other colored person in Emmanuel County. He owns a relatively large amount of property, both town property and farms, and his note for a moderate sum is as good as that of any banker in his section.

The claimant is reputed to be close, and is said to ave gotten his property by hard work and economy. It was t acquired with one fell blow, but just drifted to him the years went by and he has managed to keep it from ing away from him. He talks and reasons like a man s accustomed to own things, and handle property. He falls into any of the many traps set for colored and probably never bought a bottle of hair

Other witnesses I went to Waynesboro, Georgia and talked to Shade Allen, who is pensioned because of service in Company F of the 135 U. S. Colored Infantry. This veteran is said to be 96 years old, and his mind seemed to be in such condition that he could not remember any comrade. His daughter told me the names of some of the men her father had mentioned, as Stephny Sanders and Peter Blue, but as for the veteran himself he was not able to get his mind together, or was afraid to talk. It seems that he should be given the benefit of the doubt, and that it would not be fair to state that he was acting. At any rate I never got a statement from him, and it is easy to believe that his mind is about gone.

Under the circumstances I thought it best not to go to Olar, South Carolina to see Samuel Copeland. These Civil War veterans are all old men, and in many instances their memory is impaired.

I was not able to find anyone in the claimant's neighborhood who could testify as to where the claimant was in the year 1865, sixty-three years ago. He is reputed to

… Accounting Office also shows a Jefferson County address. The claimant states that he has never lived in Jefferson County, but has lived near that County, and lives near there now. As a matter of fact there have been periods in the claimant's life in which he never knew what his address was, no doubt, and the Special Examiner who worked the Green case may have had to find the witness' address for him.

As to the claimant's statement that he may have enlisted at Savannah it is believed that he does not fully understand the meaning of enlistment. It seems that he may have been given supplies or money that lead him to believe that he was, or might have been, enlisted at Savannah. It would seem that he only had one enlistment, and that after he had been with the troops for a short while he was put to work on the roads and worked with the same group of men and under some of the same officers that ent to make up his company. There does not seem to be ny suggestion that he was a bounty-jumper. He was most

On this 16 day of May, 19[illegible] at near Summertown county of Emanuel, State of Georgia before me, C. H. Collier, an inspector of the Bureau of Pensions, personally appeared James Hackle, who, being by me first duly sworn to answer truly all interrogatories propounded to him during this special examination of aforesaid claim for pension, deposes and says:

1 My true name is James Green. I am called Jim Green.

2 Everybody around here knows me as Green, and that is my true name. My address is Summertown, Georgia. I live about six miles from Summertown and about nine miles from Midville, Georgia. I am a farmer and own my own farm.

I was born in Emanuel County Georgia, three or four miles from here, the slave of Ned McGar. When I was a little fellow he died and they divided his slaves. I went to his daughter, Mrs. Susa Hackle, widow of John Hackle. She is dead and has been dead for years. Walker Hackle, farmer, near Summertown is her grandson. I don't think my owners kept any records of

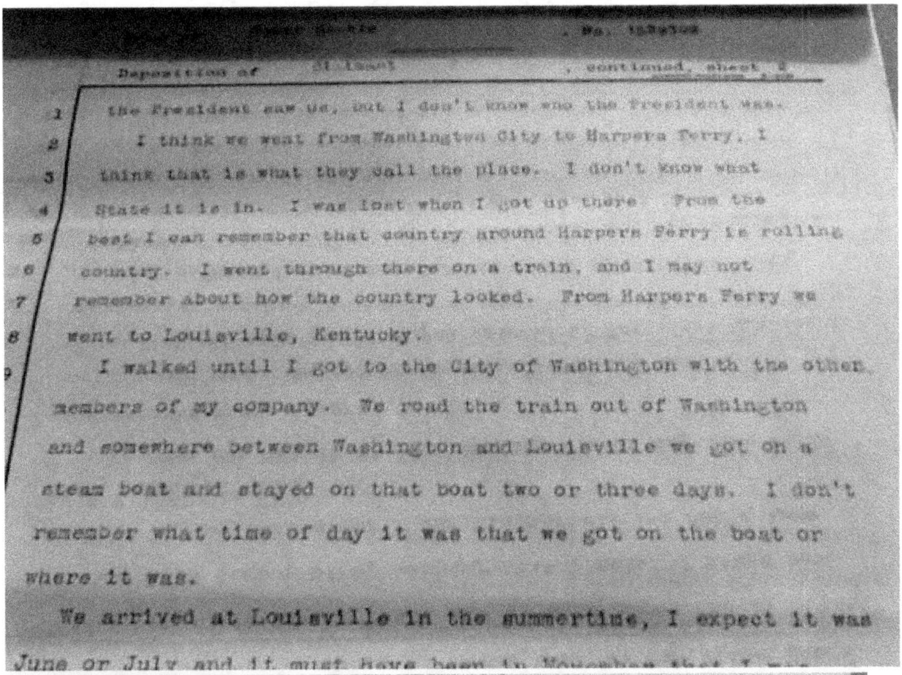

, No. [illegible]

Deposition of [illegible], continued, sheet [illegible]

the President saw us, but I don't know who the President was.

I think we went from Washington City to Harpers Ferry. I think that is what they call the place. I don't know what State it is in. I was lost when I got up there. From the best I can remember that country around Harpers Ferry is rolling country. I went through there on a train, and I may not remember about how the country looked. From Harpers Ferry we went to Louisville, Kentucky.

I walked until I got to the City of Washington with the other members of my company. We road the train out of Washington and somewhere between Washington and Louisville we got on a steam boat and stayed on that boat two or three days. I don't remember what time of day it was that we got on the boat or where it was.

We arrived at Louisville in the summertime, I expect it was

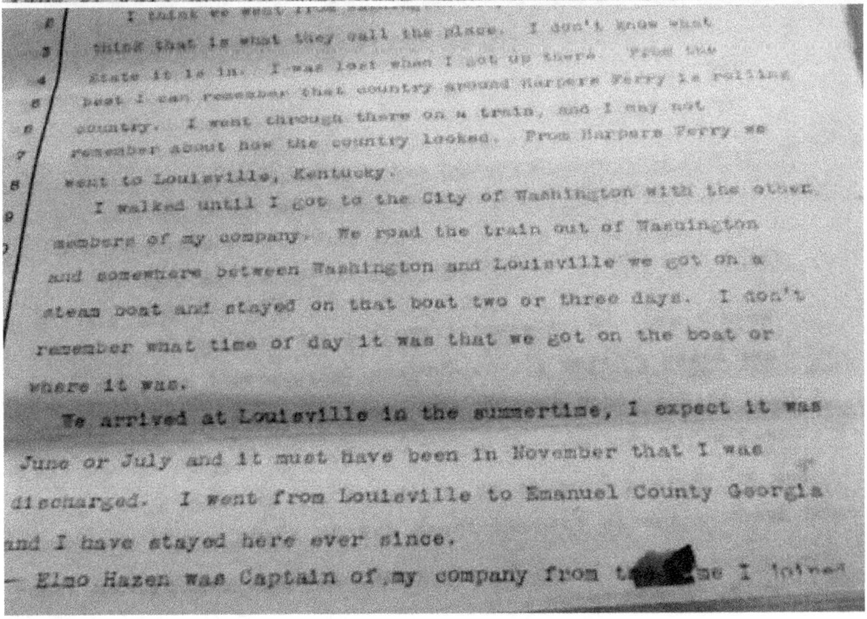

I think we went from Washington City to Harpers Ferry. I think that is what they call the place. I don't know what State it is in. I was lost when I got up there. From the best I can remember that country around Harpers Ferry is rolling country. I went through there on a train, and I may not remember about how the country looked. From Harpers Ferry we went to Louisville, Kentucky.

I walked until I got to the City of Washington with the other members of my company. We road the train out of Washington and somewhere between Washington and Louisville we got on a steam boat and stayed on that boat two or three days. I don't remember what time of day it was that we got on the boat or where it was.

We arrived at Louisville in the summertime, I expect it was
June or July and it must have been in November that I was discharged. I went from Louisville to Emanuel County Georgia and I have stayed here ever since.

— Elmo Hazen was Captain of my company from t[illegible]me I joined

[illegible]

A. Not to know it. I may have seen him when we marched passed in the City of Washington. There the officers had seats where they could look at us as we went by. When we were on the march the officers stayed off to themselves and rode horses. They sometimes just rode around in droves.

Q. Did you ever know a man by the name of Samuel Copeland?

A. I think he was a member of my company. He was an ordinary sized man, and a black man. I don't know what became of him but I think he is from Georgia. No, sir, I don't expect I would know him if I should see him now. I don't know that I would know any member of the company now, it has been so long since I last saw them.

There is a picture of me that was made four or five years fter I got out of the Army. A colored woman named Mrs. Johnson as it. She is known as Hannah Roberts. It is alright with for you to have that picture. I think I can get it from her will let you have it. She lives down on the river not far here, and her address is Midville, ...

Oct. 16, 1928.

Ctf 1581302

United States Dept. of Interier,
Bureau of Pensions,
Office of the Disbursing Clerk,
Washington, D. C.

Gentlemen:

James Green, Summertown, Ga., died on Sept. 30, 1928. Since his death there has come to Summertown, Ga., addressed to him an envelope in which you enclosed his pension check for the past month. I endorsed on this envelope, and delivered it back to the Postmaster, a notation of his ddath. I am the Executor of his will and would like to submit the necessary showing to obtain this check or so much of it as may be due.

JACOB FINLEY

William Finley gave a deposition saying "I was born and raised in Henry County, Georgia, and a slave for Mr. Jim Finley, seven miles from McDonough County. Mr. Finley's plantation was on the Butts County line. **Jacob is my half-brother,** and we had the same Mother. When Sherman's army came through Jacob, and I were in the woods caring for the horses of Mr. Finley. One day I started to go to the house, and I met the soldiers of Sherman's Army. I was carried away with them to Mr. Finley's house and while the soldiers were killing chickens and hogs, I escaped. The soldiers went out and found Jacob, Tom, and Hilles and they were carried off by them. Hallys never returned but we have heard he was in Iowa since the war. It was a year or more since I saw Jacob. He returned and said he had been a soldier in the U.S. Army."

Holloway Crockett gives an affidavit in 1901 saying that he and Jacob were in the Army together. He said "I served in the Pioneer Corps., first before we enlisted in the 135th United States Colored Troop. I was known as Holloway Lemons. My owner was John Crocket. Alex Crocket married Crocket's Daughter and I was given to the daughter. My father was a Crocket, and I was a Crocket ever since."

Holloway went on in his statement and said that "Jake/Jacob Finley and I were in the Army together and in the same company.

Jacob served under Captain Hazen's Company. He and I came home together along with Anthony Crocket, Rufus Glass, and Frank Crocket/Lemons. We all came home together. Frank Crocket is dead, Rufus Glass lives in Atlanta at Thomasville and he was in Company 'A,' also."

Jacob belonged to Jim Finley, father of Marabel Finley, during slavery. Anthony Crockett was not related but was owned by the same man (Jim Finley), during slavery.

3—295
(Old No. 3—285.)

DEPOSITION D

Case of Jacob Finley, No. 1,236,146

On this 5th day of February, 1901, at Atlanta county of Fulton State of Georgia, before me, A. B. Durkey, a special examiner of the Bureau of Pensions, personally appeared William B. Finley, who, being by me first duly sworn to answer truly all interrogatories propounded to him during this special examination of aforesaid claim for pension, deposes and says:

I am 55 years of age, occupation Trader, residence and P.O. address 1188 Markham Street, Atlanta, Georgia. Book keeper [illegible] Whitehall Street.

I was not a soldier during late war. I was born and reared in Henry County Georgia, and resided there until about 1868 or 1869. I was a slave of Mr. Jim Finley of about [illegible] miles south of McDonough. Mr. Finley's plantation was near the Butts county line.

I have been in this city since 1877.

The claimant, Jacob Finley, is my half brother. We had the same mother but different fathers. Claimant and I were owned by the same man and lived together from childhood until Sherman's army came through Georgia. At that time claimant and I were in the woods caring for the horses of Mr. Finley. One day I started up to the house of Mr. Finley and met the soldiers who belonged to Sherman's army. I was carried by them to Mr. Finley's house and while the soldiers were killing chickens, hogs etc. I escaped. The soldiers went out and found claimant, [illegible] and Phillips Finley and carried them off with them. Phillips never returned but we have heard from him in Iowa since the war. It was a year or more before I saw claimant again. He then returned home and said that he had been a soldier in the U.S. army, and

Page 16 Deposition D

No. 17

he had a discharge certificate which he showed
I was not then able to read, but I heard some
of the white members of Mr. Finley's family
read it. I am not able to state now what was
on the paper. Do not remember the date of
the discharge paper. Do not remember what
name was on the certificate. I do not remember to what company and regiment
he said he had served but he talked a great
deal about his service then.
Claimant has been residing at and around
McDonough ever since the war.
I have seen claimant frequently ever since
he returned from the army.
I have no interest in this claim. If claimant
has any disease or disability I do not
know it. In fact I do not see him often
enough to know about his physical
condition. I only see him when he comes
to this city. Claimant is about 59 years old, I suppose.
I have heard read the foregoing statement
and my answers have been correctly
recorded.

W. R. Finley
(Deponent)

Deponent.

Sworn to and subscribed before me this 7th *day of* May *1901, and I certify that the contents were fully made known to deponent before signing.*

A. B. Parker
Special Examiner.

3-446.

DEPOSITION A

Case of Jacob Guidry [illegible], No. 1,316,196

On this 8th day of February, 1901, at McDonough, county of Henry, State of Georgia, before me, A. B. Parker, a special examiner of the Bureau of Pensions, personally appeared Jacob Finley, who, being by me first duly sworn to answer truly all interrogatories propounded to him during this special examination of aforesaid claim for pension, deposes and says:

I am [illegible] years of age; my post-office address is the same. That is just like the discharge [illegible] [illegible] and it has the same reading as it which Mr Finley read.

Never was in the hospital while in service, and had no sickness [illegible] anything while in service. Never was in a battle. After we enlisted at Raleigh the regiment went on foot to Richmond and Petersburg and on to the city of Washington. We there marched before the President at the White House. When we paraded [illegible]. Then we went on the train to near Summerville. Just before we got to Summerville we took a boat and went into the city by boat. There was on one side of the river and Summerville on the other.

After discharge I came direct to this place and have lived here ever since. We got $16 or $18 a month and when discharged I had about $100. After discharge I kept my uniform in my satchel and brought them here where I bought and wore a citizens suit. Brought the [illegible] suit home and wore it [illegible].

Have been married one time only. I was married about 1870. The name of wife was [illegible] Mosely. We were married at this place by Rev. Joe [illegible]. Wife had no prior marriage. Wife and I have been separated about 8 years. She [illegible]

Page 1 of deposition A

No. 9

Atlanta. She goes by the name of Rena Finley. Do not know the street and number. She did reside near McPherson Barracks. We were never divorced from each other. We have 5 children, viz. Claude Finley, Annie Finley, Hugh Finley, [illegible] Finley and Mary Belle Finley. All the children reside in Atlanta. The youngest child Mary Belle is about 16 years old. Hugh was residing in Maryland or Washington City about 2 years ago. I became acquainted with my wife after the discharge. I caught another man with my wife and she then went off to Atlanta. She is a woman of bad character. Have never had a [illegible]. [illegible] resided at Clarksville, Tennessee and know nothing about the woman Mary Webb or Harrison Webb. Never knew such persons.

Have rheumatism of arms and legs. Have had it about two years. Do not know what caused the rheumatism. [illegible] about the [illegible]. I drink a dram but do not drink much. Had the gonorrhea about [illegible] ago but got well of it. Never had syphilis. My disabilities are not due to vicious habits. I filed a pension claim a few months ago. Mr. [illegible] of Butts County got another man a pension and told me that he could get me one. Have heard read the foregoing statement and my answers have been correctly recorded.

Attest

his
Mack X Finley
mark
Deponent

H. F. L[illegible]

Chas. M. Carmichael D.O.S.

Sworn to and subscribed before me this 4th day of Feby, 1901, and I certify that the contents were fully made known to deponent before signing.

A. R. Banks
Special Examiner.

N. B.—Examiners should be particular to have affiants sign on the line next below the closing words of their depositions so as to leave little or no space between their signatures and the end of their depositions.

3—456.

DEPOSITION A

Case of Jacob Findley, No. 1256,196

On this 8th day of February, 1901, at McDonough, County of Henry, State of Georgia, before me, A. B. Carter, a special examiner of the Bureau of Pensions, personally appeared Jacob Findley, who, being by me first duly sworn to answer truly all interrogatories propounded to him during this special examination of aforesaid claim for pension, deposes and says: I am [illegible] years of age; my post-office address is McDonough, Henry County, Georgia. I am employed by Mr. [illegible] at his livery stable.

I am not able to tell you how old I am. I am the identical person who was a soldier during the war as a private in Co. F, 133rd U.S.C. Vol. Inf. I enlisted about April 1865 and served the [illegible] with the soldiers about a year. I got with Gen. Sherman's army when it came through here and was with the Pioneer Corps some time before I enlisted. I did not have a gun and did not ~~have a gun and~~ perform the duties of a soldier until April 1865. I enlisted at Raleigh, North Carolina, and was discharged at Louisville, Kentucky. I belonged to the Pioneer Corps from the time I got with the army until it reached Raleigh and then I enlisted. I have served in any other regiment in the U.S. Army than as above and never served in the U.S. Navy or Marine Corps.

I was born in Henry County, Georgia, and have resided here all my life.

Page 1st Deposition A

Exp 5 I was born a slave of Mr. Jim Finley
now dead. Mr. Finley has a son now
residing in Jackson, Butts County Georgia.
It is [illegible] miles from this place
to the line of Butts County. When I got
out the [illegible] army I was in Butts
County [illegible] for my [illegible]. My
[illegible] had [illegible] her home to Butts
County.
The captain of my company was named
[illegible]. Our major was named [illegible]
Our lieutenants were named Adams &
[illegible]. It was Cochran instead of [illegible].
[illegible] was orderly sergeant
[illegible] a corporal of the name of [illegible]
[illegible] Some of the privates were [illegible] Green &
[illegible] Green, [illegible] [illegible] Jordan
and [illegible] [illegible]. [illegible]
the [illegible] and I remember a
part of them and some of them [illegible]
[illegible]. There are none of the members
of my company residing around
this section that I know. [illegible] members
of my regiment [illegible]
of the names of Anthony [illegible] and
[illegible] [illegible]. They reside at this
place. They have been well acquainted
with me ever since [illegible] and can
identify me as [illegible].
I was called Jake Finnell in the army.
My name was put on the rolls accidentally.
I did not know about this until I came
home and showed my discharge to [illegible]
[illegible] Mr. [illegible] Finley, dead,
and he read the name on the discharge
paper as Jacob Finnell and told me
that they did not have my name spelled
right - that my name was Jacob Finley.
[illegible] of your discharge [illegible]

A. Some 3 or 4 years after the surrender my mother had filed a claim against the Government for horses and she wanted me as a witness to show that the horses had been taken. A man called Squire McBurney who said he resided at Macon was prosecuting the claim for her. Squire McBurney asked me how I knew so much and I told him that I was a soldier. He then asked me if I had a discharge paper and I told him I had and he asked me to get it for him and he would manage to get me [illegible] acres of land. I gave him the discharge paper and have never seen it since. I do not know what became of Squire McBurney. The discharge was a yellow paper with the picture of an eagle on it. They had put my residence on the paper as Butts County. I remember that my sister [illegible] about Mr. Finley telling her that I did not reside in Butts but in Henry County, but I did not know about what he [illegible]. I was not well grown when I enlisted but I do not know my age. I am black, small, about 5 ft. 6 inch. (Claimant measured and found to be 5 ft 6 in. Barefooted) Prominent teeth [illegible] upper [illegible].

I have examined the discharge [illegible] of Jacob Finley and have heard you read it.

N I Allen — his Jacob X Finley mark, Deponent

Parks McCarney [illegible]

Sworn to and subscribed before me this 2d day of May 1897, and I certify that the contents were fully made known to deponent before signing.

A. D. Parker, Special Examiner

Page 6 Deposition A

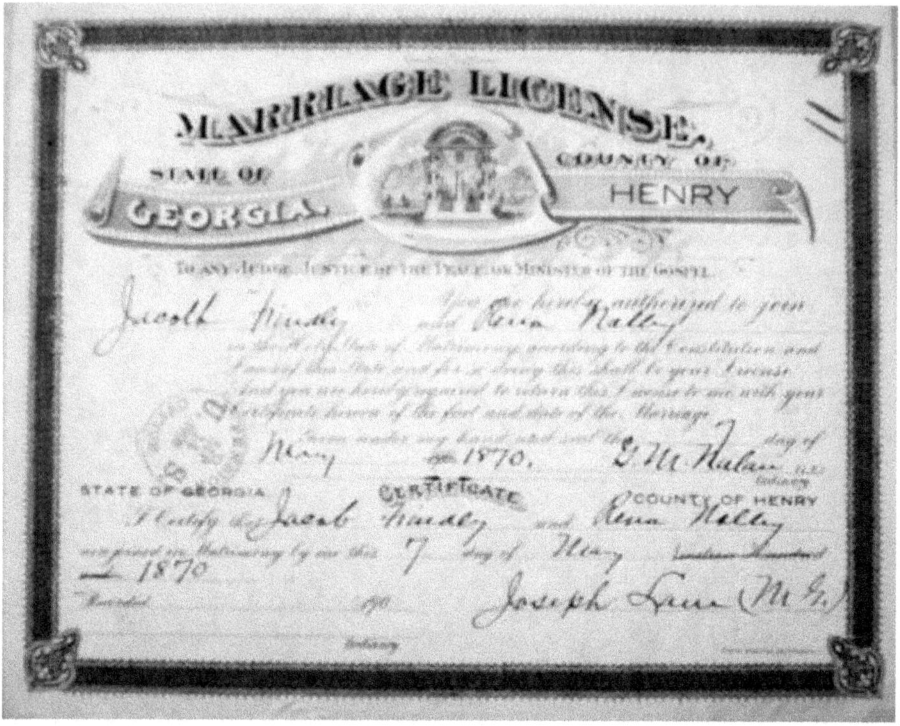

MARRIAGE LICENSE.

STATE OF GEORGIA. COUNTY OF HENRY

TO ANY JUDGE, JUSTICE OF THE PEACE OR MINISTER OF THE GOSPEL.

You are hereby authorized to join Jacob Hendley and Rena Walley in the Holy State of Matrimony, according to the Constitution and Laws of this State, and for so doing this shall be your License. And you are hereby required to return this License to me, with your Certificate hereon of the fact and date of the Marriage.

Given under my hand and seal this 7 day of May 1870. G. M. Nolan, Ordinary

STATE OF GEORGIA. CERTIFICATE. COUNTY OF HENRY

I Certify that Jacob Hendley and Rena Walley were joined in Matrimony by me this 7 day of May 1870

Joseph Lane (M.G.)

Recorded 190

Ordinary

EMANUEL WILSON

Andrew Wallace, who was the lawful guardian of Emanuel Wilson, applied for an increase in pension as Emanuel Wilson was paralyzed and helpless. "Emanuel was dense, almost to absolute vacancy." His recollections were as vague as "dreams that we dreamed." When asked about his service in the Army he said he "only served one day." Andrew said that Emanuel "knew a few motions of the gun, he walked a beat with a stick for a gun, very much like an old soldier, and saluted me as his Captain." He told us why he did not wear his uniform after service, the reason was one that "any old soldier would recognize it as genuine."

Emanuel was a slave of Mrs. Speirs' people and in 1904, lived on the plantation of Mr. Speir who looked after him as if he were a child. William Speir was a large planter, a man of affairs, and a proper person. He didn't know his age and was a full hand when the war came. He was not married when freedom came, was born and raised in the county, and belonged to Elija Wilson. After he died, he belonged to his son Steve Wilson. He said his father was Ben London and he belonged to Mobly. His mother's name was Jan Wilson. He had a brother Sam, and a sister Sella Wallace whose husband was Andrew Wallace.

Emanuel said, "I enlisted in Savannah in Company "F," 135th United States Colored Troop. Then they turned me loose the next day. I came right back and made a crop for my young boss. The Yankee doctor examined me. They stripped me naked and jammed me all over. They made me put my clothes back on and I came back home the next day." He said that he "never went back to Savannah, and had no sword or horse but had a gun. I didn't bother with it; I only had the gun one day." He used it to march and drill with. He went on and stated that he "wore blue clothes and only wore blue clothes one day. I left the blue clothes in Savannah. They were full of lice. We went to Hilton Head, we were at Raleigh, Goldsboro, Petersburg, and Washington, D.C., and mustered out at Louisville Kentucky. We went to Louisville on a steamboat. We rode a train from Louisville, Kentucky," on the way back home.

Emanuel recalled that "Doctor Hayden was my Captain. Peter Blue was an Orderly Sergeant. Bolin Miller, Orderly sergeant was a ginger cake, short man. Sergeant Wood was tall and black. The captain rode a gray horse, and the lieutenant walked. We had a heap of Colonels, about ten. We had bread, fish, and rice plus coffee. We only cooked the rice. On picket when the captain came round, we said Halt! Give the countersign. The captain would come at night to see if anyone was sleeping. If you were sleeping the captain would take the gun and put you under arrest." Emanuel remembered Jim Cross from Guyton Georgia. "Will Moore is in prison for pension fraud and is the one who started my pension discharge papers. The Yankees took Bill Moore off, they knocked him clean off." He said he thinks he "can count to ten and he never married." He does not know dollar bills and can't tell the difference between a dime and a cent. He stated he is 5' 7 ½" tall but really measures 5' 4 ½."

The examiner said that "he was not an idiot but of very low grade of intellect. He is black and has a scar on his forehead." He talked of carrying "grub" in a haversack and drinking water from a canteen while in the Army. He tells of carrying his clothes in a big haversack with a strap over each shoulder.

James Cross was also in Company "F," and gave a deposition attesting to Emanuel Wilson. He said he is sixty years of age, and resided in Guyton, Georgia, and was a private in the Civil War. He knew Emanuel Wilson, the claimant well, and served in his regiment. He was with him all the way through and was discharged with him in Louisville, Kentucky. They came home together as far as Augusta, Georgia and he was present now and he recognizes him "as the same man who served as a private in Company "F," 135th U.S.C.T.I. He is the right man beyond a doubt."

William Speirs's Deposition in the file of Emanuel Wilson said that he is harmless with no vicious habits. His sister took care of him and his money in the past, but he has been with him for twenty years. William Speirs believes he was a soldier many years ago and needs a guardian to look after him. William Speirs was part of the slave owner's family and on the property on which Emanuel was born and raised. He had lived there his whole life.

Guyton, Ga., April 12th, 192[illegible]

Department of the Interior,
Bureau of Pensions,
Washington, D.C.

Gentlemen:-

Andrew Wallace, who is the lawful Guardian of Emanuel Wilson who holds Pension Certificate No. 1,093,910 living at Tusculum, Ga. wishes to make application in behalf of his ward Emanuel Wilson for an increase of pension.

The reason for asking for the increase is that Emanuel Wilson is paralized and totally helpless. Please send to Andrew Wallace, Guardian Emanuel Wilson the proper blank for him to make application on for the increase.

Very truly yours

Clarence D Guyton

N.B. Emanuel Wilson is an idiot and cannot apply himself, except through his guardian. Send blank accordingly.

CDG

U.S. PENSION OFFICE
APR 14

Beaufort, S. C. July 17, 1904.

Hon. Com. of Pensions,

Washington, D. C.

Sir:

I have the honor to return herewith the papers in the above-cited claim for pension and to submit the following report:

This claim was sent out as to identity only. This claimant is dense, almost to absolute vacancy. His ideas and recollections are almost as vague as "dreams that we dreamed that we dreamed". A careful reading of his deposition will give one a fair idea of his capacity. I could not shake him when he said he only served one day nor could I shake him when he said he served six years. Considering his mental capacity, I deem his statement a very good one as to his service and what he did in the service. He knows a few motions of the gun, he walked a beat with a stick for a gun, very like an old soldier and saluted me as his Capt. in good style when I approached him as such. He told why he did not wear his uniform home after service and the reason was one that any old soldier will recognize as genuine. I believe he is the soldier of record. His personal description is that found in the A. G. report. If a pension is allowed this man it should be paid to a guardian. He was a slave of Mrs. ~~Weir's~~ Speir's people and now lives on the plantation of Mr. Speir who looks after him thae same as if he were a child. Should he get a little money in his own possession he has just sensed enough to go to Savannah, and then his pension, instead of being a benefit to him, would be an absolute injury. He would be much better off with the Speirs without a pension than away from them with one. William Speir is a large planter and a man of affairs and a proper person to handle this money if any should be allowed. He expressed a willingness to me to accept the trust.

I recommend reference to the Chief of the Board of Review for his consideration.

Very respectfully,

Don McClain

Special Examiner.

This man is known more as Wilson than Johnson and ctf, if issued, should issue in name of Wilson. [initials]

Case of Emanuel Wilson C. No. 1234785

On this 11th day of July 1904, at Tusculum county of Effingham State of Ga before me, Don McClain, a special examiner of the Bureau of Pensions, personally appeared Emanuel Wilson who, being by me first duly sworn to answer truly all interrogatories propounded to him during this special examination of aforesaid claim for pension, deposes and says:

I cant tell my age. I was a full hand when the war came on. I was not married when freedom came. I was born in this county the slave of Elihu Wilson. After he died I belonged to his son, Steven Wilson until freedom. I lived in this county until the war and came back here right after the war and have been here ever since. My father was named Ben London. He belonged to Mobly. I cant tell you where he got this name. That was his right name. My mother was named Jane Wilson. She belonged to my owner. Both parents are dead. I have but one brother, Sam no Sirus Rell. He gets mail at Exley, Ga. He was most a young man when I went in the army. He is only a half brother of mine. I have one sister, Silla Wallace. She lives here. Her husband is named Andrew Wallace. She is only a half sister. I and my mother titled Wilson before freedom. I enlisted at Savannah, Ga. I gave the name of Emanuel Wilson. I kept that name all through my army service. I enlisted in Co. F 160 Regt. They then turned me loose

Page 4, Deposition A

no. 5

and I came back home to this county and made a crop. Yes, I enlisted and was turned loose next day and came right back here and mad a crop. I made a crop for my young boss, Steve Wilson. I have been here ever since. Yes, I was examined when I was enlisted. The Yankey doctors examined me. They stripped me naked and jamed me all over and [illegible] me and made me put my clothes back on, and I came home the next day. Yes, I am sure I came home the next day after I was examined. I never went back to Savannah again during the war. Q. Then you were in the army only one day? A. That is all Sir. I had no sword or horse. I had a gun. I could have brought it home. I did not want to bother with it. Yes, I only had a gun one day. I used the gun to march and drill with. I never got into a fight. I wore blue clothes. I wore the blue clothes only one day. I left the blue clothes in Savannah. They were full of lice. We went on the cars. We went to Hilton Head. I cant tell where it is. We were at Raleigh, Goldsboro and Petersburg and Washington, D.C. and was mustered out at Louisville, Ky. We went to Louisville on a steamboat. We rode on a train from Louisville, Ky. I cant call the Col. Maj. or Dr. Hayden was my Capt. Johnny

Attest:

Wm. [illegible]

Emanuel his mark Wilson

DEPOSITION A

Case of Emanuel Wilson , No. 1234785

On this ___ day of ___, 190_, at
Continued county of ___
State of ___ before me, ___ a
special examiner of the Bureau of Pensions, personally appeared
Emanuel Wilson, who, being by me first duly sworn to
answer truly all interrogatories propounded to h___ during this special
examination of aforesaid claim for pension, deposes and says:

something was Lt. Peter Blue was Ord. Sergt. He put us on duty. We had three or four more Sergts. in our Co. Leonard Wood was one, Bolir Miller was one, I cant think of any more. Our Ord. Sergt was a ginger-cake man - stout. Sergt. Wood was tall and black. The Capt. was a little stout man. Lt. was about the same size. The Capt. rode a gray horse the Lt. walked. We had a heap of colonels. We had about ten I think. We had bread and fish and rice and sugar + coffee. We only cooked the rice. On picket when the Capt. came round we said halt, give the countersign. He used to come round to see if any one was asleep. If he found one asleep he took the gun and put him under arrest. I cant tell how long I was in. I think I was in about 6 years. When we quit at Louisville we all got $10.00. I think we all got a blue paper when we were discharged. We had four corporals. Leonard Wood was one, Squire Chatterman was one. Yes, we had a man named Best. (See list.) We called him Moon Best. He was a corporal. The Yorkus took him out and made a doctor of him. I dont remember Cochran. He was not a Lt.

Page 6 Deposition A

page 7
Johnny is the only Lt. I can recollect.
I cant recall Herrod, Jordan, Jones, Miller,
Landers, Townsend, Thews. yes, I remember
Cross. His name was Jim Cross. He lives at
Quitory Ga. He was in my Co. I have
never been known by any other name in
my life except Emanuel Wilson. I am
known now by that name and by
no other. Will Moore (now in prison
for pension frauds.) is the one who star
ted my pension. He said he could get
it for me. He did all my writing. The
Yankees took Bill Moore off. They knocked
him clean off. I quit him then. I cant
count a hundred. I recon I can count ten.
(Clmt. shown all kinds of money. He does
not know bills and cant tell the difference
between a dime and a cent. He cant
tell the name of the county seat or
number of months in a year.) I never
was married. (He is 5-4½ by actual measurement and not 5-7¼ as stated in circular.
He is black with scar in forehead. No
peculiarities of speech. He is not an idiot
but just of very low grade of intellect. I
drilling, &c., he shows marked signs of having
been a soldier.) We stood guard until we
were relieved. I think five hours. Jim
Cross is the only comrade I can locate.
General was the highest officer in my
Regt. We drank water out of a canteen in
the army. We carried grub in a haversack.
We carried our clothes in a big haversack
Attest: [illegible]

[illegible], Ga Georgia

Dec 2[illegible], 190[illegible]

(Date of examination)

Vertigo, Rheumatism, internal injuries, left side broken ribs, burned head and catarrh

He receives a pension of 0 dollars per month.

He makes the following statement upon which he bases his claim for Original (Original, increase, restoration, etc.)

Old and debilitated

[Atten]tion is invited to the outlines of the human skeleton and figure upon the back of this certificate, which should be used to indicate the location of a disease or injury, the entrance and exit of a missile, an amputation, etc.

We hereby certify that upon examination we find the following objective conditions:

Pulse rate, 68-72-94 [Sitting, standing, after exercise.], respiration, 18-18-20 [Sitting, standing, after exercise.], temperature, 98½, height, 5 feet 3½ inches; actual weight, 138 pounds; age, 56 years.

The soldier is intellectually of a low type, with a grinning, idiotic expression and a very limited vocabulary, aside from his mental disability he is well preserved, active and fully capable of manual labor.

No evidence of Rheumatism, all muscles, joints and tendons are well developed, supple normal in size and not tender.

The heart is normal in size, regular in action and no murmurs, the apex is 2 inches below and 2 inches to the right of left nipple; the base is behind the fourth right sterno costal articulation.

No evidence of internal injuries either thoracic or abdominal.

No evidence of broken ribs or injury to the left side.

No evidence of burn on the head; there being neither cicatrix or alopecia.

No evidence of Catarrh either nasal or pharyngeal.

No other disabilities found.

[illegible]

CHAPTER 9

THE SALKEHATCHIE WAS CROSSED UNDER HEAVY FIRE FROM REBEL INFANTRY ON THE OPPOSITE SIDE OF THE RIVER.

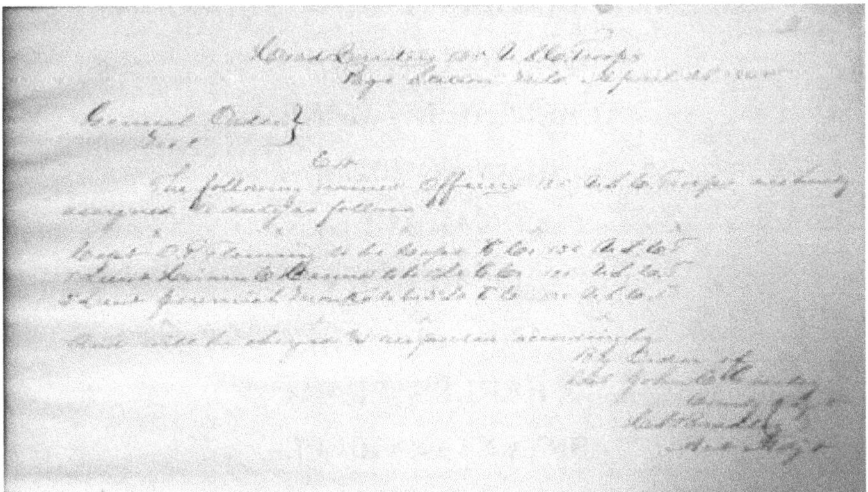

General Order #1 Identifying Officers of Company "G" 135th USCT

COMPANY “G”

INCLUDED IN THIS CHAPTER ARE EXTRACTIONS FROM THE PENSION RECORDS OF;

WILLIAM BAXTER / HARGER

JACKSON BROADUS

ALBERT BUIE / MCNIEL

SILAS COGDELL

JACOB MCMILLAN

BEN MCCREA

SANDY MCNAIR

CHARLES SPEAR

BRYANT COGDELL

WILLIAM BAXTER / HARGER

William Harger served in Company "G," under the name of William Harger, that being the same name, he entered the 135th United States Colored Troop while being a slave. It was customary for a slave to take his owner's name. He belonged to David Harger and after the army, he took his father's name, William Baxter.

J.F. Harger of Saint Matthews made an affidavit that he had known William since he was a boy because he was William's owner. He stated that William was strong and healthy up until the time he had left him to join the federal army.

William described that he enlisted when the Yankees went through, it was Sherman's Army. He joined them at Jamison's turnout about five or six miles from Saint Matthews. He enlisted in Goldsboro, North Carolina, and he was in the Pioneer Corps before Goldsboro. He did not remember much; however, he said they did pass through Virginia to get to Washington D.C.. He said that they marched all the way. He stated also he could not tell Sunday from Monday, they all seemed to run together. They stayed in Washington, DC, and did guard duty, and they were there for about a month and a half. He was in the ***Grand Review.*** From Washington they went to Louisville, Kentucky, halfway on the railroad train and the balance on the steamboat. He identified Colonel Gurley, Major Dixon, and Captain Fleming as being in charge of the Company. He went straight home after being discharged and had stayed there ever since.

William Baxter / Harger was owned by David Harger, who was dead by 1896, but Andrew, his son, resided on the old farm. Jake Harger resided a mile from the old place that was close to Jamison turnout where they all joined the union soldiers. He stated he wore his soldier clothes home and wore them until they wore out. William was married when he went into the army and had one daughter. His slave wife died and when he came home a white man took his child and carried her to Columbia. He was an Irishman. William did not know if she was dead or alive at the time. He heard from his brother that she might be dead. He had no sickness before service, and he was both a field hand and a house servant in slavery.

When stationed at Louisville Kentucky he had a lung burst. He was excused from duty some five or six times altogether. He didn't stay in the hospital but got medicine from the doctors.

After he came home, he would go from farm to farm working odd jobs. William worked for five years at R.P. Autleys in the mill from Canady's. He told us he had the mumps the second year after the war and smallpox the next year. He never really had good health after the war. The rest of his life in Orangeburg, South Carolina he wore the scars of war bravely, including losing his family.

N. B.—Examiners should be particular to have affiants sign on the line next below the closing words of their depositions so as to leave little or no space between their signatures and the end of their depositions.

(3—459)

DEPOSITION

Case of William Baxter & Wm Hunger, No. 1146481

On this 1st day of Nov 1896, at St. Mathews County of Orangeburg State of S.C. before me, E. D. Gaylord, a Special Examiner of the Pension Office, personally appeared William Baxter & William Hunger who, being by me first duly sworn to answer truly all interrogatories propounded to him during this Special Examination of aforesaid pension claim, deposes and says: My name is William Baxter I do not know my age, I am not less than 60 years old and I may be older and I reside of on Mr Evans Hills farm about five miles from St. Mathews which is my P.O. I served in Co. G 135 USCI as a private by the name of William Hunger as you can see from my certificate of discharge here handed you for inspection. I cannot read or write and I cannot tell you the year I enlisted. I went with the yankees when they came through here in Feby and it was Shermans army. I joined them at Jimmerson's turpentine about five or six miles from here (St Mathews) and I enlisted at Goldsboro, N.C. I was in the Pioneer corps from here to Goldsboro. I do not remember the name of the place I was mustered into the service. We went from Goldsboro to Washington D.C. I cannot remember the names of a single town through which we passed or stopped in North Carolina. I only know that we passed through Virginia to get to Washington. I cannot tell you of the name of a single town through which we passed or stopped in Virginia. I marched all the way from

Page 2 Deposition C

Dep , Goldsboro NC to Washington D.C. I cannot tell what Month it was then we got to Washington DC. I could not tell Sunday from Monday, they all seemed to run together. We staid in Washington about a month and a half and did Guard duty. I was in the Grand Review. (He really does not know what the Grand Review is) From Washington DC we went to Louisville Ky. Half way we travelled on Railroad train and the balance of the way by Steam boat. I do not know the name of the River on which we travelled. I do not know the name of the boat we were on. I do not know the name of the Railroad on which we travelled. I know that we run Night and day. The name of our Colonel was Gulley. Lt Col Dixon. Capt Flemming had charge of our Company. He was the only captain we had during our service. 1st Lieut Bennett. I have forgotten the name of our second Lieut. Ord Sgt Mosley. I have had the discharge paper which I gave you when I was discharged in Ky. I do not remember or rather know the year I was discharged at Louisville Ky. It was the same year I was mustered into the service in the winter and I came straight home here where I have resided ever since the service. I have no other service either in the Army or Navy of the United States. I was owned by David Horgan who resided in six miles of Harpsburg Ky. I was born and raised right there. He is dead but his sons Andrew Horgan resides at his old farm. David Horgan Jr at the old farm. Jake Horgan resides a mile from the old place.

near Summons's lumont. Mrs Kitty Robinson
a daughter resides in the same locality.
I wore my soldier clothes home and I
wore them until they were worn out.
I was a married man when I went
into the army and my wife had
had one child. My slave wife is dead
and when I came back a white man
had taken her and carried her to Columbia. He was an Irishman. I do
not remember his name. I cannot
tell how long she lived after the war
and I do not know whether she is
dead or alive. I have heard from her
brother Frank Kinley that she was dead.
My daughter Frances was living in Cokesbury
above Columbia. I heard from her
about two years ago. She is married
and she wrote me that she was married.
I do not know the name of her husband
21 and do not know the name she goes by.
I had no sickness of any kind before
the service. I was both a field hand
and house servant.
I claim pension for misery of both of my
sides and back and disease of my lungs
and for the past ten years I have suffered
from shortness of breath and a kind of
fluttering around my heart. And
that is all that ails me.

witness
J. W. Boyd
H. N. Farr

his
William X Barker
mark
Deponent

Sworn to and subscribed before me this 24 day of Nov
1896, and I certify that the contents were fully made known to deponent before signing.

E. D. Gallion
Special Examiner

Page 8 Deposition A

N. B.—Examiners should be particular to have affiants sign on the line next below the closing words of their depositions so as to leave little or no space between their signatures and the end of their depositions.

DEPOSITION

Case of William [illegible] Kruger No. 1,146,481

[illegible] day of Nov 1896, at [illegible] County of Orangeburg

State of S. C. before me, E. D. Gallion, a Special Examiner of the Pension Office, personally appeared William [illegible] Kruger, who, being by me first duly sworn to answer truly all interrogatories propounded to him during this Special Examination of aforesaid pension claim, deposes and says: I hadn't any lungs to hurt me and the small of my back and sides when in the army and when we were stationed near Louisville, Ky. I was excused from duty some four or six times all together and I was not off duty more than a week all together. I was not in hospital at all. I went to the doctor for medicine. About a month before I was discharged I suffered as I have told you and I have suffered so ever since and up to the present time.

When I came back from the army I stayed at the Kruger place for one year (1866) and went then to Thos Zimmerman's place about two miles from Kruger's place and was there two years (1867-8) and from there I came to [illegible] County at Zimmerman's [illegible] and was there two years (1869-70) and from there I went to R. P. Antley's place about a mile from Connelly's and was there about [illegible] years (1871-1876) and from there to Mrs R. P. Riley's about a mile from Antley's and I was there about five years 1877-1881 and from there to Mallard Gruyard's about a mile and

Page 4 Deposition A

a half from Mrs Riley and I was there about two years (188[illegible]-3) and from there to John Wolfe in calling distance from Grayson's and was there for two years (188[illegible]-5) and from there to Rose Kelly place three miles from Wolfe where I have resided since.
Dr J.D. Dansby who now resides at Ellisker S.C. treated me the next year (1866) after I got back for the pains in my sides back and lungs. It was in the fall of the year and he came to see me twice and I was sick in bed and often sent me medicine and I was sick over a month at that time. And Dr Hunger who resides six miles from Orangeburg S.C. next treated me for the same complaint and not quite a year after Dr [illegible] Dr Hunger visited me for the same complaint. He came to see me once and I sent for the medicine often and I was sick three weeks at that time and Dr Oskar was the next physician who treated me and it was about three years after Dr Hunger treated me he came to see me twice and I was down in the bed for two weeks and was longer up sick about a month of that. And he has been my physician since and he resides here in town.
I had measles when I was a child. I had mumps the second year after the war no one treated me except an old colored man. The third year after I came out of the army I had smallpox which lasted me about three months and I was living on Hunger place and an old man by the name of Scipio treated me. He was a colored man and

[illegible] [illegible]. It [illegible] [illegible] [illegible],
I had [illegible] since the year [illegible]
[illegible] and I have not had
any other [illegible] [illegible] since the
war.
When I went into the army I used
my owners name as [illegible] and when
I came home my father was going
by the name of Baxter and I
took his name.
Q. [illegible] can you prove that you served
as a private in Co G 135 U.S.C.T.
A. Sam Haines near St Mathews S.C. who is
now known as Sam Muller.
Wise Lake near St Mathews S.C. now known
as Wise Moak.
Frank Kitt near Mrs Zimmerman place 10 miles
from St Mathews now known as Frank
Kirby.
Jackson Antrum Orangeburg S.C. now
known as Jackson [illegible]
I have heard you read the list of comrades
and I only recognize the name of Wesley
Ellis as a member of my company.
I do not care to be present or represented
during your examination of my claim.
I understand your questions and my
answers are correctly recorded in this
deposition.

Witness
[illegible]
G. N. [illegible]

his
William X Baxter
mark
Deponent.

Sworn to and subscribed before me this 14 day of Nov
189[illegible], and I certify that the contents were fully made known to deponent before signing.

[illegible] Gibbons
Special Examiner.

Dep. C. Examination [illegible]

JACKSON BROADUS

He is from Jones County Georgia and he is a ***thousand miler.*** This means one who marched a thousand miles in Sherman's Army from Georgia, through the Carolina's and on to Washington, DC. during his service.

Jackson Broadus was a freed slave who lived in Jones County Georgia and saw Sherman's Army shortly after the Army left Atlanta Georgia. He decided to go with the army as part of the pioneer corps, and worked to clear the roads, felled the trees, and built the bridges to cross the creeks that took the Army to Savannah, Georgia. In Beaufort, South Carolina he stated that he became part of company "G." In marching to Goldsboro, North Carolina his company had to endure the harshest winter in years. It was very cold and wet and they marched through the swamps, sometimes walking with an inch of ice on the ground and that is where they slept.

The march through the rugged terrain tore his pant legs and he had shoes that he patched. It was over four hundred miles to Goldsboro where he was made a first sergeant in the 135th United States Colored Troop. They left Goldsboro after two months of replenishing their clothing and a mental rest. They moved to Raleigh, then Petersburg, Danville, Richmond, Virginia, to Washington, D.C. where they remained for four months. He tells the examiner that his duties in the Pioneer Corps consisted of clearing the roads for the wagons and soldiers to pass. For felling trees, filling holes and ditches, he received wages of twenty-four dollars per month. He stated that the name of the quartermaster of the regiment was Frank Peppins. After Washington the regiment moved to Louisville, Kentucky to do garrison duty.

In slavery Jackson belonged to Thomas Broadus. After discharge he lived in Macon and Savannah from 1865 to 1887. He then moved to Jacksonville, Florida where he ran a boarding house. He stated he was five feet eight in height. In 1901 he signed his own name to his deposition. His wife Ellen died in March of 1907. After her death he was sent to the Veterans hospital in Virginia in 1908 by his daughter. He died in the hospital May 12, 1908, **and is buried at Arlington National Cemetery, Virginia.**

GENERAL AFFIDAVIT FOR ANY PURPOSE.

STATE OF FLORIDA
COUNTY OF DUVAL } ss.

Personally appeared Jackson Broadus aged 71 years and aged years of Jacksonville, P. O., County of Duval State of Florida, who being duly sworn upon his oath declare as follows: That he is an ex-slave: that his master's name was Thomas Broadus, who resided at Monticello, Georgia; that he has no Bible-record of his age: that he entered the war in 1863; that affiant was informed by his master that he(affiant) was then between 25 and 30 years of age. And affiant further says that it was a custom before emancipation for masters to keep a record of the ages of their slaves and for slaves to enquire of their masters whenever they desired infor- fux mation as to such matters. And affiant further says that his master aforesaid is dead, and that therex are no living relatives of his said master whose whereabouts affiant is aware of.

Personally appeared Jackson Bradue [illegible] Bradtue aged 70 years

and

of Jacksonville P. O. County of Duval

State of Florida , who being duly sworn upon law oath

declare as follows: That on the 27th of March 1863 he was enrolled as first Sargent in Co. "G" 135 Regiment U.S. C Inf., in Beaufort County North Carolina. That from said date his Company moved first to Goldsboro North Carolina That said Company remained at Goldsboro about two (2) months from thence to Raleigh North Carolina where Company remained about four (4) months, at which placed he was mustered in under Major Dickson of the 135th Regiment Gurley Colonel. When his Company left Raleigh North Carolina it moved to Petersburg Virginia from Petersburg Virginia to Danville Virginia, and from Danville Virginia to Richmond Virginia from thence to Washington where he with the Company and Regiment remained for four (4) month. That his duties prior to this in the Pioneer service consisted of clearing the road for the wagons and Army to pass — Felling trees, filling up holes and Ditches; That he received as wages Twenty four ($24) Dollars per Month. That the name of the quartermaster of the regiment was Frank Pepper, That to his best knowledge and belief, he was paid his wages by the Pay master and not the Quarter Master, That to his best knowledge and belief that he was doing Pioneer duty felling trees, Filling ditches and clearing the road for wagons and the Army to pass as aforesaid on or about 2 months prior to his enlistment as a Soldier. That when his company and Regiment left Washington he moved to Louisville Kentucky where he performed Garrison duty until October 27th 1865, when he was mustered out of the service honorably.

SEE OVER.

[41]

Declaration for Restoration to the Rolls.

State of Florida, **County of** Duval, ss:

On this 31st day of August, A. D. one thousand eight hundred and Ninety Six personally appeared before me, a Notary Public within and for the County and State aforesaid, Jackson Bradae, aged about 56 years, a resident of the City of Jacksonville, County of Duval State of Florida who, being duly sworn according to law, declares that he is the identical Jackson Bradae to whom was granted Pension certificate No. 864.609 payable at the Pension Agency at Knoxville dated the 13th day of August, in the year 1897 that he makes this declaration in order to secure his restoration to the pension rolls and prays that a new certificate may be issued. That the pension was granted for Right Hernia (incomplete) which was contracted since serving as 1st Sergeant in Co. "G" 135 Regt. U.S.C. Inf Vols, and which still continues in a pensionable degree.

NOTE. The number of the original certificate with the disability and company and regiment should be given in the blank spaces.

2. He also prays additional pension for Rheumatism contracted at or near Savannah State of Georgia on or about 1890.

If the soldier has any other disability besides that for which he was pensioned, he should state so in paragraph No. 2.

That he enlisted at Beaufort S.C. on the 27 day of March 1863 and was honorably discharged at Louisville Ky October 23rd 1865 by muster out of Company. That he received an honorable discharge from the United States service. That he has no application pending under the laws of the United States relating to Pensions.

That the complaint of Rheumatism of which he complains is not due to vicious habits and is permanent in character to the best of his knowledge and belief.

He has not re-enlisted or been paid in the military, naval or marine service of the United States since the last payment of his pension; he hereby appoints, with full power of substitution and revocation, Mess Butts & Phillips of Washington D.C. his true and lawful attorney to prosecute his claim.

His post office address is Room 7 Smith Building ...

ALBERT BUIE / McNIEL

Albert Buie / McNiel was brave enough to follow many other Black men into the Pioneer Corps, with General Sherman, which began his freedom and helped to end the Civil War. On the tenth of March 1865, he enlisted in the seventeenth corps, fourth division of pioneers, Sherman's Army UST. From Philadelphus, Robeson County, North Carolina they marched to Fayetteville, North Carolina. On the 13th of March He witnessed the burning of the arsenal at Fayetteville. Albert recalled building the roads and bridges in the swamps of North Carolina until they reached Goldsboro. That is where he was sworn in and put to work in Company "G," 135th USCT. From that place the march was taken up to Petersburg, Richmond, and Alexandria, Virginia, thence to and through Washington, D.C. to camp about three miles north of the city. That was when he was sent back to the hospital at Alexandria, Virginia.

He was discharged from the hospital, and it was in the latter part of June 1865 that he arrived in Louisville, Kentucky. He performed light duty there until being discharged in November of 1865. When he arrived, his company had taken up winter quarters. He had to remain there for two or three weeks until final discharge was given. His record showed that he had measles and was followed by diarrhea and his lungs were also affected.

Albert was a slave of D.M. Buie and when he returned home from the service, he changed his name to his father's last name of McNiel. How brave Albert was to have the "GUTS" to leave his home, take that arduous and dangerous march. He then made it home, to raise a family with the health problems from the service that stayed with him his whole life.

Albert McNiel died December 22, 1915. Martha, his wife, died in 1916.

3-044

APPLICATION FOR REIMBURSEMENT.

(This application, when properly executed before some officer having authority to administer oaths for general purposes, should be forwarded, together with the pension certificate and itemized bills of all expenses, to the Commissioner of Pensions, Washington, D. C.)

State of North Carolina
County of Roberson } ss:

On this 14th day of February, A. D. one thousand nine hundred and sixteen personally appeared before me, a Recorder of Lumberton District within and for the County and State aforesaid, Alex McMillan, Admr. of Albert McNeill aged Forty-three years, a resident of Rowland, County of Robeson, State of North Carolina, who, being duly sworn according to law, makes the following declaration in order to obtain reimbursement from the accrued pension for expenses paid (or obligation incurred) in the last sickness and burial of Albert McNeill alias Albert Buie, who was a pensioner of the United States by certificate No. 1006.779, on account of the service of Albert McNeill alias Albert Buie (Name of soldier or sailor.) in G. 135 U.S. C Inf (Describe service by company and regiment, etc., if in the Army, or by the words U. S. Navy, if in the Navy.)

That pension was last paid to November 4th, 1915.

That the answers to questions propounded below are full, complete, and truthful to the best of my knowledge, information, and belief, and that no evidence necessary to a proper adjustment of all claims against the accrued pension is suppressed or withheld.

1. What was the full name of the deceased pensioner? Albert McNeill alias Albert Buie

2. In what capacity was decedent pensioned? (As invalid soldier or sailor, or as a widow, minor child, dependent relative, etc.) as a soldier

3. If decedent was pensioned as an invalid soldier or sailor—

(a) Was he ever married? (Answer yes or no.) yes

(b) How many times, and to whom? One time. Maiden name Martha McEachern

(c) If married, did his wife survive him? (Answer yes or no.) no.

(d) If so, is she still living? (Answer yes or no.) no.

(e) If not living, give full names and dates of death of all wives Been dead about 10 years Martha McNeill only wife, about 60 years when she died

(f) Was he ever divorced? (Answer yes or no.) no

(g) If so, is the divorced wife still living? (Answer yes or no.) no (If living, a copy of the decree of divorce must be filed.)

(h) If not living, give her full name and the date of her death —

4. Did pensioner leave a child under 16 years of age? (Answer yes or no.) no

5. Is any such child still living? (Answer yes or no.) no. child

6. Were any sick or death benefits paid on pensioner's account? If so, give name of society and amount paid no. not any—

GENERAL AFFIDAVIT.

State of North Carolina, County of Robeson, ss.

In the matter of Albert McNeill alias Albert Buie, Co. G. 135 U.S. Inf.

ON THIS 11th day of April, A. D. 1899, personally appeared before me a Notary Public in and for the aforesaid County duly authorized to administer oaths Albert McNeill aged about 61 years, a resident of Burnt Swamp Township in the County of Robeson and State of North Carolina well known to me to be reputable and entitled to credit, and who, being duly sworn, declared in relation to aforesaid case as follows: I enlisted in the Pioneer Corps of Sherman's army and in April 1865 after serving about one month in the Pioneer Corps I enlisted as a private in Company G. 135th Regt U.S. Infantry and served till the latter part of November 1865 when I was mustered out at Louisville Kentucky. While at Alexandria Virginia I was in the hospital about six weeks, had measles and this was followed by diarrhoea, my lungs were affected and this was followed by rheumatism which disabled me from doing any kind of labor for about 2/3, two thirds of my time.

Affiant says his name was entered on army rolls as Albert Buie on account of being formerly a slave of R. M. P. Buie — after returning home after discharge I changed my name to Albert McNeill after my father Ben McNeill.

NOTE.—Affiant should state how he gained a knowledge of the facts to which he testifies.

H[is] Post-office address is Buies, North Carolina

~~further declare that~~ no ~~interest in said case and~~ ~~not concerned in its prosecution.~~

R F Currin

A C Bowman

(If affiant signs by mark two persons who write sign here.)

Albert his McNeill alias Albert Buie
mark
(Signature of Affiant.)

State of North Carolina, County of Robeson, ss.

In the matter of Albert McNeill alias Albert Buie late of Co. G. 135 U.S.C.T.

ON THIS 16th day of Sept, A. D. 1897, personally appeared before me a Notary Public in and for the aforesaid County duly authorized to administer oaths Albert McNeill aged 59 years, a resident of Buie's in the County of Robeson and State of N.C. well known to me to be reputable and entitled to credit, and who, being duly sworn, declared in relation to aforesaid case as follows:

NOTE.—Affiant should state how he gained a knowledge of the facts to which he testifies.

On the 10th of March 1865 I enlisted in the 2nd Corps 4th Division of Pioneers Shermans Army U.S.T. at Philadelphus Robeson County N.C. From that Place we marched to Fayetteville N.C. where on or about the 18th Mch 1865 I was commissioned put to work I remained in the Pioneer Corps until some time in the following April When at Raleigh N.C. I enlisted in Co G. 135th U.S.C.T. (Capt (Oliver P. Fleming) From that Place the march was taken up to Petersburg, Richmond and Alexandria Va. thence to and through Washington D.C. about 3 miles North of the latter place, where I was sent back to the Hospital at Alexandria Va (this was in the latter part of June 1865) at where I remained on light duty until I was discharged in the latter part of Nov 1865 at Louisville Ky where my Company had to face Water Quarters When I reached that place my Co. had been discharged I had to remain there 2 or 3 weeks before my final discharge was given me

His Post-office address is

~~further declare that~~ ~~no interest in said case and~~ ~~not concerned in its prosecution.~~

Katie McN. Buie

Kate Buie.

(If affiant signs by mark two persons who write sign here)

PENSION OFFICE SEP 17 1897

Albert McNeill alias his X mark Albert Buie

(Signature of Affiant.)

FEB 1 1916
BUREAU OF PENSIONS

Lumberton, N. C.,
Jan. 31, 1916.

Department of the Interior,
Bureau of Pensions
Office of the Disbursing Clerk,
Washington, D. C.

Gentlemen:

In regard to the pension certificate of Albert McNeill Alis Albert Buie, same being No. 1, 006, 779, which went in force October 21, 1914, we wish to say that this party is dead. He died on December 21, and was buried on Dec. 22, 1915. Alex McMillan has qualified as his administrator.

We are giving you this information of his death, and wish to ascertain whether or not under the law of U. S. Pensions, if up to the time of his death there is any further amount coming to the said Albert McNeill alias Albert Buie of Buie's North Carolina. We are informed that the last payment of pension was made on or about Nov. 4, 1915. If there is any amount coming to him up to the time of his death, it will assist the administrator in paying off funeral espenses etc.

Hoping to hear from you, we remain,

Yours very respectfully,

Britt & Britt, attys -
for Alex McMillan, Admr.
of albert McNeill alias
albert Buie, deceased -

[Re]ferred to Finance Division.
FEB 2 1916

Not any in Dis Clk Off

SILAS COGDELL

Silas Cogdell was born in Sampson County, North Carolina in 1840. When the Union Army came through Goldsboro, North Carolina they enlisted about thirty men and Silas Cogdell was one of them. He stated that he was enlisted into Company "G," 10th Corps, Second Division, Cincinnati Ohio Union Division. He belonged at the time to Lewis Cogdell, and he was among about two hundred slaves from the Cogdell farm who were freed when the Union Army came to Goldsboro. Silas, his uncle, and two other Cogdells passed the physical and swore the oath of service, put on the blue uniform, and began to drill in Company "G," 135th United States Colored Troop.

Silas and the others who joined in Goldsboro and surrounding areas did not have to march through the swamps of South Carolina. When he reached Washington, DC., after marching on foot from Raleigh, North Carolina he said he marched across the long bridge before getting into Washington, and after they got into the city, they had a ***Grand Parade*** in which they were reviewed by General Grant and General Sherman. There was a very large crowd out to see their march through the city. Silas said, "some stood on the sidewalks and others on stands, both white and colored were there, men and women."

When General Sherman left Goldsboro with new men in the 135th Regiment some recalled that they continued to corduroy the roads to Raleigh and rebuild bridges, destroyed in front of them by the Confederates.

Silas remarked in his pension application, and there were two affidavits by others stating, "while in the army he fell and a very large man fell on Silas, injuring his back and hip and those injuries followed him his whole life," as quoted according to Lewis Cox.

He orally stated that he married his first wife Amanda Smith in 1866 and he had ten children with her. Amanda died in 1897. He said that Mary Jane was his second wife, whom he married in 1898, and in total he had twenty-two children. Silas Cogdell died in 1915 and is buried in the Roundabout Cemetery in Princeton, North Carolina.

(Claimant)

GENERAL AFFIDAVIT.

State of North Carolina, County of Wayne, ss:

IN THE MATTER OF Pension Claim of Silas Cogdell late Private in Co G 135th Regiment U S C Inft.

ON THIS 21 day of February, A. D. 1900, personally appeared before me, a Hugh Humphrey U S Com Eastern Dist of N C in and for the aforesaid County, duly authorized to administer oaths, Silas Cogdell aged 6[illegible] years, a resident of Princeton in the County of Johnston and State of North Carolina whose Post Office address is Princeton N C and

aged years, a resident of

in the County of and State of

whose Post Office address is

well known to me to be reputable and entitled to credit, and who, being duly sworn, declare in relation to the aforesaid case as follows:

Affiants should state how they gain a knowledge of the facts to which they testify.

I am the identical Private Soldier of Co G. 135th Regiment U S Col'd Vol's, and that I have never made a claim for pension prior or since the same was pending.
I became afflicted with Rheumatism during the year of 1866. The disease grew worse year by year until 1897, when it was worse in form and pain, from June 26th 1897 to Oct 29th 1897 and prior to and thereafter I suffered great pain from Rheumatism attacked by the disease in both legs, the joints in my right leg being swollen and more painful than in my left, yet I suffered pain in my left leg. I was confined in my bed or the house by Rheumatism nearly all the year of 1897.
I did not have any Physician on account of the condition of me, and the better reason I was poor and unable to employ and pay him. Simple country remedies was given me and for the same reason I was unable to furnish medical testimony. I also suffered with my heart. Same giving me great pain during the time from June 26 1897 to Oct 29 1897 & thence [illegible] since 1897 and am now suffering with Rheumatism & Heart Trouble.

PENSION OFFICE A FEB 23 1900 U. S.

further declare that no interest in said case and not concerned in its prosecution.

Geo. [illegible]
W. A. Dunmark

his
Silas X Cogdell
mark

If affiants sign by mark, two witnesses who can write sign here.

Princeton, N. C. 190

Silas Cogdell appeared before me this day and maketh that he is 68 years old. That he is unable to furnish any record of his birth by reason he was borned a slave and no record was made of the same. the way I am informed as to my age is what I have heard others say with whom I was raised with, and by my present looks and Condition

Sworn to and subscribed before me Nov 11, 1907
J. T. Finlayson J. P.

Silas his + mark Cogdell

6

and J K Hale residing in Johnston Co. persons whom I certify to be respectable and entitled to credit, and who, being by me duly sworn, say that they were present and saw Silas Cogdell the claimant, sign his name (or make his mark) to the foregoing declaration; that they have every reason to believe, from the appearance of the claimant and their acquaintance with him of 28 years and 40 years, respectively, that he is the identical person he represents himself to be, and that they have no interest in the prosecution of this claim.

Thos. Edwards

3-389

DEPOSITION

Case of Mary J. Cogdell, *No.* 1093,693

On this fifth *day of* July, *191*8, *at* ~~fifth~~ near Princeton, *county of* Johnston, *State of* North Carolina, *before me,* John T. Sadler, *a Special Examiner of the Bureau of Pensions, personally appeared* Mary J. Cogdell, *who, being by me first duly sworn to answer truly all interrogatories propounded to* her *during this special examination of aforesaid claim for pension, deposes and says:*

I am Almost 60 years old as well as I know, Inever did Know my age. I do any kind of work that I am able to do, and my P. O. is Princeton N.C.

I am the claimant in this case and claim pension as the widow of Silas Cogdell, who was a soldier and a pensioner when he died. He was Drawing $46.50 every thre months. My husband served in co. G, 135, U. S. C. T. I herewith hand you his discharge, (claimant produces a certificate of service J. T. S. Ex.) The soldier was much older than me, and he died December 21, 1915 at Selma this county. I was married to him almost 13 years. was born in Sampson county this State and lived there until I moved here in this county and have lived here ever since.

I was a Atkinson, my father, I have always been told that my father was Charles Williams, but I never saw him but was told by my mother that he was my father. My mothers maiden name I dont know but her name was Fannie Strickland when I first remember. Her husband was Gardner Stricland. My mother and father are both dead years ago. I have no brothers or sisters but Catherine Spells. My husband has no brothers or sisters but Squire Cogdell, and he has given me an affidavit in my claim for pension. Both me and my husband, the soldier had been married before. I was married to the soldier under the name of Mary Jane Sanders, by Preacher Spells in this county. Mr. Spells is my son-in-law, and is a regular preacher. I have been married only twice, the first time to Hardy Sanders and then to Silas Cogdell, the soldier.

The soldier had only been married the one time. His other wife was Amanda Cogdell. My first was dead long before I married the soldier.

I could not tell you to save my life the year he died, as I did not see him after he was dead. Q. Were you and your husband Hardy Sanders living together at the time of his death? A. Nosir we were not, and had

Page 1 *Deposition* A

not for a long time, and I guess it was at least ten years. He was a rover, and had been all over this country. I cant tell you when I married Sanders, but my youngest child by Sanders must now be nearly 40 years old. This child was a small girl when her father left me and never did come back to me. I had two other children by Sanders, Their names being, William who Ihave not seen for years, and do not know whether he is living or dead, and then Levitt who is at City Point Va. working at the Dupont Powder Plant. We got along alright as long as he would stay home but he would not do that and I do not know where he was or what he was doing when away from me. I never heard from him, and I never made any effort to find him as I did not know where to look, and I did not care much as he did not do much for me and the children any time he was around. What makes you think that your husband Hardie Sanders is dead? A. Now sir all the information I can give you on that is what his brother Nester Sanders told me, and thatwas , that Hardy had been killed by the cars. He just told me that Hardy had got all torn to pieces. No sir I cant tell you where he was killed as I dont know that his brother ever told me, and I never did know where it was. I dont know that his brother said on what road he got killed. I could not tell you where Nester was living at the time. Nester told me that he saw his brother after he was killed, and knew that it was him. At the time Nester told me this I was living here or near here.Q. Had you married Silas Cogdel when you learned that Sanders was dead?. A. No sir and I did not marry Cogdell until long after I heard that Sanders was dead. Oh Nester is dead and has been for years. I heard that Nester lived and died in Cumberland Co. this State, but I was never at his home and knew none of his people. I had seen Nester once before the time he came and told me about Hardy being dead. No he did not come to tell me about the death of Hardy, but was just passing by and stopped.

Attest.

Lorulter Anderson
No other witness available

Mary J. her X mark Cogdel
Deponent.

Subscribed and sworn to before me this 5th. *day of* July *1918, and I certify that the contents were fully made known to deponent before signing.*

Jno T Dale
Special Examiner.

Case of Mary J. Cogdell No. [illegible]

On this 19 day of March , 19 [illegible] near Goldsboro county of Wayne , State of North Carolina before me, R. N. Fleming , a Special Examiner of the Bureau of Pensions, personally appeared Melvin C. Atkinson , who, being by me first duly sworn to answer truly all interrogatories propounded to him during this special examination of aforesaid claim for pension, deposes and says: I am [illegible] years of age, I am a farmer and my address is Goldsboro, N. C. I have known Mary J. Cogdell for 35 or 40 years or longer. I also knew both of her husbands and knew them when they first came from Sampson Co. to this County. Her first husband was Hardy Sanders. I knew him well. I did not know him before he married her for they came here married or at least they came here as man and wife and I suppose they were married. He lived with her for some time, for two years anyway after they came here and then he got into trouble and had to go to the penitentiary for stealing old man Atkinson's ox. He was in prison for a year or so and then he came back into the neighborhood where I lived in this county but right close to the Johnson Co. line and about 7 or 8 miles south of Princeton. He was sick when he came back from prison but he wandered around a little bit and then went off to Wilmington for some reason or other. He and his wife did not live together after he came out of prison. After he had been at Wilmington for a while he was beating his way back this way on the train and the train crew got on to him and he had to jump off and he was injured in some way. I do not know just how he was injured, he was able to get back to the old neighborhood but he was sick with the injury and also with the sickness that he had when he came out of prison and it was not long before he died. He lived mostly in a house by himself but convenient to neighbors but I cannot now think of any of those old neighbors who are now living. I saw him while he was sick after he had been hurt but I did not stay with him. I saw him after he was dead and I know that he is dead. As I recollect it was about 1885 or 1886 that he died but I cannot fix

Page 11 Deposition C

Page 12

just the date. He died in this county but he was buried over in Johnson Co. about 5 or 6 miles from Smithfield among his people, for there ere a good many of the Sanders up in that part of the county but I donot know whether you could find any of the old ones up there now or not. I did not go to his burial for it was too far but I saw him after he wa s dead. I made a statement about this before a magistrate in Goldsboro some time ago. Claimant just came to me because she knew I knew about it and I went and madd it. I acknowledge my signatureto the affidavit shown me and that affidavit is correct. I am not related to this claimant. I have no interest in her pension claim. I have heard this deposition read and it is correct.

M. C. Atkinson

Sworn to and subscribed before me this 19 day of March, 1919, and I certify that the contents were fully made known to deponent before signing.

Special Examiner.

JACOB McMILLAN / DIXON

Jacob McMillan was from Cheraw, Chesterfield County, South Carolina. He said that he was born there on December 31, 1844, and belonged to Mrs. Mary Anne Dixon. He married Florence McMillan in 1866 after his return from service in the 135th United States Colored Troop. He stated he went into the army when the Union Troops came through and was in the Pioneer Corps. He recalled crossing the Pee Dee River into North Carolina and then going to Goldsboro. He said, "We got our blue uniforms and they started to drill us and made us into a regiment. When we got to Raleigh, North Carolina we were stripped naked and examined. We didn't get our guns until we got to Louisville, Kentucky."

Jacob said "When Sherman's Army came by here in 1865, they caught me and Jackson Freeman, he was then Jackson Dixon and, on the road, brought us here. Jackson was sickly and made such a fuss they turned him back but took me and put me in the Pioneer Corps."

Jacob described that when he was in the service, he lost his toes on the right foot and was also wounded in the right arm; it seemed to have happened after Raleigh, North Carolina. He lived with his disability all his life. Jacob died in 1925. He is another excellent example of an honorable soldier who had the "GUTS" to join the freedom fighters and had the valor to live a good life.

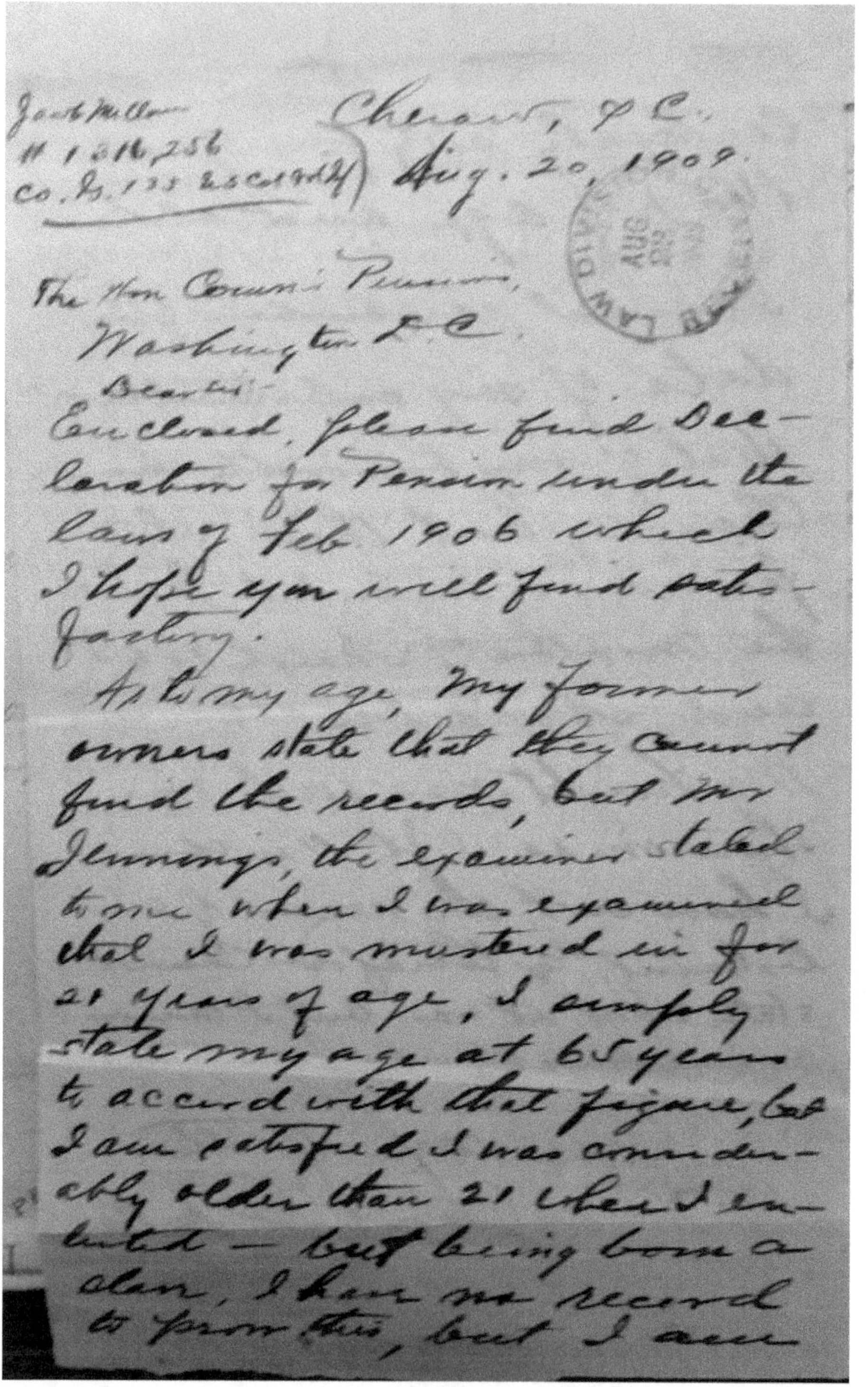

Jacob Miller
1,316,256
Co. B. 135 U.S.Col'd Inf.

Cheraw, S.C.
Aug. 20, 1909.

The Hon. Comm'r Pensions,
Washington D.C.
Dear Sir:

Enclosed, please find Declaration for Pension under the laws of Feb 1906 which I hope you will find satisfactory.

As to my age, my former owners state that they cannot find the records, but Mr Jennings, the examiner stated to me when I was examined that I was mustered in for 21 years of age, I simply state my age at 65 years to accord with that figure, but I am satisfied I was considerably older than 21 when I enlisted — but being born a slave, I have no record to prove this, but I am

Certainly sixty five years (65) of age and older

I cannot remember the date of my enlistment and that of my honorable discharge, but think the period is included between the months of March 1865 and Nov or Dec 1865 —

My height now with my shoes on is 5 ft 11 inches. I have not the record of enlistment and therefore cannot state what it was but I am considerably over five feet.

Yours respectfully
Jacob McMillen

Personally appeared before me Jacob McMillan, alias, Jacob Dixon who being duly sworn says:-

That from May 19, 1904, the date of his application for a pension under the laws of the United States and the rules of the Pension Bureau, and for several years previous, his physical condition has been such as to render him unable to perform manual labor to the extent of earning a living for himself and family; that he is a rheumatic, has lost by accident a toe, has a wound on shoulder and badly affected with kidney troubles, that these things make it possible only for him to earn a livelihood, by superintend-

shoulder and badly affected with kidney troubles, that these things make it possible only for him to earn a livelihood, by superintend-
ing his people while they work to keep him.

That is difficult, if possible, to prove by any individuals, other than his family relation his past condition except insofar as it relates to his having been confined to operations about his home, and that he has not been able to go on public works and on the turpentine farms where he has worked most of his time since the civil war.

That the reason he cannot furnish other evidence of his physical condition since his application to the present time, is the general ignorance of most professional

That in the main, he has treated himself for the complaints before mentioned except in the case of his losing his toe and that has been so long that it is impossible to get the Physicians signature who attended him

That he has been a hard worker, has been engaged in the turpentine business for years and the unusual hard work together with frequent exposures have so impaired his health that he feels and knows that he is a fit subject for a pension

Witness my hand and seal this 31st day of July 1909.

his
Jacob x McMillan

Mr. E. H. Jennings,
Special Examiner,
Charleston, S. C.

Sir:

Herewith find the papers in claim No. 1,316,256, Jacob McMillan, alias Dixon, Co. G, 138th U. S. C. I., for investigation as indicated in the accompanying Law Division letter of the 3rd instant, the purpose being to determine whether the applicant is identical with the soldier of record. If it is found that criminal features exist, the best available testimony should be secured to show responsibility for the same.

If a report be submitted, this letter and that of the Law Division should be made exhibits therein.

Very respectfully,

V. Warner.
Commissioner.

were filed through the instrumentality of Mr.Thompson,were of a fraudulent character. In the two cases in which there were genuine soldiers,the testimony showed that they had been systematically swindled by Thompson upon the allowance of their claims.

For the reasons stated you are requested to forward the papers to a special examiner whose district includes Chesterfield county, S.C.,with instructions to take the best available testimony for the purpose of determining whether the applicant is the identical soldier who performed the service. If it should appear that fraudulent acts have been committed in connection with the claim the best available testimony to establish the identity of the guilty party or parties should be had.

This letter should appear as an exhibit in the examiner's report.

Very respectfully,

BEN McCREA

Ben was born in Orangeburg, South Carolina on January 1, 1840, and was the slave of William Watts. His father was Billy McCrea and was a slave to Martin Eyrick. After the war, he went by Billy Esau and Ben Esau. He was called Esau by the white people and McCrea by the colored people.

Ben said that when he enlisted, he was stripped and examined. He said that he had a hernia while on the march from Columbia, South Carolina to Richmond, Virginia caused by a wagon that got stuck in a mud bog at Lynch's Creek, South Carolina. While helping to take the wagon out of the mud bog, he strained himself causing a very large noticeable hernia. He suffered from that hernia which continued to get worse the older he got.

Ben McCrea is another example of the brave men of the 135th USCT risking their health for their freedom and that of their families for a better life for themselves and the nation. He died July 8, 1904, at the age of sixty-four.

by GEORGE E. LEMON, of Washington, D. C., and is exclusively

at No. 5 Rose Lane Charleston, County of Charleston, State of South Carolina, who, being duly sworn according to law, declares that he is the identical Benjamin McCrea, who entered service during the War of the Rebellion under the name of Benjamin McCrea on or about the ____ day of Feby 1865, as Private in company G of the 103 regiment of U.S.C.T. commanded by Capt Fleming, and was HONORABLY DISCHARGED at Louisville Kentucky, on or about the ____ day of December, 1865, by reason of being mustered out of service; that his personal description is as follows: Age, 44 years; height, 5 feet 9 inches; complexion, dark; hair, black; eyes, black. That he is now suffering from Injury received at Lynches Creek 16 in Feb 1865 from wagon train running over his right leg at night, assisting the wagon train to cross said Lynches Creek and have been suffering from said Injury ever since my discharge at Louisville Kentucky

and that the said disability is of a permanent character, and is not the result of vicious habits, and that it incapacitates him from the performance of manual labor in such a degree as to render him unable to earn a support, and that this declaration is made for the purpose of being placed upon the pension roll, under the provisions of the Act of June 27, 1890. That he has not been employed in the military or naval service otherwise than as stated above

is prepared by GEORGE E. LEMON, of Washington, D. C., and is

---

years, a resident of Charleston in the County of Charleston and State of So Ca, whose Post Office address is 103 Hanover St. Charleston S. C. and ____ aged ____ years, a resident of ____ in the County of ____ and State of ____, whose Post Office address is ____ well known to me to be reputable and entitled to credit, and who, being duly sworn, declared in relation to the aforesaid case as follows:

That he is a cousin to the deceased soldier, Benjamin Esau, alias Mc. Cra.--- That he was at the wedding of his present widow and his ~~uncle~~ cousin Benjamin. That they were married on the 21st. day of January A. D. 1881 by the Rev. Mr. Appler. That affiant does not know of any Church or family record of marriage. That the Rev. Appler was a missionary preacher.--- That affiant was present at said ceremony of marriage.- That the Claimant had never been previously married to the date of her marraige of Benj. Esau- that affiant knew her from girlhood.- That she is still the widow of Benj. Esau.

NOTE.—Affiants should state how they gained a knowledge of the facts to which they testify.

PENSION OFFICE
SEP 9 1904

State of South Carolina } Claim of Benjamin
County of Charleston } McCra Co. G. 135th

U.S.C.T. Cf #556.393

On this 5 day of September 1896 Personally
appeared before me C.C. Murphy [illegible]
Benjamin McCra. The Claimant a citizen of
Charleston S.C. who being duly sworn, declare
in relation to aforesaid case as follows.
The incurrance of hernia of left side
took place while on march from Columbia So. Car to Richmond Virginia.

The incurrance of hernia of left side
took place while on march from Columbia So. Car to Richmond Virginia.
under following circumstances. Our
wagon train got stuck in a mud-bog
at Lynch's Creek So. Car about the month
of March 1865 and while assisting in
taking said wagon train out of
mud-bog I over strained my self
Causing a very noticable hernia to
take place while in the service from
which I suffered to some extent continuing and progressing with age, being
now of immense proportions often pros-
trating me in bed, seriously affecting me

taking said wagon train out of
mud bog I over strained my self
causing a very noticable hernia to
take place while in the service from
which I suffered to some extent continuing and progressing with age, being
now of immense proportions often pros-
trating me in bed, seriously affecting me
and rendering me totally unable to perform manual labor, for more than
3 years. is permanent in character
progressive in nature and is not
due to vicious habits.
My oral statements are made to Geo. P.
McClay at Charleston S.C. September 5th

1896 who prepared affidavit in my
presence and I did not use nor was
I aided or prompted by any written
or printed statement or recital
prepared or dictated by any other
person and not attached as an
exhibit to this testimony.
My P.O. Address is 149 Line Street

Witnesses: Benjamin his x mark McCra
E. Grant Signature of Affiant
G W Gassim

Sworn to and subscribed before me a

SANDY McNAIR / BROWN

Sandy McNair/Brown was from Robeson County, North Carolina, and he, like so many of his comrades, joined the Pioneer Corps when Sherman's Army came through. He enlisted in the 135th United States Colored Troop Goldsboro, North Carolina. Like so many of the other pioneers he was stripped naked and was made to walk around and stand in all positions and his breast was thumped and he was examined. He said, "I do not know how many fellows examined me, but I was given a uniform and sworn into Company 'G.' of the 135th United States Colored Troop."

Sandy said they started from Richmond Virginia to Washington City about the time of the surrender of General Lee to General Grant. They had been on the march for about six weeks when he got hurt. They had some skirmishes, threw up some breast works, and destroyed bridges on the way, and they couldn't travel very fast. He ruptured his right side when he fell, while on a raid during a skirmish. He stated that they stayed at Richmond, Virginia about the time of the confederate's surrender.

He recalled he fell again on his right side in the camp at Bull Run, Virginia. "While climbing the hill through the deep cut, his feet stretched apart, and he heard something tear." The doctor told him it was his back. He also said he was hurt in the Manassas gap by the rocks crossing the water.

Sandy McNair changed his name to Brown, taking it after his father's name following his freedom in 1867. In the same year he got married to his wife, Elizabeth. He told her he got a bad rupture when he was on a raid in the army, and the rupture was on his right side. Ten years after he married Elizabeth, Sandy was hauling corn to Maxton, North Carolina and his mule ran away with him, which was hitched to the cart carrying the corn. He had a young mule and "it was right skittish." The mule ran and Sandy got struck in the eye with a bush, and he couldn't see out of that eye ever again.

Sandy was fairly young when he died in 1896.

No. 3.

FOR THE AFFIDAVIT OF AN OFFICER, ORDERLY SERGEANT OR COMRADE,

As to Incurrence of Claimant's Disability or Disabilities.

☞ *The person making affidavit on this blank should be careful to fill in all the blank spaces as fully as possible. The paper may be sworn to before any officer authorized to administer oaths.*

State of North Carolina County of Robeson

In the Pension Claim No. .... *of* Sandy Brown

late a private *in Co.* G *of the* 135th *Reg't of* U.S. Col'd Infty *Vols.*

personally appeared before me, a Notary Public *in and for the aforesaid County, duly authorized to administer oaths* [illegible] McNeill *aged* 58 *years, a resident of*
(Affiant's Name here.) (Age.)

Smith Township *in the County of* Robeson *and*
(Affiant's place of residence here.) (County here.)

State of North Carolina *who being duly sworn, according to law, states that he was a* private *in Co.* G *of the* 135th *Reg't of* U.S. Col'd Infty. *Vols.*, and was well acquainted with Sandy Brown alias Sandy McNair this applicant for Pension, and
(Here affiant should state claimant's name.)

know him to be the identical person of that name who served as a private in Company G 135th Regiment of United States Col'd Infantry Vols.
(Here name the State to which Reg't was accredited, and whether Infantry, Cavalry or Artillery.)

THAT THE SAID Sandy Brown alias Sandy McNair while in the line of duty,
(Claimant's Name here.)

incurred an injury to his right side [illegible] marching towards Washington City
(Here state the wound, injury or disease claimant first incurred.)

at or near Bull Run State of Virginia on or about
(State at or near what place claimant incurred his disability.) (Name of State.)

the ...... day of April year of 1865, under the following circumstances: said Brown
(Day.) (Month or season.) (Year.) (Here state all of the circum-

was unable to travel on morning after accident. Affiant did not see him
stances under which claimant incurred the disability. Write them out as fully as you can.)

when injured but saw him when he reported that afternoon his disability to the Captain of the Co.

CLAIMANT ALSO INCURRED ....
(Here state the second disability claimant incurred, if he incurred more than one.)

at or near .... State of .... on or about
(State at or near what place claimant incurred his disability.) (Name of State.)

Post-office address: Wakulla N C

Oct 31st, 189[illegible]

SIR:

In reply to your request I have to state that I am not well enough educated to write this in my own hand writing but I know that Sandy Brown alias Sandy McNair who was a comrade of mine in Co G 135 U S C I Vols during the late War between the states was hurt on the March from Raleigh N C to Washington D C about Bull Run Va [illegible] about the latter part of April or first part of May 1865 by falling in crossing the River on Rocks and ever since he has complained of soreness in his right side low down in the body and also of Rupture This is written at my dictation at Maxton N C on the aforesaid date in my presence by Mr B F McLean

Very respectfully,

Cain his x mark McNeill

COMMISSIONER OF PENSIONS,

Washington, D. C.

United States of America

BUREAU OF PENSIONS

Former payments covering any portion of the same time to be deducted

It is hereby certified That in conformity with the laws of the United States

Sandy Brown alias Sandy McNair

who was a Private Co. G, 135th United States Colored Infantry

Dear Secretary Sandy Brown has deceased of this life he died October 5 1932

is entitled to a pension at the rate of Seventy-two dollars per month, to commence May 23, 1929 and i am his wife writing to you to let you no that he is dead i am his second wife i have been married to him 17 or 18 years. i have done my duty for him he was down helpless in bed 7 month and ben lingering four years i had to help him up night an day his age was 89

Given at the Department of the Interior this tenth day of September one thousand nine hundred and twenty-nine and of the Independence of the United States of America the one hundred and fifty-fourth

Ray Lyman Wilbur

Secretary of the Interior.

Countersigned:

A. W. Morgan

Acting Commissioner of Pensions.

OK I Married in 1911—

at all before or at my enlistment. It was
when I got the fall in the army that caused
my rupture I was not sensible of the rupture
then.

When I enlisted in the U.S. army I was Stript stark naked. Was made to walk on my all fours and stand in all positions. My breast was thumped and I was really examined. I don't know that any one saw me examined I don't know how many doctors examined me.

Question. State when, where and how you incurred rupture of right side.

Answer. We started from Richmond, Va., to Washington City about time of surrender of Gen. Grant and Gen. Lee. We had been on the march about six days when I got hurt. We had had some skirmishes - thrown up some works and destroyed bridges on our way and we couldn't travel very fast. We started from Richmond about time of the Surrender. I got my rupture of right side by a fall. I was on march at night in a cut out in a road and I was walking on rolling side of the road and I slipped and fell and in trying to catch myself with my baggage with my legs stretched apart I strained my right side and my insides came out right then and there and I fell behind - I couldn't keep up. First day I couldn't keep up and second day when I crossed the line at Bull Run I was way behind and I came up that night and my Captain Oliver P. Fleming wanted to know what was the matter and before we got to Washington I gave out. After we got to Washington we took train and went to Louisville, Ky., and there I did not do duty - any other duty than garrison duty.

Question. Who was marching by your side when you got the injury causing rupture right side?

Answer. I cannot say positively but I think

CHARLES SPEAR / McRAE

In 1908, Charles Spear/McRae gave an oral application for a pension and stated his age was about 69 years old. When he enlisted, they put him down at twenty, but he thought he was closer to twenty-five. He was born and raised in Marlboro County near Bennettsville and was owned by Ben Spears. He lived there until Sherman's Army came by and carried him off. He was first put in the Pioneer Corps and had to build roads, help the wagons, and "do such work as that" until they got to North Carolina. At Goldsboro, they started to make up the regiment and at Raleigh, "we were examined and made into the 135th USCT" and he was put into Company "G."

He said they marched from Raleigh to Washington, D.C, and passed through Richmond, Petersburg, and Alexandria, and when they reached Washington, they had a review, but he was sick and went on to camp which was on a creek on the other side of Washington. He said they "stayed there awhile, and then took a train and went some distance and then took a boat to Louisville, Kentucky, and there they camped until mustered out. When we were on our way down the river a boat sank with some horses and white officers behind us, but I don't think any of them drowned.

After they mustered out, he went by train from Louisville, then to Augusta and then walked the rest of the way home. He said he had a "brother Henry Spears, and he was in the same company, and he was dead." He was married to Phyllis in 1889 who died in 1935. Charles died in 1917, on Joshua McCall's place and is buried in a colored ground close by.

3-289

DEPOSITION

Case of Charles McRae alias Spears, No. 1369308

On this 6th. day of Dec. 1906, at Florence county of Florence State of S.C. before me, E.H. Jennings, a Special Examiner of the Bureau of Pensions, personally appeared Charles McRae who, being by me first duly sworn to answer truly all interrogatories propounded to him during this special examination of aforesaid claim for pension, deposes and says:

My age about 69. When I enlisted they put me down at 20 but I think I was nearer twenty five. I did not know my age and they just guessed at it. Farmer. P.O. Effingham, S.C.

I was born and raised in Marlboro county near Bennettsville and was owned by Mr. Wm Spears, and I lived there until Sherman's army came by and carried me off. I was first put in the Pioneer Corps and had to build roads and help the wagons and do such work as that until we got into N.C., and then at Goldsboro they started to make up a Reg. and at Raleigh we were examined and made into the 135th. U.S.C.T. and I was put in Co. G. Gurley was our Col., Dixon was our Maj., Fleming was our Capt. and Jackson something was our first sergeant.

We marched from Raleigh to Washington and passed through Richmond, Petersburg and Alexandria, and when we reached Washington they had a review but I was sick and went on to the camp which was on a creek the other side of Washington. After we staid there awhile we took a train and went some distance and then took a boat and went to Louisville, Ky. and there we were in camp until mustered out. When we were on our way down the river a boat sank with some horses and white soldiers behind us but I dont think any of the men were drowned. We were first camped out at Louisville and then were in barracks. After we were mustered out we went by train from Louisville to Augusta, Ga. and then had to walk or make our way home the best way we could. I walked part of the way and got people to bring me in wagons part of the way and then finally reached this place and have lived here and about here ever since. I never went back to my home to live. I had a brother, Henry Spears, in the same company with me, but he is dead. I have not seen any of my company since I came here, except my brother, and he is dead. I have no photograph of myself, never had one. When I came here from the army I had on my soldier clothes and went by the name of Charles Spears

Page 4 Deposition a

3-187

Page

and went by that name here until the second year after the war when we registered to vote and then I just took the name of McRae so as to have a name of my own.

I had a discharge certificate that I was given at muster out and sent it to Washington, I have had it ever since I was in the army.

That is the one you show me with my papers. I will swear that I am the man who served in company G.135th. U.S.C.T. as Charles Spears.

I have never been married but once, that was to Phillis Sanders, we were married about five miles from here by Rev. Smith about 17 years ago, I dont know the exact date. I did not know it when I gave the date to the Bureau, just guessed at it then. She had lived with a man by the name of Sanders who left her and is now in Philadelphia. I dont know whether they were married or not. During slavery I lived with a woman by the name of Agnes and when I came here from the war she was here and I took up with her again and lived with her for four or five years but never married her tho we were known as man and wife. She left me and went in the country and I dont know what has become of her. have never heard that she was dead. After she left I took with and lived with Hean Jordan as her husband but never married her. She died about two years before I married Phillis but I dont know the date of her death.

My youngest child is Maria. she is about 18. I dont know the exact date of her birth. but she is nearly grown. Phillis is her mother.

Maria is the only child that sheand I ever had. She had one for Sanders.

There are plenty of people about here who know that I came here at the close of the war with my soldier clothes on and that I then went by the name of Charles Spears and that I changed my name after I came here.

This statement has been read to me and is correct and fully understood.

Attest.

E C Worswell

A. H. Mischeaux

his
Charles X Spears now McRae.
mark

Deponent.

Subscribed and sworn to before me this 6th. *day of* Dec. 1906, *and I certify that the contents were fully made known to deponent before signing.*

E. H. Jennings
Special Examiner.

State of South Carolina.

County of Florence.

Personally appeared before me Phillis McRea, claimant, and being duly sworn, deposes and says that she is about sixty five (65) years of age and her post office address is Effingham, S. C. and that she was never married prior to the marriage with Charles McRea alias Charles Spears, also said Chaeles McRea alias Charles Spears never married prior to said marriage, that that said Charles McRea alias Charles Spears lived with and supported deponent during his life time until his death on June 5th, 1917; that the said Phillis McRea has remained single since the death of her husband and that there was only one child born to them during their wedlock, which child was named Maria McRea. She was born on October 15th 1894 and is still living, and that deponent has resided at Effingham, S. C. since the death of her husband and still resides there.

her
Phillis + McRea ....SEAL
mark

Sworn to before me this 7th day of January A.D. 1918.

C. C. [illegible]
....
Notary Public.

Civ. War Div., Wid. Orig. 1104, 546.
Phillis McRea,
Charles McRea Alias Charles Spears,
Co. G. 135 U. S. C. Inf.

BRYANT COGDELL

Bryant Cogdell voluntarily enlisted in the 135th United States Colored Troop and was placed in Company "G," at the same time as Silas Cogdell and two other Cogdell's. He said, "we all served together, were together daily, and were discharged together." This is a good example of the surname used as that of the slave owner. Here, Lewis Cogdell of Wayne County, North Carolina had two hundred slaves on his plantation, all with the name of Cogdell. When the men joined the 135th USCT they all used their slave owner's name. Are they all related by blood or by name only? In this case, Bryant Cogdell was the uncle of Silas Cogdell, and both were tent mates.

Sometime in the later part of 1865 in Kentucky, Bryant said they were "guarding a railroad bridge when a train came on, we were on the bridge in the dark. Bryant was caught between the moving rail cars and his hip was crushed badly." He suffered all the way home and was lame for the remainder of his life.

Bryant married Lucinda Cox in 1869 after returning from the service. At the time of his death in 1895, he had two children under the age of sixteen. The other two Cordell's, who entered the service at the same time, were George and Stephen Cogdell, and were most likely related by name only.

(3—449.)

DEPOSITION

Case of Lucinda Cogdell, No. 636.189

near On the 11 day of June, 1897, at Princetown, County of Johnston, State of N.C., before me, D. H. KINCAID, a Special Examiner of the Pension Office, personally appeared Silas Cogdell who, being by me first duly sworn to answer truly all interrogatories propounded to him during this Special Examination of aforesaid pension claim, deposes and says: Age 56 or 7, occupation laborer. Res 2 1/2 M f P.O. I served in Co G 135 U.S.C.T. from March 1865 to Oct 1865.

Bryant Cogdell was my uncle we were slaves & belonged to Mr. Lewis Cogdell now dead. I do not know of any sickness or injury of any kind before the war except he was cut on the arm in a fight - it did not disable him any after it was healed.

We went away together & enlisted at Goldsboro N.C and we bunked together and Geo Cogdell who has moved to some place in Miss p.o.a. not known. Yes we were stripped & thoroughly examined when we enlisted & Bryant was apparently in good health. No sir I never knew Bryant to be in hospital in service. While coming from Kentucky at Louisville we were going to guard a bridge I disremember the place & Bryant Cogdell in getting off the train was butted by the cars

Page 13 Deposition C

Page 14

running back - injuring his hips.
I did not see him when the car butted him but saw him soon afterwards & he was complaining of being hurt. I did not see any injury - don't think the skin was broken - only mashed.
This happened early one morning before daylight. He did not go on guard & he did not do any thing for a right smart while.
George Cogdell alias Stephen was present. Since thinking about it I heard that George Cogdell died in Miss.
Jacob Drew alias Cogdell was in the car with us - his pos[t]o. not known.
Bryant hobbled to the barracks, but complained of his hip.
I reckon it was along about August that Bryant was injured.
No sir no one else was injured.
I heard him say that in getting off the box car that it caught him - he running back in some way.
I now recall that Lieut Cha. Hanna had his hand mashed the same morning that Bryant was injured.
Bryant was not treated in serv

John Bucher

his
Silas X Cogdell
mark
Deponent.

Sworn to and subscribed before me this 11 day of June 1897, and I certify that the contents were fully made known to deponent before signing.

D. H. Kincaid
Special Examiner.

(3-148)

DEPOSITION

Case of Lucinda Cogdell, No. 636,189

near Princetown, 17 day of June, 1897, at County of Johnston, State of N.C., before me, D. H. KINCAID, a Special Examiner of the Pension Office, personally appeared

Silas Cogdell, who, being by me first duly sworn to answer truly all interrogatories propounded to him during this Special Examination of aforesaid pension claim, deposes and says: Age 56 or 7, occupation laborer. Res 2½ m f P.O. I served in Co G 135 U.S.C.T. from March 1865 to Oct 1865.

Bryant Cogdell was my uncle. We were slaves & belonged to Mr. Lucian Cogdell now dead.

I do not know of any sickness or injury of any kind before the war except he was cut on the arm in a fight - it did not disable him any after it was healed.

We went away together & enlisted at Goldsboro N.C. and we bunked together and Geo Cogdell who has moved to some place in Miss. does not know. Yes we were stripped & thoroughly examined when we enlisted & Bryant was apparently in good health. No sir I never knew Bryant to be in hospital in service. While coming from Kentucky, at Louisville we were going to guard a bridge I disremember the place & Bryant Cogdell in getting off the train was butted by the cars

Page 1 B. C.

Page 14

running back - injuring his hip.
I did not see him when the car butted him but saw him soon afterwards & he was complaining of being hurt. I did not see any Injury - dont think the skin was broken - only mashed.
This happened early one morning before daylight. He did not go on guard & he did not do any thing for a right smart while.
George Cogdell alias Stephen was present. Since thinking about it I heard that George Cogdell died in Miss.
Jacob Drew alias Cogdell was in the car with us - his p.o. add. not known
Bryant hobbled to the barracks, but complained of his hip.
I reckon it was along about August that Bryant was injured.
No sir no one else was injured
I heard him say that in getting off the box car that it caught him the running back in some way
I now recall that Lieut Cha. Hanna had his hand mashed the same morning that Bryant was injured.
Bryant was not treated in serv

John Bucher

his
Silas X Cogdell
mark
Deponent.

Sworn to and subscribed before me this 11 day of June, 1897, and I certify that the contents were fully made known to deponent before signing.

D. H. Kincaid
Special Examiner.

(3—448)

DEPOSITION

Case of Leanna Cogden. No. 636.189

On the Cont day of , 189 , at
County of
State of , before me, D. H. KINCAID, a
Special Examiner of the Pension Office, personally appeared
, who, being by me first duly sworn to answer
truly all interrogatories propounded to him during this Special Examination of aforesaid
pension claim, deposes and says: for the injury as we
did not have a surgeon. I don't
know that he did anything
but lay about the barracks.
Our Sgt was John Jackson poor
not known.
No sir I don't think Bryant
went on duty again - as we
went back to Louisville in about
a month & went into barracks
& it was not long before we
were mustered out.
Yes he was able to do light
duty - but we had nothing
to do.
No sir I do not recall where
the bridge was - but it seems
to me it was called "Saltcatche"
No sir he was not ruptured that
I ever heard of when he received
the injury - in fact I never heard
of him being ruptured.
No sir I do not know
of any other disease - disability
or injury he had in service - except he had the diarrhoea like
all of us had - I don't know
that it became chronic

Page 5 Deposition C

Page 16

No sir I do not Know that he had any rheumatism in service or chills & fever.

Q What was his physical condition when M.O.? Ans. I did not hear him complain of anything except his hip — which one I do not recall. He never could march like he could before he was injured. We came home together & he went to Newbern & then Kinston & I did not see him again till the year before he died when I visited him & I testified in his case.

B.J. 8 I have heard read and it is not wholly correct — We marched all the way from Kinston N.C. to Washington D.C. & I did not see Bryant when he was injured & I do not Know that his hip was dislocated. It is my best recollection that we had gone out from Louisville Ky to guard some bridge when Bryant was injured.

B.J. 2 is not wholly correct where it differs from my deposition.

B.J. 3 is not wholly correct where it conflicts with what I have told you. Q Explain the discrepancies? Ans. I do not Know of making any such statements.

Not interested. Questions understood & answers correctly recorded

Attest

John Bircher

(No other available attesting witness)

Selas his X mark Cogdell
Deponent.

Sworn to and subscribed before me this 11 day of June, 1897, and I certify that the contents were fully made known to deponent before signing.

D.H. Kincaid
Special Examiner.

CHAPTER 10

INSPIRATIONAL STORIES WITH EPIC CHALLENGES AND TRIUMPHS.

Steaming To Louisville, Kentucky

COMPANY "H"

INCLUDED IN THIS CHAPTER ARE EXTRACTIONS FROM THE PENSION RECORDS OF;

MORRIS McDUFFY
HARRY RAWLS / ROYAL / MARTIN
DAVID COX
HENRY CHESTNUT

MORRIS McDUFFIE

Sandy McDuffie was the grandson of Morris McDuffie from Marion, South Carolina. He lived in Dillon, South Carolina, and lived with Morris at the time of his death on the 12th day of September 1926. Morris left no property except for a two-horse wagon, which was given to one of his creditors at the time of his death, along with some furniture worth approximately $20.00.

Morris was married twice as per the record, the first wife being Janie, (deceased), and the second being Amie who died in 1925. He also had a son Daniel Bob McDuffie who lived in Hamer, South Carolina. Morris lived with Sandy on a nearby plantation and Daniel had seen him often.

Morris McDuffy served as a private in Company "G," 135th United States Colored Troop and was recorded as 5'-8" tall and was born about 1840 near McGrogan's, Robeson County North Carolina. In his later years, he was nearly blind and extremely feeble from old age. He had to be cared for continually due to his poor health. He complained of loss of sight in his right eye which he claims was caused while in the service of the 135th USCT, in the civil war. While working on a road near Washington, D.C., he received a "lick near his right eye from a sack" that was thrown at him on the road. It hit him by his eye, and it caused it to get inflamed which caused the eye to finally go out and he lost his sight.

In Morris's deposition, he said that he had no education and was unable to read, write, or even spell his name. Both Alfred Kinney and H.B. Bertha said that they were in the same company as Morris while in the 135th USCT. Under oath, Morris recalled that he was wounded on the right side of the head caused by a rock that was thrown at him while on the road near Georgetown not far from Washington, D.C. In addition, he had pneumonia in the month of June 1865, while on the march, and had suffered from it ever since.

The record showed that Morris died in 1926. A claim for burial expenses was submitted and by 1933 the government still had not paid the $100.00 burial expense claim.

STATE OF SOUTH CAROLINA, RE: Widow Division, C. S. 1,063,312, Morris McDuffie, H, 135 USC Inf.

COUNTY OF DILLON.

PERSONALLY APPEARED before me, Sandy McDuffie, who on being first duly sworn says: That he is thirty years of age and is a resident of Dillon County, South Carolina and that his postoffice address is Hamer, R. F. D. No. 2. That deponent is a grandson of the late Morris McDuffie who died on September 12th, 1926 and who at the time of his death was receiving a pension under certificate No. 1063312. That deponent lived with the said Morris McDuffie at the time of his death and had been living with him continuously all of deponent's life. Deponent knows that the said Morris McDuffie left no property or estate whatever except one two-horse wagon and some household furniture all of which did not exceed in value the sum of $20.00. That none of this property had any market value and nothing whatever

and is a resident of Dillon County, South Carolina and that his postoffice address is Hamer, R. F. D. No. 2. That deponent is a grandson of the late Morris McDuffie who died on September 12th, 1926 and who at the time of his death was receiving a pension under certificate No. 1063312. That deponent lived with the said Morris McDuffie at the time of his death and had been living with him continuously all of deponent's life. Deponent knows that the said Morris McDuffie left no property or estate whatever except one two-horse wagon and some household furniture all of which did not exceed in value the sum of $20.00. That none of this property had any market value and nothing whatever
has been received by the estate of Morris McDuffie for this property. Deponent delivered the wagon to one of the creditors of the said Morris McDuffie for the reason that the creditor could use it to some advantage and for the further reason that deponent was not able to sell it for anything whatever. It is possible that this property was appraised at the time of his death at a total valuation of $41.00. However, nothing was realized from it and in fact it had no market value.

IN CLAIMS FOR THE [illegible] UNDER THE ACT OF MAY 1, 1920.

In the matter of the pension claim of Morris McDuffie No. ________

State of South Carolina, County of Dillon, ss:

On this 20th day of March 1939, personally appeared before me, a Notary Public within and for the County and State aforesaid Sandy McDuffie, aged 26 years, whose post-office address is Hamer STC. Rfd # [illegible] who states in relation to the aforesaid claim as follows:

Morris McDuffie is practically blind, being able to see a very little out of one eye only; that he is very feeble on account of old age and is able to walk only a few steps at a time; that he requires the constant presence and attention of an attendant to look after him and wait on him; a great deal of the time he is not able to get up or down without assistance and all of his physical wants have to be furnished him and brought to him

[Margin: (Here state fully the kind of aid and attendance rendered pensioner.)]

[Stamp: U. S. BUREAU OF PENSIONS, MAR 26 1939, OFFICE OF THE COMMISSIONER]

Sandy McDuffie
(Affiant's Signature.)

Subscribed and sworn to before me this 20th day of March, 19[illegible] and I certify that the contents of this affidavit were fully made known and explained to the a[illegible] before the oath was administered, and that I have no interest, direct or indirect, in the prosecution [illegible]

DECLARATION FOR INVALID PENSION.

State of North Carolina, County of Robeson, ss:

On this 12th day of May, A. D. one thousand nine hundred and two personally appeared before me, J. D. Jones a Notary Public within and for the County and State aforesaid, Morris McDuffie, aged 64 years, a resident of the of Albriton County of Marion, State of S C who, being duly sworn according to law, declares that he is the identical Morris McDuffie who was ENROLLED on the 27 day of March 1865, in Co H 135 Reg U S C I as a private (Here state rank, company, and regiment in Military service, or vessel, if in the Navy.) in the service of the United States in the war of the rebellion, and served at least ninety days, and was HONORABLY DISCHARGED at Louisville K, on the 23 day of October 1865. That he has not been employed in the military or naval service otherwise than as stated above. ______ (Here state what the service was, whether prior or subsequent to that stated above, and the dates at which it began and ended.)

That he was not employed in the Military or Naval service of the United States BEFORE the 27th day of March 1865, or AFTER the 23 day of October 1865.

[NOTE.—Insert date of first enlistment and final discharge.]

That he is totally unable to earn a support by manual labor by reason of loss of (Here name ALL disease, injuries, or wounds from which disabled, and state WHEN, WHERE, and UNDER WHAT CIRCUMSTANCES each wound or injury was incurred as nearly as possible.) sight of right eye and general disability caused by age. Loss of sight of right eye occurred at his home in Marion County S.C. about 1869 from a pain in same due in his head

That said disabilities are not due to vicious habits, and are, to the best of his knowledge and belief, permanent. That he has not

the United States as a private in Co H 135 Reg army at civil war, he he received a wound on the right side of head caused by a lick from a rock which was being thrown on the road near Arlington not far from Washington which was during the month of June had Pneumonia before I received the lick or would on the head while in service in the year 1865. First attack of Rheumatism was during a march from Alexandria va to Cedar Point va. have had attacks and suffer with it more or less ever since. Morris McDuff[illegible]

Sworn to before me

[illegible] 1900

November [illegible], 1940

[illegible]

XC-2 527 405
McDUFFIE, Morris

Mrs. Flora McDuffie
Maxton, North Carolina

Dear Mrs. McDuffie:

This is in reply to your letter dated October 10, 1940, addressed to the President of the United States in connection with your charge for nursing Morris McDuffie who died on September 13, 1926.

Due to the voluminous amount of mail received by the President, it is impossible for him to answer each letter personally; therefore, your letter has been forwarded to this office for reply.

The only amount payable toward the expenses of last sickness of a pensioner is the accrued pension which may be due from the date of last payment to the date of the pensioner's death. The records show that the veteran was receiving pension at the rate of $72.00 per month. He was last paid to September 4, 1926; therefore, there was due nine days' pension at the rate of $2.40 per day, or $21.60. An award in the amount of $21.60 was approved in favor of Sandy McDuffie, R. R. #2, Box 78, [illegible], South Carolina, and forwarded for payment on January 24, 1931.

The Veterans Administration, as you will appreciate, has no alternative except to follow the explicit provisions of the governing law and, as a consequence, is without authority to authorize payment in excess of the $21.60 awarded in this case however unfortunate or extenuating the circumstances may be.

Very truly yours,

E. J. HINTON
Director
Dependents & Beneficiaries Claims Service

HARRY RAWLS / ROYAL / MARTIN

Harry Martin, as he was known, was born in Sampson County North Carolina and listed his occupation on the pension questionnaire as slave/farmer. He identified scars on his body as being on his back and right hand. His right hand was crushed while working on breastworks during the Civil War. Prior to the time of his enlistment in Company "H," of the 135th USCT, he was owned by Whitney Rawls and Lewis Martin. Although he applied for his pension under the name of Harry Rawls, he was asked if he had been known by any other name, and he listed the name, Harry Martin. The pension documents also listed his name as "Royal," most likely because of how the name was spelled from pronunciation.

The special examiner looking into Harry Rawls/Martin was doing so because of the different names regarding the pension application and the request for an increase in pension. The examiner discovered that Harry was born at the Martin Plantation in North Carolina. When one of the Martin girls married a Rawls, Harry was taken off to the Rawls Plantation. He then took up the name of Rawls and later ran away from his master to go to war. After he was discharged from the 135th USCT he went back to North Carolina to live with his mother. This is when he took up the name Martin, which was that of his mother and he had gone by that name ever since.

The examiner stated that since the people who formerly owned Harry Martin are dead, he was unable to find out from authoritative sources his true name and age. He gave his age as nineteen when he enlisted in the service but was told by Whitney Rawls that he was probably older. The examiner assumed that he had to take from the record his correct age, and "by the looks of his appearance, he judged that to be about correct." The examiner went on to document that Harry "speaks like all the negroes do here, with poor pronunciation, and it was in this way his name came to be spelled Royal." This record was signed by A.R. Smith, Special Examiner.

In the file of Harry Martin, there are declarations by Lewis Moore, Silas Cogdell, and Peter Brewer stating that Harry Rawl/Royal was the same person as Harry Martin.

The 135th USCT Research Team, Inc. has been able to find numerous descendants of Harry Martin, in fact, the farm he owned is still in the family in Wayne County, North Carolina, and they still work the land to this very day.

DECLARATION FOR PENSION.

THE PENSION CERTIFICATE SHOULD NOT BE FORWARDED WITH THE APPLICATION.

State of North Carolina, County of Wayne, ss:

On this 2nd day of Oct, A. D. one thousand nine hundred and thirteen, personally appeared before me, a Clerk Superior Court within and for the county and State aforesaid, Harry Rawl, known now as Harry Martin, who, being duly sworn according to law, declares that he is 70 years of age, and a resident of [illegible] Mount Olive, county of Wayne, State of North Carolina; and that he is the identical person who was ENROLLED at Goldsboro North Carolina, under the name of Harry Rawl, on the ___ day of March, 1865, as a Private, in Co. H. 135th Regiment U. S. Colored Volunteer Infantry

(Here state rank, and company and regiment in the Army, or vessels in the Navy.)

in the service of the United States, in the Civil war, and was HONORABLY DISCHARGED at Louisville Ky, on the Record recods the date, 18__.

(State name of war, Civil or Mexican.)

That he also served ___

(Here give a complete statement of all other services, if any.)

That he was not employed in the military or naval service of the United States otherwise than as stated above. That his personal description at enlistment was as follows: Height, 5 feet 7 inches; complexion, dark; color of eyes, dark brown; color of hair, black kinky; that his occupation was servant; that he was born about 1843, at in Sampson Co. N. C.

That his several places of residence since leaving the service have been as follows: in Wayne Co. N. C.

(State date of each change, as nearly as possible.)

That he is a pensioner under certificate No. 1,173,840. That he has ___ applied for pension under original No. ___

That he makes this declaration for the purpose of being placed on the pension roll of the United States under the provisions of

---

July [illegible]

Com Pensions
Washington D. C.
Dear Sir

I am drawing a pension of $12 per month. Pension no 1153860. I was a private Co H 135th Reg U. S. Cold Volunteer Infantry. I was formerly called & known as Harry Rawl but my name should be as my pension shows Harry Martin. I think I am entitled to an increase of pension as I learn an act was passed in 1912, I would be glad you would write me the amt of back pension on account of this increase that is due me & when you write send me blanks if there are any to fill out. I am 70 yrs of age.

Very Respectfully
Harry Martin

DEPOSITION A

Case of [illegible] known as Harry Martin, No. [illegible]

On this 18th day of February, 1909, at Mt. Olive, County of Wayne, State of N.C., before me, [illegible], a special examiner of the Bureau of Pensions, personally appeared Harry Martin, who, being by me first duly sworn to answer truly all interrogatories propounded to him during this special examination of aforesaid claim for pension, deposes and says: I am 65 years of age; my post-office address is R F D #4, Box 27 Mt. Olive, N.C. I am the identical man who served as private in Co H 135 U.S. Colored Inf. during the Civil War. I dont know the date that I was enlisted but it was in Goldsboro N.C. I served about ten months and was discharged at [illegible]ville Ky. cant remember the date of my discharge. I had a discharge certificate but it was lost. It was lost by old [illegible]

ville Ky. cant remember the date of my discharge. I had a discharge certificate but it was lost. It was lost by old [illegible]

[illegible] when I gave it to [illegible] in order to get my pension claim allowed. I think it was in March that I enlisted. I was discharged after the surrender. I had no service in either the U.S. Army or Navy before or after the before mentioned service. I have filed a [illegible] on any claims for pension the last one about twenty years ago. I dont know under what act they were filed or when. I was born in Sampson County Sampson Co N.C. I dont know when I was born and have no bible record or any kind of record showing the date of my birth. I was about 19 years of age when I enlisted. At enlistment I gave my occupation as farmer. I dont know my height at enlistment but the

Page 7 Deposition A

2

simply in office but was known as Cpl
&c. I had no permanent marks or
scars on my person and had no special
peculiarities of speech or habits. I tried
to get a copy of the date of my birth from
my former boss Whitney Rawls but he
did not have it on his records because I
was not born on his plantation. I was
born on old man Dick Martin's plantation
but he and all of the people that I knew
of are dead. My captain's name was
Brock. Lieut Powell. Sergeants Henry
Green, Cornay Kimbert & Squire Reddick.
Corporals Lewis Moore and I cannot remember the rest of them. Privates Allen
Whitney, Wilson Wellons, Henry Barry
I cannot now write. I have no picture
[illegible]
either in group or by myself. I would
further mention of the names of comrades
I have sent to you which of them would
likely be able to recall you, should they
be shown your picture. Those that you
have marked "x" would likely remember me
the men who know that I am the one and
identical man who served in Co. B 5th
U.S.C. Inf. though they were not members
of my company though of my regiment
are Silas Langley, Princeton, Johnston Co.
N.C. and Lewis Moore in my company a
my tentmate who lives at Atkinson, Pender
Co N.C. Peter Bremer of Kenner N.C. who
was in my regiment also knows that I am
the person I claim to be. Also Erving Parker
who now lives in Georgia somewhere I don't
know the name of the place that he moved to
[illegible]

Rawls I was named Harry Martin
from the time that I was a boy up until
my mistress married a Rawls; I then
changed to Martin Rawls and went by the
name of Harry Rawls. I served through
out the war as Harry Rawls and after I
was discharged I came back to my Mother
with whom I lived and was called by her
as Harry Martin and I have been so called
ever since. My I [illegible] ever since under the
name of Martin. I swear that Harry Rawls
and Harry Martin are one and the same
man. I enlisted in Goldsboro, staid here only
a short time; we then march to Raleigh
N.C. were here about a month; then we
went to Richmond Va, were here about two

and Harry Martin are one and the same
man. I enlisted in Goldsboro, staid here only
a short time; we then march to Raleigh
N.C. were here about a month; then we
went to Richmond Va, were here about two
weeks, I was sick and they hauled me in
the ambulance to Richmond. The trouble with
me was measles; from Richmond we went
to Washington, N.C. the company marched
there, we were there a month or two. We then
went to Louisville Ky. by boat. I don't know
about how long we staid at Louisville before
we were discharged but know it was nearly
all summer until fall. Our company
never did any fighting; we fell out to strike
a line of battle but it did not materialize
into a fight. I was first in the hospital
at Raleigh N.C. for the measles. I was next
in the hospital at Louisville Ky. I had
not gotten well of the measles but don't know
what my trouble was. I had no other

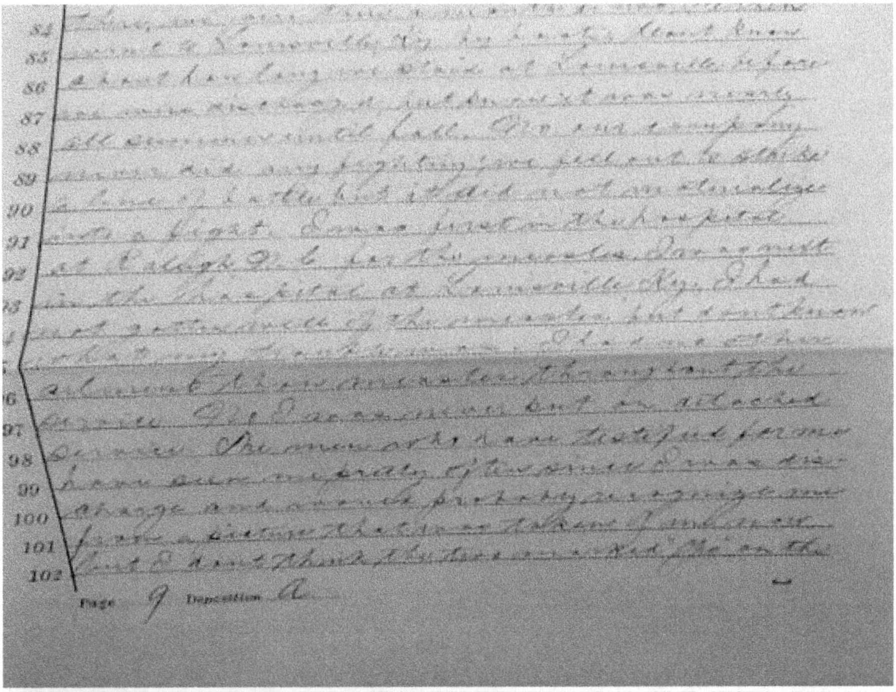

[illegible] sent to Louisville Ky. by boat. Don't know about how long we staid at Louisville before we were discharged, but we were there nearly all summer until fall. No, our company never did any fighting, we fell out to strike a line of battle but it did not develope into a fight. I was first in the hospital at Raleigh N.C. for the measles, and again in the hospital at Louisville Ky. I had not gotten well of the measles, but don't know what my trouble was. I had no other ailment that I remember through out the service. No I was never out or attached service. The men who have testified for me [illegible] have seen my [illegible] of the service I was discharged and [illegible] probably recognize me from a picture that was taken of me [illegible] but I don't think they would recognize me on the

Page 9 Deposition A

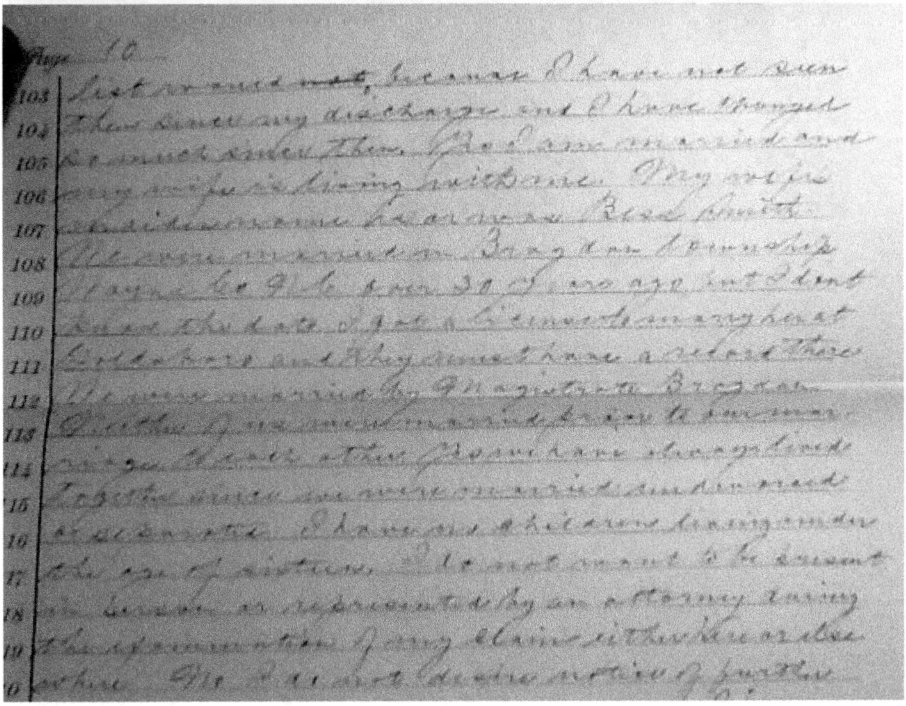

Page 10

list one now, because I have not seen them since my discharge and I have changed so much since then. No I am married and my wife is living with me. My wife's maiden name was Bess Smith. We were married in Brogden township Wayne Co N.C. over 30 years ago but I don't know the date. I got a license to marry her at Goldsboro and they must have a record there. We were married by Magistrate Brogden. Neither of us was ever married prior to our marriage. [illegible] have [illegible] together since we were married and never divorced or separated. I have no children living under the age of sixteen. I do not want to be present in person or represented by an attorney during the examination of my claim either here or elsewhere. No I do not desire notice of further

[illegible] together since we were married [illegible]. I have no children living under the age of sixteen. I do not want to be present in person or represented by an attorney during the examination of my claim either here or elsewhere. We do not desire notice of further examination either here or elsewhere. I have no attorney in my claim for pension. I have made no contracts to pay anyone any fee upon the allowance of my claim for pension. I have paid no fee to anyone. [illegible] or erasure before signing.

I have heard read the foregoing [illegible] questions have been understood and my answers are correctly recorded.

Witness:

V. C. Smith

Harry his X mark Martin

Deponent

Deponent.

Sworn to and subscribed before me this [illegible] day of February

DAVID COX

David Cox was from Darlington, South Carolina, and applied for his pension in 1901. David was in Company "H," 135th United States Colored Troop. The reason for filing a pension was given that, while in the service and when they were doing drills, the captain gave the command of "right face," that is when the man next to him turned the wrong way and the butt of his gun struck David in the head and injured his eye. He had not been able to see much out of that eye since. In addition, he had gradual suffering at times of rheumatism in his back and hip, caused by a fall he had in a skirmish one night in the Louisville area.

David's very first claim for a pension was rejected. The record indicated that under another application filed in February 1902, the soldier was allowed a pension of $6.00 a month under the act of June 27, 1890, for rheumatism and general disability. There was evidence that he further requested an increase in his pension.

The declaration by David said that he was born in Brownsville, South Carolina, and belonged to Mr. Moses Cox. After the war, David changed his name to David Williams. He indicated that he was 5' 9" tall and had a dark complexion and his occupation was as a farmer. David said that when they were in Louisville, Kentucky they had to camp in an old field part of the time and then they were moved into barracks. They helped guard the bridge part of the time while there also.

Aaron Sparks, who changed his name to Aaron Wilson after the war, said in his declaration that he was in the same Company "H," as David Cox. He said that they served under Captain Pocock and had Edward King as the Orderly Sergeant. David also said that Edward was his tent mate in service. It was also mentioned that William Evans who was in Company "H," changed his name to William Parker after the war. The record indicated that Captain Pocock was not with the company when they mustered out. He was "turned out" (released from service) just before that as they heard he had "taken a hand car and went to the depot and got in a collision breaking up the car and some other things."

David recalled that when Sherman's Army came through, they took him, Aaron Williams, and Jim McLauren and they were put in the Pioneer Corps. Upon reaching Goldsboro, North Carolina they were mustered into the 135th USCT. From Goldsboro, they marched to Raleigh and then to Washington, D.C. When they were mustered out in Louisville, Kentucky they were put on a train to Augusta, Georgia, and from there they had to walk the remainder of the way home. When David Cox returned from the army, he married Isabella and took her as his wife. They had a daughter named Theresa. Isabella died in 1895 and David died in 1912 in Darlington, South Carolina.

There has always been a debate about the black soldiers and if they carried guns. Most people thought they were only given guns when they got to Louisville Kentucky but after reading several of the pension records there are numerous examples of the men using guns for guard duty before they got to Louisville, Kentucky.

The Commissioner of Pensions.

Sir:-

The appellant, David William, alias Cox, formerly of Company H, 135th United States Colored Volunteer Infantry, enlisted March 27, 1865, and was discharged October 23, 1865. On May 16, 1900, he filed a claim for pension under the provisions of the Act of June 27, 1890, alleging permanent disability due to rheumatism and senility, which application was amended by an affidavit filed February 4, 1901, alleging disease of left eye. This claim was rejected by the Bureau, October 19, 1901, on the ground that a ratable degree of disability had not been shown since date of filing.

It appears that under an application filed August 19, 1902, soldier has been allowed $6 per month under the Act of June 27, 1890, for rheumatism and general debility.

On July 19, 1902, the attorney in the case filed an appeal in which he contended that by reason of soldier's old age and the evidence showing disability due to rheumatism, the action of the Bureau was unjust and erroneous.

Soldier appeared before a board of examining surgeons September 12, 1900, the certificate of which describes him as a

man 5 feet 10 inches in height, weighing 145 pounds, and 57 years of age, and states there is muscular rheumatism in all parts of his body, "especially the left shoulder, right knee and leg, and left side and hip." After showing that soldier's heart is normal, that there is no marked disability from sore eyes or impaired vision, the certificate concludes as follows:

> General and senile debility; He appears to be much older than age given, though there is a fair amount of vitality.

The board recommended a rating of $10 per month.

An affidavit of Dr. John H. Harden was filed October 17, 1900, in which he stated he had been acquainted with soldier for four years previous, and that he had the appearance of a dyspeptic and one who had suffered much physical pain. He further stated in part as follows:

> His features are drawn; his figure is thin and stooped. He has suffered much with rheumatism of back, hips and knees. His knee-joints are somewhat enlarged. He dates his trouble in his hips to a fall received at Louisville, Kentucky, during the last year of the war. * * * His eyes are badly affected and sometimes he is almost blind. He is often unable to perform the work required of a farm laborer and on the whole he is unfit and incapable of earning his living by any manual labor he can do.

The certificate of medical examination upon which soldier was subsequently placed upon the pension roll corroborates the previous certificate, and goes into more detail. Regarding general and senile debility it states as follows:

> He is considerably below par and is in no condition to make a support by manual labor. He looks old and lank and lean. Has worked hard and been exposed.

WASHINGTON, D.C.

Charleston, S.C., Feb. 19th. 1902.

Sir:-

Herewith I have the honor to return the papers in the claim of David Williams alias Cox, late of Co. K, 135th, U.S.C.I., No. 1242767.

This case was referred for examination as to identity and came to me for the initial investigation.

I questioned claimant and the witnesses carefully and I am satisfied from their statements that he is the man he represents himself to be. Records in my possession show that Capt. L. D. Forney was dismissed from the service on Oct. 20th. 1865.

This report is submitted for the consideration of the Chief of the Board of Review.

Very respectfully,

E. K. Jennings,

Special Examiner.

Hon. Commr. of Pensions,

Washington, D.C.

I interviewed Dave Lazure but his testimony added nothing to the case.

E. K. J.

State of South Carolina, County of Darlington, ss.

In the pension claim of David Cox

Co. K, Reg't 135th

personally came the claimant above named, who being duly sworn declares that he is the claimant in the above entitled claim; that his Post-office address is Society Hill

County of Darlington, State of South Carolina, and that

the disease of the eye was caused while in service in the following manner

while drilling at the command of the Captain, to Right face the man next to me turned the wrong way and the breech of his gun struck me on the head and since I have not been able

3 to see much out of the left eye and it has grown gradually worse ever since till now I can scarcely see out of it at all and is not able to do any work. I suffer greatly at times with rheumatism in back and hips which was caused by a fall I had in a skirmish one night at [illegible] Nashville [illegible] I [illegible] with rheumatism in my back

PENSION OFFICE U.S. FEB 4 1902

Signature by mark must be attested by two persons who write their names.

C. E. Powell.

David his x mark Cox

Affiant's signature

HENRY CHESTNUT

The fraudulent claim of Henry Chestnut and in the declaration, he claimed he could not tell who his colonel was, and he didn't remember the name of his Captain or Lieutenants, but they were all white men. Also, he did not remember the name of the Regimental Surgeon. He did believe that he was "some kind of a corporal," though as he had "some kind of stripes or something on his arm." He said the only member of his company whose name he remembered was Allen Chestnut and that "he tented with him every night and they ate and slept together." Henry said that they were "raised as boys together, Allen was his cousin, and they were both owned by old man Tom Chestnut."

They lived about three miles east of Clinton North Carolina and at the time of his declaration Henry said that old man Tom Chestnut was dead, and his wife was also dead, and didn't know of any other family. He said he was born in Clinton, North Carolina however had not lived there since the war. He recalled being twenty when he enlisted and his complexion, hair, and eyes were black.

Henry recalled that he and Allen were in the woods taking care of horses, corn, and meat and that "they had hidden out. When the Yankees came along, they took them, and they were taken to Clinton the first night." They then walked with Sherman's Army to Goldsboro. He did say that "Kilpatrick and Schofield were along with them and thought one was called General Weaver." He enlisted at Goldsboro, and they then went to Raleigh, "a place he had not seen before or since." Henry remembered he had a uniform and a musket. He was "mustered out at a place called Louisville, Kentucky."

After being mustered out Henry said he did not get home for about two years. He left Louisville and worked his way back home. He said he worked at a "sawmill at Goldsboro for a good long time." Asked by the examiner if he had been in any battles, he answered that "he hadn't but perhaps they came upon some bushwhackers occasionally and he heard some guns being fired." Henry said he never got any bounty but recalled being paid about $15.00 or $20.00 a month. He said that he had not been used to getting anything, so he didn't remember how much he got while in the service.

Henry recalled he wore a uniform and the only person who saw him wear it after mustering out was Allen Chestnut. He quit wearing it just as soon as he could get other clothes to put on after mustering out and he threw the uniform away.

Asked why he didn't claim a pension previously he answered that he did not want anyone to know he had been in the Army. He said ***"there was a lot of prejudice against colored people who had served in the Union Army and there were about fifteen killed near Clinton"*** where he was raised. When he went back there to visit, they ran him out. He went on to say that about twenty-five years previous a man shot at him, ***"he came along the road and asked who was there, and when I said 'me' he shot the ball passing over my shoulder. It was just meanness that caused him to shoot at me."***. Henry then stated that ***"times are better now,"*** regarding him being a soldier.

A remarkably interesting fact in the pension record of this soldier was the element of fraud involved following Henry's death. Henry Chestnut filed for his pension on December 11, 1890, and was pensioned under certificate #992,178. He died on February 20, 1902, and on March 3, 1902, Martha Chestnut, the alleged widow of Henry Chestnut filed her claim. These claims were filed giving a post office address being Hendersonville, North Carolina.

Now here is where the controversy comes in as on April 1, 1902, Henry Chestnut alleged service in the 135h USCT and giving a post office address at Dunn, North Carolina filed a claim under the act of June 27, 1890. As such the papers in this claim were referred to a special examination with respect to the widow Martha Chestnut under the inquiry made by the claim of Henry Chestnut. When the investigation was initiated at Dunn, North Carolina it was learned that there was no Henry Chestnut living within that mailing area, however the examiner learned from the postmaster there was a Sam Chestnut living in Newton Grove, about eighteen miles from Dunn. He was the individual who had filed claim #1,283,677 under the name of Henry Chestnut.

The confusion in this fraud case came when we learned that Sam Chestnut had in his possession the discharge certificate of Henry Chestnut and he claimed that he was the identical person who served in the war under the name of Henry Chestnut. By having the discharge certificate, Sam was able to convince Doctor Harper, who prepared the allegations of service and his disabilities, that he was in fact Henry Chestnut as shown in the fraudulent declaration.

Under investigation however, the special examiner in interviewing Sam Chestnut was able to discover that Sam was not able to identify or name any of the commanding officers in the regiment and was not able to give any information on the movement of the regiment or locations during the war. He claimed to have been wounded but didn't know where it happened and did not give the name of a single person who knew him prior to the war or who had known him since. Interestingly he also denied ever having a relative by the name of Henry Chestnut and never knew anyone by that name.

Sam Chestnut claimed that he had concealed the fact that he was a soldier for fear of physical harm and that he had thrown his uniform away as soon as he was discharged and was able to find other clothes. The examiner stated that Sam Chestnut had lived for many years in one of the best country neighborhoods he had seen in North Carolina and his neighbors spoke of him as being an industrious and law-abiding man. He noted that Sam was illiterate but of good intelligence, however, felt at the time of his interview with him that he was not being truthful.

The special examiner found out that the claimant, Sam Chestnut, was one of the children of the family of the mother, Matilda Chestnut owned as slaves by Tom Chestnut of Clinton, North Carolina, and the father was Sol Owen. The sons included Sam, Henry, and Peter and the daughters were Nannie and Easter. Henry enlisted in Company "H," 135th USCT and Sam went off with the army but soon tired and "slipped off" as detailed in the deposition of his sister Nannie.

The evidence showed that after the war Henry Chestnut returned to Clinton and then left with Matilda, his mother, along with his discharge certificate, and went to the mountains, Hendersonville, North Carolina. Later it was found that the mother, Matilda Chestnut, was living with Sam Chestnut at the time of her death and the discharge certificate fell into the hands of Sam Chestnut.

Although there was much more detailed information in the file regarding this case, in the mind of the special examiner, he was able to determine that the most recent claim by Sam Chestnut, under the name of Henry Chestnut, was fraudulent and recommended that it not be accepted and he recommended the prosecution of Sam Chestnut for attempting to defraud the Government. Unfortunately, there are other cases requiring a special examination of the pensions, where fraud was involved, some of which are also noted in this book however not all.

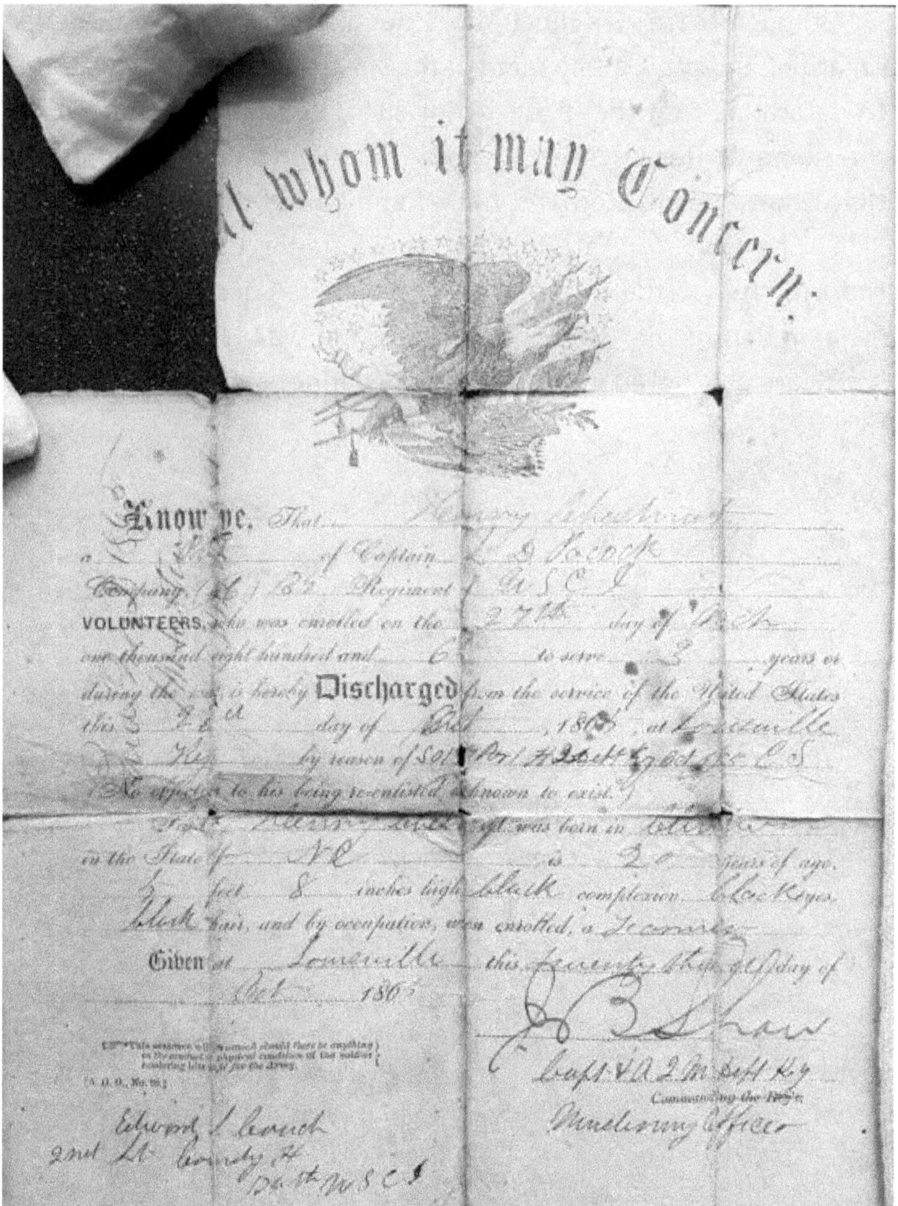

...l whom it may Concern.

Know ye, That Henry [illegible] a Pvt of Captain [illegible] Company (A) 122 Regiment U S C I VOLUNTEERS, who was enrolled on the 27th day of Oct one thousand eight hundred and 6[illegible] to serve 3 years or during the war, is hereby Discharged from the service of the United States this 23d day of Oct, 186[illegible], at Louisville Ky by reason of [illegible]

No objection to his being re-enlisted is known to exist.

Said [illegible] was born in [illegible] in the State of NC is 20 years of age, 5 feet 8 inches high, Black complexion, Black eyes, Black hair, and by occupation, when enrolled, a Farmer.

Given at Louisville this twenty third day of Oct 186[illegible]

J B Shaw

Capt & A Q M [illegible] Ky

Commanding the Reg't.

Mustering Officer

Edward [illegible]

2nd Lt [illegible]

[illegible] U S C I

N. B.—Examiners should be particular to have affiants sign on the line next below the closing words of their depositions so as to leave little or no space between their signatures and the end of their depositions.

3—290.
(Old No. 1—490.)

DEPOSITION A.

Case of Henry Chestnut, No. 1283,677.

On this 20th day of January, 1904, at Newton Grove, County of Sampson State of North Carolina, before me, John W. Hall a special examiner of the Bureau of Pensions, personally appeared Henry Chestnut, who, being by me first duly sworn to answer truly all interrogatories propounded to him during this special examination of aforesaid claim for pension, deposes and says: I am 59 years of age; my post-office address is Newton Grove, Sampson County, N.C. I gave Dunn, N.C as my P.O. address when I made my claim because I was up there when I made out my claim and the witnesses who signed for me lived there. Dr. Harper filled out my paper for me. It is about seventeen miles from here to Dunn. I never lived there.

My full name is Samuel Henry Chestnut and I am the identical person who enlisted and served during the civil war under the name of Henry Chestnut. I don't remember the company and regiment in which I served. When I was mustered out I was given a discharge certificate, which I gave to Dr. Harper of Dunn when I filed my claim. That was two years ago this coming April. I had had the paper ever since my discharge until I left it with Dr. Harper. I left it with Dr. Harper because he filled out my claim. He used to live about four miles from here and was my regular doctor. That was before he moved to Dunn. I have been to see him for medicine several times since he moved to Dunn.

Page 1. Deposition A.

6—49

Page 14 No sir, I can't tell you who my Colonel was nor do I remember the name of my Captain or Lieutenants. They were all white men. No sir, I don't remember the name of the Regimental Surgeon. I was kind of a corporal, seems to me like I had some stripes or something on my arm.

The only member of my company whose name I can remember is Allen Chestnut. I can't say positively that he was in my company, but I tented with him every night, we ate and slept together. He and I were raised as boys together, he was my cousin. We were both owned by old man Tom Chestnut who lived about 3 miles east of Clinton. He is dead now. His wife is dead and I don't know where there is any of the family. I was born at Clinton, N.C. I haven't lived there since the war. I was twenty years old when I enlisted, complexion hair and eyes black. I think I measured six feet. I was measured and examined by the Doctor when I went in the service. I don't remember that he stripped me. Allen Chestnut and I were in the woods taking care of horses, corn and meat &c which had been hid out when the Yankees came along and took us. They took us to Clinton the first night and then walked with Shermans Army to Goldsboro. I think they called it Shermans Army - I know that Kilpatrick and Schofield were along, and I think they called one General Weaver. It seems to me that I enlisted at Goldsboro, N.C. either there or at Raleigh, N.C. I went from Goldsboro to Raleigh; a place they called Raleigh - I hadn't seen it before or since. I don't remember when I got it, but I know

I had a uniform and a musket. I was mustered out at a place called Louisville, Ky. I went off in March and was mustered out in the Fall of the year. I don't know what year I went in the army but it was the year Sherman came through here. I didn't get home in about two years after discharge. I left Louisville, Ky. on muster out and worked on my way back, worked about Goldsboro in saw mill &c for good long time.

No sir, the company was not in any engagement while I was with it—perhaps we came up with bush-whackers sometimes and heard a few guns fired. We marched from Raleigh NC to Louisville, Ky., and while on the way I got a flesh wound in the left leg on the outside between the ankle and knee. I didn't get any treatment for it while in service. I don't know what place it was where I got the wound. I don't remember any place the regiment was at except Raleigh NC and Louisville, Ky. Of course it stopped while on the march but I don't remember the places.

I never got any bounty and don't know how much I was paid a month. It seems to me it was $15 or $20 per month, something along there. I hadn't been used to getting anything and don't remember how much I got while in the service. No sir, I did not drive wagon or work in the Quartermasters Department, I drilled and carried a gun. (Here I put claimant through limited manual of arms, and he seemed to understand the principal movements. JWH) I have not belonged to any military company since the war, nor have I drilled any since. I was never in the army except as shown by the discharge I gave Dr. Harper.

and I certify that the contents were fully made known to deponent before signing.

190

Page

Special Examiner.

I have no picture of myself. Had one taken about 29 years ago and my sister Easter Grady got that. I haven't seen ~~him~~ her

15

16 in about 18 years. I heard from her year before last. She was then living in Cumberland county N.C. but I dont remember her P.O. Her husband was named Isaac Groddy. I dont know what part of the county she lives in, if she is yet living. She was older than I am

The only person who ever saw me with a uniform on after muster out was Allen Chestnut. I quit wearing the uniform just as soon as I could get other clothes to put on after muster out. I threw it away.

No sir, I cant give you the name of any one who knew me before the war and since and who knows that I was in the army.

Yes sir, I thought that I was entitled to pension long before I filed my claim. I heard others talking about getting pension but I didnt want any one to know that I had been in the army is the reason I didnt claim before. There was more or less prejudice in this section against colored people who had been in the Union army. There were about fifteen killed near Clinton where I was raised and when I went ~~I went~~ back there on a visit they ran me out. About 25 years ago a man shot at me. He came along the road and asked who was there and when I said "me", he shot, the ball passing over my shoulder. It was just meanness that caused him to shoot at me. It was talked among the white people that I was a soldier but I never would own it. Times are better now, but I dont care now about them knowing I was a soldier.

With the exception of about one year when I pumped water at Bergaw, Rose Hill, Halifax and Dudley I have lived ever since

Attest: Julia A. Chesnutt — Henry his mark Chestnut

[illegible]

Inv Cf. #992.178
Henry Chestnut (deceased) H. 135 U.S.C. Inf.
W. O. #758.008
Martha S. Chestnut, Hendersonville, N.C.
Inv O. #1283.677
Henry Chestnut, H. 135 U.S.C. Inf.
P. O. Newton Grove, Sampson Co. N.C.

Raleigh, N.C. Feby. 8, 1904.

Sir:

On December 11, 1890, Henry Chestnut alleging service in H. 135 U.S.C. Inf., and giving postoffice address as Hendersonville, N.C. filed claim under the Act of June 27, 1890, and was pensioned under Certificate #992.178. January 7, 1891, he filed claim under the general law. He died on or about Feby. 20, 1902, and under date of March 3, 1902, Martha S. Chestnut, alleged widow, filed claim, her postoffice address being Hendersonville, N.C.

April 1, 1902, Henry Chestnut, alleging service in H. 135 U.S.C. Inf., and giving postoffice address as Dunn, Harnett Co. N.C. filed claim under Act of June 27 1890.

3

The papers in these several claims were referred for special examination under instructions contained in Law Division letter dated July 17 1902, with direction that the examination commence with the alleged widow, Martha S. Chestnut. The examination of that claimant having been completed, the papers come to this district for inquiry into the Invalid claim made by Henry Chestnut giving his address as Dunn, N.C.

Upon personal inquiry at Dunn I learned that there was no Henry Chestnut living within that mail delivery, but that there was a Sam Chestnut at Newton Grove, Sampson Co. N.C. some eighteen miles distant from Dunn, and that he was the person who had filed claim #1283,677 under the name of Henry Chestnut. This information I obtained from A.R. Wilson, Postmaster, and Dr. M. W. Harper of Dunn. Dr. Harper had in his possession a discharge certificate which had been given him for safe keeping by Sam Chestnut of Newton Grove at the time the declaration was executed. In fact Dr Harper prepared or wrote the allegations of service and disabilities as shown in the declaration.

Herewith is a statement made by this claimant in which he insists that his full name is Samuel Henry Chestnut and that he is the identical person who served during the civil war under the name of Henry Chestnut. He does not know the company and regiment in which he served, but states that at discharge he was given a discharge certificate which he left with Dr. Harper at time of making claim. He says the doctor "filled out" the claim.

It will be observed that this claimant denies or fails to name any of the commanding officers of the regiment and company, and the only comrade he names is Allen Chestnut, now deceased. He does

5 does not give me any history of the movements of the command —the only places mentioned being Raleigh, N.C. and Louisville, Ky.

He claims to have been wounded in the service, but does not name time or place. He does not give one the name of a single person who knew him prior to the war and who has known him since. He denies ever having a relation by the name of Henry Chestnut and says he never knew any one by that name. It will also be observed that he has, he says, always tried to conceal the fact that he was a soldier for fear of physical violence and that he threw his uniform away as soon after discharge as he could get a change of clothing.

This claimant has lived for many years in one of the best country neighborhoods I have seen in North Carolina and his neighbors speak of him as being an industrious and law abiding man. He is illiterate but of

6 good intelligence. I felt satisfied at the time I had him under examination that he

was deliberately lying to me, and I think that feeling was fully confirmed by subsequent developments.

It appears that this claimant was one of a numerous family the mother of whom was Matilda Chestnut owned as slaves by Tom Chestnut, Clinton, N.C., and the father was Sol Owen. Among the sons of Matilda were Sam, Henry and Peter and of the daughters Nannie and Easter. Henry enlisted in H. 135 U.S.C. Inf and Sam went off with the army but soon tired and "slipped off" (See deposition of Nannie Moore, sister) After the war they, Sam and Henry, returned to Sampson County, N.C. (Clinton) and Henry left with his mother Matilda his discharge certificate. He went off and the last heard of him, so far as the evidence taken by me shows, he was "on the mountains" (Dep. of Nannie Moore) no doubt he was heard from at Hendersonville, N.C. from which place he filed claim and where he died. The present claimant

after working around a few years
8 went to Johnson County, N.C. His
P.O. was Rome (His statement) ~~December~~
March 26, 1868, he married Madlina
Bennet. His name then was simply
Samuel Chestnut (Exhibit A) Rome
N.C. is not far distant from
claimants present home. Here
is the connection of the mothers
claim #343308 Matilda Chestnut filed
August 12, 1886, on account of service
of Henry Chestnut H. 135 U.S.C. Inf.,
and abandoned. It will be
noticed that the P.O. Rome was
written in the mothers application
and then changed to Harper.
At the time of the death of Matilda
Chestnut she was living with
Sam Chestnut and the discharge
certificate of Henry Chestnut
fell into the possession of
this claimant (Deps. John & Nannie
Moore) and after the death of
Henry Chestnut the claim now
under inquiry was filed - filed
almost simultaneously with that
of the alleged widow.

It is quite clear to my mind

3—1899.

M. N.

Department of the Interior,

Bureau of Pensions,

Washington, D. C., March 2, 1904.

The Honorable

The Secretary of the Interior.

Sir:

I have the honor to forward herewith the papers in the claims of

Henry Chestnut, deceased, late of Company H, 135" U.S. C.Inf., Cert.#992,178,

Matilda Chestnut, deceased mother of said soldier, Original #343,308,

Martha S. Chestnut, widow of said soldier, Original #758,006, and

Henry Chestnut, the alleged soldier of said service, Original #1283,677,

including two reports of special examination and an extract certified copy from this Bureau's records, showing fact and date of filing last mentioned claim, all for your consideration and reference to the Department of Justice, for transmission to the United States Attorney for the Eastern District of North Carolina, with a view to the prosecution of Samuel Chestnut alias Henry Chestnut, of Newton Grove, Sampson County, N.C., for the filing of false and fraudulent claim for pension in violation of section 5438, R.S.U.S.

STATEMENT OF FACTS.

The false and fraudulent claim in question was filed in this Bureau on April 1, 1902, the application having been executed in due form on March 25, 1902, before V. L. Stephens, Notary Public, at Dunn, Harnett County, N.C., and in said application the claimant alleged among other things, "that he is the identical Henry Chestnut who was enrolled on the 27th day of March, 1865, in Company H, 135" U.S.C.T., in the service of the United States in the war of the rebellion, and served at least ninety days and was honorably discharged at Louisville, Kentucky, on the 23rd day of October, 1865."

Said allegation is wholly false and fraudulent and was made in a wilful and deliberate attempt to defraud the government. This impostor, who executed and presented such fraudulent claim is Samuel Chestnut, a brother of the real soldier, Henry Chestnut, who died February 20, 1902, and who was a former husband of Martha S. Chestnut, the widow claimant above mentioned. The impostor never rendered any military or naval service, so far as can be determined, and the records of the War Department do not show his name in connection with any company of said regiment (see report from Record & Pension Office, dated 24th inst., among loose papers.) Sometime shortly after discharge Henry Chestnut turned his discharge certificate over to his mother, presumably for safe-keeping, and he left the vicinity of his old home for other parts and his whereabouts were unknown to the family for several years. In the year 1886, the mother believed that the soldier was dead and she applied for pension as a dependent mother; she was, of course, unable to prove the soldier's death and abandoned her claim; she died, as now alleged, soon after the earthquake and Samuel, this impostor, then obtained possession of the original discharge certificate of the soldier, which belonged to his brother Henry and which he has held and by the aid of which he attempted to establish his identity and his alleged service. The evidence to show this impostor"s real identity was secured on special examination and the same is summarized as follows:

Martha S. Chestnut, of Henderson, N.C., testified on September 23, 1903, before special examiner W.W. Anderson, that she was 45 years of age and the widow of Henry Chestnut, who served in Company H, 135" U.S.C.Infantry; that her husband was a pensioner at the time of his death at $6 per month (under Certificate No.992,178) and the affiant continued in part as follows: I think my husband told me his birthplace was Sampson County, N.C. + + + + + I was married to the soldier on November 15, twenty-four or twenty-five years ago at Spartanburg, S. C. + + + + My husband died on February 20, 1902. + + + My husband must have been over six feet tall, for I am five feet, seven inches and he could look down on my head; at his best he weighed 180 pounds; his complexion was dark brown; he said he had been shot in one of his ankles during the war, but I do not remember which one; there was a welt a little below the ankle on the outside, sometimes it would swell; I do not know whether the ball went into the ankle or not, he said it was the only wound he got while in the war. + + + I think Colleton was one of his bunk mates in the service and he is the only one whom I know that will know that my husband served in Company H, 135 U.S.C.Infantry. + + + + My husband's mother was named Matilda Chestnut, I heard him say so. She died at or near his old home about nineteen years ago. His sister Martha wrote to my husband that his mother had died; my husband has six or seven brothers and the same number of sisters; the names that I can remember are, John, Hardy, Samuel, Solomon, Peter, James, besides Martha, Tena, Lizzie, Easter, Nannie and Daphney; I think my husband said his old home was three or four hundred miles from here in the eastern part of the state; my husband went by his owner's name, his owner's boss was Thomas Chestnut and he took his last name.

S. of I.--5-

Sambo Colleton, of Fletchers, Henderson County, N.C., testified September 28, 1903, before special examiner W.W. Anderson, as follows: Age 56 years; occupation, farmer; I am not related to this widow claimant Martha S. Chestnut, nor interested in her pension claim; I became acquainted with her husband Henry Chestnut while in the army; we served in the same regiment; I was in Company D; I enlisted sometime in 1862 or 1863 and served to the end of the war in the same company all the time and was mustered out at Louisville, Ky. I became acquainted with Henry Chestnut after the big battle of Petersburg; he came from somewhere in the eastern part of North Carolina; he was a heavy, well built man about six inches taller than I am and I am five feet, four inches; he had no marks or scars that I remember; I saw him all the time in the army and knew him well; I saw him in the big battle at Petersburg and when we were in Kentucky; many times when we would stack arms after drilling, I would hear him complain that he had the headache and he would go off and sit down by himself until the drum beat again; I went back to South Carolina after the war; I don't know where Henry Chestnut went, as I never saw him any more after discharge until I came up here in 1868, where I have lived ever since; it was not until the year 1875 that I again saw Henry Chestnut, as it was sometime after I had moved up here; he was then living at Hendersonville, N.C., and after that I saw him often until he died; I was not at his burying, but I heard of his death in February or March, 1902, in Hendersonville; I know he was the same man whom I knew in the army, because I met him on the road the first time after discharge and I knew him and he knew me as quick as we saw each other; I don't know of any other man in the army by the name of Chestnut.

Harry Rawles, of Dudley, N.C., testifies under date of January 22, 1904, before special examiner John W. Hall, as follows: Age,60 years; occupation, farmer; I served during the civil war in Company H, 135" U.S.C.Infantry + + + + Yes sir, Henry Chestnut was in my regiment, but I don't remember that he was in my company; there was an Allen Chestnut in my company + + + + Yes sir, I knew Henry Chestnut before he went into the army, he and Allen Chestnut were both raised in Sampson County; I have not seen Henry Chestnut since the war, but I had a letter from him once, he was then up in the country in the western part of the state and he wanted me to make an affidavit in his claim for pension; Allen Chestnut is now dead. Yes sir, I think I would know Henry Chestnut if I was to meet him and talk with him. The only Chestnuts I knew in the regiment were Allen and Henry;

there was a Sam Chestnut in the same family near Clinton, N.C. but he was not in my company and regiment; he lives now not far from Newton Grove, N.C. I have seen him several times since the war, the last time two years ago; this Sam Chestnut has been in that community ever since about the close of the war and I have lived in this neighborhood ever since that time; this man Samuel Chestnut who lives now at Newton Grove, isnot the man who served with me in Company H, 135" U.S.C.Infantry during the civil war. Yes sir, I would know the Sam Chestnut who lives in Sampson County if I was to see him. No sir, the Henry Chestnut who served with me was never called Samuel. Yes sir, I knew Samuel Chestnut before the war, he lived up there near Clinton along with Henry and Allen Chestnut; these boys used to come to my house and they lived at old Tom Chestnut's; I swear most positively that the Samuel Chestnut who lives at Newton Grove, N.C. and whom I knew before the war and have known ever since, is not the man who served as Henry Chestnut in Company H, 135" U.S.C.Infantry.

John Moore, of Clinton, N.C., testified February 3, 1904, before special examiner John W. Hall, as follows: Age 69 years; I was born and raised near this place and lived in this neighborhood all my life; I was never in the United States army or navy; I lived within about three miles of Mr.Tom Chestnut before the war; I knew Allen Chestnut who was owned by Mr. Tom Chestnut and I also knew Henry, Sam and Peter Chestnut and my wife was their sister; I knew them all before the war and I married Nannie before war; I know that Allen and Henry Chestnut were in the war as soldiers, and Samuel and Peter went off with the army, but I don't know whether or not they were soldiers; Allen Chestnut is dead; I never saw any of the boys with a uniform on, but Henry had papers which showed that he had been in the war; Henry did not stay here long after he came back; before he went away he gave his army papers to his mother Matilda Chestnut and after she died, Sam, who lives at Newton Grove, got the papers and he has got the papers now; I don't know where Henry Chestnut is, when we last heard from him he was on the mountains, but I don't know what his post office address was; Samuel Chestnut, who lives at Newton Grove is a brother of Henry Chestnut and is a brother of my wife; Samuel is the only name I ever heard him called by; his name is not Samuel Henry Chestnut; Henry and Samuel were two different parties--they were brothers.

John Bunting, of Clinton, N.C., testified February 3, 1904, before special examiner J. W. Hall as follows: Age, 65 years; and affiant continued as follows: I was born and raised about four miles east of this place and about a mile from the place of Tom Chestnut; I was never in the war; I knew Allen Chestnut, I think he is dead; he was one of old lady Fannie's boys; I knew Matilda Chestnut, her husband was Solomon Owen; they had sons named Samuel, Henry, Peter and Solomon; they had a daughter Nannie and she is now the wife of John Moore and they were all owned by Tom Chestnut; Henry Chestnut was in the army that is what I heard and I was so told by those who were in the army; I never heard that Samuel Chestnut was in the army; Samuel lives at Newton Grove in the county, but I don't know where his brother lives; Samuel and Henry were brothers and they were both the sons of Matilda Chestnut; Henry Chestnut was not married when he went in the army and he was as near as I can remember about 18 years of age; he was of medium dark complexion, Samuel was the darker of the two; no sir, I never knew Samuel Chestnut who lives at Newton Grove to be known by any name except Samuel; I do not remember that I ever heard Samuel say that he was in the army; he did go off with the army, but I never heard that he was a soldier.

Peter Brewer, of Keener, Sampson County, N.C., testified February 8, 1904, before Special Examiner as follows: Age, 63 years; I served during the civil war in Company C, 135" U.S.C.Infantry; I know Allen and Henry Chestnut, who served in the same regiment with me; they were not in my company and I am not certain what company they were in, but I know they were in the same regiment; I first met them in service, and I knew them quite well in the service; I have no recollection that I have ever seen Henry or Allen Chestnut since we were mustered out. + + + + + Yes sir, I know Samuel Chestnut who lives at Newton Grove in this county and I have known him for twenty years or more; I never heard Samuel Chestnut say anything about ever being in the army and if he was ever in the army, I did not know it; he is not the man who served as Henry Chestnut in 135" U.S.C.Infantry + + + If the Samuel Chestnut who lives at Newton Grove was to tell me he served in my regiment, I would not believe him.

From the foregoing it is believed to be well shown that this alleged soldier is the brother of the genuine soldier, and that his correct name is Samuel Chestnut. To prove his identity with the person who executed the false and fraudulent application, evidence was secured as follows:

V. L. Stephens, of Dunn, Harnett County, N.C., testified January 21, 1904, before special examiner John W. Hall as follows: Age, 39 years; occupation, cashier of bank; on the 25th day of March, 1902, I was a duly qualified and commissioned Notary Public in and for Harnett County, N.C. On that day a colored man claiming to be Henry Chestnut appeared before me and executed a paper purporting to be a claim for pension against the United States on account of his military service; he signed the same in my presence by making his mark and also in the presence of J. M. Jernigan and M. L. Smith, who also signed the same in my presence and in the presence of the claimant as attesting and identifying witnesses; the oath was administered to the claimant's and witnesses just as the declaration purports to show on the date in question. I did not know him, but I knew the attesting witnesses.

M. L. Smith, of Dunn, N.C., testified January 20, 1904, before last named examiner, as follows: Age 31 years; occupation, restaurant; I am the identical M. L. Smith who appeared with the claimant Henry Chestnut and J. M. Jernigan before V. L. Stephen, Notary Public, on March 25, 1902, and signed the paper (B.J.1) which you show me. Henry Chestnut signed that paper in my presence and in the presence of the others named, by mark; the oath was administer to all of us at that time when the signatures were affixed. The man who signed the application is Henry Chestnut and was known to me as Chestnut, but I did not know his first name; he then lived and still resides at Newton Grove, N.C.

S. of I. -12

From the foregoing it appears that this offence was a bold and flagrant attempt to defraud the government by foisting upon it a false and fraudulent claim and the impostor's prosecution is vigorously recommended.

The witnesses for the government may be those above named, with special examiner J. W. Hall, who should be addressed in care of the Commissioner of Pensions, Washington, D.C., as the latter can testify that the impostor maintained before him that he was the identical person who rendered the service; that while he was known as Samuel Chestnut, his correct name was Samuel Henry Chestnut and that he was the person who had rendered the service as Henry Chestnut, and in so testifying this impostor falsely and wilfully committed perjury.

If prosecution is instituted, it is further recommended that a subpoena duces tecum be issued upon the Chief of the Record & Pension Office, War Department, directing that he or someone in his stead whom he may designate, shall appear in court with the records pertaining to Company H, 135" U.S.C. Infantry. This, to the end that the soldier's personal description may be shown and with a view to rebutting any false statements, which the accused may present.

Very respectfully,

J. C. Davenport

Acting Commissioner.

CHAPTER 11

THE SECRET OF HAPPINESS IS FREEDOM, AND THE SECRET OF FREEDOM, COURAGE!

Typical Company of USCT Soldiers

COMPANY "I"

INCLUDED IN THIS CHAPTER ARE EXTRACTIONS FROM THE PENSION RECORDS OF;

ISHAM HARRISON

LEWIS McINTYRE

WILLIAM CARRION

CALEB MALLOY

BONAPARTE DARBY / LARRYMORE

PERRY KINARD

GEORGE WOODS / BENNETT

ISHAM HARRISON

Isham Harrison was born in Beaufort, Hampton County, South Carolina, and belonged to Hard Harrison. The Bureau of Pensions record showed that Isham enlisted at Rivers Bridge, South Carolina, and became a regular soldier when the regiment reached Goldsboro, North Carolina. They then marched to Washington, D.C., and after the Grand Review, he then moved to Louisville, Kentucky. There he lived with Jesse Hodges as his tent mate.

Jesse stated, in his affidavit for Isham that they were in the same company "I," and Isham complained of head and body troubles while in camp. He could not attend drills for very long, he only attended sick calls. Isham was transferred to the hospital at Taylor Barracks and then to Jeffersonville, Indiana. Jesse knew that Isham was an "ordinarily healthy man" when he joined the Army. Isham Harrison had been a great sufferer with troubles growing out of exposure while in camp due to the cold climate.

After returning home, following his discharge from the army, the doctor reported rheumatism and malaria had been contracted by Isham due to exposure while in service. He had head troubles, kidney troubles, and bloody piles and could not work as a farmer any longer.

Isham Harrison received a pension up until his death on January 28, 1924. His wife, Rachael Harrison filed for her widow's pension on February 29, 1924, which she received, and the record showed that on June 8, 1937, a stop payment notice by the Veterans Administration was issued because of her death.

1) State of South Carolina }
County of Colleton }

Replying to Dept letter 3-079 M.G.B. June 30th 1900 Isham Harrison have to say that after being mustered out at Louisville Ky Dec 1865, he returned to South Carolina, what is now Hampton County, and resided there in at Brothers Bridge Crocketville S.C. P.O. lived there about eighteen years to about year 1883, then he moved to adjoining County of Colleton S.C.a Smoaks x Roads S.C. from 1883 to present lived there then vaguan Post Office changed to Walterboro Sclent. Was healthy when he joined Army had to go to hospital at Jefferson Barracks Ky, where he was treated for rheumatism & Malaria contracted through camp exposure since which time head troubles, Kidney troubles and bloody piles, the outgrowth of malarial troubles. Hospital treatment in 1865 since which time the ailments have grown as enumerated up to present. Do not remember Surgeons name in the Army since discharge have been treated by Drs Wyman, he is dead, Drs Lucas and Ackerman who sent statements in reference to his condition Have been debilitated for some time; within last three years trouble of ailments is so pronounced that he cannot work at all; Being a farmer he cannot now do any work in his line

Sworn to and subscribed before me this 10th day of July 1900 } Isham Harrison
H. Fryer }
Notary Public S.C. }

U.S. PENSION OFFICE JUL 13 1900

And affiant further states that he has no interest in this claim.

Isham Harrison

If affiant signs by mark two witnesses sign here. — Affiant's Signature.

Sworn to and subscribed before me on the 4th day of Feby 189_ and I hereby certify that the contents of this affidavit were fully made known to the witnesses before signing and I have no interest in this claim or its prosecution.

H. Fryer
Notary Public S.C.

L.S. — Official signature.

P. [illegible]

General Affidavit.

STATE OF [illegible] COUNTY OF Colleton

In claim No 1100 [illegible] of Esham Harrison Co. [illegible] of the 135 Regt. of U.S.C.T. Vols. Personally appeared before the undersigned, duly authorized to administer oaths within and for said County, Jesse Hodges aged 5[illegible] years, whose P. O. is Wil[illegible], County of Colleton State of So Ca. who being duly sworn, states in relation to said claim as follows to-wit:

That he knows [illegible] Esham Harrison and have been neighbors for past thirty years and am [illegible] acquainted with his habits [illegible] therefore state to the best of my knowledge and belief that his afflictions are rheumatism which keeps him down a great deal and head trouble producing dizziness preventing him from doing steady work. Knows that he has been troubled with these ailments soon after the war and the older he grows the more troublesome and frequent seem to be the diseases. That they are not due to vicious habits but affiant verily believes that they came from exposure during the war when as comrades they had to contend with all kinds of weather and climate. That this statement was dictated to Notary Public and read to affiant before signing.

And affiant further states that he has no interest in this claim.

C. Jm. Pearson

J. L. Myers

Jesse his + mark Hodges

Sworn to and subscribed before me on the 29th day of Aug 1896 and I hereby certify that the contents of this affidavit was fully made known to the witnesses before signing, and I have no interest in this claim or its prosecution.

General Affidavit.

STATE OF S. Ca. *COUNTY OF* Colleton *SS:*

In claim No. 111,200 of Isham Harrison of Co. I of the 135 Regt. of U.S. C. Inf. Vols. Personally appeared before the undersigned duly authorized to administer oaths within and for said County, Jesse Hodge aged 52 years, whose P. O. is Walterboro, County of Colleton State of S.C., who being duly sworn, states in relation to said claim as follows to-wit:

That he was a member of Co. I. 135 Reg U.S.C.T. I was a Comrade of Isham Harrison, and at one time his tent mate, That he personally know that Harrison complained of head and body troubles while in camp. That he could not attend drill for a long time, but only attend sick Calls. That the said Isham Harrison was transfered to Hospitals at Taylor Barracks and Jeffersonville Ind. Deponent knows that said Harrison was an ordinarily healthy man when he joined the Army. Since his discharge he Harrison has been a great sufferer with troubles growing out of exposure while in Camp in the cold climate of the north west. That on many occasions since our discharge had to nurse and get medicine for Harrison, being troubled with deafness Catarrh & Rheumatism

And affiant further states that he has no interest in this claim.

J. E. Myers.

Aaron F. Lee

his
Jesse Hodge
mark

Post-office address: Watterboro So Car

July 10, 1891900

SIR:

In reply to your request I have to state that Knew John Hamon for years joined U.S. Army together, same Co I, 135 Reg; were in same mess and remember that in 1865 Hamon was in Army hospital at Jefferson Barracks Ky. treated for rheumatism and Malaria. Since being mustered out they separated until twenty years ago they lived in same neighborhood. Malarial troubles continue to grow on Harrison, knows that he has head trouble Bloody piles and ailments of body. That Hamon cannot prosecute his labors as farmer is owing to his physical condition. Cannot read or write so got an official to write and who acquainted me with contents before signing. to all of which I agree

Very respectfully,

Jesse his mark Hodge

COMMISSIONER OF PENSIONS,

Washington, D. C.

I certify that I read this reply to Jesse Hodge and explained same to him — although I wrote same at his dictation —

[illegible] Notary Public [illegible]

Physician's Affidavit.

STATE OF South Carolina COUNTY OF Barnwell ss:

In claim No. 880 100 of Johnnie Harrison of Co. I of the 135 Regt. of U.S.C. Vols. Personally appeared before the undersigned duly authorized to administer oaths within and for said County, Dr. A.B. McTeer aged 32 years, whose P. O. is Ehrhardt, County of Barnwell State of S. Car. who being duly sworn, states in relation to said claim as follows to-wit:

1 Chronic disease of the brain (Cephalalgia)

2 Uraemia

3 Chronic Rheumatism

~~Of my present Condition I am not able to any thing at times~~

In his present Condition he is not able to do any thing at times

And affiant further states that he has no interest in this claim.

If affiant signs by mark, two witnesses sign here.

A. B. McTeer, M.D.

The affiant should state who wrote this affidavit and if written by any one other than himself, his ... and whether he was present and dictated its contents.

OFFICE OF

P. J. LOCKWOOD.

ATTORNEY IN PENSION CLAIMS.

Washington, D. C. April 15, 1901.

The Secretary of the Interior,

Washington, D. C.

Sir:-

I desire to appeal from the action of the Commissioner of Pensions in rejecting the claim of Isham Harrison, app. #1, 130,100, service Co. I, 135th U. S. C. Inft. under the act of June 27, 1890 as I am satisfied that an examination of the evidence will convince you that this man is entitled to the minimum rating at least under the act of 1890.

This appeal is respectfully submitted.

PJLockwood

LEWIS McINTYRE

Lewis McIntyre was a corporal in Company "I," 135th United States Colored Troop. Lewis said "I was born a slave in Marlboro County, South Carolina close to Beaver Dam, McCall. I was a slave of Archie McIntyre. I was taken by the Yankee soldiers to Handy Stanton's place which is where my wife lived. I was with the Confederate Army for about two months in 1864. I worked as a laborer but did not enlist. I was sent to Charleston by my master. After the Pioneer Corps, I enlisted in the 135th USCT in Goldsboro, next I went to Raleigh then Washington, D.C., and we went by boat to Louisville Kentucky. My Captain was Fischer."

He said his brothers Harris and Bill were in the regiment too. Lewis was the oldest of the brothers. He said that Lewis Wannamaker was his tentmate in service. He could read and write a little before enlisting and learned more when he was in the army.

Harris McIntyre said that he was a pensioner and served in Company "A," at the same time as his brother Lewis. He also said that there were six children between Lewis and himself. Harris recalled that when the soldiers came through, they took him, Lewis, Bill, Cy, Daniel, and David. He said that David, his nephew, was now dead. He went on that, they joined and marched to Fayetteville and then to Goldsboro. David ran away but the rest were in Company "A," except Lewis who was in Company "I." Lewis spent time in the hospital in Kentucky due to his illness. At the time of his declaration, he had been living within twenty miles of Harris ever since they returned home.

Lewis's brother William McIntyre did a deposition in 1904 in Bennettsville, South Carolina, and told of his service in Company "A," 135th USCT. He knew Lewis was in the regiment because he saw him almost every day. He thought Lewis was about seventy-six in 1904 as he was about a year and a half older. Once William found out about his age, he was excluded from road duty because he was able to prove how old he was.

William said that when the white soldiers came past their place, they took our owner's mules and all four of us brothers. Lewis's health was bad, and he broke down complaining while on the road march and he looked bad. William confirmed that Lewis was able to read and write.

Another soldier of the 135th USCT was James McClem who told the examiner in this case that he had known Lewis McIntyre since boyhood, and he would see Lewis on Sundays at Beaver Dam Church. He said he knew he was in his regiment because he would see him in dress parade and he did guard duty with him.

George Hamer, another soldier in the 135th USCT testified in this case and said in his deposition that the white soldiers took him when they came through and he became a cook for General Potts and then in Goldsboro, he became a soldier in the 135th USCT. He was taken ill and sent to the hospital in New Bern, North Carolina, and said that when he left the hospital he went home.

Lewis added in his deposition that he was made a corporal under General Palmer who was from Indiana. He listed his children with his wife, Betsie, as Robert, William, David, Fannie, and Henry.

This is a remarkable story of six children from the Archie McIntyre plantation at Beaver Dam, (McCall), South Carolina. How joining up with the pioneer corps with the white soldiers and subsequently enlisting in the 135th USCT turned their lives around completely. They went from slavery to free men and were able to go on to enjoy family life. This is a wonderful example of blood brothers, *with the same name and mother,* who served our country as soldiers in the 135th United States Colored Troop.

N. B.—Examiners should be particular to have affiants sign on the line next below the closing words of their depositions, so as to leave little or no space between their signatures and the end of their depositions.

3—290.

DEPOSITION A

Case of Lewis McIntyre, No. 1292404

On this 11 day of May, 1904, at Little Rock, County of Marion State of S. C. before me, R. McMorris a special examiner of the Bureau of Pensions, personally appeared Lewis McIntyre who, being by me first duly sworn to answer truly all interrogatories propounded to him during this special examination of aforesaid claim for pension, deposes and says: I am 75 years of age; my post-office address is Judson S. C.

I am a claimant for pension, having served in Co I 135th U. S. C. Infantry from March 23rd 1865 to October 23rd 1865. I never had any other service military or naval. I was a slave and was born in South Carolina Marlboro Co. near Beaver Dam. I was a slave and Archie McIntyre was my owner. When I was taken up by the Yankee soldiers I was on Handy Stanton's place, that was where my wife lived. I was owned by Archie McIntyre and she was owned by Handy Stanton. I worked on a farm. I was with the Confederate army about two months sometime in 1864. My master sent me to work for the Confederate side below Charleston S.C. I worked as a laborer. I was not enlisted. When I was at my wifes house one mile away from the McIntyre plantation, the Northern white soldiers came through, and came to my wife's house and I was ordered to go with them

Page 6 Deposition A

Dep. and I went with them as far as Goldsboro N.C. and there I enlisted I gave my name as Lewis McIntyre. I next went to Raleigh N.C. and we went through to Richmond Va on a march and to Washington D.C. and we went on a boat to Louisville Kentucky and I there was mustered out. I think I was away eight or nine months. A man named Fisher was my Captain, One Lieut was named Steele and one was named Hills. Our Colonel was named Gurley. I can remember our Orderly Sergeant but I cannot remember his name. One Sergeant was named Butler I was first a private and I was made a Corporal, One Corporal was named Brewer and one was named Peppers, No, he was a Sergeant. My brothers Harris McIntyre, and Bill McIntyre were in the Regiment but I do not know their Company. They knew I was a soldier and that I was in Co I, but I being older than they cannot remember so well, My memory is very short. Both of my brothers are pensioners. I do not know any others now living who can identify me. I lost my Discharge. My brothers came back home with me after our discharge. [illegible]

DEPOSITION C

Case of Lewis McIntyre, No. 1292 404

On this 12 day of May 1904, at Clio, county of Marlboro State of S.C., before me, R. McMorris, a special examiner of the Bureau of Pensions, personally appeared Harris McIntyre, who, being by me first duly sworn to answer truly all interrogatories propounded to him during this special examination of aforesaid claim for pension, deposes and says: I am 57 years old, P.O. Clio S.C. occupation farmer

I am a pensioner at $12 per month. I served in Co A 135th U.S.C. Infantry. Lewis McIntyre is my half brother I have known him ever since I can remember. There were six children between he and I and probably eighteen months between each child. I was born April 9th 1846. He is at least 70 years old. I lived at Archie McIntyres before the war in Marlboro S.C. about two miles from Beaver Dam and Lewis McIntyre lived on the same place and we were slaves and owned by Archie McIntyre. When the Yankee soldiers came through here, they came to the place where we lived, and they took my brothers Lewis, Bill, and Ly, Daniel and Dave, and myself. Daniel was my nephew and is dead. We went with the white soldiers to their Camp near Beaver Dam, and then we went on the march to Fayetteville, and to Goldsboro N.C. and there we enlisted and became soldiers. We were mustered in at Raleigh N.C. and were assigned to the 135th U.S.C. Infantry and I was put in Co A and Lewis

Page 15

was assigned to Co I, and Bill and Daniel were also in Co I and by and Dave ran away and went back home. Lewis and Daniel, Bill and I continued with the 135th U.S.C. Infantry We went from Raleigh N.C. to Petersburg and Richmond Va and to Washington D.C. and we went by train and boat to Louisville Ky and remained there until muster out. Lewis was with us all the time, I would see him every day. He was sick during his service and was in hospital when we were at Louisville Ky. After our discharge Lewis, Daniel Bill and I all returned home to our former place in South Carolina and Lewis lived at Bennettsville S.C and in North Carolina and he has been in Marion Co S.C. He has been within twenty miles of where he now is since 1865. He lives with one of his sons, I have seen him more or less ever since the war. There is no doubt at all but that he was a soldier and served in Co I. 135th U.S.C. Inf. Regiment. It is just as true that he so served as that I served and I am a pensioner. We enlisted the same day in March 1865 and were discharged in either October or November 1865. I was 19 years old when I enlisted and he was ten

Harris McKiye
[illegible]

DEPOSITION D

Case of Lewis McIntyre, No. 1292404

On this 12 day of May, 1904, at Beaver Dam, county of Marlboro State of S. C., before me, R. M. McMorris, a special examiner of the Bureau of Pensions, personally appeared William McIntyre, who, being by me first duly sworn to answer truly all interrogatories propounded to him during this special examination of aforesaid claim for pension, deposes and says: I am 74 years old, P. O. Bennettsville S.C. I am a pensioner at $12 per month. I served in Co A 135 U. S. C Infantry. My half brother Harris was in my Company. My half brother Lewis McIntyre was I think in Co I 135th U. S. C. Infantry. The way I know Lewis was in our Regiment is because I would see him almost every day except on a march. He would come and see us in our Company and I would visit his Company. There is no doubt or question or doubt but that he was a soldier in the 135 U S C Inf and if I am correct he was in Co I and he was an officer, he was a Corporal. Archie McIntyre was our owner up to his death, and then his widow Martha McIntyre was our owner. I was on the same place with Lewis. We were born and raised on the McIntyre place, not two miles from where I now am. Lewis is 76 years old, a year and a half older than I. According to all I know I am 74 years old. Once I had to find out my age, and I went to Daniel McIntyre and he found it in a book, and I got excused from road duty because of proving my age. The white soldiers came right past our place, and they

Page 16 Deposition D

Page

took my owners mules, and Lewis, Harris, Daniel, and I went away with the white soldiers and remained with them until we got to Goldsboro N.C. and there we enlisted, Lewis, Harris, Daniel and I enlisted. We went from Goldsboro N.C. to Washington D.C. and passed through Petersburg and Richmond Va. Lewis was with us all the time. From Washington D.C. we went by train and boat to Louisville Ky and we remained there until we were discharged. The way I know Lewis was a Corporal was because I saw the stripes on his arms. This is Beaver Dam S.C. and Lewis was born near here. I am 5 ft. 5 inches and he is taller than I. I have seen Lewis off and on until the last few years. We came home together, Harris, Lewis, Daniel and I. Lewis made a claim for pension, he told me about it. I saw him this last March when he came to find out his correct age. I never was a witness in his claim, but I know he was a soldier in our Regiment. He was a soldier just as well as I was, there is no doubt about it. Lewis' health is very bad, he is broken down, he was complaining in March and he looked bad. He could read and write a little before he was a soldier, and when he had any idle time in the army he would be trying to improve himself. I understand the questions and my answers are correctly written

John McIntyre

William his X mark McIntyre

DEPOSITION E

Case of Lewis McIntyre, No. 1292404

On this 15 day of May, 1904, at Bennettsville, county of Marlboro, State of S.C., before me, R. McMorris, a special examiner of the Bureau of Pensions, personally appeared James McLaurin, who, being by me first duly sworn to answer truly all interrogatories propounded to him during this special examination of aforesaid claim for pension, deposes and says:

I am 63 years old P.O. Bennettsville S.C. occupation carpenter
I was a private in Co K 135 U.S.C Infantry under the name of James McClenn, the recruiting officer misunderstood me, and got my name wrong. I knew Lewis McIntyre when I was a boy. He was a slave and Archie McIntyre was his owner. I lived and was raised within four miles of where he lived. I would see him at the Beaver Dam church on Sundays. He was a man, at the time of the war. He had a brother Bill McIntyre and a half brother Harris. All three of them Lewis, Harris and Bill were soldiers in the 135 U.S.C Inf. I dont know what Company Lewis was in, but he was not in Co. K. The way I know he was a soldier, is because I would see him on dress parade, and I saw him often during his service, and was on guard with him, and I would be in town at Louisville Ky with him. There is no doubt but that he was a soldier in the Regiment, I can testify to that positively. He was as much a soldier as I was. I marched with him when we were pioneers

Page 18 Deposition E

Page 19

with the white soldiers who came through South Carolina and took us with them. We continued with the white soldiers, until we arrived at Goldsboro S C and there we enlisted, and we were examined and sworn in at Raleigh N.C. We were together all the way to Washington D.C., and from there by train to Parkersburg Va and there we took a boat to Louisville Ky. When I was a lad he was a man grown, He is over 70 years old and maybe 75 years old. I have seen him occasionally since the war. His skin was dark, and he was a medium sized man in heighth. where he lived before he enlisted was near Beaver Dam S.C. I cant testify as to whether he was sick or diseased during his service, but I can testify that he was in the 135th U.S.C. Inf, and his brothers Harris and Bill are now pensioners. I did not know that Lewis had made an application for pension. I have not seen him in eight or nine years. I only knew of one Lewis McIntyre in the Regiment, and he was what I might call a neighbor before he enlisted. I understand the questions and my answers have been correctly recorded.

James L McL[illegible]

DEPOSITION F

Case of Lewis McIntyre, No. 1292404

On this 11 day of May, 1904, at Little Rock, county of Marion, State of S C, before me, R McMorris, a special examiner of the Bureau of Pensions, personally appeared Morris McDuffie, who, being by me first duly sworn to answer truly all interrogatories propounded to him during this special examination of aforesaid claim for pension, deposes and says:

I am 68 years old, light laborer, P. O. Albriton S. C.

I served in Co H. 135 U. S. C Inf and am a pensioner. I know the man before me as Lewis McIntyre. I first knew him in the army. He was in Co. I 135 U. S. C. Inf. I saw him there. I never knew him before I enlisted. I got acquainted with him in the army. I have seen him off and on since the war. At one time we worked together on a railroad. I am sure this man was in our Regiment, but I was not in his Company. His name there was Lewis McIntyre, and that has been his name since the war. I dont know any other member of his Company. I got to know this man since the war, and we talked over matters, and I know that I knew him in the Regiment. I became a witness for him in his claim for pension and I told the man I was willing to swear that Lewis McIntyre was in the next Company to Co. H, and I identified him to be the man and I now again identify the man

Page 20 Deposition F

WILLIAM CARRION

William Carrion said that he was born in Orangeburg County South Carolina by the Santee River as a slave of Doctor Wilkerson. When he was a small child, he was sold to John Easterlin. He said he "now lives nights on the plantation land and had been doing so for the last fifty years" and has never lived more than a mile from there. He said he stayed at the plantation of John Easterlin until Sherman's Army came through in 1865. He recalled when Sherman's army crossed the bridge, on the South Edisto River, the night of February 6th the next day he went with them.

The record showed that William's hair was thick and long, standing up high on the top of his head, and they measured him and found he was 5' 10 1/2". He told the enlisting officer he was twenty-four at the time he enlisted, and he was now between sixty-four and sixty-six. They went through Alexandria and crossed the bridge to get into Washington D.C. He said they went to Washington, D.C., and were in the grand review. They then camped four miles from the city. From Washington, they went by train to the Ohio River and then on boats to Louisville, Kentucky. William recalled while in Jeffersonville, John Charleston wore a corn skin cap, and everyone called him corn skin.

William Carrion was married after the war to his wife Rebecca, and it just so happened, we were able to uncover a Portrait picture of the two of them. As you can see from the picture, they appeared to be a very distinguished couple. The Easterlin family gave him and his wife fifty acres of land on which they lived together.

William Carrion 1830-1904 *Rebecca Carrion* 1850-1919

Maternal Grandparents
Marion R. Williams

DEPOSITION

Case of William Carrion alias Eastland, No. 1,116,946

On this 13 day of June 1924
near Cope, county of Orangeburg
State of SC, before me [illegible]
a special examiner of the Bureau of Pensions, personally appeared
William Carrion who, being by me first duly sworn to
answer truly all interrogatories propounded to him during this special
examination of aforesaid claim for pension, deposes and says: I am about 84
years of age; my post-office address is Cope, SC. I live about 3
miles North of Cope SC my post office. I am a
farmer. I am the William Carrion who served in
Co. I 135 U.S. Col. Inf. under the name William Eastland
and who is an applicant for pension under the act of June 27
1890. I put in my claim about ten years ago.
I was born in Orangeburg County SC on the Edisto
river as the slave of old Dr. Wilkerson. When I was a
small boy I was sold to John Eastland [illegible] and I have
lived right here on the Eastland land for the last fifty years
near Cope SC. Have not at any time during that period lived
more than a mile from the house in which I now live.
I stayed at home on the plantation of John Eastland
[illegible] until Sherman's army came through
here in February 1865 when I went to them
and they took me with them. They crossed
[illegible] bridge on South Edisto River
on the night of February 6 and the next
day I went to them. [illegible] Adam
[illegible] McMichael, Captain [illegible]
[illegible] Williams, Jack [illegible], Washington
Holmes are among the colored men who
went from this vicinity to Sherman's army.
We were put to work on the [illegible]
and kept there until we got to Raleigh
N.C. By that time the war was
[illegible] 5 [illegible]

8
Page enlisted 1865, and the 135 Regiment of Colored troops was made up and I enlisted
in Co. I of the 135th USCT. I think I enlisted in April 1865 but am not
certain as to the month. I was stripped
and examined and measured for my height.
I was six feet tall. I am old now and
do not know whether I am 6 ft tall
[illegible]. My hair was thick and long
standing up high on top and may have
caused them to measure me too high.
Claimant measured and found to be
5 ft 10½ inches, in shoes without
heels. W. H. [illegible] S.E. I do not know
my age and did not know it correctly
when I enlisted, but I know what
I told the enrolling officer. I told him
I was twenty four years old. I think
I am now about 64 or 66 years old.
I went with my regiment from Raleigh N.C.
to Richmond Va. I think we ~~made~~ made
the march in 9 or 10 days, and then on
to Washington City to the great review.
We camped four miles out of the city. We
went through Alexandria and crossed
a river (name unknown) ~~and went~~ on a bridge
to get into Washington. From Washington
we were sent on the train to the Ohio
river and then on boats to Louisville
Kentucky. From there we went to Florence
barracks Jeffersonville Ind. where we
staid a while and then back to Taylor
Barracks Louisville Ky. where
we were mustered out in November I think
1865, and I came back to this plantation
where I have lived all the time since.
The Eastertin family gave me and
my wife the fifty acres of land on
which we live. My wife was raised

in their home and wore a [illegible]

— [illegible] Jim [illegible] I think was Captain of my company [illegible] the regiment [illegible] Lt. Hayes acted as Captain [illegible] Jim (I think) Steel was also a Lieutenant in Co. I. Rev. Shaw was Chaplain of the regiment. [illegible] Butler was orderly Sergt but he was an old man and Frank [illegible] acted as orderly Sergt. [illegible] Corp. John [illegible] and Joseph [illegible] I think. He wore a coon skin cap and we called him coon skin so I may not get his name right. Our Lieutenant was named [illegible] Hayes. Isom Williams, [illegible] and — Butler were corporals. Jack [illegible] Mark Anderson, [illegible] John Allen, [illegible] Miller were some of the privates in my company.

Isom Williams [illegible] county [illegible] mate. [illegible] Isom Williams Peter Jennings (dead), [illegible] (dead) Billy [illegible] Ellis Millhouse.

Isom Williams, Jack [illegible] and Mark Anderson live in this county John Allen and Ellis Millhouse live in [illegible] county. Any of these men ought to be able to identify me as the person who served in Co. I 135 U.S.C.I. [illegible]

Attest { Annie M. Carrion
Earline K. Carrion

William his X mark Carrion
Deponent

Sworn to and subscribed before me this 13 day of [illegible], 190[illegible], and I certify that the contents were fully made known to deponent before signing.

S. F. Hampton
Special Examiner

Page 7 Deposition A

DEPOSITION

Case of William Carrion, No. 1116946

On this 13 day of June 1902 at Cope, county of Orangeburg, State of S.C., before me, [illegible], a special examiner of the Bureau of Pensions, personally appeared William Carrion who, being by me first duly sworn to answer truly all interrogatories propounded to him during this special examination of aforesaid claim for pension, deposes and says:

William Castland. When I enlisted I gave them my owner's name as my name. I gave the name Castlen, but the right name is ~~Easterlin~~ Easterlin. I got the name Carrion (by pronouncing it as if spelled Carry on) [illegible] from my father who belonged to Dr. Wilkinson, [illegible] with name Carrion. After the war when colored people were choosing names for themselves and registering [illegible] I [illegible] the name Carrion for my surname and I still hold to that name and my [illegible] go by that name. I know of no other people white or colored by that name. I have no marks or scars about me by which I could be identified. I have no picture of myself made while I was a soldier.

I claim pension for kidney trouble and rheumatism and for about six years I have had dyspepsia. None of my disease is due to any bad habits. I do not drink.

I married my present and only wife Rebecca the last year of the war on the Easterlin place. We had the permission of our white folks and we were married under slave customs by an old colored preacher, Will Darby, long since dead. Juno Mitchell, Ben Johnson, Gabriel Tyler and Henry Johnson, P.O. Cope, S.C. were present and saw my marriage to Rebecca Easterlin my present wife. We have no children under sixteen years old.

I first had [illegible] Washington D.C. for my attorney but now my attorneys are Milo B. Stevens & Co., Washington D.C. They are to have the lawful fee of my claim is allowed, ten dollars I think. I have not paid any fee to any one for work on my claim.

Dep. 8 Deposition A

GENERAL AFFIDAVIT.

State of South Carolina
County of Orangeburg

In the matter of the claim for widows Pension

Rebecca Carrion wife of William Carrion [illegible]

Personally came before me, a Notary Public in and for the

County and State aforesaid, D. J. Hydrick M.D. Orangeburg S.C.

That Rebecca Carrion is the wife of deceased, Wm Carrion

That the said Wm Carrion died suddenly of heart disease on the 13th Feb 1904 in the town of Cope S.C. & that he held the post mortem in the capacity of the official investigating & inquest physician for the County of Orangeburg in State of S.C. That even before making the post mortem on the above date, he also attended the deceased Wm Carrion on several occasions and treated & diagnosed his case as one of valvular disease of the heart.

That deponent further says he is a regular licensed practicing physician living in the City of Orangeburg S.C.

CALEB MALLOY

Caleb was born in 1828 in Stewartsville Township, Laurinburg, North Carolina, and died in 1908 in Maxton, North Carolina. "In slave time" his wife Polly belonged to Daniel McKinnon in Stewartsville, Scotland County North Carolina and Caleb belonged to Dr. John Malloy three miles away. They lived together a short time before Caleb joined with the Union Army. When he came home, they were married by Peter McRae at the Caledonia Church in Richmond County.

Caleb was thirty-four when he enlisted in the army. In April of 1865 while on the march to Washington, D.C., Caleb was injured by falling from a bridge which affected his back and chest. He ended up in the hospital in Alexandria, Virginia because of the injuries sustained in the fall. W.A. Lowe in his Affidavit said that from 1890 to 1896 Caleb Malloy was disabled to do manual labor to half which would be fifty percent disabled. He stated further that he had been a close neighbor, and the disabilities of Caleb Malloy "were not due to vicious habits."

PHYSICIAN'S AFFIDAVIT

3-472

SOUTHERN DIVISION

W. invgl. 909.149.
Caleb Malloy.
Co. E, 135 Regt U.S.C. Vol. Inf.

A. E. K. Ex'r.

Department of the Interior,

BUREAU OF PENSIONS.

Washington, D. C., Dec 21, 1908.

MADAM: In your above-entitled claim you are required to give answers to the following questions in the blank space after each question. You will please return this circular under cover of the inclosed envelope which requires no postage.

Very respectfully,

Mrs Polly A. Malloy,
Blackout,
N.C.

J. L. Davenport
Commissioner.

1. Where were you born? Answer. Richmond County N.C. in portion now Scotland Co. 3 M N of new Maxton N.C. 7 M S.E. Laurinburg N.C.
2. Where did you live at the time you became acquainted with the soldier? Answer. When I was born
3. How long had you known the soldier before you were married to him? Answer. since Childhood
4. When, where, and by whom were you married to the soldier? Answer. We were married as slaves and were remarried after the war by Peter McRae J.P. at Caledonia Church
5. Where have you lived since your marriage to the soldier? Give the date of each change of residence. Have always lived in 3 miles of place where raised
6. Were you married before your marriage to the soldier? Answer. No
7. Have you married since the soldier's death? Answer. No
8. Were any children born to you and the soldier? If so, state their names and the dates of their birth. No.
9. Were you a slave? If so, state the names of all your owners, particularly the name of your owner at the date of your marriage to the soldier, and all names by which you have been known. Daniel McKinnon
10. Where was the soldier born? Answer. Richmond County N.C. in what is now Scotland County
11. Where did the soldier live when you became acquainted with him? Answer. Richmond County N.C.
12. Where did the soldier enlist? Answer. Raleigh N.C.
13. When did the soldier enlist? Answer. March 27th 1865
14. Where had he lived before enlistment? Answer. Richmond County N.C.
15. What was the soldier's age at enlistment? Answer. about 34 years His occupation? Farm Laborer
His height? about 5 feet, 8 inches. The color of his skin? Black
16. Were you his only wife? Answer. Yes
17. Was the soldier a slave? If so, state the names of all his owners, and particularly of his owners at the date of his marriage to you, and at his enlistment, and all names by which he was known. Arch'd McCormic owned him to boyhood then Dr John Malloy to time he was freed

Polly A. Malloy (her mark)

ATTEST: 1. A. L. Jones
2. D. M. Wilkinson
(Witnesses who can write sign here.)

Date: January 1st, 1909

SPECIAL NOTICE. The civil officer before whom this affidavit is executed should be careful to fill in all spaces both in the caption and jurat.

GENERAL AFFIDAVIT.

State of N. C., County of Robeson, ss:

In the matter of Claim #669.582 Caleb Malloy Pvt. Co. 135 U.S.C.T.

ON THIS 13th day of August, A.D. 1898 personally appeared before me a Notary Public in and for the aforesaid County, duly authorized to administer oaths W A Lowe aged 64 years, a resident of Maxton in the County of Robeson and State of N C whose Post-Office address is Maxton N. C. A H Currie aged years, a resident of Stewartsville Township in the County of Richmond and State of N C, whose Post-Office address is Maxton N C

Filed in claims under GENERAL LAW and under ACT JUNE 27, 1890.

well known to be reputable and entitled to credit, and who being duly sworn, declared in relation to aforesaid case as follows: W A Lowe that he is well acquainted with, Caleb Malloy and has been since 1883 and that from September 27th 1890 to November 18th 1896 and to the present date that the said Caleb Malloy has been disabled to do manual labor at least 1/2 that the cause of his disability, is attributable to misery in his breast, injury to his back and general debility. That his his chance for obtaining this information have been that during the entire time he has lived a close neighbor to him and has had frequent and constant chances to observe the ability of said Caleb Malloy to perform manual labor. He states further that the said disabilities of said Caleb Malloy are not due to vicious habits.

A H Currie that he knows the facts above set forth by W A Lowe to be true and that he concurs in the same. That he has been acquainted with Caleb Malloy all his life and has been a near neighbor to him and has had frequent and regular opportunities to observe his disability

PENSION OFFICE U. S. AUG 17 1898

they further declare that they have no interest in said case and that they are not concerned in its prosecution.

A. H. Currie

W. A. Lowe

(If Affiants sign by mark, two witnesses who can write sign here.) (Signature of Affiants.)

SPECIAL NOTICE. The civil officer before whom this affidavit is executed should be careful to fill in all spaces, both in the caption and jurat.

Claimant's

~~GENERAL~~ AFFIDAVIT.

State of North Carolina, County of Robeson, ss:

In the matter of Claim of Polly A. Malloy Widow of Caleb Malloy Co. I 135 USCI

ON THIS 14 day of January, A. D. 1909, personally appeared before me a Notary Public in and for the aforesaid County, duly authorized to administer oaths Polly A. Malloy aged 65 years, a resident of Stewartsville Township in the County of Scotland, and State of North Carolina whose Post-office address is Maxton, N. C. well known to be reputable and entitled to credit, and who, being duly sworn, declared in relation to aforesaid case as follows: That she is the widow of the soldier, Caleb Malloy, who died on the 14th day of November 1908. That prior to emancipation she was

(NOTE.—Affiant should state how he gains a knowledge of the facts to which he testifies.)

a slave, the property of Daniel McKinnon who resided in what is now Stewartsville Township, Scotland County, N. C. That her said husband, the soldier above mentioned was also a slave and owned by Dr John Malloy who resided in said territory and within 3 miles of affiants master. That affiant and the soldier lived and cohabited as man and wife for a short time before the soldier enlisted in the United States Army and after his return lived together again and under the Reconstruction period were married at Caledonia Church in Richmond County by Peter McRae, Justice of the Peace. That she has not been able to find any record of the mariage, but affiant was the only wife the soldier ever had and the soldier was the only husband the affiant ever had. Affiant knows of her own knowledge that the soldier was never married to anyone except herself and that she has never been married to anyone except the soldier. Also that they lived together as man and wife without any seperation, except the time the soldier was in the Army of the United States from the time they agreed to be man and wife when they were slaves prior to 1865 to the death of the soldier on November 14th 1908

~~Further declares that ... no interest in said case and ... not concerned in its prosecution.~~

A. F. Jones
D. K. Wilkinson

(If Affiant signs by mark, two witnesses who can write sign here.)

Polly A. her mark Malloy
(Signature of Affiant.)

Claimant

PENSION OFFICE U. S. JAN 27 1909

NOTICE. The civil officer before whom this affidavit is executed should be careful to fill in all spaces, both in the caption and jurat.

GENERAL AFFIDAVIT.

State of North Carolina, County of Robeson, ss:

In the matter of Claim of Polly A Malloy widow of Caleb Malloy Co. I 135 USCI

ON THIS 14th day of January, A. D. 1909, personally appeared before me a Notary Public in and for the aforesaid County, duly authorized to administer oaths J. A. Sutherland aged 68 years, a resident of Stewartsville Township, in the County of Scotland and State of North Carolina whose Post-office address is Maxton, N. C. and D. A. Patterson, aged 48 years, a resident of Stewartsville Township, in the County of Scotland, and State of North Carolina, whose Post-office address is Maxton, N. C.

well known to be reputable and entitled to credit, and who, being duly sworn, declared in relation to aforesaid case as follows: The said J. A. Sutherland; That he knew both the soldier, Caleb Malloy and the widow, Polly Ann Malloy. That the soldier was a

(Note.—Affiants should state how they gain a knowledge of the facts to which they testify.)

slave, the property of Dr John Malloy and the widow was a slave the property of Daniel McKinnon, both of whom lived in the neighborhood where affiant lives and where he was raised. That he knows that the said soldier and the claimant lived together as man and wife while they were slaves and that as soon as the soldier returned from the army in 1865 they went to live together again and so continued to live up to the death of the soldier. That affiant knows that neither the soldier nor the widow were ever married to anyother person.

D.A.Patterson that he has known the soldier and the claimant since his childhhod and that they lived together all that time, up to the death of the soldier as man and wife. That the widow, the claimant has not married since the date of her husband's, the soldiear's death. Both affiants state that they have always lived in the neighborhood where the soldier and the widow lived as man and wife, they having lived a good portion of the time on the farms of affiants and that they were known as man and wife and that neither had or claimed anyother as husband or wife and lived and acted as husband and wife during all that time.

They further declare that they have no interest in said case and are in no way not concerned in its prosecution.

PENSION OFFICE U. S. JAN 27 1909

J. A. Sutherland
D A Patterson

(If Affiants sign by mark two witnesses who can write sign) (Signatures of Affiants.)

JAN 26 1909

BONAPARTE DARBY / LARRYMORE

Bonaparte Darby also known as Bonaparte Larrymore, from Fort Matte, South Carolina said he entered the service of the 135th regiment as Bonaparte Darby. In the General Affidavit of N.S. Darby he stated that Bonaparte was owned by his father, and at the time he was deceased. He knew that he was in the Union Army as a soldier but could not say what regiment or company he was in. His father's plantation was near Fort Matte, Orangeburg County, South Carolina. He saw him soon after discharge and until the last three years saw him quite often. He said he visited Bonaparte about six months previous and conversed with him about his pension claim. There was no doubt in the world that Bonaparte Larrymore was the identical Bonaparte Darby as claimed by him. It was quite common for ex-slaves to change their names after slavery.

In the service, he said he was exposed to the rain and cold and developed rheumatism in his knees and left side which disabled him from manual labor. In 1860, prior to service, he was married to Williby Darby by the reverend Sherick Evans. He listed his children as Novinia Larrymore born in 1870, Henrietta born in 1871, Lidia born in 1872, and Luisia born in 1873.

According to the pension record Bonaparte ended up living in Monrovia, Montserrado County, Liberia however it showed in 1907 he lived in St. Matthews, South Carolina which was known as Buck Head or High Hill Creek. It is on record that in 1907 his official address was listed as Montserrado County, Liberia.

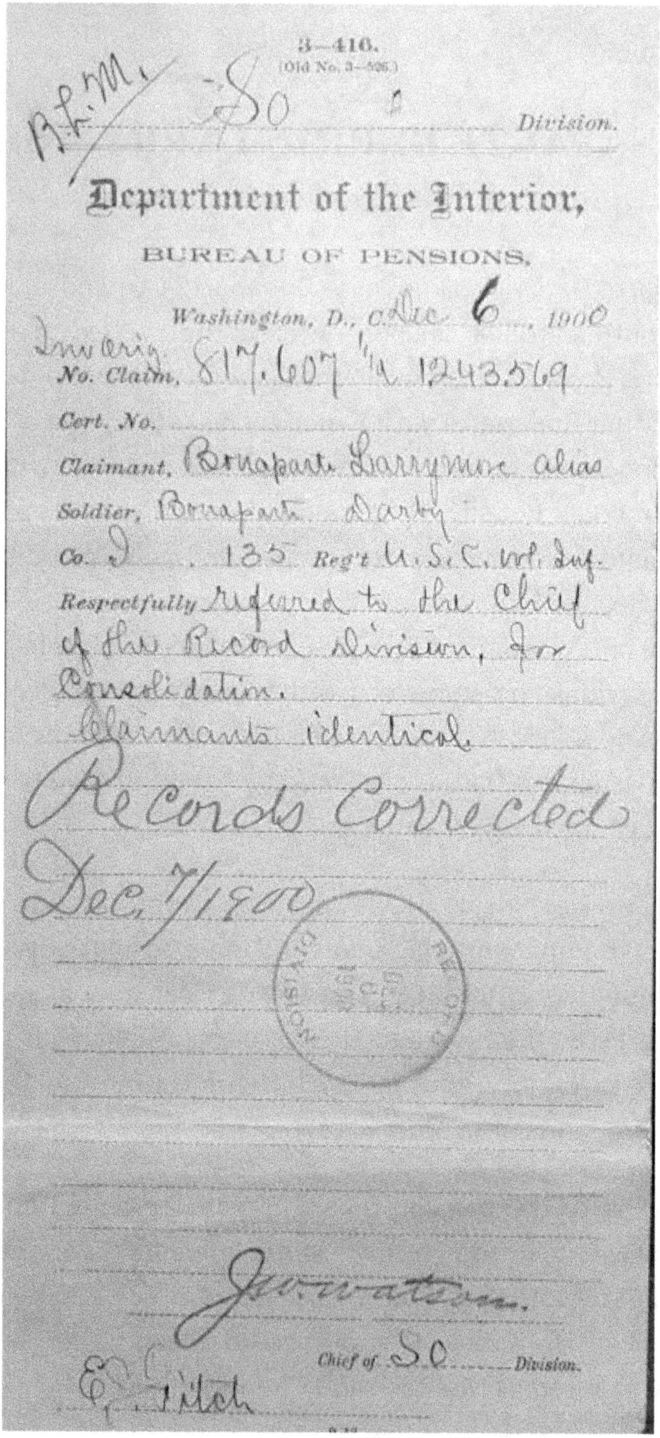

3—416.
(Old No. 3—526.)

B.L.M. / S.O. Division.

Department of the Interior,

BUREAU OF PENSIONS,

Washington, D. C. Dec 6, 1900

Inv orig
No. Claim, 817.607 & 1243569

Cert. No.

Claimant, Bonapart Larrymore alias

Soldier, Bonapart Darby

Co. I, 135 Reg't U. S. C. Vol. Inf.

Respectfully referred to the Chief of the Record Division, for Consolidation.
Claimants identical.

Records Corrected
Dec. 7/1900

J. W. Watson.

Chief of S.O. Division.

E. Fitch

GENERAL AFFIDAVIT.

~~State of~~ District Columbia, County of Washington, ss:

IN THE MATTER OF Pension Claim No. 817,607 filed June 2nd 1890 of Bonaparte Larramore alias Darby Co. [illegible] 135th Regt. U.S. Col. Troops

on this .... day of October A. D. 1891, personally appeared before me, a Notary Public in and for the aforesaid County, duly authorized to administer oaths, [illegible] aged [illegible] years, whose Post Office address is [illegible] Street Washington County of Washington ~~State of~~ D.C., who, being duly sworn, declared in relation to said case as follows:

I have known Bonaparte Larramore alias Darby all of my life. He was owned by my father, now deceased. I know he was in the Union Army as a soldier but cannot say of my own knowledge what Co. and Regt. he belonged to. My father's plantation was near Fort Motte, Orangeburg County S.C. from which place or near there Bonaparte enlisted. I seen him soon after his discharge, and until the past three years saw him quite often. Three years ago I left Orangeburg Co. S.C. and have resided ever since in Washington City. About six months ago I visited my old home in S.C. and conversed with Bonaparte about his Pension Claim. There is no doubt in the world but that Bonaparte Larramore is the identical Bonaparte Darby as claimed by him. It was quite common for ex-slaves to change their names.

Affiant further declares that he has no interest in said case, and is not concerned in its prosecution.

Hy. S. Darby
Signature of Affiant.

If affiant sign by mark, two persons who can write sign here.

The officer before whom this is executed must not witness X signature of affiant.

3-173.

Southern — Div.
Sms. No. 817.607
Bonaparte Larramore
Co. I, 135 Reg. U.S. C. Vol. Inf.

Ex'r.

Department of the Interior,

BUREAU OF PENSIONS.

Washington, D. C., June 5, 1898

Sir:

Will you kindly answer, at your earliest convenience, the questions enumerated below? The information is requested for future use, and it may be of great value to your family.

Very respectfully,

Bonaparte Larramore
Fort Motte
Orangeburg Co. S.C.

H. Clay Evans
Commissioner.

No. 1. Are you a married man? If so, please state your wife's full name, and her maiden name.

Answer: Yes my wife name was Killiby Darby

No. 2. When, where, and by whom were you married? Answer: was married in 1860 and was remarried after the war 1868 by Rev. Shedrick Evans

No. 3. What record of marriage exists? Answer: a marriage certificate

No. 4. Were you previously married? If so, please state the name of your former wife and the date and place of her death or divorce. Answer:

I had no other wife except my present one

No. 5. Have you any children living? If so, please state their names and the dates of their birth. Answer:

Novinia Larymore born 1870
Henrietta Larymore " 1871
Lidia Larymore " 1872
Luisia Larymore " 1873

Date of reply, July 11, 1898

B Larrymore
(Signature.)

CLAIMANT'S AFFIDAVIT.

Republic ~~State~~ of Liberia, County of Montserrado, ss:

In the matter of Bonaparte Dorby late of Co. I, 135 U.S.C. Infantry.

ON THIS 27 day of August A.D. 1900, personally appeared before me Owen L. H. Smith U.S.C. Genl in and for the aforesaid County, duly authorized to administer oaths Bonaparte Dorby age 55 years, whose Post Office address is Monrovia, Montserrado County, Liberia who, being duly sworn, declares in relation to said case as follows: I am the identical

[Note.—Affiants should state how they gain a knowledge of the facts to which they testify.]

Bonaparte Dorby. Was born May 1845. enlisted a private in 1st Lieut. C. J. Hales' Company (I) 135. Reg. U.S.C. Infantry Vol. Was enrolled May 12, 1865, near Columbia S.C. Am five feet, seven inches high, Black complexion, Black eyes, Black hair and when enrolled was by occupation a Farmer. Was discharged at Louisville Ky, October 23, 1865. After my discharge I returned to Fort Motte, Orangeburg County S.C. and again engaged in farming. I resided continuously in the neighborhood of Fort Motte S.C. until my departure for Liberia Africa January 1877. My Post Office address was Fort Motte S.C. I have never applied for Pension before this effort. I did apply for Back pay and Bounty (through Samuel J. Price Esq. of Washington D.C.) which was disallowed by settlement No 165,002 March 3, 1872.

Sarthea Vaughn

E. L. Parker

(If Affiant signs by mark, two persons who can write must sign here.)

10.11.00

Bonaparte his x mark Dorby

(Signature of Affiant.)

SOUTHERN DIVISION. 3—493. B Ex'r.

Inv. No. [illegible]
Bonifast Lawrence, Darby
Co. [illegible] Reg't U.S. [illegible]

Department of the Interior,

BUREAU OF PENSIONS,

Washington, D. C., June 15, 1898

Sir:

In your above-entitled claim for pension you are required to answer the following questions in the blank spaces prepared for that purpose, and return the same to this Bureau at your earliest convenience.

Very respectfully,

H. Clay Evans
Commissioner.

Bonifaste Lawrence
Fort Motte
Orangeburg S. C.

First. What is your actual residence at the present time, and what is the nearest post-office?

Answer. Orangeburg County State S.C. Post Office Fort Motte

Second. Where did you live from date of discharge until you moved to your present place of residence, and what were the dates of the various changes? If in a city, state name of street and number of house.

Answer. As soon as discharged went to the present place where I live now, and was born here in this County

Third. What post-office was nearest to each of your several places of residence?

Answer. Fort Motte

Fourth. What has been your occupation since date of discharge.

Answer. Farming

Fifth. Have you ever been known by any name other than that given in your application for pension? If so, state it in full.

Answer. Bonifast Darby

Sixth. Were you in the military or naval service under a name different from that by which you are now known? If so, state what it was.

Answer. Bonifast Darby

Date of reply, July 11, 1898

B Lawrence
(Claimant's signature.)

[illegible] 8-2

In the Matter of the Application for Pension of Bonaparte Darby.

Now comes one Bonaparte Darby, age about 63, and whose post office address is now at Monrovia, Liberia, c/o the American Legation, who first being duly sworn deposes and says that to the best of his knowledge and belief he makes the following affidavit:

FIRST: That on May 12th, 1865, as a private he enlisted in Company I, 135 Regiment of the United States Colored Infantry Volunteers at Organgeburg, South Carolina, where he was born, and was honorably discharged from said service October the 23, 1865, at Louisville, Kentucky. That his Captain was J.B.Shaw with C.J.Hales as 1st Lieutenant.

SECOND: That during said service in the said Union Army the deponent was very much exposed to rain, from which has developed the rheumatism, settling in his knees and left side, which disables him now from manual labor, his only means of support. That aside from the above service he has not served in the Army or Navy of the United States of America.

THIRD: That as far as known by the affiant none of his fellow soldiers are now residing in the Republic of Liberia. But he recalls the names of several of his comrades who at one time resided in the County of Orangeburg, South Carolina: Jackson Frederick, Helliot Brunson, Randal Bowman, Washington Anderson, and Lewis Wanamaker.

FOURTH: That the surname of the deponent's master was Darby, and at the time of his enlistment he was going by the name of Bonaparte Darby, and enlisted under that name. And that after his discharge and the Colored People were granted the right of suffrage, numbers of them thruout the Southern States of the Union changed their surname from the surname of their masters to their father's name for various reasons, but that the affiant changed his name from Bonaparte Darby to Bonaparte Laramore, from the surname of his former master to that of his father, for the reason that after his freedom he did not wish longer to bear the name of his former master, and joined in what then seemed to be the custom of the time. Further that since that time he has been known by both names: Bonaparte Darby and Bonaparte Laramore; but that he is the same identical Bonaparte Darby, having possession of his original discharge, who more than 42 years ago enlisted as a private in the Union Army at Orangeburg, South Carolina, and subsequently honorably discharged at Louisville, Kentucky.

FIFTH: That if under the age law passed in 1907, if under the law of 1890, or any of the other laws effecting those who have served in the Union Army, the aforesaid deponent is entitled to a pension under the foregoing statement of facts, he respectfully requests that the same be granted. He further requests the Department to designate in these quarters a competent physician to examine him in regard to his present disabilities, and that Messrs. S.I.Wright and Comapny, of Washington, D.C., are duly appointed as his attorneys in the prosecution of this claim.

Bonaparte X Darby
Deponent.

Witness:

Ernest [illegible]

Annabel [illegible]

This is to certify that the above deponent Bonaparte Darby, alias Bonaparte Laramore, personally appeared before me, Secretary of the Legation of the United States for Liberia, and gave the foregoing affidavit, and after hearing the same read and read and acknowledging he understood the same, affirmed that the same to his best knowledge and belief is true, Wherefore this 11th day of June A.D.1907, in testimony of which I affix the seal of the Legation of the United States.

George W. E[illegible]

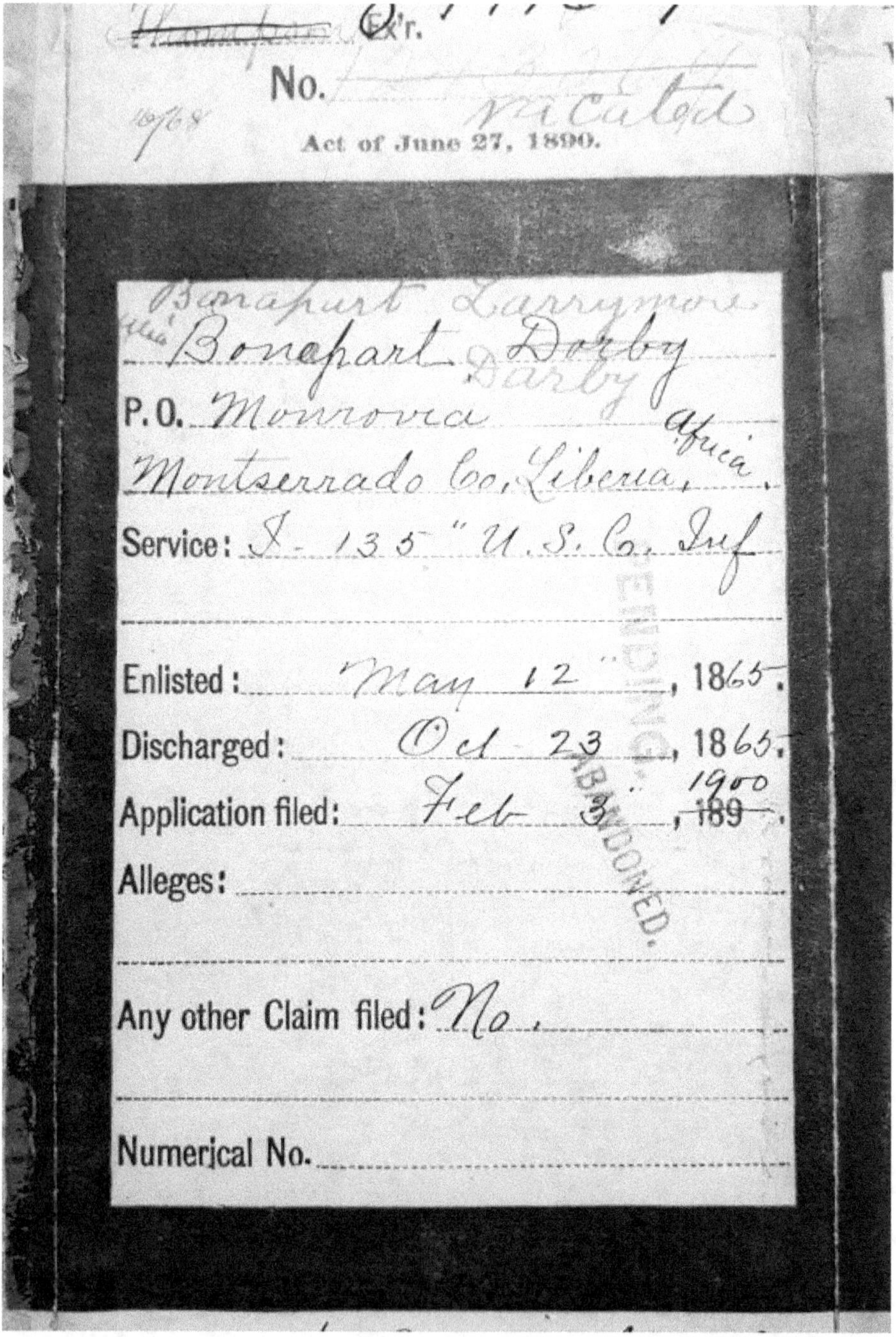
Ctf'r.

No. Vacated

Act of June 27, 1890.

Bonapart Larrymore

alias Bonapart ~~Dorby~~ Darby

P.O. Monrovia

Montserrado Co. Liberia. Africa

Service: I. 135" U.S.C. Inf

Enlisted: May 12", 1865.

Discharged: Oct 23, 1865.

Application filed: Feb 3", ~~189~~ 1900.

Alleges:

Any other Claim filed: No.

Numerical No.

PENDING.

ABANDONED.

PERRY KINARD

Perry Kinard was from Kearse South Carolina, and it shows he died March 31, 1886. In slave time his owner was Mr. Jacob Kinard. His wife Elsie, whose father was Jack Copeland, belonged to Mr. Jake Copland who had the adjacent plantation to Jacob Kinard.

Perry joined the Pioneer Corps at Rivers Bridge when Sherman's army was marching north from Savannah, Georgia to Columbia, South Carolina. He served as a corporal in Company "I," of the 135th United States Colored Troop.

Soon after the war ended Perry and Elsie were married. They were married by the Reverend Nash Bradham at the house of Elsie's father, Jake Copeland. Perry and Elsie lived together until his death as evidenced in several of the declarations in his file. When Perry died, he left approximately fifty acres of land to Elsie of which only fifteen acres could be cultivated. The rest of the acreage was timberland. The total land value at the time was estimated to be worth about three dollars per acre.

GENERAL AFFIDAVIT.

State of South Carolina, County of Barnwell, ss:

In the matter of Mrs Elsie Renard's claim for pension

On this 17 day of [illegible] A. D. one thousand eight hundred and ninety-[illegible], personally appeared before me a Notary Public within and for the County and State aforesaid, duly authorized to administer oaths, Stepheney Kearse aged 67 years, a resident of Kearse County of Barnwell and State of South Carolina well known to me to be reputable and entitled to credit, and who, being duly sworn, declared in relation to aforesaid case as follows:

That the soldier Perry Renard

(NOTE.—Affiants should state how they gain a knowledge of the facts to which they testify.)

served as Corporal, in Co. I Regt No 135 U.S.C.T. from the time of his enlistment near Goldsboro N.C. during the month of March A.D. 1865 and remained in the U.S. military service until honorably discharged by reason of the declaration of peace) about the [illegible] of November 1865 when he was mustered out of service. That the soldier therefore served in the aforesaid capacity from March 1865 as stated, until mustered out. He has not been in service of the U.S. since the date of his discharge.

His Post-Office address is Kearse Barnwell Co S.C.

He further declare that he has no interest in said case and is not concerned in its prosecution.

David H. Kearse

(If affiants sign by mark, two witnesses who write sign here.)

Stepheney Kearse

(Signature of Affiant.)

no Pvt service

Deal

W.H.S.

AUG 12 1892

CLAIMANT'S AFFIDAVIT.

State of South Carolina County of Barnwell ss.

In the matter of Mrs Elsie Kinard's claim for Pension

ON THIS 1 day of Aug A. D. 1892, personally appeared before me, a Notary Public in and for the aforesaid County, duly authorized to administer oaths, Mrs Elsie Kinard aged — years, a resident of Kearse in the County of Barnwell and State of South Carolina whose Post Office address is Kearse well known to me to be reputable and entitled to credit, and who, being duly sworn declared in relation to said case as follows:

The soldier Perry Kinard died on 26th day of March 86 in stead of the 31st March. That the error was in all probability a mistake of the writer who filled out the original application, being herself unable to read or write. She further states that the time of marriage as testified to by the affidavits of [illegible] and Jack Copeland was correct, for it was not until after the soldier's return from the military service of the U.S. at the close of the war, that they were married, and that the error is also due to the party who filled the application. She also affirms that her husband remained in the service of the U.S. until discharged, which to the best of her recollection was about 1st November 1865. That she applied for pension through [illegible] Atty early after the death of the soldier—

David H. Kearse
[If Affiant sign by mark, two persons who can write sign here.]
Susan B. Kearse

Elsie her X mark Kinard
(Signature of Affiant.)
Claimant.

GENERAL AFFIDAVIT.

State of South Carolina, County of Barnwell, ss:

In the matter of Mrs Elsie Kinard's claim for Pension

On this 17 day of August A. D. one thousand eight hundred and ninety-two, personally appeared before me a Notary Public within and for the County and State aforesaid, duly authorized to administer oaths, Rev David H. Kearse aged 27 years, a resident of Kearse County of Barnwell and State of South Carolina well known to me to be reputable and entitled to credit, and who, being duly sworn, declared in relation to aforesaid case as follows:

Pub. to his personal knowledge —

(NOTE.—Affiants should state how they gain a knowledge of the facts to which they testify

Having lived nearly all of his life in the immediate vicinity of Jerry Kinard the soldier. That Mrs Elsie Kinard the soldiers widow has not remarried since the death of her husband. That she has no means of support other than tilling a small farm. the estate of her deceased husband Perry Kinard That the taxable property now in her possession is not over $200 worth That he is secretary of the church with which the soldier was connected and with which he held membership. he can clearly affirm that there is no church or public record showing date etc of soldiers marriage to the widow That the person who is said to have performed the marriage ceremony is dead

His Post-Office address is Kearse Barnwell Co SC

I further declare that he has no interest in said case and is not concerned in its prosecution.

S. B. Kearse
(If affiants sign by mark, two witnesses who write sign here.)

David H. Kearse
(Signature of Affiants.)

Removed to Spartanburg S.C.

|| no remge. Dependence.

Exd.
Sdec.

W. H. P.
Clk

3—289.
(Old No. 9—46.)

DEPOSITION C

Case of Elsey Kinard, No. [illegible]

On this 25th day of Sept, 1901, at Kearse county of Bamberg State of South Carolina, before me, W. H. Stovall, a special examiner of the Bureau of Pensions, personally appeared Daniel Copeland, who, being by me first duly sworn to answer truly all interrogatories propounded to him during this special examination of aforesaid claim for pension, deposes and says:

I am 54 years old. Occupation farmer. Post Office Kearse Bamberg Co. S. C.

I have known Perry Kinard all my life. I belonged on an adjoining plantation to him during slavery. Since freedom we have always been neighbors.

Elsey Kinard is my sister. Elsey was never previously married and neither was Perry. He had no wife during slavery. He had no children by any person before he had some by his present widow. Elsey has never had any children except those by Perry.

They were married by ceremony the year after the soldiers left their camps. I was present. Noah Bradham performed the ceremony of marriage at old man Jake Copelands plantation.

Perry and Elsey never separated. They lived together as husband and wife until his death.

I cant state the number of children they had for I never kept up with that. Three of the children are dead. I do not know the ages of their children. I dont want to guess at their ages.

I saw the body of Perry Kinard soon after his death. Cant state the date of his death, can only say it was about 15 years ago.

Page 13 Deposition C

Page 14

Elsey never remarried. She has never lived with any man as his wife since she became a widow.

Perry left Elsey about 50 acres of land worth I would judge about $3.00 per acre. He left little or no personal property. I considered him to be a poor man.

(Former affidavit of witness read to him)

Answer. That affidavit I believe to be correct. Those dates were furnished me by Elsey when I made it.

Have heard the above read. It is correct.

Attest.
Geo W. Kincad
(None other
near.)

Samuel Copeland
his
mark

Deponent.

Sworn to and subscribed before me this 23rd day of Sept, 1901, and I certify that the contents were fully made known to deponent before signing.

W. H. [illegible]
Special Examiner.

GEORGE WOODS / BENNETT

In the 1900 deposition of George Woods, he stated he was living in "Leflora, Mississippi and was a farmer." He entered the 135th United States Colored Troop as George Woods but first enlisted in the Pioneer Corps at Brunswick, Georgia. He was discharged in November 1865, as he could remember, as it had been thirty-five years. He was recruited into the 15th Pioneer Corps under Captain Fischer and said "in about three months I drew arms in the 135th and became a regular soldier. I got one hundred dollars as bounty while in the 135th regiment."

He said his Colonel was Mr. Gullion, Major was Dixon, Surgeon, Doctor, and the other officers he had forgotten. George stood about 5′ 7" tall with broad shoulders, ginger cake color with a big voice according to his comrades. George remarked about Captain Fischer as being tall and slender, and mentioned he remembered Lieutenant Hale and Steele. Company comrades consisted of John Howell, and Charly Burke, "a yellow cross-eyed man." He said he had four sergeants, Kiles, one called "coonskin" (who was a short Black man), and Brutal Butler from Savannah, Georgia.

(Ned) Edward Washington (Jamison) From Orangeburg, South Carolina, in his deposition talked about being a slave, only free when the soldiers of the Yankee Army passed through. They cleared and repaired roads in what they called the Pioneer Corps, "we were put into companies and had officers," Ned said. He did not recognize George Bennett from the photograph, but he did know a George Woods in his company. William Green after the war became a "scavenger cart guy" in Avondale. Ben Mc Millan, and Lewis Mc Entire, from Dillon, South Carolina, didn't recognize George from the photograph. George mentioned that Jack Wall got shot in Augusta, but George did not know if he was dead or alive. Charles Kenneday had a stroke but was still alive. All these men were part of George Woods experience in the 135th USCT and all vouched for him.

Once home in Madison, Georgia, George married Lucy Ann Poster, a yellow woman, in 1866. His parents were Simon and Charlotte Woods from the Jack Wood plantation in Morgan County, Georgia.

John F. Woods, Jack's son, testified for Goerge who had applied for a pension under the 1890 rules. Together, George and Lucy raised ten children in both Georgia and Mississippi, where they moved and are on the 1900 census where they owned land.

Case of George Wood, No. 635,159.

On this 27th day of January, 1911, at Deponent's Home, county of Morgan, State of Georgia, before me, N. D. Avis, a Special Examiner of the Bureau of Pensions, personally appeared John F. Wood, who, being by me first duly sworn to answer truly all interrogatories propounded to him during this special examination of aforesaid claim for pension, deposes and says:

I am 65 years of age. I am a farmer. I live about six miles from Buckhead, Georgia. I have lived here in Morgan County all my life. I am known as Jack Wood.

Before he stated a name in connection with his business the examiner present showed me a tintype (the one with the case. Examiner) but I failed to recognize the picture as one of a person whom I have known. The examiner asked me if any of my former colored people lived in Mississippi and I stated that George Bennett does and that I see that this tintype is a picture of him.

George Bennett's parents were Simon + Charlotte. They belonged to my father, John C. Wood. George was born in this county, the property of my father, about 12 miles from Madison, the county seat. His parents and he belonged to my father until they were freed early in 1865 and the only surname that any of them had then was Wood. When Sherman's army passed through here, George went off with it and he came back here in a year's time, maybe. After he got back here, he told me that he had been a soldier in the Yankee army and that he was put to helping fix roads for the passage of wagons and artillery. I don't remember that he ever told me what number was given to the regiment in which he was.

Upon coming back here after he had

Page 7 Deposition B

been with the army, George took the name Bennett. His father had taken that name after he became free and George took it also. George married in this county a yellow woman who had belonged to the Pastor family and who was named Lucy. George & Lucy lived around here and near this community - until something like ten years ago when they moved to Mississippi. A few years ago, George was back here on a visit. I don't know his Mississippi address.

George is younger than I. I was born in 1841 and he is something like five years younger - I don't know his exact age and there is no record of the date of his birth. He is about 64 - possibly 65 - years old. He is the oldest of Simon's living children. He has a sister Alice Henry near here who is a great deal younger than he; his brother Will is the youngest of them.

I understood the foregoing as it was read by the examiner and my statements are correctly recorded.

John T. Wood

3-200.

DEPOSITION A

Case of George Bennett, No. 1385159.

On this 17th day of Feb 1910, at Greenwood, County of Leflore, State of Miss, before me, W. T. [illegible], a special examiner of the Bureau of Pensions, personally appeared George Bennett, who, being by me first duly sworn to answer truly all interrogatories propounded to him during this special examination of aforesaid claim for pension, deposes and says: I am 72 years of age; my post-office address is Hilandale Miss.

Occupation farmer. I served in Co I 135th U.S. Col. Inf. under the name of George Cook and enlisted at [illegible] in January 1865 and was discharged at Taylor's Barracks in Louisville Ky sometime in November 1865 as near as I can now recollect it. I had no other service military or naval. I was in the 10th Pioneer Corps under Capt Fisher about three months before I drew arms for the 135th. I was not a regular soldier then and don't know that any company in the Pioneer Corps had any particular name. I have never drawn a pension. I got one hundred dollars in bounty while in the 135th regiment. My Colonel was [illegible] Jackson. Maj. Dickerson was the surgeon doctor and the other regimental officers I forget. My Captain in Co I was [illegible], Wm Fisher, John [illegible] 1st Lieut, and 2nd Lieut [illegible]

Page 6 Deposition A

His name was something like Steele. [illegible] was 2nd Lieut Richardson [illegible] and John Howell a yellow fellow humped shouldered and long jawed from Columbia SC. was 1st Sergt of my company. I forget the names of the other Sergeants or the Corporals I served with and the private soldiers were Charlie Burke, Jack Wall & Mitchell Tate, [illegible] all I can name. I slept with Mitchell Tate & Charlie Burke and Burke was a yellow fellow and cross eyed. I had no favorite messmate. I had no particular associates except the men named. I have not been a member of my company since discharged. I lost my discharge [illegible] in Georgia eight years after I got it. My regiment was made up at Savannah and went from there out toward Beaufort up the river soon after I joined it - six weeks after I joined it - and to Salem Church on the Ridge Road where they examined us again while stark naked and mustered us in. We went rapidly across the country

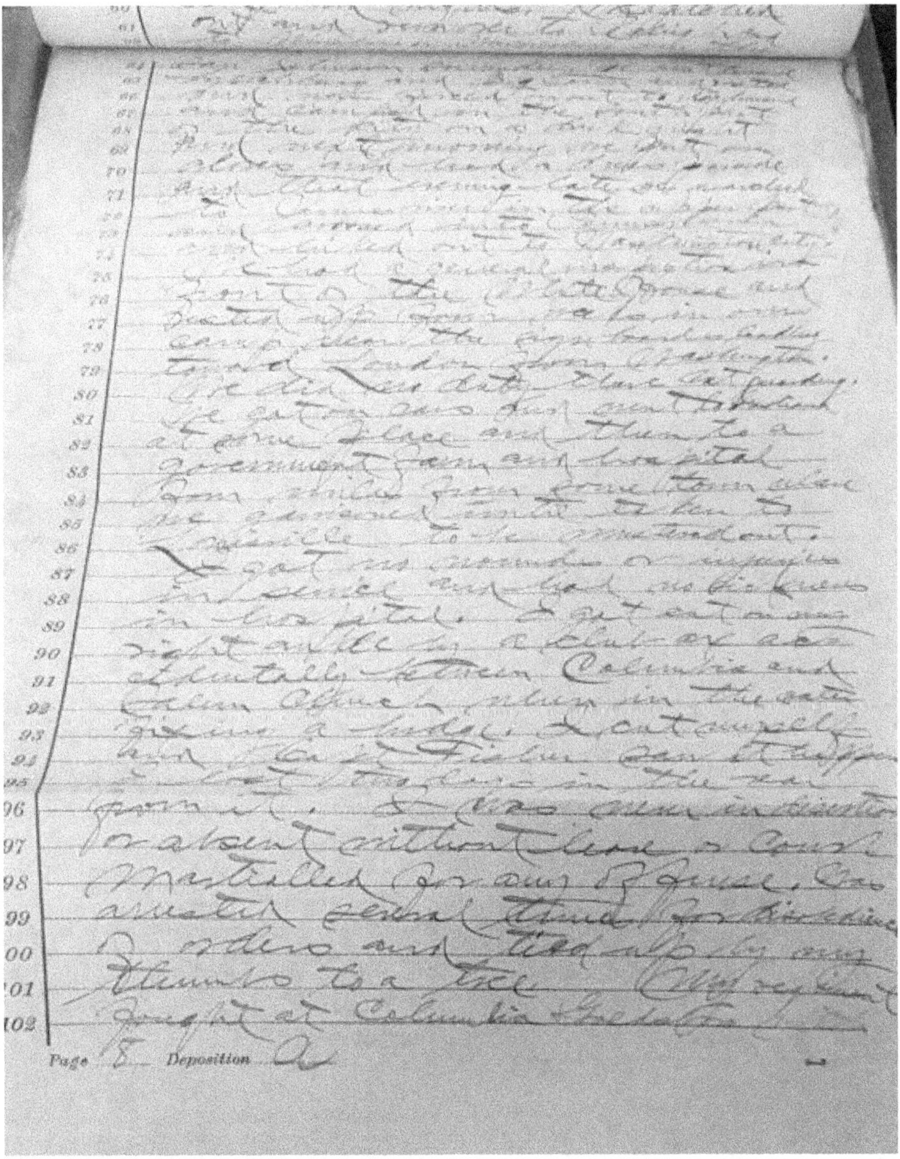

[illegible] out and [illegible] to [illegible]

[illegible] the White House and [illegible] camp [illegible] the [illegible] toward London from Washington. We did [illegible] there [illegible]. We got on cars and went to [illegible] at some place and then to a government farm and hospital [illegible] miles from some town where we [illegible] taken to [illegible]ville to be mustered out.

I got no wounds or injuries in service and had no sickness in hospital. I got cut on my right ankle by a club or axe accidentally between Columbia and [illegible] when in the water [illegible] a bridge. I cut myself and [illegible] Fisher [illegible] in the [illegible] from it. I was once in [illegible] for absent without leave & Court Martialled for any [illegible]. Was arrested several times for disobeying orders and tied up by my thumbs to a tree. [illegible] fought at Columbia [illegible]

Page 8 Deposition A

Page 9

Johnson and Whitesmen. We were in the 15th Corps all the way through. We had quite a number of men killed and wounded but none from my company. I can't bring back in mind any particular incidents of any battles or camp life to [illegible] my [illegible].

I was born on the plantation of my owner John C. Woods twelve miles west of Madison Morgan Co. Ga in February 1839 and stayed there until captured by the Yankees when hiding out in the woods with a bunch of Masters mules and got into the Pioneer Corps and from there into the 135th Regiment and my parents was Simon & Charlotte Bennett of that same Woods place and I have gone by their name since muster out and the name I took in the army came from my old Master and I have had no other name at any time in my life.

I gave in my age as 22 at enlistment. I have no record of my date of birth and am just telling you what my mammy said which was that I was

his
George [mark] Bennett

Attest.

[illegible]

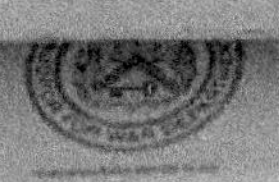

WASHINGTON ,Sept.16,1909.

RPH.422.

The Hon. Commissioner of Pensions.
Washington, D.C.

Sir:

George Woods alleges in his application filed August 15, 1907, that his P.O.address is Hilandale, Mississippi; that his age is 67 years, born Feby. 16, 1840, in Morgan Ga., that he was a private in Co.I. 135th U.S.C.T.; that he joined the army at Brunswick, Georgia ; that he " went from Brunswick to Buford S.C. from Buford to Columbus S.C. from Columbus to Charlotte, N.C. from Charlotte to Goldsborough, from Goldsborough to Raleigh, from Raleigh to wignsborough from Wignsborough to Petersburg Va. from Petersburg to Richmond Va. from Richmond Va. to Washington D.C., from Washington his Regt. went West on train to some point on the Ohio river, where their Regt. took transport and went to Louisville, Ky. after which affiant Co.I. with two more companies of said Regt. went into R arracks at Louisville, Ky. from which place affiant was Discharged on or about Nov. 1865!" He further alleges that he took part in the battles of Columbus S.C. and Goldsborough, and that his discharge "was burned up in 1864 with his dwelling house ,and all contents therein." His cross mark signature is witnessed by E.C. Clegg and Simon Jones, their P.O.address Gunnison, Mississippi.

Respectfully.

B. F. HARPER
Auditor,

By 6666-

C.I. 361843
P.C. 1,385159.

PENSION OFFICE H SEP 18 1909 U. S.

CHAPTER 12

AMERICA WITHOUT HER SOLDIERS WOULD BE LIKE GOD WITHOUT HIS ANGELS.

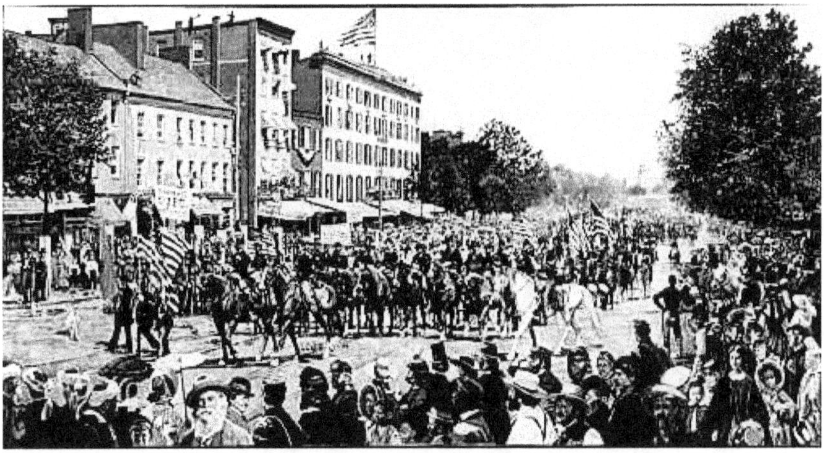

Grand Parade Through Washington, DC

COMPANY “K”

INCLUDED IN THIS CHAPTER ARE EXTRACTIONS FROM THE PENSION RECORDS OF;

PETER MIDDLETON
JACOB HOBBS
ALEXANDER SCOTT
TOBIAS CARROL / SIMMONS
JULIUS JOHNSON / CLINTON

PETER MIDDLETON

This pension record for Peter and Rachel Middleton is quite the story of how fraud was perpetrated against the union-colored soldiers after the war was over. Peter was a slave to Pinkney's Plantation and Rachel belonged to the Bellinger Plantation. They were slaves on adjoining plantations in Barnwell County, South Carolina. Rachel was a young girl when they were married in the white people's house by a colored preacher, and they had one child before the "war of the rebellion." Peter stated that, after they were married, he went to Charleston to join the Union Army. In the fall of 1865, Peter came home and complained that he had been wounded from a gunshot in the hip and somewhere in his head. His injuries bothered him for the remainder of his short life. Peter died of consumption after one year of being in bed on February 8, 1885. After Peter died Rachel applied for, and drew a widow's pension of $8.00 a month, under the act of June 27, 1890.

On the widow's application of 1901, Rachel stated to a special examiner that Tobias Carrol was the man who filled out all the paperwork for her widow's pension and she paid him $10.00 for doing so, but Tobias Carrol could not read or write. In fact, it was essentially Mr. George McClay, who did the paperwork. He was Tobias's roommate and claimed to be an attorney.

Due to inconsistencies a special investigator was assigned to this case and others in the area. Upon investigation, George McClay was found out to have defrauded not only Rachel's application but also that of Tobias Carrol's, Ben McCray's, and Alexander Scott's along with his wife's.

Mr. George McClay was sentenced to the penitentiary because of the fraud and delay of pension for Rachel Middleton. Because of his actions, Rachel had to move seventeen times in her lifetime throughout the city of Charleston. She died in August of 1925 in Charleston, South Carolina.

Case of [illegible]

On this 15th day of Oct., 1901, at Charleston, county of Charleston, State of S.C., before me, R. J. Austin, a special examiner of the Bureau of Pensions, personally appeared Clarence Palmer, who, being by me first duly sworn to answer truly all interrogatories propounded to him during this special examination of aforesaid claim for pension, deposes and says:

My age is 56 years. Occupation dairyman P.O. & residence No. 20, Clifford St. this City. I am not acquainted with any one named Rachel Middleton. I know Geo. P. McClay now in the penitentiary. I see the signature "Clarence Palmer" signed as an attesting witness to the mark of Alexander Scott signed to an affidavit executed June 6, 1896 and I acknowledge the signature to be mine, I wrote it. I cannot recollect appearing before McClay and seeing Alexander Scott make his mark but I am sure he did make his mark in my presence or I would not have signed as a witness.

I do not know Benjamin McCra but I acknowledge the signature "Clarence Palmer" signed as an attesting witness, in the claim of Rachel Middleton, to the mark of Benjamin McCra as being my signature. I wrote it but I cannot recollect going before Geo. P. McClay and seeing Benjamin McCra make his mark but I am sure I did see him make his mark to said affidavit purporting execution on June 6 1896 which you show me for I know

Page 23 Deposition D

I would not have signed as an attesting witness if I had not seen the Indian Make his mark.

I am positive that A. J. McClay the wife of George P. McClay was not present when either of the two affidavits mentioned was executed. She was not present when I signed the papers you show me.

I cannot say where I was when I signed these papers. Sometimes he would come down to the dairy and get me to sign his papers but I have no recollection where I was when I signed these papers.

I am not related to the client. I have no interest in the case.

I have thoroughly understood all your questions and my answers are correctly recorded herein as I have heard you read them.

Clarence Palmer

Deponent.

... before me this 15" day of Oct.

Case of Rachel Middleton et al, No. 386,192.

On this ______ day of ______, 190__, at ______ county of Contin[ued] State of ______, before me, ______, a special examiner of the Bureau of Pensions, personally appeared Rachel Middleton, who, being by me first duly sworn to answer truly all interrogatories propounded to h____ during this special examination of aforesaid claim for pension, deposes and says:

When I signed my application but I dont know Ben McBra, I cannot write & I cant say whether the papers you show me are the the ones I sworn to before McClay or not. I dont know how many times Tobias Carroll went with me to sign before McClay. Yes Joseph Simmons saw me sign but I dont know whether Simmons ~~saw~~ signed his name as a witness or not. I am not acquainted with Alexander Scott. Tobias Carroll and Chas. F. Smith witness in this claim are both dead.

I do not know Ben McBra.

I do not care to be present when you take further testimony in this case. I have understood your questions and my answers are correctly recorded herein.

Attest
Dan McClain

her
Rachel X Middleton
mark

Sworn to & subscribed before me this 14 day of Oct 1901 and I certify that the contents were fully made known to deponent before signing.

R. J. Austin
Special Exam.

Page 18 Deposition A

3—289.

DEPOSITION

Case of Rachel Middleton Wf No. 386 192.

On this 21 day of Oct, 1901, at Charleston county of Charleston State of S.C, before me, R.J. Austin, a special examiner of the Bureau of Pensions, personally appeared Alexander Scott, who, being by me first duly sworn to answer truly all interrogatories propounded to him during this special examination of aforesaid claim for pension, deposes and says:

I am about 54 yrs, for I was born in 1847. Occupation wood sawing. Residence corner King & Ray st. (No number) Charleston S.C. I am a pensioner. I was a private in K 135 U.S.C.T. I do not know Rachel Middleton. I think I sorter knew Peter Middleton and I think he was in my regiment but I dont think he was in my company. I did not know Peter Middleton until I met him in the service. I have only seen him once since I was discharged from the service and that was about two years ago here in Charleston. No, I never made an affidavit for Peter Middleton nor for Rachel Middleton the claimant never was a witness for either one of them. When I met Peter two years ago I would not have known him if he had not made himself known to me. Yes, I can recollect seeing him in the service but I cant recollect that there was any thing the matter with him. No, I cannot think he was in my company. When I met him two years ago he said he was

Page 2d Deposition E

No. 26

in poor health, had a pain in his back and he said all of his limbs hurt him. I did not notice that he had a cough and if he had any consumption or any symptoms of consumption I did not notice it either while he was in the service or two years ago when I met him. Oh no, I am positive I never made an affidavit for Peter or Rachel Middleton.

I do not know Clarence Palmer. I knew Geo McClay now in the penitentiary. No, I never appeared before Geo P. McClay and swore to anything in this Middleton case that you are asking me about. I cannot write my name. I hear you read what purports to be an affidavit made by me on the 6th of June 1896 and sworn to before Geo P. McClay with my mark witnessed by Clarence Palmer and A. J. McClay and I say that it is a forgery for I did not sign said paper nor did I authorize anyone to sign my name or make my mark for me to said paper. So far as I know Peter Middleton was in good health while he was in the service and if he contracted lung disease in the U.S. service or had lung disease while he was in the war I know nothing about it. I know I never saw this paper with my name to it before. If Peter made an affidavit in my claim I don't know it. I am not related to claimant, and not interested in this claim. I hear you read this deposition, I have understood your questions & my answers are correctly recorded herein.

Attest,

J. E. Armstrong

Alexander his X mark Scott
Deponent

Sworn to and subscribed before me this 21st day of Oct.,

OFFICER'S OR COMRADE'S TESTIMONY.

I, Alexander Scott, a resident of Charleston in the County of Charleston State of South Car. late Private of Company K of the 135 Regiment of U.S.C.T. on oath, depose and say, that I was well acquainted with Peter Middleton late a member in Company K of the 135 Regiment of U.S.C.T. of the war of 1861; that at the time of his enlistment, said Peter Middleton was a man of sound Physical health

and while in the military service of the United States, in the line of his duty, and without fault or improper conduct of his own, on or about the month day of March 1865 near Columbia in the State of So. Car. to Richmond Va. marching continuously until June 1865 exposed in much rain and having to wade in much water and with wet clothes continuously on he contracted lung disease. My oral statements are made to Geo. C. McClay at Charleston S. Car. June 6th 1896 who prepared affidavit in my presence and I did not use nor was I aided or prompted by any written or printed statement or recital prepared or dictated by any other person and not attached as an exhibit to this testimony.

I know these facts from having been with command on march and I have no interest whatever in the prosecution of this claim for pension.

Two witnesses when signed by mark: Clarence Palmer; A. J. McClay [illegible]

Alexander his x mark Scott

Sworn to and subscribed before me this sixth day of June 1896 at Charleston in the County of Charleston State of So. Car. I certify that I am disinterested, that the affiant is to me well known, and is respectable, and worthy of full credit as a witness, and that the contents of the affidavit were made known to him before execution.

Geo. C. McClay
Notary Public
S.C.

3

JACOB HOBBS

Jacob stated that he was born on August 8, 1840, in Sampson County, North Carolina. He told, in his oral deposition for a pension, that he enlisted in Goldsboro where they camped for about a month and then went to Raleigh. From Raleigh they went to Richmond, Virginia, and then on to Washington, D.C. They were in Washington until about June 11, 1865, and then went to Louisville, Kentucky, and remained there until he was discharged.

Jacob said he was sick in Goldsboro a few days after enlistment and that he had diarrhea. He did not go to the hospital and then he stated he was taken sick on the march from Raleigh to Weldon, North Carolina. He was then taken up in an ambulance and was carried to Richmond and put in the hospital. "I was a very sick man," he said. Jacob did not know what ailed him, and just before they reached Richmond, they were caught in a very severe rainstorm; he got wet, and it made him worse. When they got "sight of Richmond" a soldier who was riding with them in the ambulance died but "what his name was, he did not know." They stopped along the way and buried him. Jacob said that he had a terrible cough and a pain in his left ear. From Richmond, he was put on a steamer and carried to Alexandria, Virginia. After getting better from all his sickness he was then sent to Louisville, Kentucky and he recalled he performed guard duty there.

While in Louisville, Kentucky Jacob said that he tripped over his tent mate and was injured in the privates and said how badly it hurt at the time. Jacob was mustered out of the Army on October 23, 1865, and returned home. Later in 1887, he became completely blind by a disease in the head and was sent to the National Soldiers home in Elizabeth City, Virginia. He died at the Soldiers Home there in Virginia in 1913.

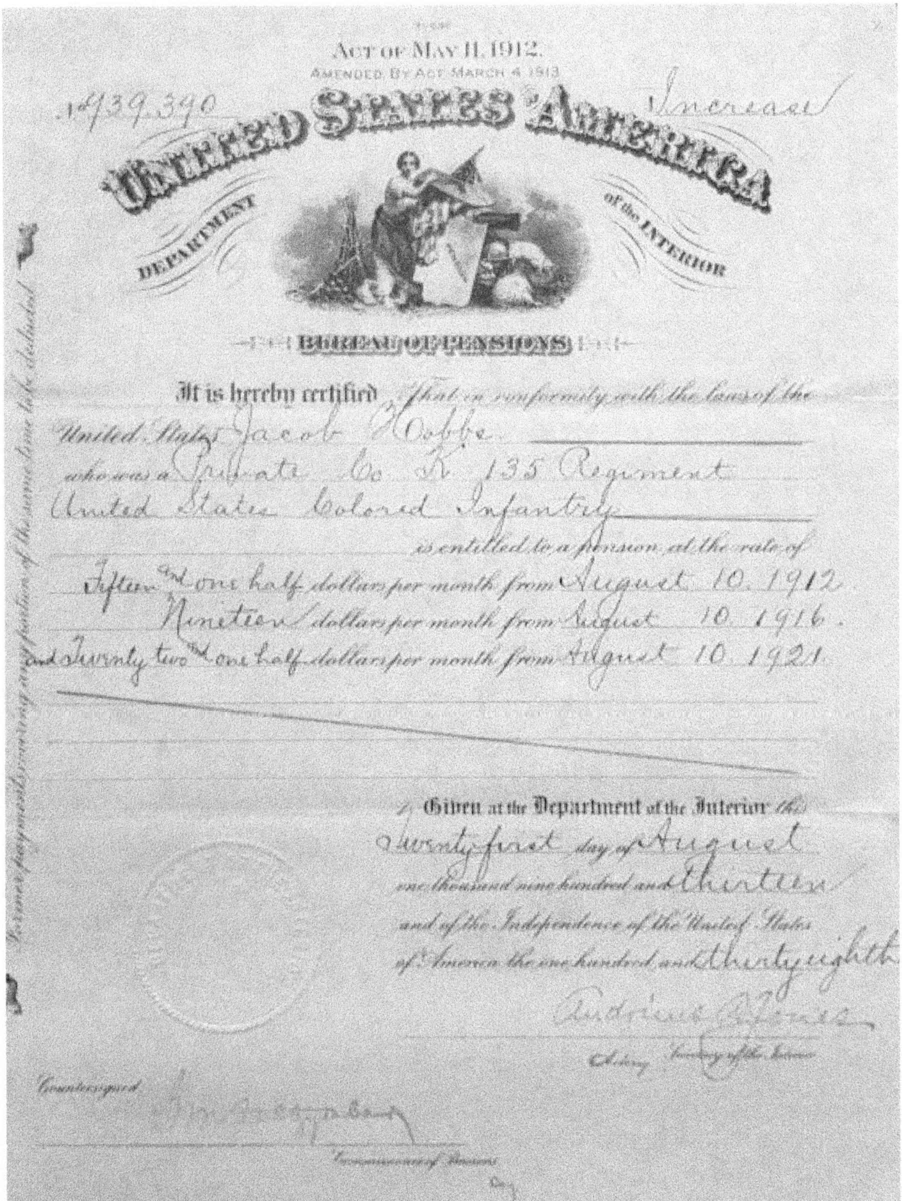
Act of May 11, 1912.
Amended By Act March 4, 1913

No 939.390 Increase

UNITED STATES OF AMERICA

DEPARTMENT of the INTERIOR

BUREAU OF PENSIONS

It is hereby certified That in conformity with the laws of the United States Jacob Hobbs who was a Private Co K 135 Regiment United States Colored Infantry is entitled to a pension at the rate of

Fifteen and one half dollars per month from August 10 1912

Nineteen dollars per month from August 10 1916.

and Twenty two and one half dollars per month from August 10 1921

Given at the Department of the Interior this Twenty first day of August one thousand nine hundred and thirteen and of the Independence of the United States of America the one hundred and thirty eighth

[illegible signature]

Acting Secretary of the Interior

Countersigned

[illegible signature]

Commissioner of Pensions

Declaration for Pension

Act of May 11, 1912.

The Pension Certificate should not be forwarded with the application.

INSTRUCTIONS —This form may be used for Original Pensions or Increase of Pensions. Declaration and testimony in support of same to be executed before some officer of a court of record having custody of its seal, a notary public, justice of the peace, or other officer authorized to administer oaths for general purposes. If such officer is not required by law to have and use a seal, his official character, signature and term of office must be certified by the proper State, County, or city officer under his official seal, unless such certificate has been filed in the Bureau of Pensions for general reference.

State of Virginia **, County of,** Elizabeth City **ss:**

On this 17 day of [illegible], A. D. one thousand nine hundred and twelve personally appeared before me, a Notary Public, within and for the County and State aforesaid, Jacob Hobbs, who, being duly sworn according to law, declares that he is 66 years of age, and a resident of Phoebus County of Elizabeth City, State of Virginia; and that he is the identical person who was **ENROLLED** at Goldsboro N.C. under the name of Jacob Hobbs on the 26 day of April 1865 as a Private in Co. K 135th Regt U.S. Col Troops (Here state rank and company and regiment in the Army, or vessels if in the Navy.)

in the service of the United States, in the Civil War, and was ***Honorably Discharged*** at Louisville Ky on the 23 day of Oct 1865

That he also served................ (Here give a complete statement of all other services, if any.)

That he was not employed in the military or naval service of the United States otherwise than as stated above. That his personal description at enlistment was as follows: Height, 5 feet 6 inches; complexion, Black, color of eyes, Black, color of hair, Black; that his occupation was Laborer, that he was born Aug 10 1846, 18... at Sampson County N.C. Now totally blind as result of service

That his several places of residence since leaving the service have been as follows: N.C. Natl Soldiers Home, Va. Phoebus Va (State the date of each change as nearly as possible.)

That he is ...... a pensioner. That he has .... heretofore applied for pension Certificate No. 939.290. (If a pensioner, the certificate number only need be given. If not, give number of former application if one was made.)

That he makes this Declaration for the purpose of being placed on the Pension Roll of the United States, under the provisions of the Act of May 11, 1912. for age and blindness

That he appoints, with full power of substitution and revocation.................. of .... County of .... State of ...., his true and lawful attorney, to prosecute his claim, and requests and directs that ......be allowed and paid, upon the issuance of a Certificate thereafter, such fee as may be hereafter provided by law, NOT EXCEEDING TEN DOLLARS.

His post office address is Phoebus ...... County of Elizabeth City State of Virginia

PENSION OFFICE U.S. MAY 18 1912

Claimant's Signature, Jacob his mark Hobbs

Attest 1. John T Byrd

2. Gould P. Austin

(Two witnesses who can write must sign here.)

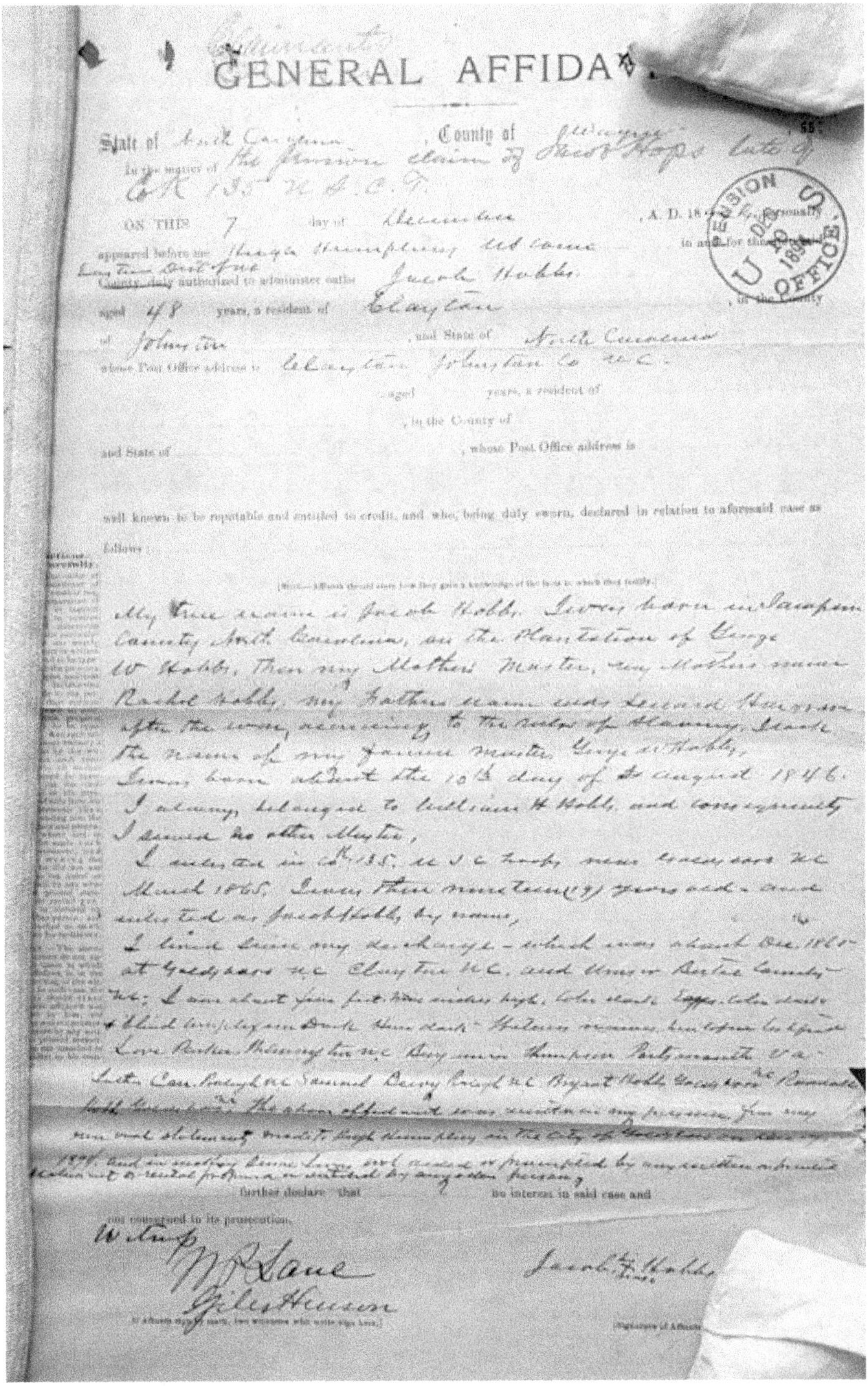

GENERAL AFFIDA[illegible]

State of North Carolina, County of [illegible], ss.

In the matter of the pension claim of Jacob Hobbs late of Co. K 135 U.S.C.T.

ON THIS 7 day of December, A. D. 1894, personally appeared before me Hugh Humphrey US Com[illegible] in and for the [illegible] County, duly authorized to administer oaths Jacob Hobbs aged 48 years, a resident of Clayton, in the County of Johnston, and State of North Carolina whose Post Office address is Clayton Johnston Co N.C.

aged years, a resident of , in the County of and State of , whose Post Office address is

well known to be reputable and entitled to credit, and who, being duly sworn, declared in relation to aforesaid case as follows:

My true name is Jacob Hobbs. I was born in Sampson County North Carolina, on the Plantation of George W Hobbs, Then my Mother's Master, my Mother's name Rachel Hobbs, my Father's name was [illegible] Harrison after the war, according to the [illegible] of slavery, I took the name of my former master George W Hobbs,

I was born about the 10th day of August 1846.

I always belonged to William H Hobbs, and consequently I served no other Master,

I enlisted in Co. K 135. U S C Troops near Goldsboro NC March 1865. I was then nineteen (19) years old – and enlisted as Jacob Hobbs by name,

I lived since my discharge – which was about Dec. 1865 at Goldsboro N.C. Clayton N.C. and [illegible] County NC; I am about five feet [illegible] inches high, color dark, [illegible] color dark & [illegible] [illegible]

[illegible]

The above affidavit was written in my presence, from my own oral statement, made to Hugh Humphrey in the City of Goldsboro on [illegible] 1894 and in making same I was not aided or prompted by any written or printed statement or recital prepared or dictated by any other person,

further declare that no interest in said case and not concerned in its prosecution.

Witness
W R Lane
Giles Henson

[If affiant signs by mark, two witnesses who write sign here.]

Jacob his mark Hobbs

[Signature of Affia

12

Nat. Mil. Home Va. Jany 3/87

Dear Doctor,

I need your Cfg. as to my physical condition when in the Service & at the time of my discharge.

You treated me aug. 1865 for Injury of the head & injury of the privates, resulting in total blindness. Place Louisville Ky. My Injury of the head causing running from the ears & nose. (catarrh) was caused by exposure. My Injury of the privates caused by a kick from one work in a scuffle.

Please do what you can for your old friend to help him get his pension. and God will reward you. Send me a bill for blanks chgs.

Yours in F. C. & L.

Jacob Hope,

Co. K, 135 U.S.C.I.

N. M. Home Va.

31

HOSPITAL STATEMENT.

Here give the No. of the claim, if known, and the letter of Co. and No. of Regt.

I hereby certify that I am claimant for Pension No. 566785 I was late of Company "K" 135 Regiment U.S. C.T. Volunteers, and the following is a full, true, and correct statement of all treatment received by me while in the service of the United States, to the best of my recollection:

NOTICE.

Here give a full and complete statement of all the treatment you received while in the service. State the names, numbers, and location of all hospitals in which you received treatment, and state whether general, brigade, regimental, division, post, corps, or field hospital. State date of entering each, and date of leaving. If not treated in the service state the fact.

I was disabled Louisville Ky. or in the field near Louisville Ky. by an injury in my privates caused by a kick by our Cook (Manson) in Aug. 65. Also by an injury or rupture of the head caused by a severe cold on a long march from Rawley to Washington D.C. resulting in total blindness. Treated in Regimental Hosp.

State here the present Post Office address of claimant.

Given this 3 third day of Jany, 1887.

and I further state my Post Office address is Nat. Mil. Home, County of Eliz. City, State of Virginia.

his
Jacob X Foss
mark
Claimant's Signature.

This statement must be signed by claimant himself, and need not be sworn to.

ALEXANDER SCOTT

He was in Company "K," of the 135th United States Colored Troop and stated he lived at 495 King Street in Charleston, South Carolina. He died on April 5, 1911, and is buried in the Colored Lutheran Cemetery and there is no headstone. Alexander said that his owner was Patrick Carson, in slavery, and he lived two miles from Orangeburg, South Carolina. In February of 1865, Sherman's Army of 60,000 men came through the state and he left along with more than sixty young Black men who joined up with the army in the Pioneer Corps at the time.

Alexander recalled that in Raleigh, North Carolina he enlisted with a fellow slave, Pino Butler, from near Lone Star, South Carolina. Wendy Glover, also a fellow slave, and Jamison, both living near Lone Star, enlisted. He said he was about seventeen years of age 5'-4 ½", and born in Orangeburg, South Carolina, on Patrick Carson's Plantation. His father's name was James Scott and said that he assumed his father's name in 1867. In 1902, on his application for pension, he stated that he broke his left arm and wrist while in the service at Lynch's Creek, South Carolina, lifting a government wagon out of a bog.

Alexander also became part of the fraudulent scandal involving Mr. George P. McClay who ended up in prison for false witness, false testimony, and stealing from the colored soldiers who could not read or write.

PLACE OF DEATH
County of Charleston
Township of
or
City of Charleston

Standard Certificate of Death

~~STATE OF SOUTH CAROLINA~~
Bureau of Vital Statistics
~~State Board of Health~~
Health Department, City of Charleston
Registration District No.
(No. 5 Sheppard St. Ward)
(If death occurred in a Hospital or institution give its NAME instead of street and number.)

File No.—For State Registrar Only

Registered No. 9 -520
(For use of Local Registrar.)

FULL NAME Alexander Scott
Residence—In City. Yrs. Mos. Days

PERSONAL AND STATISTICAL PARTICULARS

SEX: Male
4. COLOR OR RACE: Colored
5. Single, Married, Widowed, or Divorced (write the word): Married

If married, widowed, or divorced HUSBAND of (or) WIFE of ——————

DATE OF BIRTH (Month, day, and year) ———

AGE: Years 49 | Months | Days | If less than 1 day, hrs. or min.

8. Trade, profession, or particular kind of work done, as spinner, sawyer, bookkeeper, etc.: Laborer
9. Industry or business in which work was done, as silk mill, saw mill, bank, etc.: ———
10. Date deceased last worked at this occupation (month and year)
11. Total time (years) spent in this occupation

BIRTHPLACE (city or town) (State or country): So.Caro.

13. NAME [OF FATHER]: James Scott
14. BIRTHPLACE (city or town) (State or country): S.C.
15. MAIDEN NAME [OF MOTHER]: ————————
16. BIRTHPLACE (city or town) (State or country): ———————

INFORMANT ——————
(Address) —————————

BURIAL, CREMATION, OR REMOVAL
Place Col. Lutheran Cem. ———— 19

UNDERTAKER E.Gadsden
(Address) ————

FILED ———— 19 ———————— Registrar.

MEDICAL CERTIFICATE OF DEATH

21. DATE OF DEATH (month, day, and year) April.5, 1911

22. I HEREBY CERTIFY, That I attended deceased from Mch.30.1911, 19 to Apr. 5,1911 19

I last saw h[im] alive on Apl.5.1911, 19 , death is said to have occurred on the date stated above, at 2 P. m.

The principal cause of death and related causes of importance in order of onset were as follows: Date of onset

Pneumonia

Contributory causes of importance not related to principal cause:

Name of operation Date
What test confirmed diagnosis? Was there an autopsy?
23. If death was due to external causes (violence) fill in also the following:
Accident, suicide, or homicide? Date of injury , 19
Where did injury occur? (Specify city or town, and state)
Specify whether injury occurred in industry, in home, or in public place.

Manner of injury
Nature of injury
24. Was disease or injury in any way related to occupation of deceased?
If so, specify

(Signed) J.M.Thompson M.D. 4/6/11
(Address) 53 Radcliff St.

State of South Car Claim of Alexander Scott Co.
County of Charleston
U.S.C.T. On this 29th day of September 1897
appeared before me a Notary Public within
the State and County aforesaid Benjamin M.
54 a citizen of Charleston S.C. who being by me
sworn declare in relation to above entitled claim
member of Co. G. 133rd U.S.C.T. and was present w
on long march from Columbia S.C. Spring of 1865
claimant while on said march at Lynchs Creek N.C. assi
wagon train out of mud bog got struck on his left
near the Wrist by a piece of scantlin or stick
of the men assisting said wagon train out of bog
tioned. and causing him much suffering during co
of march and untill now. And along with Rh
of a general nature and other complaints he
wholly and permanently unable to perform a
labor whatever from prior to April 17th 189
by reason thereof a physical wreck of the conf
house and bed where he has been so confi
for longer than the last month in destitute
stances upon the Charity of friends and
a feeble wife. and that none of his compl
are to vicious habits, professions in nature pe
character. I have no interest in this case
concern in its prosecution. P.O. Address 2 mile
ting St Road.

witness to mark
1. A.W. Curry
2.

Signature of
Benjamin his X mark M.

[illegible]

Sworn to and subscribed before me at Charleston S.
of September 1897 by above named affiant
claimant was fully made known who is a cre
person entitled to belief and I have no int
claim

G.O. [illegible]
Notary Pu

Declaration for Invalid Pension

5

...te of S. C. County of Charleston ss:

ON THIS 16th day of December, A. D. one thousand nine hundred and two

...re me, a Notary Public in and for the County

...State aforesaid, personally appeared Alexander Scott

...56 years, a resident of Charleston, county of Charleston

...e of S. C., who being duly sworn according to law, declares that he is the

...tical Alexander Scott who was enrolled on the 27

...of March, 1865, as Private in Co. K. 135 Reg't U. S. C. T. Vols.
(Here state rank, company and regiment, if in the Military service, or vessel, if in the Navy.)

...e service of the United States during the war of the rebellion, and served at least ninety days, and was

...rably discharged at or near Louisville K. Y.

...e State of K. Y., on the 23 day of October, 1865.

That he is Partially (Partially or totally.) unable to earn a support by reason of my left arm (Here state the nature and extent of every disability)

having been broken while in the service of

the U. S. at Lynches Creek S. C. while

...tting government wagons out of the bog.

PENS...
U
DEC
23
1902

That said disabilities are not due to vicious habits, and are to the best of his knowledge and belief permanent.

That he has not been employed in the U. S. military or naval service otherwise than as stated above.

...other service, here state in what organization, and when it began and ended.)

That he has not been in the military or naval service of the United States since the 23 day of Oct. 1865.

That he has received applied for a pension. is now pensioned by certificate
(If pensioned, state your name, number of certificate, and the rate.)

...766023 at $6.00 per month.
(...plied for it. If you have applied, but not received pension, state when and for what disability, and give number of claim.)

That he makes this declaration for the purpose of being placed on the pension roll of the United States ... the provisions of the Act of May 9, 1900, amending the Act of June 27, 1890.

...He hereby appoints **J. W. MORRIS, of Washington, D. C.**, his attorney to prosecute his claim with ... of substitution. That his post-office address is 9 Sumter St. Charles...

...ty of Charleston, State of S. C.

Julius Meyers

Shadrick Riley

Two witnesses who can write, must sign here.

Alexander his x mark Scott
Signature of Claimant.

...listed March 27, 186.., honorably discharged ..., 1...

...listed ..., 186.., honorably discharged ...

...nsioned at $ 6 per month. Last paid to ...

3—289.
(Old No. 4—446.)

DEPOSITION

...se of Alexander Scott, No. 966,023.

On this 20 day of Nov, 1901, at Charleston, county of Charleston, ...te of S. C., before me, R. J. Austin, a ...ial examiner of the Bureau of Pensions, personally appeared ...enjamin McCra, who, being by me first duly sworn to ...wer truly all interrogatories propounded to him during this special ...mination of aforesaid claim for pension, deposes and says:

I am 62 years of age, a ... laborer, P.O. and residence 27 ... Blow Meeting St. Road. I was a member of Co. G 135th U.S.C.I. Alexander Scott did not belong to my Co. but did belong to my Regt. I think he was a member of Co "K". I never testified in Alexander Scotts case to the best of my recollection. I dont know any thing about his case, except what he told me. I saw him with his arm in a "sling" and I asked him what was the matter and he said he had hurt his arm. I dont recollect how he said he got his arm hurt. I dont know whether he lost any time from duty on this act or not. If there was anything else the matter with him I dont know it. I think he was sick but I dont know what was the matter. I cannot tell whether I made an affidavit in this case before Geo. P. McClay or not. I may have done so. No, I never sign my name. I always make my mark.

Page 40 Deposition L

3–289.
(Old No. 3–446.)

DEPOSITION

[C]ase of Alexander Scott No. 966023

On this 16th day of Nov., 1904, at Charleston, county of Charleston, [S]tate of S. C., before me, R. L. Allen, a [sp]ecial examiner of the Bureau of Pensions, personally appeared [A]lexander Scott, who, being by me first duly sworn to [an]swer truly all interrogatories propounded to him during this special [exa]mination of aforesaid claim for pension, deposes and says:

I was born in 1847 I live at the corner of Race and King Sts this city. I am laborer. I am positively the Alexander Scott who served as a private in Co. K 135 regt. U.S.C. Inf. I enlisted at Raleigh N.C. I cannot say what date I enlisted but I served about ten months and was mustered out at Louisville Kentucky. No I cannot now remember the date of my muster out. It was in the spring when I enlisted and the next fall when mustered out. My Capt. William Johnson 1st Lieut. John Orman 2nd Lt. was Fifer, Orderly sergt. was Wesley Carroll. My bunk mate were Joseph Flower, Merritt White and Clem Walton. They were all Georgia men & I cannot tell where they are. I do not know where any of my officers are. The following were in my company Ben McCra, Manuel Chavis, Orangeburg S. C. Isaac Thompson P.O. Lone Star S.C. Cedric Morgan P.O. Orangeburg S.C. Windy Pauling P.O. Summerville S.C. Sampson Shuler P.O. Orangeburg S.C.

Page 9 Deposition A

33

Fogel P.O. Orangeburg S.C. Ben
a is the only Comrade living in
which that I know of. We
from Raleigh to Washington
We stayed there about a
t. We next went to Louisville
and spent the balance of our
We were not in any fights.
one of our men were desperate.
My Owner was Patrick Carson
lived about 20 miles from Orange
S.C. When Shermans Army
through this State I left
and went with the army
Raleigh N.C. when I enlisted.
fellow slaves were Pinis Butler
was living near Lone Star S.C.
ar or so ago. Windy Glover
also a fellow slave and
Jamison both living near
Star S.C. I was between
17 years of age when I enlisted
five feet and three inches
enlisted. The last time I was
measured I was five ft 4 inches
height. Hair and eyes black
brown. I was born in
geburg County S.C. on Patrick
son's plantation. My father
was James Scott who
ged to a man named Irick
father was called Scott and I

laim

his
Alexander X Scott
mark
Deponent.

to and subscribed before me this 16 day of Nov,
I certify that the contents were fully made known to deponent
ng.

R. J. Austin,
Special Examiner.

3–289.
(Old No. 3–446.)

DEPOSITION

Case of Alexander Scott, No. 966,023.

On this .... *day of* Cont*inued*, *190*–, *at* .... *county of* .... *State of* ...., *before me,* ...., *a special examiner of the Bureau of Pensions, personally appeared* Alexander Scott, *who, being by me first duly sworn to answer truly all interrogatories propounded to h*.... *during this special examination of aforesaid claim for pension, deposes and says:*

wrote the same name when I enlisted. I was a laborer when I enlisted.

The first application I ever filed for a pension was about two years before I drew my pension first and was under the new law. I next filed an application for an increase. I think I filed this a year ago last August. Geo. E. McClay wrote the application for me. I was sworn to this application by Geo. McClay. He had me hold up my hand and sworn me. Two men signed at the same time. I said to witnesses that they knew me and saw me make my mark. Yes I touched the pen. I cannot recall the names of the witnesses that signed that application with me. They both belonged to my regt. but not to my Co. or company. They were colored men and both tall men and both darker than I am. We all signed this application and were sworn at Solomon Brown's barber shop. You misunderstood me for it was Solomon Brown

Page 11 Deposition A

12 and Mr. McClay w
who swore me as attorney. I would k
the names of the attesting witnes
I heard them. No, Paul B
was not a witness. No, Tobe a
Carroll was not one of them.
I dont think one was named
Logan. No one was not nam
Vanderhorst. Yes, I know
a man named David Logan and I
believe he was one of the witne
who signed that application,
could not think who the other witne
was. I do not know any man
named Charles S. Vanderhorn
Do you know any man named
er? Ans, Thats the man I am
trying to think of — Isam Brewer
Isam Brewer and David Logan sa
me make my mark and saw m
sworn and I saw both of them swo
and both wrote their names,
dont know whether they signed o
both sides of the application or no
If any man named Vande
horst was present I dont reca
it. I am sure I saw Solom
Brown affix or inspect his sea
to that application. We were
all sworn at the same time, one
by one. I was examined by the
doctor in this case and I got a m
Attest: his
on McClain Alexander X Scott
mark Deponent

Sworn to and subscribed before me this 16 day of Nov
1901, and I certify that the contents were fully made known to deponent
before signing.

R. J. Ancient
Special Examiner

his .... day of Continued, 190 ..,
.... county of ....
.... before me, ...
aminer of the Bureau of Pensions, personally appeared ....
..nder Scott, who, being by me first duly sworn
ruly all interrogatories propounded to h...... during this speci
ion of aforesaid claim for pension, deposes and says:

..ed Johnson who lived on Commis..
..ed to write for me about ..
..dont know what he wrote, ..
..t say whose name he signed ..
..t letter. The applications men..
..ed that is the application on
..h my pension was allowed a..
.. application for increase fi..
..st Aug. a year ago are ..
..y applications I ever filed.
No, I have never asked a pensi..
..der the General Law or the Ol..
.. Yes I know what you m..
.. filing an application under ..
.. Law. You have to prove un..
..t law that you was han..
.. disabled while in the ser..
..e and are still disabled fr..
..at disability. No, I did not ..
..pension of that kind for I ..
..as not in the hospital a..
..at I could not make the
..oof. No, I did not file ..
.. claim and did not authorize ..
..y to file it for me. No I ..
..t sworn to an old law appl..
.. by Geo A McClay. No I did
.. appear before Geo A McCl..
..th Paul Blunt, Jefferson Pa..
..13 Deposition a

3—289.
(Old No. 3—486.)

DEPOSITION

...se of Alexander Scott, C. No. 966,023

On this .... day of ...., 190 , at .... county of ....ate of ...., before me, ..., a ...cial examiner of the Bureau of Pensions, personally appeared ...lexander Scott, who, being by me first duly sworn to ...wer truly all interrogatories propounded to h...... during this special ...mination of aforesaid claim for pension, deposes and says:

Dr. John Thompson made an af...
...idavit for me but I cannot
say whether he was sworn or
not. The first application I fi...
was for the pension I now draw and
Geo. C. McClay swore me to the applica...
Yes I held up my hand and was
sworn. I think it was at Geo. C.
McClay's house when I was sworn.
Yes, I remember I touched the
pen and made my mark to the
application but I cannot tell
when it was nor can I tell
who signed that application as
me as witnesses. The only
persons present when I signed that
first application, the one I draw pen...
under (Ex. No. 1) was myself, Geo. C. McCl...
and Alfred Simmons. No one
named L. Jackson or Adam Finley
or Benjamin McCra or Isam Bro...
was there when I signed that
application. I know all these per...
sons except L. Jackson and know
they were not present.
I cannot tell how many times
I was sworn by McClay. I
recollect that Tom Blunt witness...
my mark one time but I don't

Page 17 Deposition A

18

recollect any body by the name
of Ad Currie. Pace Blunt
witnessed my mark more than
once but I can't tell how many
times. I cannot say whether
Tobias Carroll and Benjamin McL
were sworn in the old law
claim or not for I did not
file that claim and know
nothing about it.

I have heard this statement
read I have only one claim
pending now and that is a
claim for increase under
the new law. I have ~~the~~
thoroughly understood all your
questions and my answers
are correctly recorded here.

Attest.
Dow McLelain

his
Alexander X Scott
mark

TOBIAS CARROL / SIMMONS

He was born in Bamberg, South Carolina in 1839 and belonged to the Pinkney Plantation, eight miles from Bamburg. His father's name was Frank Carrol, owned by the same Plantation as himself. Tobias had two half-brothers. Richard Bellinger, who was a carpenter, and Stewart who was a preacher in Oakley, South Carolina and they had a different father who was a white man. Tobias entered the Union Army at the age of eighteen and was in Company "K," 135th United States Colored Troop. We find that he died February 17, 1901, in Charleston, South Carolina where he worked as a plasterer.

Tobias's wife Elizabeth born in 1839 belonged to Lacins Bellinger, a Methodist Preacher. She married Tobias in 1878. She stated in her oral deposition that, after the war, Tobias complained about a pain in his side. He looked healthy enough, however all the toes on his right foot were gone. He never did say how he lost them, but it could very possibly have been due to frostbite. The doctor stated, on the record, that he died of kidney trouble and that is why he had a small pension.

When Tobias was alive and living in Charleston, he was one of George P. McClay's cases of fraud which caused the pension bureau to send a special examiner to investigate and uncover several other cases of fraud. This resulted in George P. McClay going to the penitentiary.

Elizabeth said in her written deposition that she and Tobias had nine children together. She died in February of 1921.

B–280.

DEPOSITION D

Case of Elizabeth Simmons, No. 737217

On this 3rd day of March, 1902, at Charleston, county of Charleston, State of South Carolina, before me, Geo. T. Clements, a special examiner of the Bureau of Pensions, personally appeared Alexander Roth, who, being by me first duly sworn to answer truly all interrogatories propounded to him during this special examination of aforesaid claim for pension, deposes and says:

I am about 55 years of age. My Post Office Address is Corner of King & Blake Sts Charleston S.C. I was a private in Co "K" 35th U.S.C. Troops. I was enlisted in March 1863 and was mustered out of service in October 1865 at which time the whole Regiment was discharged. I knew Tobias Carroll who was a private in my company. I never knew him by any other name in the Army [illegible] the Tobias Carroll. I never knew him until I met him in Co "K" 35th. I knew him all through my service. We were discharged at Louisville Ky. We joined the Army at Orangeburg S.C. and marched through with the Army as Pioneers cutting down the trees and fixing the roads for the Artillery and when we got to Raleigh N.C. we enlisted. He was with us at Orangeburg and marched through to Raleigh N.C. as a pioneer. When we came home from Louisville we came by train to Augusta Ga, and then came home by foot. When we got to Barnwell Court House Tobias Carroll left us to go to his old home at Bamberg Barnwell Co S.C. and I went on to Orangeburg Orangeburg Co S.C. After that I did not see him again until I met him here in Charleston S.C. about ten years ago. I knew his face as soon as I saw him and I knew him afterwards up to his death about a year ago. I visited him

Page 5 Deposition D

[illegible] 16

by Reade Post G.A.R. When I met him in
Seale that he was known as Tobias Simmons
so I always knew him as Tobias Simmons
afterwards. He was known as Tobias Simmons
up to his death. I met his wife at his house
I was only at his house twice. He had quite
a crowd of children but I didn't know any
of them, just seen them in the house. She
looked to be a much younger person
than he was. She was a dark complexioned
woman. I never knew her name I
only called her Mrs. Carroll. I never
called her Mrs. Simmons. I never called
him by any other name than Carroll but
other people called him Simmons. He
was receiving a pension before he died
I do not know when he first got it.
I do not know where he lived at the
time of his death. [not after 1882 I think] I visited at
his house. He lived on Charlestone Alley

only called her Mrs. Carroll. I never
called her Mrs. Simmons. I never called
him by any other name than Carroll but
other people called him Simmons. He
was receiving a pension before he died
I do not know when he first got it.
I do not know where he lived at the
time of his death. [not after 1882 I think] I visited at
his house. He lived on Charlestone Alley

just off King Street. I have not
seen Tobias wife since he died. I
know that Tobias Carroll whom I knew
in the Army and Tobias Simmons whom
I met in Charleston. He were both the
same person as I always called him
Carroll. I have understood your
questions. My answers are properly
recorded

his
Alexander X Scott
mark

Witness
A. F. Scott
Gary Scott
Witness

Deponent.

Sworn to and subscribed before me this 3rd day of March
[illegible] that the contents were fully made known to deponent

AFFIDAVIT OF CLAIMANT.

State of South Carolina, County of Charleston, ss:

In the pension claim of Elizabeth Simmons widow of Tobias Simmons late of Co. K – 135th Reg't U. S. C. Inf. Vols.

personally came the claimant above named, who being duly sworn declares that she is the claimant in the above entitled claim, that her Postoffice address is 5 Duncan St. Charleston County of Charleston State of S.C. and that

That she cannot furnish proff of her marriage from the Public record for the reason records were not kept in Barnwell County and especially at the time she married Tobias Simmons.

That the record of the birth of the children has been given by the preacher of the Church in which the children were baptised; that there is no public record to be found that she knows of; that she is still the widow of Tobias Simmons. That she has no who is legally bound to support her; that she is dependent on her own labor for support.

PENSION FEB 5 U. S.

State of South Carolina,

County of Charleston.

This is to certify that I joined in holy wedlock at Bamberg, in the County of Barnwell, State of South Carolina, Elizabeth Handy to Tobias Simmons, on the 19th, day of October 1878, while Pastor of Orange Grove ~~African~~ M. E. Church. That said service was made a part of the Record of said Church at time of performance of the ceremony.

Sworn and subscribed to before me this 19th, day of March 1901 at Charleston. S. C.

W. F. Bailey

Presiding [illegible] Methodist Protestant [illegible]

L. M. Fennell
Notary Public
Charleston S.C.

PENSION FEB 5 U. S.

JULIUS JOHNSON / CLINTON

On the twenty fourth of April 1906 at Bennettsville, Marlboro, County, South Carolina, Julius gave an oral deposition in front of E. H. Jennings. He was a special examiner for the Bureau of Pensions, and stated that he was born in Anson County, North Carolina, and was owned by Colonel William Johnson. He sold him long before the war to Colonel Allen McFarland of Cheraw, South Carolina, and in 1857 he was sent to the plantation that Colonel McFarland owned in Chesterfield County, South Carolina.

Julius recalled that when Sherman's Army came through, he went with them and he was put in the Pioneer Corps until they got to Goldsboro, North Carolina. Goldsboro is where they started to make up the 135th USCT, and when he got to Raleigh, North Carolina, he was put into Company "K". He said from there they marched to Washington, D.C. and camped in the Maryland highlands. They next took a train to somewhere on the Ohio River, and from there on a boat to Louisville, Kentucky where they camped until they were mustered out. Julius served with doctors at the hospital in Louisville, Kentucky most of the time. His officers were Colonel Gurley, Lt. Colonel Bud Long, and Major Dixon. His Captain was Johnson, and his lieutenants were Auman and Pfeiffer. Parks was the surgeon and Shoals was his assistant and they all knew him as Clinton in Service and later knew him as Johnson.

When mustered out Julius said he went by train to Augusta, Georgia, and from there he had to work his way home through the country, as the railroads had been torn up. He said his name was Clinton before the war but as Mr. McFarland owned him some of the people called him by that name.

When Julius applied for a pension, he said his soldier's name was Clinton, however, William Townsend, who sent for his papers, and was a know it all, insisted that he must have gone by his owner's name in the service. That being the case he just let him put his name down that way, as McFarland. When the answer came back that they could not find his name, he then told him if he would put down Clinton then they would find his name. That he did and they were able to then find him in the 135th USCT.

Julius said at the time that he was sure he was sixty-five years old, and he told them he knew that because all his life his father told him that he was born October 2, 1940. He was twenty-four when he entered the Army and was twenty-five when he mustered out. He said that there was no record of his birth and there was no one living that knew of when he was born. This is a good example of how he was able to prove that he was who he said he was, that he served in the 135th United States Colored Troop, who he married, and the birth dates of his children. It is so hard to prove anything that occurred during "slave time" as most did not read or write, and there were very few records. Also, the fact that in 1867 they could change their names from their slave owners' name to their father's name, which made it harder to prove who they were, especially if they did not apply for a pension until later in life.

Julius Johnson married Malina Johnson in December 1860, and on the 1880 census, they had six children listed. Julius Johnson Died in 1912 in Red Bluff, Marlboro County, South Carolina.

Charleston, S.C. May 3rd, 1906.

Sir:-

Herewith I have the honor to return the papers in the claim of Julius Clinton now Johnson, late of Co. K. 135th. U.S.C.T. No. 1302329.

This case was referred for examination to determine identity, age and physical condition from time of filing to date of examination.

Claimant was served with the usual notice and waives notice of any further examination.

Claimant's statement and the testimony shows that he is the soldier of record. He served as Clinton and has been known as Johnson nearly ever since muster out; the name of McFarland does not belong in his case and should not be used. It was used in his application under his protest.

He says that he was born on Oct. 2nd. 1840, and the testimony and records show that the Bureau can safely accept that date as correct.

The testimony also shows that claimant has been about one half disabled for manual labor, on account of age and rheumatism, ever since he filed his claim, that his physical condition was the same from the date of filing until he was examined. The physican referred to by claimant is Dr. J.C. McKenzie, he did live at Parkton, N.C. but is reported to have gone to Fla. and his address in that state could not be ascertained. Dr. McKenzie is said to have left South Carolina just prior

records show that the Bureau can safely accept that date as correct.

The testimony also shows that claimant has been about one half disabled for manual labor, on account of age and rheumatism, ever since he filed his claim, that his physical condition was the same from the date of filing until he was examined. The physican referred to by claimant is Dr. J.C. McKenzie, he did live at Parkton, N.C. but is reported to have gone to Fla. and his address in that state could not be ascertained. Dr. McKenzie is said to have left South Carolina just prior
to the time claimant filed his application, and has never treated him since, therefore, I do not think that his testimony will add anything to the case; and, hence, submit this report for the consideration of the Chief of the Board of Review.

Very respectfully,

Hon. Comr. of Pensions.
Washington, D.C.

Special Examiner.

Isaac Williams is a preacher and was away from home, and it was not known when he would return. Judge McLaurin says that he testified positively before him that he knew claimant in service as Clinton.

DEPOSITION

Case of Julius Clinton *No.* 1302329

On this 25th. *day of* April, 1906 *at* Bennettsville *county of* Marlboro *State of* S.C. *before me,* S.H.Jennings *a Special Examiner of the Bureau of Pensions, personally appeared* Daniel Flinn now Davis. *who, being by me first duly sworn to answer truly all interrogatories propounded to* him *during this special examination of aforesaid claim for pension, deposes and says:*

My age 61. Not at work. P.O. as above.

I served in Co.K.135th.U.S.C.T. I am a pensioner.

I was born in Darlington Co. but came here when four years old. At the time the war started I was owned by Mr.Allen McFarland and had belonged to him for several years.

I know Julius Johnson, have known him since long before the war. He was also owned by Mr.Allen McFarland. Before the war he went by the name of McFarland and in the army he went by the name of Clinton but after the war he took the name of Johnson and he is now known by that name. Yes sir, he was a soldier, I will swear that he is the man who served in Co.K.135th. with me as Julius Clinton. He went in the army with me and came home with me. I have known him for fifty years or more, we were owned by the same man, and I have seen him every month since the war, and I know that what I say is true. You can ask any of

name of McFarland and in the army he went by the name of Clinton but after the war he took the name of Johnson and he is now known by that name. Yes sir, he was a soldier, I will swear that he is the man who served in Co.K.135th. with me as Julius Clinton. He went in the army with me and came home with me. I have known him for fifty years or more, we were owned by the same man, and I have seen him every month since the war, and I know that what I say is true. You can ask any of

the old 135th. men about here and they will tell you that he was in the Reg. I dont know his age exactly, but he is about four years older than I. We were boys together and he was always four years older than I. My mother told me that I was born in Dec.1844.

Claimant has been weak and in bad health for five or six years. I see him often and know that during that time he has not been able to do any work. You can see that he is too weak and painful to work.

He has complained of rheumatism in all his limbs for five years. Says that he is in pain all the time, and he looks like it. I am sure that he has not been able to do any manual labor of any kind since he filed his claim in June 1903.

Yes sir, I am positive that he was in the same Co. and Reg. with me. I am not related, have no interest in this claim and this statement is correct and fully understood.

Attest. Daniel his X Flinn now Davis.
mark

Milton McL[illegible]

Page 6 *Deposition* 13

7

CHAPTER 13

"THEY MARCHED DAY AND NIGHT, WERE FED FROM THE WAGON TRAIN, AND KNEW NO SUNDAYS."

AUTHORS DISTINGUISHED CHOICES

INCLUDED IN THIS CHAPTER ARE EXTRACTIONS FROM THE PENSION RECORDS OF;

SAMPSON PRINGLE

WESLEY CRUMMEDY

JOHN DURDEN

STEPHEN WATKINS

LAWRENCE McCOOK

SAMPSON PRINGLE

Sampson Pringle was born at Pringles Ferry, near Georgetown, South Carolina. In his oral deposition for pension, he spoke about how he was owned by William Bull Pringle, Jr., whose grandfather was the Attorney General to George Washington. In the early stages of the war, he was sent by his master to "work for the confederate government." He helped build fortifications at Fort Sumter for about a year. Next, he was sent to Marlboro County, South Carolina at Cheraw, to one of Pringles plantations on the Pee Dee River. We discovered that William Bull Pringle Jr. owned about 142 slaves, according to the 1860 slave schedule. Sampson is listed on both the 1850 and 1860 slave schedules.

In 1865, Sherman's Army marched through South Carolina, and when they reached Cheraw, they recruited many freed slaves, Sampson Pringle being among them. He was asked by the pension examiner; "how many Pringle slaves ran away and joined the Union Army at the same time you did." He answered, "Two, Thomas and Scipio." Sampson was put in Company "H," 135th United States Colored Troop. Thomas was also put in the same company, however, Scipio was put in Company "F."

Sampson said that he was in Company "H," the entire time and was never on detached duty. He said Gurley was his Colonel, Bud Long was the Lt. Colonel, and he didn't remember the major. Pocock was Captain, Penwick was the 1st Lieutenant, and Horace West acted as Sergeant. Sampson recalled that they were first used in the Pioneer Corps, building corduroy roads so that the ten-mile Army train, supply wagons, and ambulances could move with the army until they reached Goldsboro, North Carolina. That is when they were enlisted in the 135th United States Colored Troop. He said that they were then given their blue uniforms with brass eagle buttons, and their one important task was to drill and drill and drill. To enter the 135th USCT, he recalled, they were stripped naked and examined, given their new clothes, including new boots and socks. The regiment then learned to drill together company by company.

Sampson testified that, "Being a slave of Bull Pringle, born and raised about five miles from Georgetown as a house slave, I was pretty much raised in town. My father's name was Richard Pringle, and both were titled after our owner. I think I was forty-two when I enlisted in Goldsboro, North Carolina."

On the march, leaving Goldsboro, about halfway between Raleigh and Alexandria, Virginia, "I was struck down by a large pain, immediately I was picked up by four members of the regiment and put in an ambulance which carried me to a US transport boat, not a great distance, which took me to Alexandria, Virginia and there I entered the general hospital. I remained in the hospital under medical treatment for about two months."

Sampson went on to say "Sergeant Thomas Pringle and Scipio Pringle were my tent mates mostly. I was in all the fighting in front of Richmond, Virginia. I was wounded in the neck and the back. We lost lots of men killed and wounded in front of Richmond. Cohen was killed, and I helped bury him. Thomas Pringle, my roommate, was killed there."

Later Sampson continued, "I applied for a pension in May of 1891, under the act of June 27, 1890, at $6.00 a month for the loss of my right eye and partial loss of my left eye, rheumatism, and general disability to do hard work." Jim Lingo was Sampson's witness, and Thomas Lawrence and an old soldier signed Sampson's pension application. Sampson said, "These witnesses signed that they knew me as a soldier." Mr. R.B. Anderson filled out his pension application. Sampson was examined for an increase in his pension in front of the South Carolina pension board. "W.B. King was my attorney. He made me swear and touch the pen and then he charged me $0.50."

In his pension application Sampson added, "I have been married twice. My first wife died in childbirth, and I married Hager Baker, my second wife. She is the widow of Baker. Her husband was dead when I married her. I knew he was dead when I married her. I attended the funeral. Reverend Ephram Johnson married us. We had a boy who was a soldier in the Spanish American war. We have but one child under sixteen, Rebecca. It's down in the book."

Mr. Pringle said in 1901, "I am sixty-five years of age and reside as before laboring when able. Milo B. Stephens is my attorney in Washington, DC. They took out ten dollars to pay R.B. Anderson, our postmaster here, who is my local agent. He did all of my writing and the swearing of witnesses for me. I pay him fifty cents each time he draws a paper. I never fail to pay him. When my pension was allowed and my check came with my first payment, Anderson went with me to the bank to cash the check. Anderson carried the check and took the money from the man at the bank. He gave me my money and kept out his. He showed me how much money he kept for himself; it was thirty dollars. He was well satisfied; I think it was in ten-dollar bills. The check was for five hundred dollars and something, but I sent three hundred and fifty dollars to the bank in

Charleston. I brought home ninety dollars and Anderson kept the balance which was five hundred and ninety dollars." This is a case that was referred to a special examiner and then was referred to the chief of the law division for fraud.

Sampson told the examiner that he trusted Anderson to go to the bank with his first check and instructed him to send the money to the Charleston bank. At the bank, Anderson said "he gave me ten or fifteen dollars for what I had done for him, the first check was about two hundred dollars." Sampson filed a suit against R.B. Anderson in Georgetown, South Carolina, on July 3, 1901. He also filed for an increase in pension which he received five hundred and ninety dollars, but claimed he only got ninety dollars and Anderson kept the balance. Mr. F.M. Dagrenton, the bank manager at the Bank of Charleston, stated he had a client named Sampson Pringle, who resided in Georgetown, who did not read or write. He opened an account on December 16, 1899, and made a deposit of two hundred dollars. Further investigation developed the fact that the pensioner deposited three hundred and fifty dollars into the bank on June 9, 1899.

In 1867, after he received the right to vote Sampson said, "I changed my name to my father's, and I am now known as Sampson Richardson." Sampson worked for many years for one of the wealthiest families in South Carolina.

We found that Bull Pringle graduated from West Point, and his father was a state senator. Sampson was a well-known person in Georgetown and when he died, they buried him on the plantation he was born on, (Pringles Ferry). We have included his picture and obituary, which is rare, here in his record. His picture also is shown in Chapter 19, (Soldiers Pictures,). Sampson Pringle is a man of great courage, integrity, and a man of valor.

3—289.
(Old No. 3—188.)

DEPOSITION A

Case of Sampson Pringle, Inv. Ctf., No. 980985

On this 23 day of March, 1901, at Georgetown county of Georgetown, State of N.C., before me, Don McClaire, a special examiner of the Bureau of Pensions, personally appeared Sampson Pringle, who, being by me first duly sworn to answer truly all interrogatories propounded to him during this special examination of aforesaid claim for pension, deposes and says:

I am 65 years of age, P.O. and residence as above, laborer, I am the same Sampson Pringle who served as a private in Co. H - 135 U.S.C. Inf. and was pensioned under the Act of June 27, 1890 at $6 a month for loss of sight of eye and partial loss of left and rheumatism and general disability to do hard work. I was born in 5 miles of this place but was pretty much raised right in town. I cant tell what year I was born in. I get my age from my owner, Bill Pringle, whose slave I was born and was his slave until freedom. My master lived here until the war. My father was named Richard Pringle. We both titled after our owner. I have never been known by any other name than Sampson Pringle. I think I was 42 when I enlisted. I enlisted at Goldsboro, N.C. I cant give the year. Capt. Pocock enlisted me. They carried me and had me examined before the doctor. They had something like a clock and examined my whole body and then they put me down on the book. I was discharged at Louisville, Ky. Nat'l Barracks after the war more than a year. I cant give the year. Since the war I have

Page 4 Deposition A

lived no place except in Georgetown all the time. I gave I my discharge to Atty. McPheley to get my back pay and bounty. I never did see it any more. He is dead. (Pensioner is 5-7 by actual measurement, no mark or scars, & black) Co. H- 135 was my only U.S. service. I was not in the confederate army in any capacity. I was with my Co. all the time. I never was on detached duty. Gully was Col. Budlong was Lt. Col. I don't remember the Maj. Pocock was Capt. Renwick was 1st Lt. I have forgotten 2nd Lt. Horace West acted Ord. Sergt. Thomas Pringle and Scipio Pringle were my tent mates mostly. I was in all the fighting in front of Richmond. I was wounded there in the neck and in the back. We lost lots of men killed and wounded in front of Richmond. Cohen was killed. I helped to bury him. Thomas Pringle, my tent mate, was killed there. Here are my pension papers. I always keep them in my own possession. I have never pledged either for money or thing of value. (May voucher and certif. exhibited voucher O.K. Certif. shows, issued May 10th 1899, at six dollars a month commencing Jun. 24, 1891, partial inability to earn a support by manual labor. Knoxville Agency.) When I put in for a pension R.B. Anderson, Thomas Lawrence and

Attest:
B. I. Lazard

Sampson his X mark Pringle
Deponent.

Sworn to and subscribed before me this 23rd day of March, 1901, and I certify that the contents were fully made known to deponent before signing.

Dow McClain

3-289.
(Old No. 3-446.)

DEPOSITION B

Case of Sampson Pringle, No. 980986

On this 23 day of March, 1901, at Georgetown county of Georgetown State of S.C., before me, Clow McClain, a special examiner of the Bureau of Pensions, personally appeared R. B. Anderson, who, being by me first duly sworn to answer truly all interrogatories propounded to him during this special examination of aforesaid claim for pension, deposes and says:

I am 43 years of age, P.O. and residence as above, Postmaster of Georgetown, S.C. I am well acquainted with Sampson Pringle. I represented him as his local agent when he was prosecuting his claim for pension. His Washington Atty. was Milo B. Stevens. I was not sub agent to Stevens, had no arrangement or agreement with him as to a division of the fee and received no part of Stevens fee. I had no contract with Pringle but when his first check came I went to the bank with him and instructed him about sending some of his money to a Charleston Bank and he gave me, at the bank $10 or $15 for what I had done for him. I made him no charge whatever. He gave me the amount of his own motion. He owed me nothing for borrowed money or on any other account. I have heard my answers and they are correct. He asked me to go to the bank with him to instruct him about sending his money to Charleston.

R. B. Anderson

Page 10 Deposition B

page 15

When he received his money at the bank in this city he paid me voluntarily, ten or fifteen dollars. I do not recollect the exact amount. I made no charge whatever. I did not charge him the ordinary notarial fees for drawing his papers and swearing ~~swearing~~ his witnesses. I did all that free because he was old and poor. I went with him to the bank because he asked me to do so. I think he paid me in paper money but I cant state the size of the bills. I do not recollect whether any one was with us or not at the bank. I think there was not. I kept no account of the work I did for him. I cant tell how many papers I drew or how many witnesses I swore or what I did. I know he came to me from time to time as his claim progressed and I always did what there was to do to advance the claim. I paid out no money for him and did not go on any trips to procure testimony for him. The money was paid to me while we were out in the bank. I did not go to the bank to get him to pay me money, for I made him no charges, but I went to assist him. I have heard my answers ~~at his request~~ and they are correct.

R. D. Anderson
Deponent

Attest:
A. T. Horry

Sworn to and subscribed before me this 11 day of July 1901, and I certify that the contents were fully made known to deponent before signing.

Dow McClain
Special Examiner.

3—289.
(Old No. 3—418.)

DEPOSITION A

Case of Sampson Pringle Inv. ctf., No. 980785

On this .... day of ...., 190 , at
Continued, county of ....
State of ...., before me, ..., a
special examiner of the Bureau of Pensions, personally appeared
Sampson Pringle, who, being by me first duly sworn to answer truly all interrogatories propounded to h— during this special examination of aforesaid claim for pension, deposes and says:

Lin Lingo were my witnesses. Thomas Lawrence was an old soldier and I signed his paper for a pension. I also signed Ligno's papers for a pension. R.B. Ander was P.M. He knew me for 40 years. These witnesses only signed that they knew that I was a soldier. That was all they did. I did the same for them. I paid some of my witnesses 25¢ and some 50. I gave Anderson nothing. I did not pay them at the time. I paid them when my pension came. I was examined before the Board last Jan. I have applied for increase. I was before the Charleston S.C. Board. My claim under the old law was rejected. (Letter shown "no record") I have no claim pending before the Bureau except my claim for increase under the new law. C. & W. B. King were my attorneys in Washington. R.B. Andlerson was my local agent. They took out $10 for King. I paid Anderson, I think I paid him $30. He went to the bank with me. He stand with me to the very last. He took the money from the bank and gave me my money and kept his. He said he was well satisfied. No one was present but the men in the bank. I dont know

Page 6 Deposition A

whether they saw the transaction or not. He gave me no receipt for the money he kept. I execute my voucher before R.B. Anderson, N.P. and P.M. I only carry the two papers. He makes me swear and touch the pen and charges me 50¢. I have been married twice. My first wife died and I then married Hager Baker. She was the widow Baker. Her husband was dead when I married her. I know her husband was dead when I married her, I attended the funeral. Rev. Ephraim Johnson married me and my present wife. I cant tell exactly when we were married but we had a boy who was a soldier in the Spanish war. We have but one child under 16, Rebecca. I think she very close to 16 - may be a little over. It is down in the book. I have heard my answers and they are correct.

Sampson his X mark Pringle

Attest:
B.I. Hazard

Sworn to and subscribed before me this 23 day of March

190[illegible] and I certify that the contents were fully made known to deponent

3—289.
(Old No. 3—466.)

DEPOSITION A

Case of Sampson Pringle, Inv. late No. 980985

On this 13 day of July, 1901, at Georgetown, county of Georgetown, State of S.C., before me, Dor McClain, a special examiner of the Bureau of Pensions, personally appeared Sampson Pringle, who, being by me first duly sworn to answer truly all interrogatories propounded to him during this special examination of aforesaid claim for pension, deposes and says:

I am 65 years of age, P.O. and residence as above. Laborer when able. I am the pensioner in the above-cited claim. Milo B. Stevens was my Washington attorney. They took out $10 to pay him when my pension was allowed. R. B. Anderson, our postmaster here, was my local agent. He did my writing and swore my witnesses for me. I paid him each time he drew a paper or swore a witness for me. Each time I paid him 50¢. I never failed to pay him at the time he did the work. When my pension was allowed and my check came for the first payment, Anderson went with me to the bank to cash the check. Anderson carried the check and took the money from the man at the bank. He gave me my money, and kept out his. He showed me how much he kept for himself and it was $30. He was well satisfied. I think it was ten-dollar bills. No one was present except the bank man. I do not know which of the bank men paid the money. I sent some, $300 I think, to Charleston, brought $70 home and Anderson got the balance. I sent the $300 to the Charleston Savings Bank.

Page 8 Deposition A

Page 9

I am real sure I brought $90 ho[me]
The check was for five hundred and
something. I cant tell how much ove[r]
five hundred. I remember now. I sen[t]
$350 to the Charleston Savings Bank,
brought $90 home and gave Anderson
the balance. I mean he kept the balance
(Ctf. issued May 10-1899- to commence
Jan. 24-1891- at $6 a month making in
all $590.) He kept the money out. I
did not give it to him at all. No
one counted my money after I got
home. I can count money but I did
not count the money Anderson kept.
He said it was $30 and that is all
I know about it. I have heard
my answers and they are correct.

Samphson his x mark Pringle

Attest:
Rebecca Pilchord

Deponent.

Inv. Ctf. 980985
Sampson Pringle
H-135 U.S.C.V.I.
Act June 27, 1890
Knoxville Agency.

Charleston, S.C.,
July 23, 1901.

Hon. Com. of Pensions,
Washington,
D.C.

Sir:

In the "slip" investigation of the Charleston, S.C. it was developed that the pensioner in the above-cited claim paid R.B. Anderson, P.M. of Georgetown, S.C. a fee of ten or fifteen dollars. Anderson admits that he received the fee of about that amount. I think it not at all improbable that he received much more. Anderson handled the money at the bank and took his fee and returned the pensioner the balance. The pensioner took $90 home and sent $850 to a Charleston bank. This leaves about $60 unaccounted for. After getting a statement from the bank, Dep. C,

I procured the No. of pensioner's bank book and with this data made another investigation at the bank and learned that the pensioner did deposit $350 in the bank June 9 - 1899. The pensioner is very ignorant and my second visit to him shows that he is not a man who could stand a very rigid cross examination. In my judgment a prosecution in this case would be unwise unless brought with a number of others. Pensioner insisted that he paid Anderson $30 when I first saw him. On my second visit he was uncertain but thought it was $30.

I recommend reference to the Chief of the Law Division for his consideration.

Very respectfully
Dow McClain,
Special Examiner.

Health Department of the City of Georgetown.

CARRY THIS CERTIFICATE TO REGISTRAR FOR BURIAL PERMIT.

Copy

CERTIFICATE OF DEATH

1. Full name of Deceased, (Write legibly and spell correctly. If an infant not named give parents name.) Samson Richards

2. Age, 65 years, ... months, ... days. Color, Black

3. ~~Single~~, Married, ~~Widower or Widow~~, (Cross legibly the words not required in this line.) 4. Occupation Laborer

5. Birthplace, (State or County.) SC. How long in the United States, if of Foreign birth.

6. How long Resident in this City 30 years

7. Father's Birthplace, (State or County.) SC.

8. Mother's Birthplace, (State or County.) SC.

9. Place of Death, (If an institution, please state the name.) No. ....
Prince Street. Ward.

10. I Hereby Certify, That I attended deceased from Aug 9 1902, to Aug 21 1902; that I last saw him alive on the 21 day of Aug 1902; that he died on the 18 day of September 1902, about .... o'clock, A. M. or P. M., and that the Cause of his death was:

H... Hypertrophy

TIME FROM ATTACK TILL DEATH:

Write opposite each cause: if unknown it should be so

Obituary.

HE LIVES IN OUR MEMORY.

Georgetown, S. C., Sept 18, 02

Brother Samson Pringle departed this life, aged 77 years, he being one of the veteran soldiers. He went to Charleston to be examined by the doctors July 29; he came back home Aug. 1, and on the 4th of said month he was taken sick, but bore his afflictions like Job. He was a member of Wesley M. E. Church—a class leader, steward and exhorter. He left a benevolent wife, three daughters, one son, and a host of friends to mourn. He died in the faith. Servant of God, well done. Thy glorious warfare is passed. The battle is fought, the race is won, and thou art crowned at last.

J. T. Wilson, Pastor.

... Black M. D.
Medical Attendant.
... Georgetown S.C.

PENSION
DEC 23 1902
U. S.
OFFICE

Attention is invited to the outlines of the human ... and they should be used whenever it is possible to indicate precisely the location ... as amputation, &c.

WESLEY CRUMMEDY

Wesley Crummedy became a Buffalo Soldier after the Civil War. He originally enlisted in the Army in 1865 and gave his age at the time at 18 years old and claimed he was born on March 27th, 1847, in Sampson County, North Carolina. He was from Clinton, North Carolina, when he first enlisted in Company "E," in the 135th United States Colored Troop at Goldsboro, North Carolina. His service in the 135th USCT was significant., as he served the Regiment as the trumpeter. This role he took on would follow him throughout his service history.

In his Declaration for Pension dated May 23, 1912, in Pueblo, Colorado Wesley claimed to be 65 years of age. He documented that he was the identical person who was enrolled at Goldsboro, N.C. under the name of Wesley Crummedy. He enrolled on March 27, 1865, as a private in Co. "E," 135th Regt. U.S. Col. Troop or Infantry Volunteer and listed his occupation as a farmer.

Following the war, and after being discharged from the army, Wesley gave reference in his pension record that he listed several places of residence to include about three years in Greenville and Jonesborough, Tennessee, until 1872, and then in El Paso, Texas, from 1883 to 1887, and Pueblo, Colorado ever since to 1912. Following the Civil War, and when he was a Buffalo Soldier, he married Virginia Kenady on May 15, 1877, at Prairie, Grant County, New Mexico.

From May 7, 1872, Mr. Crummedy served as a Buffalo Soldier Trumpeter in Co. "B," 9th U.S. Cavalry, until 1877. He then reenlisted in the same regiment from February 21, 1878, to February 20, 1883, all the while being the Trumpeter. His pension documents showed that he received $8.00 per month for his time spent in the service of the United States.

There is a reference in the applicant's pension file from the House of Representatives that Mr. Crummedy had been turned down several times due to previous conflicting statements regarding his age. Therefore, there was a temporary hold on his application in 1910. There appeared to be eleven previous statements regarding his age. The examiner pointed out that a statement made by Wesley in February 1899 stated his age as being forty-four years old. The examiner pointed out that he enlisted in 1865, which would have made him ten years of age at the time. The examiner explained how that would be ridiculous and indicated Wesley would hardly know his exact age based on his physical appearance.

To help resolve the age conflict, Colonel Irving F. Stanton, one of Pueblo Colorado's leading ex-soldier citizens, wrote to the House of Representatives to verify Wesley Crummedy's service and attempted to resolve the dispute regarding his age as there was a ten-year discrepancy in his file. As substantiation to his actual age, there appears a Notarized statement of fact in the file that there was a family bible on which is recorded that Wesley Crummedy was born on March 27, 1847, in Sampson County, North Carolina.

Following his time in the Service, Wesley Crummedy was an active member of the Pueblo G.A.R., where he served as their Bugler/Trumpeter, and "His tall figure was familiar in G.A.R. parades." One of his duties, that he was proud of, was the sounding of "taps" at the graves of departed comrades. He was well known in the community for being a kind and generous man. He was known as the Trumpeter of the Pueblo Post of the Grand Army of the Republic, always on hand when the Post was to appear in Pueblo.

Wesley Crummedy died on December 28, 1917, and is himself buried in the cemetery on the north side of the G.A.R. plot in Pueblo, Colorado. Virginia Kenady Crummedy, his wife, died in January 1914.

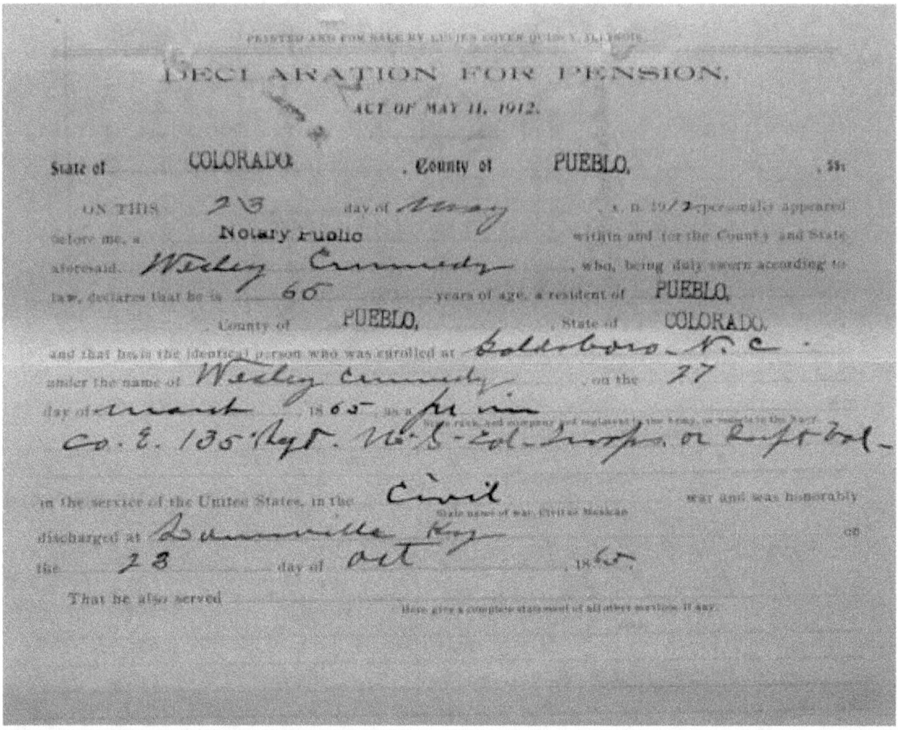

PRINTED AND FOR SALE BY ... QUINCY, ILLINOIS.

DECLARATION FOR PENSION.

ACT OF MAY 11, 1912.

State of COLORADO, County of PUEBLO, ss:

ON THIS 23 day of May, A. D. 1912 personally appeared before me, a Notary Public within and for the County and State aforesaid, Wesley Kennedy, who, being duly sworn according to law, declares that he is 66 years of age, a resident of PUEBLO, County of PUEBLO, State of COLORADO, and that he is the identical person who was enrolled at Goldsboro N. C. under the name of Wesley Kennedy, on the 27 day of March 1865 as a pvt in Co. E. 135 Regt. U. S. Col. Troops or Inft Vol. in the service of the United States, in the Civil war and was honorably discharged at Louisville Ky on the 23 day of Oct, 1865.

That he also served ... Here give a complete statement of all other services, if any.

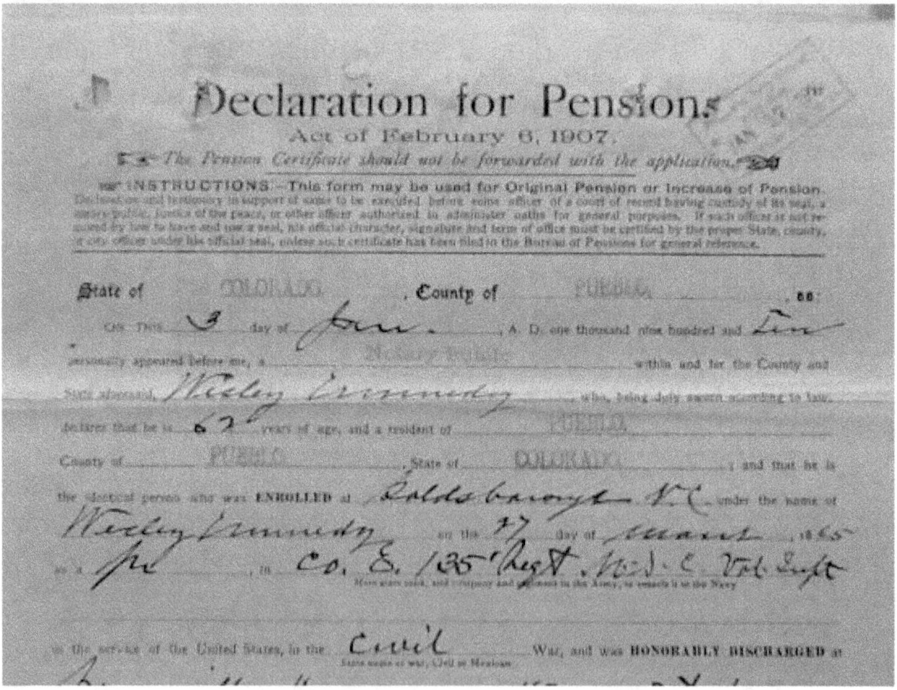

Declaration for Pension

Act of February 6, 1907.

The Pension Certificate should not be forwarded with the application.

INSTRUCTIONS.—This form may be used for Original Pension or Increase of Pension. Declaration and testimony in support of same to be executed before some officer of a court of record having custody of its seal, a notary public, justice of the peace, or other officer authorized to administer oaths for general purposes. If such officer is not required by law to have and use a seal, his official character, signature and term of office must be certified by the proper State, county, or city officer under his official seal, unless such certificate has been filed in the Bureau of Pensions for general reference.

State of COLORADO, County of PUEBLO, ss:

ON THIS 3 day of Jan., A. D. one thousand nine hundred and Ten personally appeared before me, a Notary Public within and for the County and State aforesaid, Wesley Kennedy, who, being duly sworn according to law, declares that he is 62 years of age, and a resident of PUEBLO, County of PUEBLO, State of COLORADO, and that he is the identical person who was ENROLLED at Goldsborough N. C. under the name of Wesley Kennedy on the 27 day of March, 1865 as a pvt, in Co. E. 135 Regt. U. S. C. Vol. Inft in the service of the United States, in the Civil War, and was HONORABLY DISCHARGED at

ON THIS 3 day of Jan., A. D. one thousand nine hundred and ten personally appeared before me, a Notary Public within and for the County and State aforesaid, Wesley Crumedy, who, being duly sworn according to law, declares that he is 62 years of age, and a resident of Pueblo County of Pueblo, State of Colorado, and that he is the identical person who was ENROLLED at Goldsborough N.C. under the name of Wesley Crumedy on the 27 day of March 1865 as a pvt in Co. E. 135 Regt. U.S. C. Vol. Inft

in the service of the United States, in the Civil War, and was HONORABLY DISCHARGED at Louisville Ky. on the 23 day of October 1865

That he also served Co. B. 9th U.S. Cav. from May 7th 1872 to May 7th 1877 & reenlisted in same Co. & Regt. from Feb. 21st 1878 to Feb. 20 1883 [illegible]

That he was not employed in the military or naval service of the United States otherwise than as stated above. That his personal description at enlistment was as follows: Height, 5 feet 6 inches; complexion, dark; color of eyes, black; color of hair, black; that his occupation was servant; that he was born March 27, 1847, at Sampson County N.C.

That his several places of residence since leaving the service have been as follows: Mitchell Co. N.C. about 3 years, at [illegible] & [illegible]borough [illegible] until 1872 El Paso Tex. from 1883 to 1887 [illegible] Colo. [illegible]

HOUSE OF REPRESENTATIVES

WASHINGTON

JAN 1 [illegible] 1910

Jan. 11,1910

Hon. J. L. Davenport,

Commissioner of Pensions,

Washington, D. C.

JAN 1 [illegible]

Dear Sir:

I enclose Declaration for Pension of Wesley Crumedy, Co. E, 135th U. S. Colored Volunteer Infantry and other services, certificate No. 808264. Mr. Crumedy has been turned down a number of times on account of conflicting statements as to age and I will ask you to temporarily withhold action on this case.

Very truly yours,

[illegible signature]

State of , County of , ss:

In the Matter of Inc. of Pension of Wesley Crumedy late Co. E. 135th U.S.C. Inft. (also Co. B. 9th U.S. Cav.)

ON THIS 23d day of December, A.D. one thousand nine hundred and nine personally appeared before me, a Notary Public within and for the County and State aforesaid, duly authorized to administer oaths, Wesley Crumedy aged 62 years, a resident of No. 908 N. Santa Fe ave. PUEBLO, County of PUEBLO, State of COLORADO, well known by me to be reputable and entitled to credit, and who, being duly sworn according to law, declares, in relation to the aforesaid case as follows: when I enlisted in the Army in the year 1865, I gave my age as 18 years, which was from the information received from my Mother: that she informed me at that time, that I was 18 years of age, and that I was born on March 27th, and I have always believed and now believe, that to be my age at that time, making my present age, 62, years on the 27th day of March, 1909. At the time of my enlistments, since 1865, I have no recollection what was said as to my age, but if the War Records show my age differently, than what I have stated above, it is an error on the part of some one, and how that error occured, I do not know. The statement given herewith, as to my age, I received from my Mother, which I have every reason to believe and do believe, is correct.

Washington, D. C.

Dear Sir:

I enclose a letter from Colonel Irving W. Stanton of Pueblo, Colorado, one of Colorado's leading ex-soldier citizens, in behalf of Wesley Crumedy and will now ask you to consider it in connection with his declaration of pension received by you on Jan. 12, 1910 with my letter of Jan. 11. The case has certificate No. [illegible]. Mr. Crumedy was a former slave and, as I have heretofore pointed out, could hardly be expected to know his exact age. E 135 U.S.C. Inf. B 9 U.S. Cav.

I have personally examined the files of his case in the Pension Bureau, which disclose that prior to the time of filing his new declaration on Jan. 12, he had made eleven statements as to his age, most of which would make him appear to be still under sixty-two. In this connection, I would like to call your attention to a statement of the soldier's age made by him in Feb. 1899, when he stated his then age to be forty-four years. As there is no question about his having enlisted first in 1865, he would have been, according to the statement made in Feb. 1899, but ten years of age. This is ridiculous and ought to be sufficient to show that he did not in 1899 know what his age was. He has simply lost track of the years. He gave his age as eighteen when he enlisted, which was, of course, the enlistment

Pueblo Colorado
May 3. 1910

Hon John A. Martin
M. C. Washington D.C.
Dear Sir

Wesley Crummedy (colored) now receiving a pension of eight dollars per month. Original Pension Certificate No 808264 Act June 27. 1890 for Military service rendered from March 27. 1865 to October 27. 1865, as private of Co. E. 135th Regiment U.S. Colored Troops discharged by reason of muster out of Company at Louisville Kentucky on last above named date, is an applicant for increase of pension to which I believe him to be lawfully entitled.

Crummedy states that he was eighteen years of age when he enlisted as above set forth; this fact the muster rolls of his Company will disclose, and at this late

of muster out of Company at Louisville Kentucky on last above named date, is an applicant for increase of pension to which I believe him to be lawfully entitled.
Crummedy states that he was eighteen years of age when he enlisted as above set forth; this fact the muster rolls of his Company will disclose, and at this late
day I do not believe there is any other way to establish it, and under existing circumstances this should be satisfactory evidence.

If at the date of his enlistment he was eighteen years of age he is now past sixty three, and is entitled to a pension of twelve dollars per month, under the present pension act.

Wesley Crummedy served two enlistments of five years each in the regular Army as follows. First enlistment May 7. 1872 discharged May 7. 1877 while holding the grade

of Trumpeter in Troop B. 9th Regiment U.S. Cavalry.
Second enlistment February 21st 1878, discharged on the 20th
day of February 1883, by reason of expiration of service
at Fort Hays Kansas while holding the grade of Trumpeter
Troop B. 9th Regiment U.S. Cavalry making in all ten
years and seven months honorable service for his
Country.
Wesley Crumedy has lived in Pueblo for twenty three or
twenty four years, I have known him well for more
than twenty years. I presume you know and will
remember him as the Trumpeter of the Pueblo Post
of the Grand Army of the Republic, always on hand when
the Post is to appear in public. He is well known in the
community as a kindly generous man but is not able
physically to perform hard manual labor.
I shall esteem it a personal favor if you can assist

[illegible]

Department of the Interior,
BUREAU OF PENSIONS.

Adjutant General's Office
APR 6 1892

Washington D.C. April 6, 1892

Respectfully referred to the
Adjutant General
U.S.A. requesting a
report as to the
within named soldier's
alleged service in Co
B 9 U.S. Cav from
May 7, 1872, to May 7, 1877,
and from Feb 21, 1878 to
Feb 20, 1883

Inv. No. 1068571
Wesley Crumedy
Co E 135 U.S.C. Inf
Co B 9 U.S. Cav

Green B. Raum
Commissioner.

War Department,
ADJUTANT GENERAL'S OFFICE,
Washington, April 6th, 1892.

Respectfully returned to the Commissioner
of Pensions.

Wesley Crumedy
Troop B 9 U.S. Cav,
Enlisted May 7 1872,
at Jonesboro, Tenn.
Discharged May 7/77,
at Fort Craig N.M., by
exp. of ser. a Trumpeter.
Again enlisted in same
troop Feby 21st 1878.
Discharged Feby 20 1883
at Fort Hays, Ks, by
exp. of ser. a Trumpeter.
Born in Bladen Co N.C.
Aged 21 years occupation
farmer, black hair, black
eyes, black complexion
5 feet [illegible] inches high.

PENSION OFFICE

[illegible] Kelton
Adjutant General.

OBITUARY

The funeral of Wesley Crumedy will be held this afternoon at 2:30 in the Davis & Vories' chapel. Rev. Mr. Harding will officiate. The Woman's Relief Corps and G. A. R. will exemplify their burial service and the members of Puritan lodge No. 2762, I. O. O. F. will attend in a body. Interment will be in the north side G. A. R. plot. Mr Crumedy served during the war in Company E, 135th Reg., S. C. colored volunteers and had lived in Pueblo for the past thirty-five years.

Wesley Crumedy, 67 years old, member of the local post of the G. A. R., died yesterday at a local hospital. Altho a negro, Crumedy served with the Union army in the Civil war. He was the bugler for the local post and his duties included the sounding of "taps" at the graves of departed comrades. His tall figure was familiar in G. A. R. parades, and he was proud of his soldier uniform and his record with the Union army during the great Civil war. He had been ill several weeks at a local hospital. The body is in care of Davis and Vories and the

JOHN DURDEN

John Durden was born in Sampson County, North Carolina, and in slavery his owner was William, (Billy) Durden according to the Bureau of Pension records. He claimed to be from "about sixteen miles north of Clinton, North Carolina," and at the time he enlisted in the army, he didn't know his age.

When Sherman's Army came through, where John Durden was living, on the Durden property, he went off with the army in the Pioneer Corps but wasn't a soldier. Upon reaching Goldsboro, North Carolina, he was mustered into Company "G," 135th United States Colored Troop, but only after being inspected by the doctor. He was *"stripped stark naked,"* and at the time, didn't have any shoes. At enlistment, he was measured but didn't know his height, however, the documents show him as six feet tall, and he said his complexion is a "ginger cake color, some call it copper," and his age at 21 years old.

At Goldsboro, John Durden recalled being quartered in tents and that they drilled and drilled, and they unloaded train cars of rations. Soon after that they marched to Raleigh, North Carolina, where they had tents and stayed in the pine woods about two miles out. He remembers next marching to Washington D.C. and being fed on the march from the wagon train. They marched only in the daytime and sometimes at nighttime and ***"didn't know any Sundays."***

Near Washington, D.C., they drilled, as he recalled, and then remembered being in a march through Washington that was called the "General Inspection." That was the time they went on through to camp about six miles outside the city in tents. The camp referred to was Camp Kearney, which was one of the guard post camps that surrounded Washington, D.C.

He recalled from Washington, they went to Louisville, Kentucky, and that is where his company guarded a railroad bridge. They were quartered in a barracks that he referred to as a "long house." From there, they went back to Louisville and they were there for a brief period of time before being mustered out of the army.

John Durden returned to the Durden place after leaving the army and stayed there for about one year. He then went to Halifax County for about five years, then back to Sampson County. In 1878 he went to Midway, Georgia, a town between Walterboro and Macintosh Georgia.

In 1905, we found that John first traveled to Savannah for examination, and then took the train to Brunswick, Georgia. He stated in the declaration that when he went to Brunswick, he "was right smart worse than I was when I went to Savannah." He said he wasn't in good health when he went to Savannah, and he kept getting worse and worse when he went to Brunswick. He claimed of being laid up for two weeks with the chills there.

John said that, prior to the date of his deposition in 1905, "Several years ago, fifteen or more, I reckon – I married Dianna Jeems in this county. Dianna had been twice married before I married her. Her first husband was Tinny Wilson, and her second husband was Israel Jeems." He went and stated "Wilson died at E.P.

Millers and Jeems died at this place where I now live. Both died before I knew Dianna." John ends by saying he had no children.

The Deposition closes "I understand the foregoing as it was read, and my statements are correctly recorded." It is signed with an "X" at his name, John Durden, and attested.

John Durden died in 1915, in Mcintosh County, Georgia, and Dianna Durden (Deridon) filed for her widow's pension on October 20, 1917.

DEPOSITION

Case of John Durant (Soldier Durden), No. 1,322,431.

On this 17th day of October, 1907, at near McIntosh, County of Liberty, State of Georgia, before me, [illegible], a special examiner of the Bureau of Pensions, personally appeared John Durden, who, being by me first duly sworn to answer truly all interrogatories propounded to him during this special examination of aforesaid claim for pension, deposes and says: I am years of age; my post-office address is Riceboro, Liberty County, Georgia. I am a farmer. According to what my old master told me before I left him, I will be 67 years old next March. I was told that I was born in 1840-something — somewhere along there.

My understanding always has been that my surname is Durden though some write the name a little different. But my master's name was Billy Durden, though I don't know how the surname is spelled.

write the name a little different. But my master's name was Billy Durden, though I don't know how the surname is spelled.

I am the person that has claimed pension as a member of "Co. I, 135th United States Colored Infantry". I have known that it was Co. G, 135th all the time since I was in the army.

I enlisted at Goldsboro, North Carolina, in February 1865 and I was discharged at Louisville, Kentucky, within a month or so of Christmas in the same year.

I was never in the United States navy and I was never an enlisted man in the army at any time other than when I was in the 135th Colored Infantry; but I was taken along by a pioneer corps before I enlisted. I wasn't a soldier

Deposition

in the pioneer corps and I don't know my name or designation for the pioneer corps. I went from the pioneer corps with the 135th. with the same officers.

I was born in Sampson County, North Carolina. The county seat is Clinton and I was born about 16 miles from Clinton. At the time I enlisted I stated that I didn't know my age; what they supposed me to be I don't know. I was full grown then. I was measured but I don't remember what my height was said to be. I won't be certain whether I have grown any since. I was stripped stark naked but I don't remember whether I was measured then or when I was discharged. I must then have been 21 years old or older.

I am about 6 feet high now.

My color has always been about as it

In the company I was called John Durden. I had no nickname.

I never have had a name other than John Durden and never have borne any other name.

I have no picture of myself as a soldier. I don't know of there being a picture of me in existence.

I have no certificate of discharge and no paper relating to my service as a soldier, that I received while I was a soldier or at the time I was discharged. I had a discharge but it was lost.

After I enlisted, I remained with the regiment, at Goldsboro, for something like four or five weeks, as I remember and we were quartered in tents. We were drilled some and we unloaded cars that brought in food for the soldiers. Next we went to Raleigh — marched — and we stayed there until two or three

the regiment at Goldsboro for something like four or five weeks, as I remember and we were quartered in tents. We were drilled some and we unloaded cars that brought in food for the soldiers. Next we went to Raleigh - marched - and we stayed there until two or three or four weeks after Johnson surrendered at Greensboro or Greenville (whichever it was). At Raleigh, we were in tents out in the pine woods, about two miles as nigh as I can remember, from Raleigh. We there went through the exercises of drilling - nothing else particularly. We next went to Washington, D.C.; we marched and, as near as I can remember, we were six weeks going. There were a good many regiments - colored & white marching. We were fed on the march by rations from the wagon trains. We marched sometimes only in the day and sometimes in the day time and night time

Page 7 Deponent [signature]

Page 8

and we didn't know any Sunday. We marched through Washington and went out about six miles and camped in tents; I don't remember the name of the camp. We drilled while we were near Washington. We were there a good while but I can't remember how long. I was in a march through Washington that was called general inspection; that was the time we went on through and out to the camp. That was the only time I marched in Washington.

From Washington, we went to Louisville Kentucky; Co. I went from there to Shepherdsville where we guarded a railroad bridge and the company there was quartered in frame barracks - a long house! From there we went back to Louisville and we were dis-out to the camp ... time I marched to Washington. From Washington, we went to Louisville, Kentucky; I went from there to Shepherdsville where we guarded a railroad bridge, and the company there was quartered in frame barracks — a long house. From there we went back to Louisville and we were discharged soon after we got back.

From Washington, we went by train to some point on the Ohio River and there marched but not very far. From Louisville to Shepherdsville we went by train and went back by train. We rode in coaches.

I don't remember the names of any of the officers of the regiment. The captain of our company was named Captain Fleming. He was, I think, as tall as

Attest:

Daniel Becontt

Willoby Jones

his
John X Duncan
mark
Deponent.

Sworn to and subscribed before me this ________ day of ________, and I certify that the contents were fully made known to deponent ... signing.

the company and I have forgot them. I don't know where Kelly lived.

I don't remember any of those whose names (from list, exhibition) the examiner has read to me, except Jacob Coppedell; there were Jake and Silas and, if I don't make a mistake, Bryan Coppedell. I got acquainted with all of them after I joined the company; their home, I learned, was not so very far from Goldsboro. Jake was tall & thin. Silas was not so tall but he was stouter than Jake; the 3d one was between Jake & Silas in height, as I remember, and he wasn't as slim as Jake. Jake was the lightest in color — he was light brown; the others were not real black — were a dark brown. I don't know where any of them lives now.

Nothing happened to me and nothing particular occurred that I remember by which other members of the company should remember me. I was not wounded or otherwise hurt; I was

[illegible]

me from Mr. Durden's place. They took also Romy Durden. He ran away & went back home and I never saw him again.

My brothers were Simon (dead), Monge (lived not far from Durden place when I last knew of him), George (lived somewhere there also), Alec (there also), Wylie (there also); my sisters were Chaney (wife of Nelson Durden), Milly, Lucinda. They are all dead. My father was Moses Durden & my mother Lucy Durden.

My recollection is that Benjamin Durden was about my age: the four brothers of his younger than me.

My brother Simon and my sister Chaney were older than I; I was next to Chaney in age.

The Coppell boys knew me in the army: we talked about knowing each other while

Page 12 Deposition A

Page 13

people before we had gone into the army. We lived too far apart for us colored people to know one another.

I don't think of any other in the company whose white people I had known.

Silas (we called him Sile), a cousin of mine, belonged to Co. B—he's dead. Sam Durden (raised on Billy Durden's plantation—as Sile was also) belonged to Co. B. Sam is dead too.

I don't desire to be present or represented by another—I can't be—when testimony shall be taken in this claim—not here nor elsewhere.

I went first to Savannah for examination and then to Brunswick. When I went to Brunswick, I was right smart worse than I was when I went to Savannah. I did not certainly break

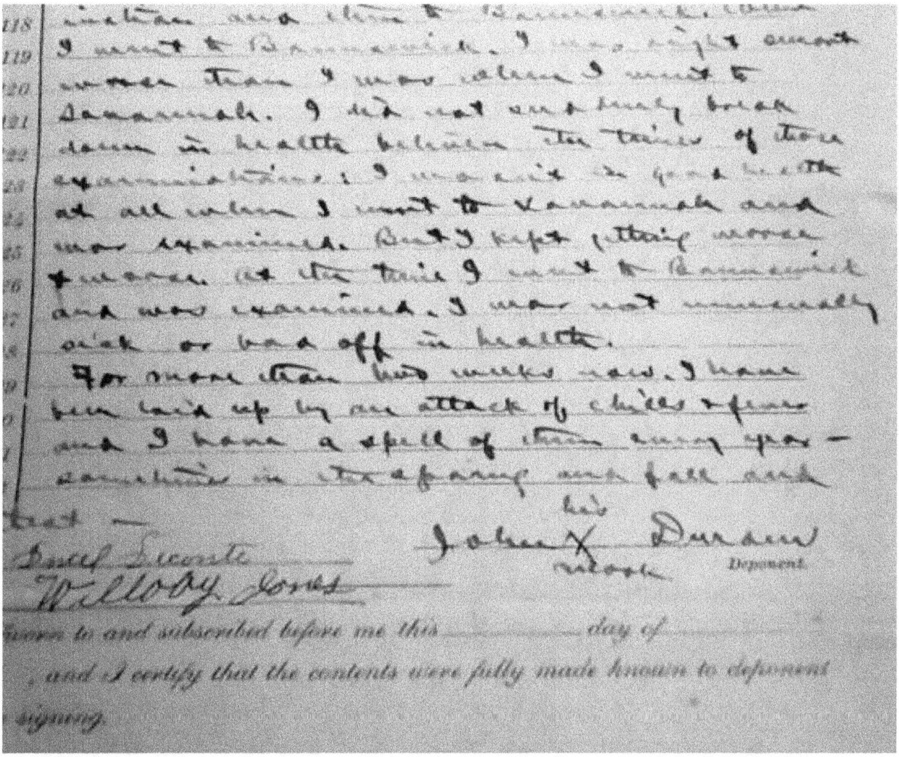

...ination and then to Brunswick. When I went to Brunswick, I was right smart worse than I was when I went to Savannah. I did not suddenly break down in health between the times of those examinations; I was not in good health at all when I went to Savannah and was examined. But I kept getting worse & worse. At the time I went to Brunswick and was examined, I was not unusually sick or bad off in health.

For more than two weeks now, I have been laid up by an attack of chills & fever and I have a spell of them every year — sometimes in the spring and fall and that —

his
John X Durden
mark
Deponent

Basil Leconte
Willoby Jones

worn to and subscribed before me this ______ day of ______, and I certify that the contents were fully made known to deponent ... signing.

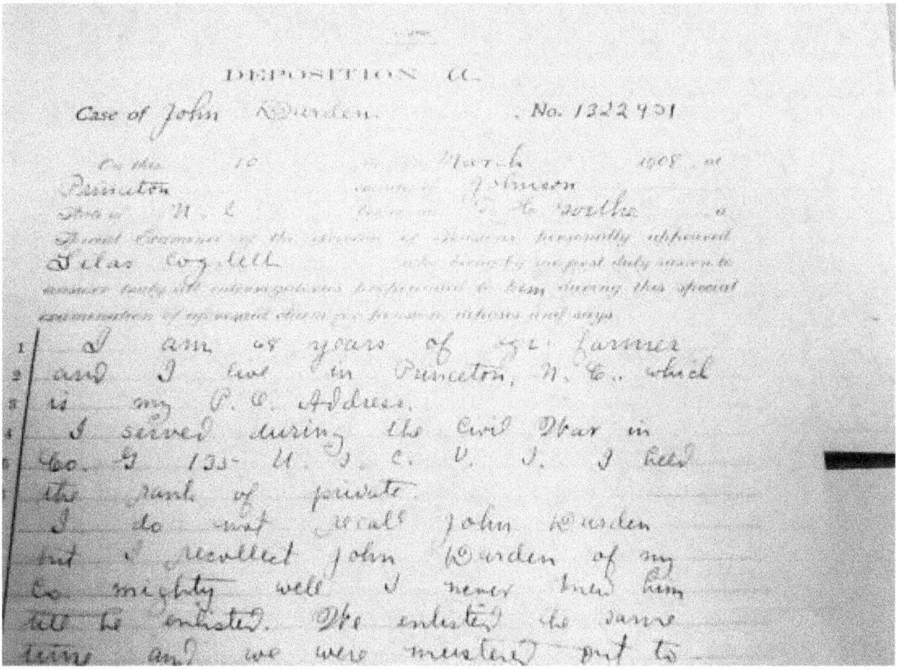

DEPOSITION C.

Case of John Durden, No. 1322491

On the 10 day of March 1908, at Princeton county of Johnson State of N. C. before me, F. H. Wolfe, a Special Examiner of the Bureau of Pensions, personally appeared Silas Coghill who, being by me first duly sworn to answer truly all interrogatories propounded to him during this special examination of aforesaid claim for pension, deposes and says:

I am 68 years of age; farmer and I live in Princeton, N. C., which is my P. O. Address.

I served during the Civil War in Co. G 135 U. S. C. V. I. I held the rank of private.

I do not recall John Durden but I recollect John Durden of my Co. mighty well. I never knew him till he enlisted. We enlisted the same time and we were mustered out to-

Co. G 135 U. S. C. I. I was the rank of private. I do not recall John Worden but I recollect John Warden of my Co mighty well. I never knew him till he enlisted. We enlisted the same time and we were mustered out together. We enlisted in March and were discharged in Oct. 1865.

John Warden was from Sampson Co. N. C. and said he had been a slave. He was tall - nearly six feet and was light complexioned - was light ginger cake color. I know he was from Sampson Co because he told me so. We were the best of friends in the army but I have never seen him since muster out. I have often inquired for him since our muster out but could never locate him. John Warden was younger than I was - was about 18 I would suppose in service.

No, I never knew a John Werden in G Co.

I have heard clmts statement read. I am fully satisfied that he served in G Co.

Page Deposition A

as he states he recollects things about our service more accurately than I do. Charley Hanna was the 1st Lt. He is the man he refers to as Lt. Charley. The other Cogdells are all dead. I do not believe that any man after these long years could make a much more accurate statement than clmt has done. His description of the men as to height and color is about perfect and what he says as to our movements after enlistment is correct. There can be no doubt but what he is the genuine soldier for unless he had been there he could not know so much about the service. I have heard read the above deposition. I have fully understood your questions and my answers have been correctly recorded.

Silas his X mark Cogdell

Attest
Catharine richardson
P. T. Howell

STEPHEN WATKINS

In his deposition, Stephen said "I do not know my correct age, but I have a letter here from my mother who is now dead that shows that I am sixty-six. I am a farmer and I live near Snow Hill, NC, which is my post office address. During the Civil War, I served in Company 'G,' 135th United States Colored Infantry. I held the rank of private. I enlisted in March, about the close of the war, and served a few months. I think I received my discharge about November. I was only in the Army the one time and was never in the Navy."

Stephen went on and said, "I was born in Alamance County, North Carolina. When I was a child, I was sold as a slave to Neil Watkins of Sampson County, North Carolina. He lived in between Treadwell and Clinton. My name was Siler before I was sold to Mr. Watkins, but after that sale, I always went by Watkins." In the deposition of D.C. McPherson, it's said that his father was John McPherson, and he owned some slaves named Siler. Sarah was the mother of the family, and she had three sons, Viz, Stephen, and Perron.

Stephen was sold when he was about ten or twelve years old, and he was a little black short boy when he was sold. In Stephen's deposition, he said he was about 10 years of age when he was sold on the farm in Sampson County and then remained with Mr. Watkins, who bought him until the Northern soldiers came through about the last of the war and that is when he joined them. He said he then went to Goldsboro and then to Raleigh, and in Raleigh, he was regularly enlisted. Stephen recalled that they were not given guns until they got to Louisville.

Further in Stephen's deposition he said, "they first made us act as a Pioneer Corps and drilled us with axes, and shovels." He said that they got knapsacks and their blue uniforms with brass buttons at Goldsboro. "We marched on foot all the time from Raleigh to Washington, but from Washington, we took a train and went to someplace I think called Spartanburg, and took a boat that carried us to Louisville, Kentucky. After we got to Louisville, they took away our axes, spades, and shovels, and gave us guns, and then drilled us with them. Gurly was our Colonel. Budlong was our Lieutenant Colonel, but I do not recall the first names of either."

Stephen clearly stated that ***"when we got to the edge of the city of Washington, we laid over for a while. We then marched into the city and had a general review. We marched in front of the White House, there were seats for ladies to sit on like there is in a circus, and I never before, in all my life, saw such crowds. There were boys and men up in the trees, and people were packed in every place they could be. They said that General Grant and General Sherman were there, but I did not know them. It was in the front of the White House, where there was a great stand on which there were many people, but there were many other stands, and when you talk about women folks, there they were. After the big parade, we marched out of the city but camped only a short distance away for a few days, and then took the train to Louisville, as I stated. In the big parade in Washington, the white Troops Marched 1st, the Colored Troops brought up the end of the parade."***

In the deposition of Silas Cogdell, he wrote in support of Stephen Watkins about marching in the Grand Review and said the following: "There was a very big crowd out to see us march. Some stood on the sidewalk and others on stands both white and colored were there, men and women. I do not know Stephen Watson but there was a little low colored man in my company who we called Stephen Watkins. He was short in the army, and he is still short."

In the deposition of Needham Lewis, he testified in support of Stephen Watkins. He recalled Stephen Watkins in Company "G," 135th USCT, and that he suffered from piles and his hernia busted. Needham said that "Stephen's statements are all true as he goes on about the grand parade in Washington. The big stands were there just as stated. A great concourse of people were there to see us march by."

Aron Jones, another soldier in the company with Stephen Watkins, recalled, "from time to time, we were on guard together. The only thing I think he is mistaken about is our marching as a Pioneer Corps from Raleigh to Washington, D.C., for I always thought we went as regular soldiers."

As Stephen stated, "I have heard the depositions of Needham Lewis, Aaron Jones, and Silas Cogdell, as well as the deposition of DC McPherson. I am satisfied and have no complaints. I cannot recollect another soul who could testify for me."

Stephen Watkins lived until 1936 and is buried in Snow Hill North Carolina, at the Saint Peter Church Cemetery. There is a picture of his headstone in this book in "Chapter 18," with the other headstones of the men of the 135th USCT that we have been able to locate.

On this [illegible] *day of* January 1918 *191* , *at* Snow Hill , *county of* Greene

State of N. C. *before me,* Thos. H. Goethe , *a Special Examiner of the Bureau of Pensions, personally appeared* [illegible] Watkins *who, being by me first duly sworn to answer truly all interrogatories propounded to h— during this special examination of aforesaid claim for pension, deposes and says:*

I do not know correct age but I have a letter here from my mother who is now dead that shows that I am [illegible]; farmer and I near Snow Hill, N. C., which is my post office address.

During the Civil War I served in Co. G, 135 U. S. C. Inf. I held the rank of private. I enlisted in March about the close of the war and served a few months. I think I received my discharge about November. I was only in the army the one time and was never in the Navy.

I was born in Alamance Co. N. C., but when I was a child I was sold as a slave to Neil Watkins of Sampson Co. N. C. We lived between Treadwell and Clinton. My name was Ellis before I was sold to Mr. Watkins but after that sale I always went as Watkins.

Personal description of soldier: Height, five feet four and one half inches; complexion, hair and eyes, black. No marks or scars. I was never in a hospital while in service. I was about eleven years of age when I was sold on the farm in Sampson Co. I then remained with Mr. Watkins till the Northern soldiers came through

sold to Mr. Watkins but after that sale I always went as Watkins.
Personal description of soldier: Height, five feet four and one half inches; complexion, hair and eyes, black. No marks or scars. I was never in a hospital while in service. I was about eleven years of age when I was sold on the farm in Sampson Co. I then remained with Mr. Watkins till the Northern soldiers came through

about last of war and then I joined them and came along as a camp follower. We went to Goldsboro and then to Raleigh and in Raleigh I was regularly enlisted. We were not given guns, however, till we got to Louisville, Ky. They first made us act as a pioneer corps and drilled us with axes, shovels, etc. We marched on foot all the time from Raleigh to Washington but from Washington we took a train and went to some place I think called Spartanburg and took a boat that carried us to Louisville, Ky. After we got to Louisville they took away our axes, spades, and shovels and gave us guns and then drilled us with them. No, we were not in any fights. No men were killed out of my company. Gurley was our Colonel. Budlong was the Lt. Col. Do not recall the first name of either. I do not recall

Page 5 *Deposition* A

[illegible] over N. C. before the war. He used to sell horses down there. No, I never went as Wilson. My parents are dead. The only living relative I have is a brother. I do not know his street or number. He lives in Indianapolis, Ind., and his name is Jasper Siler. He is younger than I am. My owners are all dead. I have a cousin Annie Prunes of Kinston. Her husband's name is [illegible]. [illegible] knew nothing about me in slave days. [illegible] in the pioneer corps till we got to Louisville, Ky. I carried an axe till I got that far. After we got to Louisville I got a gun. We got knap sacks at Goldsboro. We got our uniforms at Goldsboro. We wore blue uniforms with brass buttons. So far as I can remember our regiment was not divided. I am mistaken too for we split when we were going to Richmond. As I remember my company and company [illegible] went together. So many companies would follow so many wagons. Don't recollect just how many companies went together but not many before there would be more wagons and then more companies. They made us carry axes and shovels to repair the road. I had a discharge paper but lost it [illegible]. I lost it moving around. It was a sort of brown paper. My discharge was handed me by my captain. He told me to keep it but did not give any special reason for my doing so. I am sure that I carried an axe and no gun in going to Washington. I carried my axe in the great parade in Washington. No, I had not been issued a gun up to that time. My only sister is dead. I only have the one brother. After my discharge I

Page 7 Deposition A

Elias Cogdell ... who, being by me first duly sworn to answer truly all interrogatories propounded to h... during this special examination of aforesaid claim for pension, deposes and says:

I am 70 years of age; keep a restaurant and I live as stated above. I am in no wise relatedto claimant and haveno interest in the prosecution of his pension claim.

I served during the Civil War in Co. G, 135th U. S. C. Vol. Inf. I enlisted when the company was made up and was mustered out at Louisville, Ky. with the regiment. I was a private soldier. We were organized at Goldsboro and then went to Raleigh and from there we marched to Washington, D. C. We got guns at Louisville. We carried axes and acted as Pioneer Corps till we got to Washington and after we got there we went on a Grand parade. We were reviewed by GeleralSherman General Grant. There was a great crowd to see us. I remember Stephen Wadkins. (He pronounces the name as I have spelled it. THG) He was a private of my company. I have only seen him once since he left the army. He cme here about one week ago. He came to my house at night and asked me if I knew him. I first told him no, and then I looked carefully and then I called his name. He is still the little short man

Pioneer Corps till we got to Washington and after we got there we went on a Grand parade. We were reviewed by GeleralSherman General Grant. There was a great crowd to see us. I remember Stephen Wadkins. (He pronounces the name as I have spelled it. THG) He was a private of my company. I have only seen him once since he left the army. He cme here about one week ago. He came to my house at night and asked me if I knew him. I first told him no, and then I looked carefully and then I called his name. He is still the little short man
he was in the army. In the army we were great friends and while here he told me things that would have made me know that he was the man he claimed to be even if I had not recollected his resemblance. I have heard claimant's statement. He has given a straight statement. Stephen told me that he now lives near Snow Hill in Greene Co. N. C. I have never seen him but the one time nor had I heard from him prior to that time since our discharge. I can and do swear positively that the man who visited me a week ago and called himself Stephen Wadkins is the same man who served under that name in my Co. I could not possibly be mistaken in his identity. I have heard read the

Page 9 Deposition ...

DEPOSITION C

Case of Stephen Watkins, alias Watson, No. 1074219

On this 29 day of January 1919 191 , at Snow Hill, county of Greene State of N. C. before me, Thos. H. Goethe, a Special Examiner of the Bureau of Pensions, personally appeared [illegible], who, being by me first duly sworn to answer truly all interrogatories propounded to h during this special examination of aforesaid claim for pension, deposes and says:

I am 69 years of age; laborer and I reside as stated above. I am in no wise related to claimant and have no interest in the prosecution of his pension claim. I served during the Civil War in Co. C, 135 U. S. C. Vol. Inf. I enlisted in March and was discharged towards the last of the year. I know Stephen Watkins well. I first met him while I was in the 135th. He also belonged to that regiment but I do not recollect what company he was in. I saw him frequently in service and knew him as Stephen Watkins there. I knew him then under the same name that he now goes under. I have been knowing him ever since he left the army. After his discharge he moved to Goldsboro and I saw him anyway within a year after his discharge and have been seeing him at times ever since--in fact for several years he has lived here around me.

Q Men of one company in service don't often know anything about men from another company--how did you come to know claimant

belonged to that regiment but I do not recollect what company he was in. I saw him frequently in service and knew him as Stephen Watkins there. I knew him then under the same name that he now goes under. I have been knowing him ever since he left the army. After his discharge he moved to Goldsboro and I saw him anyway within a year after his discharge and have been seeing him at times ever since--in fact for several years he has lived here around me.

Q Men of one company in service don't often know anything about men from another company--how did you come to know claimant

when he was not in your company?

A At times we used to be on guard together and I got to knowing him in that way. I guess I would have forgotten him had I never seen him since discharge but being so much with him since service has made me recollect him well in the army. No, I am not mistaken in the man. I can and do swear solemnly that the man who is now present and goes as Stephen Watkins served in my regiment but at present I do not recollect the company that he was in.

Our regiment was made up in Goldsboro and from there we went to Raleigh where we were examined by the doctors, two of them, and then we were regularly sworn in.

Q Where were you when guns were issued to your regiment?

Page 11 Deposition C

A I do not recollect whether we drew them when we enlisted or when we got to Louisville. I know we got them somewhere on that route.

Q After you left Raleigh did you ever carry an axe, a hoe, a spade or anything of that character?

A I do not recollect doing so.

Q Claimant says you all acted as pioneer corps men between Raleigh and Washington and that he carried an axe?

A I do not recollect that. My recollection is that at Raleigh we were made regular soldiers. I have heard claimant's statement read. He tells many things which are so. What he says is true as to the grand review in Washington, crossing a long bridge, going part of the way to Louisville by boat but I do not recall that we carried axes, shovels, etc. He may remember that but I don't. No, I cannot name any one else who was in claimant's company. I have heard read the above deposition. I have fully understood your questions and my answers have been correctly recorded.

his
Aaron X Jones
mark

ts

...za Jone...

Case of Stephen Watkins, No. 1094217

On this 15th day of March 1913 191 , at Selma, county of Johnson, State of N. C., before me, Thos. H. Goethe, a Special Examiner of the Bureau of Pensions, personally appeared Needham Lewis, who, being by me first duly sworn to answer truly all interrogatories propounded to h— during this special examination of aforesaid claim for pension, deposes and says:

I will soon be 67; farmer and I live as stated above. I served during the Civil War in Co. C, 135th U. S. C. Inf. I held the rank of private. We were organized at Goldsboro but we were not sworn in till we got to Raleigh, N. C. I was with the regiment from its organization to its close.

We got no guns till we got to Louisville, Ky. We marched on foot from Raleigh to Washington, D. C. We carried axes, hoes and spades on that march and acted as a Pioneer Corps. We never drilled what I would call drill till we got our guns at Louisville. No, I do not recollect a man named Stephen Watson or Stephen Watkins. I have no recollection ever knowing a man of that name or making an

on foot from Raleigh to Washington, N. C. We carried axes, hoes and spades on that march and acted as a Pioneer Corps. We never drilled what I would call drill till we got our guns at Louisville. No, I do not recollect a man named Stephen Watson or Stephen Watkins. I have no recollection ever knowing a man of that name or making an affidavit for him. I have heard what purports to be my former affidavit read. I cannot bring a thing of it to mind and am still unable to recall the man. I have heard the deposition of Stephen Watkins read. His deposition is true and he must certainly have been a soldier in my regiment as he states. What he says is so about marching on foot to Washington, acting as Pioneer Corps, taking train from Washington to Louisville part of the way and going the remainder by boat. Only a man who was with us could give the information that he has given. I have heard read the above deposition. I have fully understood yur questions and my answers have been correctly recorded.

his
Needham X Lewis
mark

Attests
Needham R. Lewis

Special Examiner of the Bureau of Pensions, personally appeared Silas Dogdell, who, being by me first duly sworn to answer truly all interrogatories propounded to h___ during this special examination of aforesaid claim for pension, deposes and says:

I am 70 years of age; keep a restaurant and I reside in Selma, N. C., which is my post office address. I am in no wise related to claimant and have no interest in the prosecution of his pension claim. I served during the Civil War in Co. G, 135th Inf. U.S.C. I was a private soldier. I enlisted in March about the time the war closed and served a few months. We organized at Goldsboro, then went to Raleigh and from there marched on foot to Washington, D. C. and on the march we acted as Pioneer Corps and carried axes, spades, etc. We aided on that march in making roads. We marched across the long bridge before getting in Washington and after we got in the city they had a grand parade in which we were reviewed by General Grant and General Sherman. There was a very large crowd out to see us march. Some stood on the side walk and others stands--both white and colored were there, men and women. I do know Stephen Watson but there was a little low colored man in my pany who we called Stephen Wadkins. He was like myself a private dier. I have only seen him one time since our discharge and then

D. C. and on the march we acted as pioneer corps and carried, axes, spades, etc. We aided on that march in making roads. We marched across the long bridge before getting in Washington and after we got in the city they had a grand parade in which we were reviewed by General Grant and General Sherman. There was a very large crowd out to see us march. Some stood on the side walk and others on stands--both white and colored were there, men and women. I do not know Stephen Watson but there was a little low colored man in my company who we called Stephen Wadkins. He was like myself a private soldier. I have only seen him one time since our discharge and then he came here about a week before you were here last month. When he first came he asked me if I knew him. I answered no, but on looking at him carefully I called him Stephen Wadkins for I then recognized him as being the man who served in my company under that name. He was the only man of that or similar name in the company. I know him by his looks and his talk. He was short in the army and he is short still. At enlistment he looked about grown and that was all, still I do not know his age at that time. In service we were very great friends, but I do not recall from what county he said he was from. As I remember he was from somewhere in Eastern North Carolina. He tells me that he now lives at Snow Hill. I have heard the deposition of Stephen Watkins, alias Watson read. He tells

Page 10 Deposition

Page 11

all straight regarding our acting [illegible] Corps till we got to Washington, D. C. I can swear and do swear solemnly that the man who called on me a few weeks ago served with me in Co. G, 135 U. S. Inf., and that I knew him in that company as Stephen Wadkins and that he was the only man of that or similar name in the company. There is absolutely no chance for me to be mistaken as to his identity for while with me I not only recognized his voice and his looks but he told me many things about our service which I know to be so. We did not get guns till we got to Louisville, Ky., and it was from that place that we were discharged. From discharge up to a few weeks ago I never laid eyes on Stephen and do not know where he was all that time except he told me that he had been about Snow Hill. "Stephen is the man for I know him as good as I know my brother". Claimant's statement is correct where he states that we marched through Petersburg and Richmond on our way to Washington. I have heard read the above deposition. I have fully understood your questions and answers have been correctly recorded.

his

on foot and acted as pioneer corps [illegible]

From Washington, we went to Louisville, KY., and staid there till we were mustered out. I cannot recall a man named Stephen

Warsaw, county of Duplin

State of N. C., before me, Thos. H. Goethe, a Special Examiner of the Bureau of Pensions, personally appeared Sandy Grady, alias McNair, who, being by me first duly sworn to answer truly all interrogatories propounded to h— during this special examination of aforesaid claim for pension, deposes and says:

I am 84 years of age; feed stock and farm and I live five miles from Warsaw, N. C., which is my post office address.

I served during the Civil War in Co. G, 135th U. S. C. Vol. Inf. I held the rank of private. I was with the company from muster in till muster out. We were enlisted at Raleigh but we were in service some days before that. From Raleigh we marched on foot and acted as pioneer corps till we got to Washington, D. C. From Washington, we went to Louisville, Ky., and staid there till we were mustered out. I cannot recall a man named Stephen Watkins or Stephen Watson or similar name. I have heard his statement read. He must have been with us for he tells our movements correctly and also correctly names the Col. Lt. Col. and Capt. He tells what is so about marching over a long bridge before we got to Washington and about the parade in Washington and also about our not getting guns till we got to Louisville. I remember Silas Cogdell and Gatling Campbell but cannot recall Stephen Watson. I have heard read the above deposition. I have fully understood your questions and my answers have been correctly recorded.

Sandy B Grady alias McNair

[illegible]

during the Civil War in Co. G, 135th U. S. C. Inf. I held the rank of private. I do not recall a man named Stephen Watson, Watkins or similar name. I only recall one Stephen in my company and his name was Stephen Brown but he is dead. He died near here several years back. He has been dead over twenty years. He never got a pension. He was a low chunky man. No, he never went as Watson. He was raised here. I have heard claimant's statement read. He names the three officers correctly, tells what is so about our acting as pioneer corps till we got to Washington, tells what is so about marching over the long bridge just before we got into Washington and also tells what is so about our not getting guns till we got to Louisville, KY. He certainly gave it straight about the big parade in Washinging, about the big crowds to see us pass in review so I believe that the man was with us. He must be the man he claims to be for unless he had been there he could not know all those things. I have heard read the above deposition. I have fully understood your questions and my answers have been correctly recorded.

his
Lewis X McNeill
mark

Attest:
A. H. McKenzie
Albert Jordan

Burlington, county of Alamance

State of N. C., before me, Thos. H. Goethe, a Special Examiner of the Bureau of Pensions, personally appeared D. C. McPherson, who, being by me first duly sworn to answer truly all interrogatories propounded to h___ during this special examination of aforesaid claim for pension, deposes and says:

I am 70 years of age; farmer and I live two miles from Burlington, N. C., which is my post office address. My father was John McPherson. I had a brother James but he is dead. Father owned some slaves named Siler--Sarah was the mother of the family. She had three sons, viz., Stephen, Perron and I do not recall the name of the youngest. Stephen was sold when he was a boy of about ten or twelve years old. I do not know to whom he was sold. He was sold from the block and I have never seen him since nor do I know where he was carried after he was sold. I have a brother in Randolph Co. Isaac P. McPherson is his name. He lives at Franklinville. My father did not live in Randolph Co., but he lived near the line before the war. Stephen was a little black short boy when he was sold and he was a little younger than I am but I do not know his correct age. We have no record of the ages of our slaves in existence. I do not know exact difference between my age and that of Stephon but I think

was John McPherson. I had a brother James but he is dead. Father owned some slaves named Siler--Sarah was the mother of the family. She had three sons, viz., Stephen, Perron and I do not recall the name of the youngest. Stephen was sold when he was a boy of about ten or twelve years old. I do not know to whom he was sold. He was sold from the block and I have never seen him since nor do I know where he was carried after he was sold. I have a brother in Randolph Co. Isaac P. McPherson is his name. He lives at Franklinville. My father did not live in Randolph Co., but he lived near the line before the war. Stephen was a little black short boy when he was sold and he was a little younger than I am but I do not know his correct age. We have no record of the ages of our slaves in existence. I do not know exact difference between my age and that of Stephon but I think
I was about three or four years the oldest. I do not know where any of the Silers are now. Stephen was sold alone. I have heard read the above deposition. I have fully understood your questions and my answers have been correctly recorded.

D. C. McPherson

LAWRENCE McCOOK

He started his journey in General Sherman's Army on Daniel McCook's plantation about ten miles from Milledgeville, Georgia. Lawrence said he was about twenty-three years old, and his mother's name was Hanna. He stated he joined Sherman's Army in Macon not far from home. He was not a camp follower but was recruited into the Pioneer Corps, clearing, and building corduroy roads for the supply wagons. When they reached the Ogeechee River outside of Savannah, they had troops in the rice ponds and on picket duty and they were in the process of overtaking Fort McAllister. That was when one of his peers declared they were surrounded by the rebels. Lawrence stated at the time he was a color bearer.

They were on a drain between two ponds and our Captain said, "the time has come when we must kill or be killed." We fell in line and marched and fired. This dam which we were on is a strip of land about forty feet wide, separated by two ponds. He stated that he did not know what they were doing when he was shot first in the left hand and then shot in the head. Some soldiers picked me up and moved me to the house, now a hospital, on the bend of the Ogeechee River. It was a framed building two and a half stories high. "The doctor treated me by putting a silver dollar in my head which has stayed there." Lawrence said he could still feel it. He also recalled a white woman waited on him in the hospital who was called ***Aunt Becky Young***.

After spending about a month in the hospital, Lawrence rejoined his company, the Pioneer Corps, in Savannah, Georgia, and when Sherman's Army moved into South Carolina and then onto North Carolina, Lawrence was with them. In Goldsboro, he was enlisted in the 135th United States Colored Troop with his company, put on the uniform of a regular union soldier, and began the march following Confederate General Johnston. As they waited in Raleigh, North Carolina, drilling, and drilling, as a regiment, they received orders to start the march to Washington, D.C., which was about four hundred and eighty miles passing through Virginia.

At Petersburg, Virginia, Lawrence had an interesting story of his time serving in the 135th USCT and recalled being shot and stabbed several times. One of his stories memorialized in his deposition was "I got shot in the left foot at Petersburg, we were crawling on our hands and knees. At the time, we were sent there to take a fort and had been marching along by the ditch. After I got shot, I was taken prisoner. Half of my company was captured at the same time. I was stabbed in the body, clear through, by a wounded rebel. I was in the ditch and there were some logs there, and cotton bales on top of the logs, and sacks of sand on top of the cotton. I was smothering in the ditch, and I wanted to pull a sack of sand off the cotton bale. I would crawl up on the bale, and then I could get some air. A rebel boy was there, wounded in the foot, I think it had been blown up." I said to the rebel, "I am wounded, and so are you. Don't you hurt me, and I won't you. I wanted to throw this sack of sand over you so that I could get up on this bale of cotton to get some air. I jerked the boy and the sand off and just then the wounded rebel struck his bayonet through me."

He recalled that was all he could remember about that. Lawrence said "I also got my right ear shot in at the same time, but I can't tell how, when, or where. I was also cut twice in the right wrist by a sword, in the hands of a rebel cavalry man. I think this was done at the same time I got the bayonet stabbed through the body." I remembered the rebel said to me, "there you damn S of a B. I will kill you fighting against your master, and he struck me with his sword, and that is all I can tell you about that."

Lawrence is one of the few soldiers in the 135th USCT, who did not go home to Georgia, after being mustered out. He crossed over the Ohio River from Louisville, Kentucky, to Indiana, and continued to live and work there. He also worked in Illinois before he finally ended up in Des Moines, Iowa. He eventually ended up living at the Veterans Home in Marshalltown, Iowa, where he died on the 6th of October 1892. Lawrence is buried there in the Veterans Home Cemetery.

Co. "F" 135th U.S.C.T.,) Rejection affirmed.
No. 408,115.)
P.O. Rockton, Iowa.)

The Commissioner of Pensions.

Sir:-

Herewith are returned the papers which accompanied your report of April 13,1891, in the original claim for pension of Lawrence Mc.Cook,Co."F",135th,U.S.C.T.,No.408,115,on appeal from the action of rejection by your Bureau.

The records of the War Department show that the soldier enlisted March 27,1865, and was discharged October 23,1865. No prior service is shown.

July 14,1880,he filed a claim for pension alleging that at the battle of Richmond,Va.,in 1864, he received gun shot wounds

-2-

in head and right side.

In a declaration filed January 8,1887, he alleged gun shot wound of head, right temple, left foot and hand, and bayonet wound of right side at Petersburg,Va.,about June 1864. In other affidavits he alleges other times and places for incurrence.

His claim was rejected April 8,1890, on the ground of no record and failure of claimant to prove origin in the service and line of duty,and that the records of the War Department do not afford any additional information.

From this adverse action claimant appeals.

The claim was sent out for Special Examination on August 29,1889.

The claimant's statement taken by the Special Examiner shows that he has a very poor recollection of his army service, or that he feigned or was really ignorant. His statements are contradictory, and are entirely inconsistent with his service as

net wound of right side at Petersburg,Va.,about June 1864. In other affidavits he alleges other times and places for incurrence.

His claim was rejected April 8,1890, on the ground of no record and failure of claimant to prove origin in the service and line of duty,and that the records of the War Department do not afford any additional information.

From this adverse action claimant appeals.

The claim was sent out for Special Examination on August 29,1889.

The claimant's statement taken by the Special Examiner shows that he has a very poor recollection of his army service, or that he feigned or was really ignorant. His statements are contradictory, and are entirely inconsistent with his service as shown by the records.

He says that at the time the war broke out he was a slave which is probably true. He says he enlisted in the Fall when the Yankees came and took him away and says this was at Macon, Ga. He says he was shot in the night and taken to a hospital in

of 1864, and that he remained in said hospital for a few weeks; that when he was brought to hospital he was suffering with a severe bayonet wound of right side and a gun shot wound of head; that she waited on him while there and remembers his case well; that he was so severely wounded he thought he would die; that the doctors said he could not live; that when the claimant called on her shortly before making her affidavit, that she recognized him at once as the same man she had nursed in the hospital; that he was treated in the hospital by Dr.Hayes who came from Philadelphia; that her name at the time was Sarah A.Palmer.

In reply to an office inquiry as to how she recollected or identified claimant when he called upon her, she said:

"You ask me how I remember McCook; after twenty years. "If one had asked me how I remembered that there was a war, I "could have answered as readily. This man, if any one had seen "him one day, they could not have forgotten him; he was bayoneted in the side and wounded in the head and suffered terribly;

that he was so severely wounded he thought he would die; that the doctors said he could not live; that when the claimant called on her shortly before making her affidavit, that she recognized him at once as the same man she had nursed in the hospital; that he was treated in the hospital by Dr.Hayes who came from Philadelphia; that her name at the time was Sarah A.Palmer.

In reply to an office inquiry as to how she recollected or identified claimant when he called upon her, she said:

"You ask me how I remember McCook; after twenty years. "If one had asked me how I remembered that there was a war, I "could have answered as readily. This man, if any one had seen "him one day, they could not have forgotten him; he was bayonet-"ed in the side and wounded in the head and suffered terribly; "was very nervous and thought he was going to die, when I was in "the tent he would repeat, 'Oh! Misses, I'me gwine to die. Pray "for me', so that it would ring in my ears from day to day. He "was as great a big horrible negro as I ever saw. I had not seen "him since he was taken away from City Point until one day last

"Spring he came up on my porch; I stepped to the door and saw "him, and I said 'Oh! Misses I'se gwine to die!'; he knew I was "the one that took care of him. There are a great many soldiers "that I took care of that write me to make or sign statements to "aid them in getting pensions whom I do not recall to my mind. "There was a man by name of Stevens that had the fever, and in "delirium would say that I drank his brandy, and would say so to "the doctor; such are not forgotten by me. I was with the sol-"diers three years and was away only eight days."

In the affidavit of W.H.Jones he swears to seeing the claimant before and after the battle of Richmond,Va.,and that claimant was a member of Co."F" 1st U.S.C.T.,and fixes the date Sept.29, & 30 1864. It cannot be true that the claimant was in the service in Co."F" 135th U.S.C.T.,at any time in 1864. The regiment was not organized until March 1865.

If claimant had a prior service in Co."F" 1st U.S.C.T., or in any other organization it is not shown. The A.G.Record

that I took care of that write me to make or sign statements to
"aid them in getting pensions whom I do not recall to my mind.
"There was a man by name of Stevens that had the fever, and in
"delirium would say that I drank his brandy, and would say so to
"the doctor; such are not forgotten by me. I was with the sol-
"diers three years and was away only eight days."

In the affidavit of W.H.Jones he swears to seeing the claimant before and after the battle of Richmond,Va.,and that claimant was a member of Co."F" 1st U.S.C.T.,and fixes the date Sept.29, & 30 1864. It cannot be true that the claimant was in the service in Co."F" 135th U.S.C.T.,at any time in 1864. The regiment was not organized until March 1865.

If claimant had a prior service in Co."F" 1st U.S.C.T., or in any other organization, it is not shown. The A.G.Report, shows that a thorough search of the records of all organizations in which it was in any degree probable that the claimant served, has been made and no record of any prior service of claimant found. The claimant could not have participated as a Union sol-

That the claimant joined Sherman's army on its March to the Sea, and became a camp-follower, and while such, was afterward, while with or near the army shot and bayonetted by some confederate soldier is the only theory consistent with the testimony of Sarah J.Young and the only one that will reconcile the conflicting testimony in the case, if it can be reconciled at all.

The claimant, when he left his master's plantation and followed in the wake of Sherman's army may have imagined himself a soldier and that impression may have clung to him ever since. The Special Examiner who took his statement in Marshall County, Iowa says that claimant had been there but a short time; that he is either actually or purposely entirely ignorant of his army history and that his statement is worthless.

In any event the claim is not made out. It is shown conclusively that he could not have received the wounds and injuries complained of while a member of Co."F" 135th U.S.C.T.

Your action of rejection is affirmed.

It appears that the soldier has been pensioned under the

-7-

Act of June 27, 1890, at $12 per month on injury to left index finger and slight deafness of both ears.

Very respectfully,

Cyrus Bussey

Assistant Secretary.

(3—456.)

DEPOSITION A

Case of Lawrence McCook, No. 408115

On this 29th day of Aug. 1889, at Marshalltown, County of Marshall, State of Iowa, before me, F. G. Loomis, a Special Examiner of the Pension Office, personally appeared Alias Lawrence McCook, who, being by me first duly sworn to answer truly all interrogatories propounded to him during this Special Examination of aforesaid pension claim, deposes and says: I cannot tell my age but when the war broke out, or rather when I went in the army, I was 23 years old. Occ. common labor. Residence and P.O. as above.

When the war broke out I was the slave of Daniel McCook and lived on his place 19 miles east of Milledgeville Ga. The Yankee soldiers came there and took me to Savannah Ga. where a Colored Regiment was formed (No. of regmt not known) and I went in to Co. F. Capt. Hazel and a Lt. which they called Johnnie. I remember Berry Dunnigan. Jim Duncan

and [illegible] deposes and says: I cannot tell my age
but when the war broke out, or rather
when I went in the army, I was 23
years old. occ common labor. Residence
and P.O. as above.
When the war broke out I was the
slave of Daniel McCook and lived
on his place 9 miles east of Milledgeville
Ga. The Yankee Soldiers came there
and took me to Savannah Ga.
where a Colored Regiment was formed
(No. of regmt not known) and I went in
to Co. I. Capt. Hazel and a Lt. which
they called Johnnie. I remember
Berry Dunnigan, Jim Duncan,
Thomas McLaughlin, Squire Chapman,
Clark Scrutchin and Sam Tobin
who was 1st Sergt. I can't tell what
time in the year I enlisted but I
think it was in the fall when the
Yankees came and took me away
from the Plantation. I don't
remember ever being at Goldsboro
N.C. but I was in N.C. at some place.
I also remember being in Macon Ga.
I first got shot in fore finger of
left hand. I can't tell whether it was

and took me to Savannah Ga.
where a Colored Regiment was formed
(No. of regmt not known) and I went in
to Co. I. Capt. Hazel and a Lt. which
they called Johnnie. I remember
Berry Dunnigan, Jim Duncan,
Thomas McLaughlin, Squire Chapman,
Clark Scrutchin and Sam Tobin
who was 1st Sergt. I can't tell what
time in the year I enlisted but I
think it was in the fall when the
Yankees came and took me away
from the Plantation. I don't
remember ever being at Goldsboro
N.C. but I was in N.C. at some place.
I also remember being in Macon Ga.
I first got shot in fore finger of
left hand. I can't tell whether it was
in N.C. or S.C. but it was where there
was

Page 8 Deposition G

9

rice ponds and moss hanging from the trees. We were on a dike between two ponds. It was in the night and the Rebels surrounded us and our boss said the time had come when we must kill or be killed. I was color bearer and did not fire, but our men fell in line and marched and fired. This dam which we were on was a strip of land some 10 feet wide and separated the two rice ponds. I don't know what we were doing there but I was shot in left hand first and then I was shot again - in the same night - in my head at temple. After that some soldiers from Wis. and Ind. came and captured the rebels and us too. We were in the middle with the rebels all around us. I was taken to a hosp. in a bend of the Ogeechee River - so they said. It was a frame building 1½ stories high, and looked like

be killed. I was color bearer and did not fire, but our men fell in line and marched and fired. This dam which we were on was a strip of land some 10 feet wide and separated the two rice ponds. I don't know what we were doing there but I was shot in left hand first and then I was shot again - in the same night - in my head at temple. After that some soldiers from Wis. and Ind. came and captured the rebels and us too. We were in the middle with the rebels all around us. I was taken to a hosp. in a bend of the Ogeechee River - so they said. It was a frame building 1½ stories high, and looked like
a store building. The Dr. treated me, put a silver half dollar in my head which is in there now, and you can feel it. I don't know that it was money but it looked like money that the Dr. put in my head. Yes. there was a hole in my head. I also had the small pox

separated the two rice ponds. I
don't know what we were doing there
but I was shot in left hand first
and then I was shot again — in the
same night — in my head at temple.
After that some soldiers from
Wis. and Ind. came and captured
the rebels and us too. We were in
the middle with the rebels all
around us. I was taken to a hosp.
on a bluff of the Appomatic River — so
they said. It was a frame building
1½ stories high, and looked like
a stone building. The Dr. treated me,
put a silver half dollar in my
head which is in there now,
and you can feel it. I don't know
that it was money but it looked
like money that the Dr. put in
my head. Yes. there was a hole in
my head. I also had the small pox
while in that hosp. I can't tell
how long I was in that hosp. but

I think for over a month. A white
woman waited on me and I have
seen her since — Aunt Becky Young,
I saw her in Des Moines. I did
not remember her but she said she
remembered me, and said she was
the woman who waited on me.
I am sure a white lady waited on me
at the hosp. at Appomatic River.
I got shot through the left foot
at Petersburg. We were crawling on
our hands and knees at the time.
We were sent there to take a fort, and
had been marching along by a ditch
After I got shot I was taken prisoner,
half of my Co. were captured at same
time. I was stabbed in the body —
clear through by a wounded rebel.
I was in the ditch and there were
some logs there and cotton bales on
top of the logs, and sacks of sand on
top of the cotton. I was smothering
in the ditch and I wanted to pull
a sack of sand off the cotton bale so
I could crawl up on the bale and
get some air. A rebel lay there wounded.

[illegible]

I got shot through the left foot at Petersburg. We were crawling on our hands and knees at the time. We were sent there to take a fort and had been marching along by a ditch. After I got shot I was taken prisoner. Half of my Co. were captured at same time. I was stabbed in the body clear through by a wounded rebel. I was in the ditch and there were some logs there and cotton bales on top of the logs, and sacks of sand on top of the cotton. I was smothering in the ditch and I wanted to pull a sack of sand off the cotton bale so I would crawl up on the bale and get some air. A rebel boy there wounded. I think a fort had been blown up. I said to the rebel, "I am wounded and so are you. Don't you hurt me and I won't you. I want to throw this sack of sand over you so that I can get up on this bale of cotton to get some air." I jerked the bag of sand off and just then the wounded rebel stuck his bayonet through me.

After I got shot I was taken prisoner, half of us boys were captured at same time. I was stabbed in the body clear through by a wounded rebel. I was in the ditch and there were some logs there and cotton bales on top of the logs and sacks of sand on top of the cotton. I was smothering in the ditch and I wanted to pull a sack of sand off the cotton bale so I would crawl up on the bale and get some air. A rebel boy there wounded I think a fort had been blown up. I said to the rebel "I am wounded and so are you. Don't you hurt me and I won't you. I want to throw this sack of sand over you so that I can get up on this bale of cotton to get some air". I jerked the bag of sand off and just then the wounded rebel stuck his bayonet through me

Page 10 Deposition A

2

11

Page and I don't remember anything further. I don't know anything about what was done with me. I don't remember about being in the hosp'l or being treated for my wounded foot or for the bayonet wound. Can't tell a thing about it. I remember being in Washington. And I know I was discharged at Louisville, Ky. I think I was in the army about 1½ years. I also got my right ear shot in some way and at some time but I can't tell how or when or where. I was also cut twice in right wrist by a sword in the hands of a rebel cavalry man. I think this was done at the same time I got the bayonet stab through the body. I remember the rebel said 'Here you damn S. of a b. I will kill you, fighting against your master,' and he struck at me with his sword, and that is all I can tell about it. At the time I was mustered out at Taylor Barracks, Louisville, my wounds

bayonet wound. Can't tell a thing about it. I remember being in Washington, and I know I was discharged at Louisville, Ky. I think I was in the army about 1½ years. I also got my right ear shot in some war ahead at some time but I can't tell how or when or where. I was also cut [illegible] in right wrist by a sword in the hands of a rebel cavalry man. I think this was done at the same time I got the bayonet stab through the body. I remember the rebel said "here you dam S. of a b, I will kill you, fighting against your master" and he struck at me with his sword, and that is all I can tell about it. At the time I was mustered out at Taylor Barracks, Louisville, my wounds were all healed up and there was nothing apparently the matter with me. I went across the river to Ft Madison, where I lived with my uncle, Henson May, for about 3 years. I sawed wood and did any work I could. Bob. Blue (colored) and his brother John Blue lived at Fratton Station

Witnesses
[illegible]

his
Lawrence x McCook
mark
Deponent

State of ..., before me, ... a Special Examiner of the Pension Office, personally appeared Clint ..., who, being by me first duly sworn to answer truly all interrogatories propounded to h... during this Special Examination of afore-said pension claim, deposes and says: North of Ft Madison. Bob. Blue worked with me in a Hide house for a man named Hinkles (I think that was his name) in Ft Madison. My work was handling hides, tying them up and placing them on the scales to be weighed etc. My uncle Henson May had a daughter named Rachel May. I can't call to mind any other person in Ft Madison. I went to Indianapolis from Ft Madison and I staid there 2 seasons. I worked for Col. Streight, 3 or 4 miles east of Indianapolis, worked on a farm part of 2 seasons. Julius Caesar (colored) also worked for the Col. While working for the Col, he took me up to Woodland, Ind. where I worked on his farm 2 mos or so. I got sick while there and was doctored. The Dr. said it was caused from lifting. I can't name the Dr. I then went back to Indianapolis

[illegible]
at Ft Madison. His work was handling
hides etc. tieing them up and
placing them on the scales to be
weighed etc. My Uncle Hugson
may had a daughter named
Rachel May. I can't call to mind
any other person in Ft Madison.
I went to Indianapolis from
Ft Madison and I stayed there
2 seasons. I worked for Col
Straight, 3 or 4 miles east of
Indianapolis worked on a farm
part of 2 seasons. Julius Caesar
(colored) also worked for the Col
While working for the Col. he took
me up to Woodland. Ind. when I
worked on his farm I was or so,
I got sick while there and was
doctored. The Dr. said it was caused
from lifting. I can't name the Dr.
I then went back to Indianapolis
and boarded 3 or 4 weeks with
Mrs. Overstreet (colored) She kept a
boarding house near St. Louis Circle

Page 12 Deposition [illegible]

3

[illegible] and Ohio depot. I left Ind. and
went to Coles Co. Ill. about 2 miles
south west of Mattoon. I took up
with a blacksmith named
Burk Kilburn. He lived in a
house owned by Bob. Sawyer.
Bob and his brother Isaac Sawyer
were two farmers. Kilburn run
a country blacksmith shop.
He let me live with him about one
season. I grubbed, chopped, and
cut hazelbrush. Jim Trimble
was a farmer I worked for also
for John Eldridge (farmer) lived
6 miles south of Mattoon.
I next went to Woodlawn.
Jefferson Co. Ill. and worked for
Sawyer Bros. also for Mr. Hartline
3 miles S. W. from Woodlawn.
also for Bert. Lacy and his brother
south of St Louis. I staid there
for a year or two and there was
where I first tried to get a pension.
John D Bowland was [illegible]

was a farmer I worked for also
for John Etheridge (farmer) lived
6 miles south of Mattoon.
I next went to Woodlawn,
Jefferson Co. Ill. and worked for
Dwyer Stees. also for Mr. Hashline
3 miles S. W. from Woodlawn.
also for Bent. Lacy and his brother
South of W. Lawn. I staid there
for a year or two and there was
where I first tried to get a pension.
John W. Bowland was my lawyer
in Woodlawn. I can't tell how
long I did live at Woodlawn. but
a good while. and I am well known
there. While in Indianapolis
working for Col. Streight. I passed
clotted blood. from the bayonet wound
and the Dr. gave me some medicine
for it in Ind. But the Dr. at
Woodland said I had over done
I can't give the names of the Drs.

While at Woodlawn, Ill. I had a
breaking out across my abdomen.
where I was bayoneted. and the Dr.
who treated me was a son-in-law of
Bent. Lacy but I can't give his
name. Blood came through me then
The Dr said it was from over
lifting and from the wound
I marked at Richview, while
living at Woodlawn
I don't know any one by the name
of William H. Jones. I never
lived in Mt Vernon. Ill. but used
to go there before the clerk to have
papers made out. I was down sick
several times while I lived at
Woodlawn and the Dr. came to
see me but never would tell me
what ailed me. I lived in
Decatur. Ill. a few months only
I was also in Clinton. Ill. a few
mos. and then in Bloomington Ill

where I was bayoneted. And the Dr
who treated me was a son-in-law of
Brent Lacy but I can't give his
name. Blood came through me then
The Dr said it was from over
lifting and from the wound.
I preached at Richview while
living at Woodlawn.
I don't know any one by the name
of William H. Jones. I never
lived in Mt Vernon Ill. but used
to go there before the clerk to have
papers made out. I was down sick
several times while I lived at
Woodlawn and the Dr came to
see me but never would tell me
what ailed me. I lived in
Decatur Ill. a few months only
I was also in Clinton Ill. a few
mos. and then in Bloomington Ill.
from whence I went to Des Moines Ia.
thence to Indianola Ia. I then came
back to Des Moines. My side "riz"
(swelled) and Dr. Homs and his
partner treated me. Right there
(points to the bayonet scar in front)
was where it swelled and right there
(points to scar on back, where bayonet
is said to have come out) is where it

lived in Mt Vernon Ill. but used
to go there before the clerk to have
papers made out. I was down sick
several times while I lived at
Woodlawn and the Dr came to
see me but never would tell me
what ailed me. I lived in
Decatur Ill. a few months only
I was also in Clinton Ill. a few
mos. and then in Bloomington Ill.
from whence I went to Des Moines Ia.
thence to Indianola Ia. I then came
back to Des Moines. My side "riz"
(swelled) and Dr. Homs and his
partner treated me. Right there
(points to the bayonet scar in front)
was where it swelled and right there
(points to scar on back, where bayonet
is said to have come out) is where it
broke. I was staying at the house
of Henry Bell (colored), when
Dr. Homs treated me. The Dr
ran something in to my back

page 19 deposition [illegible]

... in the Poor House
in Des Moines a while. I was sent
out there to die. I had no medical
treatment in the Poor House. I staid
there a week or two, and then
crawled away from there. I was too
weak to walk. I went to Colfax, Ia.
Shehole in my back kept running
for a long time. I staid in Colfax
and worked in a hotel, peeled potatoes
for $11. a month. I then went to
Newton Ia. thence to Grinnell
where I preached and got married
for the first time. my wound in
the back was still discharging.
thence went to Belle Plaine Ia.
where they put me in the calaboose,
thought I was a thief and robber.
I then went to Eldora Ia. then
to Toledo Ia. then to Grinnell: then
to Oskaloosa Ia. to see John Lacy.
and tell Lacy to have them help me
on my pension. thence to New
Sharon: thence up here to
Marshalltown. Stopping a short
time in a place preaching and
working as best I could.

Shehole in my back kept running
for a long time. I staid in Colfax
and worked in a hotel, peeled potatoes
for $11. a month. I then went to
Newton Ia. thence to Grinnell
where I preached and got married
for the first time. my wound in
the back was still discharging.
thence went to Belle Plaine Ia.
where they put me in the calaboose,
thought I was a thief and robber.
I then went to Eldora Ia. then
to Toledo Ia. then to Grinnell: then
to Oskaloosa Ia. to see John Lacy.
and tell Lacy to have them help me
on my pension. thence to New
Sharon: thence up here to
Marshalltown. Stopping a short
time in a place preaching and
working as best I could.

Witnesses
Goodwin
Ward

his
Lawrence McCook
mark.

Deponent.

Sworn to and subscribed before me this 29 day of Aug.
, and I certify that the contents were fully made known to deponent before signing.

[illegible]

DEPOSITION 66

Case of Lawrence McCook, No. 408115

On this ______ day of Continued, 188_, at ______, County of ______, State of ______, before me, ______, a Special Examiner of the Pension Office, personally appeared Same, who, being by me first duly sworn to answer truly all interrogatories propounded to h___ during this Special Examination of aforesaid pension claim, deposes and says: I have never been in any fights or rows since I left the army and I have never been shot or hurt or cut in any fights since I came out of the army. Nr. I had no scar on my back until doctor cut it open to let the matter out of me. I dont think the bayonet went clear through me, I think it stopped near the back bone, and I think that rising on me was from the effects of the bayonet. My mother, Hannah McCook still lives at Iorg, Ga. and the old man Paul McCook has children living there yet, but my old master is dead. I dont know

[illegible] since the war. I would be sure to tell you a lie. I have tramped all over the country and I dont know myself where I have been. I used to fish in Stuartsville, Mo. one season - stopped with a colored man named Scott and with James and Andrew Ray (Kay).

I dont remember that I was ever in the hosp at City Point. I dont remember of being in any hosp except at (Aqueduct old Brickley) River.

I think I got hurt in my head and in my hand and in my body at the Rice Ponds as I have told you. that is my idea. I dont know anything about when I got that shot in my right leg.

I think I got that bayonet stab at Petersburg. I am sure of that. I think I got the cuts in my right wrist at the same place but I am not sure. I dont remember having any treatment for bayonet wound while in service. I worked for Mr. Reynolds (or Randal) in Des Moines. He sells plows etc. [illegible]

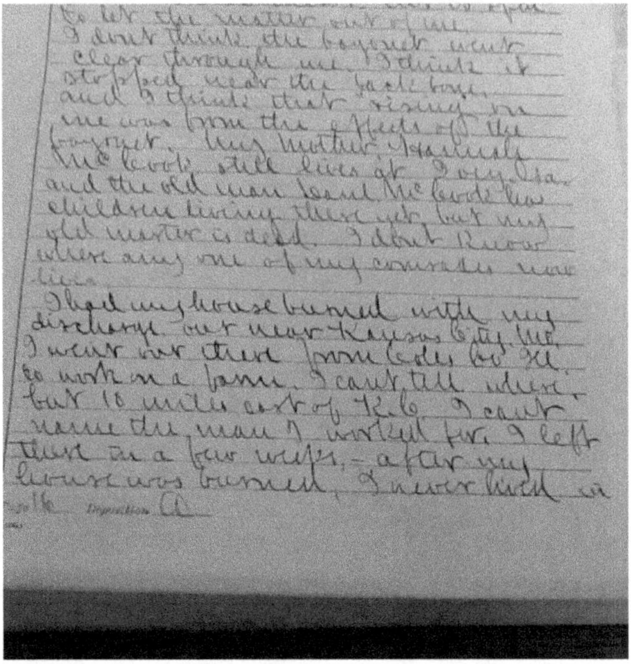

to let the matter out of me.
I dont think the bayonet went
clear through me. I think it
stopped near the back bone,
and I think that rising on
me was from the effects of the
bayonet. My mother Hannah
McCook still lives at [illegible]
and the old man Daniel McCook has
children living there yet, but my
old master is dead. I dont know
where any one of my comrades now
lives.
I had my house burned with my
discharge out near Kansas City Mo.
I went out there from Coles Co Ill.
to work on a farm. I cant tell where,
but 10 miles east of K.C. I cant
name the man I worked for. I left
there in a few weeks, after my
house was burned. I never lived in

Deposition A

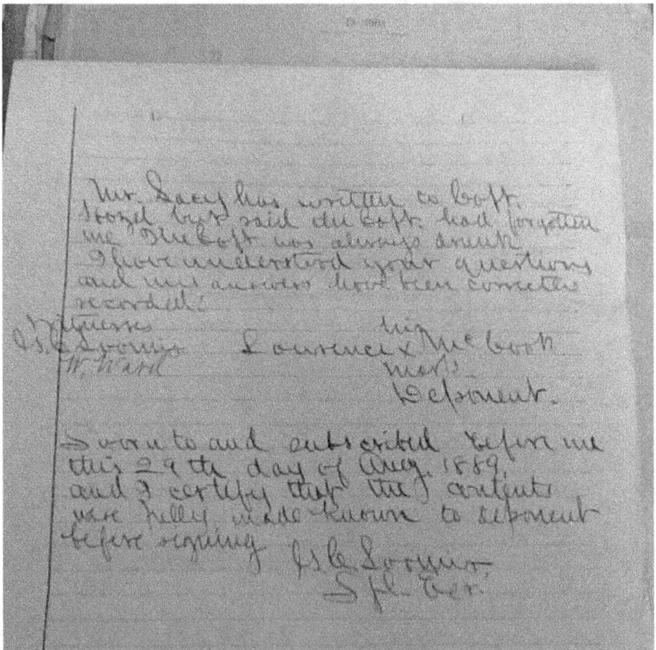

Mr. [illegible] has written to Capt.
[illegible] but said the Capt. had forgotten
me. The Capt. was always drunk.
I have understood your questions
and my answers have been correctly
recorded.

Witnesses
[illegible]
W. Ward

his
Lawrence x McCook.
mark
Deponent.

Sworn to and subscribed before me
this 29th day of Aug. 1889,
and I certify that the contents
were fully made known to deponent
before signing.
[illegible],
Spl. Ex.

CHAPTER 14

INTRODUCTION TO WIDOW'S PENSION'S

THE LIFE OF A WIDOW AFTER HER SOLDIER OF THE 135th UNITED STATES COLORED TROOP HAS PASSED.

The forgotten heroes of the Civil War are the young men of the 135th USCT who arrive home in the winter of 1865. The records show that quite a few marry within three years after the war, though some marry in the custom of slavery and have no written proof of marriage. Others have a ceremony with a preacher in someone's home or on the plantation and as time marches on, there will be licenses issued and written proof of weddings.

When applying for a widow's pension, they must first show evidence of the soldier's service, mostly with their discharge certificate or an affidavit from another soldier or neighbors who knew them before service, during service, and after serving in the regiment. This will take time, maybe a year or two. The widows with or without children under the age of sixteen support themselves and their children with only their labor in the cotton fields or as washerwoman, house housekeepers, or cooks. They must prove that they were married to the soldier, and without written proof, it was like moving a mountain. If they were older, according to the pension records, they may tell the pension lawyer that all witnesses to the marriage ceremony were dead in many of the cases. I have not seen more than a small handful that can read or write, or do they know how their name is spelled? To prove the date of the wedding, dates of children's births, or events that have happened like before or after the earthquake. This is mind blowing but the widows never gave up in their attempt for their rightful pension.

The next requirement was the children and their birth dates. Widows used several ways to give the birth dates and ages of their children. One was having midwives or friends who had a child close to or the same age, which helped prove their birth date. There could be as many as a dozen people who stated under oath that the child was hers and the date of the birth as close as possible. Sometimes, the white people helped to prove a birth date, or once in a while, they had a bible record with the family information in it.

Today, we talk about living paycheck to paycheck, but can you imagine living without a husband? You would go from one farm job to another, or if you were clever and lived on a plantation, maybe you could be the cook or the laundress. So, these small payments of pension money were a huge help. A good example was a woman whose husband returning from the war moved the family to Charleston and he died shortly after the move. She was forced to move seventeen times in her remaining lifetime due to lack of support. They were the underground heroes of the freed slaves. No one worked harder to move their family from slavery to freedom.

We cannot forget to mention that so many of the wives die in childbirth, which is why you would see so many of the soldiers often had more than one wife. Maya Angelou said, "How important it is for us to recognize and celebrate our Heroes and Sheroes!"

Proving the soldier had died and the date of his death was a challenge for most widows prior to 1901. It could take up to six years before the pension bureau would start the monthly payments. One of the things they had to show the pension board, if the soldier died before 1915, was proof of death. Friends, family, and white persons who knew the soldier, and saw the body, made an affidavit, testifying he died and the date of the death. In some cases, the merchant in town who sold the coffin would be able to make a true statement for the widow. Today, if you look at the pension card in the National Archives, you will see the widow's application date which will give you a clue as to the date of the soldier's death.

Now, there is another reason we want to highlight these women, remembering that they did not read or write, they had mostly lived in the same location all of their lives. They had to ask someone they knew and trusted to help them apply for the pension, as it could be a clerk whom they purchased supplies from, or their husbands did business with before they died. It could be an attorney in town, the postmaster, or even a man who came to the house saying he could get her a pension, if she could trust him. Another case was widows who did not know their husband had died in service. The widow would be made aware of a bounty years later and that they could apply for and collect a pension on his behalf.

The widows had to hire a white man to write the pension bureau, fill out the necessary paperwork, get the required depositions; in order to prove their claim so they could receive a pension. The pension check would then be sent to them. Some amounts are as high as four thousand dollars plus they would receive a monthly payment. The next trust that could be broken, was to help the widow get a bank account (in both names,) it was not legal though. When monthly checks would come, the widow would have to go to town and touch the paper, and he, (the white man,) would have to put an X at her name. The check would be deposited into the bank, and he would take his cut (illegally). Some of these trusted white men took more than others. As the children grew up, and were able to read and write, they would discover what had happened and they could confront the "trusted white man" and demand he give back the money he had taken illegally. The trusted man would lie to the widow, so she would complain to the pension board, and they would send a special investigator who would come and interview all parties, and as a result, many of these trusted men would go to the penitentiary.

These widow stories we've uncovered are heart gripping and still apply in today's world. In Chapter fourteen, we highlighted several examples of these "Sheroes!"

WIDOW PENSIONS

SELECT WIDOW PENSIONS INCLUDED IN THIS CHAPTER ARE EXTRACTIONS FROM THE WIDOW PENSION RECORDS OF;

LOUISA HUFF

HAGAR JENNINGS

LAVINIA HARPER

LUCINDA McCALL

AMY GIBSON

THE ANDREW WALLACE WIVES

LOUISA HUFF
WIDOW OF DANIEL HUFF

Louisa Huff's story is a simple but beautiful love story that touches everyone's heart.

Louisa was born and raised close to Dublin, Georgia, and belonged to the Huff plantation. Louisa states that she was fourteen years old when the Civil War ended. Her father was Alex Huff, and her mother was Amy Huff. Louisa's husband, Daniel Huff, went by the name Nazareth, and he said in slave days he belonged to some "white people" named Nazareth. Daniel said, his "dady" would move down by her "dady" and we all had the same last name, but we were not kin.

Louisa said she has always been a Huff and recounts how she met Daniel. She being young and Daniel coming home as a freedom fighter ***"on a Saturday and I met him that night, he came from the war wearing a blue uniform with brass buttons."*** She said she got married the next year and they got married on a Sunday in the church and the church was full. He always said, "He never had another wife or woman until he had me." She stated that they lived together until he died in 1917. As man and wife, they raised twelve children together. Louisa died in 1930 and she and Daniel Huff are both buried in Dublin, Georgia, at the William Chapel Baptist Church Cemetery.

3-289a.
(For typewriter.)

Gordon Bradshaw Place

Case of Louisa Huff No. 1120140

On this 19 day of January , 1921, at Dublin county of Laurens , State of Ga. before me, Thos. H. Goethe , a Special Examiner of the Bureau of Pensions, personally appeared Louisa Huff , who, being by me first duly sworn to answer truly all interrogatories propounded to her during this special examination of aforesaid claim for pension, deposes and says:

I do not know age but was fourteen when the Civil War ended; house keeping and I reside at 802 Decatur St., Dublin, Ga.

I claim pension as the widow of Daniel Nazareth who was known after he left the army under the name of Daniel Huff. My husband died on Wednesday night beforethe Third Sunday of May 1918. We were together when he died. He passed away a mile from here. We had lived as husband and wife from marriage to his death and had never been divorced or legally separated. I buried him and I have not re-married since his death.

My father was Alex Huff. My mother was Amy Huff. Huff was always my name for I married a Huff.

Q When and where did you marry?

A I married in McDuffey Co. Ga. and I think we were about eight miles from the town of Thompson. We were on the farm of Mrs. Mary McGaha. We were married on a Sunday in Chruch and the Church was full. However, I only know one person who is now alive who saw the ceremony performed and that is George Powell who lives this side of Bartow. He was living in the neighborhood where we lived at the time and was in Church. Now my sisters were all there but I don't know that they are alive. I left them in McDuffey. My sister Emily married Dick Bradshaw, Daisey married Major Barser? Hannah married Frank Bradshaw. Annie married Frank Thomspon. I have heard from none of them for fifty years. Rev. Jessey Rong, a Baptist Minister married us. My husband has it wrong if he

Page 2 Deposition A.

states wewere married by Romanus Moore. I knew Jessey Roney well. No, I cannot think of any one else who saw us married.

After our marriage my husband and I lived for three years near Thompson, Ga. and then we moved to Johnson Co.

Q Give me the date of your marriage?

A I cannot give the exact date but my husband came out one year and we married the next. He came from the War on a Saturday and I met him that night. He came from the war wearing a blue uniform with brass buttons.

Q Where did you live in Johnson Co.

A Near Ennis or Kite. We lived for years on the place of Jack Minton and then we moved to Jefferson Co. We were there two years and then moved here and have been here ever since. In Jefferson we lived near Bartown. George Powell was one of our neighbors. Mrs. Lula Minton has known me ever since I left McDuffey. She still knows me. I saw her Chrstmas. It was on the place of her husband where we used to live. My husband and myself lived as husband and wife from from marriage to his death and we were known to all as being such and we raised twelve children and I not only have grand children but great grand children as well. I have never been back to McDuffey since I left there. I have never received a letter from my sisters since I left. I had a brother Searborn Huff, Solomon Huff and Jesse Huff. They were all in McDuffey when I left. My husband has one sister Mandy Hill. She lives in Sparta. Her husband is dead. I saw her last year. My husband had been out of the war just about a year as near as I can come at it when we married. He always said he never had a wife or woman till he had me. All our children were born after we left McDuffey. Lawrence Barser, some white folks named Jackson used to live near us. Preacher did not give us a marriage paper. Thompson was the biggest place near us and was called eight miles from our home.

her
Louisa X Huff
mark

attest
Cora Jacob

BRIEF JACKET INDEX 3-366 SPECIAL EXAMINATION DIVISION

GER

DEPARTMENT OF THE INTERIOR

BUREAU OF PENSIONS

Wid.Orig.1123140 No. Louise Huff, widow of Daniel Nazareth, known as Huff, Co. K, 135 U.S.C.I.

Widow, Sep.8,1916

In cases submitted for special examination the papers should be indexed to show page numbers, names and addresses of claimants and witnesses, dates of filing, and subjects covered, a separate index being required for each brief. In indexing surgeons' certificates, dates of examination, not of filing, should be stated.

1 Claimant, Dublin, R.R.1, Ga.,Jul 5,1918, declaration.
2 do Oct.14,1918,husband sometimes called Nazareth-served in Co. K, 135 U.S.C.Inf.;neither divorced, lived together to May 1918; neither married before.
3 Claimant, Oct.7,1920, no relative in World war.
3½ E.B.Claxton,M.D. Laurens Co.,Ga.,Oct. 14,1918, attended soldier last illness, died May 17,1918.
4 George Powell, p.o.box 32,Bartow, Ga.,May 26,1919, Daniel Huff and Louisa Huff were married in 1868 by Jessie Roney and lived together until death of soldier.
5 J.B.Gamble, Laurens Co.,Ga.,Oct. 14, 1918,lived together,no separation
6 Ordinary McDuffie Co.,Ga.,May 26,1920,no marriage record.
7 do Columbia Co.,Ga.,Aug.18,1920, no record of marriage.
8 do Warren Co.,Ga.,Sep.1,1920, do
9 Soldier's family data statement,July 7,1903,wife Louisa Huff,married in Feb.,1868,in McDuffie Co.,Ga.,by Romanus Moore; ordinary of McDuffie County has record.

10 Soldiers family data circular, Sep. 27,1912, same as No. 9.

11 do Apr.22,1915,

12 W.A.Burnley, Dublin, Laurens Co.,Ga.,Jun.8,1920,knew claimant and soldier from date of their marriage to 1903;never separated or divorced.

13 Mrs Lila Minton,Kite,Ga.,Mar.6,1920, same as No.12.

Georgia Jefferson County

Personally appeared before me A. J. Harman N.P. & Ex off J.P. in and for said County Richard Howell, who on oath says he knows Daniel Nazreth who now goes by name of Daniel Kemp, that he knows that this Daniel Kemp is the original Daniel Nazreth who enlisted in Co K 135 Reg. U.S.C.I. That he knew him as Daniel Nazreth before he enlisted and that he was owned as a slave by Frank Nasworthy of said State & County. That he went off with Shermans army and enlisted in the 135th Reg. U.S.C.I. Co K. Richard Howell the deponent further says that he was enlisted under the name of Richard Howell in Co K 34th Reg U.S.C.I.

Sworn to and subscribed before me this 4th Nov 1903
A. J. Harman N.P. & Ex off J.P.

Richard his + mark Howell

PENSION A NOV 16 1903 U.S. OFFICE

So Div

Int. Dept No 1090617

Daniel Nazreth,
now Daniel Kniff
K 135 U.S. C Infy

Georgia Jefferson County

Before me N T Harman ? offic in and for said County comes Daniel Kniff formerly Daniel Nazreth who on oath says that he was born in Columbia County Ga. I was enlisted at Savannah Ga, I was twenty five years old and I was a slave owned by Frank Newsome of Jefferson County Ga. I was five feet seven inches high, black complexion Black eyes and black hair, scar on right thumb caused by a bone felon.

I have since I was discharged I lived in McDuffie County Ga seven years. Then in Warren County Ga six years, then in Hancock County twenty years, then in Wrightsville Johnson County Ga four years. And now in Jefferson County from 1st Jan 1903

Sworn to and subscribed before me this 14th Sept 1903
N T Harman N.P. Ex off J.P.

Daniel his mark Kniff
formerly
Daniel his mark Nazreth

HAGAR JENNINGS
WIDOW OF ADAM JENKINS

After burying her husband and trying to survive on her own, on September 17, 1901, a special investigator W.L. Harris was sent to take up the claim of Hagar Jennings brought on by the Black community.

The investigation showed clearly that the pensioner had illegitimate relations with a colored man named William Williams. Mr. Harris stated that it was quite difficult to obtain testimony in the case, for the man was a sort of local preacher, and a foreman on the plantation where some seventy hands are employed.

Hagar claimed she was sixty-four years old, lived on Edisto Island, South Carolina, and was a farmer. She was born to slave parents whose master was William Eddings, a planter on Edisto Island. She said her father was Bob Brisbane. Her husband was tall, a yellow man, and a farmer. He had no marks except the one on his back caused by whipping while he was a slave. Hagar's husband was born and raised on Parris Island, South Carolina. "We were married by Reverend Johnson (White), in his house on Edisto Island. His discharge certificate was destroyed by fire when the house was burned." She let the investigator know that she had only been married once to Adam and was married to him until his death.

Will Williams, a colored man who lived on the Legare Plantation, next to the plantation on which Hagar lived, and whose foreman was Mr. Seabrook, said that Will Williams "commenced to cohabitate with

Hagar as soon as her husband died." Hagar stated she has had nothing to do with Will Williams since she got her pension. Hagar lived alone in her house which was close to her married daughter. "Mr. Will Williams used to haul wood and do plowing for me. Sometimes he would give me money for sugar and groceries." Hagar testified. "He hasn't done anything for me since I received my pension. I did sleep with Mr. Williams from when my husband died until I got my pension. I have lived by myself and supported myself by my own labor." Hagar had a very small house and eight acres of land, where she grew vegetables and truck for a living.

Hagar said, "I had a witness for my claim for a pension. I proved that Adam was in the service, we were married, and that I was a lawful widow. I paid each witness fifty cents when I got my pension. Mr. Stevens, a notary public and storekeeper at the steamboat wharf, did all my writing for my application. I never paid Mr. Stevens until I got my first pension check. Mr. Stevens had it sent to him, and he paid me one hundred and fifty dollars, I think. No one was present when Mr. Stevens paid me the money." Mr. Stevens told Hagar that he had taken out of her pension money what she owed him for his writings and his trouble. Hagar did not know how much Mr. Stevens took out but her nephew, Spia Brisbane of Edisto Island, went with her to Mr. Stevens' back room, where Hagar got paid. Her nephew could read and write. Hagar went to Mr. Stevens on the fourth of every month with her pension certificate. She said, "Mr. Stevens has always had my pension vouchers." Hagar would touch the pen and swear that it was her signing the "X." Hagar now always had to pay two witnesses and Mr. Stevens took one dollar each time she got her pension. She then received twenty-two dollars every three months and Mr. Stevens couldn't steal from her after the investigation.

In 1901, the pension bureau had still not settled this case surrounding Mr. Stevens and the money he had been taking from Hagar. Hagar died in 1903 and is buried on Edisto Island.

3—289.
(Old No. 3—446.)

DEPOSITION

Case of Hagar Jennings, wid. No. 469227

On this 5th day of September, 1901, at Edisto Island county of Barnwell Charleston Co State of South Carolina before me, R. E. Roberts, a special examiner of the Bureau of Pensions, personally appeared Hagar Jennings who, being by me first duly sworn to answer truly all interrogatories propounded to her during this special examination of aforesaid claim for pension, deposes and says: I am 64 years of age, and reside on Edisto Island, S.C. Occupation farming. I was born of slave parents whose master was named Wm Eddings a planter living on Edisto Island, S.C. My father name was Bob Brisbane. I don't know how he got that name but my name was Hagar Brisbane before my marriage. My husbands full name was Adam Jennings, and he had no other name and I have never been known or called by any other name than Hagar Jennings since my marriage to Adam Jennings. I don't know what Company or regiment my husband served in. My husband was a "tall slim yellow man," black hair and eyes. Occupation a farmer No marks that had scars on his back caused by whipping while a slave. My husband was born on Parris Island S.C. and I think he was about 65 years of age when he died. I have never been married but once and that was two years after the war, and then I married Adam Jennings. We were married by the Rev. Johnson, (white) in his house on Edisto Island S.C. We had a marriage certificate but it was burned when our house was destroyed by fire. I was not parted or divorced from my husband during the time from our marriage up to his death. My husband never had any other wife except me, and I never had any other husband except Adam Jennings. Will Williams a colored man who lives on the Legare plantation next to the plantation on which I live and who is the foreman for Mr Seabrook commenced to cohabit with me soon after my husband died. I did not have anything to do with Will Williams before my husband died and have not had anything to do with him since I first got my pension. This Will Williams and I used to go to bed together in my house. I live alone in my house which is close to the house of my married daughter whose husband is named Abraham Wright. — Will Williams used to haul wood for me and plow for me after my husband died and sometimes he would send his boys to haul wood and do plowing for me. Some times he would give me a little money to buy sugar and groceries I had

Attest:-
G. W. Seabrook
Ezekill Bowens

Hagar her X mark Jennings
Deponent.

Sworn to and subscribed before me this 5th day of Sept., 1901, and I certify that the contents were fully made known to deponent before signing.

R. E. Roberts
Special Examiner.

3-289.
(Old No. 3-408.)

DEPOSITION

Case of Hagar Jennings et al No. 469227.

On this .... *day of* .... , *190* ..., *at* ....
county of ....
State of .... , *before me,* .... , *a special examiner of the Bureau of Pensions, personally appeared* .... *who, being by me first duly sworn to answer truly all interrogatories propounded to h.... during this special examination of aforesaid claim for pension, deposes and says:*

to have someone to do things for me, Since I drawn my pension I dont have anything to do with Will Williams or any other man. I had no money and I just used to go bed with this Will Williams and he would give me groceries and do work on my farm to pay me for this pleasure, but I am not married to him because he has a wife and had a wife when he "had me" after my husband died, Will Williams and I slept together off and on from the time of my husbands death up to when I first got my pension money. I think it was in about "one half a month" after my husband died when Will Williams and I first slept together this was in my own house and in my bed We would take our clothes off when we went to bed together, but Williams would not stay with me all night because he had to go home, I think he would go home about 10 o'clock at night, I never had a child for 6 years before my husband died and did not have any baby and was not

Page 7 Deposition A

in the family way by Will Williams.
I have lived by myself and supported
myself by my own labor, since my
husband died. Since I got my pension
I live on that mostly. I have my
house and 8 acres of land and I raise
vegetables and truck to live on. —
I have but two children both of whom
are married. My husband died
5 years ago this January coming at
the house where I now live. My
husband died of rheumatism in
8 days after he was taken sick, and
no doctor attended him in his last
illness. My husband was a sickly
man when I married him and
he always complained of a
pain in his breast.
I have no claim pending for pension
under any law. I have lived where
I now live ever since my husband
died. My witnesses in my pension
claim. Will Williams. Moses Brown
(deceased) Moses Brown and my husband
was in the army together. William and
Sarah Bailey also testified for me. I
now recollect that Isaac Birall was also
a witness. These witnesses testified
that I was the lawful widow
of Adam Jennings. I paid each
of my witnesses 50cts after I got
my pension. A Mr Stevens, a Notary

Attest:
G.W. Seabrook
Ezekiel Bowles

Hagar her X mark Jennings
Deponent.

Sworn to and subscribed before me this 5th day of Sept, 1901, and I certify that the contents were fully made known to deponent before signing.

R. E. Roberts
Special Examiner.

3—280.
(Old No. 1—468.)

DEPOSITION

Case of Hagar Jennings widow No. 469227.

On this .... *day of* ...., 190.., *at* ...., *county of* ....

State of .... Continued *before me*, ..., *a special examiner of the Bureau of Pensions, personally appeared* ...., *who, being by me first duly sworn to answer truly all interrogatories propounded to h.... during this special examination of aforesaid claim for pension, deposes and says:*

Public and a Store keeper at the Steamboat Wharf on Edisto Island S.C. did all of my writing for me when I was applying for pension, I dont know what Mr Stevens first name is. this Mr Stevens swore me and my witnesses, I never paid Mr Stevens, anything until I got my first pension money, I did not have my first pension Check. Mr Stevens had it and he paid me $150.00 I think it was $150.00. No one was present when Mr Stevens paid me this money, we were in a room off from his store room and no one saw him pay me this money. Mr Stevens told me that he had taken out of my pension money what was due him for writing and trouble which he had with my pension claim. I dont know how much he took out, but my Nephew "Ezra Brisbane, of Edisto Island S.C. was with me at Mr Stevens Store, and after I came out of the room where Mr Stevens paid me, I had him count the money Mr Stevens gave me, and he will know just how much it was, because he can read and write. I go to Mr Stevens on the 4th of the month when my pension is due, I have my pension Certificate

Page 9 Deposition A

Page 10

now, but Mr Stevens has always had it most of the time, since I got it. I never have my pension voucher. Mr Stevens always has them, I touch the pen and he swears me, I have to and always do pay two witnesses 50 cts. each every time I get my pension money and I suppose Mr Stevens takes $1.00 each time because I only get $22.00 and my pension is $24.00 every three months. I have never pawned my pension Certificate and have never borrowed any money on it, from any person for any purpose whatever. —

My husband was some times called Adam Bolles, but I don't know how he came to be called by that name. I married him under the name of Bolles, but after he applied for a pension they wrote to him from Washington D.C. that he must take the name under which he served in the Army and then he took the name of Adam Jennings. —

I have heard your questions and have fully understood them and my answers have been correctly recorded, I make this statement of my own free will and without coercion on the part of any one,

Attest: her
Hagar x Jennings
mark

R. E. W. Seabrook

Ezekill Bowles

Deponent.

Sworn to and subscribed before me this 5th day of Sept, 1907, and I certify that the contents were fully made known to deponent before signing.

R. E. Roberts
Special Examiner.

LAVINIA HARPER
WIDOW OF WILLIAM KEITT

Lavinia Harper, widow of William Keitt, was born and raised in Orangeburg County, South Carolina. She was owned by Mr. George Bowman and was given to his daughter when she married Mr. William Murray. From then on, until freedom, George Bowman's daughter was Lavinia's owner.

In 1871, Lavinia married William Harper/William Keitt in Branchville, South Carolina, by Mr. Reedish. Willaim Keitt, her husband, was born in Saint Mathews and was owned by Mr. Keitt. She met William when he came to live about a mile from Lavinia's house. They lived together as husband and wife until he died in 1906, and she never married again. She stated that she had ten children by her late husband and five are still alive. Lavinia had no property or income of any kind. Ola was Lavinia's youngest child, however Lavinia stated she previously had one child in slavery on the plantation when she was very young. The father was Jake Phillips. He got Lavinia in that fix and her mother went to his house and told him he could never come to Lavinia's house, or she would have him arrested.

William Keitt/Harper was owned by Mr. Jacob Keitt before the war. Lavinia's maiden name was Jamison, which was her father's name as well. To prove that William Keitt is now Harper, and that he was in the 135th USCT, and that they were married, she had to have more than five people make affidavits swearing that the background and history she gave were all true. Glover Jamison, who was her son, before she was married to Willaim Keitt, also submitted his affidavit. Glover testified and showed the bible record from slavery that was old and genuine. Glover stated his mother had no property and had to work for a living. William Harper's death date was April 24, 1906.

This is a sad example of how badly some widows were treated. Most could not read or write, and they would have to rely on the men in town to prove their worth. The pension board asked Lavinia for proof and clarifications to her widow pension request, year after year, from 1906 to 1929. She never received the increase in widow's pension that she so desperately needed, and she died destitute in 1929.

Branchville, S.C.

Jan 25, 19[illegible]

In re- Lavinia Harper, Widow Division
W.C. 630193. William Harper,
G. 135 U.S.C. Vol- Inf.

United States
Department of the Interior
Bureau of Pensions
Washington, D.C.

Dear Gentleman:-

About the first of Dec, 1929. I sent you a Telegram asking you to please let me know why the delay of so long a time in the way of fowarding back pay check for Increase in the pension of Mrs. - Lavinia Harpers, of Branchville, S.C.

I have up to date not heard any thing from you what ever since I mailed you the Affidavit Signed by my self before a Notary Public, stating that Mr. Colliers, age was found to be correct as he had always kept his family age in his familey Bible. He states that he does know that Mrs. Harper is (80) Eighty years of age, and over. Now I urgently request that you please let me hear from you at, once as to what consideration has been given this claim for Increased pensation that she has been Entitled to since the change in the Laws, to Increase the pensations.

Please note that this old lady is not able now to get about hardly any, and is in bad health and if this is not sent to her soon she will not live to draw any Increase much less her retroactive pay due her. Trusting that you will mail this check to her Address by return mail.

Very truly yours,

March 17, 1930.

See statements made by pensioner that her parents changed their surname to Jamison, and that she was known as Lavinia Jamison, and was married to soldier under that name; that she had a child named Glover Jamison prior to her marriage to soldier. In Special Examiner's report dated May 25, 1907, there is found the testimony of Glover Jameson, who says he is the son of Lavinia. It is believed that the report from the Census Bureau filed March 12, 1930, refers to this pensioner, and that she was born in at least 1853.

J. V. D.
Ex'r

U.S. Pension Bureau
Washington, D.C.

Mrs. Lavinia Harper
No. 630193

Oct 30th 1927.

Dear Sir:-

I have been requested to write you in regards to the pension claim of Mrs. Lavinia Harper No. 630193 Widow of the said Veteran, William (Keith) afterwards known as William Harper. private. Co. G 135th Reg. U.S. Colored Volunteer Infantry. This Widow is under the impression that she is entitled to a raise in monthly compensation, and she also wants her address changed from Rowesville, S.C. to R.F.D. #1. Branchville, S.C. please give this your early attention and let her know if she is due a raise in compensation.

Very truly yours,

W. E. Tiller
Service Officer. American Legion Post #1
Branchville, S.C.

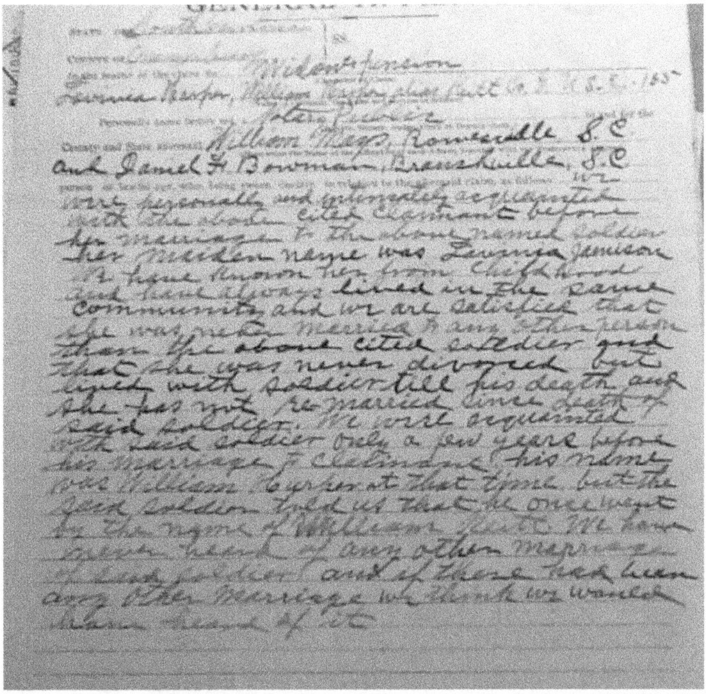

State of South Carolina
County of Orangeburg } ss.
In the matter of the claim for Widow's pension
Levinia Harper, William Harper alias Keitt Co. [illegible] U.S.C. 135
Personally came before me a Notary Public
in and for the County and State aforesaid William Mays, Rowesville S.C
and Daniel F. Bowman Branchville, S.C
persons of lawful age, who being duly sworn, declare in relation to the aforesaid claim as follows: We were personally and intimately acquainted with the above cited claimant before her marriage to the above named soldier her maiden name was Levinia Jamison We have known her from childhood and have always lived in the same community and we are satisfied that she was never married to any other person than the above cited soldier and that she was never divorced but lived with soldier till his death and she has not re married since death of said soldier. We were acquainted with said soldier only a few years before his marriage to claimant, his name was William Harper at that time but the said soldier told us that he once went by the name of William Keitt. We have never heard of any other marriage of said soldier and if there had been any other marriage we think we would have heard of it

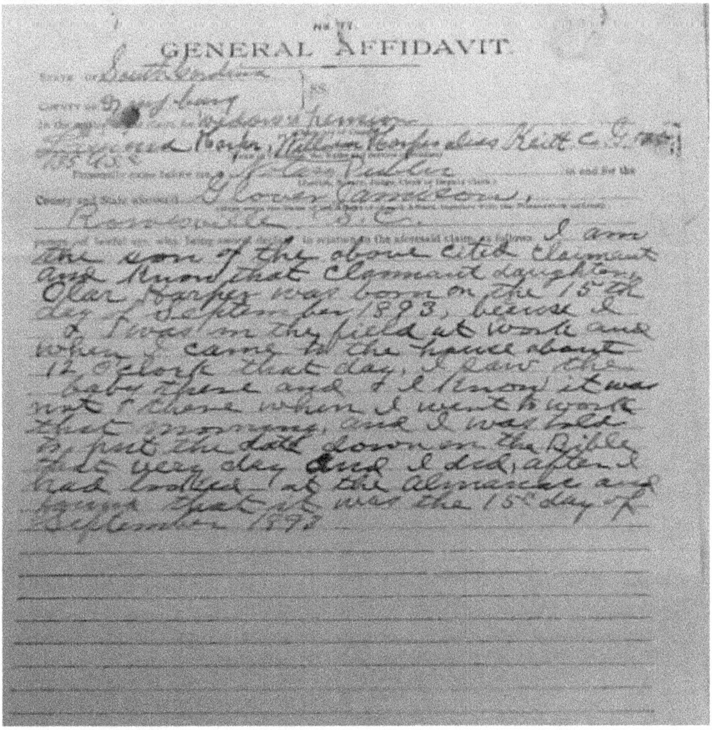

GENERAL AFFIDAVIT.

State of South Carolina
County of Orangeburg } ss.
In the matter of the claim for Widow's Pension
Levinia Harper, William Harper alias Keitt Co. [illegible]
135 U.S.C.
Personally came before me a Notary Public in and for the
County and State aforesaid Glover Jamison,
Rowesville S.C.
persons of lawful age, who being duly sworn, declare in relation to the aforesaid claim as follows: I am the son of the above cited claimant and know that claimant daughter Olar Harper was born on the 15th day of September 1893, because I I was on the field at work and when I came to the house about 12 O'clock that day, I saw the baby there and I know it was not there when I went to work that morning, and I was told to put the date down on the Bible that very day and I did, after I had looked at the almanac and found that it was the 15th day of September 1893

LUCINDA McCALL
WIDOW OF DAVID McCALL

Lucinda has an interesting story in the pension record of David McCall. We found that she was David's third wife as his previous two wives died. In the deposition of Boston Bethea, he testified that David's first wife, during slavery, was Miley and when he returned from the Army, he lived with her until she died. Boston said that she died about fifteen years after the war. David then married Kittie and he lived with her until she died. Boston doesn't recall when she died, however, he believed she had been dead for about fifteen years. This deposition by Boston was in July of 1906.

After the death of David's second wife, Boston Bethea said that David married Lucinda Gadbold about a year later and testified that he witnessed their marriage. Boston went on to say that Lucinda had just one husband, before David McCall, who was Mitchell Gadbold and he had been "killed by a mob just before the big shake." Lucinda was not married, nor had she been with a man after Michell had been killed until she married David McCall.

David McCall, also known as David Hamer, applied for and received a pension in his later years. After he died, Lucinda applied for and was granted her widow's pension. In support of Lucinda, Hector Stackhouse gave a deposition testifying that he knew she was the wife of David McCall, also known as David Hamer, and that she had not remarried after David died. Hector Stackhouse said he served with David in Company "H," of the 135th United States Colored Troop during the war. He had known David and Lucinda for many years and that they lived together as husband and wife until he died, and if she had remarried after his death, he would certainly have been aware of it as they lived not far apart.

Lucinda McCall did receive her widow's pension after providing the necessary paperwork and numerous depositions justifying that she was the wife of David McCall and that she had not remarried after his death. She began receiving a pension of twenty-five dollars a month in 1917, and in 1919, a special examiner was sent to investigate as in February of 1919 she claimed not to have received her check. Upon the special examiners' investigation into the matter, it was discovered that the check for Lucinda had, in fact, been endorsed by someone and paid for by the bank. Lucinda claimed to never have received the payment and, as the investigator questioned the bank employees to determine who had cashed the check, they claimed not to recall any particular person cashing the check. There was a copy of the check in the file with the endorsement on the back by Lucinda McCall, however, she claims not to have ever seen the check and never authorized anyone else to receive or cash the check.

There was no final disposition of whatever became of the alleged cashing of the check by someone other than Lucinda, however, it would appear the matter was resolved as there are no further disputes.

Lucinda died as a widow on December 23, 1932, in Dillon, Manning Township, South Carolina.

On this 4th day of Oct., 1917, at Dillon county of Dillon, State of S. C. before me, Thos. H. Goethe, a Special Examiner of the Bureau of Pensions, personally appeared Willie McNeill, who, being by me first duly sworn to answer truly all interrogatories propounded to him during this special examination of aforesaid claim for pension, deposes and says:

I am 31 years of age; farmer and I reside near Dillon, S. C., which is my post office address.

Nine years ago I married the daughter of Lucinda McCall but I knew her all my life--grew up in the same neighborhood with her. She makes her home with me and has been doing so ever since I married her daughter. Before our marriage my wife and Claimant lived together. I have direct and personal knowledge of the fact that she has not remarried since the death of David McCall. I would know it had she done so but know positively that she has contracted no marriage since soldier passed away nor has she lived with a man. She has gone only as Lucinda McCall and my wife and I have furnished her a living. That is we did so since our marriage and before our marriage my wife aided her to live. My wife before our marriage was a cook for the white folks--cooked for Dr. Davis and helped her mother all she was able. Claimant has worked all she could to help herself but she is old and cannot do a great deal. With the help we give her she has managed to get along fairly well. The above deposition has been read to me and my answers have been correctly recorded.

Willie McNeill
Deponent

Subscribed and sworn to before me this 25th day of Oct. 1917 and I certify that contents were fully made known to deponent before signing.

[illegible]
Special Examiner

Page 8 Deposition B

Case of [illegible] McCall No. 245572

On this 25 day of Oct., 19 17 at Dillon County of Dillon, State of S. C. before me, [illegible], a Special Examiner of the Bureau of Pensions, personally appeared Hector Stackhouse, who, being by me first duly sworn to answer truly all interrogatories propounded to him during this special examination of aforesaid claim for pension, deposes and says:

I am [illegible] 64; farmer and I reside near Dillon, S. C., which is my post office address.

I am in no wise related to Lucinda McCall and have no interest in the prosecution of her pension claim.

Her husband David Hagor or McCall served with me during the Civil War in Co. H, 135 U. S. C. Inf.

I have known Lucinda for many years--knew her before David married her and have known her continuously since his death. She has lived in from one to three miles of me ever since the soldier died and I have seen her from time to time. She has not re-married since David died. Had she re-married I would have been sure to have learned of it for a thing, like a marriage spreads in the country. She has not lived with a man and her reputation has been good. Her name has not been mixed with a scandall of any kind. She is well respected by those who know her. Since the soldier's death she has gone simply as Lucinda McCall. I never heard of her having any other name since the soldier passed away. The above deposition has been read to me and my answers have been correctly recorded.

his
Hector ✕ Stackhouse
mark

Attests
J. F. Martin

Subscribed and sworn to before me this 25th day of Oct. 1917 and I certify that contents were fully made known to deponent before signing.

Th. Hewitt
Special Examiner

Page 14 Deposition 6

On this 25 day of Oct., , 19 17 at Dillon county of Dillon , State of S. C. before me, Thos. H. Goethe , a Special Examiner of the Bureau of Pensions, personally appeared Neill E. Bethea , who, being by me first duly sworn to answer truly all interrogatories propounded to him during this special examination of aforesaid claim for pension, deposes and says:

I am 58 to 59 years of age; farmer and I reside near Dillon, S. C., which is my post office.

I am in no wise related to claimant and have no interest in the prosecution of her pension claim.

I have known her all my life. I have lived as her next door neighbor for fifteen years. She has not re-married since the death of her husband David Hamer or McCall. Claimant has been known only as Lucinda McCall since the death of David. She bears a good name. There has been no scandall connected with her name and I know I am competent to testify upon that point for I have known her day in and day out. She has had no men hanging around her. She is well respected by all who know her. The above deposition has been read to me and my answers have been correctly recorded.

Neill E. Bethea
Deponent

Subscribed and sworn to before me this 25th day of October 1917 and I certify that contents were fully made known to deponent before signing.

Thos. Goethe
Special Examiner

Thos. H. Goethe , a Special Examiner of the Bureau of Pensions, personally appeared Lucinda McCall , who, being by me first duly sworn to answer truly all interrogatories propounded to her during this special examination of aforesaid claim for pension, deposes and says:

I am about 78 years of age; house keeping and I reside as stated above. I was born somewhere in the Charleston section but cannot tell just where. I really should have said Savannah and if I said Charleston before to Mr. Jennings I got it wrong. I was only a girl when we left there so I cannot describ the locality. We were nearer Savannah than anywhere else. My father was Ben Manning. My mother was Hager Manning. My sister Charlotte was the oldest child and I was next to her. Dinnah followed me and Rachel was after her. My brother Sipp was the last. He was the baby. When I was about fifteen we were all brought to Clio. Bill Medley who owned us brought us to Clio and he sold us to Manning and we were then his slaves till Freedom come.

Q How far was Savannah from you before you were brought to Clio?

A It was so near that we could go and come in a night on the boat.

My first husband was Mitchell Godbolt but he died and then I married David McCall and he had been a soldier and he drew a pension.. He died near Dillon. I was living with him at time of his death. We were never divorced or legally separated. I was his lawful wife when he died.

No, I have not re-married since his death nor have I lived with a man. I have gone only as Lucinda McCall. It is the only name I have been known under since my husband died.

Page 6 Deposition

Columbia, S. C., Oct. 26, 1917.

Hon. Commissioner of Pensions,

Page 7

I have lived in this neighborhood ever since he passed away and am known to all the people around here. You can see any you please. I would like to be present when you see the witness around here but not elsewhere. Lawyer Lane of Dillon has been doing my writing. He did not say what he would charge. I have only paid him two dollars up to date. I have no formal contract with him.

My husband David McCall died years ago but just how many years I cannot say positively but my daughter who is present says he died sixteen years back.

The above deposition has been read to me and my answers have been correctly recorded.

her
Lucinda X McCall
mark

Attests
J. F. Martin

Subscribed and sworn to before me this 25th day of Oct. 1917 and I certify that contents were fully made known to deponent before signing.

[illegible signature]
Special Examiner

Case of Lucinda McCall No. 834051

On this 23 day of August, 1919, at Clio county of Marlboro, State of S. C. before me, Thos. H. Goethe, a Special Examiner of the Bureau of Pensions, personally appeared William E. Anderson, who, being by me first duly sworn to answer truly all interrogatories propounded to him during this special examination of aforesaid claim for pension, deposes and says:

I am 26 years of age; Cashier First National Bank of Clio, S. C.

I do not know any one named Lucinda McCall or Lucinda Hamer.

I have examined the photostat copy of check No. 3558551, dated February 4, 1919, to the order of Lucinda McCall of Dillon, Dillon Co. S. C.. That check was paid by my Bank on February 8, 1919, but to whom paid I do not remember. I do not know the party and do not remember a single thing connected with the cashing of same. The President of the Bank Mr. Henry L. Galloay is now in the mountains. If he was here he might possibly be able to throw some light upon the matter for it is possible that he may have cashed the check, or it may possibly have been cashed by my assistant Miss Kity May Snipes. If she and Mr. Galloay can give no information then I do not see how it will be possible to ever find the party who received the money for said check for as I said I have not the remotest recollection of the affair. The above deposition has been read to me. I have fully understood your questions and my answers have been correctly recorded. That is our endorsement stamp all right. We paid it.

William E. Anderson

Jurat over

Page B Deposition B

county of Dilion , State of S. C. before me, Thos. H. Goethe , a Special Examiner of the Bureau of Pensions, personally appeared Lucinda McCall , who, being by me first duly sworn to answer truly all interrogatories propounded to her, during this special examination of aforesaid claim for pension, deposes and says:

I do not know age but was born a long time before the Big War; house keeping and I reside on the place of Dr. David three and a half miles from Dilion, S. C.

I draw a pension of twenty five dollars a month but do not recall under what number I get it. I get it as the widow of David McCall or David Hamer. He died a few years ago but I do not remember the exact date of his death. My pension commenced last year and I have received all checks due except the February check which I never received. I never got it from the Post Office and don't know who did. I never authorised any one else to do so. I cannot write. I always sign my name by mark. I have no idea who received the check and cashed it. I never at any time instructed any one else to get my check from the Post Office. I never go to Clio. I have not been there since the close of the Civil War. I do not know what company and regiment my husband was in but he got a pension and was drawing it at the time of his death. I again say that I have not the slightest idea who got my check out of the Post Office last February and cashed same at the bank in Clio. No, sir, I know that my children did not do that. It was some one aside from any member of my family. Who it was though I do not know. The above depositin has been read to me. I have fully under tood your questions and my answers have been correctly recorded.

her
Lucinda x McCall
mark

Attests G. S. Alford

Page 5 Deposition A L Manning

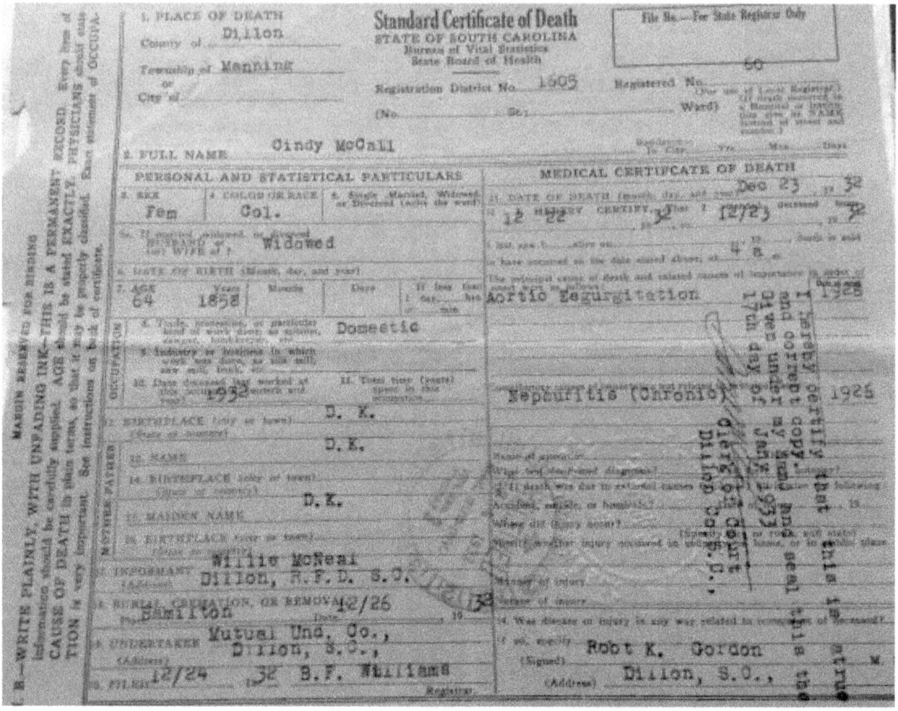

Standard Certificate of Death
STATE OF SOUTH CAROLINA
Bureau of Vital Statistics
State Board of Health

1. PLACE OF DEATH
County of Dillon
Township of Manning
or
City of

Registration District No. 1605
Registered No. 66
File No.—For State Registrar Only

2. FULL NAME Cindy McCall

PERSONAL AND STATISTICAL PARTICULARS

3. SEX Fem
4. COLOR OR RACE Col.
5. Single, Married, Widowed or Divorced (write the word) Widowed
7. AGE 64 Years 1858
8. Trade, profession, or particular kind of work done Domestic
10. Date deceased last worked at this occupation 1932
12. BIRTHPLACE (city or town) D. K.
13. NAME D. K.
15. MAIDEN NAME D. K.
INFORMANT Willie McNeal (Address) Dillon, R.F.D. S.C.
BURIAL, CREMATION, OR REMOVAL Place Hamilton Date 12/26 1932
UNDERTAKER Mutual Und. Co., (Address) Dillon, S.C.,
FILED 12/24 1932 B.F. Williams Registrar

MEDICAL CERTIFICATE OF DEATH

21. DATE OF DEATH (month, day, and year) Dec 23 1932
22. I HEREBY CERTIFY, That I attended deceased from 12 22 1932 to 12/23 1932
... death is said to have occurred on the date stated above, at 4 a.m.
The principal cause of death and related causes of importance in order of onset were as follows: Aortic Regurgitation 1925
Contributory causes of importance not related to principal cause: Nephuritis (Chronic) 1925
(Signed) Robt K. Gordon
(Address) Dillon, S.C.,

I hereby certify that this is a true and correct copy. Given under my hand and seal this 17th day of Jan 1933
Clerk of Court
Dillon Co., S.C.

AMY GIBSON
WIDOW OF JAMES GIBSON

Amy Gibson was a smart savvy woman who lived on the Nelson Gibson plantation all her life along with James Gibson. ***She was the cook in the big house.*** James returned from the war to the Gibson plantation in 1865. He married Amy in July of 1870 by the Reverend Neil Newton. In 1902, when Amy applied for her widow's pension, Reverend Newton's grandson testified for her. He testified that she and James were married and the correct date of their wedding. As you know, there are so many things a widow must prove before getting a widow's pension.

James applied for his pension in 1885 and received his first check in 1889. As we found out from the pension record, James came home from the Army sick but did not know what he had. James struggled to work and feed his family and Amy had to work as well. James complained that his heart hurt, he had rheumatism in his legs, and his arms hurt at the same time. Eventually, it became that he was not able to work, and finally, only walked on crutches. Twelve people gave affidavits as proof that he was ill. James died of tuberculosis on June 13, 1902.

Amy Gibson, James Gibson's widow, applied for a widow's pension in 1902 and she stated that she had known James since she was a little girl and married him in 1869.

In May 1902, just before James died, Nellie Britt testified that Mr. F. Luther Carrie, who attended the pension claim, rode out to the

Gibson house on a Saturday night and stated that he had been advised that James's claim was allowed. The next afternoon, Carrie and his brother William drove up to the house and took James aside; after they left, James told Amy he would be receiving forty-one dollars, which was his pension money. James had to give five dollars to Carrie which left James with thirty-five dollars in paper and silver, however, James's first payment was eighty-two dollars. Afterward, James received eighteen dollars per quarter and James brought home one half of that amount.

On one occasion, Carrie was shared (given) nine dollars, so he drove to the Gibson house one night accompanied by Daniel McLaurin. Carrie and Daniel demanded James give him nine more dollars and, out of fear, James, being too weak to argue with him, gave him the money, even though he knew what they had demanded of him was illegal.

After James died, and for Amy to get her widow's pension, she had to work with Mr. Carrie to write the application and get the necessary witnesses to prove to the pension bureau her worthiness for a pension. She paid the witnesses fifty cents each and Mr. Carrie stated to Amy "I'll get paid after you get your pension." After Amy received her third eighteen-dollar check, a few days later, Carrie came to the house and said he came for his money. Amy only had six dollars left so she gave it to him. Carrie then told Amy "You will have to pay me three dollars more."

Shortly after, Amy was in the Calhoun store where Carrie worked as the storekeeper, he told her she still owed him three dollars, and Amy refused to pay him. She stated that while she agreed to give him one half of her first payment and had kept faith in doing so, she never agreed to give him one half of subsequent payments, and did not propose to do so any longer. Thereupon, Carrie got mad and said that he would have Amy arrested. Amy told him to "go ahead."

The original checks are now herewith forwarded, the checks for the order of Amy Gibson were paid through the New York clearing house on July 18, 1903.

Here within is transmitted the original telegram received by the commissioner of pensions from Amy Gibson on July 15, 1903, which witnesses the following statement, *"F.L. Carrie still holds my check for nine hundred and fourteen dollars. Claims one half for himself. Please act and act at once."*

E.F. Ware, commissioner stated "This is an extremely profitable method of earning a living if the government had not interfered."

The special examiner D.H. Alexander arrived at Cleo, South Carolina, on October 14, 1903, and the next day, the check for nine hundred and fourteen dollars was placed in Amy Gibson's hands. It was delivered to Amy's house by attorney Boocher. Carrie accused Amy and her son of borrowing money from him to buy horse feed. However, after testimony from the Calhoun store accountant that Carrie could not produce proof of the money borrowed, it seemed Carrie concealed the idea that he had the right to collect from each succeeding payment.

It was under this application for the accused's (Amy Gibson) pension that the United States Pension Bureau directed the US pension agent at Knoxville, Tennessee, to make payments to Amy Gibson.

In December of 1903, the books of the Calhoun store proved that Amy owed one hundred and twenty-three dollars and seventy-two cents and that she paid the bill in cotton and cash. So, this was a false statement made by Mr. Carrie. Amy Gibson received the rest of her pension checks without any further difficulties.

Amy Gibson died on June 17, 1917, and is buried in Crossroads Cemetery, Cleo, South Carolina.

for himself. Please act and act at once."

Amy Gibson, of Clio, S.C., testifies that she is the widow of James Gibson, the soldier who died June 15, 1902; that she has known the soldier since she was a little girl and knows that he was never married before he married her in 1869 or '70 at Gibson Station, N.C., Rev. Neil Newton performing the ceremony; that in June, 1903, a pension certificate was issued to her and in July, 1903, she received through the mail a letter containing two pension checks, one for $70.27 and the other for $914.00; the first check being the amount due witness as soldier's widow and the second check being amount due soldier at time of his death; that F. Luther Currie, of Clio, S.C., was the local agent or attorney in her deceased husband's claim, and her husband paid him fifty cents for the preparation and execution of each paper filed in support of his claim down to the time of his death, and after his death, witness employed Currie to prosecute her claim and offered him fifty cents for the preparation and execution of each paper, but he said no, that he would get his money when the

Gibson No. 383,985, dated July 11, 1903. The original checks are herewith forwarded. The check to the order of Amy Gibson was paid through the New York clearing house on July 18, 1903.

Herewith is transmitted the original telegram received by the Commissioner of Pensions from Amy Gibson on July 15, 1903, which contains the following statement:

"F.L.Currie still holds my check for $914. Claims one-half for himself. Please act and act at once."

Amy Gibson, of Clio, S.C., testifies that she is the widow of James Gibson, the soldier who died June 15, 1902; that she has known the soldier since she was a little girl and knows that he was never married before he married her in 1869 or '70 at Gibson Station, N.C., Rev. Neil Newton performing the ceremony; that in June, 1903, a pension certificate was issued to her and in July, 1903, she received through the mail a letter containing two pension checks, one for $70.27 and the other for $914.00; the first check being the amount due witness as soldier's widow and the second check being amount due soldier at time of his death; that F. Luther Currie, of Clio, S.C., was the local agent or attorney in her deceased

that after witness had the proceeds of the third $18 check a few days Currie came to his house and said, "Britt, I come for that money;" that witness only had $6 left, so he gave the $6 to the accused and the accused said "you will have to pay me $3 more;" that shortly after this witness was in Calhoun's store and Currie said something about the $3, and witness refused to pay him, stating that while he had agreed to give him one-half of the first payment and had kept faith in so doing, he never did agree to give him one-half of the subsequent payments and did not propose to do so any longer, thereupon the accused got mad and said he would have witness arrested, so witness told him to go ahead, but he did not and the witness has had nothing to do with him since, that Luther Currie has never refunded any portion of the money which he collected from witness for his services in the prosecution of this pension claim;

that witness has never had any business dealing with him in connection with any other matter than the pension claim;that witness has never bought any property from him,and has never been in his debt,and he has never rendered witness any service of any character except with reference to the pension claim;that witness worked for the father of the accused,and was square when he quit working there,and that when witness got his first money Currie did not say anything to him about applying for increase until long after he had paid witness $41;that witness was not sworn by Currie to an application for increase.

Nellie Britt, wife of Everitt Britt, Clio, S.C.,testifies that F.Luther Currie attended to her husband's pension claim, which was ~~easy~~ allowed in May,1902; that one Saturday evening in May or June of that year her husband came home,stating that he had been advised that his claim was allowed;that the next afternoon, which was Sunday, F.Luther Currie and his brother,William,drove

Nellie Britt, wife of Everitt Britt, Clio, S.C., testifies that F.Luther Currie attended to her husband's pension claim, which was ~~only~~ allowed in May,1902; that one Saturday evening in May or June of that year her husband came home,stating that he had been advised that his claim was allowed;that the next afternoon, which was Sunday, F.Luther Currie and his brother,William,drove up to the house and F.Luther Currie took her husband aside;that after he left,witness'husband showed her $41,which they counted together;that her husband then took five dollars of the money and gave her $36;that $35 of the money was in paper,and six dollars in silver,and her husband told her that was the pension money that Currie had given him;that previous to this her husband had said

5 D 13

the first payment was about $82,but he had agreed to give Currie one half of that for getting the pension,and her husband told her that afterwards he was to get $18 a quarter,and when the first $18 payment was made her husband came home and said he had half of that amount;that when the next payment was made he told the same story, and witness thought this was wrong,and made a fuss about it;and when the third eighteen-dollar check came her husband did not go to Currie with it,but on that occasion he brought the full eighteen dollars home,and three days'later Currie,accompanied by Daniel F. McLaurin,drove up to the house at night and Currie demanded of her husband nine dollars,one-half the amount of the check, and after some discussion her husband came to her and said that Currie was after the money,and witness counted out six dollars and gave it to her husband,and he carried it to the buggy and gave it to Currie,and that her husband referred to having been threatened by Currie at the time.

F.Luther Currie asked witness to take a drive with him at night, after business hours, and they drove to the home of Everett Britt, whereupon Currie called Britt out of the house and said to him, "I have come after that money"; that Britt went back into his house and in a few minutes returned and handed Currie 3,4,5 or 6 dollars in silver (witness cannot state the exact amount, but knows that it was more than one or two dollars); that witness does not remember any of the conversation that took place on thatoccasion; that the only conversation witness recalls having heard between Currie and Britt with reference to the money was the conversation he had heard that night; that witness cannot remember anything that was said that night that indicated how Britt came to owe Currie.

William F. Cross, cashier of the Bank of Clio, Clio, S.C. testifies that, as shown by the bank ledger, F.Luther Currie did not have an account with the Bank of Clio in June, 1902, but opened an account on Sep.30, 1902; that witness identifies checks No.360, ... Assistant Treasurer of the

period from Jan.1st to Dec.16,1902; that in explanation of this account, referring to the debit sheet, the word check"on line 2 means trade check issued to patrons of the store, and the amount paid out, this being a simple method of giving credit, saving the bookkeeper the work of charging to the patrons a long list of small items; that as shown by the corrected sheet Britt made no payments on account during June and July, 1902; that the entire account, with the exception of $13,10, was paid in cotton, and the credit of $40, 40 on Sep.10,1902, means one bale of cotton, and the credit of $24,34, a part bale of cotton; of $33,76, one bale of cotton etc.

NOTE:- the account presented by this witness, taken from the books of the store, shows that pensioner purchased goods to the amount of $123,72, and that he paid in cotton and in cash the sum of $123,72, this being material to the case in this, that it appears to prove the falsity of the statement made by the accused with reference to his transactions with the pensioner.

Charles H. Evans of Landrum, S.C., testifies that he is acquainted with Everett Britt and has been acquainted with F.Luther Currie two years; that he was employed as a clerk in Calhoun's store at Clio, S.C. during the year 1902, and identifies as genuine

Pension Agent at Knoxville, Tenn., to make payment to Amy Gibson.

The paper marked No.2 in the brief is the unexecuted voucher which was forwarded by the U.S.Pension Agent at Knoxville,Tenn., to the deceased soldier, for the sum of $937.27, covering the period from August 5, 1890, to August 4, 1902; this voucher was not executed by the soldier by reason of the fact that he died on June 15, 1902, before the paper reached his home. The accrued voucher on its face purports execution by Amy Gibson before F. Luther Currie on July 6, 1903, for the sum of $924.47, in payment of pension for the period from August 5, 1890, to June 16, 1902, under the invalid claim, $914.47 being payable to Amy Gibson and $10 being payable to W.B.Tierney, attorney of record, for his fee as provided by Section4, of the Act of June 27, 1890.

As is shown by the receipts attached to the voucher, the $10 fee was paid by check No.383,986, dated July 11, 1903, and the $914.47 was paid by check drawn to the order of Amy

WIVES OF ANDREW WALLACE

In 1912, a declaration for pension was made by Andrew Wallace, of Company "K," 135th United States Colored Troop, in Bennettsville, South Carolina. He stated that he was born June 5, 1834, and that he was five foot six tall. In 1890, he left Bennettsville and moved to Maxton, North Carolina, where he made his living as a traveling preacher.

Alice Wallace, the third wife of Andrew, testified that she was the widow of Andrew Wallace, and that she married him in Saint Charles, South Carolina, in 1923, in Lee County. They were married for about four years, and it was in Saint Charles where she nursed Andrew until he died. She buried him in Saint Charles after he died on April 10, 1926. In her quest for a pension, Alice testified that she knew he was living in Maxton, North Carolina, before he came to Saint Charles as a preacher. People in Saint Charles said Andrew would come to visit a woman that he said was his granddaughter but not related.

The widow in Maxton, North Carolina, was Sallie Wallace, Andrew's second wife. Claims were referred for an opinion showing which of either of the claimants was the legal widow of the soldier. The claim was undergoing a special examination to determine who is the rightful widow of Andrew Wallace. The examiner stated that there were no divorces granted in South Carolina before 1912. Sallie

Wallace stated that she and Andrew were married February 26, 1895. The Examiner said that there seemed to be no evidence of a marriage in 1923.

Sallie lived in Maxton, and she was "a person of fair reputation and had not remarried or had marital relationships" since the separation or since the soldier died. The soldier deserted his wife, Sallie, without any apparent cause. It was said that the soldier was childless and that he and Sallie had words over mortgaging the homeplace and he walked off.

Andrew's first wife, Cilla, died in South Carolina in 1890. Her children are Carrie DeBerry and Walter Wallace. Andrew's daughter Carrie was born in Marlboro County, South Carolina, and she stated that when she was very young, her father married Sallie Gilchrist. Carrie testified that she had lived with Sallie ever since. Her mother was Priscilla Wallace, and she was buried in the Mathew Chapel Cemetery.

Sallie Wallace, Andrew's second wife, lived with the family of Frank Patterson in Brooklyn near Maxton after Andrew deserted her. Sallie died on July 16, 1930, and received a widow's pension until the day she died.

The last they could determine was that Alice, the third wife, ended up living in Bishopville, South Carolina.

ACT OF MAY 11, 1912

~~ACT OF FEBRUARY 6, 1907.~~

DECLARATION FOR PENSION.

THE PENSION CERTIFICATE SHOULD NOT BE FORWARDED WITH THE APPLICATION

State of N. C. } ss.
County of Robeson }

On this 15 day of June, A. D. one thousand nine hundred and twelve, personally appeared before me, a Notary Public within and for the county and State aforesaid Andrew Wallace, who, being duly sworn according to law, declares that he is 72 years of age, and a resident of Maxton county of Robeson State of N.C.; and that he is the [illegible] Andrew Wallace on the 27 day of March, 1865, as a Private in Co K 135 Regt U.S. Col Troops Vols

(Here state rank, and company and regiment in the Army, or vessels if in the Navy.)

in the service of the United States, in the Civil war, and was HONORABLY DISCHARGED

(State name of war, Civil or Mexican.)

at Louisville Ky, on the 23 day of October, 1865.

That he also served

(Here give a complete statement of all other services, if any.)

That he was not employed in the military or naval service of the United States otherwise than as stated above. That his personal description at enlistment was as follows: Height, feet inches; complexion, Dark; color of eyes, Black; color of hair, Black; that his occupation was Farm Laborer; that he was born, 18 , at Bennettsville, Marlboro County S.C.

That his several places of residence since leaving the service have been as follows: Bennettsville S.C. to 1890 and Maxton N.C. since that date

(State date of each change, as nearly as possible.)

That he is a pensioner That he has heretofore applied for pension under Cert # 825,570

(If a pensioner, the certificate number only need be given. If not, give the number of the former application, if one was made.)

That he makes this declaration for the purpose of being placed on the pension roll of the United States under the provisions of the ~~act of February 6, 1907.~~ ACT OF MAY 11, 1912

That he hereby appoints, with full power of substitution and revocation, **W. W. DUDLEY & CO., of Washington, D. C.**, his true and lawful attorney to prosecute his claim.

That his post-office address is Maxton, County of Robeson, State of N.C.

Andrew his X mark Wallace
(Claimant's signature in full.)

Attest: (1) Geo McQueen
(2) J. S. McQueen

PENSION E JUN 18 1912 U. S.

Case of Sallie Wallace No. 1582019.

On this 22 day of January , 19 29 at Bishopville county of Lee , State of South Carolina before me, E. F. Fewell , an inspector of the Bureau of Pensions, personally appeared Alice Wallace , who, being by me first duly sworn to answer truly all interrogatories propounded to h er during this special examination of aforesaid claim for pension, deposes and says:

My age is 50. Residence and mail address, Bishopville, S. C. I am a nurse and I work for Mr s. Luther Moore here.

I am the widow of Andrew Wallace who was a soldier in the Civil war and a pensioner. I was married to him about 4 years before he died. He died at St. Charles in this county and I was living with him at the time of his death. I got the pension money that was due him at the timeof his death, that is I got $16 and the rest of the money I paid to people to get the pa ers fixed up.

I had known Andrew Wallace for about 5 years before we were married and when I first met him he was living at Maxton, N. C., and he used to come down here to visit a woman that he raised and that he called his grand daughter but who was no kin to him.

After we were married I heard that he had a wife living at Maxton and the name of that wife was Sallie. I never saw her and the first I heard of any such woman was when a letter came to Andrew Wallace from her. I had a woman read the letter and she said it was from Sallie Wallace who was his wife. I got after him about Sallie and at first he would not own up to it but after a while he told me that he was married to Sallie and that he left her because he saw her misbehaving with another man. That is all he ever told me about it Later his daughter came down here from Maxton and I asked her about Sallie and she told me that he and Sallie were married and that she did not know why he left Sallie and knew of no reason why he should have left her. He never got a divorce from Sallie as far as I know.

The soldier had a wife before he marr ed Sallie and he told me t that that first wife was dead but I do not know where that wife died.

I do not remember her name and I do not know whether it was Cilla or not.

About a month after I married the soldier he got in such a shape that I had to look after him like he was a baby and I had to take care of him right along then until he died.

I know of no other wife that the soldier had and I do not know any place he lived before he came to St. Charles except Maxton, N. C.

I h ve heard the foregoing read and it is correct.

Lewis Hamilton
Witness to mark.
Only one available.

her
Alice X Wallace.
mark
Deponent.

Subscribed and sw rn to before me this 22 day of January 192 , and I certify th t the contents were fully made known to deponent before signing.

E. F. Fewell
Inspector.

Memorandum, S. E. Division.

Subject. 1582019. Wallace.

Claim is undergoing special examination to determine whether the claimant ~~xx~~ was ever divorced from the soldier, how often and to whom each had been married prior to marriage to each other, and how and when former marriages were dissolved; alsowhether claimant has entered into marital relations with another since separation from soldier.

It is shown by evidence that claimant was never married prior to her marriage to soldier and that she has not entered into marital relations with another since separation from the soldier. It does not appear that she applied for a divorce. The testimony also tends to show that soldier had a former wife Cilla or Pricilla who died near Bennettsville, S. C. It is not known whether he was married prior to his marriage to Cilla. It is also shown that he contracted a marriage with one Alice Ford and the accrued pension was paid to her. This marriage is shown to have taken place June 23, 1923, in Lee County, S. C.

Reference. Further examination as recommended in summary of report No. 1, is approved for the purpose of securing the testimony of the last wife Alice Wallace or Alice Ford who is said to be now living at Bishopville, Lee Co., S. C.

Then to Marlboro Co., S. C., as to prior marital history of soldier, for the testimony of Noah Maloy and Frank Poe of Bennettsville, and others as may be thought necessary.

No divorces are granted in South Carolina and there are no marr age records prior to about 1912.

E. F. Fewell
Reviewer.

IN REPLY REFER TO
Board of Review
W.O. 1582019
Sallie, widow
Andrew Wallace
Co. K, 135 U.S.C.Inf.
****
Address: Maxton, N.C.

3—1865

UNITED STATES
DEPARTMENT OF THE INTERIOR
BUREAU OF PENSIONS
WASHINGTON

RECEIVED
MAR 21 1928
S. E. D. FILES

March 20, 1928

Chief of the
Special Examination Division

Papers in claim are referred for special examination to determine whether the claimant was ever divorced from the soldier, how often and to whom each had been married prior to their marriage to each other, and how and when former marriages were dissolved; also whether the claimant has entered into marital relations with another since separation from the soldier.

The claimant alleges marriage to the soldier February 26, 1895, and furnishes evidence apparently proving such fact. She further alleges no divorce, and furnishes corroborative evidence, but following the death of the soldier on April 10, 1926, the accrued pension due in his case was paid to one Allace Wallace, of St. Charles, South Carolina, on evidence showing ceremonial marriage June 25, 1923. In the examination to be had we should have a statement from this later wife as to divorce of soldier from the present claimant.

A. H. Henderson
Chief, Board of Review.

Examination approved:
Winfield Scott
Commissioner.

Case of Sallie Wallace No. 1582019

On this 9 day of June, 1928, at Maxton county of Robeson, State of North Carolina before me, W. H. Stovall, an inspector of the Bureau of Pensions, personally appeared Sallie Wallace, who, being by me first duly sworn to answer truly all interrogatories propounded to her during this special examination of aforesaid claim for pension, deposes and says:

I am 58 or 59 years old I guess, am living in this town with my step daughter Sarrie Deberry, and post office address is Maxton N C. I claim pension as the widow of Andrew Wallace and I was married to him at Floral College N C not so far from this town with a license and by Aaaron McNeise a Methodist preacher. I lived with Wallace at the College for two years and then we moved to a farm close to this town and then in town. Wallace was a preacher and used to go about. He was from South Carolina and like to go there to preach, he went backwards and forth to South Carolina as long as I lived with him. I did not try to procure any divorce from Andrew Wallace and I was not thinking about any divorce. He died at St Charles S C and was buried there. I never saw him buried and was not able to go to the funeral. I had not seen Wallace in several months before his death. I was born up above Floral College on Mr Tom Purcells place and my parents were Toney and Amanda Gilchrist, both deceased, and I had one brother, Oscar Gilchrist, who died ten or fifteen years ago, and three sisters but one sister is dead. The sisters living are Hannah Jane Pleasant, widow of John Pleasant, living in Fayetteville N C, and Mary McCrea the wife of Ed McCrea, farmer, living near Parkton N C. I had lived around Floral College up to my marriage to Andrew Wallace and Marshall Deberry, Adam Evans, Nelson Graham, knew me in those days. The soldier Andrew Wallace was born I guess in South Carolina and had lived there before coming to Floral College N C. He was a preacher and went about considerably and I had known him just a year before we were married. He said he had lived in Marlboro S C. I dont know anything about his parents or his family except one sister, Louisa Wallace, the wife of ----, forget her husbands name, who lived with me a good while but went back South before she died. I am unable to give names of people who knew Andrew Wallace prior to his location at Floral CollegN C.

Q. How many times have you been married?

A. Just one time and that was to Andrew Wallace. I had given birth to no children prior to my marriage to Andrew Wallace and had lived most of the time with a cousin, Mary Ann McNair, deceased, after the death of my father. I must have been 26 years old when I was married to Andrew Wallace.

Q. How many times was Andrew Wallace married?

A. I do not know sir. He had a wife before marrying me as I knew her children but not the woman herself. The name of that former wife is said to have been Priscilla and Carrie Deberry says she is dead. Wallace had no wife in North Carolina except me. After he went to South Carolina shortly before dying they say he got married to some other woman but I dont know her name or anything about her. I was never divorced from my husband and never thought about such a thing. My husband and I had some words about the land he wanted to put a mortgage on and I would not agree to it so he walked off. Since he left me I have lived with Carrie Deberry and been supported by my labor on the

Attest: Ely Leggett
E. Stella Jones

her
Sallie X Wallace
mark
Deponent.

Case of Sallie Wallace, No. 1582019

Deposition of Sallie Wallace, continued, sheet

farms of different people living close to Maxton and chopping cotton.

The children of Andrew Wallace by his first wife are Carrie Deberry, Walter Wallace, living in the country somewhere and a Spanish War soldier, and Andrew Wallace up North at Altoona. I had three children by Andrew Wallace and all died as babies. I have made no attempt to marry any man since Wallace went back to South Carolina.

No member of my immediate family served in the World War and I have no claim to the benefits of the War Risk Act. I understand the object of this special examination and the privileges I am entitled to which I will waive as I cannot afford to incur further expense in this maber. William Fletcher of Washington D C is my attorney. I was sworn to the declaration. I paid the notarial fees and for copies of public records. If Andrew Wallace attempted to procure a divorce from me after returning to South Carolina I never heard anything about it. Carrie Deberry was with him in South Carolina and should know where Wallace lived. I have heard the foregoing deposition read and it is correct.

Attest: Lillie Leggett

Estella Jones

her
Sallie X Wallace
mark
Deponent.

Subscribed and sworn to before me on this the 9 day of June 1928, and I certify the contents were fully made known to deponent before signing.

M H Glover, Inspector.

July 14, 1941.

YOUR FILE REFERENCE:

IN REPLY REFER TO: 5AC-B-X

State Registrar of Vital Statistics,
Raleigh, North Carolina.

WALLACE, Sallie
WC-1,582,019
Civil War

Dear Sir:

Information is on file that Sallie Wallace, widow of Andrew Wallace, whose last address was Maxton, North Carolina died July 26, 1930.

It is requested that a certified copy of the public record of the death of the pensioner be furnished. It is officially certified that a certified copy of the aforestated public record is required by the Veterans Administration of the United States in order that the pension account in her favor may be properly closed.

Very truly yours,

H V Stirling

H. V. STIRLING,
Director of Finance.

RECEIVED JUL 26 1941

1407
215

JUL 16 1941

SEP 18 1941

CHAPTER 15

LT. JOHN AUMAN'S JOURNAL

The following journal was provided to the 135th USCT Research Team, Inc., by Cindi Pratt who's Great, Great Grandfather was 1st Lieutenant John Auman of Company "K," 135th USCT. He gave a first-hand account of his life in the army prior to becoming a member of the 135th USCT, and during his time in the Regiment. We are so appreciative of being able to include his record of events during his service. We are also extremely thankful to Cindi and her mother for sharing his journal and artifacts and allowing us to include it in our book to complete the story.

(A sketch of the life of John Auman written by himself mostly from memory)

"My father, Phillip Auman, of whose history we know but little (we don't even know to a certainty how he spelled his name: Auman or Aumand); we never saw any papers or books wherein he wrote his name. Mother always said the latter was right and we wrote it so for years, but executors of father's estate always wrote it the former way and so we finally adopted it. He was of Russian descent either from the nobility or a deserter from the army for these were the only ones who could get away from Russia at that time; his father also took part in the freedom of our country by enlisting in the army and taking part in the Revolutionary War.

Father was born in the city of Lancaster, PA., in the year 1796 where he learned the millwright trade and made it his life's business.

My mother's maiden name was Christianna Noacker from a German descent of whose history I know nothing; she was born in Berks County, Pa., in the year 1806.

They were married in Contor County in 1825 and settled in the village of Aaronsburg, same county, and state, and lived in a little brick house on the east side of Main Street; they made this their home while father lived. To them were born seven children: Mary, who died in infancy of scarlet fever; Susan, Sarah, William R., Charles B., John, and Catherine for the family record as near complete as can be made at this time, so in the back part of this book.

My father died in Feb. 1839. Mother at once made arrangements by selling the house and all personal property that she could not take with her and moved to western Illinois with her uncle Jacob Neidigh and a colony of nine families started in Michigan on wagons as far as Pittsburgh, where she bought new furniture for the new house, consisting of one bedstead, four chairs, and a stove. Cookstoves were not known then, this was a box stove with an oven on top.

Here we took cat down Ohio, and up the Mississippi and landed at Savannah, where we again traveled by wagon thirty-five miles and settled in Stephenson County five miles north of Freeport on a farm of two hundred acres, on the border of a large prairie, where we were exposed to annual prairie fires and several times suffered the loss of some property such as fences and other minor property. Here we spent our days of childhood and youth in many checkered scenes of frontier want and poverty until some of us were large enough to help mother to provide for the family. This was our family home 'til the spring of 1864; in the meantime, Sarah was married to Daniel Deischer, William to Miss Susan Latig, Charles B. to Mary Sheller, and Catharine to F. L. Scott. Susan never married.

I worked on the farm with the exception of part of two summers when I worked at carpentering and one summer attended school.

October 1st, 1861, I enlisted in the community that was being recruited for the Civil War by William Young and T. J. Vood. It is not the intention of this sketch to give a history of the Civil War, not even a history of the part that the command took with which I was connected; only so much of it as may be necessary to give an intelligent account of that part of the army with which I was connected.

We were sworn in the military service in Freeport, Ill. Oct. 8th, 1861 after which William Young was elected Captain, T.J. Wood 1st Lieutenant, and Moses R. Tompson 2nd Lieutenant. At 9 o'clock we took the train for camp of instruction, at Clear Lake 7 miles west of Springfield, Ill., where we arrived on the 9th. On the 10th we were physically examined, then sworn in the service for three years; then drew our clothing, which was two wool shirts, two pair of drawers, one pair. pants, a pair of shoes, two pair of socks, a good heavy jacket, overcoat and cap, and the other outfit which was a blanket, knapsack, haversack, canteen, and one wedge tent to four men.

Then commenced the regular routine of camp life. Squad, palation, company and regimental drills, guard and police duties. (Police in camp means cleaning streets and camp in general.).

Some three weeks after the beginning of camp life I was a detailed nurse in the regimental hospital. Two large sized tents were used for this purpose. About the first of December, we moved to the new barracks or Oprap Butler; we remained here 'til February 12th when our regiment left for Fort Donelson. Our regiment was organized soon after we were mustered in with five companies from Stephenson County and one company from the southern part of the state; these companies were A, B, C, F, Gand K, and were numbered 46th Il. Vol. Infantry. A short time before the Regiment left, four companies were sent from Dixon' to fill the regiment. At that time a regiment was composed of ten companies with one hundred men, but few companies were full even at the organization. When the regiment Left, we had 31 sick in the hospital most all measles cases. I was left in charge with 3 other men to assist me: one cook and two nurses. Two weeks later, all but nine were able to Join the regiment which we did at Fort Henry, Tenn.; the nine I left in the General post hospital.

Our regt. was not the first to board the boat with the expedition up the river, landing at Pittsburgh Lending. We went in camp about a mile from the landing; as others came up, they camped farther out until the camp extended about three miles in advance of us. Everything remained quiet (till the evening of April 4th, when some pickets were fired on, regiments were ordered to division headquarters but returned at about midnight and again all was quiet 'till the morning of the 6th, we heard the first firing at about 7 o'clock and were not ordered to the front. It was my time on duty at the hospital; the other nurses went with the regiment. At about 10 o'clock the wounded began to come in, then we had all we could do to dress the wounded and care for them.

The Major was among the first that came in and as our lines retreated and the rebels came so near that the stray balls began to fly pretty thick, the Major ordered the hospital to be moved to the river, where we continued the work not confining ourselves to our regiment but any that were wounded taking them on board the boats as fast as we could. The night was dark and it rained hard, the hill was steep to the river, after midnight, I took a few hours rest in the wagon, where in a half sitting position, wet and cold, I took a little rest. In the morning the battle again opened. Oh! What a dreadful day, when all day long the wounded and dying were brought in from the field 'till it seemed all available space was full and the means of assistance seemed but mockery to the awful result of a two days hard fought battle; in the evening the word came book that the rebels were falling back and our troops were in possession of the battlefield. After a night's rest came the burial of the dead and caring for the rest of the wounded; all available boats were used to transport the wounded back to the established hospitals. Then began the slow siege of Corinth. My health began to break down when we landed, or even before but now I grew worse and not able for any kind of duty.

After the siege of Corinth, we marched to the interior of Tenn., camped at LaGrange awhile then went to Memphis, where we camped for about two months then marched back in the interior and camped at Bolivar, Tenn.

Oct. 4th our division received marching orders; they went out to the Wachee River where they engaged General Price's army as they retreated from the second battle of Corinth. I was not able to go on such a forced march so with other sick I was left in comp. Our Col. John A. Devis was wounded at Shiloh and not able to be with this command all summer but he returned to us only about three weeks before this, and on account of his wound had no use of his right arm at all; at this battle, he was again wounded and so was the 1st Lieutenant of our Company: M.R. Thompson. (They both died five days after.) I was one of the six who were detailed to escort their bodies to their home, where they were buried with military honors at Freeport, Ill.

I immediately took medical treatment with our family physician who pronounced my disability chronic liver complaint and on his certificate of my disability and sent the regiment I was allowed to remain at home until about the middle of Dec., when I again rejoined my regiment near Holly Springs, Miss.

At this time General Grant moved his army South, while General Sherman attacked Vicksburg (5/22/163) but when the rebels came in our rear and took and destroyed our supplies at Holly Springs, Sherman fell back to Vicksburg; General Grant moved the army back into Tenn., our brigade was camped at LaGrange and Germantown all winter. (1862 '63)

One time when we moved camp there were about three inches of snow; we scraped the snow away and pitched our tent, without straw or any kind of bedding, spread out a blanket on the frozen ground, and had one for cover. In the spring we marched to Memphis; here with five or six other mechanics, I was detailed in a pioneer corps of the fourth division of the 17th Army Corps. We were not with the main army that went to Gibson (5/1/63) and Jackson (5/14/63) then followed the rebel army to Vicksburg, (7/4/63) but we immediately Joined the army at Vicksburg and were there through the siege. We were on the extreme left; after the surrender, we were with that part of the army commanded by General & Sherman who went to Jackson against a rebel force that was stationed there probably for the purpose of attacking us in the roar. When we returned, we were camped in Vicksburg then went to Natchez where we worked on the fortifications till about the middle of Jan., 1864. Here I enlisted as a veteran, this was in accordance with an order from the War Department that any of the soldiers that had served two years or more could re-enlist and for another term of three years or during the war, we were to have forty days' furlough and four hundred dollars bounty. Many of our regiment re-enlisted and had gone to Vicksburg before our command came up. When we got there, they had gone home on their furlough so we got individual furloughs and soon started for home.

This was a sad furlough for me; when I arrived at Freeport I found brother Chas. in bed with inflammatory rheumatism. Mother was sick at the old home and on Feb 23rd (1864) she died. I didn't know that either of them was sick until I got home. When I returned to my command I met the pioneer corps at Helena, Ark., who was on the way to Cairo, Ill., at this point we were camped for several weeks, then went up the Tenn. River to Clifton, from here we marched to Athens then Huntsville, then back to Athens, and Roam and joined the main army to Altona Pass. We took our place on the line round Kennesaw mountains, then Mariette, and crossed the river about five miles below Marietta. Then followed the siege of Atlanta on the 22nd of July (1864) the day Gen McPherson was killed. We were on the extreme left when the rebels came 'round on our left and rear; thirteen of our pioneer corps were taken prisoners while we were throwing up a fort. The rest of us would have been taken but we were a little farther along the line. We ran into the bush and thus made our escape. This, I think, was the hardest contested battle that I witnessed while I was in the service.

After this battle, I was forced to assist in the field hospital, to dress wounds, until the men could be taken back to the established hospitals, until August 10th when I returned to my command. Then followed the usual duties of pioneer corps building forts, some breast works, putting in order, building bridges, etc., the forts were built in a different manner usually with convenient size logs a crib like structure sometimes straight and sometimes on an angle as conditions required then throw the earth from the rear to the front, leaving openings or port holes to shoot through. (The forts are for the use of artillery.)

Aug. 28th a large force marched on Jonesborough, destroying railroads, bridges, etc. Atlanta was evacuated Sept. 2nd, 1864, first blowing up large magazines which we heard and saw the light in the distance of about thirty miles; at the same time, they evacuated Jonesborough. We followed this retreating army then on the fourth, we started back toward Atlanta. We enjoyed this expedition at this time of the year for the corn was just in good roasting ear it was such a decided change after having lived so long on pork and hardtack. We got Brook to Atlanta on Sept. 9th. On Oct. 1st started a three days expedition. Started again to the rear via Marietta after Woods' army who were marching north; on the 9th we stopped at Kennesaw Mountain. I went up to view the country which could be seen at a great distance all 'round.

On the 11th at midnight started, marched all night, and stopped for two hours for breakfast. We were now in the rear of Woods' (Reb. Gen.) army which was hurrying to the north on this chase we went through Altona pass, Carterville, Kingston, Bearsville, Rasaku, and through Snake Creek Gap; this Gap is about six miles long and some places, quite narrow. The rebels had filled trees across it in every conceivable shape which we had to chop and roll out of the road before we could get teams and artillery through, then to Lafayette, Summerville, and Gainesville, Ala; here we camped till Oct. 29th when we started back toward Atlanta via Cedar Bluff, Cove Springs, Cedartown, Dallas, Loss Mountain, and Marietta. Here we camped til Nov, 13th, 1864. Marched toward Atlanta where we arrived the next day and camped one mile from town. Nov. 15th started south on another campaign which proved to be the beginning of the noted: "Sherman's march to the sea" we marched from ten to twenty miles a day without any particular event to change the usual tramp in line and in foraging except skirmishing in front and rear; on the 22nd we passed through Gordon 23rd through Toomsburg. The nights were cool (ice froze 1/2 inch thick); on the 28th our squad of foragers were taken prisoner except one who hid himself and escaped after the night.

Dec. 5th, I took command of a squad of negroes and worked them with the pioneer corps. On the 10th we came within four miles of Savannah; here the rebel army made a bold stand considerable fighting all along the line. The rice fields and ditches were flooded, this is done by letting the water in at high tide then close the floodgates and thus hold the water on the fields and ditches.

On this march, we were first put on half rations, then quarter, and now none, depending on foraging but now, about everything was eaten up except rice in the straw which had to be first pounded off the straw then put in mortar and stamped to remove the hulls then fan it in the wind. (This was about all we had for ten days until communication was opened to the Sea Port.)

Our troops took possession of the city of Savannah, Ga., Dec 21, 1864.

We camped in the city for a few days then moved down the river nine miles; here we started to organize our colored men into a pioneer regiment, but we did not long enough at this one to complete it. Capt. John H. Davis of the Pioneer Corps was to be Colonel. About the tenth of Jan., 1865, we moved to Bufort, S. C. While in camp here, John E. Gurley was sent to take command of our proposed pioneer regiment as Col. He reorganized the regiment. I was assigned 1st Lt. of Co. K, but marching orders again interfered with perfecting the organization. We came from ThunderBolt, our camp on the Savannah River, to Bufort. On an ocean steamer, which was a new experience for me, we were out for twelve hours which was all I could stand without losing my breakfast.

About Feb. 1st, Sherman's army was again under marching orders. In a few hours, we reached the river. This is a skimpy country. The river has many channels and small islands. These we were obliged to ford, for the rebels held the road that was graced and bridged. We went into the river at about 1 o'clock, the water being just about at a freezing temperature. When I first stepped in the water it seemed I could not go any farther, but there was no other way. Some of the channels were shallow while some were waist deep, so we waded through water and mud 'till night. All the time it was raining hard. There was hardly a dry spot on us. The rebs fell back with the teams. We built a log fire, so we warmed ourselves. We did not dry much, for it rained all night, and so on, day after day through mud and rain, sometimes getting in camp at 5, 10 or 11 o'clock at night, wet and cold. Then after making and drinking a cup of hot coffee, and perhaps quarter rations of "hard tack" and a little fat pork. Stand at the fire, heat a wet blanket, wrap it 'round us and lay down and go to sleep. Sometimes working all night, building or repairing a bridge so as to get the wagon train across the next day, I sometimes felt that the favored soldier was the one that was killed in the first battles. Our course was northwest, through Orangeburg, then on to Columbia. The city was almost deserted at our advance; and soon after dark, in fact all night, many buildings were set on fire. The buildings were mostly built of pitch pine lumber and were only set on fire. The next morning it was a different looking place from what it was the day before. It seemed like a total destruction, stopping only a day. We advanced on the road leading to Fayetteville, N.C., then on to Goldsburough, where we camped long enough to complete the organization of our regiment and receive our commissions. It was numbered the 135 U.S.C. Troop and we were assigned as a pioneer Regiment of the 17th Army Corps.

Then in April we again took up the line of march through Raleigh and camped about five miles Southwest of the city. While here in this one we heard the good news of Lee's surrender and a few more of the same nature. Then came the terrible news of the assassination of President Lincoln, which cast a gloom over soldiers' faces. Then the surrender of J. E. Johnson on the 26th, we felt that the war was now over and we were happy.

Now our army was again under marching orders on the road to Petersburg then to Richmond. Here we stopped for a day and it gave us an opportunity to see the city and most noted places, some of which were the Capital, Jef Davis' residence, the old Libby prison down near the river, its awful history is now a part of the history of the Civil War.

Then the army again moved toward Washington, D. C. We halted for several days at Alexandria. Here we had rations issued to us but no clothing. We had no chance or money to procure an officer's outfit. I presume this was so planned and they wanted to see our review just as we came through on the long march. Some were almost, if not quite, barefooted, the clothing wanted to be "tattered and torn." Some, the pants so worn that they did not meet the stockings; the rest of the cloth in like state of rags. We who had lately been commissioned wore shoulder straps on private suits that were worn; which caused many commendations that we were out for the good of our country and not on dress parade.

Following each regiment were the pack mules loaded with camp equipment: kettles, frying pans, sacks and boxes of provisions, rolls of blankets, etc., etc. In this condition, we paraded the streets of Washington on May 24th, 1865, which took about three hours. They gave us a great reception, many flags, and banners flying from every building and across the streets such as "Welcome!", "Welcome Western Heroes," "Welcome Sherman's Army," and many similar banners.

People from all over the country came to witness the great review. Crowds of people on either side of the streets, as far as we could see, greeted us with cheer after cheer, all along the line of march.

We camped about three miles northeast of the city. In a few days, we drew all our private pay. This was the first pay I received since I re-enlisted Jan. 4th, 1864. (17 months) My pay amounted to over three hundred dollars.

A few days after this we went down to the city and bought our officers' outfit consisting of the uniform suit, what was known as a fatigue suit, a common military hat, coat or blouse, pants, vest, and shirts and valise; sword and belt and sesh. At a cost of about eighty-five dollars.

I visited the city two or three times after this in company with some officers of our regiment. The places of most interest were the Smithsonian Institute, the post office, the patent office, the Capitol, and the Treasury building, where we had drawn our pay a few days before. There was too much to look at and remember in so short a time.

Being in camp about three weeks we again got marching orders. At the Baltimore and Ohio R.R. depot we were crowded into box cars like cattle going to market but this was more desirable than marching as had done so long and hard. The Scenery along this R. R. is very interesting; the places where some of the battles of the late war were fought Harper's Forry where John Brown and his party were executed on account of their raid into Virginia, then the natural scenes over the mountains. There are twenty-one tunnels on the west side of the mountains. At Parkersburg we went on board of a boat down the river to Louisville, Ky.; there we camped about three miles south of the city. After three or four weeks, we moved closer to the city; my captain was detailed on the court martial downtown, which left me in command of the Company. From here I got a leave of absence for twenty days from September 20th which time I spent at home in Ill.

In October we received orders to be mustered out. Our papers were dated October 23rd, 1865. But there were so many papers to be made out a complete muster roll which must give an account of every man that was a member of the Company at any time, and other reports. Then after we received transportation for our colored men, we had to see them on the cars; some went to Ga., some to S. C., some to N. C., we left for home Nov. 6th and arrived in Freeport, Ill. Nov. 8th, 1865, just four years and one month from the day I left.

The following winter I spent attending a commercial school in Freeport and in visiting some old friends.

In the spring and summer, I worked at carpentering; in the fall I bought a one third interest in a tannery in Rockford, Ill.; to this business, I gave my attention 'til the spring of 1869 when I sold out and went to Dokotn, Ill. in the grain and lumber business with my brother William."

THE END

FOOTNOTES

BY GRANDSON EVERITT SHELDON:

Grandpa's Journal breaks off abruptly at this point. I would guess that he once intended to write further chapters of his life since the notebook in which he wrote remains to this day less than half filled. Perhaps a certain reticence or shyness kept him from writing about the events of his marriage and family life or maybe he was waiting for the leisure of old age, which never arrived. At any rate, while he states above that in the spring of 1869 he began a new business enterprise with his brother, William, he relegates to the Family Record in the back of the notebook the fact that late in that same April he was married to Martha Lucilla Mayberry, at White Rock Center, Ogle Co., Illinois.

It could be argued that marriage and family were not exceptional events, since most people get married, but that in four years of the Civil War, most of the time in combat, is exceptional and deserves to be written down while fresh in memory.

Looking back, 100 years later, we agree that the events were indeed important to record, and we are glad that Grandpa didn't let his lack of education stand in the way. Later generations could correct the spelling and punctuation if they wished, but only an eyewitness could accurately record the events.

I don't know how Grandpa kept the dates and places so clearly, but every name and date that I have checked from his Journal squares exactly and accurately with the records of professional historians.

We are indebted to my grandmother, Martha Lucilla Mayberry Auman, and to my aunt, Anna Mary Auman, for carefully preserving the Journal, as well as his sword and scabbard and sash. I suppose the officer's uniform gradually was worn and used until it disappeared, or did it? From my childhood, I remember the "old blue cape" which was once a part of Grandpa's dress uniform and wore extraordinarily well as a handy protection from cold and rain, some 70 years after the time of its purchase.

FAMILY RECORD

MARRIAGE

John Auman and Martha Lucilla Mayberry were married on April 29th, 1869. At White Rock Center, Ogle Co., Ill. By Rev. W. H. Weller

BIRTHS

Calvin Mabry Auman was born February 19th, 1870. Son of John and Martha L. Auman, at Dakota, Ill.

Martha Theodora Auman, daughter of John and Martha L. Auman, was born February 19th, 1873, at Tecumseh, Neb.

Anna Kary Auman was born August 30th, 1875 in Tecumseh, Neb., the daughter of John and Martha L. Auman.

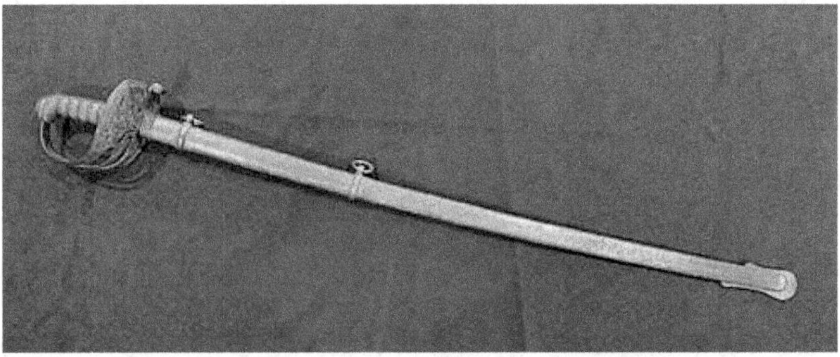

Lt. John Auman's Sword in Scabbard

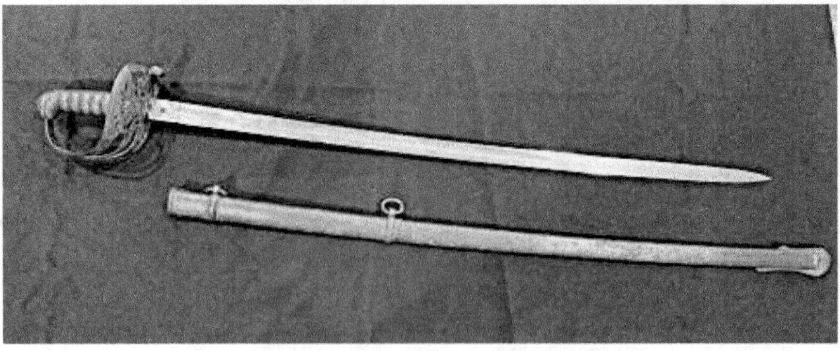

Lt. John Auman's actual Sword from the Civil War

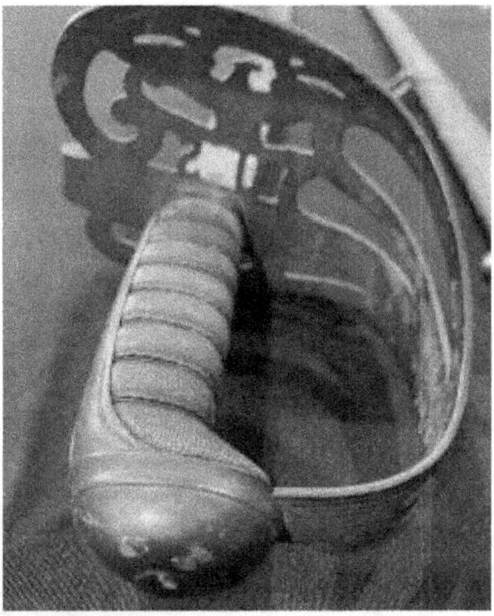

Lt. John Auman's Diary

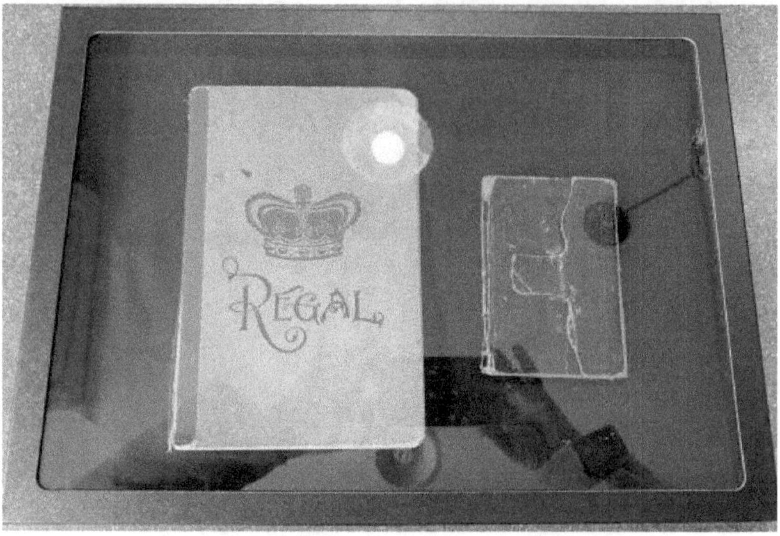

Lt. John Auman's Journal/Diary

CHAPTER 16

THEIR RELIGION AND GENEALOGY

IMPORTANCE OF RELIGION TO THE MEN WHO WERE BORN AND LIVED IN SLAVERY AND DIED IN FREEDOM.

We are adding a chapter on religion because we and Dr. Reginald Hildebrand agree that it deserves more attention than it has received in other stories of Black soldiers. We don't think that Black soldiers were absorbed by religion, or they spent all of their free time in worship and prayer. As they were young men, they were not saints. However, a distinctive black Civil War theology played an important role in shaping the worldview of "the Black troops."

Freed Black slaves emancipated by the Civil War believed God was real. They knew him. They met Him personally in many a wild orgy of religious frenzy, and in the wild stillness of the night. "His plan for them was clear; they were to suffer and be denigrated, and then afterward, by divine edict, raised to manhood and power; and so, on 1 1 1863, he made them free." Stated by W.E.B. DuBois in 1935.

One notable Black Chaplain who composed religious music was John N. Mars. During the flag presentation ceremony of North Carolina's first regiment (which later became the 35th US Colored Infantry), Chaplain John N. Mars introduced a hymn of his composition:

All men are equal in God's sight,
The bond, the freed, the black, the white;
He made them all, then freedom consciousness;
He made the man, man made the slave.

Even battle songs of the Black soldiers sometimes reflected the importance of religion in their lives. The regiments of the A.M.E. Chaplains Henry McNeal Turner and William H. Hunter both sang variations of this combat ditty:

We are gallant fourth, (or first)
Who slightly have been tried;
When ordered to a battle,

Take Jesus for our guide.

According to Colonel Higginson, one song was sung “perhaps twice as often as any other.” Its words are simple and hopeful;

Hold your light, Bruder Robert,
Hold your light,
Hold your light on Canaan’s shore.

A similar song spoke of the deliverance of a whole army:

My army cross over,
My army cross over,
O’Pharoah’s army drowned!
My army cross over.

Religion is included herein as it was found to be important in their lives at that time, more so than it seems in recent years, and, therefore, deserves mentioning.

Reverend George Stetson Shaw, Chaplain, 135th United States Colored Troop background.

"At the age of seven, he was put out to live on a farm in East Freetown, Mass. At sixteen, he returned to New Bedford, and for two years worked with his father at ship and house, carpentering. Later, until he was twenty-one, he was an apprentice to Ebenezer Keen, of the firm of Pierce & Keen, of New Bedford. His early education was in the district schools. At twenty-one, he entered the Meadville, Penn., Theological School. He graduated on June 26, 1862, and was ordained to the Christian ministry on November 9th of that year.

His first impulse toward the ministry, which has been his life’s work, was his desire to become a foreign missionary. In November 1862, he was appointed chaplain of the Missouri State Penitentiary at Jefferson City. In 1864, he enlisted in Company C, 27th Missouri Infantry; his first battle was at Resaca, Ga., where a bullet from the enemy destroyed the gun in his hands. He was with the army during the siege of Atlanta, and in Sherman's march to the sea and through the Carolinas. At Raleigh, N. C., he was promoted to the chaplaincy of the 135th U. S. Colored Infantry, which was discharged at Louisville, Kentucky, on November 2, 1865. For the next two years, he remained in the West, acting as a missionary or settled pastor in Wisconsin, Minnesota, Illinois, and Michigan. Returning to Massachusetts, he came to Ashby for a single Sunday on July 18, 1868, and has now been a pastor there for thirty-eight years [40 years at the time of his death]. During his residence, he has been active and earnest not only for his church but for the community at large. He was instrumental in founding the Free Public Library, and has always been interested in the schools, visiting them freely whether on the Committee or otherwise. He has served in many ways, not only his own townsmen but the people of the neighboring towns, and is a true friend to all who are in trouble of any kind." ~ from "Silas Gates, of Stow, Mass., and the Descendants of His Son, Paul Gates, of Ashby, Mass." Compiled by Julius Kendall Gates and Samuel Pearly Gates, printed for private circulation, 1907.

CHAPTER 17

REGIMENTAL ROLLS
OF THE
135TH UNITED STATES COLORED TROOP

The following pages are from the certified rolls of the 135th United States Colored Troop as taken from the official records and certified by the National Archives in Washington, DC. We feel they are as complete and authentic as can be verified through our extensive research of this regiment.

NAME	COMPANY	INFO
Moore, Andrew J (Captain)	A	"C" Company 23rd Regiment Indiana Inf. Volunteers
Morse, Willard N (1st Lieutenant)	A	"A" Company 64th Regt. Illinois Volunteer Infantry
Ray, Joseph (2nd Lieutenant)	A	"A" Company 53rd Regt. Illinois Volunteer Infantry
Timanus, John M (Sgt. Major)	A	Hamilton County, Davenport Ohio
Mason, George W (Sergeant)	A	Jasper County, Georgia
Ringer, Thomas (Sergeant)	A	Montgomery, Alabama
Wade, Washington (Sergeant)	A	Columbia, South Carolina
Walker, Daniel (Sergeant)	A	Barnwell, South Carolina
Childs, Alexander (Corporal)	A	North Carolina
Dixon, Arthur (Corporal)	A	Hancock County, Georgia
Flernvis, Alexander (Corporal)	A	Jefferson County, Georgia
Grant, Edward(Corporal)	A	Greensboro, Georgia
Hanks, Henry (Corporal)	A	Oglethorpe County, Georgia
Kinney, Spencer (Corporal)	A	Marlboro County, South Carolina
Shepard, Alford (Corporal)	A	Newton County, Georgia
Stokes, Charles (Corporal)	A	Orangeburg, South Carolina
Barbery, Charles	A	South Carolina
Barnes, Francis/Frank*	A	Orangeburg, South Carolina
Blair, Jesse	A	South Carolina
Brady, Giles	A	Marion, South Carolina
Brauns, Anotin	A	
Brown, Austin	A	Barnwell South Carolina
Brown, John	A	Virginia
Bullard, Glasgow	A	Sandersville, Georgia
Casson/Corson, Warren	A	Orangeburg, South Carolina
Clark, Judge	A	Moore County, Georgia

Cobb, Amos	A	Robeson County, North Carolina
Coffea, Thomas	A	
Cogdell Abraham	A	Goldsboro, North Carolina
Conner, Robert	A	Screven County, Georgia
Cox, Oscar	A	Henderson, North Carolina
Craig, Edward	A	Winnsboro, South Carolina
Davis, Samuel	A	Newberry, South Carolina
Dixon, Nathan	A	Hancock County, Georgia
Dortry/Dorty, Samuel	A	Screven County, Georgia
Dortry, Mathew	A	Screven County, Georgia
Drake, John	A	Virginia
Foster, Alexander	A	Columbia, South Carolina
Foster, Solomon	A	North Carolina
Frank, Henry	A	Moore County, North Carolina
Fuller, Asa	A	Washington, DC
Garrett, Nero	A	
Gibson, James	A	
Giles, Jasper	A	Mississippi
Glass, Rufus	A	Newton County, Georgia
Gregory, Granville*	A	Clio, South Carolina
Grissell, Patrick	A	Screven, Georgia
Hane/Howe, Alson/Alison	A	Camden, South Carolina
Hane/Howe, Henry*	A	Camden, South Carolina
Harper, Jesse	A	Henry County, Georgia
Herd, Giles	A	Concord, North Carolina
Holton/Hofton, Allen	A	North Carolina

Howe, Henry	A	
Jefferson, David	A	Griffin County, Georgia
Johnson, Frank*	A	Richmond, Virginia
Jorden, James	A	Jasper County, Georgia
Kimey/Kinney, Alfred	A	Marlboro County, South Carolina
Kinney, Aaron	A	Marlboro County, South Carolina
Lagget/Leggett, James	A	South Carolina
Lauton/Lawton, James	A	South Carolina
Leggett, Truss	A	Fayetteville, North Carolina
Lyons, Peter*	A	Marlboro County, South Carolina
Mackey, Thomas	A	Savannah. Georgia
Manley, Henry	A	Sampson County, North Carolina
Manning, Daniel	A	Robeson County, North Carolina
Manning, Henry	A	Marion County, South Carolina
Manning, John	A	Marlboro County, South Carolina
Maten/Moten, Henry	A	
McCall, Daniel	A	Marlboro County, South Carolina
McCall, James	A	
McClerin, Silas	A	Marlboro County, South Carolina
McClerin, Vander	A	Red Bluff, South Carolina
McConigan/McCunigall, John	A	Wayne County, North Carolina
McEntyre/McEntire, Daniel aka Paul	A	Marlboro County, South Carolina
McEntyre, Harris	A	Marlboro County, South Carolina
McEntyre, William	A	Marlboro County, South Carolina
Mingle, Josephus	A	Burke County, Georgia
Mingle, Shephard	A	Burke County, Georgia

Moore, John	A	Marlboro County, South Carolina
Moten, Henry	A	Augusta, Georgia
Murphy, Depholis	A	Burke County, Georgia
Nelson/Wilson, John	A	Jones County, Georgia
Newton, Andrew	A	Screven County, Georgia
Newton, William aka Phillips William	A	Screven County, Georgia
Olford, James	A	South Carolina
Pecor, John	A	Newton County, Georgia
Pettigrew, Lewis	A	Screven County, Georgia
Prestly, Ephram	A	Putnam County, Georgia
Qualt, Monroe	A	Richmond, Virginia
Rains, Thomas**	A	Hancock, Georgia
Riddle, George	A	Sandersville Georgia
Robertson, James	A	New Bern, North Carolina
Robison, Butler	A	South Carolina
Savington, Thomas	A	Georgia
Scott, George	A	Charleston, South Carolina
Shepard/Shephard, William	A	Bates County, Georgia
Sigler/Seeler, Moses*	A	Lawrenceburg, North Carolina
Simmons/Simonds, Frank	A	Columbia South Carolina
Stephens, Cato	A	South Carolina
Stephens, John	A	Atlanta, Georgia
Summer, Edward	A	
Thomas, Amos	A	Bryant County, Georgia
Thompson, Isaac	A	Sampson County, Georgia
Walker, Benjamin	A	Robeson County, North Carolina

Walker, Henry	A	Davidson County, North Carolina
Washington, Hollin	A	Columbia, South Carolina
Whitis, Peter	A	Georgia
Williams, James	A	Chesterfield, South Carolina
Wilson, Willis	A	Bennettsville, South Carolina
Woods, Samuel	A	Hampton, Virginia

*Indicates died in Service.

**Indicates deserted the Company.

NAME	COMPANY	INFO
Whitney, George W (Captain)	B	
Westfall, Charles H (1st Lieutenant)	B	"B" Company 15th Illinois Infantry
Buck, Noble H (2nd Lieutenant)	B	"H" Company 11th Iowa Infantry
Polley, Silas H (2nd Lieutenant)	B	14th Illinois Infantry
Brown, Rix (Sergeant)	B	Richmond, Virginia
Campbell, Edmond (Sergeant)	B	Cheraw, South Carolina
Miller, Bacheus (Sergeant)	B	Savannah, Georgia
Peddy, George (Sergeant)	B	Jasper County, Georgia
Williams, Jesse (Sergeant)	B	Lawrence, South Carolina
Coden, Robert (Corporal)	B	Kershaw District, South Carolina
Fort, Reuben (Corporal)	B	Clinton, North Carolina
Hicks, Michael (Corporal)	B	Simpson County, North Carolina
Hunter, Isiah (Corporal)	B	Macon, Georgia
Keller, William Corporal)	B	Charleston, South Carolina
Lawrence, James (Corporal)	B	Barnwell, South Carolina
Lemons, Frank (Corporal)	B	Lancaster District, South Carolina
McMichael, William (Corporal)	B	Orangeburg, South Carolina
Pitts, Edmund (Corporal)	B	Jones County, Georgia
Asher, Rayford	B	North Carolina
Bangs, George	B	Washington, North Carolina
Barentine, Aaron	B	Mulberry District, South Carolina
Barnet, Daniel	B	North Carolina
Bertha, John*	B	North Carolina
Birch/Burch, Postel	B	Winnsboro, South Carolina
Bouy/McNeil	B	Robeson County, North Carolina
Bowen, James	B	Jones County, Georgia
Brodus/Brodas, Lewis	B	Duplin County, Georgia
Burke, Edmund	B	Cheraw, South Carolina

Burns, Andrew	B	Cheraw, South Carolina
Burns, Ira	B	Emanuel County, Georgia
Burns/Burnes, Moses	B	Cheraw, South Carolina
Burns, Samuel	B	Screven County, Georgia
Clemmens, William**	B	McDonough County, Georgia
Covington, Manuel/Emmanuel	B	South Carolina
Curtis, Alexander/Alexandria	B	Gloucester County, Virginia
Durden, Cyrus	B	Sampson County, North Carolina
Durden, Thomas	B	Sampson County, North Carolina
Eli, Ephraim	B	South Carolina
Evans, Buck	B	Fayetteville, North Carolina
Fazen, Amos	B	Duplin County, North Carolina
Fazen, Dennis	B	Duplin County, North Carolina
Fazen, Solomon	B	Duplin County, North Carolina
Flanagan, David	B	Fairfield District, South Carolina
Gates, Joseph	B	Charleston, South Carolina
Glover, James	B	Charleston, South Carolina
Glover, Richard	B	Charleston, South Carolina
Gooden, William	B	Mulberry District, South Carolina
Grant, Jackson	B	Beaufort, South Carolina
Green, William	B	Beaufort, South Carolina
Griswold, Talbert	B	Jones County, Georgia
Grover, William	B	Charleston, South Carolina
Hadley, Ruffin	B	Johnson County, South Carolina
Hagrove John	B	Sampson County, North Carolina
Hicks, William	B	Samson County, North Carolina
Hill, Nelson	B	Manchester, Virginia
Hopkins, Cato	B	Savannah, Georgia

Howard, William Henry**	B	Hanover District, North Carolina
Hubbard, Jerry	B	Mulberry District, South Carolina
Hutchins, Henry	B	Macon, Georgia
Hyte, Robert	B	Burke County, Georgia
Jamison/Jannison, Stephen	B	Orangeburg, South Carolina
Johnson, Henry	B	Emanuel County, Georgia
Jones, Nicodemus	B	Burke County, Georgia
Kesick/Kessick, Hardee	B	Jones County, Georgia
Law, Aaron	B	Orangeburg, South Carolina
Lemons, Anthony	B	Henry County, Georgia
Lemons, Halloway/Holliway	B	Henry County, Georgia
Mathews, Daniel**	B	Owensville, South Carolina
Maye, Samuel	B	Jefferson County, Georgia
Miller, Benjamin	B	Jones County, Georgia
Millhouse, Joseph	B	Barnwell, South Carolina
Moore/More, Henry	B	Mulberry District, South Carolina
Moore/More, John	B	Mulberry District, South Carolina
Moore/More, Philip/Phillip	B	Mulberry District, South Carolina
Murphy, Carolina*	B	Hanover County, Virginia
Murphy, Elias	B	Sampson County, North Carolina
Murphy, Isley/Irby/Isaack	B	Sampson County, North Carolina
Murphy, Richard	B	Samson County, North Carolina
Murphy, Stephen**	B	Samson County, North Carolina
Murphy, William**	B	Simpson County, North Carolina
Parmer, Wesley	B	Warren County, North Carolina
Peddy, Thomas	B	Jasper County, Georgia
Pitts, Wilson	B	Jones County, Georgia
Price, Henry	B	Charleston, South Carolina

Rodwell, Joseph	B	Warren County, North Carolina
Sandy, Arthur	B	Simpson County, North Carolina
Shoate, George	B	Jones County, Georgia
Simmons, Joseph	B	Charleston, South Carolina
Sopshier/Sapshire, Mack	B	Jasper County, Georgia
Spearman, Jackson	B	Sampson County, North Carolina
Stanford, William	B	Jasper County, Georgia
Thomson, Isaac	B	Charleston, South Carolina
Thompson, John	B	Sampson County, North Carolina
Thompson, Jacob	B	Sampson County, North Carolina
Thompson, Peter	B	Sampson County, North Carolina
Thompson, Rayford	B	Sampson County, North Carolina
Thompson, Robert	B	Sampson County, North Carolina
Thompson, Sona/Sena	B	Sampson County, North Carolina
Thompson, Willis	B	Sampson County, North Carolina
Wetherly, Hartley**	B	Mulberry District, South Carolina
Wetherly, Jessie	B	Mulberry District, South Carolina
Wetherly, Robert	B	Mulberry District, South Carolina
Whaly, Charles	B	Orangeburg, South Carolina
Williams, Silas	B	Screven County, Georgia
Williams, Frank**	B	Raleigh, North Carolina
Williams, James **	B	Chesterfield, South Carolina

*Indicates died in Service.

**Indicates deserted the Company.

NAME	COMPANY	INFO
Mitchell, Thomas L. (Captain)	C	"E" Company 53rd Illinois Volunteer Infantry
Ball, Basil R (1st Lieutenant)	C	"H" Company 3rd Iowa Volunteer Infantry
Ferguson, David L. (2nd Lieutenant)	C	"G" Company 53rd Illinois Volunteer Infantry
Lester, Elijah (Sergeant)	C	Jones County, Georgia
Marshal, John (Sergeant)	C	Hardin, Tennessee
McMikel, Joseph (Sergeant)	C	Orangeburg, South Carolina
Peppers, Francis (Sergeant)	C	Clinton, North Carolina
Thomas, John (Sergeant)	C	Bennettsville, South Carolina
Brown, John (Corporal)**	C	Effingham County, Georgia
Glover, Christopher (Corporal)*	C	Monticello, Georgia
Jones, Willson (Corporal)	C	Gordon County, Georgia
Kerkendoll, Jesse (Corporal)	C	Triggs, Kentucky
Lamar, Abraham (Corporal)	C	Jones County, Georgia
Luckey, Henry (Corporal)	C	Newton County, Georgia
Smith, Hilliard (Corporal)	C	Washington, Georgia
Wirick, George (Corporal)	C	Columbia, South Carolina
Beacher, Calvin	C	Orangeburg, South Carolina
Beach, Nelson	C	Malbry District, South Carolina
Blow, Thadius	C	Jones County, Georgia
Bookman, William B.	C	Winnsboro, South Carolina
Bostick, James	C	Buck County, Georgia
Brewer, Isom	C	Sampson County, North Carolina
Brewer, Peter	C	Sampson County, North Carolina
Buller, Osborne	C	Virginia
Butler, Samuel	C	Orangeburg, South Carolina
Chestner, Daniel*	C	Sampson County, North Carolina
Chestnut, Allen	C	Sampson County, North Carolina

Clay, Gabrel	C	Wilkinson County, Georgia
Clay, Green	C	Wilkinson County, Georgia
Clay, Wiet	C	Wilkinson County, Georgia
Clay, Winfield	C	Wilkinson County, Georgia
Culer, Asbury*	C	Orangeburg, South Carolina
Cup, Henry	C	Morgan County, Georgia
Daughtry, Alexander	C	Sampson County, North Carolina
Facen, Allen	C	Duplin County, North Carolina
Facen, Henry*	C	Duplin County, North Carolina
Grear, Henry	C	Bucks County, Georgia
Grear, Med./Mede	C	Jones County, Georgia
Hager, Josey	C	Orangeburg, South Carolina
Hill, Washington	C	Mercer County, Kentucky
Hobbs, Amos	C	Sampson County, North Carolina
Hobbs, Thomas*	C	Sampson County, North Carolina
Hobbs, William	C	Sampson County, North Carolina
Holmes, Francis*	C	Clinton, North Carolina
Hook, Toney	C	Lexington, South Carolina
Inmon, George	C	Washington, Georgia
Inmon, Henry	C	Buck County, Georgia
Johnson, Thomas	C	Sampson County, North Carolina
Jones, Aaron	C	Snow Hill, North Carolina
Jones, Richard	C	Butts County, Georgia
Keit, Franklin	C	Orangeburg, South Carolina
Keit, Thomas	C	Orangeburg, South Carolina
Keit/, Wandy	C	Orangeburg, South Carolina
Lamar, Edward	C	Jones County, Georgia

Lamar, Stephen	C	Jones County, Georgia
Laval, Simon	C	Sampson County, North Carolina
Lewis/Louis, Benjamin	C	Wayne County, North Carolina
Lewis/Louis, Needham	C	Wayne County, North Carolina
Linch, James	C	Jasper County, Georgia
Marsh, Daniel	C	Clinton, North Carolina
Mathews, Allen	C	Sampson County, North Carolina
McCline, Mingo**	C	Mabry County, South Carolina
McCullum, Conley	C	Mabry County, South Carolina
McKiney, Nathan	C	Robeson County, North Carolina
McKiney, William	C	Bucks County, Georgia
Moseley, Joseph	C	Sampson County, North Carolina
Muler/Muller, Alexander	C	Sampson County, North Carolina
Newton, Amos	C	Lexington, South Carolina
Odem, Ezeakel	C	Sampson County, North Carolina
Owens, Elias	C	Fayetteville, North Carolina
Parker, Columbus*	C	Sampson County, North Carolina.
Parker, Ervin/Irvin	C	Sampson County, North Carolina
Parker, Franklin*	C	Sampson County, North Carolina
Pate, Alford**	C	Goldsboro, North Carolina
Quick, Andrew	C	Shelby, South Carolina
Quick, Ebenezer	C	Shelby, South Carolina
Quick, London	C	Marlboro, South Carolina
Raford, James	C	Jefferson County, Georgia
Smith, Francis	C	Washington, Georgia
Smith, Oren	C	Washington, Georgia
Smith, Scott	C	Marion District, South Carolina
Smith, Thomas	C	North Carolina

Lamar, Stephen	C	Jones County, Georgia
Laval, Simon	C	Sampson County, North Carolina
Lewis/Louis, Benjamin	C	Wayne County, North Carolina
Lewis/Louis, Needham	C	Wayne County, North Carolina
Linch, James	C	Jasper County, Georgia
Marsh, Daniel	C	Clinton, North Carolina
Mathews, Allen	C	Sampson County, North Carolina
McCline, Mingo**	C	Mabry County, South Carolina
McCullum, Conley	C	Mabry County, South Carolina
McKiney, Nathan	C	Robeson County, North Carolina
McKiney, William	C	Bucks County, Georgia
Moseley, Joseph	C	Sampson County, North Carolina
Muler/Muller, Alexander	C	Sampson County, North Carolina
Newton, Amos	C	Lexington, South Carolina
Odem, Ezeakel	C	Sampson County, North Carolina
Owens, Elias	C	Fayetteville, North Carolina
Parker, Columbus*	C	Sampson County, North Carolina.
Parker, Ervin/Irvin	C	Sampson County, North Carolina
Parker, Franklin*	C	Sampson County, North Carolina
Pate, Alford**	C	Goldsboro, North Carolina
Quick, Andrew	C	Shelby, South Carolina
Quick, Ebenezer	C	Shelby, South Carolina
Quick, London	C	Marlboro, South Carolina
Raford, James	C	Jefferson County, Georgia
Smith, Francis	C	Washington, Georgia
Smith, Oren	C	Washington, Georgia
Smith, Scott	C	Marion District, South Carolina
Smith, Thomas	C	North Carolina

Sparrow, John	C	Beaufort, South Carolina
Stanton, Franklin**	C	Malbry District, South Carolina
Stanton, Louis	C	Malbry District, South Carolina
Thomas., Samuel	C	Savannah, Georgia
Thompson, Alfred	C	Wayne County, North Carolina
Townsend, Joshua	C	Charleston, South Carolina
Townsend, Richard	C	Charleston, South Carolina
Townsend, William	C	Charleston, South Carolina
Vaughn, Joseph	C	Columbia, South Carolina
Weatherly, Trotto	C	Malbry, South Carolina.
Weston, June	C	Columbia, South Carolina
Weatherly, Richard	C	Bennettsville, South Carolina
Whaley, Cesar	C	Orangeburg, South Carolina
White, Floid	C	Jones County, Georgia
White, Haywood	C	Sampson County, North Carolina
Williams, Isaiah	C	Davidson, Tennessee
Willingham, Solomon	C	Fairfield, South Carolina
Wirick, John	C	Columbia, South Carolina
Wirick, Nicholas	C	Guyton, Georgia
Wolf, Wallace	C	Sumter South Carolina

*Indicates died in Service.

**Indicates deserted the Company.

NAME	COMPANY	INFO
Klock, John I. (Captain)	D	32nd Regt. Wisconsin Volunteer Infantry
Stone, Charles W (1st Lieutenant)	D	Iowa Infantry Volunteers
Ware, Joseph (2nd Lieutenant)	D	Co. "C" 41st Illinois Volunteer Infantry
Allen, Ben (Sergeant)	D	Jones County, Georgia
Erwin, Manuel (Sergeant)	D	Screven County, Georgia
Grant, James (Sergeant)	D	Savannah, Georgia
Hooper, James (1st Sergeant)	D	Fayetteville, North Carolina
Roggers, Marshall (Sergeant)	D	Washington County, Georgia
Wilson, Richardson (Sergeant)	D	Promoted from Corporal
Benson, Paul (Corporal)	D	Richland County, South Carolina
Evans, Robert (Corporal)	D	Fayetteville, North Carolina
Hill, Joshua (Corporal)	D	Mississippi
Martin, Jerry (Corporal)	D	Burke County, Georgia
Michael, Peter (Corporal)	D	Edisto Island, South Carolina
Simms, William D. (Corporal)	D	Augusta, Virginia
Washington, John (Corporal)	D	Warren County, Georgia
Abells, Daniel	D	Richmond, Virginia
Belcher, Abram	D	Burke County, Georgia
Belcher, Isaac	D	South Carolina
Best, Isaac	D	Screven County, Georgia
Blunt, David	D	St. Matthews, South Carolina
Blunt, Thomas	D	Screven County, Georgia
Boston, Andrew	D	Georgia
Burnett, Allison	D	Fayetteville, North Carolina
Bush, Joseph	D	Maryland
Butler, Peter	D	Cumberland County, North Carolina
Carter, William	D	Murray County, Georgia
Cease, Alick*	D	Barnwell County, South Carolina

Chavis, John	D	Johns Island, South Carolina
Cody, Harry	D	Hancock, Georgia
Cody, Jacob	D	Marion, Georgia
Collington, Sambo	D	South Carolina
Coon, Richard	D	Columbia, South Carolina
Crossley, Isaac	D	Marion, South Carolina
Crossley, Tom	D	Virginia
Crossley, Toney	D	South Carolina
Davis, Richard	D	Walton, Georgia
Doyle, Charles	D	Effingham County, Georgia
Ely, Richard	D	Barnwell County, South Carolina
Evans, Mars	D	Fayetteville, North Carolina
Fulton, Thomas	D	Fayetteville, North Carolina
Gibson, John	D	Marlboro County, South Carolina.
Gibson, Simon	D	Richland County, South Carolina
Gaston, Peter	D	South Carolina.
Gibson, John	D	Marlboro County, South Carolina
Gibson, Simon	D	Richland County, South Carolina
Gilmore, Andrew	D	Bladen County, North Carolina
Gilmore, Henry	D	Fayetteville, North Carolina
Gilmore, Joseph	D	Fayetteville, North Carolina
Green, Isaac	D	Columbia, South Carolina
Green, Sonco/Sanco	D	South Carolina
Hardy, William	D	South Carolina
Henry, Isaac	D	Fayetteville, North Carolina
Hill, Alick	D	Mississippi
Hill, Manuel	D	Putnam County, Georgia
Howell, Alfred	D	Richland County, South Carolina

Huger, Newell	D	South Carolina
Jacobs, Edmond	D	South Carolina
Jennings, Green	D	Georgia
Jones, Noah	D	Kershaw, South Carolina
Linkhorn, Julius	D	Sampson County, North Carolina
Lurk, Simon	D	Columbia, South Carolina
Mack, Perry	D	Midway, South Carolina
Martin, Peter*	D	Jefferson County, Georgia
McCrea/McRae, Adam	D	Fayetteville, North Carolina
McCrea, Henry	D	Fayetteville, North Carolina
McCrea, James	D	Fayetteville, North Carolina
McCrea, Mingo	D	Fayetteville, North Carolina
McDaniel, Nero	D	Richland, South Carolina
McKibben, Oliver	D	Butts County, Georgia
Mews, Ned	D	Barnwell County, South Carolina
Mews, Pompey	D	Barnwell County, South Carolina
Michael, John	D	Edisto Island, South Carolina
Nelson, Sam/Samuel	D	Columbia, South Carolina
Oliver, Anthony	D	Lexington, South Carolina
Parker, Adam	D	Effingham, Georgia
Parker, George	D	Effingham, Georgia
Pattison, David	D	Barnwell County, South Carolina
Pattison, John*	D	Barnwell County, South Carolina
Pope, Burrel	D	Georgia
Powell, Lewis/Louis*	D	Robeson County, North Carolina
Powell, Washington	D	Robeson County, North Carolina
Price, Edward	D	Columbia, South Carolina
Psalter, Anthony	D	Sampson County, North Carolina

Quick, London	D	Marlboro County, South Carolina
Riles, Handy	D	Simpson County, North Carolina
Robberts, James	D	Richmond, Virginia
Robbin, Peter	D	Fairfield, North Carolina
Rollins/Rolin, John	D	Alamance, North Carolina
Sherwood, Jack	D	Wayne County, North Carolina
Snipes, April	D	Edisto Island, South Carolina
Stephens, Thomas	D	Fairfield, South Carolina
Thomas, Sam	D	Savannah, Georgia
Tidwell, Charles	D	Virginia
Walker, David	D	Fayetteville, NC
Watson, Thomas	D	Hancock County, Georgia
Weston, William	D	Greenville, South Carolina
Whitehead, Oliver	D	Bladen County, North Carolina
Whithead, Tom/Thomas	D	Bladen County, North Carolina
Wilkinson, Berry	D	Butts County, Georgia
Williams, Fred	D	Beaufort, South Carolina
Wilson, James	D	Johns Island, South Carolina
Winks, William*	D	South Carolina

*Indicates died in Service.

**Indicates deserted the Company.

NAME	COMPANY	INFO
Johnson, George W. (Captain)	E	"K" Company 32nd Illinois Volunteer Infantry
Jackson, John (1st Lieutenant)	E	"B" Company 10Th Illinois Volunteer Infantry
Buch, Noble (2nd Lieutenant)	E	"K Company 2nd Illinois Volunteer Infantry
Talbert, Micajah (1st Sergeant)	E	National Cemetery, Natchez, Mississippi
Hull, Joshua (Sergeant)	E	Williamson County, Tennessee
Smith, Thomas (Sergeant)	E	Bertie County, North Carolina
Smith, Henry (Sergeant)	E	Petersburg, Virginia
Audrey, Ned (Sergeant)	E	Sampson County, North Carolina
Boller, Osborne (Corporal)	E	Winnsboro, South Carolina
Coleman, Washington (Corporal)*	E	Savannah, Georgia
Hayes, Jasper (Corporal)	E	Washington County, Georgia
Ingram, John (Corporal	E	Lancaster County, South Carolina
Jones, Belcer (Corporal)	E	Beaufort, South Carolina
Miller, Alexander Corporal)	E	Washington County, Georgia
Miller, Isaac (Corporal)	E	Charleston, South Carolina
Smith, Henry (Corporal)	E	Petersburg, Virginia
Suffold, Henry (Corporal)	E	Athens, Georgia
Tributs, Adam (Corporal)	E	Columbia, South Carolina
Whitley, Haywood (Corporal)	E	Johnson County, North Carolina
Andrews, Shadrack	E	Orangeburg, South Carolina
Barton, Hampton	E	Orangeburg, South Carolina
Beckham, Fletcher*	E	Lancaster County, South Carolina
Bike, John	E	Orangeburg, South Carolina
Bleu/Blew, Lewis	E	Robeson County, North Carolina
Boice, Moses**	E	Union County, North Carolina
Boker, Stephen	E	Orangeburg, South Carolina
Bond, Jacob	E	Monticello, Georgia
Bond, Thomas	E	Macon, Georgia

Bradley, Benjamin	E	Richland County, South Carolina
Burnett, Peter	E	Fayetteville, North Carolina
Canthon/Canton/Cauthon, Richard	E	Lancaster South Carolina
Carters/Carter, Sanney/Sonny	E	Sapelo Island, Georgia
Coker, William	E	Columbia, South Carolina
Collins, Alfred	E	Nash County, North Carolina
Covington, Wallace*	E	Marlboro County, South Carolina
Craig, Henry	E	Winnsboro, South Carolina
Cremety, Wesley	E	Bladen County, North Carolina
Durham, Henry	E	Fairfield District, South Carolina
Drake, Matthew	E	Robeson County, North Carolina
Edmondson, James	E	Green County, North Carolina
Fears, Nelson	E	Jasper County, Georgia
Ford, Charles	E	Winnsboro, South Carolina
Fort, Huycen	E	Bladen County, North Carolina
Fort, Phillip	E	Wayne County, North Carolina
Hamilton, Jackson*	E	Savannah, Georgia
Ingram, George	E	Landcaster County, South Carolina
Ingram, Henry	E	Landcaster County, South Carolina
Johnson, Jacob	E	Camden, South Carolina
Johnson, James	E	Franklin County, North Carolina
Johnson, Scipio	E	Charleston, South Carolina
Jones, Peter	E	Beaufort, South Carolina
Keneley, George	E	Columbia, South Carolina
Keneley, Marcellus	E	Columbia, South Carolina
Lane, Edward*	E	Bladen County, North Carolina
Leech, Berry	E	Fayetteville, North Carolina
Lively, Edward W	E	Putnam County, Georgia

Manley, Henry	E	Sampson County, North Carolina
Manning, Andrew	E	Clarendon District, South Carolina
Manning, Brutus	E	Clarendon District, South Carolina
Manning, Lewis	E	Camden, South Carolina
Manning, March	E	Clarendon District, South Carolina
Manning, Pompey	E	Bush Point, South Carolina
McCarter, Ceasar	E	Lumberton, North Carolina
McDaniels, Abraham	E	Cumberland County, North Carolina
McGee, Lewis/Louis	E	Richmond, Virginia
McKeeven, Moses	E	Bennettsville, South Carolina
McKeler, Colon	E	Marion County, South Carolina
McKenzie, Thomas	E	Orangeburg, South Carolina
McMichael, Richard	E	Butts County, Georgia
McMillen, Edward	E	Wake County, North Carolina
McNeal, Wilson	E	Fayetteville, North Carolina
Moore, William	E	Cheraw, South Carolina
Myrande, Cyrus	E	Baldwin County, Georgia
Newton, Charles	E	Monticello, Georgia
Nott, Sancho	E	Richland County, South Carolina
Owens, Joseph	E	Richmond, Virginia
Owens, Preston	E	Sampson County, North Carolina
Palmer, Samuel	E	Columbia, South Carolina
Parker, James	E	Sampson County, North Carolina
Parker, Samuel	E	Williamson County, Georgia
Parker, Thomas	E	Sampson County, North Carolina
Pea, Carolina	E	Fairfield County, South Carolina.
Phillips, George	E	Lancaster County, South Carolina
Raymond, Archer	E	Hardeeville, South Carolina

Raymond, Marion	E	Hardeeville, South Carolina
Rove, Alfred	E	Orangeburg, South Carolina
Sellers, Benjamin	E	Robeson County, North Carolina
Spell, Allen**	E	Sampson County, North Carolina
Stevens, Samuel	E	Franklin, Alabama
Strange, Harrison	E	Washington County, Georgia
Strange, Ralph	E	Washington County, Georgia
Temples, Washington	E	Baldwin County, Georgia
Tributs, Jonas	E	Lancaster County, South Carolina
Walton, Daniel	E	Greenville County, Virginia
Warren, Branson	E	Sampson County, North Carolina
Whaley/Whayley, David	E	Orangeburg District, South Carolina
Whaley/Whayley, Moses	E	St. Matthews, South Carolina
Williams, Alexander	E	Screven County, Georgia

*Indicates died in Service.

**Indicates deserted the Company.

NAME	COMPANY	INFO
Hazen, Elmore (Captain)	F	"E" Company 3rd Iowa Infantry
Adams, Noah F. (1st Lieutenant)	F	"D" Company 68th Regiment Ohio Infantry Volunteers
Cochrane, John A (2nd Lieutenant)	F	"I" Company 45th Regiment Ohio Infantry Volunteers
Hemphill, John (Sergeant)	F	Floyd County, Georgia
Lewis, Jerry (Sergeant)	F	Jones County, Georgia
Russell, Samuel (Sergeant)	F	Knox County, Tennessee.
Sanders, Stephen (Sergeant)	F	Barnwell County, South Carolina
Wood, Lennon (Sergeant)	F	Union County, North Carolina
Bess, Gilbert (Corporal)	F	Barnwell County, South Carolina
Blue, Peter (Corporal)	F	Charleston, South Carolina
Crawford, Allen (Corporal)	F	Barber County, Georgia
Hamer, Harry (Corporal)	F	Marlboro County, South Carolina
Miller, Balding (Corporal)	F	Baldwin County, Georgia
Musk, Daniel (Corporal)	F	Marlboro County, South Carolina
Quattlebaum, Hamton (Corporal)	F	Marlboro County, South Carolina
Russell, James (Corporal)	F	Charleston, South Carolina
Parks, Hinton F (Surgeon)	F	Promoted to Surgeon 31 May 1865
Shoales, George A (Asst. Surgeon)	F	Assigned to duty in the Rgmt. 28 Apr. 1865
Baltimore, Arnold	F	Jones County, Georgia
Brown, Samuel	F	Robeson County, North Carolina
Brown, Stephen	F	Robeson County, North Carolina
Burney, Francis	F	Morgan County, Georgia
Casey, Robert	F	Bibbs County, Georgia
Chapman, Squire	F	South Carolina
Clark, Edward**	F	Buck County, Georgia
Cook, Samuel	F	Burke County, Georgia

An original Volunteer Enlistment record that was found at the Huntington Library in San Marino, (Pasadena) California. We found that all of the enlistment documents for Company I are strored there.

VOLUNTEER ENLISTMENT.

STATE OF North Carolina — TOWN OF Goldsboro

I, Moses Humphrey, born in Robinson County in the State of North Carolina, aged Twenty Three years, and by occupation a Farmer, Do hereby acknowledge to have volunteered this Twenty Seventh day of March, 1865, to serve as a **Soldier** in the **Army of the United States of America**, for the period of *THREE YEARS*, unless sooner discharged by proper authority: Do also agree to accept such bounty, pay, rations, and clothing, as are, or may be, established by law for volunteers. And I, Moses Humphrey, do solemnly swear, that I will bear true faith and allegiance to the ***United States of America,*** and that I will serve them honestly and faithfully against all their enemies or opposers whomsoever; and that I will observe and obey the orders of the President of the United States, and the orders of the officers appointed over me, according to the Rules and Articles of War.

Sworn and subscribed to, at Goldsboro N.C. this 27th day of March, 1865. Before D. Dijon 1st Lieut 28th U.S.C. Infty

Moses his mark Humphrey

I CERTIFY, ON HONOR, That I have carefully examined the above-named Volunteer, agreeably to the General Regulations of the Army, and that, in my opinion, he is free from all bodily defects and mental infirmity, which would in any way disqualify him from performing the duties of a soldier.

H. T. Parks
A. A. Surg U.S.A.
EXAMINING SURGEON.

I CERTIFY, ON HONOR, That I have minutely inspected the Volunteer Moses Humphrey previously to his enlistment, and that he was entirely sober when enlisted; that, to the best of my judgment and belief, he is of lawful age; and that, in accepting him as duly qualified to perform the duties of an able-bodied soldier, I have strictly observed the Regulations which govern the recruiting service. This soldier has Black *eyes,* Black *hair,* Black *complexion,* is Five *feet* four *inches* high.

~~Sergeant~~ Theodore F. [illegible] Captain
135th ~~[illegible]~~ *Regiment of* ~~Ohio~~ U.S.C.T. ~~Volunteers,~~
RECRUITING OFFICER.

(A. G. O. No. 74 & 76.)

Mustered into the service of the United States, for three years or during the war, from date of enlistment, in Company ___ 135 Regiment of U.S.C.T. Volunteers, on the 26 day of April 1865, at Raleigh N.C.

[illegible] 12th Lieut [illegible] A.C.M. [illegible]

Copland, Samuel	F	Barnwell County, South Carolina
Cosins, Francis	F	Morgan County, Georgia
Danrick, Elijah**	F	South Carolina
Eaves/Evans, Sebron	F	Burnell County, South Carolina
Erby, Flanders	F	Robeson County, North Carolina
Fay, James	F	Virginia
Finlay, Jacob	F	Butts County, Georgia
Furlough, Harry	F	Morgan County, Georgia
Giles, Albert	F	Butts County, Georgia
Green, John	F	Fairfield District, South Carolina
Green, Osa/Ossie/Assie	F	Marlboro, South Carolina
Green, Shade	F	Waynesboro, Georgia
Greene, Barney	F	Baldwin County, Georgia
Hackle, James	F	Manual County, Georgia
Harris, Prince	F	Barnwell County, Georgia
Herring/Hewin, Henry	F	Winnsboro, South Carolina
Hicks, Elias	F	Wilkinson County, Georgia
Hines, Robert	F	Burke County, Georgia
Houstrander, Richard	F	Liberty County, South Carolina
Howell, George	F	Morgan County, Georgia
Howell, Moses	F	Morgan County, Georgia
Hugar, Adam	F	Orangeburg, South Carolina
Jackson, Aaron	F	Marlboro, South Carolina
Jackson, Thomas**	F	Winnsboro, South Carolina
Jamison, Abraham	F	Barnwell County, South Carolina
Jamison, Ned	F	Barnwell County, South Carolina
Jamison, Moses	F	Barnwell County, South Carolina

Jennings, Anthony	F	Sumter South Carolina
Jorden, Doss	F	Morgan County, Georgia
Kurse, Henry	F	Barnwell County, South Carolina
Lain/Lane, Jerry	F	Wilkinson County, Georgia
Mack, Adam	F	Barnwell County, South Carolina
Mathews, Martin	F	Manchester, Virginia
McCarter, Irwin/Erwin	F	Robeson County, North Carolina
McCarter, Fortune	F	Robeson County, North Carolina
McCarter, Prince	F	Robeson County, North Carolina
McCoad/McCode, Lewis/Louis	F	Orangeburg, South Carolina
McCook, Lawrence	F	Jones County, Georgia
McKesicks/McKesics, Henry	F	Jasper County, Georgia
McLain/McLane, Isaac	F	Maxton, North Carolina
McLaughlin, Thomas	F	Robeson County, North Carolina
McMellin/McMillon, Neil/Neal	F	Robeson County, North Carolina
McMillon, Emanuel/Manuel	F	Robeson County, North Carolina
McMillon, Samuel	F	Robeson County, North Carolina
McMullen, Thomas	F	Robeson County, North Carolina
Miller, Charles	F	Screven County, Georgia
Miller, John	F	Florence, Alabama
Miller, Washington	F	Sampson County, North Carolina
Parker, Monday	F	Screven County, Georgia
Patterson, Mansfield	F	Robeson County, North Carolina
Pearson, Austin	F	Jasper County, Georgia
Pie, Charles	F	Jasper County, Georgia
Pie, George	F	Monticello, Georgia
Ralls/Rools, Judson	F	Sampson County, North Carolina

Roberts, Silas	F	Darlington County, South Carolina
Rools, Dallis/Dalas	F	Sampson County, North Carolina
Rools, Joseph	F	Sampson County, North Carolina
Sanders, Isaac	F	Barnwell County, South Carolina
Simmons, Lawrence	F	Branchville, South Carolina
Simmons/Simons/Simms, Thomas	F	Winnsboro, South Carolina
Smith, Francis	F	Johns Island, South Carolina
Smith, Toney/Tony	F	Robeson County, North Carolina
Stokes, Sippio**	F	Manchester, Virginia
Thears/Thiers/Theirs/Theris, Julius	F	Beaufort, South Carolina
Townsand/Townsend, Adam**	F	Marlboro County, South Carolina
Townsand/Townsend, Daniel	F	Marlboro County, South Carolina
Townsand/Townsend, Dock**	F	Marlboro County, South Carolina
Townsand/Townsend, Duncan	F	Marlboro County, South Carolina
Townsand/Townsend, Francis	F	Marlboro County, South Carolina
Townsand/Townsend, James/Julius	F	Marlboro County, South Carolina
Townsand/Townsend, Noah	F	Marlboro County, South Carolina
Townsand/Townsand, Perry	F	Marlboro County, South Carolina
Townsand/Townsend, William*	F	Marlboro County, South Carolina
Townsand, William	F	Marlboro County, South Carolina
Waley/Willey, James	F	Goldsboro, North Carolina
Washington, George	F	Butts County, Georgia
White, John	F	North Carolina
Williams, Jerry	F	Stanley County, North Carolina
Wilson, Manuel	F	Screven County, Georgia
Wise, John	F	Manual County, Georgia

*Indicates died in Service.

**Indicates deserted the Company.

NAME	COMPANY	INFO
Fleming, Oliver P (Captain)	G	"I" Company 15th Iowa Volunteer Infantry
Hanna, Hiram (1st Lieutenant)	G	"H" Company 11th Iowa Volunteer Infantry
Monks, Jeremiah (2nd Lieutenant)	G	"C" Company 23rd Indiana Infantry
Broadtus, Jackson (Sergeant)	G	Washington, DC
Brooks, Charles (Sergeant)	G	Macon, Georgia
Habersham, Jacob (Sergeant)	G	Savannah, Georgia
Mackey, Syrus/Sirus (Sergeant)	G	Savannah, Georgia
Peoples, Stepney (Sergeant)	G	Pocotaligo, South Carolina
Brooks, Greenberry (Corporal)	G	Macon, Georgia
Carrol, William (Corporal)	G	Mobile, Alabama
Hurger, James (Corporal)	G	Columbia, South Carolina
Isley, Alfred (Corporal)	G	Orangeburg, South Carolina
Kennedy, Sephus (Corporal)	G	Orangeburg, South Carolina
West, Dock (Corporal)	G	Savannah, Georgia
Whitfield, Alfred (Corporal)	G	Goldsboro, North Carolina
Bankston, George	G	Mayweather, Georgia
Brinkle, Stepney	G	Suffolk County, Virginia
Black, Simon	G	Robeson County, North Carolina
Bragg, Freeman	G	Savannah, Georgia
Buoy, Albert	G	Robeson County, North Carolina
Buoy, Aleck	G	Raleigh, North Carolina
Campbell, Abraham*	G	Columbia, South Carolina
Campbell, Gadley	G	Goldsboro, North Carolina
Copely, Anthony	G	Robeson County, North Carolina
Carroll, Edward	G	Mobile, Alabama
Clay, Richard**	G	Greenville County, Virginia
Cogdel, Bryant	G	Wayne County, North Carolina

Cogdel, George	G	Wayne County, North Carolina
Cogdel, Jacob	G	Wayne County, North Carolina
Cogdel, Silas	G	Wayne County, North Carolina
Copely, Anthony	G	Columbia, South Carolina
Crawley, Jack	G	Robeson, County, North Carolina
Davis, Henry**	G	Columbia, South Carolina
Deridon/Durden, John	G	Sampson County, North Carolina
Dickson/Dixon, Jacob	G	Cheraw, South Carolina
Drake, Evans	G	Columbia, South Carolina
Drake, Osborn	G	Richland, Virginia
Drake, Peter	G	Columbia, South Carolina
Dudley, Joseph	G	Columbia, South Carolina
Dun, Robert	G	Wake County, North Carolina
Ellis, Wesley	G	Orangeburg, South Carolina
Eps, Levi	G	Marion County, Georgia
Eps, Toby	G	Twiggs County, Georgia
Fletcher, John	G	Sparksville, Virginia
Gardner, Solomon	G	Burke County, Georgia
Hamer, David	G	Little Rock, South Carolina
Hanes, Samuel	G	Orangeburg, South Carolina
Harris, Gilbert	G	Atlanta, Georgia
Hunter, Lewis	G	Winnsboro, South Carolina
Hurger, Cesar/Ceasar	G	Columbia, South Carolina
Hurger, William	G	Columbia, South Carolina
Irby, Charles	G	Baltimore, Maryland
Jackson, John	G	Savannah, Georgia
Johnson, Isah	G	Orangeburg, South Carolina

Johnson, Robert	G	Cheraw, South Carolina
Johnson, Wayman	G	Cheraw, South Carolina
Kelly, Hope	G	Orangeburg, South Carolina
Kit, William	G	Orangeburg, South Carolina
Kitrale, Simon	G	Orangeburg, South Carolina
Lin, Henry	G	Raleigh, North Carolina
Lin, Kennedy	G	Wake County, North Carolina
Low, King	G	Wake County, North Carolina
Lucas, Willie	G	Bennettsville, South Carolina
Lurick, George	G	Columbia, South Carolina
Magaha, Albert	G	Fayetteville, North Carolina
Mason, Andrew	G	Petersburg, Virginia
McDaniels, Aaron	G	Cumberland County, South Carolina
McRay, Benjamin	G	Orangeburg, South Carolina
McNeal, Cane	G	Wake County, North Carolina
McNeal, Lewis	G	Robeson County, North Carolina
McNeal, Ramsey*	G	Robeson County, North Carolina
McNear/McNair, Sandy	G	Robeson County, North Carolina
McNear, Winslow	G	Robeson County, North Carolina
Mertic, Gibson	G	Cheraw, South Carolina
Mickel, Dudley*	G	Cheraw, South Carolina
Mickel/Mickle, Hampton	G	Camden, South Carolina
Mikel, Moses	G	Camden, South Carolina
Mikel/Mickle, Nathan	G	Camden, South Carolina
Mikel/Mickle, Paul	G	Fairfield County, South Carolina
Mikel, Richard	G	Camden, South Carolina
Mikel/Mickle, Samuel	G	Camden, South Carolina

Mikel/Mickle, William	G	Camden, South Carolina
Morgan, Shadrack	G	Orangeburg, South Carolina
Murphy, Harry/Henry*	G	Robeson County, North Carolina
Muse, July	G	Barnwell County, South Carolina
Myers, Morris	G	Springfield, Georgia
Navinett, Adam**	G	Columbia, South Carolina
Navinett, Gabriel	G	Orangeburg, South Carolina
Palmer, Essic	G	Columbia, South Carolina
Seigler/Siglar, Cato	G	Orangeburg, South Carolina
Sellers/Cellars, Hillard	G	Orangeburg, South Carolina
Spears, Charles	G	Bennettsville, South Carolina
Spears, Henry	G	Bennettsville, South Carolina
Stewart. Lock	G	Lumberton, North Carolina
Summerville, Charles	G	Clarksville, Virginia
Sutten/Sutton, Thomas	G	Kinston, North Carolina
Thomas, William	G	Huntsville, Georgia
Tucker, George	G	Savannah, Georgia
Watson, Stephen	G	Randolph, North Carolina
Weathers, Charles	G	Raleigh, North Carolina
Weatherspoon, Samuel	G	Raleigh, North Carolina
Willis, Daniel**	G	Bennettsville, South Carolina
Wooden, Jack	G	Barnwell County South Carolina
Zimmond, Erry	G	Orangeburg, South Carolina
Ziggers, Marcum	G	Chesterfield, South Carolina

*Indicates Died in Service.

**Indicates deserted the Company.

NAME	COMPANY	INFO
Pocock, Lloyd D (Captain)	H	"C" Company, 16th Iowa Infantry Regiment
Couch, Edward, L (2nd Lieutenant)	H	"C" Company 1st Iowa Infantry Regiment
Brown, Joseph (Sergeant)	H	Charleston, South Carolina
Cane, Edward (Sergeant)	H	Orangeburg, South Carolina
Humbert, Prince (Sergeant)	H	Pocatalico, South Carolina
Lucas, Henry (Sergeant)	H	Savannah, Georgia
Smith, Robert (Sergeant)	H	Clinton, North Carolina
West, Horace (Sergeant)	H	Vicksburg, Mississippi
Brock, James (Corporal)	H	Lumberton, North Carolina
Holmes, Squire (Corporal)	H	Clinton, North Carolina
Johnson, Charles (Corporal)	H	Robertsville, South Carolina
McThey, Samuel (Corporal)	H	Little Rock, South Carolina
Moore, Lewis (Corporal)	H	Clinton, North Carolina
Roads, King (Corporal)	H	Warsaw, North Carolina
Watters, Ase (Corporal)	H	Little Rock, South Carolina
Write, Nickolas (Corporal)	H	Cheraw, South Carolina
Bathey, Henry	H	Adamsville, South Carolina
Bathey, Paterick	H	Adamsville, South Carolina
Bathey, Peator**	H	Little Rock, South Carolina
Bea, Handy	H	Beaufort, South Carolina
Brim, John	H	Henderson County, North Carolina
Burges, Albert	H	Warren County, North Carolina
Burges, Siras/Cyrus	H	Warren County, North Carolina
Chestnut, Henry	H	Clinton, North Carolina
Cocks, David	H	Brownsville, South Carolina
Cocks, John**	H	Brownsville, South Carolina
Dent, Frank	H	Columbia, South Carolina

Dent, Isaac/Isac	H	Columbia, South Carolina
Dick, Thomas aka Dick Thomas	H	Smithville, Virginia
Draik/Drake, Samuel	H	Columbia, South Carolina
Dudley, Nelson**	H	Bennettsville, South Carolina
Easterland/Esterland, Ely**	H	Marlboro, South Carolina
Easterly, Trust**	H	Columbia, South Carolina
Erby, Edwin	H	Marlboro, South Carolina
Essac, Spewer	H	Washington, North Carolina
Evans, Beb**	H	Marlboro, South Carolina
Evans, Perry	H	Marlboro, South Carolina
Evans, William	H	Marlboro, South Carolina
Garratt, Richard	H	Macon, Georgia
Gauddy, Boston	H	Little Rock, South Carolina
Gauddy, Jack	H	Little Rock, South Carolina
Greene, Jefferson B.	H	Savannah, Georgia
Hamer, Martin	H	Little Rock, South Carolina
Hamer, Alexander/Elick	H	Cleo, South Carolina
Hamer/Hayman, Arthur*	H	Cleo, South Carolina
Hamer, David	H	Cleo, South Carolina
Hamer, Ephraim	H	Cleo, South Carolina
Hamer/Haymer, Nathan	H	Cleo, South Carolina
Hamer, Peator	H	Cleo, South Carolina
Holmes, Haywood**	H	Sampson County North Carolina
Hamer, Tan	H	Cleo, South Carolina
Hill, Henry*	H	Washington, North Carolina
Jefferson, Green	H	Milledgeville, Georgia
Johnson, Henry	H	Robeson County, North Carolina

Johnson, Jerry	H	Millen, Georgia
Johnson, Peator	H	Robeson County, North Carolina
Kierce, Isaac	H	Charleston, South Carolina
Logan, David	H	Charleston, South Carolina
Luther, Martin	H	Little Rock, South Carolina
Manin/Mannon, Jack aka Jack Warren*	H	Little Rock, South Carolina
McClem, Ely	H	Mulberry, South Carolina
McClem, Jack	H	Clinton, North Carolina
McClem, James	H	Cheraw, South Carolina
McClem, Sky*	H	Mulberry, South Carolina
McCloud, Manil**	H	Marlboro, South Carolina
McDuffy, Moris/Morrice	H	Fayetteville, North Carolina
McMullen, Benjamin/Ben	H	Fayetteville, North Carolina
McQuain, Wade	H	Columbia, South Carolina
Melvin, Nelson	H	Little Rock, South Carolina
Moore, Dimond	H	Clinton, North Carolina
Palmer, June**	H	Surgeon
Pathey, Danil	H	Richmond, Virginia
Polstran, John	H	Mulberry, South Carolina
Pringall, Cipio	H	Georgetown, South Carolina
Pringall, Sampson	H	Georgetown, South Carolina
Pringall, Thomas	H	Georgetown, South Carolina
Rawl, Harry	H	Sampson County, North Carolina
Rence, James	H	Mulberry, South Carolina
Robson, James	H	Mulberry, South Carolina
Rogers, Charles**	H	Bennettsville, South Carolina
Rogers, Prince**	H	Bennettsville, South Carolina

Sampson, John**	H	Clinton, North Carolina
Sheltin/Shelton, William	H	Savannah, Georgia
Siggler, Frederick	H	Orangeburg, South Carolina
Smith, Edward	H	Clinton, North Carolina
Spalding, Fullar	H	Saphelo Island, Georgia
Sparks, Aron	H	Mulberry, South Carolina
Sparks, Hamilton**	H	Mulberry, South Carolina
Sparks, Jerry**	H	Mulberry, South Carolina
Sparks, July**	H	Mulberry, South Carolina
Sparks, King	H	Mulberry, South Carolina
Sparks, Nelson	H	Mulberry, South Carolina
Sparks, Peator	H	Mulberry, South Carolina
Sparks, Preston**	H	Mulberry, South Carolina
Sparks, Richard**	H	Mulberry, South Carolina
Sparks, William	H	Mulberry, South Carolina
Spearman, Owen	H	Fayetteville, North Carolina
Spencer/Sprewer, Esaac/Essex	H	Marion, South Carolina
Stackhouse, Hector	H	Marion, South Carolina
Stackhouse, John**	H	Raleigh, North Carolina
Stoaks, Peater*	H	Bennettsville, South Carolina
Thompson, General*	H	Little Rock, South Carolina
Thompson, James	H	Charleston, South Carolina
Townsman, Alfred	H	Bennettsville, South Carolina
Watters/Walters, Jacob	H	Little Rock, South Carolina
West, Handy	H	Vicksburg, Mississippi
Willis, John	H	Atlanta, Georgia
Wright/Write, Ceasor**	H	Bennettsville, South Carolina

* Indicates this person died in service.

** Indicates this person Deserted the Company.

NAME	COMPANY	INFO
Fisher, Theodore F. (Captain)	I	"H" Co., 32nd Regt. Ohio Vet. Volunteer Infantry
Hale, Christopher J. (1st Lieutenant)	I	"A" Co., 53rd Regt. Indiana Vet. Volunteer Infantry
Steele, Joseph H (2nd Lieutenant)	I	"H" Co., 45th Regt. Ohio Volunteer Infantry
Butler, Brutus (Sergeant)	I	Savannah, Georgia
Charlton, John (Sergeant)	I	Savannah, Georgia
Cooper, Charles (Sergeant)	I	Columbia, South Carolina
Kyles, Frank (Sergeant)	I	Milledgeville, Georgia
Shaw, Joseph (Sergeant)	I	Boliver, Tennessee
Armstrong, George (Corporal)	I	Summerville, Tennessee
Breuer, Louis (Corporal)	I	Montgomery, Georgia
Butler, Aaron (Corporal)	I	Eaton, Georgia
Butler, Martin (Corporal)	I	Newburg Village, South Carolina
Kinard, Perry (Corporal)	I	Barnwell County, South Carolina
Rice, July (Corporal)	I	Colleton County, South Carolina
Singleton, John (Corporal)	I	Chester, South Carolina
Williams, Isom (Corporal)	I	Colleton County, South Carolina
Wiley, Postler/Postel (Corporal)	I	Winnsboro, South Carolina
Allen, Boston**	I	Duncanville, South Carolina
Allen, John	I	Charleston, South Carolina
Anderson, Washington	I	Orangeburg, South Carolina
Beson, Handy	I	Bullock County, Georgia
Blue, David*	I	Moore County, Georgia
Booker, Jacob	I	Fayetteville, North Carolina
Bouman/Bowman, Randel	I	Orangeburg, South Carolina
Brady/Bredy, Taylor	I	Fayetteville, North Carolina
Brinson, Alexander	I	Savannah, Georgia
Burk, Charles	I	Washington, DC
Butler. London	I	Savannah. Georgia

Cementen, Philip	I	Beaufort, South Carolina
Chapin, Flander	I	Georgetown, South Carolina
Cloy, Willis	I	Newberry Village, South Carolina
Coon, Henry	I	Richland County, South Carolina
Curse, James	I	Barnwell County, South Carolina
Curse/Kearse, Stepney	I	Barnwell County, South Carolina
Darby, Bonaparte/Bonepart	I	Barnwell County, South Carolina
Dave, King	I	Barnwell County, South Carolina
Earley/Erley, Boston	I	Barnwell County, South Carolina
Fedrick/Fredrick/Fedrica, Jackson	I	Orangeburg, South Carolina
Fogg, Julius	I	Fairfield District, South Carolina
Fuk/Fulk, Ransom	I	Colleton County, South Carolina
Fuk/Fulk, Washington	I	Colleton County, South Carolina
Fulk, Peter	I	Colleton County, South Carolina
Fulk/Falk, Stepney	I	Colleton County, South Carolina
Gilmore, Franklin	I	Richmond, Virginia
Hampton, Joseph	I	Burke County, Georgia
Harrison, Isom	I	Beaufort, South Carolina
Harrison, Smart	I	Beaufort, South Carolina
Hodges, Jessie	I	Bullock County, Georgia
Hughes, Ramsey*	I	Richmond County, North Carolina
Hughes, Thomas	I	Richmond County, North Carolina
Jackson, Andrew*	I	Richmond County, North Carolina
Jaminson/Jamison/Janinson, Oulan	I	Orangeburg, South Carolina
Jennings, Adam	I	Beaufort, South Carolina
Jennings, Moses	I	Edisto Island, South Carolina
Jennings, Peter	I	Richmond, Virginia

Johnson, Isaac	I	Orangeburg, South Carolina
Johnson, Louis	I	Orangeburg, South Carolina
Jones, Lord W	I	Green County, Kentucky
Kane, Jaco	I	Orangeburg, South Carolina
Kennedy, Charles	I	Fairfield, South Carolina
Kennedy, Willis	I	Fairfield District, South Carolina
Kinard, William	I	Barnwell County, South Carolina
King, Heridie	I	Buckingham, Virginia
Knapper, Waldon	I	Milledgeville, Georgia
Lan/Lau, Wiat	I	Orangeburg, South Carolina
Malloy, Calep	I	Stewartsville, North Carolina
Marshall, John	I	Buck County, Georgia
McClain, Jackson	I	Robeson County, North Carolina
Michael, John	I	Edisto Island, South Carolina
Miller, Enoch	I	Harris Neck, Georgia
Miller, John	I	Florence, Alabama
Millhous, Ellis	I	Orangeburg, South Carolina
Morfit, Isaiah	I	Newburg District, South Carolina
Moss, William	I	Barnwell County, South Carolina
Owens, John	I	Richmond, Virginia
Richardson, Jackson	I	Charleston, South Carolina
Robinson, James	I	Winnsboro, South Carolina
Robinson, Rolin	I	Richmond, Virginia
Roseberg, Charles	I	Fairfield District, South Carolina
Rush, Efphraim* (28 May 1865)	I	Buried, Arlington National Cemetery
Scott, Kit	I	Beaufort, South Carolina
Shivers, John	I- from G	Orangeburg, South Carolina

Sigler, Alexander*	I	Orangeburg, South Carolina
Smith, Berry	I	Columbia, South Carolina
Smith, Calvin	I	Columbia, South Carolina
Smith, William	I	Columbia, South Carolina
Stacks, Jerry/Jerrie	I	Columbia, South Carolina
Steedley/Studley, Charles	I	Orangeburg, South Carolina
Taylor, Henry	I	Nashville, Tennessee
Taylor, John	I	Savannah, Georgia
Tribus, Alexander	I	Lexington, South Carolina
Turner, Isaac	I	Greenville, North Carolina
Umphrey, Moses*	I	Robeson County, North Carolina
Vaughn, Henry	I	Memphis, Tennessee
Walker, Stephen	I	Memphis, Tennessee
Walls, Jackson	I	Athens, Alabama
Wannamaker, Frank	I	Orangeburg, South Carolina
Wannamaker, Irvin/Ervin	I	Orangeburg, South Carolina
Waterman, Lewis/Louis	I	Orangeburg, South Carolina
Wells, William/James	I	Columbia, South Carolina
Woods, George	I	Madison, Georgia
Eastland, William	I	Orangeburg, South Carolina

* Indicates this person died in service.

** Indicates this person Deserted the Company.

NAME	COMPANY	INFO
Johnson, William (Captain)	K	"D" Company, 13th Iowa Veteran Volunteer Infantry
Auman, John (1st Lieutenant)	K	"G" Company 46th Regt. Illinois Vet. Volunteer Infantry
Pfeiffer, William (2nd Lieutenant)	K	"B" Company 39th Ohio Veteran Volunteer Infantry
Carroll, Ashley F (Sergeant)	K	Charleston, South Carolina
Bailey, Lewis (Sergeant)	K	Orangeburg, South Carolina
Collins, Benjamin (Sergeant)	K	Richmond, Virginia
Johnson, Alexander (Sergeant)	K	Greenville, South Carolina
Smith, Charles (Sergeant)	K	Charleston, South Carolina
Parks, Thomas (Sergeant)**	K	Wilkinson County, Georgia
Glenn, Thomas (Corporal)	K	McCannon, Georgia
Graham, John (Corporal)	K	McPhearson, South Carolina
Hatcher, Augustus (Corporal)	K	Burrel, Kentucky
Hollins, James (Corporal)	K	Monticello, Georgia
Kelley/Kelly, John (Corporal)	K	Jasper County, Georgia
Minigen, Hammon (Corporal)	K	Orangeburg, South Carolina
Nazareth, Daniel (Corporal)	K	Warrenton, Georgia
Solomon, Willas/William (Corporal)**	K	Abbeville, South Carolina
Whiters, Lafayette (Corporal)	K	Cassville, Georgia
Arnold, John	K	Morgan County, Georgia
Ashfort, Simon	K	Sampson County, North Carolina
Bailey, William	K	Orangeburg, South Carolina
Bishop, Toney	K	Barnwell County, South Carolina
Bonden/Bouden, Jones	K	Sampson County, North Carolina
Brooks, Floyd	K	Jones County, Georgia
Butsale, Andrew	K	Butts County, Georgia
Campbell, Cornelius	K	Bennettsville, South Carolina
Carroll, Frank	K	Cowpens, South Carolina

Carroll, Tobias	K	Barnwell County, South Carolina
Ceas/Sease, Isaac or Israel	K	Barnwell County, South Carolina
Cease/Sease, Major	K	Barnwell County, South Carolina
Ceas/Sease, Thomas	K	Barnwell County, South Carolina
Clinton, Julius	K	Anson County, North Carolina
Copelan/Coplin, Henry	K	Barnwell County, South Carolina
Dalens/Dolens/Dollens, Henry	K	Savannah, Georgia
David, Cyrus	K	Marlboro County, South Carolina
Davis, Charles	K	Lumberton, North Carolina
Davis, Simon	K	Effingham County, Georgia
Eastner, Adam *	K	Orangeburg, South Carolina
Evans/Evens, Wilson	K	Jefferson County, Georgia
Fearrer/Farer, Charles**	K	Putnam County, Georgia
Flinn, Daniel	K	Darlington County, South Carolina
Flinn, William**	K	Colleton County, South Carolina
Flowers, Burrell	K	Wayne County, North Carolina
Flowers, Joseph	K	Columbia, South Carolina
Fogle, William	K	Orangeburg, South Carolina
Free, Jackson	K	Duncan, South Carolina
Galasfort, George	K	Cheraw, South Carolina
Hilton, Allen	K	Lancaster, South Carolina
Holman, Redney J	K	Orangeburg, South Carolina
Holmes, Haywood	K	Sampson County, North Carolina
Holmes, Prince	K	McPhearson, South Carolina
Hops/Hobbs, Jacob	K	Sampson County, North Carolina
Houser/Howser, Daniel	K	Orangeburg, South Carolina
Houser/Howser, Vandy	K	Orangeburg, South Carolina

Inman, Dennis	K	Burke County, Georgia
Jennings, Benjamin	K	Orangeburg, South Carolina
Jennings, Garvin**	K	Orangeburg, South Carolina
Johnson, Alexander	K	Greenville, South Carolina
Jones, Peter	K	Louisville County, South Carolina
Keith, James	K	Lexington, South Carolina
King, Henry	K	Marlboro County, South Carolina
Kirklasure, Peter	K	Orangeburg, South Carolina
Lawrence, Sandy	K	Screven County, Georgia
Lloyd/Loyd, Henry	K	Liberty, Georgia
Lucas, William	K	Screven County, Georgia
Marshall, Edward	K	Barnwell County, South Carolina
McCall, Henry	K	Smith County, Tennessee
McCannon, Henry	K	Richmond, Virginia
McCloud, John	K	James Island, South Carolina
McFarlin, Abraham	K	Marlboro County, South Carolina
Michael, Alexander	K	James Island, South Carolina
Michael/Mikell, Cyrus	K	Edisto Island, South Carolina
Michael, James	K	Edisto Island, South Carolina
Michael, Samuel	K	Edisto Island, South Carolina
Middleton, Peter	K	Barnwell County, South Carolina
Millhouse, Alexander	K	Orangeburg, South Carolina
Mobley, Adam	K	Winnsboro, South Carolina
Mood, Joseph	K	Columbia, South Carolina
Nicholus, Columbus *	K	Richmond, North Carolina
Nicholus, Edmund	K	Richmond, North Carolina
Oden, Lemon	K	Marlboro County, South Carolina

Page, Patrick	K	Wayne County, North Carolina
Parker, Anthony	K	Washington, Georgia
Parker, Love	K	Clinton, North Carolina
Pipkins, Vandy	K	Marlboro County, South Carolina
Prinkle, Benjamin	K	Georgetown, South Carolina
Robertson, Furgeson	K	Milledgeville, Georgia
Ryles, John	K	Sampson County, North Carolina
Shuyler, Sampson	K	Orangeburg, South Carolina
Scott, Alexander	K	Beaufort, South Carolina
Sheilds/Shields, George**	K	Flat Rock, South Carolina
South, Manton/Manson	K	Atlanta, Georgia
Spivey, Henry	K	Jefferson, Georgia
Wallace, Andrew	K	Bennettsville, South Carolina
Walton, Clemm	K	Morgan County, Georgia
Weston, Israel	K	Charleston, South Carolina
Williams, Abraham	K	Lexington, South Carolina
Williams, Dudley *	K	Marlboro County, South Carolina
Williams, Isaac	K	Cheraw, South Carolina
Williams, Taylor	K	Cheraw, South Carolina
Zimmer, Caleb	K	Orangeburg, South Carolina
Zimmer, Wesley	K	Orangeburg, South Carolina

*Represents died in service.

**Indicates Deserted the Company.

135TH UNITED STATES COLORED INFANTRY, STAFF

Gurley, John E (Colonel) F & S Capt. "C" Co., 33rd Wis. Infantry Volunteers

Budlong, David H (1st lieutenant) F & S "C" Company 33rd Wisconsin Infantry Volunteers (Promoted To Lt. Colonel)

Hooper, William F (1st Lieutenant) F & S Regt. Quartermaster 2nd Iowa Infantry Volunteers

Bradley, Horace S (1st Lieutenant) F & S Adjutant "C" Co. Vet. Battalion 14th Ill. Inf., Vol.

Crossman, Lyman C (Hosp. Steward & S "F" Co. 17th Wis. Vet. Vol. Inf. Druggist)

Shaw, George S (Chaplain)F & S "C" Company 29th Missouri Volunteer Infantry

Parks, Hinton F. (Surgeon)F & S 1st & 5th State Militia Cavalry, Missouri

Shoales, George A. (Asst. Surgeon) F & S Official Army Register of Volunteer Force & part of the African American Civil War Memorial

REGISTER OF DEATHS/DESERTIONS
135TH UNITED STATES COLORED TROOP
COMPANY "A"
DEATHS

Frank Barnes Died June 9, 1865, Alexandria, Virginia

Henry HaneDied June 28, 1865, Alexandria, Virginia

Frank Johnson Died June 6, 1865, Alexandria, Virginia

Peter Logan Died June 26, 1865, Louisville, Kentucky

Moses Sigler Died July 9, 1865, Louisville, Kentucky

COMPANY "B"
DISCHARGED IN RICHMOND, VIRGINIA

Louis Broadus

Manuel Covington

Stephen Jamison

Jackson Spearman

DEATHS

Carolina Murphy

John Bertha

COMPANY "D"

DEATHS

William MickleDied May 11, 1865, Manchester, Virginia

Alexander CeaseDied July 24, 1865, Louisville, Kentucky

Peter MartinDied July 12, 1865, Louisville, Kentucky

John PattisonDied June 11, 1865, Alexandria, Virginia

Louis PowellDied July 21, 1865, Jeffersonville, Indiana

COMPANY "E"

DEATHS

Wallace Covington Died Fort Kearney

Fletcher Becham Died May 28, 1865, Alexandria, Virginia

Jackson Hamilton Died June 30, 1865, Louisville, Kentucky

Edward James Died July 1, 1865, Alexandria, Virginia

Washington Coleman Died July 3, 1865, Alexandria, Virginia

COMPANY "F"

DEATHS

William Townsend Died May 6, 1865, Near Raleigh, North Carolina

DESERTED

Adam Townsend Deserted Louisville, Kentucky

Dock Townsend Deserted Louisville, Kentucky

COMPANY "G"

DEATHS

Abraham Campbell

Dudley Nickel

Ramsey McNeil

Henry Murphy

COMPANY "H"

DEATHS

Sky Mc Clem Died April 27, 1865, Raleigh, North Carolina

Henry Hill Died June 8, 1865, Alexandria, Virginia

Arthur Haines Died June 30, 1865, Alexandria, Virginia

John Manner Died July 3, 1865, Richmond, Virginia

Peter Stokes Died July 24, 1865, Louisville, Kentucky

General Thompson Died September 9, 1865, Louisville, Kentucky

COMPANY "I"

DEATHS

Moses Umphrey Died May 15, 1865, on the Po River, Virginia

David Blue Died June 8, 1865

Ramsey Hughes Died June 18, 1865, Floating Hospital, Louisville, Kentucky

Julius Fogg Died June 16, 1865, In Hospital, Richmond, Virginia

Alexander Sigler Died June 3, 1865, Camp Kearney, Washington, DC

Andrew Jackson Died May 24, 1865, Washington, D.C..

Ephraim Rush Died May 27, 1865, Washington D.C.

COMPANY "K"

DEATHS

Gordon Liman Died May 11, 1865, Manchester, Virginia

Dudley Williams Died July 16, 1865, Louisville, Kentucky

Adam EastnerDied Alexandria, Virginia

Columbus Nicholus Died June 12, 1865, Alexandria, Virgini

CHAPTER 18

HEADSTONES

INTRODUCTION TO THE HEADSTONES OF THE MEN OF THE 135TH UNITED STATES COLORED TROOP

Upon learning of the 135th United States Colored Troop being formed in Goldsboro, North Carolina, toward the end of the Civil War, we began our search to find out more about this "lost troop." Our initial thoughts were to find pictures of the men that belonged to the 135th USCT, however, we quickly discovered that there were few pictures taken during the war, especially of individual Black troops. To our dismay, it became readily apparent that we would be truly fortunate to be able to find actual photographs of the men of this troop.

As we researched the 135th USCT further, we discovered that there were hundreds of pension records for these men at the National Archives in Washington, D.C. Over our eight plus years researching this regiment, we have been able to obtain over four hundred pension records of these soldiers. Since we had such a challenging time trying to find pictures of the men, we did find several over the years, so we started our quest to try to find where the men were buried and to see if they had a headstone.

Our search for headstones of the men of the 135th USCT has been surprisingly successful. We have traveled all over the country, including Georgia, South Carolina, North Carolina, Virginia, Washington, D.C., Kentucky, Indiana, and as far as California in our search for the records and headstones of these men. To date, we have been fortunate enough to obtain photographs of over ninety of the men. The following pages include pictures of the actual headstones of these courageous men and where they are located.

We have included the regular soldiers of the regiment, most of them privates in the army, and we have also included the headstones of the white officers that we have been able to locate. Our way of honoring these men was to visit their graves and place a flag on the headstones. You will see the pictures of their headstones on the following pages.

 ! Anthony Crockett, McDonough Memorial Cemetery, McDonough, Henry Co. Ga	 Benjamin Esau Mc Cray, Charleston, SC
 Berry Leech, Beauty Spot United Methodist Church Cemetery, Robeson County, NC	 Christopher Glover, Military Cemetery, Alexandria, VA
 Amos Cobb, Mount Mariah Cemetery, Chancellor, Geneva Co., Alabama	 Jno Hewitt Drake Cemetery, Pasquotank County Virginia

 Francis Barnes, Military Cemetery, Alexandria, Va	 Elias Murphy, Haley Cemetery, Bedford Co. Tennessee
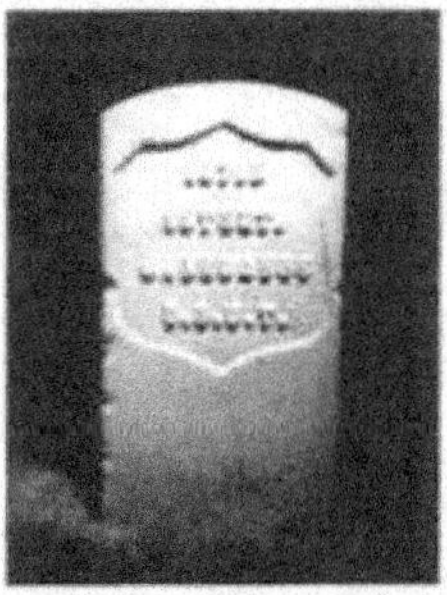 Jackson Broadus, Arlington National Cemetery, Arlington, VA. Sec 23	 Noble H. Buck, Original Headstone,-Carroll Hill Cemetery, Fairfax, Franklin Co., VT.
 Noble H. Buck, Replacement Headstone, - Carroll Hill Cemetery, Fairfax, Franklin Co., VT.	 Rix Brown Richmond National Cemetery, Va

Aron Jones
Snow Hill, Green Co.,
North Carolina

Daniel Chestner
New Albany National
Cemetery, IN

Franklin Parker
Military Cemetery,
Alexandria, VA

Lit Parker
Military Cemetery,
Alexandria, VA

Needham Lewis
Selma Colored Cemetery,
Selma, Johnston Co. NC

Thomas Hobbs
Military Cemetery,
Alexandria, VA

William Hobbs
Military Cemetery,
Alexandria, VA

Alexander Cease
New Albany National
Cemetery, IN

Isaac Green
Barnwell Cemetery
Columbia, South Carolina

John Chavis
St. Stephens AME
Church, Johns Island,
Charleston Co., SC

Peter Martin
New Albany National
Cemetery, IN

Sambo Colleton Fletcher
Saint John Baptist Church
Cemetery Henderson NC

 Abram McDaniels Military Cemetery, Alexandria VA	 Thomas Parker Parker Cemetery, Worth County, GA
 W. H. Johnson Hookerton Cemetery, Green County, North Carolina	 Washington Coleman Military Cemetery, Alexandria, VA
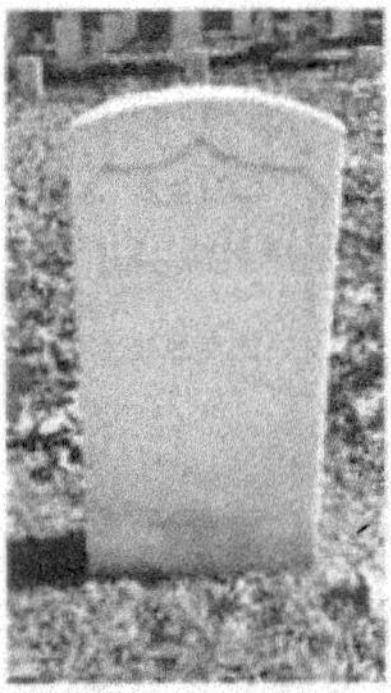 William Miller Military Cemetery, Alexandria, VA	 Aaron Scurlock aka McDaniel, Elmwood Cemetery, Cumberland Co. NC

 Albert McNeill aka Buie or Buoy, Panthersford Church Cemetery, Red Springs Robeson County, NC	 Cain McNeill Maxton United Methodist Cemetery, Zion, NC
 Evans Drake, Drake Cemetery, Acme, Columbus Co. NC	 Ramsey McNeil Military Cemetery, Alexandria, VA
 Aaron Wilson aka Sparks, Macedonia Missionary Baptist Church Cemetery, Bennettsville, Marlboro County, South Carolina	 Cyrus Burges Odell Baptist Church Cemetery, Warren County, North Carolina

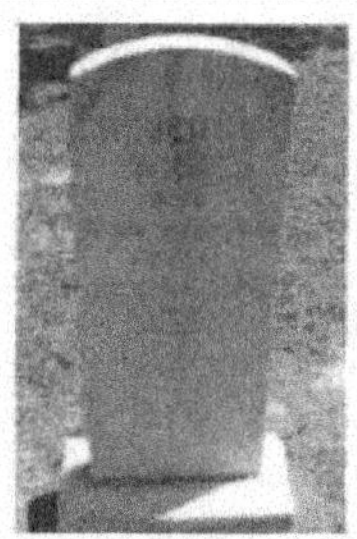

 Moses Sigler New Albany National Cemetery, New Albany, Floyd County, Indiana	 David Blue Military Cemetery, Alexandria, VA
 Ephriam Rush Arlington National Cemetery, Arlington, VA	 George Mason Military Cemetery, Alexandria, VA
 Perry Kinard Three Mile Creek Christian Church Cemetery, Bamberg, SC	 Adam Mobley Oakland Cemetery, Navasota, Grimes Co., TX

Dudley Williams
New Albany National Cemetery, IN

Daniel Mason,
Alexandria National Cemetery, Alexandria, VA

Fletcher Beckham
Military Cemetery, Alexandria, VA

Francis Holmes
Military Cemetery, Alexandria, VA

Frank Kyles, Memorial Hill Cemetery, Milledgeville, Baldwin Co., GA

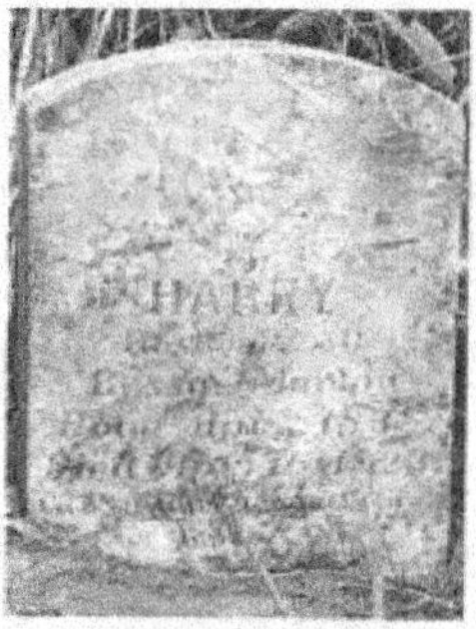

Harry Martin
Martin Family Cemetery, Mount Olive, Wayne County, North Carolina

Henry Hill
Pine Forest Cemetery, Wilmington, New Hanover County, NC

Henry Howe
Military Cemetery, Alexandria, VA

Henry McRea
Wilmington National Cemetery, North Carolina

Holloway Crockett, McDonough Memorial Cemetery, McDonough, Henry County, Ga

Jack Sherrod
Jack Sherrod Family Cemetery, Watery Branch, Wayne County, NC

Jackson Hamilton
New Albany National Cemetery, Indiana

 Jacob McMillan Cheraw, Fisher Hill Community Cemetery, South Carolina	 Jacob Thompson, Wilmington National Cemetery, North Carolina
 James Green Cross and Green Cemetery, Colemans Lake, Emanuel County, GA	 James Hatcher, Lewis Cemetery #2, Marion, Crittenden Co., Kentucky
 John Bertha New Albany National Cemetery, Indiana	 Lawrence McCook Iowa Veterans Home Cemetery, Marshalltown, Iowa

 Moses Humphrey Fredericksburg National Cemetery, Virginia	 Perry Townsend, Maxton, Scotland, County, North Carolina
 Peter Bright New First Missionary Baptist Church, Edisto Island, South Carolina	 Philip Fort Fort Family Cemetery, Wayne County, NC
 Prince Holmes Beaufort National Cemetery, Beaufort, SC	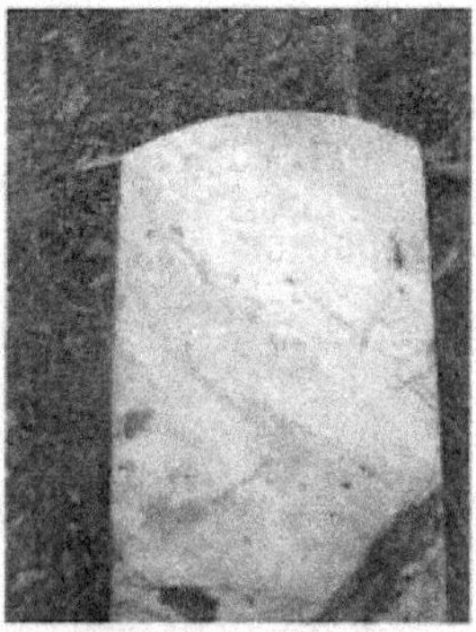 Ransom Folk Folk-Heyward Cemetery, Colleton County, SC

Sam Barber
Government Cemetery
Hopkins, SC

Simon Gibson
Gibson Cemetery,
Scotland County, NC

Stepany Sanders,
Bethlehem Baptist Church
Cemetery, Bamberg,
South Carolina

Stephen Watkins
Saint Peter Church
Cemetery, Snow Hill,
Greene, County, NC

Thomas W. Keit
Randolf Cemetery,
Richland, County, SC

John M. Timanus, Sgt.
Major, US Soldiers &
Airman's Home National
Cemetery, Washington
DC.

!st Lt. Hiram Hanna, Greenwood Cemetery, Muscatine, Iowa

1st Lt. Basil R, Ball, Forest Lawn Memorial Park, Omaha, Nebraska

1st Lt. Charles W. Stone, San Francisco National Cemetery, San Francisco, CA

1st Lt. John Auman, Wyuka Cemetery, Lincoln, Lancaster Co., Nebraska

2nd Lt. Edward Couch, Greenwood Cemetery, Muscatine, Iowa

2nd Lt. Joseph Ware, Riverside Cemetery, Mahomet, Illinois

 LT. Charles W. Leeds, Leeds and Grenville United Co. Ontario, Canada	 LT. Christopher Hale, Pioneer Cemetery, Boise, ADA Co. Idaho
 Lt. Col. David Budlong, Greenwood Memorial Park, San Diego, Ca	 Lt. Joseph Steele, Greenwood Cemetery, Decatur, Macon Co., IL
 Lt. Oliver Fleming Maple Hill Cemetery, Osceola, Clarke Co. Iowa	 Maj. Gen. John Logan US Soldiers and Airmans Home National Cemetery, Washington, DC

Capt. Silas H. Polley, Freeport City Cemetery, Freeport, Steppenson Co., IL

Capt. Loyd D. Pocock, Wood National Cemetery, Milwaukee, Wisconsin

Capt. Elmore Hazen, Mountain Home National Cemetery, Washington County, TN.

Capt. Klock, Washington Veterans Home Cemetery, Retsil, Kitsap Co. Washington

Capt. Theodore F Fisher, Oakwood Cemetery, Warsaw, Indiana

Capt. Thomas L. Mitchell, Marshall Cemetery, Marshall, Illinois

Chaplain George Stetson Shaw, Glenwood Cemetery, Ashby, Massachusetts

Col John Gurley
Pine Mound Cemetery,
La Salle, Co. Illinois

Amos Hobbs
Bryant Cemetery
7750 Laurel Way
Leland, North Carolina

CHAPTER 19

SOLDIERS PICTURES

The following are the only pictures of the soldiers of the 135th United States Colored Troop that we have been able to compile through our years of research.

William Eastland Carrion

Holloway Crocket

Soloman Gardner

Harry Martin

Stepany Peoples

Sampson Pringle

July Rice

Jack Sherrod

John Taylor

George Woods

CHAPTER 20

OFFICERS PICTURES

The following pictures are of the Officers of the 135th United States Colored Troop that we have been able to locate through our years of research. The Junior Officers' pictures were taken in Louisville, Kentucky after the war and provided to us by Cindy Pratt.

General William Tecumseh Sherman

Col. John Edgar Gurley

George S. Shaw, Chaplain

Capt. Andrew Moore, Co. C

Capt. Thomas L. Mitchell, Co. C

Captain John I. Klock, Co. D

Captain William Johnson, Co. K

1st Lt. Basil R. Ball, Co. C

1st Lt. Charles Westfall, Co. B

1st Lt. Hiram Hanna, Co. G

2nd Lt. Joseph Ray, Co. A

2nd Lt. Noble H. Buck, Co. B

George A. Shoales, Assistant Surgeon

APEX

MANUAL FOR THE INSTRUCTION OF CIVIL WAR PIONEER TROOPS

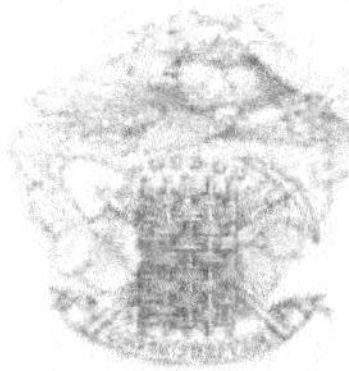

DUTIES, ORGANIZATION & EQUIPMENT OF INFANTRY PIONEERS

COMPILED FOR LIVING HISTORIANS, REENACTORS, AND EDUCATORS

"It is, however, of importance, when an army is moving, that pioneers and sappers accompany the advanced guard, to increase the number of practicable roads, to remove obstructions, throw small bridges across creeks, if necessary, and secure the means of easy communication between the different corps of the army"

BARON DE JOMINI MILITARY ENGINEERING

"HOW NOW, CAPTAIN MACMORRIS?
HAVE YOU QUIT THE MINES?
HAVE THE PIONEERS GIVEN O'ER?"

The Art of War embraces a variety of disciplines including Strategy, Tactics, Intelligence, Transportation, and Engineering. Since antiquity, large armies have organized a portion of their forces to include men skilled in trades and professions that are useful in the successful accomplishment of construction and demolition tasks. These men are sometimes referred to as "sappers and miners," "pontooniers," and "pioneers," but all may be generally described as "engineers." Their duties included road and bridge construction, fortification, mining, and general construction, in camp, on the march and under fire, in the field. The purpose of these operations is the same as for all other branches of service, which is the defeat of the enemy. Building or improving roads and bridges speeds transportation that delivers mortal force to the enemy's front. Fortification and siege work provide cover for an attacking force while bringing it as near as possible to its target. Where the enemy is strongly entrenched, a direct assault by infantry may fail without the support of mining and demolition, or the construction of parallel saps to conduct an attacking force to a place from which the enemy's works can be taken by storm. Working under the covering fire of skirmishers, engineers remove or destroy obstacles from the path of the army's advance. Engineers contribute to military intelligence by means of reconnaissance, topographical surveys, and producing maps required for strategic planning and tactical operations.

The outbreak of sectional hostilities, in 1861, required a growing army to organize more engineer support than could be provided by a few companies of regulars. Creating this added support occurred when a number of volunteer engineer units were raised from New York, Michigan, Kentucky, and Missouri. Where military operations could not benefit from these organizations, a regiment might be assigned to service as "acting engineers" or "pioneers." Loyal civilians, often freed slaves, were taken into service and placed under the command of a qualified officer. At times when no officer or noncommissioned officer could be found with the necessary skills, supervision of the pioneers might go to a civilian. Engineer regiments and companies attached to Army command were exempt from duties other than that of their "immediate profession."

They carried arms for their own protection, but were not expected to serve as line troops. Engineer regiments might be assigned to support Army operations, but their official orders came from departmental command behind the lines. The time required to process paperwork and approve orders often delayed the usefulness of engineers in situations requiring a rapid response. A solution to this administrative problem was found when Army of the Cumberland commander, William S. Rosecrans, assigned his chief engineer, Captain James St.Clair Morton, to organize a brigade of pioneer infantrymen whose civilian professions suited them to perform engineer tasks, drawn from the ranks and organized into companies led by similarly skilled officers. Perhaps out of deference to brigade commander Morton's regular rank of Captain, the brigade's company officers were all lieutenants. Morton was later promoted to Brigadier General of Volunteers, but after a falling out with Rosecrans in 1863, he resigned his general's commission and was promoted to the regular rank of Major, in a post at the Engineer Bureau in Washington City, under Chief Engineer General John Barnard. Requesting a field assignment, the energetic Morton was assigned chief engineer, IX Army Corps. He was killed in action on June 17, 1864, at the head of the IX Corps assault against Confederate trenches at Petersburg. Morton's creation, the Pioneer Brigade, was designated the "Engineer Brigade" during the last year of the war, serving with distinction. In his memoir, General Hazen complained that while the Pioneer Brigade provided a useful service to the army, its existence caused morale to suffer. The best and brightest men in the ranks tended to be those selected as "extra duty" men, depriving their home units of their personal example.

The term "pioneer" denotes one who goes before the rest, blazing trails and making way for others who follow. In military parlance, the word has long described soldiers engaged in road and bridge construction. A military "pioneer" is nothing more or less than any person in military service, whether or not they are enlisted, commissioned, or a civilian performing the tasks of a military engineer. Most pioneers were infantrymen serving in this capacity. The role of a pioneer soldier is that of an engineer soldier, except that pioneers are subject to the direct orders of field command, and their officers are not governed by the Articles of War (No. 63), Article XLVI, Section 1357 of the Revised Regulations for the Army (1861), or Article II, Section 10 of the 1863 Regulations, including the Engineer Supplement (Article XLVI). Each corps provided a battalion of pioneers. These were divided into ten or twelve companies of eighty or one hundred men, based on the strength of those brigades from which they were drawn. The senior ranking lieutenant served as Lieutenant Colonel commanding the battalion, the next ranking lieutenant as Major, and the ranking lieutenant in each company served as Captain of that company. This model applied to noncommissioned officers. The ranking Sergeant served as Sergeant Major, etc. Unlike the Volunteer and Regular Engineer organizations, the Pioneers were directly subject to infantry command. When a company of pioneers was attached to a brigade, corps, division, or army, its place in formations was adjoining and immediately following the skirmishers, in advance of the main force. They assumed the same place in the advance of division, corps, and army formations. Engineers, on the other hand, were placed at the center of a formation, with the artillery. It is an important distinction. As the war dragged on and attrition depleted the ranks of many a regiment, the mode of assigning and deploying pioneers changed, reflecting changes in unit strength and integrity. Methods differed between eastern and western commands, even after eastern commands had been given over to western commanders in 1864. The Pioneers' established equipment was designated as follows:

Equipage for Twenty Men Estimate for a Regiment:

Six Felling axes
Six Hatchets
Two Cross cut Saws
Two Cross cut Files
Two Hand Saws
Four Hand saw Files
Six Spades
Two Shovels
Three Picks
Six Hammers
Two Half Inch Augers
Two Inch Augers
Twenty lbs. Nails, assorted
Forty lbs. Spikes, assorted
One coil rope
One wagon, with four horses or mules

It is hoped that all regimental commanders will see the obvious utility of this order, and do all in their power to render it as efficient as possible.

By command of Major General Rosecrans.

ARMY OF THE POTOMAC PIONEERS

On April 5, 1864, General Order # 15 called for a pioneer corps to be drawn from the ranks, based on the Army of the Cumberland model, with a few changes. Instead of two men per company, one man in fifty was drawn from the brigade's ranks based on his skill, energy, and experience. A shift in method reflecting the attrition witnessed by many regiments in the Army of the Potomac. This reflects a tremendous concern for the mobility and celerity of engineering resources, despite the Army of the Potomac's being served by a brigade of engineers. As with the Army of the Cumberland, the pioneers traveled in advance of each brigade, division, and corps. Instead of using wagons, tools were carried by panniered mules.

This is further evidence of the grim urgency that attended their duties.

"GENERAL ORDERS NO. 15,

HEADQUARTERS, ARMY OF THE POTOMAC, APRIL 5, 1864"

Excerpt:

"II. The following is established as the organization and equipment of the pioneer parties of this army:

First, the unit of organization will be by brigade. In each brigade, 1 man shall be selected for every 50 men equipped for duty in it; for every ten men, thus selected, a corporal shall be detailed, and for every 20, a sergeant, and for each brigade, 1 lieutenant.

For each division, a first lieutenant of the old date or a captain shall be detailed to command the pioneers of the division, who will be a member of the division staff, and be furnished with a horse and equipment by the quartermaster's department.

The pioneers will be armed as they were in their regiments, and men and officers will be especially selected for fitness for the duty.

They will be excused from all guard and picket duty and from ordinary fatigue details. The tools will be furnished in the following proportions: viz, five tenths' axes, three tenths' shovels, two tenths pick and be carried on pack mules during the march, each mule carrying the tools for 40 pioneers.

The quartermaster's department will provide the necessary mules and appropriate panniers for this service.

Brigade and division commanders are directed to give special attention to the prompt formation and equipment of their pioneer parties.

In camp, the pioneer parties will make the ordinary repairs to roads, bridges, etc. On the march, they will move at the head of the infantry column and promptly put in order all parts of the route where artillery and wagons have to pass, whether for their own command or for troops to follow.

Second. Corps commanders will cause 1 noncommissioned officer and 25 efficient men to be selected and placed under the chief quartermaster of the corps to serve as a mounted pioneer party to accompany the trains, and to be provided with 10 axes, 10 spades, and 5 picks. The horses and equipment for the pioneers for the trains will be furnished by the quartermaster's department.

By command of Major General Meade: S. Williams, Assistant Adjutant General"

The Official records, etc.

IX ARMY CORPS ENGINEERS

Until May 1864, IX Army Corps (AC) was a nominally independent organization under Ambrose Burnside's command. It possessed its own "acting engineer" forces and would continue using these infantry regiments as a rotating engineer corps after IX Corps was placed under Meade's command in May 1864. While IX AC was subject to G.O. no.15, Burnside, perhaps with Morton's encouragement, appears to have ignored it in practice. The following infantry regiments were assigned to engineer duty:

35th Massachusetts Infantry, assigned "Acting engineer troops" for the Overland Campaign, 1864.

48th Pennsylvania Infantry, Mining beneath Elliot's Salient, July 1864.

17th Michigan Infantry, Construction of fortifications before Petersburg; June 1864 March 1865.

PIONEER INSIGNIA

1863 Army Revised Regulations, article LI, section 1585: "Chevrons...for a Pioneer two crossed hatchets of cloth, same color and material as the edging of the collar, to be sewed on each arm above the elbow in the place indicated for a chevron (those of a corporal to be just above and resting on the chevron), the head of the hatchet upward, its edge outward, of the following dimensions: viz: Handle four- and one-half inches long, one fourth to one third of an inch wide. Hatchet: two inches long, one inch wide at the edge."

The specific contours of this insignia were not standard, and many variations are to be found. One interesting example is a metallic insignia (pp20) at Snake Creek Gap, near Resaca, Georgia. Illustrated in Civil War Relics of the Western Campaigns, by Charles S. Harris on page 212. The two crossed hatchets are not identical; one of common pattern and the other resembling a shingle hatchet. It is uncertain how this was worn, but eyelets suggest that it was sewn to cloth, perhaps as a cap insignia.

Fatigue" 1865 Q.M. Manual; note the "doe foot" ax handle design"

In the 1866 Quartermaster Report, the "Fatigue" uniform illustrated includes an 1858 forage cap with a yellow metal insignia that could portray crossed hatchets worn just above the visor.

Pioneer chevrons were required by regulation to be the same as the branch of service, but in the case of the Army of the Cumberland, infantry pioneers wore the device in yellow, which was the branch of service color designating engineers and not blue, which was the branch of service color for infantry. Another color variant is the piping for engineer officer trousers. According to regulation, they should be fashioned of gold bullion, for staff corps. New York State regulations specify buff piping for engineer officers but make no mention of pioneer chevrons.

10. PIONEER TOOLS

The US Army Quartermaster Reports describe tools recommended for use by the Army. Hand tools carried by military pioneers were no different than one would find on any farm or construction site. Tool patterns have changed little, but fabrication methods have changed drastically. Hand-forged axes will show evidence of hammer-welding and folding the metal to shape. Cast axe-heads will not, but surface porosity can betray a cast item. Selecting tools for reenacting purposes can best be directed by consulting Civil War period QM Reports and buying tools according to specification guidelines, given below.

1865 Quartermaster Specifications:

Pick-Axes
"Pick-axes—to be of two sizes, 23 and 25 inches long, made of he best American iron and steel, he eye at the center, to be 2 ¾ inches by one and seven eighths inches outside, and inside 2 ½ by one and five eighths inches in the clear; blade of the hoe end one and five eighths inches wide, and the pick end a square point; each end to be steeled 4 inches and polished bright, without lacquer or paint; to weigh 61/4 to 6 ½ pounds"

Felling Axes
"Felling axes to be of three sizes, and to be made of the best American iron and steel; blade to be well steeled to the edge; for medium sized axe, length of blade 7 ¾ inches; width of pole (poll) 3 and seven sixteenths inches; thickness of pole, seven eighths of an inch; width on the edge, 4 ¾ to 5 inches; of eye 2 ¾ by ¾ inches, oval in shape. The other sizes to correspond proportionally and with the above specifications, and to all average in weight 56 pounds to the dozen".

A full description of this army shovel and sling—both designed by Henry Benham, later commander of the Engineer Brigade, is found in the Fort Snelling manual. The entry is too lengthy to include in this text. Contact Historic Fort Snelling in Saint Paul, Minnesota for information.

11. TOOL SLINGS

When troops were moving at a distance from the supply wagons, they were able to carry tools by means of sling-carriages prescribed by Quartermaster Reports. Dover press reprinted the 1889 Quartermaster Manual, which illustrates a variety of tool-slings that are identical to those used during the Civil War, with a few changes. The '89 specifications call for a slightly longer sling-strap than is described in 1860's QM Manuals. One suggested

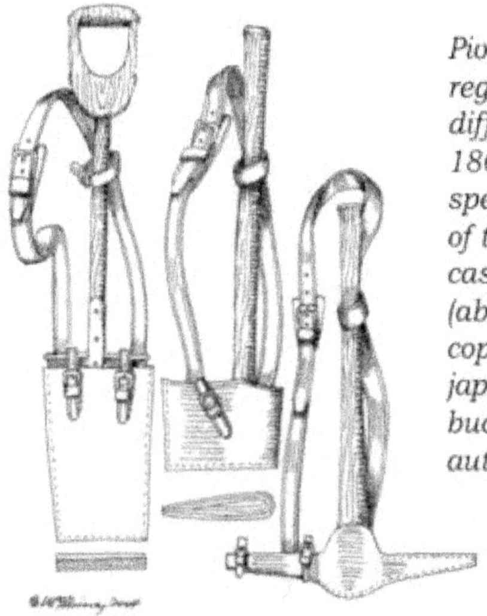

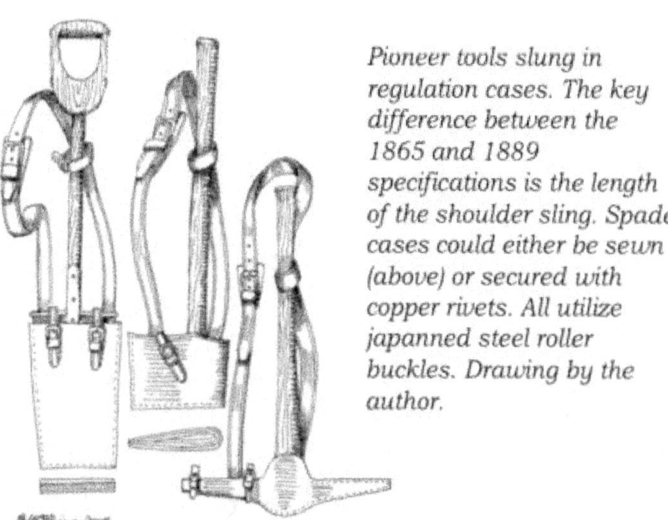

Pioneer tools slung in regulation cases. The key difference between the 1865 and 1889 specifications is the length of the shoulder sling. Spade cases could either be sewn (above) or secured with copper rivets. All utilize japanned steel roller buckles. Drawing by the author.

explanation is that added sling-length was due to the increased use of mounted infantry, a fact that I have yet to confirm. Please consult the attached copies of the 1865 QM Manual for correct dimensions. While official orders prescribe the movement of tools via wagon or mule-pannier, slings were undoubtedly used, like Colonel

Hatchets

"To be of the best American iron and steel, well steeled at the edge; five and one eighth inches long; pole one and seven eighths inches long by five eighths of an inch in thickness; eye oval, 1 ½ by three eights of an inch in size; blade 2 ¾ inches on the edge; weight 18 ounces

Axe Handles

"To be made of good, seasoned hickory wood, 34 to 36 inches long, and free of knots or shakes"

Spades

"Three sizes, Nos. 1,2 and 3, made of the best American or Swedish bar iron, pointed with steel 5 inches deep from the cutting edge. No 2, plain back, medium size, length of blade 11 ¾ inches; width at top seven and an eighth inches; width of edge six and seven eighths inches; thickness of blade at top, No. 14 wire gauge; at edge and middle, No. 10 wire gauge; handle of ash wood, 2 feet 5 ½ inches long, secured at top, "D" with 2 iron rivets, and in the socket of the blade with 3 iron rivets. Weight, 3 ¾ to 4 ½ pounds.

Shovels

Three sizes, 1 , 2 and 3; made of the best American or Swedish bar iron pointed with steel 5 inches deep from the cutting edge. No. 2, medium size, plain back, with "D" handle; blade 11 ½ inches long; 9 ½ inches wide at the bottom, eight and three eighths inches wide at the top; handle of ash wood 2 feet 5 ½ inches long, secured in the socket with 3 iron rivets; in top, through the "D: with 2 iron rivets. Weight 4 ½ pounds"

From The Fort Snelling Manual—

Picket Shovel

Used by men on picket and guard duty to entrench themselves quickly and protect them from the sharpshooters of the enemy. To be made of No. 16 wire gauge cast steel, polished and concave in form of the same shape as the old scoop or long handled shovel.

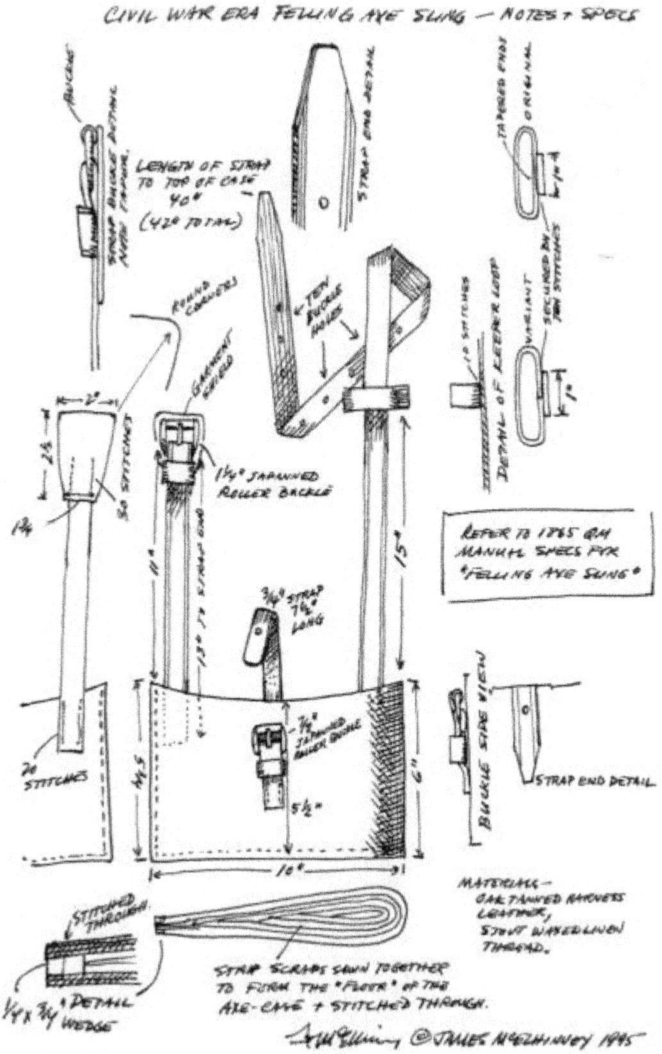

Author's 1995 drawing of an original Civil War felling-axe sling, now in a private collection. Dimensions conform to 1865 Quartermaster Report specs.

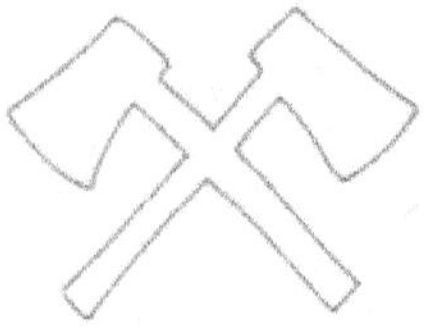

Standard pioneer chevron pattern
H: 3.5 inches;
W: 5 Inches

Variant pioneer chevron pattern
H:3.2 inches;
W: 4.75 inches

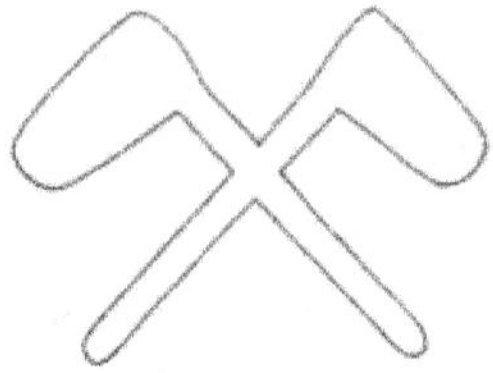

GLOSSARY

Abatis (abba tee) - An obstacle in front of a fortified position made of trees with sharpened branches pointing outward.

Balk (bahk) - Heavy beams used in building pontoon bridges

Banquette (bang ket) - A narrow elevated platform running behind the revetment of a work.

Bastion (bass chun) - A four-sided enclosure projecting the corner of a larger work beyond its normal plan.

Birago (Bee rah go) - A type of bridge in which the roadway is suspended from a trestle, used for crossing waterways and defiles.

Bomb proof - An underground shelter built to protect troops from shelling

Breastwork - Any defensive fortification behind which soldiers may find cover while fighting.

Chess - The planks used to build a roadway across a pontoon bridge.

Chevaux de Frises (Shay vo duh Freeze) - A kind of obstacle made by attaching sharpened poles to a central log. Name translated literally; "Friesien Horses" (the Friesiens had no cavalry).

Corduroy - Popular term for a wooden paving, made by laying saplings and smaller timber side by side, at a right angle to the direction of traffic, as distinct from a "plank" road.

Counterscarp - The wall of the ditch in front of a fortified position below the glacis

Coup de l'oeil militaire (koo d' oo y mili tare) - Literally, a "military stroke (stratagem) of the eye." The ability to see the military use of the land.

Cremellaire - A zigzag design used in laying out trenches and works

Dead man - A buried log or beam to secure a heavy rope or cable used in bridge construction.

Declination - The angle expressing the difference between magnetic north and true north.

Degree - A unit of measure. The compass possesses 360, with 90 between each of the basic directions

Embrasure (Em bray shoor) - The opening in a fortified wall, through which the muzzle of a cannon may pass and fire. Literally a "hug."

Entanglement - An obstacle against infantry created by making snares of cordage or telegraph wire, secured to stumps or trees

Face - The wall or section of a fortified position built in the same direction.

Fascine (Fah seen) - Longitudinal bundles of brush bound into 12-foot lengths, fabricated logs from brush, for use in field construction. Also known as "faggots" when burned as fuel.

Fraises (Frazes) - A line of sharpened stakes, set into the earth, often in a fortified ditch or embankment, as an obstacle against infantry

Gabion (Gay bee on) - A four-foot-high cylinder made of woven brush and vines, placed and filled with earth for use in field construction.

Gorge - The open part of a bastion or salient, facing the rear; the part of a three-sided work that is not enclosed.

Glacis (Glay sis) - The inclined outer edge of a ditch in front of earthworks, triangular in section, slightly elevated above the natural surface of the terrain.

Head Log - A wooden log or beam laid along the rampart of a work to afford protection from hostile small arms fire

Lashing - Methods of securing parts of a structure to one another with cordage

Loophole - An opening in a fortified wall through which small arms may be fired

Military Crest - That part of inclined terrain just below the summit, which from the bottom appears to be the highest point. A suitable place for entrenching.

Miner - A person expert in explosives and the construction of tunnels.

Orientation - The process of aligning a map upon the ground it portrays; literally "to face east."

Palisade - A wall of pointed posts, usually about 12 feet high, set into the earth, side by side as a wall, or as part of a stockade.

Pannier - A wicker basket or wooden box hung on either side of a pack frame, mounted on a horse or mule, upon which tools, weapons, and bundles may be carried.

Pioneer –A soldier skilled in construction and demolition who belongs to the detachment moving ahead of the battalion, to clear the way and throw up obstacles against the enemy; an infantryman acting as an engineer soldier.

Pioneer Corporal - A staff noncommissioned officer in control of the pioneer detachment for a regiment. Like the Sergeant Major and Ordnance Sergeant, the Pioneer Corporal is part of the regimental staff chain of command

Plank Road - A muddy thoroughfare made passable by paving its surface with sawn planks, as distinct from a "corduroy" road.

Plumb - True vertical, ascertained by hanging a pointed weight from the intersecting point of a tripod.

Ponton also "pontoon." - A flat-bottomed boat, square stern, and aft, used as supports for balk and chess bridges across waterways.

Rampart - The upper surface of a fortified embankment, often inclined toward the front, in line with the surface of the glacis.

Ravelin (Rahv lin) - A triangular outer work, usually in front of the ditch surrounding a bastion

Redan (Re dahn) - Triangular enclosure built to cover a field piece and its crew.

Revetment (Re vet ment) - Method of stabilizing the interior wall of an earthwork using either timber, lumber, gabions, fascines, sandbags, or sod. A retaining wall.

Rigging - Methods of positioning, moving, and elevating heavy objects using cordage, block, and tackle.

Salient (Say lee ent) - Part of an entrenched line projected beyond the line, usually having two or three faces.

Sap - A trench or covered way built to convey attacking troops as close as possible to the fortified target.

Sapper - A soldier expert in digging trenches and covered ways under fire

Sap Roller - An oversized gabion, usually with a smaller one inside, packed with wood, to protect sappers from small arms fire

Scarp - The front face or wall of a work, behind the ditch.

Slashing - An obstacle created by gathering a hedge of brush and branches at a distance before a fortified position.

Stockade - A simple fortified enclosure made up of palisades; a prison pen.

Stringers - Wooden rails placed under head logs, the other end resting behind a trench; to protect men fighting in the trench from head logs falling into the trench.

Tennille - A line of inverted redans.

Terreplein (Tar plane) - Literally "open ground." The platform of a rampart, for the cannon, behind the parapet.

Topographical Engineers - An independent corps of officers, skilled in science, engineering, surveying, and mapping who conducted the majority of western explorations, reconsolidated in 1863 with the Army Corps of Engineers.

Traverse - Part of an earthwork slightly higher or the same height as the rampart, running perpendicular to it, to limit collateral damage caused by artillery shells or enfilading fire.

Trestle - A framework using triangular structures to elevate, reinforce, support, and extend other structures, such as bridges, over dry defiles and waterways.

Tripod - Three-legged platform used to support plane tables, transits, vernier compasses, telescopes, and other surveying equipment.

Trou de loup (True d loo) "Wolf pit" - A conical hole with sharp stakes set points upward.

The 135th United States Colored Troop Marched in the Grand Review in Washington D.C. on May 24, 1865 as we have discovered through primary sources and official records.

Special Orders, No. 105.

SPECIAL ORDERS, No. 105.

HDQRS. SEVENTEENTH ARMY CORPS, *Jones', N. C., April 25, 1865.*

* * * * * *

II. The movement to-morrow will be via Green Level and Trades Hill to near the Haw River. The Ninth Illinois Mounted Infantry will move forward at 5.30 a. m. The bridge train, Lieutenant-Colonel Tweeddale commanding, will move forward at 6 a. m. Brig. Gen. M. F. Force, commanding First Division, will detach two regiments from his command, one to move in advance of the bridge train, the other to move with it as guard. The First Division will follow the bridge train. The Fourth Division, Bvt. Maj. Gen. G. A. Smith commanding, will follow the First Division. The Third Division, Bvt. Maj. Gen. M. D. Leggett commanding, will follow the Fourth Division. The troops will move on the right of the train.

III. Col. John E. Gurley, commanding One hundred and thirty-fifth U. S. Colored Troops, will divide his command among the divisions of the corps as follows: To the First Division, three companies; to the Third Division, three companies; to the Fourth Division, four companies. He will assign competent officers to the command of each detachment.

By command of Maj. Gen. F. P. Blair:

C. CADLE, JR.,
Assistant Adjutant-General.

Special Orders, No. 106.

SPECIAL ORDERS, No. 106.

HDQRS. SEVENTEENTH ARMY CORPS, *Jones', N. C., April 26, 1865.*

* * * * * *

VIII. The command will move back to Raleigh to-morrow, and will occupy their old camp. The Ninth Illinois Mounted Infantry will move at 6.30 a. m. The First Division, Brig. Gen. M. F. Force commanding, will move at 7 a. m. The Fourth Division, Bvt. Maj. Gen. G. A. Smith commanding, will follow the First Division. The Third Division, Bvt. Maj. Gen. M. D. Leggett commanding, will follow the Fourth Division. The One hundred and thirty-fifth U. S. Colored Troops, Col. John E. Gurley commanding, will follow the Third Division. The pontoon train, Lieutenant-Colonel Tweeddale commanding, will follow the train of the command. The First Regiment Michigan Engineers and Mechanics, Col. J. B. Yates commanding, will follow the pontoon train. The trains of the command, with a small guard, will move together next after the One hundred and thirty-fifth U. S. Colored Troops in the order of their respective divisions.

By command of Maj. Gen. F. P. Blair:

C. CADLE, JR.,
Assistant Adjutant-General.

Special Orders, No. 131.

SPECIAL ORDERS, No. 131. HDQRS. SEVENTEENTH ARMY CORPS, *Near Alexandria, Va., May 22, 1865.*

* * * * * * *

X. In order to carry out the orders from military division and army headquarters for the review on the 24th instant, the following orders are made: The Ninth Illinois Mounted Infantry will move in advance, following the Fifteenth Army Corps, being prepared to move at 6 a. m. The Third Division will follow the Ninth Illinois Mounted Infantry. The Fourth Division will follow the Third Division. The First Division will follow the Fourth Division. The artillery of the corps under Maj. Fred. Welker, chief of artillery, will follow the First Division. The command will be supplied with two days' rations (cooked) from Wednesday morning. The order of march will be in accordance with the orders from military division and army headquarters. The trains of the command in the same order that the divisions move in will move to the camp already designated as soon as the review is over. The detachments of the One hundred and thirty-fifth U. S. Colored Troops with each division will move next after the pioneer corps. The knapsacks of the command will be loaded in wagons and hauled to the new camp.

By command of Maj. Gen. F. P. Blair:

C. CADLE, Jr.,
Assistant Adjutant-General.

We have also found numerous pension records of the soldiers where they talked about marching through Washington, D.C., passing the White House, and passing the president of the United States. They spoke of how proud they were to have marched in the Grand Review after the Civil War.

General Orlando M. Poe

Born in Ohio in 1832, Orlando Poe came to prominence after graduating 6th in his class at West Point in 1856. Five years later he served as a Lieutenant under General George McLellan. His small, early victory with the controversial McLellan earned him command as Colonel of the 2nd Michigan Volunteer Infantry. Conducting several successful campaigns with his brigade of volunteers but not having been confirmed for promotion by Congress, Poe's rank reverted to that of Captain assigned to the Engineers of the regular Army. With this post Poe was attached to the 1st Michigan Mechanics and Engineers.

The 1st Michigan Mechanics and Engineers was formed in 1861 with William Powers Innes as Colonel who mentioned Poe in his resignation letter at the end of his enlistment. In 1863 Poe was promoted Chief Engineer of the Army of the Ohio. By 1864 he had been tapped by William Tecumseh Sherman to be his chief engineer for the capture of Atlanta, seizure of Savannah, and Sherman's Carolina campaign.

They engaged in fierce fighting at Atlanta with extensive losses of men killed, wounded, and missing but not the city. Despite their losses the army was buoyed by the outcome. Following the destruction and seizure of Atlanta, in September 1864, Ulysses Grant recounted in 1885 that Sherman had 60,000 fit and able troops to make his move toward Savannah. At the time Sherman conveyed to Grant his concerns about "...finding provisions and ammunition..." along the way.

The sandy soil before them lent itself to poor forage. It failed to discourage the army including its two hundred forty black pioneers guided by Poe who were ready to honor their enlistment commitment. They did, fortunately, find rice straw. The grain added to the troops' diets; the stalks fed the livestock.

From Grant we know that: "The troops, both of the right and left wings, made most of their advance along the line of railroads, which they destroyed. The method adopted to perform this work was to burn and destroy all the bridges and culverts, and for a long distance, at places, to tear up the track and bend the rails. Soldiers to do this rapidly would form a line along one side of the road with crowbars and poles, place these under the rails and, hoisting all at once, turn over many rods of road at one time. The ties would then be placed in piles, and the rails, as they were loosened, would be carried and put across these log heaps. When a sufficient number of rails were placed upon a pile of ties it would be set on fire. This would heat the rails very much more in the middle, that being over the main part of the fire, than at the ends, so that they would naturally bend of their own weight; but the soldiers, to increase the damage, would take tongs and, one or two men at each end of the rail, carry it with force against the nearest tree and twist it around, thus leaving rails forming bands to ornament the forest trees of Georgia. All this work was going on at the same time, there being a sufficient number of men detailed for that purpose. Some piled the logs and built the fire; some put the rails upon the fire; while others would bend those that were sufficiently heated: so that, by

the time the last bit of road was torn up, that it was designed to destroy at a certain place, the rails previously taken up were already destroyed."

Further records of their work along with Poe's importance are revealed in Sherman's 1889 revision of his memoirs: "...I give the best maps which I believe have ever been prepared, compiled by General O. M. Poe, from personal knowledge and official surveys, and what I chiefly aim to establish is the true cause of the results which are already known to the whole world...." November 9, 1864, Sherman's orders were: "The organization, at once, of a good pioneer battalion for each army corps, composed if possible of negroes, should be attended to. This battalion should follow the advance-guard, repair roads and double them if possible, so that the columns will not be delayed after reaching bad places. Also, army commanders should practice the habit of giving the artillery and wagons the road, marching their troops on one side, and instruct their troops to assist wagons at steep hills or bad crossings of streams. Captain O. M. Poe, chief-engineer, will assign to each wing of the army a pontoon-train, fully equipped and organized; and the commanders thereof will see to their being properly protected at all times."

Poe's special task at that time was destruction, using a large force to level selected targets. "Each division was preceded by its corps of black pioneers...." as instructed by Sherman. Poe's preparations for the march to Savannah included assignment of 70 "negroes" to each division's pioneer corps. An average of 490 black pioneers. The Michigan Engineers and Mechanics train of 20 wagons were loaded with tools while pontoon wagons were organized in separate trains.

Marching out of Atlanta, "Colonel Poe had provided tools for ripping up the rails and twisting them when hot...," echoing, in short, Grant's description of the process. Bivouacked at Covington that night Sherman recalled saying "...we could receive a few of their young, hearty men as pioneers." Poe and his troops – engineers and pioneers - engaged in more than destroying and repairing railroads, bridges, and armories. He laid-off lines of defense and located redoubts, was responsible for "...reconnoitering the ground around Fort McAllister..." to "...prepare it so as to make a fortified camp large enough to accommodate the vast herd of mules and horses that would thus be left behind" in the event that Sherman was to join General Grant in Virginia before reaching Savannah.

Sherman found Savannah well entrenched and garrisoned when the army approached in early December. The siege began on the 10th. Capturing Fort McAllister opened supply lines to steamboats. On the 16th Poe wrote to his wife that "...we have just marched three hundred miles through the heart of the enemy's country." All communication during the march had ceased. Loneliness seeped into his letters as it must have for all soldiers.

The Confederate Army evacuated during the night of the 20st. Once in Savannah, Poe was tasked with determining which captured forts were to be used by Union forces and

which were to be dismantled and destroyed. Colonel Poe also "reconnoitered and laid off new lines of parapet, which would enable a comparatively small garrison to hold the place, and a heavy detail of soldiers was put to work thereon...." The work was completed by the middle of January, except for reprovisioning.

Plans for moving the Army north to join General Grant were drafted. Part of those plans included Colonel Poe accompanying Sherman in recognition of the effectiveness of discharging his duties thus far. Grant though changed his mind. This allowed Sherman to, as he stated, "...sally forth with my army resupplied, cross the Savannah, feign on Charleston and Augusta, but strike between, breaking en route the Charleston & Augusta Railroad, also a large part of that from Branchville and Camden toward North Carolina, and then rapidly to move for some point of the railroad from Charleston to Wilmington, between the Santee and Cape Fear Rivers...."

"Woe to South Carolina!" Poe wrote. "We are on her borders, ready to carry fire & sword into every part of that state." On the first day of the new year his letter contained the assurance that the "...the troops have been reviewed, clothing & provisions distributed, and the bugles are ready to sound the advance." Weather on their march became so bad, though, that water froze almost instantly. They were marching without tents. On the flip-side, the hard freeze allowed wagons and artillery to make headway.

In February 1865 Poe and a large detachment destroyed the arsenal at Columbia, South Carolina, reaching their first objective. At Columbia Poe had to "...repair and corduroy the roads and rebuild the bridges" to ensure progress to their second objective of Fayetteville, North Carolina. Coordinating movements to support Sherman's march Grant cautioned one commander that the movement he proposed was, perhaps, ill-advised because Sherman's large army "...was eating out the vitals of South Carolinas."

Sherman marched north toward Winnsboro once Columbia was secured. There he converged with his left wing. His right wing was then turned eastward to North Carolina to meet the final objective of the campaign, Goldsboro. Crossing the Pee Dee River on March 6th they advanced straight toward Fayetteville where they reprovisioned, without the desired clothing supplies. As he had done in Columbia, Poe by "the clang of hammers & axes, wielded by more than a thousand men..." destroyed the Fayetteville arsenal, commenting to his wife that it "was a beautiful place...."

On March 15th the move was on to Goldsboro. Progress was cautious, vigilant, deliberate. They were nearing Lee's army led by General Joseph Johnston. Skirmishes and losses were inevitable, notably on the 16th, 19th and 20th. They were also hampered by heavy rains requiring corduroying long stretches of road, slogs through swamps, communication and biological (i.e., water moccasins and alligators) challenges, and 20,000 to 30,000 followers. It took six weeks to reach Fayetteville from Columbia.

They covered four hundred twenty-five miles from Savannah to Goldsboro in fifty days all while fording five navigable rivers in brutal, mid-winter weather. In that time the black pioneer ranks had grown by 600 in South Carolina. Another 250 joined in North Carolina.

The Union Army converged on Goldsboro on March 22, 1865. General Sherman arrived on the 23rd. Poe too. That day Poe told his wife that, by virtue of his brevet promotions, he was now a Colonel in the regular army, also – "...our army is large and the demands constant." Plans were laid to move toward Grant on April 18th. Encamped they rested, resupplied, repaired rail lines with an eye toward future movements and opened muster rolls to form the 135th United States Colored Troops.

None of this would have been possible without the sheer determination and skills of the engineer and pioneer corpsmen like those that served under Poe. Considering that one estimate of the necessary kit to equip twenty men per regiment was rudimentary - Six Felling Axes, Six Hammers, Six Hatchets, Two Half-Inch Augurs, Two Cross-Cut Saws, Two Inch Augurs, Two Cross Cut Files, Two Two-Inch Augurs, Two Hand-Saws, Twenty lbs. Nails (Assorted), Two Hand-Saw Files, Forty lbs. Spikes (Assorted), Six Spades, One Coil Rope, Two Shovels, Three Picks, One Wagon (with four horses, or mules) - it is impossible to underestimate the degree of their accomplishments.

Poe provided some context of what was involved in their endeavors. Writing about the campaign of Savannah to Goldsboro, in Goldsboro, on April 1, 1865, he recounted the extent of labor involved in moving the army across the varied terrains and through the extant circumstances they encountered. Clearly, armies destroyed infrastructure when in retreat. While on the offensive armies built and rebuilt infrastructure, as well as destroying what was deemed necessary at each point in their plan.

According to Poe's report, leaving Savannah the pontonniers (pontoon bridge builders) accompanied the 15th Corps. The remaining engineering troops were transported by water to Beaufort. Due to torrential rains and flooding 700 feet of bridging was constructed just to cross the Savannah River, 1,000 feet of trestle bridging, and miles of corduroying were also necessary. All totaled, both wings of the army constructed more than 7,700 feet of pontoon bridges. Trestle bridging and corduroying roads along this section of the campaign, Poe recounted, was all performed by the "...Michigan Engineers, the pioneers, and several sub-divisions of the Army."

In South Carolina, Poe and his men built 22 bridges, each about 25 feet in length, over a mile in the swamp; the road through the swamp was completely corduroyed. All done overnight, by the light of the moon and torch. More bridges were built, 400 miles of corduroy roads were laid as the army pressed on toward Goldsboro. Sherman's army continually engaged in skirmishes, burning ties and twisting rail to disable railroads, destroying water stores, dismantling depots, with a long list of other laborious tasks in pursuit of the ultimate goal.

Expertise and energy were necessities as the army moved from Goldsboro to Raleigh then to Washington D.C. The 135th United States Colored Troop were integral to this leg of the march. As freedom fighters these men risked their lives with the

understanding that they had an opportunity to build something better for themselves and their families.

To take advantage of the opportunity, men in General Poe's charge faced a work-a-day life that demanded physical stamina and mental fortitude. Building bridges and roads qualified on both counts.

Corduroying roads was timber-heavy construction that accounted for the lion's-share of the work of the corps. Logs of sufficient length and diameter were laid in closely spaced parallel rows perpendicular to the direction the army traveled, akin to placing dowels of a similar diameter side-by-side. These roads were in essence land bridges. They were by their nature permanent, critical installations for troops and wagons (though they were potentially dangerous to horses) to cross swampy or muddy terrain. And they could be covered with soil, planks, moss or other materials to minimize bumps and hazards.

Pre-war truss bridges of steel were replaced by wooden trestle bridges which could be built quickly throughout the course of the war. Intended as temporary structures they had to be strong enough to support the weight of locomotives and rail cars filled with supplies, livestock, and to transport troops. With nothing more than simple tools the pioneers did the hard work of felling trees of sufficient size to give structural support to the triangular shaped tripods that were the underpinnings of the deck upon which the trains traveled. The trestle itself had to be anchored deep enough in the riverbed to be secure for purpose.

According to Poe, "whenever it was deemed necessary to use a bridge for a greater length of time than forty-eight hours the pontoon bridges were invariably replaced by wooden trestle bridges constructed from materials at hand, either by engineer troops or the pioneer forces."

Pontoon bridges were also temporary river-crossing structures. Sherman used the Cumberland pontoon extensively on his campaigns. They were canvas covered, foldable and could be transported in standard supply wagons, unlike earlier versions. The men would have to stand in the river to construct and anchor the pontoons, so they didn't float away. Yet, they needed to be quick enough to assemble to allow troops and supply trains to cross and disassemble to prevent being used by Confederate forces.

This falls short of detailing the logistics of planning, placement and providing the number of wagons to move the pontoons into place. Consideration of the available supplies, number of wagons necessary to haul the pontoons, the relative distance they needed to cover in a specified time, the length of the wagon train, and how to protect them all had to be evaluated. It, of course, fell to Poe.

Vast quantities of timber were necessary as well, if it could be supplied or found as the campaign advanced. The trees had to be felled by ax or saw and moved into place. Thousands and thousands and thousands of trees! By Confederate General Beauregard's estimate the Union laid twelve miles of road a day, if not more. Where no

trees were available or stands had already been cleared, the corps cannibalized fence posts, rails, and boards found at nearby plantations or farms.

Giving just a glimpse at what the men endured, Private Rice Buell noted in his diary that "It was not a pleasant job in our wet clothes with water up to our knees but we had the work done...." Up to it they were, for the most part. They had been subjected to extreme hardship and exposure. Upon arrival in Goldsboro 1/6 of the army was without shoes and other clothing.

The Pioneer Corps and tool trains remained as they were on the Savannah to Goldsboro campaign when the army was reorganized for the march to Washington D.C. Except, as Poe, said "...that it was extended to the additional force that had joined us." The immensity of this leg of the campaign required that a "...hundred thousand men..." have entrenching tools.

In all the pioneers and engineers laid 3.37 miles of pontoon bridges, built 1.7 miles of trestle bridges, and corduroyed 580 miles of road moving from Atlanta to the U.S. capitol.

The soldiers, obviously, were not unscathed. A list of maladies of the sick and dead soldiers of the 135th is no doubt applicable to the black pioneers at large. Their maladies, other than casualties, included – fever, chronic and acute diarrhea, dysentery, inflammation, lung disease, pneumonia, typhoid, scurvy, consumption (tuberculosis), dropsy, jaundice, nephritis, piles, bronchitis. Daniel Townsend, for example, lost his lower left arm, was considered totally disabled and discharged. Like Townsend the sick may have been mustered-out because of the severity of their illness. Others went AWOL for reasons known to them.

General Poe recapitulated the contents of his Goldsboro letter in October and expanded upon it to include the entire campaign, pre-Atlanta and post-Goldsboro. In the throes of the war, he wrote regularly to his wife. Most understandably were devoid of military interest. The maps (printed on linen to make them easy to carry), books, letters from others, and the mementos he took away from the meeting of Generals Sherman and Johnston that he mentions sending to her might be of more interest.

In less than eight short weeks the newly enlisted men, the 135th, Poe referred to in Goldsboro, and the rest of the army would march in the six-hour long Grand Review that marked the end of four years of conflict. A memorable day, May 25th, for Poe and the men of the 135th.

Were indebted to Marian Maytan for her kind assistance in providing copies of General Poe's 1865 letter from the O.M. Poe Papers, 1853, 1878, Clarke Historical Library, Central Michigan University

The Memoirs of General W. T. Sherman, Complete.

The flag of the 135th United States Colored Troop as described in the Special Orders of the Headquarters Seventeenth Army Corps.

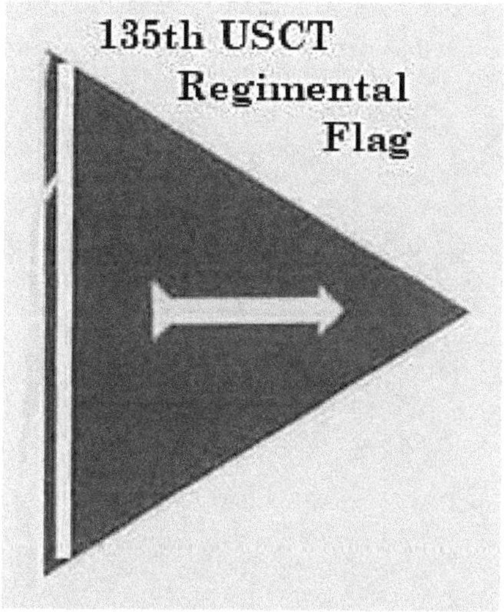

135th USCT Campaign Flag

The 135th United States Colored Troop

Civil War Trails Marker

Leading the Way!

Making history in Goldsboro, North Carolina.
"They led the way," is the title for the Civil War Trails sign in Goldsboro, North Carolina which was installed there on March 27, 2023, on the 158th anniversary of the historic enlistment of the 135th United States Colored Troop, (Infantry). The Civil War Trails marker is installed at 201 Center Street in the heart of downtown Goldsboro as a remembrance to the men of the 135th USCT and in their honor.

The story of this infantry Regiment was largely forgotten until around 2016. The 135th USCT Research Team, Inc. which was formed by Jay and Amy Bauer, and which was made up of descendants and regional historians spent innumerable hours exploring archives, traveling the country and delving into online sources and tirelessly analyzing historical documents searching for information about the men who would ultimately serve in this infantry Regiment. Lt. Col. (retired) Deborah Jones, a descendant and secretary of the team expressed, "It is exciting to see these once enslaved men recognized for their back breaking endeavors to provide Freedom for all!"

The sign is part of the Civil War Trails program which connects visitors to over 1,400 sites. As Drew Gruber, the Executive Director of the Civil War Trails, Inc. explained "These Black men entered town as formerly enslaved people and marched out as Federal employees, soldiers in the United States Army."

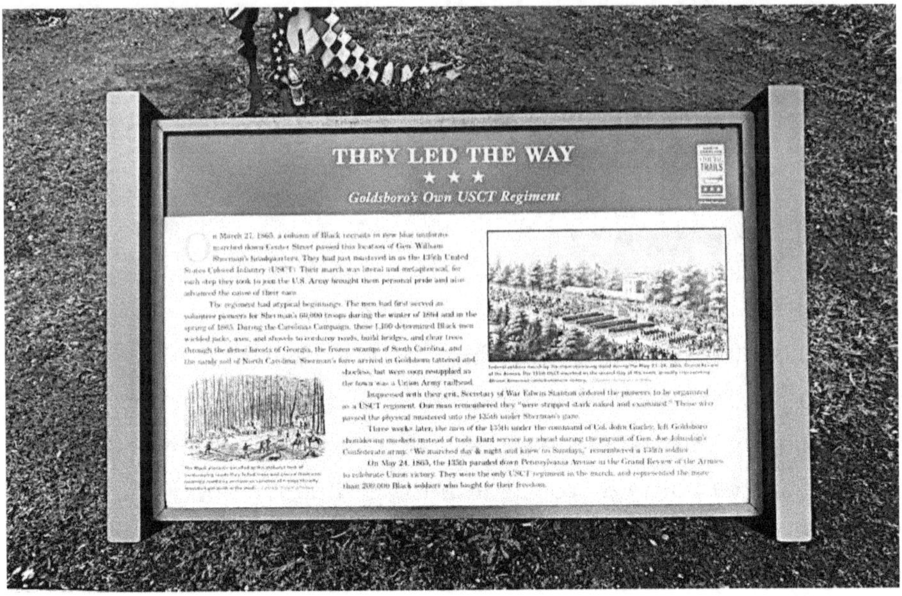

201 South Center Street, Goldsboro, North Carolina.

Dedication - March 27, 2023

Civil War Trails Marker

ACKNOWLEDGMENTS

Board of Directors 135th USCT Research Team, Inc

Jay Bauer, President
Amy Bauer, Vice President
Trista Jorges, 2nd Vice President
Deborah Jones, Secretary
Leonard Paul Sherrod, Treasurer
Regina Lesnau, (Retired) Treasurer
Board of Advisers
Benjamin F. Speller, Jr. PhD.
Dr. Reginald F. Hildebrand
Earl Ijames, Curator of NC Museum of History
Dr. Malcolm Beech, President, - U.S.C.T. Living History Assoc.
David Winslow

Team Members 135th USCT Research Team, Inc.

Ann Clark Hurrey
Audrey McKinney
Sussie Sutton
Cheryl Richardson
Donald Harmon
James Jones
Elizabeth Martin/Meggett & Family
Sandra Fort/Kemp
Stephanie Fort/Kent
Lloyd Townsend
Larry and Sharon Laboda
Angel McKnight
Louise Johnson
Parthenia Cogdell
Dr. Pamela Monk

Dr. Anita Locus Sanders

Special Thanks

35th USCT Reenactors

37th USCT Reenactors

135th USCT Reenactors

Battery B, 2nd Regiment USCT Light Infantry, Inc

18th Corps Civil War Reenactors

Rev. Dr. Louis S. Leigh Jr. First African Bapt. Ch., Goldsboro, NC

The Adrian and Selena Worrell Family

Dr. Frank Smith PhD. Dir. of African American Civil War Museum,

Representative John R. Bell NC House Majority Leader

Cindy Pratt & Teddy Harrington (The John Auman diary)

Hari Jones in Memoriam

Goldsboro ROTC – Col Curtis Inman, USA(Retired)

The City of Goldsboro, North Carolina

Jim Hinnant

Chuck Allen in Memoriam

Margaret Oman

Glenn Aycock, Goldsboro City Council Retired

Julie Metz

Downtown Goldsboro Development Corporation

Jennifer Kuykendahl Executive Director Wayne County Museum

Ashlin Glatthar Goldsboro Wayne Tourist Board

North Carolina Humanities

Civil War Trails Drew Gruber, Executive Director

The Freedom Seekers Heritage Chorale

(Living History Weekend April 6, 2018)

Hilda Watson Banks, Conductor

Lori Williams Grant, Concert Pianist & Creative Coordinator

Bernard George, Narrator

Majesty Rose

Bryson Rogers Hill, Drummer

Hiawatha Jones

Ida Adams
Shirley Hamilton Carter
Charlyne Edwards
Eunice Whitted Hudson
Pier Protz
Gwendolyn G. Shipman
Faye Smith
Mary Emma Steven
G. Patricia L. Stokes
Annetta Stokes Streater
Polly Walker
MaeBelle White
Gloria Williams
Eddie Charles Atkins
Michael Blount
Danny Lewis
Charles H. Moore
Nancy Wooten Coor
Kaye Newsome Cox
Marjorie Holloway
Cynthia Reynolds
Yvonne Stovall Rouse
Susie Shepherd
Sussie Sutton
JoAnne Young
James Eaddy
Eddie Edwards
Adell Hall
Hugh Jones
Glen Little
Vernon Kornegay in Memoriam
Carl Martin
Kim McClarin
Maxwell William

Bring the good old bugle boys,
We'll sing another song.
Sing it with a spirit that will
Start the world along.
Sing it as we used to sing it
Fifty Thousand Strong
As we're marching Through Georgia

Author Autobiographies

Amy and Jay Bauer have detailed a personal, true and historic document to memorialize the men of the 135th United States Colored Troop. *"It's all about GUTS,"* are the personal life stories of the soldiers compiled after eight years of research and "in their own words." This is their second book following the publication of *"Where Eagles Come From,"* about a young girl in search of her roots and she discovers her ancestor was a soldier in the 135th USCT.

Amy's education includes attending St. Vincent's Academy, in Savannah, Georgia and Georgia Southern University. Amy was a successful real estate agent in Southern California and later was the owner of Bauer Insurance Services. Jay attended Bishop Garcia Diego High School, and college in Santa Barbara, California before entering the US Army. Captain Bauer was a fixed wing Army aviator in Vietnam receiving two Distinguished Flying Crosses, the Vietnam Cross of Gallantry with Palm, and 19 Air Medals. Following his military service, he spent 40 years working as Vice President of a Commercial Construction Company in Southern California before retiring in 2013.

www.ingramcontent.com/pod-product-compliance
Lightning Source LLC
Chambersburg PA
CBHW051456150726
47997CB00001B/1
* 9 7 9 8 9 9 1 0 6 6 3 1 0 *